CONTENTS.

THE RULE AND EXERCISES OF HOLY LIVING.

▲ 2

HOLY LIVING AND DYING

With Prayers Containing the Whole Duty of a Christian

JEREMY TAYLOR

COSIMOCLASSICS

NEW YORK

HOLY LIVING AND DYING: With Prayers Containing the Whole Duty of a Christian
Cover © 2007 Cosimo, Inc.

For information, address:

Cosimo, P.O. Box 416
Old Chelsea Station
New York, NY 10113-0416

or visit our website at:
www.cosimobooks.com

HOLY LIVING AND DYING: With Prayers Containing the Whole Duty of a Christian was originally published in 1883.

Cover design by www.kerndesign.net

ISBN: 978-1-60206-550-5

CHAP. IV.—*Of Christian Religion.*

THE RULE AND EXERCISES OF HOLY DYING.

TO THE RIGHT HONOURABLE

AND TRULY NOBLE

RICHARD LORD VAUGHAN,

EARL OF CARBERY, KNIGHT OF THE HONOURABLE
ORDER OF THE BATH.

My Lord,

I have lived to see religion painted upon banners, and thrust out of churches; and the temple turned into a tabernacle, and that tabernacle made ambulatory, and covered with skins of beasts and torn curtains; and God to be worshipped, not as he is, "the Father of our Lord Jesus," (an afflicted Prince, the King of sufferings,) nor as the "God of peace," (which two appellatives God newly took upon him in the New Testament, and glories in for ever,) but he is owned now rather as "The Lord of hosts," which title he was pleased to lay aside, when the kingdom of the gospel was preached by the Prince of peace. But when religion puts on armour, and God is not acknowledged by his New Testament titles, religion may have in it the power of the sword, but not the power of godliness; and we may complain of this to God, and amongst them that are afflicted, but we have no remedy but what we must expect from the fellowship of Christ's sufferings, and the returns of the God of peace. In the mean time, and now that religion pretends to stranger actions upon new principles; and men are apt to prefer a prosperous error before an afflicted truth; and some will think they are religious enough if their worshippings have in them the prevailing ingredient; and the ministers of religion are so scattered that they cannot unite to stop the inundation, and from chairs or pulpits, from their synods or tribunals, chastise the iniquity of the error, and the ambition of evil guides, and the infidelity of the willingly seduced multitude; and that those few good people who have no other plot in their religion but to serve God and save their souls, do want such assistances of ghostly counsel as may serve their emergent needs, and assist their endeavours in the acquist of virtues, and relieve their dangers when they are tempted to sin and death; —I thought I had reasons enough inviting me to draw into one

body those advices which the several necessities of many men must
use at some time or other, and many of them daily; that by a collection of holy precepts they might less feel the want of personal
and attending guides, and that the rules for conduct of souls might
be committed to a book which they might always have; since they
could not always have a prophet at their needs, nor be suffered to
go up to the house of the Lord to inquire of the appointed oracles.

I know, my Lord, that there are some interested persons who
add scorn to the afflictions of the church of England; and, because
she is afflicted by men, call her "forsaken of the Lord;" and because her solemn assemblies are scattered, think that the religion is
lost, and the church divorced from God, supposing Christ (who was
a man of sorrows) to be angry with his spouse when she is like him
[for that is the true state of the error]; and that he who promised
his Spirit to assist his servants in their troubles, will, because they
are in trouble, take away the Comforter from them; who cannot
be a comforter but while he cures our sadnesses, and relieves our
sorrows, and turns our persecutions into joys, and crowns, and
sceptres. But, concerning the present state of the church of
England, I consider, that because we now want the blessings of
external communion in many degrees, and the circumstances of a
prosperous and unafflicted people, we are to take estimate of ourselves with single judgments, and every man is to give sentence
concerning the state of his own soul by the precepts and rules of
our Lawgiver, not by the after-decrees and usages of the church;
that is, by the essential parts of religion, rather than by the uncertain significations of any exterior adherences: for, though it be uncertain when a man is the member of a church whether he be a member to Christ or no, because in the church's net there are fishes
good and bad; yet we may be sure that, if we be members of Christ,
we are of a church to all purposes of spiritual religion and salvation; and in order to this, give me leave to speak this great truth —

That man does certainly belong to God, who, 1. Believes and is
baptized into all the articles of the Christian faith, and studies to
improve his knowledge in the matters of God, so as may best make
him to live a holy life. 2. He that, in obedience to Christ, worships God diligently, frequently, and constantly, with natural religion; that is, of prayer, praises, and thanksgiving. 3. He that
takes all opportunities to remember Christ's death by a frequent
sacrament, (as it can be had,) or else by inward acts of understanding, will, and memory, (which is the spiritual communion,) supplies
the want of the external rite. 4. He that lives chastely; 5. And
is merciful; 6. And despises the world, using it as a man, but never
suffering it to rifle a duty; 7. And is just in his dealing, and diligent in his calling. 8. He that is humble in his spirit; 9. And obedient to government; 10. And content in his fortune and employment. 11. He that does his duty because he loves God; 12. And

especially if, after all this, he be afflicted, and patient, or prepared to suffer affliction for the cause of God : the man that hath these twelve signs of grace and predestination, does as certainly belong to God, and is his son as surely, as he is his creature.

And if my brethren in persecution and in the bonds of the Lord Jesus can truly show these marks, they shall not need be troubled that others can show a prosperous outside, great revenues, public assemblies, uninterrupted successions of bishops, prevailing armies, or any arm of flesh, or less certain circumstance. These are the marks of the Lord Jesus, and the characters of a Christian : this is a good religion; and these things God's grace hath put into our powers, and God's laws have made to be our duty, and the nature of men and the needs of commonwealths have made to be necessary. The other accidents and pomps of a church are things without our power, and are not in our choice : they are good to be used when they may be had, and they help to illustrate or advantage it; but if any of them constitute a church in the being of a society and a government, yet they are not of its constitution, as it is Christian and hopes to be saved.

And now the case is so with us that we are reduced to that religion which no man can forbid; which we can keep in the midst of a persecution ; by which the martyrs, in the days of our fathers, went to heaven; that by which we can be servants of God, and receive the spirit of Christ, and make use of his comforts, and live in his love, and in charity with all men : and they that do so cannot perish.

My Lord, I have now described some general lines and features of that religion which I have more particularly set down in the following pages ; in which I have neither served nor disserved the interest of any party of Christians, as they are divided by uncharitable names from the rest of their brethren; and no man will have reason to be angry with me for refusing to mingle in his unnecessary or vicious quarrels; especially while I study to do him good by conducting him in the narrow way to heaven, without intricating him in the labyrinths and wild turnings of questions and uncertain talkings. I have told what men ought to do, and by what means they may be assisted ; and in most cases I have also told them why; and yet with as much quickness as I could think necessary to establish a rule, and not to engage in homily or discourse. In the use of which rules, although they are plain, useful, and fitted for the best and worst understandings, and for the needs of all men, yet I shall desire the reader to proceed with the following advices.

1. They that will with profit make use of the proper instruments of virtue, must so live as if they were always under the physician's hand. For the counsels of religion are not to be applied to the distempers of the soul as men used to take hellebore: but they must

dwell together with the spirit of a man, and be twisted about his understanding for ever; they must be used like nourishment, that is, by a daily care and meditation; not like a single medicine, and upon the actual pressure of a present necessity: for counsels and wise discourses, applied to an actual distemper, at the best are but like strong smells to an epileptic person; sometimes they may raise him, but they never cure him. The following rules, if they be made familiar to our natures and the thoughts of every day, may make virtue and religion become easy and habitual; but when the temptation is present, and hath already seized upon some portions of our consent, we are not so apt to be counselled, and we find no gust or relish in the precept: the lessons are the same, but the instrument is unstrung, or out of tune.

2. In using the instruments of virtue, we must be curious to distinguish instruments from duties, and prudent advices from necessary injunctions; and if by any other means the duty can be secured, let there be no scruples stirred concerning any other helps: only if they can, in that case, strengthen and secure the duty, or help towards perseverance, let them serve in that station in which they can be placed. For there are some persons in whom the Spirit of God hath breathed so bright a flame of love, that they do all their acts of virtue by perfect choice and without objection, and their zeal is warmer than that it will be allayed by temptation; and to such persons mortification by philosophical instruments, as fasting, sackcloth, and other rudenesses to the body, is wholly useless; it is always a more uncertain means to acquire any virtue, or secure any duty; and if love hath filled all the corners of our soul, it alone is able to do all the work of God.

3. Be not nice in stating the obligations of religion; but where the duty is necessary, and the means very reasonable in itself, dispute not too busily whether, in all circumstances, it can fit thy particular; but "super totam materiam," upon the whole make use of it. For it is a good sign of a great religion, and no imprudence when we have sufficiently considered the substance of affairs, then to be easy, humble, obedient, apt, and credulous in the circumstances, which are appointed to us in particular by our spiritual guides, or, in general, by all wise men in cases not unlike. He that gives alms does best not always to consider the minutes and strict measures of his ability, but to give freely, incuriously, and abundantly. A man must not weigh grains in the accounts of his repentance; but for a great sin have a great sorrow, and a great severity; and in this take the ordinary advices, though, it may be, a less rigour might not be insufficient; ἀκριβοδίκαιον, or arithmetical measures, especially of our own proportioning, are but arguments of want of love and of forwardness in religion; or else are instruments of scruple, and then become dangerous. Use the rule heartily and enough, and there will be no harm in thy error if any should happen.

4. If thou intendest heartily to serve God, and avoid sin in any one instance, refuse not the hardest and most severe advice that is prescribed in order to it, though possibly it be a stranger to thee; for whatsoever it be, custom will make it easy.

5. When many instruments for the obtaining any virtue, or restraining any vice, are propounded, observe which of them fits thy person or the circumstances of thy need, and use it rather than the other; that by this means thou mayest be engaged to watch and use spiritual arts and observation about thy soul. Concerning the managing of which, as the interest is greater, so the necessities are more, and the cases more intricate, and the accidents and dangers greater and more importunate; and there is greater skill required than in the securing an estate, or restoring health to an infirm body. I wish all men in the world did heartily believe so much of this as is true; it would very much help to do the work of God.

Thus, my Lord, I have made bold by your hand to reach out this little scroll of cautions to all those, who, by seeing your honoured name set before my book, shall, by the fairness of such a frontispiece, be invited to look into it. I must confess it cannot but look like a design in me, to borrow your name and beg your patronage to my book, that, if there be no other worth in it, yet at least it may have the splendour and warmth of a burning-glass, which, borrowing a flame from the eye of heaven, shines and burns by the rays of the sun its patron. I will not quit myself from the suspicion, for I cannot pretend it to be a present either of itself fit to be offered to such a personage, or any part of a just return; but I humbly desire you would own it for an acknowledgment of those great endearments and noblest usages you have past upon me; but so men in their religion give a piece of gum, or the fat of a cheap lamb, in sacrifice to Him that gives them all that they have or need; and unless He, who was pleased to employ your Lordship as a great minister of his providence, in making a promise of his good to me, the meanest of his servants, "that he would never leave me nor forsake me," shall enable me, by greater services of religion, to pay my great debt to your honour, I must still increase my score; since I shall now spend as much in my needs of pardon for this boldness, as in the reception of those favours by which I stand accountable to your Lordship in all the bands of service and gratitude; though I am, in the deepest sense of duty and affection,

My most honoured Lord,
Your Honour's most obliged
And most humble Servant,
JER. TAYLOR.

THE

RULE AND EXERCISES

OF

HOLY LIVING, &c.

CHAPTER I.

CONSIDERATION OF THE GENERAL INSTRUMENTS AND MEANS SERVING
TO A HOLY LIFE, BY WAY OF INTRODUCTION.

IT is necessary that every man should consider, that, since God
hath given him an excellent nature, wisdom and choice, an
understanding soul, and an immortal spirit; having made him
lord over the beasts, and but a little lower than the angels;
he hath also appointed for him a work and a service great
enough to employ those abilities, and hath also designed him
to a state of life after this, to which he can only arrive by that
service and obedience. And therefore, as every man is wholly
God's own portion by the title of creation, so all our labours
and care, all our powers and faculties, must be wholly employed
in the service of God, and even all the days of our life ; that,
this life being ended, we may live with him for ever.

Neither is it sufficient that we think of the service of God
as a work of the least necessity, or of small employment, but
that it be done by us as God intended it ; and that it be done
with great earnestness and passion, with much zeal and desire ; that we refuse no labour ; that we bestow upon it much
time ; that we use the best guides, and arrive at the end of
glory by all the ways of grace, of prudence, and religion.

And, indeed, if we consider how much of our lives is taken
up by the needs of nature ; how many years are wholly spent,
before we come to any use of reason ; how many years more,
before that reason is useful to us to any great purposes ; how
imperfect our discourse is made by our evil education, false

B

principles, ill company, bad examples, and want of experience ;
how many parts of our wisest and best years are spent in eating and sleeping, in necessary businesses and unnecessary vanities, in worldly civilities and less useful circumstances, in the
learning arts and sciences, languages, or trades ; that little
portion of hours that is left for the practices of piety and religious walking with God, is so short and trifling, that, were
not the goodness of God infinitely great, it might seem unreasonable or impossible for us to expect of him eternal joys
in heaven, even after the well spending those few minutes
which are left for God and God's service, after we have
served ourselves and our own occasions.

And yet it is considerable, that the fruit which comes from
the many days of recreation and vanity is very little ; and,
although we scatter much, yet we gather but little profit : but
from the few hours we spend in prayer and the exercises of a
pious life, the return is great and profitable ; and what we sow
in the minutes and spare portions of a few years, grows up to
crowns and sceptres in a happy and a glorious eternity.

1. Therefore, although it cannot be enjoined, that the
greatest part of our time be spent in the direct actions of devotion and religion, yet it will become, not only a duty, but
also a great providence, to lay aside, for the services of God
and the businesses of the Spirit, as much as we can ; because
God rewards our minutes with long and eternal happiness ;
and the greater portion of our time we give to God, the more
we treasure up for ourselves ; and "no man is a better merchant than he that lays out his time upon God, and his money
upon the poor."

2. Only it becomes us to remember, and to adore God's
goodness for it, that God hath not only permitted us to serve
the necessities of our nature, but hath made them to become
parts of our duty ; that if we, by directing these actions to
the glory of God, intend them as instruments to continue our
persons in his service, he, by adopting them into religion, may
turn our nature into grace, and accept our natural actions as
actions of religion.   God is pleased to esteem it for a part of
his service,[1] if we eat or drink ; so it be done temperately,

---

[1] Πυθομένου τινὸς, πῶς ἐστὶν ἐσθίειν ἀρεστῶς θεοῖς ; εἰ δικαίως ἐστὶν,
ἔφη, καὶ εὐγνωμόνως, καὶ ἴσως, καὶ ἐγκρατῶς, καὶ κοσμίως, οὐκ ἔστι καὶ
ἀρεστῶς τοῖς θεοῖς.—Arrian, Epict. l. i. c. 13.

and as may best preserve our health, that our health may enable our services towards him: and there is no one minute of our lives, (after we are come to the use of reason,) but we are or may be doing the work of God, even then when we most of all serve ourselves.

3. To which if we add, that in these and all other actions of our lives we always stand before God, acting, and speaking, and thinking in his presence, and that it matters not that our conscience is sealed with secrecy, since it lies open to God; it will concern us to behave ourselves carefully, as in the presence of our Judge.

These three considerations, rightly managed, and applied to the several parts and instances of our lives, will be like Elisha stretched upon the child, apt to put life and quickness into every part of it, and to make us live the life of grace, and do the work of God.

I shall, therefore, by way of introduction, reduce these three to practice, and show how every Christian may improve all and each of these to the advantage of piety, in the whole course of his life; that if he please to bear but one of them upon his spirit, he may feel the benefit, like an universal instrument, helpful in all spiritual and temporal actions.

SECT. I. *The first general Instrument of Holy Living, Care of our Time.*

HE that is choice of his time will also be choice of his company, and choice of his actions; lest the first engage him in vanity and loss; and the latter, by being criminal, be a throwing his time and himself away, and a going back in the accounts of eternity.

God hath given to man a short time here upon earth, and yet upon this short time eternity depends; but so, that for every hour of our life (after we are persons capable of laws, and know good from evil) we must give account to the great Judge of men and angels. And this is it which our blessed Saviour told us, that we must account for every idle word; not meaning, that every word which is not designed to edification, or is less prudent, shall be reckoned for a sin; but that the time which we spend in our idle talking and unprofitable discoursings, that time which might and ought to have been employed to spiritual and useful purposes, that is to be accounted for.

B 2

For we must remember, that we have a great work to do, many enemies to conquer, many evils to prevent, much danger to run through, many difficulties to be mastered, many necessities to serve, and much good to do; many children to provide for, or many friends to support, or many poor to relieve, or many diseases to cure; besides the needs of nature and of relation, our private and our public cares, and duties of the world, which necessity and the providence of God have adopted into the family of Religion.

And that we need not fear this instrument to be a snare to us, or that the duty must end in scruple, vexation, and eternal fears, we must remember, that the life of every man may be so ordered (and indeed must) that it may be a perpetual serving of God: the greatest trouble and most busy trade and worldly encumbrances, when they are necessary, or charitable, or profitable in order to any of those ends which we are bound to serve, whether public or private, being a doing God's work. For God provides the good things of the world to serve the needs of nature, by the labours of the ploughman, the skill and pains of the artisan, and the dangers and traffic of the merchant: these men are, in their calling, the ministers of the Divine Providence, and the stewards of the creation, and servants of a great family of God, the world, in the employment of procuring necessaries for food and clothing, ornament, and physic. In their proportions, also, a king, and a priest, and a prophet, a judge, and an advocate, doing the works of their employment according to their proper rules, are doing the work of God; because they serve those necessities which God hath made, and yet made no provisions for them but by their ministry. So that no man can complain that his calling takes him off from religion; his calling itself, and his very worldly employment in honest trades and offices, is a serving of God; and, if it be moderately pursued, and according to the rules of Christian prudence, will leave void spaces enough for prayers and retirements of a more spiritual religion.

God hath given every man work enough to do, that there shall be no room for idleness; and yet hath so ordered the world, that there shall be space for devotion. He that hath the fewest businesses of the world is called upon to spend more time in the dressing of his soul; and he that hath the most affairs may so order them that they shall be a service of

God; whilst at certain periods, they are blessed with prayers and actions of religion, and all day long are hallowed by a holy intention.

However, so long as idleness is quite shut out from our lives, all the sins of wantonness, softness, and effeminacy are prevented, and there is but little room left for temptation; and, therefore, to a busy man temptation is fain to climb up together with his businesses, and sins creep upon him only by accidents and occasions; whereas to an idle person they come in a full body, and with open violence, and the impudence of a restless importunity.

Idleness is called "the sin of Sodom and her daughters,"[2] and indeed is "the burial of a living man;"[3] an idle person being so useless to any purposes of God and man, that he is like one that is dead, unconcerned in the changes and necessities of the world; and he only lives to spend his time, and eat the fruits of the earth: like a vermin or a wolf, when their time comes they die and perish, and in the mean time do no good; they neither plough nor carry burdens; all that they do either is unprofitable or mischievous.

Idleness is the greatest prodigality in the world; it throws away that which is invaluable in respect of its present use, and irreparable when it is past, being to be recovered by no power of art or nature. But the way to secure and improve our time we may practise in the following Rules.

Rules for employing our Time.

1. In the morning, when you awake, accustom yourself to think first upon God, or something in order to his service; and at night also, let him close thine eyes: and let your sleep be necessary and healthful, not idle and expensive of time, beyond the needs and conveniences of nature; and sometimes be curious to see the preparation which the sun makes, when he is coming forth from his chambers of the east.

2. Let every man that hath a calling be diligent in pursuance of its employment, so as not lightly or without reasonable occasion to neglect it in any of those times which are usually, and by the custom of prudent persons and good husbands, employed in it.

3. Let all the intervals or void space of time be employed

<hr>

[2] Ezek. xvi. 49   [3] Senec.

in prayers, reading, meditating, works of nature, recreation, charity, friendliness and neighbourhood, and means of spiritual and corporal health; ever remembering so to work in our calling, as not to neglect the work of our high calling; but to begin and end the day with God, with such forms of devotion as shall be proper to our necessities.

4. The resting days of Christians, and festivals of the church, must, in no sense, be days of idleness; for it is better to plough upon holy days, than to do nothing or to do viciously: but let them be spent in the works of the day, that is, of religion and charity, according to the rules appointed.[4]

5. Avoid the company of drunkards and busy-bodies, and all such as are apt to talk much to little purpose; for no man can be provident of his time that is not prudent in the choice of his company; and if one of the speakers be vain, tedious, and trifling, he that hears, and he that answers, in the discourse, are equal losers of their time.

6. Never walk with any man, or undertake any trifling employment, merely to pass the time away;[5] for every day well spent may become a "day of salvation," and time rightly employed is an "acceptable time." And remember, that the time thou triflest away was given thee to repent in, to pray for pardon of sins, to work out thy salvation, to do the work of grace, to lay up against the day of judgment a treasure of good works, that thy time may be crowned with eternity.

7. In the midst of the works of thy calling, often retire to God[6] in short prayers and ejaculations; and those may make up the want of those larger portions of time, which, it may be, thou desirest for devotion, and in which thou thinkest other persons have advantage of thee; for so thou reconcilest the outward work and thy inward calling, the church and the commonwealth, the employment of the body and the interest of thy soul: for be sure that God is present at thy breathings and hearty sighings of prayer, as soon as at the longer offices of less busied persons; and thy time is as truly sanctified by a trade, and devout though shorter prayers, as by the longer offices of those whose time is not filled up with labour and useful business.

[4] See Chap. iv. Sect. 6.   [5] S. Bern. de Triplici Custodia.
[6] Laudatur Cæsar apud Lucanum,
—— media inter prælia semper
Stellarum cœlique plagis, superisque vacavi.—x. 186.

8. Let your employment be such as may become a reasonable person; and not be a business fit for children or distracted people, but fit for your age and understanding. For a man may be very idly busy, and take great pains to so little purpose, that, in his labours and expense of time, he shall serve no end but of folly and vanity. There are some trades that wholly serve the ends of idle persons and fools, and such as are fit to be seized upon by the severity of laws and banished from under the sun; and there are some people who are busy, but it is, as Domitian was, in catching flies.

9. Let your employment be fitted to your person and calling. Some there are that employ their time in affairs infinitely below the dignity of their person; and, being called by God or by the republic to help to bear great burdens, and to judge a people, do enfeeble their understandings and disable their persons by sordid and brutish business. Thus Nero went up and down Greece, and challenged the fiddlers at their trade. Aeropus, a Macedonian king, made lanterns. Harcatius, the king of Parthia, was a mole-catcher: and Biantes, the Lydian, filed needles. He that is appointed to minister in holy things must not suffer secular affairs and sordid arts to eat up great portions of his employment: a clergyman must not keep a tavern, nor a judge be an innkeeper: and it was a great idleness in Theophylact, the patriarch of C. P., to spend his time in his stable of horses, when he should have been in his study, or the pulpit, or saying his holy offices. Such employments are the diseases of labour, and the rust of time, which it contracts, not by lying still, but by dirty employment.

10. Let our employment be such as becomes a Christian; that is, in no sense mingled with sin : for he that takes pains to serve the ends of covetousness, or ministers to another's lust, or keeps a shop of impurities or intemperance, is idle in the worst sense : for every hour so spent runs him backward, and must be spent again in the remaining and shorter part of his life, and spent better.

11. Persons of great quality, and of no trade, are to be most prudent and curious in their employment and traffic of time. They are miserable, if their education hath been so loose and undisciplined as to leave them unfurnished of skill to spend their time: but most miserable are they, if such misgovernment and unskilfulness make them fall into vicious and baser

company, and drive on their time by the sad minutes and periods of sin and death.   They that are learned know the worth
of time, and the manner how well to improve a day; and they
are to prepare themselves for such purposes, in which they
may be most useful in order to arts or arms, to counsel in public, or government in their country; but for others of them,
that are unlearned, let them choose good company, such as may
not tempt them to a vice, or join with them in any; but that
may supply their defects by counsel and discourse, by way of
conduct and conversation.   Let them learn easy and useful
things, read history and the laws of the land, learn the customs of their country, the condition of their own estate, profitable and charitable contrivances of it: let them study prudently to govern their families, learn the burdens of their
tenants, the necessities of their neighbours, and in their proportion supply them, and reconcile their enmities, and prevent their lawsuits, or quickly end them; and in this glut of
leisure and disemployment, let them set apart greater portions
of their time for religion and the necessities of their souls.

12. Let the women of noble birth and great fortunes do the
same things in their proportions and capacities; nurse their
children, look to the affairs of the house, visit poor cottages,
and relieve their necessities; be courteous to the neighbourhood, learn in silence of their husbands or their spiritual
guides, read good books, pray often and speak little, and
"learn to do good works for necessary uses;" for by that
phrase St. Paul expresses the obligation of Christian women
to good housewifery, and charitable provisions for their family
and neighbourhood.

13. Let all persons of all conditions avoid all delicacy and
niceness in their clothing or diet, because such softness engages
them upon great misspendings of their time, while they dress
and comb out all their opportunities of their morning devotion, and half the day's severity, and sleep out the care and
provision for their souls.

14. Let every one of every condition avoid curiosity, and all
inquiry into things that concern them not.   For all business
in things that concern us not, is an employing our time to no
good of ours, and therefore not in order to a happy eternity.
In this account our neighbours' necessities are not to be reckoned; for they concern us, as one member is concerned in the

grief of another: but going from house to house, tattlers and busy-bodies, which are the canker and rust of idleness, as idleness is the rust of time, are reproved by the apostle in severe language, and forbidden in order to this exercise.

15. As much as may be, cut off all impertinent and useless employments of your life, unnecessary and fantastic visits, long waitings upon great personages, where neither duty, nor necessity, nor charity obliges us; all vain meetings, all laborious trifles, and whatsoever spends much time to no real, civil, religious, or charitable purpose.

16. Let not your recreations be lavish spenders of your time; but choose such which are healthful, short, transient, recreative, and apt to refresh you; but at no hand dwell upon them, or make them your great employment; for he that spends his time in sports, and calls it recreation, is like him whose garment is all made of fringes, and his meat nothing but sauces; they are healthless, chargeable, and useless. And therefore avoid such games which require much time or long attendance, or which are apt to steal thy affections from more severe employments. For to whatsoever thou hast given thy affections, thou wilt not grudge to give thy time. Natural necessity, and the example of St. John, who recreated himself with sporting with a tame partridge,[7] teach us that it is lawful to relax and unbend our bow, but not to suffer it to be unready or unstrung.

17. Set apart some portions of every day for more solemn devotion and religious employment, which be severe in observing: and if variety of employment, or prudent affairs, or civil society, press upon you, yet so order thy rule, that the necessary parts of it be not omitted; and though just occasions may make our prayers shorter, yet let nothing but a violent, sudden, and impatient necessity make thee, upon any one day, wholly to omit thy morning and evening devotions; which, if you be forced to make very short, you may supply and lengthen with ejaculations and short retirements in the day-time, in the midst of your employment or of your company.

18. Do not the "work of God negligently"[8] and idly: let not thy heart be upon the world when thy hand is lifted up in prayer; and be sure to prefer an action of religion, in its place and proper season, before all worldly pleasure, letting secular

[7] Cassian. Collat. 24. c. xxi.   [8] Jer. xlviii. 10.

things, that may be dispensed with in themselves, in these
circumstances wait upon the other: not like the patriarch,
who ran from the altar in St. Sophia to his stable, in all his
pontificals, and in the midst of his office, to see a colt newly
fallen from his beloved and much-valued mare Phorbante.
More prudent and severe was that of Sir Thomas More, who,
being sent for by the king when he was at his prayers in public, returned answer he would attend him when he had first
performed his service to the King of kings. And it did honour
to Rusticus,[9] that, when letters from Cæsar were given to
him, he refused to open them till the philosopher had done
his lecture. In honouring God and doing his work, put forth
all thy strength; for of that time only thou mayest be most
confident that it is gained, which is prudently and zealously
spent in God's service.

19. When the clock strikes, or however else you shall measure the day, it is good to say a short ejaculation every hour,
that the parts and returns of devotion may be the measure of
your time: and do so also in all the breaches of thy sleep;
that those spaces which have in them no direct business of
the world, may be filled with religion.

20. If, by thus doing, you have not secured your time by
an early and fore-handed care, yet be sure by a timely diligence
to redeem the time; that is, to be pious and religious in such
instances[10] in which formerly you have sinned, and to bestow
your time especially upon such graces, the contrary whereof
you have formerly practised, doing actions of chastity and
temperance with as great a zeal and earnestness as you did
once act your uncleanness; and then, by all arts, to watch
against your present and future dangers, from day to day securing your standing: this is properly to redeem your time,
that is, to buy your security of it at the rate of any labour
and honest arts.

21. Let him that is most busied set apart some "solemn
time every year,"[11] in which, for the time, quitting all worldly
business, he may attend wholly to fasting and prayer, and the
dressing of his soul by confessions, meditations, and attend

<hr>

[9] Plutarch. de Curiosit. c. xv.
[10] Οἱ ἐν αὐτοῖς εὐδοκιμοῦντες, οἷς ἥμαρτον, εὐπρεπεστέραν τὴν ἀπωλο
γίαν εἰσαεὶ φέρονται.—Procop. 2. Vandal.
[11] 1 Cor. vii. 5.

ances upon God; that he may make up his accounts, renew his vows, make amends for his carelessness, and retire back again, from whence levity and the vanities of the world, or the opportunity of temptations, or the distraction of secular affairs, have carried him.

22. In this we shall be much assisted, and we shall find the work more easy, if, before we sleep, every night,[12] we examine the actions of the past day with a particular scrutiny, if there have been any accident extraordinary; as long discourse, a feast, much business, variety of company. If nothing but common hath happened, the less examination will suffice; only let us take care that we sleep not without such a recollection of the actions of the day, as may represent any thing that is remarkable and great, either to be the matter of sorrow or thanksgiving: for other things a general care is proportionable.

23. Let all these things be done prudently and moderately, not with scruple and vexation. For these are good advantages, but the particulars are not Divine commandments; and, therefore, are to be used as shall be found expedient to every one's condition. For, provided that our duty be secured, for the degrees and for the instruments every man is permitted to himself, and the conduct of such who shall be appointed to him. He is happy that can secure every hour to a sober or a pious employment: but the duty consists not scrupulously in minutes and half-hours, but in greater portions of time; provided that no minute be employed in sin, and the greater portions of our time be spent in sober employment, and all the appointed days, and some portions of every day, be allowed for religion. In all the lesser parts of time, we are left to our own elections and prudent management, and to the consideration of the great degrees and differences of glory that are laid up in heaven for us, according to the degrees of our care, and piety, and diligence.

The Benefits of this Exercise.

This exercise, besides that it hath influence upon our whole lives, it hath a special efficacy for the preventing of, 1. beggarly sins: that is, those sins which idleness and beggary

---

[12] Μηδ' ὕπνον μαλακοῖσιν ἐπ' ὄμμασι προσδέξασθαι, Πρὶν τῶν ἡμερινῶν ἔργων τρὶς ἕκαστον ἐπελθεῖν· Πῇ παρέβην; τί δ' ἔρεξα; τί μοι δέον οὐκ 'τελέσθη;—Pythagor. Aur. Carm.

usually betray men to; such as are lying, flattery, stealing, and dissimulation.   2. It is a proper antidote against carnal sins, and such as proceed from fulness of bread and emptiness of employment.   3. It is a great instrument of preventing the smallest sins and irregularities of our life, which usually creep upon idle, disemployed, and curious persons.   4. It not only teaches us to avoid evil, but engages us upon doing good, as the proper business of all our days.   5. It prepares us so against sudden changes, that we shall not easily be surprised at the sudden coming of the day of the Lord: for he that is curious of his time will not easily be unready and unfurnished.

SECT. II. *The general Instrument of Holy Living, Purity of Intention.*

THAT we should intend and design God's glory in every action we do, whether it be natural or chosen, is expressed by St. Paul,[1] " Whether ye eat or drink, do all to the glory of God." Which rule when we observe, every action of nature becomes religious, and every meal is an act of worship, and shall have its reward in its proportion, as well as an act of prayer. Blessed be that goodness and grace of God, which, out of infinite desire to glorify and save mankind, would make the very works of nature capable of becoming acts of virtue, that all our lifetime we may do him service.

This grace is so excellent that it sanctifies the most common action of our life; and yet so necessary that, without it, the very best actions of our devotion are imperfect and vicious. For he that prays out of custom, or gives alms for praise, or fasts to be accounted religious, is but a Pharisee in his devotion, and a beggar in his alms, and a hypocrite in his fast. But a holy end sanctifies all these and all other actions which can be made holy, and gives distinction to them, and procures acceptance.

For as to know the end distinguishes a man from a beast, so to choose a good end distinguishes him from an evil man. Hezekiah repeated his good deeds upon his sick-bed, and obtained favour of God, but the Pharisee was accounted insolent for doing[2] the same thing: because this man did it to upbraid

---

[1] 1 Cor. x. 31.

[2] Atticus, eximie si cœnat, lautus habetur;
 Si Rutilus, demens.   Juven. Sat. 11.

his brother, the other to obtain a mercy of God. Zacharias questioned with the angel about his message, and was made speechless for his incredulity; but the blessed Virgin Mary questioned too, and was blameless; for she did it to inquire after the manner of the thing, but he did not believe the thing itself: he doubted of God's power, or the truth of the messenger; but she, only of her own incapacity. This was it which distinguished the mourning of David from the exclamation of Saul; the confession of Pharaoh from that of Manasses; the tears of Peter from the repentance of Judas: "for the praise is not in the deed done, but in the manner of its doing.[3] If a man visits his sick friend, and watches at his pillow for charity's sake, and because of his old affection, we approve it; but if he does it in hope of legacy, he is a vulture, and only watches for the carcass. The same things are honest and dishonest: the manner of doing them, and the end of the design, makes the separation."

Holy intention is to the actions of a man that which the soul is to the body, or form to its matter, or the root to the tree, or the sun to the world, or the fountain to a river, or the base to a pillar: for without these the body is a dead trunk, the matter is sluggish, the tree is a block, the world is darkness, the river is quickly dry, the pillar rushes into flatness and a ruin; and the action is sinful, or unprofitable and vain. The poor farmer that gave a dish of cold water to Artaxerxes was rewarded with a golden goblet; and he that gives the same to a disciple in the name of a disciple, shall have a crown: but if he gives water in despite, when the disciple needs wine or a cordial, his reward shall be to want that water to cool his tongue.

But this duty must be reduced to rules :—

Rules for our Intentions.

1. In every action reflect upon the end; and in your undertaking it, consider why you do it, and what you propound to yourself for a reward, and to your action as its end.

2. Begin every action in the name of the Father, of the Son, and of the Holy Ghost; the meaning of which is, 1. that we be careful that we do not the action without the permission or warrant of God: 2. that we design it to the glory of God, if not in the direct action, yet at least in its consequence; if not

* Seneca.

in the particular, yet at least in the whole order of things and
accidents: 3. that it may be so blessed, that what you intend
for innocent and holy purposes may not by any chance, or
abuse or misunderstanding of men, be turned into evil, or made
the occasion of sin.

3. Let every action of concernment be begun with prayer,
that God would not only bless the action, but sanctify your
purpose; and make an oblation of the action to God: holy and
well-intended actions being the best oblations and presents we
can make to God; and, when God is entitled to them, he will
the rather keep the fire upon the altar bright and shining.

4. In the prosecution of the action, renew and re-enkindl
your purpose by short ejaculations to these purposes: "Not
unto us, O Lord, not unto us, but unto thy name let all praise
be given:" and consider, "Now I am working the work of
God; I am his servant, I am in a happy employment, I am
doing my Master's business, I am not at my own dispose, I am
using his talents, and all the gain must be his:" for then be
sure, as the glory is his, so the reward shall be thine. If thou
bringest his goods home with increase, he will make thee ruler
over cities.

5. Have a care that, while the altar thus sends up a holy
fume, thou dost not suffer the birds to come and carry away the
sacrifice: that is, let not that which began well, and was intended for God's glory, decline and end in thy own praise, or
temporal satisfaction, or a sin. A story told to represent the
vileness of unchastity, is well begun; but if thy female auditor
be pleased with thy language, and begins rather to like thy
person for thy story than to dislike the crime, be watchful lest
this goodly head of gold descend in silver and brass, and end
in iron and clay, like Nebuchadnezzar's image; for from the
end it shall have its name and reward.[4]

6. If any accidental event, which was not first intended by
thee, can come to pass, let it not be taken into thy purposes, nor
at all be made use of; as if, by telling a true story, you can do
an ill turn to your enemy, by no means do it; but when the
temptation is found out, turn all thy enmity upon that.

7. In every more solemn action of religion join together
many good ends, that the consideration of them may entertain
all your affections; and that, when any one ceases, the purity

[4] Qui furatur ut mœchetur, mœchus est magis quam fur.—Arist. Eth.

of your intention may be supported by another supply. He
that fasts only to tame a rebellious body, when he is provided
of a remedy either in grace or nature, may be tempted to leave
off fasting.   But he that in his fast intends the mortification
of every unruly appetite, and accustoming himself to bear the
yoke of the Lord, a contempt of the pleasures of meat and
drink, humiliation of all wilder thoughts, obedience and humility, austerity and charity, and the convenience and assistance to devotion, and to do an act of repentance; whatever
happens, will have reason enough to make him to continue his
purpose, and to sanctify it.   And certain it is, the more good
ends are designed in an action, the more degrees of excellency
the man obtains.

8. If any temptation to spoil your purpose happens in a religious duty, do not presently omit the action, but rather strive
to rectify your intention, and to mortify the temptation.   St.
Bernard taught us this rule : for when the devil, observing him
to preach excellently and to do much benefit to his hearers,
tempted him to vain-glory, hoping that the good man, to avoid
that, would cease preaching, he gave this answer only, "I neither began for thee, neither for thee will I make an end."

9. In all actions which are of long continuance, deliberation, and abode, let your holy and pious intention be actual ;
that is, that it be, by a special prayer or action, by a peculiar
act of resignation or oblation, given to God : but in smaller
actions, and little things and indifferent, fail not to secure a
pious habitual intention ; that is, that it be included within
your general care, that no action have an ill end ; and that it
be comprehended in your general prayers, whereby you offer
yourself and all you do to God's glory.

10. Call not every temporal end a defiling of thy intention,
but only, 1. when it contradicts any of the ends of God; or, 2.
when it is principally intended in an action of religion.   For
sometimes a temporal end is part of our duty ; and such are
all the actions of our calling, whether our employment be religious or civil.   We are commanded to provide for our family:
but if the minister of divine offices shall take upon him that
holy calling for covetous or ambitious ends, or shall not design
the glory of God principally and especially, he hath polluted
his hands and his heart ; and the fire of the altar is quenched,
or it sends forth nothing but the smoke of mushrooms or un-

pleasant gums. And it is a great unworthiness to prefer the interest of a creature before the ends of God the Almighty Creator.

But because many cases may happen in which a man's heart may deceive him, and he may not well know what is in his own spirit; therefore by these following signs we shall best make a judgment whether our intentions be pure and our purposes holy.

Signs of Purity of Intention.

1. It is probable our hearts[5] are right with God, and our intentions innocent and pious, if we set upon actions of religion or civil life with an affection proportionate to the quality of the work; that we act our temporal affairs with a desire no greater than our necessity; and that, in actions of religion, we be zealous, active, and operative, so far as prudence will permit; but, in all cases, that we value a religious design before a temporal, when otherwise they are in equal order to their several ends: that is, that whatsoever is necessary in order to our soul's health be higher esteemed than what is for bodily; and the necessities, the indispensable necessities of the spirit, be served before the needs of nature, when they are required in their several circumstances; or plainer yet, when we choose any temporal inconvenience rather than commit a sin, and when we choose to do a duty rather than to get gain. But he that does his recreation or his merchandise cheerfully, promptly, readily, and busily, and the works of religion slowly, flatly, and without appetite, and the spirit moves like Pharaoh's chariots when the wheels were off; it is a sign that his heart is not right with God, but it cleaves too much to the world.

2. It is likely our hearts are pure and our intentions spotless, when we are not solicitous of the opinion and censures of men; but only that we do our duty, and be accepted of God. For our eyes will certainly be fixed there from whence we expect our reward: and if we desire that God should approve us, it is a sign we do his work, and expect him our paymaster.

3. He that does as well in private, between God and his own soul, as in public, in pulpits, in theatres, and market-places, hath given himself a good testimony that his purposes are full of honesty, nobleness, and integrity. For what Helkanah said to the mother of Samuel, "Am not I better to thee

* See Sect. I. of this Chapter, Rule 18.

than ten sons ?" is most certainly verified concerning God ; that he, who is to be our judge, is better than ten thousand witnesses. But he that would have his virtue published studies, not virtue, but glory. "He is not just[6] that will not be just without praise : but he is a righteous man that does justice, when to do so is made infamous ; and he is a wise man who is delighted with an ill name that is well gotten." And indeed that man hath a strange[7] covetousness, or folly, that is not contented with this reward, that he hath pleased God. And see what he gets by it. He that does good works[8] for praise or secular ends, sells an inestimable jewel for a trifle ; and that which would purchase heaven for him he parts with for the breath of the people ; which at best is but air, and that not often wholesome.

4. It is well, also, when we are not solicitous or troubled concerning the effect and event of all our actions ; but that being first by prayer recommended to him is left at his dispose : for then, in case the event be not answerable to our desires, or to the efficacy of the instrument, we have nothing left to rest in but the honesty of our purposes ; which it is the more likely we have secured, by how much more we are indifferent concerning the success. St. James converted but eight persons, when he preached in Spain ; and our blessed Saviour converted fewer than his own disciples did : and if thy labours prove unprosperous, if thou beest much troubled at that, it is certain thou didst not think thyself secure of a reward for thine intention ; which thou mightest have done, if it had been pure and just.

5. He loves virtue for God's sake and its own that loves and honours it wherever it is to be seen ; but he that is envious or angry at a virtue that is not his own, at the perfection or excellency of his neighbour, is not covetous of the virtue, but of its reward and reputation ; and then his intentions are polluted. It was a great ingenuity in Moses that wished all the people might be prophets ; but if he had designed his own honour, he would have prophesied alone. But he that desires only that the work of God and religion shall go on, is pleased with it, whosoever is the instrument.

6. He that despises the world, and all its appendant vani-

---

[6] Seneca, Ep. 113.   [7] St. Chrys. l. ii. de Compun. Cordia.
[8] St. Greg. Moral. 8, cap. xxv.

c

ties, is the best judge, and the most secured of his intentions: because he is the furthest removed from a temptation. Every degree of mortification is a testimony of the purity of our purposes; and in what degree we despise sensual pleasure, or secular honours, or worldly reputation, in the same degree we shall conclude our heart right to religion and spiritual designs.

7. When we are not solicitous concerning the instruments and means of our actions, but use those means which God hath laid before us, with resignation, indifferency, and thankfulness; it is a good sign that we are rather intent upon the end of God's glory than our own conveniency, or temporal satisfaction. He that is indifferent whether he serve God in riches or in poverty, is rather a seeker of God than of himself; and he that will throw away a good book because it is not curiously gilded, is more curious to please his eye than to inform his understanding.

8. When a temporal end consisting with a spiritual, and pretended to be subordinate to it, happens to fail and be defeated, if we can rejoice in that, so God's glory may be secured, and the interests of religion, it is a great sign our hearts are right, and our ends prudently designed and ordered.

When our intentions are thus balanced, regulated, and discerned, we may consider, 1. That this exercise is of so universal efficacy in the whole course of a holy life, that it is like the soul to every holy action, and must be provided for in every undertaking; and is of itself alone sufficient to make all natural and indifferent actions to be adopted into the family of religion.

2. That there are some actions, which are usually reckoned as parts of our religion, which yet, of themselves, are so relative and imperfect, that without the purity of intention they degenerate: and unless they be directed and proceed on to those purposes which God designed them to, they return into the family of common, secular, or sinful actions. Thus, alms are for charity, fasting for temperance, prayer is for religion, humiliation is for humility, austerity or sufferance is in order to the virtue of patience: and when these actions fail of their several ends, or are not directed to their own purposes, alms are misspent, fasting is an impertinent trouble, prayer is but lip-labour, humiliation is but hypocrisy, sufferance is but vexation; for such were the alms of the Pharisee, the fast of Jezebel, the prayer of Judah reproved by the prophet Isaiah, the

humiliation of Ahab, the martyrdom of heretics ; in which nothing is given to God but the body, or the forms of religion ;
but the soul and the power of godliness is wholly wanting.

3. We are to consider that no intention can sanctify an unholy or unlawful action.   Saul, the king, disobeyed God's
commandment, and spared the cattle of Amalek to reserve the
best for sacrifice ; and Saul, the Pharisee, persecuted the church
of God, with a design to do God service ; and they that killed
the apostles had also good purposes, but they had unhallowed
actions.   When there is both truth in election, and charity in
the intention ;[9] when we go to God in ways of his own choosing or approving, then our eye is single, and our hands are
clean, and our hearts are pure.   But when a man does evil
that good may come of it, or good to an evil purpose, that
man does like him that rolls himself in thorns that he may
sleep easily ; he roasts himself in the fire that he may quench
his thirst with own sweat ; he turns his face to the east that
he may go to bed with the sun.   I end this with the saying of
a wise heathen :[10] " He is to be called evil that is good only for
his own sake.   Regard not how full hands you bring to God,
but how pure.   Many cease from sin out of fear alone, not
out of innocence or love of virtue ;" and they, as yet, are not to
be called innocent, but timorous.

SECT. III. *The third general Instrument of Holy Living ; or
the Practice of the Presence of God.*

THAT God is present in all places, that he sees every action,
hears all discourses, and understands every thought, is no
strange thing to a Christian ear who hath been taught this
doctrine, not only by right reason and the consent of all the
wise men in the world, but also by God himself in Holy Scripture.   " Am I a God at hand, saith the Lord, and not a God
afar off ? Can any hide himself in secret places that I shall not
see him ? saith the Lord.   Do not I fill heaven and earth ?"[1]
" Neither is there any creature that is not manifest in his
sight ; but all things are naked and open to the eyes of him
with whom we have to do."[2] " For in him we live, and move,
and have our being."[3] God is wholly in every place ; included in no place ; not bound with cords except those of love ;

---

[9] St. Bern. lib. de Præcept.   [10] Publius Mimus.
[1] Jer. xxiii. 23, 24.   [2] Heb. iv. 13.   [3] Acts xvii. 28.

not divid·d into parts, not changeable into several shapes;
filling heaven and earth with his present power and with his
never absent nature. So St. Augustine[4] expresses this article.
So that we may imagine God to be as the air and the sea;
and we all enclosed in his circle, wrapped up in the lap of his
infinite nature; or as infants in the wombs of their pregnant
mothers : and we can no more be removed from the presence
of God than from our own being.

Several Manners of the Divine Presence.

The presence of God is understood by us in several manners, and to several purposes.

1. God is present by his essence ; which, because it is infinite, cannot be contained within the limits of any place; and
because he is of an essential purity and spiritual nature, he
cannot be undervalued by being supposed present in the places
of unnatural uncleanness ; because as the sun, reflecting upon
the mud of strands and shores, is unpolluted in its beams, so
is God not dishonoured when we suppose him in every of his
creatures, and in every part of every one of them ; and is still
as unmixt with any unhandsome adherence as is the soul in
the bowels of the body.

2. God is every where present by his power.[5] He rolls the
orbs of heaven with his hand ; he fixes the earth with his foot;
he guides all the creatures with his eye, and refreshes them
with his influence ; he makes the powers of hell to shake with
his terrors, and binds the devils with his word, and throws
them out with his command; and sends the angels on embassies
with his decrees; he hardens the joints of infants, and con-
firms the bones, when they are fashioned beneath secretly in
the earth. He it is that assists at the numerous productions
of fishes ; and there is not one hollowness in the bottom of the
sea, but he shows himself to be Lord of it by sustaining there
the creatures that come to dwell in it: and in the wilderness,
the bittern and the stork, the dragon and the satyr, the unicorn
and the elk, live upon his provisions, and revere his power,
and feel the force of his almightiness.

3. God is more specially present, in some places, by the
several and more special manifestations of himself to extraor-

---

[4] Lib. vii. de Civit. c. xxx.   [5] Θεὸς περιέχει τῇ βουλήσει τὸ πᾶν,
μείζων τοῦ παντὸς ὥσπερ τῇ οὐσίᾳ, οὕτως καὶ τῇ ἀξίᾳ.—Resp. ad Orthod.

dinary purposes. First, by glory. Thus, his seat is in heaven, because there he sits encircled with all the outward demonstrations of his glory, which he is pleased to show to all the inhabitants of those his inward and secret courts. And thus, they that " die in the Lord," may be properly said to be " gone to God ;" with whom although they were before, yet now they enter into his courts, into the secret of his tabernacle, into the retinue and splendour of his glory. That is called walking with God, but this is dwelling or being with him. " I desire to be dissolved and to be with Christ ;" so said St. Paul. But this manner of the Divine presence is reserved for the elect people of God, and for their portion in their country.

4. God is, by grace and benediction, specially present in holy places,[6] and in the solemn assemblies of his servants. If holy people meet in grots and dens of the earth, when persecution or a public necessity disturbs the public order, circumstance, and convenience, God fails not to come thither to them : but God is also, by the same or a greater reason, present there, where they meet ordinarily, by order, and public authority ; there God is present ordinarily, that is, at every such meeting. God will go out of his way to meet his saints, when themselves are forced out of their way of order by a sad necessity : but else, God's usual way is to be present in those places where his servants are appointed ordinarily[7] to meet. But his presence there signifies nothing but a readiness to hear their prayers, to bless their persons, to accept their offices, and to like even the circumstance of orderly and public meeting. For thither the prayers of consecration, the public authority separating it, and God's love of order, and the reasonable customs of religion, have in ordinary, and in a certain degree, fixed this manner of his presence ; and he loves to have it so.

5. God is especially present in the hearts of his people, by his Holy Spirit : and indeed the hearts of holy men are temples in the truth of things, and, in type and shadow, they are heaven itself. For God reigns in the hearts of his servants : there is his kingdom. The power of grace hath subdued all his enemies : there is his power. They serve him night and day, and give him thanks and praise : that is his glory. This is the religion and worship of God in the temple. The temple itself is the heart of man ; Christ is the High Priest, who from thence

[6] Matt. xviii. 20 ; Heb. x. 25.   [7] 1 Kings v. 9 ; Psal. cxxxviii. 1, 2.

sends up the incense of prayers, and joins them to his own intercession, and presents all together to his Father; and the
Holy Ghost, by his dwelling there, hath also consecrated it
into a temple;"[8] and God dwells in our hearts by faith, and
Christ by his Spirit, and the Spirit by his purities; so that we
are also cabinets of the mysterious Trinity; and what is this
short of heaven itself, but as infancy is short of manhood, and
letters of words? The same state of life it is, but not the same
age. It is heaven in a looking-glass, dark, but yet true, representing the beauties of the soul, and the graces of God,
and the images of his eternal glory, by the reality of a special
presence.

6. God is especially present in the consciences of all persons, good and bad, by way of testimony and judgment: that
is, he is there a remembrancer to call our actions to mind, a
witness to bring them to judgment, and a judge to acquit or
to condemn. And although this manner of presence is, in
this life, after the manner of this life, that is, imperfect, and
we forget many actions of our lives; yet the greatest changes
of our state of grace or sin, our most considerable actions, are
always present, like capital letters to an aged and dim eye:
and, at the day of judgment, God shall draw aside the cloud,
and manifest this manner of his presence more notoriously,
and make it appear that he was an observer of our very
thoughts, and that he only laid those things by, which, because we covered with dust and negligence, were not then
discerned. But when we are risen from our dust and imperfection, they all appear plain and legible.

Now, the consideration of this great truth is of a very
universal use in the whole course of the life of a Christian.
All the consequents and effects of it are universal. He that
remembers that God stands a witness and a judge, beholding
every secrecy, besides his impiety, must have put on impudence, if he be not much restrained in his temptation to sin.
"For the greatest part of sin is taken away,[9] if a man have a
witness of his conversation: and he is a great despiser of God
who sends a boy away, when he is going to commit fornication,
and yet will dare to do it though he knows God is present,
and cannot be sent off: as if the eye of a little boy were more
awful than the all-seeing eye of God. He is to be feared in

⁸ 1 Cor. iii. 16; 2 Cor. vi. 16.   ⁹ S. Aug. de verbis Dominicis, c. iii

public, he is to be feared in private: if you go forth, he spies you; if you go in, he sees you: when you light the candle, he observes you; when you put it out, then also God marks you. Be sure, that while you are in his sight, you behave yourself as becomes so holy a presence." But if you will sin, retire yourself wisely, and go where God cannot see; for no where else can you be safe. And certainly, if men would always actually consider, and really esteem this truth, that God is the great eye of the world, always watching over our actions, and an ever-open ear to hear all our words, and an unwearied arm ever lifted up to crush a sinner into ruin, it would be the readiest way in the world to make sin to cease from amongst the children of men, and for men to approach to the blessed estate of the saints in heaven who cannot sin, for they always walk in the presence and behold the face of God. This instrument is to be reduced to practice, according to the following rules.

Rules of exercising this consideration.

1. Let this actual thought often return, that God is omnipresent, filling every place; and say with David,[10] "Whither shall I go from thy spirit, or whither shall I flee from thy presence? If I ascend up into heaven, thou art there: if I make my bed in hell, thou art there," &c. This thought, by being frequent, will make an habitual dread and reverence towards God, and fear in all thy actions. For it is a great necessity and engagement to do unblamably, when we act before the Judge,[11] who is infallible in his sentence, all-knowing in his information, severe in his anger, powerful in his providence, and intolerable in his wrath and indignation.

2. In the beginning of actions of religion, make an act of adoration, that is, solemnly worship God, and place thyself in God's presence, and behold him with the eye of faith; and let thy desires actually fix on him, as the object of thy worship, and the reason of thy hope, and the fountain of thy blessing. For when thou hast placed thyself before him, and kneelest in his presence, it is most likely, all the following parts of thy devotion will be answerable to the wisdom of such an apprehension, and the glory of such a presence.

3. Let every thing you see represent to your spirit the pre-

---

[10] Psal. cxxxix. 7, 8.   [11] Boeth. 1. v. de Consol.

sence, the excellency, and the power of God; and let your conversation with the creatures lead you unto the Creator; for so shall your actions be done, more frequently, with an actual eye to God's presence, by your often seeing him in the glass of the creation. In the face of the sun you may see God's beauty; in the fire you may feel his heat warming; in the water, his gentleness to refresh you: he it is that comforts your spirit when you have taken cordials; it is the dew of heaven that makes your field give you bread; and the breasts of God are the bottles that minister drink to your necessities. This philosophy, which is obvious to every man's experience, is a good advantage to our piety; and, by this act of understanding, our wills are checked from violence and misdemeanour.

4. In your retirement, make frequent colloquies, or short discoursings, between God and thy own soul. "Seven times a day do I praise thee: and in the night season also I thought upon thee, while I was waking." So did David; and every act of complaint or thanksgiving, every act of rejoicing or of mourning, every petition and every return of the heart in these intercourses, is a going to God, an appearing in his presence, and a representing him present to thy spirit and to thy necessity. And this was long since by a spiritual person called, "a building to God a chapel in our heart." It reconciles Martha's employment with Mary's devotion, charity and religion, the necessities of our calling and the employments of devotion. For thus, in the midst of the works of your trade, you may retire into your chapel, your heart; and converse with God by frequent addresses and returns.

5. Represent and offer to God "acts of love and fear," which are the proper effects of this apprehension, and the proper exercise of this consideration. For, as God is every where present by his power, he calls for reverence and godly fear: as he is present to thee in all thy needs, and relieves them, he deserves thy love: and since, in every accident of our lives, we find one or other of these apparent, and in most things we see both, it is a proper and proportionate return, that, to every such demonstration of God, we express ourselves sensible of it, by admiring the Divine goodness, or trembling at his presence; ever obeying him because we love him, and ever obeying him because we fear to offend him. This is that which Enoch did, who thus "walked with God."

6. Let us remember that God is in us, and that we are in him: we are his workmanship, let us not deface it; we are in his presence, let us not pollute it by unholy and impure actions. God hath "also wrought all our works in us:"[12] and, because he rejoices in his own works, if we defile them, and make them unpleasant to him, we walk perversely with God, and he will walk crookedly towards us.

7. " God is in the bowels of thy brother;" refresh them, when he needs it, and then you give your alms in the presence of God, and to God; and he feels the relief which thou providest for thy brother.

8. God is in every place: suppose it therefore to be a church ; and that decency of deportment and piety of carriage which you are taught by religion, or by custom, or ·by civility and public manners, to use in churches, the same use in all places: with this difference only, that in churches let your deportment be religious in external forms and circumstances also; but there and every where let it be religious in abstaining from spiritual indecencies, and in readiness to do good actions ; that it may not be said of us, as God once complained of his people, " Why hath my beloved done wickedness in my house ?"[13]

9. God is in every creature: be cruel towards none, neither abuse any by intemperance. Remember, that the creatures, and every member of thy own body, is one of the lesser cabinets and receptacles of God. They are such which God hath blessed with his presence, hallowed by his touch, and separated from unholy use, by making them to belong to his dwelling.

10. He walks as in the presence of God that converses with him in frequent prayer and frequent communion ; that runs to him in all his necessities, that asks counsel of him in all his doubtings ; that opens all his wants to him; that weeps before him for his sins ; that asks remedy and support for his weakness ; that fears him as a judge ; reverences him as a lord ; obeys him as a father ; and loves him as a patron.

The Benefits of this Exercise.

The benefits of this consideration and exercise being universal upon all the parts of piety, I shall less need to specify any particulars; but yet, most properly, this exercise of considering the Divine presence is, 1. An excellent help to prayer,

[12] Isa. xxvi. 12.   [13] Jer. xi. 15. secund. vulg. edit.

producing in us reverence and awfulness to the Divine Majesty of God, and actual devotion in our offices.   2. It produces a confidence in God, and fearlessness of our enemies, patience in trouble, and hope of remedy ; since God is so nigh in all our sad accidents, he is a disposer of the hearts of men and the events of things, he proportions out our trials, and supplies us with remedy, and, where his rod strikes us, his staff supports us.   To which we may add this ; that God, who is always with us, is especially, by promise, with us in tribulation, to turn the misery into a mercy, and that our greatest trouble may become our advantage, by entitling us to a new manner of the Divine presence.   3. It is apt to produce joy and rejoicing in God, we being more apt to delight in the partners and witnesses of our conversation ; every degree of mutual abiding and conversing being a relation and an endearment : we are of the same household with God ; he is with us in our natural actions, to preserve us ; in our recreations, to restrain us ; in our public actions, to applaud or reprove us ; in our private, to observe us ; in our sleeps, to watch by us ; in our watchings, to refresh us : and if we walk with God in all his ways, as he walks with us in all ours, we shall find perpetual reasons to enable us to keep that rule of God, " Rejoice in the Lord always, and again I say rejoice."   And this puts me in mind of a saying of an old religious person,[14] " There is one way of overcoming our ghostly enemies ; spiritual mirth, and a perpetual bearing of God in our minds."   This effectively resists the devil, and suffers us to receive no hurt from him.   4. This exercise is apt, also, to enkindle holy desires of the enjoyment of God, because it produces joy, when we do enjoy him ; the same desires that a weak man hath for a defender ; the sick man, for a physician ; the poor, for a patron ; the child, for his father ; the espoused lover, for her betrothed.   5. From the same fountain are apt to issue humility of spirit, apprehensions of our great distance and our great needs, our daily wants and hourly supplies, admiration of God's unspeakable mercies : it is the cause of great modesty and decency in our actions ; it helps to recollection of mind, and restrains the scatterings and looseness of wandering thoughts ; it establishes the heart in good purposes, and leadeth on to perseverance ; it gains purity and perfection, (according to the saying of God to Abraham, " walk

[14] In Vita S. Anton.

before me and be perfect,") holy fear, and holy love, and indeed every thing that pertains to holy living: when we see ourselves placed in the eye of God, who sets us on work and will reward us plenteously, to serve him with an eye-service is very pleasing ; for he also sees the heart : and the want of this consideration was declared to be the cause why Israel sinned so grievously, " for they say, The Lord hath forsaken the earth, and the Lord seeth not :"[15] therefore " the land is full of blood, and the city full of perverseness."[16] What a child would do in the eye of his father, and a pupil before his tutor, and a wife in the presence of her husband, and a servant in the sight of his master, let us always do the same ; for we are made a spectacle to God, to angels, and to men ; we are always in the sight and presence of the all-seeing and almighty God, who also is to us a father and a guardian, a husband and a lord.

Prayers and Devotions, according to the religion and purposes of the foregoing considerations.

I.—*For grace to spend our time well.*

O eternal God, who from all eternity dost behold and love thy own glories and perfections infinite, and hast created me to do the work of God after the manner of men, and to serve thee in this generation and according to my capacities ; give me thy grace that I may be a curious and prudent spender of my time, so as I may best prevent or resist all temptation, and be profitable to the Christian commonwealth, and, by discharging all my duty, may glorify thy name.   Take from me all slothfulness, and give me a diligent and an active spirit, and wisdom to choose my employment: that I may do works proportionable to my person and to the dignity of a Christian, and may fill up all the spaces of my time with actions of religion and charity ; that, when the devil assaults me, he may not find me idle; and my dearest Lord at his sudden coming may find me busy in lawful, necessary, and pious actions ; improving my talent intrusted to me by thee, my Lord; that I may enter into the joy of my Lord, to partake of his eternal felicities, even for thy mercy's sake, and for my dearest Saviour's sake.   Amen.

[15] Psal. x. 11.   [16] Ezek. ix. 9.

Here follows the devotion of ordinary days; for the right employment of those portions of time which every day must allow for religion.

The first Prayers in the morning, as soon we are dressed.

Humbly and reverently compose yourself, with heart lift up to God, and your head bowed, and meekly kneeling upon your knees, say the Lord's Prayer: after which use the following collects, or as many of them as you shall choose. —"Our Father, which art in heaven," &c.

1. *An Act of Adoration, being the song that the angels sing in heaven.*

Holy, holy, holy, Lord God Almighty, who was, and is, and is to come:[17] heaven and earth, angels and men, the air and the sea, give glory, and honour, and thanks to him that sitteth on the throne, who liveth for ever and ever.[18] All the blessed spirits and souls of the righteous cast their crowns before the throne, and worship him that liveth for ever and ever.[19] Thou art worthy, O Lord, to receive glory, and honour, and power; for thou hast created all things, and for thy pleasure they are, and were created. Great and marvellous are thy works, O Lord God Almighty: just and true are thy ways, thou King of saints.[20] Thy wisdom is infinite, thy mercies are glorious; and I am not worthy, O Lord, to appear in thy presence, before whom the angels hide their faces. O holy and eternal Jesus, Lamb of God, who wert slain from the beginning of the world, thou hast redeemed us to God by thy blood out of every nation, and hast made us unto our God kings and priests, and we shall reign with thee for ever. Blessing, honour, glory, and power, be unto him that sitteth on the throne, and to the Lamb, for ever and ever. Amen.

2. *An Act of Thanksgiving, being the song of David, for the morning.*

Sing praises unto the Lord, O ye saints of his, and give thanks to him for a remembrance of his holiness. For his wrath endureth but the twinkling of an eye, and in his pleasure is life; heaviness may endure for a night, but joy cometh in the morning. Thou, Lord, hast preserved me this night

[17] Rev. xi. 17.   [18] Rev. v. 10, 13.   [19] Rev. iv. 10.   [20] Rev. xv. 3.

from the violence of the spirits of darkness, from all sad casualties and evil accidents, from the wrath which I have every day deserved; thou hast brought my soul out of hell; thou hast kept my life from them that go down into the pit; thou hast showed me marvellous great kindness, and hast blessed me for ever: the greatness of thy glory reacheth unto the heavens, and thy truth unto the clouds. Therefore shall every good man sing of thy praise without ceasing. O my God, I will give thanks unto thee for ever. Hallelujah!

3. *An Act of Oblation, or presenting ourselves to God for the day.*

Most holy and eternal God, lord and sovereign of all the creatures, I humbly present to thy Divine Majesty myself, my soul and body, my thoughts and my words, my actions and intentions, my passions and my sufferings, to be disposed by thee to thy glory; to be blessed by thy providence; to be guided by thy counsel; to be sanctified by thy Spirit; and, afterwards, that my body and soul may be received into glory: for nothing can perish which is under thy custody; and the enemy of souls cannot devour what is thy portion, nor take it out of thy hands. This day, O Lord, and all the days of my life, I dedicate to thy honour, and the actions of my calling to the uses of grace, and the religion of all my days to be united to the merits and intercession of my holy Saviour Jesus; that in him and for him I may be pardoned and accepted. Amen.

4. *An Act of Repentance or Contrition.*

For, as for me, I am not worthy to be called thy servant; much less am I worthy to be thy son: for I am the vilest of sinners and the worst of men; a lover of the things of the world, and a despiser of the things of God; proud and envious, lustful and intemperate, greedy of sin, and impatient of reproof, desirous to seem holy, and negligent of being so; transported with interest; fooled with presumption and false principles; disturbed with anger, with a peevish and unmortified spirit, and disordered by a whole body of sin and death. Lord, pardon all my sins for my sweetest Saviour's sake: thou, who didst die for me, holy Jesus, save me and deliver me: reserve not my sins to be punished in the day of wrath and eternal vengeance; but wash away my sins and blot them out of thy

remembrance, and purify my soul with the waters of repentance and the blood of the cross; that, for what is past, thy
wrath may not come out against me; and, for the time to come,
I may never provoke thee to anger or to jealousy. O just and
dear God, be pitiful and gracious to thy servant. Amen.

5. *The Prayer or Petition.*

Bless me, gracious God, in my calling to such purposes as
thou shalt choose for me, or employ me in: relieve me in all
my sadnesses; make my bed in my sickness; give me patience
in my sorrows, confidence in thee, and grace to call upon thee
in all temptations. O be thou my guide in all my actions;
my protector in all dangers; give me a healthful body, and a
clear understanding; a sanctified and just, a charitable and
humble, a religious and a contented spirit; let not my life be
miserable and wretched; nor my name stained with sin and
shame; nor my condition lifted up to a tempting and dangerous fortune: but let my condition be blessed, my conversation
useful to my neighbours, and pleasing to thee; that, when my
body shall lie down in its bed of darkness, my soul may pass
into the regions of light, and live with thee for ever, through
Jesus Christ. Amen.

6. *An Act of Intercession or Prayer for others, to be added
to this or any other office, as our devotion, or duty, or their
needs, shall determine us.*

O God of infinite mercy, who hast compassion on all men,
and relievest the necessities of all that call to thee for help,
hear the prayers of thy servant, who is unworthy to ask any
petition for himself, yet, in humility and duty, is bound to
pray for others.

For the Church.

O let thy mercy descend upon the whole church; preserve
her in truth and peace, in unity and safety, in all storms, and
against all temptations and enemies; that she, offering to thy
glory the never-ceasing sacrifice of prayer and thanksgiving,
may advance the honour of her Lord, and be filled with his
Spirit, and partake of his glory. Amen.

For the King.

In mercy, remember the king; preserve his person in health

and honour; his crown, in wealth and dignity; his kingdoms, in peace and plenty; the churches under his protection, in piety and knowledge, and a strict and holy religion: keep him perpetually in thy fear and favour, and crown him with glory and immortality. Amen.

For the Clergy.

Remember them that minister about holy things; let them be clothed with righteousness, and sing with joyfulness. Amen.

For Wife or Husband.

Bless thy servant [my wife or husband] with health of body and of spirit. O let the hand of thy blessing be upon *his* [or *her*] head, night and day, and support *him* in all necessities, strengthen *him* in all temptations, comfort *him* in all *his* sorrows, and let *him* be thy servant in all changes: and make us both to dwell with thee for ever in thy favour, in the light of thy countenance, and in thy glory. Amen.

For our Children.

Bless my children with healthful bodies, with good understandings, with the graces and gifts of thy Spirit, with sweet dispositions and holy habits; and sanctify them throughout in their bodies, and souls, and spirits, and keep them unblamable to the coming of the Lord Jesus. Amen.

For Friends and Benefactors.

Be pleased, O Lord, to remember my friends, all that have prayed for me, and all that have done me good. [*Here name such whom you would especially recommend.*] Do thou good to them, and return all their kindness double into their own bosom, rewarding them with blessings, and sanctifying them with thy graces, and bringing them to glory.

For our Family.

Let all my family and kindred, my neighbours and acquaintance [*here name what other relations you please*], receive the benefit of my prayers, and the blessings of God; the comforts and supports of thy providence, and the sanctification of thy Spirit.

For all in Misery.

Relieve and comfort all the persecuted and afflicted; speak

peace to troubled consciences; strengthen the weak; confirm the strong; instruct the ignorant; deliver the oppressed from him that spoileth him, and relieve the needy that hath no helper; and bring us all, by the waters of comfort, and in the ways of righteousness, to the kingdom of rest and glory, through Jesus Christ our Lord.   Amen.

To God, the Father of our Lord Jesus Christ; to the eternal Son, that was incarnate and born of a virgin; to the Spirit of the Father and the Son, be all honour and glory, worship and thanksgiving, now and for ever.   Amen.

Another Form of Prayer, for the Morning.

In the name of the Father, and of the Son, and of the Holy Ghost.   Our Father, &c.

I.

Most glorious and eternal God, Father of mercy, and God of all comfort, I worship and adore thee with the lowest humility of my soul and body, and give thee all thanks and praise for thy infinite and essential glories and perfections, and for the continual demonstration of thy mercies upon me, upon all mine, and upon thy holy catholic church.

II.

I acknowledge, dear God, that I have deserved the greatest of thy wrath and indignation; and that, if thou hadst dealt with me according to my deserving, I had now, at this instant, been desperately bewailing my miseries, in the sorrows and horrors of a sad eternity.   But, thy mercy triumphing over thy justice and my sins, thou hast still continued to me life and time of repentance; thou hast opened to me the gates of grace and mercy, and perpetually callest upon me to enter in, and to walk in the paths of a holy life, that I might glorify thee, and be glorified of thee eternally.

III.

Behold, O God, for this thy great and unspeakable goodness, for the preservation of me this night, and for all other thy graces and blessings, I offer up my soul and body, all that I am, and all that I have, as a sacrifice to thee and thy service; humbly begging of thee to pardon all my sins, to defend me from all evil, to lead me into all good; and let my portion be amongst thy redeemed ones, in the gathering together of the saints in the kingdom of grace and glory.

IV.

Guide me, O Lord, in all the changes and varieties of the world; that in all things that shall happen I may have an evenness and tranquillity of spirit; that my soul may be wholly resigned to thy divinest will and pleasure, never murmuring at thy gentle chastisements and fatherly correction; never waxing proud and insolent, though I feel a torrent of comforts and prosperous successes.

V.

Fix my thoughts, my hopes, and my desires, upon heaven and heavenly things; teach me to despise the world, to repent me deeply for my sins; give me holy purposes of amendment and ghostly strength, and assistances to perform faithfully whatsoever I shall intend piously. Enrich my understanding with an eternal treasure of Divine truths, that I may know thy will: and thou, who workest in us to will and to do of thy good pleasure, teach me to obey all thy commandments, to believe all thy revelations, and make me partaker of all thy gracious promises.

VI.

Teach me to watch over all my ways, that I may never be surprised by sudden temptations or a careless spirit, nor ever return to folly and vanity. Set a watch, O Lord, before my mouth, and keep the door of my lips, that I offend not in my tongue, neither against piety nor charity. Teach me to think of nothing but thee, and what is in order to thy glory and service: to speak nothing but of thee, and thy glories; and to do nothing but what becomes thy servant, whom thy infinite mercy, by the graces of thy Holy Spirit, hath sealed up to the day of redemption.

VII.

Let all my passions and affections be so mortified and brought under the dominion of grace, that I may never, by deliberation and purpose, nor yet by levity, rashness, or inconsideration, offend thy Divine Majesty. Make me such as thou wouldest have me to be: strengthen my faith, confirm my hope,

D

and give me a daily increase of charity, that, this day and ever, I may serve thee according to all my opportunities and capacities, growing from grace to grace; till, at last, by thy mercies, I shall receive the consummation and perfection of grace, even the glories of thy kingdom, in the full fruition of the face and excellences of God the Father, the Son, and the Holy Ghost; to whom be glory and praise, honour and adoration, given by all angels, and all men, and all creatures, now, and to all eternity. Amen.

¶ To this may be added the prayer of intercession for others, whom we are bound to remember, which is at the end of the foregoing prayer; or else you may take such special prayers which follow at the end of the fourth chapter [for parents, for children, &c.].

After which, conclude with this ejaculation.

Now, in all tribulation and anguish of spirit, in all dangers of soul and body, in prosperity and adversity, in the hour of death and in the day of judgment, holy and most blessed Saviour Jesus, have mercy upon me, save me, and deliver me and all faithful people. Amen.

¶ Between this and noon, usually, are said the public prayers appointed by authority; to which all the clergy are obliged, and other devout persons that have leisure, to accompany them.

¶ Afternoon, or at any time of the day, when a devout person retires into his closet for private prayer or spiritual exercises, he may say the following devotions.

An exercise to be used at any time of the day.

In the name of the Father, and of the Son, &c.   Our Father, &c.

The Hymn, collected out of the Psalms, recounting the excellences and greatness of God.

O be joyful in God, all ye lands; sing praises unto the honour of his name, make his name to be glorious.   O come hither, and behold the works of God, how wonderful he is in his doings towards the children of men.   He ruleth with his power for ever.[21]

He is the Father of the fatherless, and defendeth the cause of the widow, even God in his holy habitation.   He is the God that maketh men to be of one mind in a house, and bringeth the prisoners out of captivity; but letteth the runagates continue in scarceness.[22]

It is the Lord that commandeth the waters; it is the glorious God that maketh the thunder.   It is the Lord that ruleth the sea: the voice of the Lord is mighty in operation; the voice of the Lord is a glorious voice.[23]

Let all the earth fear the Lord: stand in awe of him, all ye that dwell in the world.[24]   Thou shalt show us wonderful things in thy righteousness, O God of our salvation; thou art the hope of all the ends of the earth, and of them that remain in the broad sea.[25]

Glory be to the Father, &c.

Or this:

O Lord, thou art my God, I will exalt thee; I will praise thy name, for thou hast done wonderful things; thy counsels of old are faithfulness and truth.[26]

Thou, in thy strength, settest fast the mountains, and art girded about with power.   Thou stillest the raging of the sea, and the noise of his waves, and the madness of his people.[27]

They, also, that remain in the uttermost parts of the earth shall be afraid at thy tokens; thou, that makest the outgoings of the morning and evening to praise thee.

O Lord God of hosts, who is like unto thee? thy truth, most mighty Lord, is on every side.[28]   Among the gods there is none like unto thee: O Lord, there is none that can do as thou doest.   For thou art great, and doest wondrous things; thou art God alone.[29]

God is very greatly to be feared in the council of the saints, and to be had in reverence of all them that are round about him.[30]

Righteousness and equity are in the habitation of thy seat; mercy and truth shall go before thy face.   Glory and worship are before him; power and honour are in his sanctuary.[31]

[21] Psal. lxvi. 1, 4, 6.   [22] Psal. lxviii. 5, 6.   [23] Psal. xxix. 3, 4.
[24] Psal. xxxiii. 8.   [25] Psal. lxv. 5.   [26] Isa. xxv. 1.
[27] Psal. lxv. 6—8.   [28] Psal. lxxxix. 9.   [29] Psal. lxxxvi. 8, 9.
[30] Psal. lxxxix. 8, 15.   [31] Psal. xcvi. 6.

36 — DEVOTIONS FOR ORDINARY DAYS.

Thou, Lord, art the thing that I long for; thou art my hope, even from my youth. Through thee have I been holden up, ever since I was born; thou art he that took me out of my mother's womb; my praise shall be always of thee.[32]

Glory be to the Father, &c.

¶ After this may be read some portion of Holy Scripture, out of the New Testament, or out of the Sapiential books of the Old, viz., Proverbs, Ecclesiastes, &c., because these are of great use to piety, and to civil conversation. Upon which, when you have awhile meditated, humbly composing yourself upon your knees, say as followeth.

Ejaculations.

My help standeth in the name of the Lord, who hath made heaven and earth.[33]

Show the light of thy countenance upon thy servant, and I shall be safe.[34]

Do well, O Lord, to them that be true of heart, and evermore mightily defend them.[35]

Direct me in thy truth, and teach me; for thou art my Saviour, and my great Master.[36]

Keep me from sin and death eternal, and from my enemies visible and invisible.

Give me grace to live a holy life, and thy favour, that I may die a godly and happy death.

Lord, hear the prayer of thy servant, and give me thy Holy Spirit.

The Prayer.

O eternal God, merciful and gracious, vouchsafe thy favour and thy blessing to thy servant: let the love of thy mercies, and the dread and fear of thy majesty, make me careful and inquisitive to search thy will, and diligent to perform it, and to persevere in the practices of a holy life, even till the last of my days.

II.

Keep me, O Lord, for I am thine by creation; guide me, for I am thine by purchase; thou hast redeemed me by the blood of thy Son; and loved me with the love of a father, for I am thy child by adoption and grace: let thy mercy pardon my sins, thy providence secure me from the punishments and

[32] Psal. lxxi. 5, 6. [33] Psal. cxxiv. 8. [34] Psal. lxxx. 7.
[35] Psal. cxxv. 4. [36] Psal. xxv. 5.

evils I have deserved, and thy care watch over me, that I may never any more offend thee: make me, in malice, to be a child; but in understanding, piety, and the fear of God, let me be a perfect man in Christ, innocent and prudent, readily furnished and instructed to every good work.

III.

Keep me, O Lord, from the destroying angel, and from the wrath of God: let thy anger never rise against me, but thy rod gently correct my follies, and guide me in thy ways, and thy staff support me in all sufferings and changes. Preserve me from fracture of bones, from noisome, infectious, and sharp sicknesses; from great violences of fortune and sudden surprises: keep all my senses entire till the day of my death, and let my death be neither sudden, untimely, nor unprovided: let it be after the common manner of men, having in it nothing extraordinary, but an extraordinary piety, and the manifestation of thy great and miraculous mercy.

IV.

Let no riches make me ever forget myself, no poverty ever make me to forget thee: let no hope or fear, no pleasure or pain, no accident without, no weakness within, hinder or discompose my duty, or turn me from the ways of thy commandments. O, let thy Spirit dwell with me for ever, and make my soul just and charitable, full of honesty, full of religion, resolute and constant in holy purposes, but inflexible to evil. Make me humble and obedient, peaceable and pious; let me never envy any man's good, nor deserve to be despised myself: and if I be, teach me to bear it with meekness and charity.

V.

Give me a tender conscience; a conversation discreet and affable, modest and patient, liberal and obliging; a body chaste and healthful, competency of living according to my condition, contentedness in all estates, a resigned will and mortified affections; that I may be as thou wouldest have me, and my portion may be in the lot of the righteous, in the brightness of thy countenance, and the glories of eternity. Amen.

Holy is our God. Holy is the Almighty. Holy is the Immortal. Holy, holy, holy Lord God of Sabaoth, have mercy upon me.

A Form of Prayer for the Evening, to be said by such who have not time or opportunity to say the public prayers appointed for this office.

Evening Prayer.

I.

O eternal God, great Father of men and angels, who hast established the heavens and the earth in a wonderful order, making day and night to succeed each other; I make my humble address to thy Divine Majesty, begging of thee mercy and protection this night and ever. O Lord, pardon all my sins, my light and rash words, the vanity and impiety of my thoughts, my unjust and uncharitable actions, and whatsoever I have transgressed against thee this day, or at any time before. Behold, O God, my soul is troubled in the remembrance of my sins, in the frailty and sinfulness of my flesh, exposed to every temptation, and of itself not able to resist any. Lord God of mercy, I earnestly beg of thee to give me a great portion of thy grace, such as may be sufficient and effectual for the mortification of all my sins, and vanities, and disorders: that, as I have formerly served my lust and unworthy desires, so now I may give myself up wholly to thy service and the studies of a holy life.

II.

Blessed Lord, teach me frequently and sadly to remember my sins; and be thou pleased to remember them no more: let me never forget thy mercies, and do thou still remember to do me good. Teach me to walk always as in thy presence: ennoble my soul with great degrees of love to thee, and consign my spirit with great fear, religion, and veneration of thy holy name and laws; that it may become the great employment of my whole life to serve thee, to advance thy glory, to root out all the accursed habits of sin; that in holiness of life, in humility, in charity, in chastity, and all the ornaments of grace, I may by patience wait for the coming of our Lord Jesus. Amen.

III.

Teach me, O Lord, to number my days, that I may apply my heart unto wisdom; ever to remember my last end, that I may not dare to sin against thee. Let thy holy angels be ever present with me, to keep me in all my ways from the malice and violence of the spirits of darkness, from evil company, and the occasions and opportunities of evil, from perishing in popular judgments, from all the ways of sinful shame, from the hands of all mine enemies, from a sinful life, and from despair in the day of my death. Then, O brightest Jesu, shine gloriously upon me, let thy mercies and the light of thy countenance sustain me in all my agonies, weaknesses, and temptations. Give me opportunity of a prudent and spiritual guide, and of receiving the holy sacrament; and let thy loving spirit so guide me in the ways of peace and safety, that with the testimony of a good conscience, and the sense of thy mercies and refreshment, I may depart this life in the unity of the church, in the love of God, and a certain hope of salvation through Jesus Christ our Lord and most blessed Saviour. Amen.

Our Father, &c.

Another Form of Evening Prayer, which may also be used at bed-time.

Our Father, &c.

I will lift up my eyes unto the hills, from whence cometh my help.[37]

My help cometh of the Lord, which made heaven and earth.

He will not suffer thy foot to be moved: he that keepeth thee will not slumber.

Behold, he that keepeth Israel shall neither slumber nor sleep.

The Lord is thy keeper; the Lord is thy shade upon thy right hand.

The sun shall not smite thee by day, neither the moon by night.

The Lord shall preserve thee from all evil; he shall preserve thy soul.

The Lord shall preserve thy going out and thy coming in, from this time forth for evermore.

Glory be to the Father, &c.

I.

Visit, I beseech thee, O Lord, this habitation with thy mercy, and me with thy grace and salvation. Let thy holy angels pitch their tents round about and dwell here, that no

[37] Psal. cxxi. 1, &c.

illusion of the night may abuse me, the spirits of darkness may
not come near to hurt me, no evil or sad accident oppress me ,
and let the eternal Spirit of the Father dwell in my soul and
body, filling every corner of my heart with light and grace.
Let no deed of darkness overtake me ; and let thy blessing,
most blessed God, be upon me for ever, through Jesus Christ
our Lord. Amen.

II.

Into thy hands, most blessed Jesu, I commend my soul and
body, for thou hast redeemed both with thy precious blood.
So bless and sanctify my sleep unto me, that it may be temperate, holy, and safe; a refreshment to my wearied body, to
enable it so to serve my soul that both may serve thee with a
never-failing duty. O, let me never sleep in sin or death
eternal, but give me a watchful and a prudent spirit, that I
may omit no opportunity of serving thee ; that whether I sleep
or wake, live or die, I may be thy servant and thy child : that
when the work of my life is done, I may rest in the bosom of
my Lord, till by the voice of the archangel, the trump of God,
I shall be awakened, and called to sit down and feast in the
eternal supper of the Lamb.   Grant this, O Lamb of God, for
the honour of thy mercies, and the glory of thy name, O most
merciful Saviour and Redeemer Jesus. Amen.

III.

Blessed be the God and Father of our Lord Jesus, v ho hath
sent his angels, and kept me this day from the destruction
that walketh at noon, and the arrow that flieth by day ; and
hath given me his Spirit to restrain me from those evils to
which my own weaknesses, and my evil habits, and my unquiet enemies, would easily betray me. Blessed and for ever
hallowed be thy name for that never-ceasing shower of bless
ing by which I live, and am content and blessed, and provided
for in all necessities, and set forward in my duty and way to
heaven. Blessing, honour, glory, and power, be unto Him
that sitteth on the throne, and to the Lamb, for ever and ever.
Amen.

Holy is our God. Holy is the Almighty. Holy is the
Immortal. Holy, holy, holy Lord God of Sabaoth, have
mercy upon me.

Ejaculations and short Meditations to be used in the night,
when we awake.

Stand in awe and sin not; commune with your own heart upon your bed and be still. I will lay me down in peace and sleep: for thou, Lord, only makest me to dwell in safety.[38]

O Father of spirits, and the God of all flesh, have mercy and pity upon all sick and dying Christians, and receive the souls which thou hast redeemed returning unto thee.

Blessed are they that dwell in the heavenly Jerusalem, where there is no need of the sun, neither of the moon, to shine in it: for the glory of God does lighten it, and the Lamb is the light thereof.[39] And there shall be no night there, and they need no candle; for the Lord God giveth them light, and they shall reign for ever and ever.[40]

Meditate on Jacob's wrestling with the angel all night; be thou also importunate with God for a blessing, and give not over till he hath blessed thee.

Meditate on the angel passing over the children of Israel, and destroying the Egyptians for disobedience and oppression. Pray for the grace of obedience and charity, and for the Divine protection.

Meditate on the angel who destroyed in a night the whole army of the Assyrians for fornication. Call to mind the sins of thy youth, the sins of thy bed; and say, with David, " My reins chasten me in the night season, and my soul refuseth comfort." Pray for pardon and the grace of chastity.

Meditate on the agonies of Christ in the garden, his sadness and affliction all that night; and thank and adore him for his love, that made him suffer so much for thee; and hate thy sins, which made it necessary for the Son of God to suffer so much.

Meditate on the four last things. 1. The certainty of death. 2. The terrors of the day of judgment. 3. The joys of heaven. 4. The pains of hell; and the eternity of both.

Think upon all thy friends who are gone before thee; and pray that God would grant to thee to meet them in a joyful resurrection.

" The day of the Lord will come as a thief in the night;[4] in

---

* Psal. iv. 4, 9.   [39] Rev. xxi. 23.   [40] Rev. xxii. 5.
                    [41] 2 Pet. iii. 10

the which the heavens shall pass away with a great noise, and the elements shall melt with fervent heat; the earth also, and the works that are therein, shall be burnt up. Seeing, then, that all these things shall be dissolved, what manner of persons ought we to be, in all holy conversation and godliness, looking for and hastening unto the coming of the day of God?"

Lord, in mercy remember thy servant in the day of judgment.

Thou shalt answer for me, O Lord my God. In thee, O Lord, have I trusted: let me never be confounded. Amen.

¶ I desire the Christian reader to observe, that all these offices or forms of prayer (if they should be used every day) would not spend above an hour and a half; but because some of them are double (and so but one of them to be used in one day) it is much less: and by affording to God one hour in twenty-four, thou mayest have the comforts and rewards of devotion. But he that thinks this is too much, either is very busy in the world, or very careless of heaven. I have parted the prayers into smaller portions, that he may use which and how many he please in any one of the forms.

Ad Sect. 2.

A Prayer for holy intention in the beginning and pursuit of any considerable action, as Study, Preaching, &c.

O eternal God, who hast made all things for man, and man for thy glory, sanctify my body and soul, my thoughts and my intentions, my words and actions, that whatsoever I shall think, or speak, or do, may be by me designed to the glorification of thy name; and by thy blessing it may be effective and successful in the work of God, according as it can be capable. Lord, turn my necessities into virtue; the works of nature into the works of grace, by making them orderly, regular, temperate, subordinate, and profitable to ends beyond their own proper efficacy: and let no pride or self-seeking, no covetousness or revenge, no impure mixture or unhandsome purposes, no little ends and low imaginations, pollute my spirit, and unhallow any of my words and actions; but let my body be a servant of my spirit, and both body and spirit servants of Jesus; that, doing all things for thy glory here, I may be partaker of thy glory hereafter; through Jesus Christ our Lord. Amen.

Ad Sect. 3.

A Prayer meditating and referring to the Divine presence.

¶ *This Prayer is specially to be used in temptation to private sin.*

O Almighty God, infinite and eternal, thou fillest all things with thy presence; thou art every where by thy essence and by thy power, in heaven by glory, in holy places by thy grace and favour, in the hearts of thy servants by thy Spirit, in the consciences of all men by thy testimony and observation of us. Teach me to walk always as in thy presence, to fear thy majesty, to reverence thy wisdom and omniscience; that I may never dare to commit any indecency in the eye of my Lord and my Judge; but that I may with so much care and reverence demean myself that my Judge may not be my accuser, but my advocate; that I, expressing the belief of thy presence here by careful walking, may feel the effects of it in the participation of eternal glory; through Jesus Christ. Amen.

CHAP. II. OF CHRISTIAN SOBRIETY.

SECT. I. *Of Sobriety in the general sense.*

CHRISTIAN religion, in all its moral parts, is nothing else but the law of nature, and great reason; complying with the great necessities of all the world, and promoting the great profit of all relations, and carrying us, through all accidents of variety of chances, to that end which God hath from eternal ages purposed for all that live according to it, and which he hath revealed in Jesus Christ: and, according to the apostle's arithmetic, hath but these three parts of it; 1. Sobriety, 2. Justice, 3. Religion. " For the grace of God, bringing salvation, hath appeared to all men; teaching us that, denying ungodliness and worldly lusts, we should live, 1. Soberly, 2. Righteously, and 3. Godly, in this present world, looking for that blessed hope and glorious appearing of the great God and our Saviour Jesus Christ." The first contains all our deportment in our personal and private capacities, the fair treating of our bodies and our spirits. The second enlarges our duty in all relations to our neighbour. The third contains the offices of direct religion, and intercourse with God.

Christian sobriety is all that duty that concerns ourselves in the matter of meat, and drink, and pleasures, and thoughts; and it hath within it the duties of, 1. Temperance, 2. Chastity, 3. Humility, 4. Modesty, 5. Content.

It is a using severity, denial and frustration of our appetite, when it grows unreasonable in any of these instances: the necessity of which we shall to best purpose understand, by considering the evil consequences of sensuality, effeminacy, or fondness after carnal pleasures.

Evil consequences of Voluptuousness or Sensuality.

1. A longing after sensual pleasures is a dissolution of the spirit of a man, and makes it loose, soft, and wandering; unapt for noble, wise, or spiritual employments; because the principles upon which pleasure is chosen and pursued are sottish, weak, and unlearned, such as prefer the body before the soul,[1] the appetite before reason, sense before the spirit, the pleasures of a short abode before the pleasures of eternity.

2. The nature of sensual pleasure is vain, empty, and unsatisfying, biggest always in expectation, and a mere vanity in the enjoying, and leaves a sting and thorn behind it, when it goes off. Our laughing, if it be loud and high, commonly ends in a deep sigh; and all the instances of pleasure have a sting in the tail, though they carry beauty on the face and sweetness on the lip.

3. Sensual pleasure is a great abuse to the spirit of a man, being a kind of fascination or witchcraft, blinding the understanding and enslaving the will. And he that knows he is free-born, or redeemed with the blood of the Son of God, will not easily suffer the freedom of his soul to be entangled and rifled.[2]

4. It is most contrary to the state of a Christian, whose life is a perpetual exercise, a wrestling and warfare, to which sensual pleasure disables him, by yielding to that enemy with whom he must strive if ever he will be crowned.[3] And this argument the apostle intimated: "He that striveth for mas-

---

[1] Tu si animum vicisti potiùs quàm animus te, est quod gaudeas. Qui animum vincunt, quam quos animus, semper probiores cluent.—Trinum. ii. 2. 29. [2] Μόνον σκέψαι, πόσου πωλεῖς τὴν σεαυτοῦ προαίρεσιν, ἄνθρωπε· εἰ μηδὲν ἄλλο, μὴ ὀλίγου αὐτὴν πωλήσῃς.—Arrian, c. 2. l. i.

[3] Θέλεις Ὀλύμπια νικῆσαι; Δεῖ σ' εὐτακτεῖν, ἀναγκοτροφεῖν, ἀπέχεσθαι πεμμάτων, γυμνάζεσθαι πρὸς ἀνάγκην, κ.τ.λ. Epict. c. 29. 2. ed. Schw.

teries is temperate in all things: now they do it to obtain a corruptible crown, but we an incorruptible."[4]

5. It is by a certain consequence the greatest impediment in the world to martyrdom: that being a fondness, this being a cruelty to the flesh; to which a Christian man, arriving by degrees, must first have crucified the lesser affections: for he that is overcome by little arguments of pain, will hardly consent to lose his life with torments.

Degrees of Sobriety.

Against this voluptuousness, sobriety is opposed in three degrees.

1. A despite or disaffection to pleasures, or a resolving against all entertainment of the instances and temptations of sensuality; and it consists in the internal faculties of will and understanding, decreeing and declaring against them, disapproving and disliking them, upon good reason and strong resolution.

2. A fight and actual war against all the temptations and offers of sensual pleasure in all evil instances and degrees: and it consists in prayer, in fasting, in cheap diet and hard lodging, and laborious exercises, and avoiding occasions, and using all arts and industry of fortifying the spirit, and making it severe, manly, and Christian.

3. Spiritual pleasure is the highest degree of sobriety; and in the same degree in which we relish and are in love with spiritual delights, the hidden manna,[5] with the sweetness of devotion, with the joys of thanksgiving, with rejoicing in the Lord, with the comforts of hope, with the deliciousness of charity and alms-deeds, with the sweetness of a good conscience, with the peace of meekness, and the felicities of a contented spirit; in the same degree we disrelish and loathe the husks of swinish lusts, and the parings of the apples of Sodom, and the taste of sinful pleasures is unsavoury as the drunkard's vomit.

Rules for suppressing Voluptuousness.

The precepts and advices which are of best and of general use in the curing of sensuality, are these:

1. Accustom thyself to cut off all superfluity in the provisions of thy life, for our desires will enlarge beyond the

---

[4] 1 Cor. ix. 25.   [5] Apoc. ii. 17.

present possession so long as all the things of this world are unsatisfying: if, therefore, you suffer them to extend beyond the measures of necessity or moderated conveniency, they will still swell: but you reduce them to a little compass when you make nature to be your limit.   We must more take care that our desires should cease[6] than that they should be satisfied: and, therefore, reducing them to narrow scantlings and small proportions is the best instrument to redeem their trouble, and prevent the dropsy, because that is next to a universal denying them: it is certainly a paring off from them all unreasonableness and irregularity.   For "whatsoever covets unseemly things, and is apt to swell into an inconvenient bulk, is to be chastened and tempered: and such are sensuality, and a boy,"[7] said the philosopher.

2. Suppress your sensual desires in their first approach;[8] for then they are least, and thy faculties and election are stronger; but if they, in their weakness, prevail upon thy strengths, there will be no resisting them when they are increased, and thy abilities lessened.   "You shall scarce obtain of them to end, if you suffer them to begin."

3. Divert them with some laudable employment, and take off their edge by inadvertency, or a not-attending to them. For, since the faculties of a man cannot at the same time, with any sharpness, attend to two objects, if you employ your spirit upon a book, or a bodily labour, or any innocent and indifferent employment, you have no room left for the present trouble of a sensual temptation.   For to this sense it was, that Alexander told the Queen of Caria, that his tutor Leonidas had provided two cooks for him;[9] " Hard marches all night, and a small dinner the next day:" these tamed his youthful aptnesses to dissolution, so long as he ate of their provisions.

4. Look upon pleasures, not upon that side that is next the sun, or where they look beauteously; that is, as they come towards you to be enjoyed, for then they paint and smile, and dress themselves up in tinsel and glass gems, and counterfeit imagery; but when thou hast rifled and discomposed

---

[6] Desideria tua parvo redime; hoc enim tantum curare debes, ut desinant.—Senec.   [7] Lib. iii. Eth. c. 12. p. 129. ed. Wilk.
[8] Facilius est initia affectuum prohibere, quàm impetum regere.— Senec. Ep. 86.   [9] Νυκτοπορίαν καὶ ὀλιγαριστίαν.

them with enjoying their false beauties, and that they begin to go off, then behold them in their nakedness and weariness.[10] See, what a sigh and sorrow, what naked unhandsome proportions, and a filthy carcass, they discover ; and the next time they counterfeit, remember what you have already discovered, and be no more abused. And I have known some wise persons have advised to cure the passions and longings of their children by letting them taste of every thing they passionately fancied ; for they should be sure to find less in it than they looked for, and the impatience of their being denied would be loosened and made slack : and when our wishings are no bigger than the thing deserves, and our usages of them according to our needs, (which may be obtained by trying what they are, and what good they can do us,) we shall find in all pleasures so little entertainment, that the vanity of the possession will soon reprove the violence of the appetite. And if this permission be in innocent instances it may be of good use : but Solomon tried it in all things, taking his fill of all pleasures, and soon grew weary of them all. The same thing we may do by reason which we do by experience, if either we will look upon pleasures as we are sure they look when they go off, after their enjoyment ; or if we will credit the experience of those men who have tasted them and loathed them.

5. Often consider and contemplate the joys of heaven, that, when they have filled thy desires, which are the sails of the soul, thou mayest steer only thither, and never more look back to Sodom. And when thy soul dwells above, and looks down upon the pleasures of the world, they seem like things at distance, little and contemptible ; and men running after the satisfaction of their sottish appetites seem foolish as fishes, thousands of them running after a rotten worm, that covers a deadly hook ; or at the best, but like children with great noise pursuing a bubble rising from a walnut-shell, which ends sooner than the noise.

6. To this the example of Christ and his apostles, of Moses, and all the wise men of all ages of the world, will much help ; who, understanding how to distinguish good from evil, did

[10] Voluptates abeuntes fessas et pœnitentia plenas, animis nostris natura subjecit, quo minus cupide repetantur.—Seneca. Læta venire Venus, tristis abire solet.

choose a sad and melancholy way to felicity, rather than the broad, pleasant, and easy path to folly and misery.

But this is but the general. Its first particular is temperance.

SECT. II. *Of Temperance in Eating and Drinking.*

SOBRIETY is the bridle of the passions of desire[1], and temperance is the bit and curb of that bridle, restraint put into a man's mouth, a moderate use of meat and drink, so as may best consist with our health, and may not hinder but help the works of the soul by its necessary supporting us, and ministering cheerfulness and refreshment.

Temperance consists in the actions of the soul principally: for it is a grace that chooses natural means in order to proper, and natural, and holy ends; it is exercised about eating and drinking, because they are necessary; but therefore it permits the use of them, only as they minister to lawful ends; it does not eat and drink for pleasure, but for need, and for refreshment, which is a part or a degree of need. I deny not that eating and drinking *may be*, and in healthful bodies *always is*, with pleasure; because there is in nature no greater pleasure than that all the appetites which God hath made should be satisfied: and a man may choose a morsel that is pleasant, (the less pleasant being rejected as being less useful, less apt to nourish,) or more agreeing with an infirm stomach, or when the day is festival by order, or by private joy. In all these cases it is permitted to receive a more free delight, and to design it too, as the less principal: that is, that the chief reason why we choose the more delicious be the serving that end for which such refreshments and choices are permitted. But when delight is the only end, and rests in itself, and dwells there long, then eating and drinking is not a serving of God, but an inordinate action; because it is not in the way to that end whither God directed it. But the choosing of a delicate before a more ordinary dish is to be done as other human actions are, in which there are no degrees and precise natural limits described, but a latitude is indulged; it must be done moderately, prudently, and according to the accounts of wise, religious, and sober men: and then God, who gave us such variety of creatures, and our choice to use

[1] Ἐγκράτεια, ἀπὸ τοῦ ἐν κράτει ἔχειν τὴν ἐπιθυμίαν.

which we will, may receive glory from our temperate use, and thanksgiving; and we may use them indifferently without scruple, and a making them to become snares to us, either by too licentious and studied use of them, or too restrained and scrupulous fear of using them at all, but in such certain circumstances, in which no man can be sure he is not mistaken.

But temperance in meat and drink is to be estimated by the following measures.

Measures of Temperance in Eating.

1. Eat not before the time, unless necessity, or charity, or any intervening accident, which may make it reasonable and prudent, should happen. Remember, it had almost cost Jonathan his life, because he tasted a little honey before the sun went down, contrary to the king's commandment; and although a great need which he had excused him from the sin of gluttony, yet it is inexcusable when thou eatest before the usual time, and thrustest thy hand into the dish unseasonably, out of greediness of the pleasure, and impatience of the delay

2. Eat not hastily and impatiently, but with such decent and timely action that your eating be a human act, subject to deliberation and choice, and that you may consider in the eating : whereas, he that eats hastily cannot consider particularly of the circumstances, degrees, and little accidents and chances, that happen in his meal ; but may contract many little indecencies, and be suddenly surprised.

3. Eat not delicately or nicely, that is, be not troublesome to thyself or others in the choice of thy meats or the delicacy of thy sauces. It was imputed as a sin to the sons of Israel, that they loathed manna and longed for flesh : " the quails stunk in their nostrils, and the wrath of God fell upon them." And for the manner of dressing, the sons of Eli were noted of indiscreet curiosity ; they would not have the flesh boiled, but raw, that they might roast it with fire. Not that it was a sin to eat it, or desire meat roasted ; but that when it was appointed to be boiled, they refused it : which declared an intemperate and a nice palate. It is lawful in all senses to comply with a weak and a nice stomach ; but not with a nice and curious palate. When our health requires it, that ought to be provided for ; but not so our sensuality and intemperate longings. Whatsoever is set before you, eat ; if it be provided

E

for you, you may eat it, be it never so delicate; and be it
plain and common, so it be wholesome, and fit for you, it must
not be refused upon curiosity: for every degree of that is a
degree of intemperance.   Happy and innocent were the ages
of our forefathers, who ate herbs and parched corn, and drank
the pure stream, and broke their fast with nuts and roots;[2]
and when they were permitted flesh, ate it only dressed with
hunger and fire; and the first sauce they had was bitter
herbs, and sometimes bread dipped in vinegar.   But in this
circumstance, moderation is to be reckoned in proportion to
the present customs, to the company, to education, and the
judgment of honest and wise persons, and the necessities of
nature.

4. Eat not too much: load neither thy stomach nor thy
understanding.   "If thou sit at a bountiful table, be not
greedy upon it, and say not there is much meat on it.   Remember that a wicked eye is an evil thing: and what is
created more wicked than an eye?   Therefore it weepeth
upon every occasion.   Stretch not thy hand whithersoever it
looketh, and thrust it not with him into the dish.   A very
little is sufficient for a man well nurtured, and he fetcheth not
his wind short upon his bed."

Signs and Effects of Temperance.

We shall best know that we have the grace of temperance
by the following signs, which are as so many arguments to
engage us, also, upon its study and practice.

1. A temperate man is modest: greediness is unmannerly
and rude.   And this is intimated in the advice of the son of
Sirach, "When thou sittest amongst many, reach not thy
hand out first of all.   Leave off first for manners' sake, and
be not insatiable, lest thou offend."   2. Temperance is accompanied with gravity of deportment: greediness is garish, and
rejoices loosely at the sight of dainties.[3]   3. Sound but
moderate sleep is its sign and its effect.   Sound sleep cometh
of moderate eating; he riseth early, and his wits are with

---

[2] Felix nimium, prior ætas, contenta fidelibus arvis;
    Facili quæ serâ solebat, jejunia solvere glande.—Boeth. de Cons. lib. i.
    Arbuteos fœtus, montanaque fraga legebant.—Ov. M. i. 104.
[3] Cicero vocat Temperantiam ornatum vitæ, in quo decorum illud et
honestum situm est.

him. 4. A spiritual joy and a devout prayer. 5. A suppressed and seldom anger. 6. A command of our thoughts and passions. 7. A seldom-returning and a never-prevailing temptation. 8. To which add, that a temperate person is not curious of fancies and deliciousness. He thinks not much and speaks not often of meat and drink; hath a healthful body and long life, unless it be hindered by some other accident: whereas to gluttony, the pain of watching and choler, the pangs of the belly, are continual company. And therefore Stratonicus said handsomely concerning the luxury of the Rhodians, "They built houses as if they were immortal; but they feasted as if they meant to live but a little while." And Antipater, by his reproach of the old glutton Demades, well expressed the baseness of this sin; saying, that Demades, now old,[4] and always a glutton, was like a spent sacrifice, nothing left of him but his belly and his tongue; all the man besides is gone.

Of Drunkenness.

But I desire that it be observed, that because intemperance in eating is not so soon perceived by others as immoderate drinking, and the outward visible effects of it are not either so notorious or so ridiculous, therefore gluttony is not of so great disreputation amongst men as drunkenness; yet, according to its degree, it puts on the greatness of the sin before God, and is most strictly to be attended to, lest we be surprised by our security and want of diligence; and the intemperance is alike criminal in both, according as the affections are either to the meat or drink. Gluttony is more uncharitable to the body, and drunkenness to the soul, or the understanding part of man; and therefore in Scripture is more frequently forbidden and declaimed against than the other; and sobriety hath by use obtained to signify temperance in drinking.

Drunkenness is an immoderate affection and use of drink. That I call immoderate that is besides or beyond that order of good things for which God hath given us the use of drink. The ends are, digestion of our meat, cheerfulness and refreshment of our spirits, or any end of health; besides which if we go, or at any time beyond it, it is inordinate and criminal —it is the vice of drunkenness. It is forbidden by our blessed

[4] Plutarch. de Cupid. Divit.

E 2

Saviour in these words:[5] " Take heed to yourselves, lest at
any time your hearts be overcharged with surfeiting and
drunkenness:" surfeiting, that is, the evil effects, the sottishness and remaining stupidity of habitual or of the last night's
drunkenness. For Christ forbids both the actual and the habitual intemperance; not only the effect of it, but also the
affection to it; for in both there is sin. He that drinks but
little, if that little make him drunk, and if he know beforehand his own infirmity, is guilty of surfeiting, not of drunkenness.[6] But he that drinks much, and is strong to bear it, and
is not deprived of his reason violently, is guilty of the sin of
drunkenness. It is a sin not to prevent such uncharitable
effects upon the body and understanding; and therefore a
man that loves not the drink is guilty of surfeiting if he does
not watch to prevent the evil effect: and it is a sin, and the
greater of the two, inordinately to love or to use the drink,
though the surfeiting or violence do not follow. Good therefore is the counsel of the son of Sirach, " Show not thy
valiantness in wine ; for wine hath destroyed many."[7]

Evil Consequents to Drunkenness.

The evils and sad consequents of drunkenness (the consideration of which are as so many arguments to avoid the sin) are
to this sense reckoned by the writers of Holy Scripture, and
other wise personages of the world. 1. It causeth woes and
mischief,[8] wounds and sorrow, sin and shame;[9] it maketh
bitterness of spirit, brawling, and quarrelling ; it increaseth
rage and lesseneth strength ; it maketh red eyes, and a loose
and babbling tongue. 2. It particularly ministers to lust, and
yet disables the body; so that in effect it makes man wanton
as a satyr, and impotent as age. And Solomon, in enumerating the evils of this vice, adds this to the account,[10] " thine
eyes shall behold strange women, and thine heart shall utter
perverse things:" as if the drunkard were only desire, and
then impatience, muttering and enjoying like an eunuch em-
bracing a woman. 3. It besots and hinders the actions of the

[5] Luke xxi. 34.   [6] Κραιπάλη ἀπὸ προτεραίας aut ἀπό χθιζῆς
οἰνοποσίας.—Schol. in Aristoph. Idem fere apud Plutarch. Vinolentia
animi quandam remissionem et levitatem, ebrietas futilitatem significat.
—Plutarch. de Garrul.   [7] Ecclus. xxxi. 25.   [8] Prov. xxiii. 29;
Ecclus. xxxi. 26.   [9] Multa faciunt ebrii, quibus sobrii erubescunt.--
Senec. Ep. lxxxiii. 17.   [10] Prov. xxiii. 33.

understanding, maketh a man brutish in his passions, and a
fool in his reason; and differs nothing from madness, but that
it is voluntary, and so is an equal evil in nature, and a worse
in manners.[11] 4. It takes off all the guards, and lets loose the
reins of all those evils to which a man is by his nature or by his
evil customs inclined, and from which he is restrained by reason and severe principles. Drunkenness calls off the watch-
men from their towers; and then all the evils that can proceed from a loose heart, and an untied tongue, and a dissolute
spirit, and an unguarded, unlimited will, all that we may put
upon the accounts of drunkenness. 5. It extinguisheth and
quenches the Spirit of God, for no man can be filled with the
Spirit of God and with wine at the same time. And therefore St. Paul makes them exclusive of each other:[12] "Be not
drunk with wine, wherein is excess; but be filled with the
Spirit."[13] And since Joseph's cup was put into Benjamin's
sack, no man had a divining goblet. 6. It opens all the
sanctuaries of nature, and discovers the nakedness of the soul,
all its weaknesses and follies; it multiplies sins and discovers
them; it makes a man incapable of being a private friend or
public counsellor. 7. It taketh a man's soul into slavery and
imprisonment more than any vice whatsoever,[14] because it
disarms a man of all his reason and his wisdom, whereby he
might be cured, and therefore commonly it grows upon him
with age; a drunkard being still more a fool and less a man.
I need not add any sad examples, since all story and all ages
have too many of them. Amnon was slain by his brother
Absalom when he was warm and high with wine. Simon,
the high priest, and two of his sons, were slain by their brother at a drunken feast. Holofernes was drunk when Judith
slew him; and all the great things that Daniel spake of Alexander[15] were drowned with a surfeit of one night's intemperance: and the drunkenness of Noah and Lot are upon record

[11] Insaniæ comes est ira, contubernalis ebrietas.—Plutarch.
————— Corpus onustum
Hesternis vitiis animum quoque prægravat.—Horat.
Ebrietas est voluntaria insania.—Senec.
[12] Ephes. v. 18.
[13] Οἶνός σε τρώει μελιήδης, ὅς τε καὶ ἄλλους
Βλάπτει, ὃς ἄν μιν χανδὸν ἕλῃ, μηδ' αἴσιμα πίνῃ.—Hom. Od. φ'. 293.
[14] Prov. xxxi. 4.
——— Οὐδεὶς δὲ μεθύων, ἂν σκοπῆς, Ὃς οὐχὶ δοῦλός ἐστι τοῦ πεπω-
κέναι.—Philem. p. 344. ed. Clerc.   [15] Alexandrum intempe-

to eternal ages, that in those early instances, and righteous persons, and less criminal drunkenness than is that of Christians in this period of the world, God might show that very great evils are prepared to punish this vice; no less than shame, and slavery, and incest; the first upon Noah, the second upon one of his sons, and the third in the person of Lot.

Signs of Drunkenness.

But if it be inquired concerning the periods and distinct significations of this crime; and when a man is said to be drunk; to this I answer, that drunkenness is in the same manner to be judged as sickness. As every illness or violence done to health, in every part of its continuance, is a part or degree of sickness; so is every going off from our natural and common temper and our usual severity of behaviour, a degree of drunkenness. He is not only drunk that can drink no more; for few are so: but he hath sinned in a degree of drunkenness who hath done any thing towards it beyond his proper measure. But its parts and periods are usually thus reckoned: 1. apish gestures; 2. much talking; 3. immoderate laughing; 4. dulness of sense; 5. scurrility, that is, wanton, or jeering, or abusive language; 6. an useless understanding; 7. stupid sleep; 8. epilepsies, or fallings and reelings, and beastly vomitings. The least of these, even when the tongue begins to be untied, is a degree of drunkenness.

But that we may avoid the sin of intemperance in meats and drinks, besides the former rules of measures, these counsels also may be useful.

Rules for obtaining Temperance.

1. Be not often present at feasts, nor at all in dissolute company, when it may be avoided, for variety of pleasing objects steals away the heart of man; and company is either violent or enticing, and we are weak or complying, or perhaps desirous enough to be abused. But if you be unavoidably or indiscreetly engaged, let not mistaken civility or good-nature engage thee either to the temptation of staying, (if thou understandest thy weakness,) or the sin of drinking inordinately.

2. Be severe in your judgment concerning your proportions, and let no occasion make you enlarge far beyond your

rantia bibendi, et ille Herculaneus ac fatalis scyphus perdidit.—Senec. Ep. lxxxiii. 21.

ordinary. For a man is surprised by parts; and while he thinks one glass more will not make him drunk, that one glass hath disabled him from well discerning his present condition and neighbour danger. "While men think themselves wise, they become fools:" they think they shall taste the aconite and not die, or crown their heads with juice of poppy and not be drowsy; and if they drink off the whole vintage, still they think they can swallow another goblet.[16] But remember this, whenever you begin to consider whether you may safely take one draught more, it is then high time to give over. Let that be accounted a sign late enough to break off; for every reason to doubt is a sufficient reason to part the company.

3. Come not to table but when thy need invites thee; and, if thou beest in health, leave something of thy appetite unfilled, something of thy natural heat unemployed, that it may secure thy digestion, and serve other needs of nature or the spirit.

4. Propound to thyself (if thou beest in a capacity) a constant rule of living, of eating and drinking, which, though it may not be fit to observe scrupulously, lest it become a snare to thy conscience, or endanger thy health upon every accidental violence; yet let not thy rule be broken often nor much, but upon great necessity and in small degrees.

5. Never urge any man to eat or drink beyond his own limits and his own desires. He that does otherwise is drunk with his brother's surfeit,[17] and reels and falls with his intemperance; that is, the sin of drunkenness is upon both their scores, they both lie wallowing in the guilt.

6. Use St. Paul's instruments of sobriety: "Let us who are of the day be sober, putting on the breast-plate of faith and love, and, for an helmet, the hope of salvation." Faith, hope, and charity, are the best weapons in the world to fight against imtemperance. The faith of the Mahometans forbids them to drink wine, and they abstain religiously, as the sons of Rechab; and the faith of Christ forbids drunkenness to us, and therefore is infinitely more powerful to suppress this vice, when we remember that we are Christians, and to abstain from drunkenness and gluttony is part of the faith and discipline of Jesus, and that with these vices neither our love to God, nor our hopes of heaven, can possibly consist; and, therefore,

[16] Senec. Ep. lxxxiii. Chi ha bevuto tutto il mare, può bere ancor' un tratto.   [17] Nil interest, faveas sceleri an illud facias.—Senec.

when these enter the heart, the others go out at the mouth; for this is the devil that is cast out by fasting and prayer, which are the proper actions of these graces.

7. As a pursuance of this rule, it is a good advice, that, as we begin and end all our times of eating with prayer and thanksgiving, so, at the meal, we remove and carry up our mind and spirit to the celestial table, often thinking of it, and often desiring it; that, by enkindling thy desire to heavenly banquets, thou mayest be indifferent and less passionate for the earthly.

8. Mingle discourses, pious, or, in some sense, profitable, and in all senses charitable and innocent, with thy meal, as occasion is ministered.

9. Let your drink so serve your meat as your meat doth your health; that it be apt to convey and digest it, and refresh the spirits; but let it never go beyond such a refreshment as may a little lighten the present load of a sad or troubled spirit, never to inconvenience, lightness, sottishness, vanity, or intemperance; and know, that the loosing the bands of the tongue, and the very first dissolution of its duty, is one degree of the intemperance.

10. In all cases be careful that you be not brought under the power of such things which otherwise are lawful enough in the use. "All things are lawful for me; but I will not be brought under the power of any," said St. Paul. And to be perpetually longing, and impatiently desirous of any thing, so that a man cannot abstain from it, is to lose a man's liberty, and to become a servant of meat and drink, or smoke.—And I wish this last instance were more considered by persons who little suspect themselves guilty of intemperance, though their desires are strong and impatient, and the use of it per-petual and unreasonable to all purposes, but that they have made it habitual and necessary, as intemperance itself is made to some men.

11. Use those advices which are prescribed as instruments to suppress voluptuousness, in the foregoing section.

Sect. III. *Of Chastity.*

READER, stay, and read not the advices of the following sec-tion, unless thou hast a chaste spirit, or desirest to be chaste, or at least art apt to consider whether you ought or no. For there are some spirits so atheistical, and some so wholly possessed with a spirit of uncleanness, that they turn the most prudent and chaste discourses into dirty and filthy apprehensions; like choleric stomachs, changing their very cordials and medicines into bitterness, and, in a literal sense, turning the grace of God into wantonness. They study cases of conscience in the matter of carnal sins, not to avoid, but to learn ways how to offend God and pollute their own spirits; and search their houses with a sunbeam, that they may be instructed in all the corners of nastiness. I have used all the care I could, in the following periods, that I might neither be wanting to assist those that need it, nor yet minister any occasion of fancy or vainer thoughts to those that need them not. If any man will snatch the pure taper from my hand and hold it to the devil, he will only burn his own fingers, but shall not rob me of the reward of my care and good intention, since I have taken heed how to express the following duties, and given him caution how to read them.

Chastity is that duty which was mystically intended by God in the law of circumcision. It is the circumcision of the heart, the cutting off all superfluity of naughtiness, and a suppression of all irregular desires in the matter of sensual or carnal pleasure. I call all desires irregular and sinful that are not sanctified, 1. by the holy institution, or by being within the protection of marriage; 2. by being within the order of nature; 3. by being within the moderation of Christian modesty. Against the first are fornication, adultery, and all voluntary pollutions of either sex. Against the second are all unnatural lusts and incestuous mixtures. Against the third is all immoderate use of permitted beds, concerning which judgment is to be made, as concerning meats and drinks, there being no certain degree of frequency or intention prescribed to all persons; but it is to be ruled as the other actions of a man, by proportion to the end, by the dignity of the person in the honour and severity of being a Christian, and by other circumstances of which I am to give account.

Chastity is that grace which forbids and restrains all these, keeping the body and soul pure in that state in which it is placed by God, whether of the single or of the married life; concerning which our duty is thus described by St. Paul: "For this is the will of God, even your sanctification, that ye should abstain from fornication; that every one of you should know how to possess his vessel in sanctification and honour, not in the lust of concupiscence, even as the Gentiles which know not God." [1]

Chastity is either abstinence or continence. Abstinence is that of virgins or widows; continence, of married persons. Chaste marriages are honourable and pleasing to God; widow. hood is pitiable in its solitariness and loss, but amiable and comely when it is adorned with gravity and purity, and not sullied with remembrances of the passed licence, nor with present desires of returning to a second bed. But virginity is a life of angels, the enamel of the soul, the huge advantage of religion, the great opportunity for the retirements of devotion; [2] and, being empty of cares, it is full of prayers; being unmingled with the world, it is apt to converse with God; and by not feeling the warmth of a too forward and indulgent nature, flames out with holy fires till it be burning like the cherubim and the most ecstasied order of holy and unpolluted spirits.

Natural virginity, of itself, is not a state more acceptable to God; but that which is chosen and voluntary, in order to the conveniences of religion and separation from worldly encumbrances, is therefore better than the married life, not that it is more holy, but that it is a freedom from cares, an opportunity to spend more time in spiritual employments; it is not allayed with businesses and attendances upon lower affairs: and if it be a chosen condition to these ends, it containeth in it a victory over lusts, and greater desires of religion, and self-denial; and therefore is more excellent than the married life, in that degree in which it hath greater religion, and a greater mortification, a less satisfaction of natural desires, and a greater fulness of the spiritual: and just so is to expect that little coronet, or special reward, which God hath prepared (extraordinary and besides the great crown of all faithful souls) for those "who have not defiled themselves with women, but follow the" virgin "Lamb for ever." [3]

But some married persons, even in their marriage, do better please God than some virgins in their state of virginity; they, by giving great example of conjugal affection, by preserving

---

[1] 1 Thess. iv. 3—5.　　[2] Virginitas est, in carne corruptibili, incorruptionis perpetua meditatio.—St. Aug. l. de Virg. c. 13.　　[3] Apoc. xiv. 4.

their faith unbroken, by educating children in the fear of God, by patience and contentedness, and holy thoughts, and the exercise of virtues proper to that state, do not only please God, but do in a higher degree than those virgins whose piety is not answerable to their great opportunities and advantages.

However, married persons, and widows, and virgins, are all servants of God, and co-heirs in the inheritance of Jesus, if they live within the restraints and laws of their particular estate chastely, temperately, justly, and religiously.

The Evil Consequents of Uncleanness.

The blessings and proper effects of chastity we shall best understand, by reckoning the evils of uncleanness and carnality.

1. Uncleanness, of all vices, is the most shameful. " The eye of the adulterer waiteth for the twilight, saying, No eye shall see me ; and disguiseth his face. In the dark they dig through houses, which they had marked for themselves in the day-time ; they know not the light, for the morning is to them as the shadow of death. He is swift as the waters ; their portion is cursed in the earth ; he beholdeth not the way of the vineyards."[4] Shame is the eldest daughter of uncleanness.[5]

2. The appetites of uncleanness are full of cares and trouble, and its fruition is sorrow and repentance. The way of the adulterer is hedged with thorns ;[6] full of fears and jealousies, burning desires and impatient waitings, tediousness of delay, and sufferance of affronts, and amazements of discovery.[7]

3. Most of its kinds are of that condition that they involve the ruin of two souls ; and he that is a fornicator or adulterous steals the soul, as well as dishonours the body, of his neighbour ; and so it becomes like the sin of falling Lucifer, who brought a part of the stars with his tail from heaven.

4. Of all carnal sins, it is that alone which the devil takes delight to imitate and counterfeit ; communicating with witches and impure persons in the corporal act, but in this only.

5. Uncleanness, with all its kinds, is a vice which hath a professed enmity against the body. "Every sin which a man doth is without the body ; but he that committeth fornication sinneth against his own body."[8]

Job xxiv. 15, &c.   [5] Ἄτιμα πάθη.   [6] Hos. ii. 6.
[7] Appetitus fornicationis anxietas est, satietas verò pœnitudu.- -[8] Hieron.   [8] 1 Cor. vi. 18.

6. Uncleanness is hugely contrary to the spirit of government,[9] by embasing the spirit of a man, making it effeminate,
sneaking, soft, and foolish, without courage, without confidence.   David felt this after his folly with Bathsheba; he
fell to unkingly arts and stratagems to hide the crime; and
he did nothing but increase it, and remained timorous and
poor-spirited, till he prayed to God once more to establish
him with a free and a princely spirit.[10]   And no superior dare
strictly observe discipline upon his charge, if he hath let himself loose to the shame of incontinence.

7. The gospel hath added two arguments against uncleanness which were never before used, nor, indeed, could be.
Since God hath given the Holy Spirit to them that are baptized, and rightly confirmed and entered into covenant with
him, our bodies are made temples of the Holy Ghost, in which
he dwells; and therefore uncleanness is sacrilege, and defiles
a temple.   It is St. Paul's argument, "Know ye not that
your body is the temple of the Holy Ghost?"[11] and "He that
defiles a temple, him will God destroy.[12]   Therefore glorify
God in your bodies;" that is, flee fornication.   To which,
for the likeness of the argument, add, that "our bodies are
members of Christ; and therefore God forbid that we should
take the members of Christ, and make them members of a
harlot."   So that uncleanness dishonours Christ, and dishonours the Holy Spirit: it is a sin against God, and, in this
sense, a sin against the Holy Ghost.

8. The next special argument which the gospel ministers,
especially against adultery, and for the preservation of the
purity of marriage, is, that marriage is by Christ hallowed
into a mystery, to signify the sacramental and mystical union
of Christ and his church.[13]   He, therefore, that breaks this
knot, which the church and their mutual faith have tied, and
Christ hath knit up into a mystery, dishonours a great rite
of Christianity, of high, spiritual, and excellent signification.

9. St. Gregory reckons uncleanness to be the parent of
these monsters,[14] blindness of mind, inconsideration, precipi-
tancy or giddiness in actions, self-love, hatred of God, love of
the present pleasures, a despite or despair of the joys of religion here, and of heaven hereafter.   Whereas, a pure mind

---

[9] Φθαρτικαὶ τῶν ἀρχῶν.   [10] Spiritu principali me confirma.—Psal. li.
[11] 1 Cor. vi. 19.   [12] 1 Cor. iii. 17.   [13] Eph. v. 32.   [14] Moral.

in a chaste body is the mother of wisdom and deliberation, sober counsels and ingenuous actions, open deportment and sweet carriage, sincere principles and unprejudicate understanding, love of God and self-denial, peace and confidence, holy prayers and spiritual comfort, and a pleasure of spirit infinitely greater than the sottish and beastly pleasures of unchastity. "For to overcome pleasure is the greatest pleasure: and no victory is greater than that which is gotten over our lusts and filthy inclinations."[15]

10. Add to all these, the public dishonesty and disreputation that all the nations of the world have cast upon adulterous and unhallowed embraces. Abimelech, to the men of Gerar, made it death to meddle with the wife of Isaac; and Judah condemned Thamar to be burnt for her adulterous conception: and God, besides the law made to put the adulterous person to death, did constitute a settled and constant miracle to discover the adultery of a suspected woman,[16] that her bowels should burst with drinking the waters of jealousy. The Egyptian law was to cut off the nose of the adulteress, and the offending part of the adulterer. The Locrians put out both the adulterer's eyes. The Germans (as Tacitus reports) placed the adulteress amidst her kindred naked, and shaved her head, and caused her husband to beat her with clubs through the city. The Gortynæans crowned the man with wool, to shame him for his effeminacy; and the Cumani caused the woman to ride upon an ass, naked and hooted at, and for ever after called her by an appellative of scorn, "a rider upon the ass:"[17] all nations, barbarous and civil, agreeing in their general design, of rooting so dishonest and shameful a vice from under heaven.

The middle ages of the church were not pleased that the adulteress should be put to death:[18] but in the primitive ages, the civil laws by which Christians were then governed gave leave to the wronged husband to kill his adulterous wife if he took her in the fact:[19] but because it was a privilege indulged to men rather than a direct detestation of the crime, a consideration of the injury rather than of the uncleanness, there-

[15] St. Cyprian. de Bono Pudicitiæ. [16] Numb. v. 14. [17] Ὀνόβατις.
[18] Concil. Tribur. c. 46. Concil. Aurel. 1. sub Clodovæo.
[19] Cod. de adulteriis, ad legem Juliam, l. 1. et Cod. Theod de adulteriis, c. placuit.

fore it was soon altered; but yet hath caused an inquiry,
Whether is worse, the adultery of the man or the woman?

The resolution of which case, in order to our present affair,
is thus: 1. In respect of the person, the fault is greater in a man
than in a woman, who is of a more pliant and easy spirit, and
weaker understanding, and hath nothing to supply the unequal
strengths of men, but the defensative of a passive nature and
armour of modesty, which is the natural ornament of that sex.
And "it is unjust that the man should demand chastity and
severity from his wife which himself will not observe towards
her,"[20] said the good emperor Antoninus: it is as if the man
should persuade his wife to fight against those enemies to
which he had yielded himself a prisoner. 2. In respect of
the effects and evil consequents, the adultery of the woman is
worse, as bringing bastardy into a family, and disinherisons
or great injuries to the lawful children, and infinite violations
of peace, and murders, and divorces, and all the effects of rage
and madness. 3. But in respect of the crime, and as relating
to God, they are equal, intolerable, and damnable: and since
it is no more permitted to men to have many wives than to
women to have many husbands, and that in this respect their
privilege is equal, their sin is so too. And this is the case of
the question in Christianity. And the church anciently refused to admit such persons to the holy communion, until they
had done seven years' penances in fasting, in sackcloth, in
severe inflictions and instruments of chastity and sorrow, according to the discipline of those ages.

Acts of Chastity in general.

The actions and proper offices of the grace of chastity in
general, are these:

1. To resist all unchaste thoughts: at no hand entertaining
pleasure in the unfruitful fancies and remembrances of uncleanness, although no definite desire or resolution be entertained.

2. At no hand to entertain any desire,[21] or any fantastic
imaginative loves, though by shame, or disability, or other
circumstance, they be restrained from act.

[20] Apud Aug. de Adulter. Conjug. Plut. Conjug. Præcept.
[21] —— Casso saltem delectamine amare quod potiri non licet.
                                                        Poeta.

3. To have a chaste eye and hand: for it is all one with what part of the body we commit adultery; and if a man lets his eye loose and enjoys the lust of that, he is an adulterer.[22] "Look not upon a woman to lust after her."[23] And supposing all the other members restrained, yet if the eye be permitted to lust, the man can no otherwise be called chaste than he can be called severe and mortified that sits all day long seeing plays and revellings, and out of greediness to fill his eye, neglects his belly. There are some vessels which, if you offer to lift by the belly or bottom, you cannot stir them, but are soon removed if you take them by the ears. It matters not with which of your members you are taken and carried off from your duty and severity.

4. To have a heart and mind chaste and pure; that is, detesting all uncleanness; disliking all its motions, past actions, circumstances, likenesses, discourses: and this ought to be the chastity of virgins and widows, of old persons and eunuchs especially, and generally of all men, according to their several necessities.

5. To discourse chastely and purely;[24] with great care declining all indecencies of language, chastening the tongue and restraining it with grace, as vapours of wine are restrained with a bunch of myrrh.

6. To disapprove by an after-act all involuntary and natural pollutions: for if a man delights in having suffered any natural pollution, and with pleasure remembers it, he chooses that which was in itself involuntary; and that which, being natural, was innocent, becoming voluntary, is made sinful.

7. They that have performed these duties and parts of chastity will certainly abstain from all exterior actions of uncleanness, those noonday and midnight devils, those lawless and ungodly worshippings of shame and uncleanness, whose birth is in trouble, whose growth is in folly, and whose end is in shame.

But besides these general acts of chastity, which are common to all states of men and women, there are some few things proper to the severals.

[22] Patellas *luxuriæ oculos*, dixit Isidorus. Ἀλγηδόνας ἀνθρώπων, alius quidam. [23] Time videre unde possis cadere, et noli fieri perversâ simplicitate securus.—St. Aug. [24] Sp. Minucius Pontifex Posthumium monuit, ne verbis vitæ castimoniam non æquantibus uteretur.— Τὰ... de Cap. ex Inim. Utilit.

Acts of Virginal Chastity.

1. Virgins must remember, that the virginity of the body is only excellent in order to the purity of the soul; who therefore must consider, that since they are in some measure in a condition like that of angels, it is their duty to spend much of their time in angelical employment; for in the same degree that virgins live more spiritually than other persons, in the same degree is their virginity a more excellent state. But else, it is no better than that of involuntary or constrained eunuchs, a misery and a trouble, or else a mere privation, as much without excellency as without mixture.

2. Virgins must contend for a singular modesty; whose first part must be an ignorance in the distinction of sexes, or their proper instruments; or if they accidentally be instructed in that, it must be supplied with an inadvertency or neglect of all thoughts and remembrances of such difference; and the following parts of it must be pious and chaste thoughts, holy language, and modest carriage.

3. Virgins must be retired and unpublic: for all freedom and looseness of society is a violence done to virginity, not in its natural, but in its moral capacity; that is, it loses part of its severity, strictness, and opportunity of advantages, by publishing that person whose work is religion, whose company is angels, whose thoughts must dwell in heaven, and separate from all mixtures of the world.

4. Virgins have a peculiar obligation to charity: for this is the virginity of the soul; as purity, integrity, and separation is of the body: which doctrine we are taught by St. Peter: " Seeing ye have purified your souls in obeying the truth through the Spirit unto unfeigned love of the brethren, see that ye love one another with a pure heart fervently."[25] For a virgin that consecrates her body to God, and pollutes her spirit with rage, or impatience, or inordinate anger, gives him what he most hates, a most foul and defiled soul.

These rules are necessary for virgins that offer that state to God, and mean not to enter into the state of marriage; for they that only wait the opportunity of a convenient change, are to steer themselves by the general rules of chastity.

[25] 1 Pet. i. 22.

Rules for Widows, or Vidual Chastity.

For widows, the fontanel of whose desires hath been opened by the former permissions of the marriage-bed, they must remember,

1. That God hath now restrained the former licence, bound up their eyes and shut up their heart into a narrower compass, and hath given them sorrow to be a bridle to their desires. A widow must be a mourner; and she that is not cannot so well secure the chastity of her proper state.

2. It is against public honesty to marry another man so long as she is with child by her former husband; and of the same fame it is in a lesser proportion, to marry within the year of mourning; but anciently it was infamous for her to marry till by common account the body was dissolved into its first principle of earth.

3. A widow must restrain her memory and her fancy, not recalling or recounting her former permissions and freer licences with any present delight; for then she opens that sluice which her husband's death and her own sorrow have shut up.

4. A widow that desires her widowhood should be a state pleasing to God, must spend her time as devoted virgins should, in fastings and prayers, and charity.

5. A widow must forbid herself to use those temporal solaces, which in her former estate were innocent, but now are dangerous.

Rules for Married Persons, or Matrimonial Chastity.

Concerning married persons, besides the keeping of their mutual faith and contract with each other, these particulars are useful to be observed.[26]

1. Although their mutual endearments are safe within the protection of marriage, yet they that have wives or husbands must be as though they had them not; that is, they must have an affection greater to each other than they have to any person in the world, but not greater than they have to God; but that they be ready to part with all interest in each other's person rather than sin against God.

2. In their permissions and licence, they must be sure to

[26] Nisi fundamenta stirpis jacta sint probè, Miseros necesse est esse deinceps posteros.—Eurip.

F

observe the order of nature, and the ends of God. "He is an ill husband that uses his wife as a man treats a harlot,"[27] having no other end but pleasure. Concerning which our best rule is, that although in this, as in eating and drinking, there is an appetite to be satisfied which cannot be done without pleasing that desire, yet, since that desire and satisfaction was intended by nature for other ends, they should never be separate from those ends, but always be joined with all or one of these ends, "with a desire of children, or to avoid fornication, or to lighten and ease the cares and sadness of household affairs, or to endear each other;" but never with a purpose, either in act or desire, to separate the sensuality from these ends which hallow it. Onan did separate his act from its proper end, and so ordered his embraces that his wife should not conceive, and God punished him.

3. Married persons must keep such modesty and decency of treating each other,[28] that they never force themselves into high and violent lusts, with arts and misbecoming devices; always remembering, that those mixtures are most innocent which are most simple and most natural, most orderly and most safe.

4. It is a duty of matrimonial chastity to be restrained and temperate in the use of their lawful pleasures; concerning which, although no universal rule can antecedently be given to all persons any more than to all bodies one proportion of meat and drink, yet married persons are to estimate the degree of their licence according to the following proportions. 1. That it be moderate, so as to consist with health. 2. That it be so ordered as not to be too expensive of time, that precious opportunity of working out our salvation. 3. That when duty is demanded, it be always paid (so far as is in our powers and election) according to the foregoing measures. 4. That it be with a temperate affection, without violent, transporting desires, or too sensual applications. Concerning which a man is to make judgment by proportion to other actions, and the severities of his religion, and the sentences

[27] Non debemus eodem amico uti et adulatore; nec eâdem uti uxore et scorto.—Plut. Conjug. Præcept.   [28] Non rectè est ab Herodoto dictum, simul cum tunicâ mulierem verecundiam exuere. Quæ nam casta est, positâ veste, verecundiam ejus loco induit, maximèque verecundiâ conjuges tesserâ maximi invicem amoris utuntur.—Plut. Conjug. Præcept.

of sober and wise persons; always remembering, that marriage is a provision for supply of the natural necessities of the body, not for the artificial and procured appetites of the mind. And it is a sad truth, that many married persons, thinking that the flood-gates of liberty are set wide open without measure or restraint, (so they sail in that channel,) have felt the final rewards of intemperance and lust, by their unlawful using of lawful permissions. Only let each of them be temperate, and both of them be modest. Socrates was wont to say, that those women to whom nature had not been indulgent in good features and colours, should make it up themselves with excellent manners; and those who were beautiful and comely should be careful that so fair a body be not polluted with unhandsome usages. To which Plutarch[29] adds, that a wife, if she be unhandsome, should consider how extremely ugly she would be if she wanted modesty; but if she be handsome, let her think how gracious that beauty would be if she superadds chastity.

5. Married persons by consent are to abstain from their mutual entertainments at solemn times of devotion; not as a duty of itself necessary, but as being the most proper act of purity, which, in their condition, they can present to God, and being a good advantage for attending their preparation to the solemn duty and their demeanour in it. It is St. Paul's counsel, that, "by consent for a time they should abstain, that they may give themselves to fasting and prayer."[30] And though when Christians did receive the holy communion every day,[31] it is certain they did not abstain, but had children; yet, when the communion was more seldom, they did with religion abstain from the marriage-bed during the time of their solemn preparatory devotions, as anciently they did from eating and drinking, till the solemnity of the day was past.

6. It were well if married persons would, in their peniten-

---

[29] De Conjug. Præcept.   [30] 1 Cor. vii. 5.   [31] Hoc etiam ex more Christianorum. Tertul. suadens fœminis Christianis ne Paganis nubant, ait, Quis denique solennibus Paschæ abnoctantem securus sustinebit?—Tertul. ad Uxor. 2. 1. Et ex more etiam Gentilium. Plut. Sympos. 3. q. 6. Nobis autem, si leges civitatis rectè colimus, cavendum est, ne ad templa et sacrificia accedamus, paulò antè re venereâ usi. Itaque expedit, nocte et somno interjecto, justoque intervallo adhibito, mundos rursum quasi de integro, et ad novum diem nova cogitantes (ut ait Democritus) surgere.

tial prayers and in their general confessions, suspect themselves, and accordingly ask a general pardon for all their indecencies, and more passionate applications of themselves in
the offices of marriage: that what is lawful and honourable
in its kind may not be sullied with imperfect circumstances;
or if it be, it may be made clean again by the interruption
and recallings of such a repentance, of which such uncertain
parts of action are capable.

But, because of all the dangers of a Christian none more
pressing and troublesome than the temptations to lust, no enemy
more dangerous than that of the flesh, no accounts greater than
what we have to reckon for at the audit of concupiscence, therefore it concerns all that would be safe from this death to arm
themselves by the following rules, to prevent or to cure all the
wounds of our flesh made by the poisoned arrows of lust.

Remedies against Uncleanness.

1. When a temptation of lust assaults thee, do not resist it
by heaping up arguments against it and disputing with it, considering its offers and its dangers, but fly from it;[32] that is,
think not at all of it, lay aside all consideration concerning it,
and turn away from it by any severe and laudable thought of
business.   St. Jerome very wittily reproves the Gentile superstition, who pictured the virgin-deities armed with a shield
and lance, as if chastity could not be defended without war
and direct contention.   No; this enemy is to be treated otherwise.   If you hear it speak, though but to dispute with it, it
ruins you; and the very arguments you go about to answer,
leave a relish upon the tongue.   A man may be burned if he
goes near the fire, though but to quench his house; and by
handling pitch, though but to draw it from your clothes, you
defile your fingers.

2. Avoid idleness, and fill up all the spaces of thy time with
severe and useful employment; for lust usually creeps in at
those emptinesses where the soul is unemployed, and the body is
at ease.   For no easy, healthful, and idle person was ever
chaste, if he could be tempted.   But of all employments
bodily labour is most useful, and of greatest benefit for the
driving away the devil.

[32] Contra libidinis impetum apprehende fugam, si vis obtinere victoriam.
—St. Aug.   Nella guerra d' amor chi fuge vince.

3. Give no entertainment to the beginnings, the first motions and secret whispers of the spirit of impurity. For if you totally suppress it, it dies ;[33] if you permit the furnace to breathe its smoke and flame out at any vent, it will rage to the consumption of the whole. This cockatrice is soonest crushed in the shell; but if it grows, it turns to a serpent, and a dragon, and a devil.

4. Corporal mortification, and hard usages of our body, hath, by all ages of the church, been accounted a good instrument, and of some profit against the spirit of fornication. A spare diet, and a thin coarse table, seldom refreshment, frequent fasts, not violent, and interrupted with returns to ordinary feeding, but constantly little, unpleasant, of wholesome but sparing nourishment: for by such cutting off the provisions of victual, we shall weaken the strengths of our enemy. To which if we add lyings upon the ground, painful postures in prayer, reciting our devotions with our arms extended at full length, like Moses praying against Amalek, or our blessed Saviour hanging upon his painful bed of sorrows, the cross, and (if the lust be upon us, and sharply tempting) by inflicting any smart to overthrow the strongest passion by the most violent pain, we shall find great ease for the present, and the resolution and apt sufferance against the future danger. And this was St. Paul's remedy, " I bring my body under ;" he used some rudenesses towards it. But it was a great nobleness of chastity which St. Jerome reports of a son of the king of Nicomedia,[34] who, being tempted upon flowers and a perfumed bed with a soft violence, but yet tied down to the temptation, and solicited with circumstances of Asian luxury by an impure courtesan, lest the easiness of his posture should abuse him, spit out his tongue into her face; to represent that no virtue hath cost the saints so much as this of chastity.[35]

5. Fly from all occasions, temptations, loosenesses of company, balls and revellings, indecent mixtures of wanton

[33] ――――― Quisquis in primo obstitit
      Pepulitque amorem, tutus ac victor fuit:
      Qui blandiendo dulce nutrivit malum,
      Serò recusat ferre, quod subiit, jugum.—Senec. Hippol. 133.

[34] In vitâ S. Pauli.   [35] Benedictus in spinis se volutavit, S. Martinianus faciem et manus. S. Johannes, cognomento Bonus, calamos acutos inter ungues et carnem digitorum intrusit. S. Theoctistus in silvis more ferarum vixit, ne inter Arabes pollueretur.

dancings, idle talk, private society with strange women, starings upon a beauteous face, the company of women that are singers, amorous gestures, garish and wanton dresses, feasts and liberty, banquets and perfumes,[36] wine and strong drinks, which are made to persecute chastity ; some of these being the very prologues to lust, and the most innocent of them being but like condited and pickled mushrooms, which, if carefully corrected and seldom tasted, may be harmless, but can never do good ; ever remembering that it is easier to die for chastity than to live with it : and the hangman could not extort a consent from some persons from whom a lover would have entreated it. For the glory of chastity will easily overcome the rudeness of fear and violence ; but easiness and softness and smooth temptations creep in, and, like the sun, make a maiden lay by her veil and robe, which persecution, like the northern wind, makes her hold fast and clap close about her.

6. He that will secure his chastity, must first cure his pride and his rage. For oftentimes lust is the punishment of a proud man,[37] to tame the vanity of his pride by the shame and affronts of unchastity ; and the same intemperate heat that makes anger does enkindle lust.

7. If thou beest assaulted with an unclean spirit, trust not thyself alone ; but run forth into company whose reverence and modesty may suppress, or whose society may divert thy thoughts : and a perpetual witness of thy conversation is of especial use against this vice, which evaporates in the open air like camphire, being impatient of light and witnesses.

8. Use frequent and earnest prayers to the King of purities, the first of virgins, the eternal God, who is of an essential

---

[36] Στέφος πλέκων ποθ' εὗρον
Ἐν τοῖς ῥόδοις Ἔρωτα,
Καὶ τῶν πτερῶν κατασχών,
Ἐβάπτισ' εἰς τὸν οἶνον,
Λαβὼν δ' ἔπιον αὐτόν·
Καὶ νῦν ἔσω μελῶν μου
Πτεροῖσι γαργαλίζει.—Julian.

Venus rosam amat propter fabellam quam recitat.—Labanius.
Venter mero æstuans citò despumatur in libidines.—St. Hieron.
Il fuoco che non mi scalda, non voglio che mi scotti.

[37]   ———numquid ego à te
Magno prognatam deposco consule ———
Velatamque stolâ, mea cùm conferbuit ira?—Horat. Serm. .. i. Sat. 2

purity, that he would be pleased to reprove and cast out the unclean spirit. For beside the blessings of prayer by way of reward, it hath a natural virtue to restrain this vice: because a prayer against it is an unwillingness to act it; and so long as we heartily pray against it our desires are secured, and then this devil hath no power. This was St. Paul's other remedy: "For this cause I besought the Lord thrice." And there is much reason and much advantage in the use of this instrument; because the main thing that in this affair is to be secured, is a man's mind.[38] He that goes about to cure lust by bodily exercise alone (as St. Paul's phrase is) or mortifications, shall find them sometimes instrumental to it, and incitations of sudden desires, but always insufficient and of little profit; but he that hath a chaste mind shall find his body apt enough to take laws; and let it do its worst, it cannot make a sin, and in its greatest violence can but produce a little natural uneasiness, not so much trouble as a severe fasting-day, or a hard night's lodging upon boards. If a man be hungry he must eat; and if he be thirsty he must drink in some convenient time, or else he dies: but if the body be rebellious, so the mind be chaste, let it do its worst, if you resolve perfectly not to satisfy it, you can receive no great evil by it. Therefore the proper cure is by application to the spirit and securities of the mind, which can no way so well be secured as by frequent and fervent prayers, and sober resolutions, and severe discourses. Therefore,

9. Hither bring in succour from consideration of the Divine presence and of his holy angels, meditation of death, and the passions of Christ upon the cross, imitation of his purities, and of the Virgin Mary, his unspotted and holy mother, and of such eminent saints, who, in their generations, were burning and shining lights, unmingled with such uncleannesses which defile the soul, and who now follow the Lamb whithersoever he goes.

10. These remedies are of universal efficacy in all cases extraordinary and violent; but in ordinary and common, the remedy which God hath provided, that is, honourable marriage,[39] hath a natural efficacy, besides a virtue by Divine

---

[38] Mens impudicam facere, non corpus solet. [39] Danda est opera ut matrimonio devinciantur. quod est tutissimum juventutis vinculum.— Plut. de Educ. Lib.

blessing, to cure the inconveniences which otherwise might afflict persons temperate and sober.

SECT. IV. *Of Humility.*

HUMILITY is the great ornament and jewel of Christian religion; that whereby it is distinguished from all the wisdom of the world; it not having been taught by the wise men of the Gentiles, but first put into a discipline, and made part of a religion, by our Lord Jesus Christ, who propounded himself imitable by his disciples so signally in nothing as in the twin sisters of meekness and humility. Learn of me, for I am meek and humble; and ye shall find rest unto your souls.

For all the world, all that we are, and all that we have, our bodies and our souls, our actions and our sufferings, our conditions at home, our accidents abroad, our many sins and our seldom virtues, are as so many arguments to make our souls dwell low in the deep valleys of humility.

Arguments against Pride by way of consideration.

1. Our body is weak and impure, sending out more uncleannesses from its several sinks than could be endured, if they were not necessary and natural; and we are forced to pass that through our mouths, which as soon as we see upon the ground, we loathe like rottenness and vomiting.

2. Our strength is inferior to that of many beasts, and our infirmities so many that we are forced to dress and tend horses and asses, that they may help our needs and relieve our wants.

3. Our beauty is in colour inferior to many flowers, and in proportion of parts it is no better than nothing; for even a dog hath parts as well proportioned and fitted to his purposes, and the designs of his nature, as we have; and when it is most florid and gay, three fits of an ague can change it into yellowness and leanness, and the hollowness and wrinkles of deformity.

4. Our learning is then best when it teaches most humility but to be proud of learning is the greatest ignorance in the world. For our learning is so long in getting, and so very imperfect, that the greatest clerk knows not the thousandth part of what he is ignorant; and knows so uncertainly what he seems to know, and knows no otherwise than a fool or a child even what is told him or what he guesses at, that except

those things which concern his duty, and which God hath revealed to him, which also every woman knows so far as is
necessary, the most learned man hath nothing to be proud of,
unless this be a sufficient argument to exalt him, that he uncertainly guesses at some more unnecessary things than many
others, who yet know all that concerns them, and mind other
things more necessary for the needs of life and commonwealths.

5. He that is proud of riches is a fool. For, if he be exalted above his neighbours, because he hath more gold, how
much inferior is he to a gold mine! How much is he to give
place to a chain of pearl, or a knot of diamonds! For certainly
that hath the greatest excellence from whence he derives all
his gallantry and pre-eminence over his neighbours.

6. If a man be exalted by reason of any excellence in his
soul, he may please to remember that all souls are equal; and
their differing operations are because their instrument is in
better tune, their body is more healthful or better tempered;
which is no more praise to him than it is that he was born in
Italy.

7. He that is proud of his birth is proud of the blessings of
others, not of himself: for if his parents were more eminent
in any circumstances than their neighbours, he is to thank
God, and to rejoice in them; but still he may be a fool, or unfortunate, or deformed; and when himself was born, it was
indifferent to him whether his father were a king or a peasant,
for he knew not any thing nor chose any thing: and most
commonly it is true, that he who boasts of his ancestors, who
were the founders and raisers of a noble family, doth confess
that he hath in himself a less virtue and a less honour, and
therefore that he is degenerated.

8. Whatsoever other difference there is between thee and
thy neighbour, if it be bad it is thine own, but thou hast no
reason to boast of thy misery and shame: if it be good, thou
hast received it from God; and then thou art more obliged to
pay duty and tribute, use and principal to him: and it were
a strange folly for a man to be proud of being more in debt
than another.

9. Remember what thou wert before thou wert begotten.
Nothing. What wert thou in the first regions of thy dwelling, before thy birth? Uncleanness. What wert thou for

many years after? Weakness. What in all thy life? A great sinner. What in all thy excellences? A mere debtor to God, to thy parents, to the earth, to all the creatures. But we may, if we please, use the method of the Platonists,[1] who reduce all the causes and arguments for humility, which we can take from ourselves, to these seven heads. 1. The spirit of a man is light and troublesome. 2. His body is brutish and sickly. 3. He is constant in his folly and error, and inconstant in his manners and good purposes. 4. His labours are vain, intricate, and endless. 5. His fortune is changeable, but seldom pleasing, never perfect. 6. His wisdom comes not till he be ready to die, that is, till he be past using it. 7. His death is certain, always ready at the door, but never far off. Upon these or the like meditations if we dwell, or frequently retire to them, we shall see nothing more reasonable than to be humble, and nothing more foolish than to be proud.

Acts or Offices of Humility.

The grace of humility is exercised by these following rules.

1. Think not thyself better for any thing that happens to thee from without. For although thou mayest, by gifts bestowed upon thee, be better than another, as one horse is better than another, that is, of more use to others; yet, as thou art a man, thou hast nothing to commend thee to thyself but that only by which thou art a man, that is, by what thou choosest and refusest.

2. Humility consists not in railing against thyself, or wearing mean clothes, or going softly and submissively; but in hearty and real evil or mean opinion of thyself. Believe thyself an unworthy person heartily, as thou believest thyself to be hungry, or poor, or sick, when thou art so.

3. Whatsoever evil thou sayest of thyself, be content that others should think to be true: and if thou callest thyself fool, be not angry if another says so of thee. For if thou thinkest so truly, all men in the world desire other men to be of their opinion; and he is a hypocrite that accuses himself before others, with an intent not to be believed. But he that calls himself intemperate, foolish, lustful, and is angry when his neighbours call him so, is both a false and a proud person.

[1] Apuleius de Demon. Socratis.

4. Love to be concealed, and little esteemed :[2] be content to want praise, never being troubled when thou art slighted or undervalued; for thou canst not undervalue thyself, and if thou thinkest so meanly as there is reason, no contempt will seem unreasonable, and therefore it will be very tolerable.

5. Never be ashamed of thy birth,[3] or thy parents, or thy trade,[4] or thy present employment, for the meanness or poverty of any of them; and when there is an occasion to speak of them, such an occasion as would invite you to speak of any thing that pleases you, omit it not, but speak as readily and indifferently of thy meanness as of thy greatness. Primislaus, the first king of Bohemia, kept his country shoes always by him, to remember from whence he was raised: and Agathocles, by the furniture of his table, confessed that from a potter he was raised to be the king of Sicily.

6. Never speak any thing directly tending to thy praise or glory; that is, with a purpose to be commended, and for no other end. If other ends be mingled with thy honour, as if the glory of God, or charity, or necessity, or any thing of prudence be thy end, you are not tied to omit your discourse or your design, that you may avoid praise, but pursue your end, though praise come along in the company. Only let not praise be the design.

7. When thou hast said or done any thing for which thou receivest praise or estimation, take it indifferently and return it to God; reflecting upon him as the giver of the gift, or the blesser of the action, or the aid of the design : and give God thanks for making thee an instrument of his glory, for the benefit of others.

8. Secure a good name to thyself by living virtuously and humbly ; but let this good name be nursed abroad, and never be brought home to look upon it : let others use it for their own advantage; let them speak of it if they please ; but do not thou at all use it, but as an instrument to do God glory, and thy neighbour more advantage. Let thy face, like Moses's, shine to others, but make no looking-glasses for thyself.

9. Take no content in praise when it is offered thee; but let thy rejoicing in God's gift be allayed with fear, lest this

[2] Ama nesciri et pro nihilo reputari.—Gerson.
[3] Il villan nobilitado non cognosce parentado.
[4] Chi del arte sua si vergogna, sempre vive con vergogna.

good bring thee to evil. Use the praise as you use your pleasure in eating and drinking; if it comes, make it do drudgery, let it serve other ends, and minister to necessities, and to caution; lest by pride you lose your just praise, which you have deserved, or else, by being praised unjustly, you receive shame into yourself with God and wise men.

10. Use no stratagems and devices to get praise. Some use to inquire into the faults of their own actions or discourses, on purpose to hear that it was well done or spoken, and without fault;[5] others bring the matter into talk, or thrust themselves into company, and intimate and give occasion to be thought or spoke of. These men make a bait to persuade themselves to swallow the hook, till by drinking the waters of vanity they swell and burst.

11. Make no suppletories to thyself, when thou art disgraced or slighted, by pleasing thyself with supposing thou didst deserve praise, though they understood thee not, or enviously detracted from thee: neither do thou get to thyself a private theatre and flatterers,[6] in whose vain noises and fantastic praises thou mayest keep up thine own good opinion of thyself.

12. Entertain no fancies of vanity and private whispers of this devil of pride; such as was that of Nebuchadnezzar: "Is not this great Babylon, which I have built for the honour of my name, and the might of my majesty, and the power of my kingdom?" Some fantastic spirits will walk alone, and dream waking of greatnesses, of palaces, of excellent orations, full theatres, loud applauses, sudden advancement, great fortunes, and so will spend an hour with imaginative pleasure; all their employment being nothing but fumes of pride, and secret indefinite desires and significations of what their heart wishes. In this, although there is nothing of its own nature directly vicious, yet it is either an ill mother or an ill daughter, an ill sign or an ill effect; and, therefore, at no hand consisting with the safety and interests of humility.

13. Suffer others to be praised in thy presence, and entertain their good and glory with delight; but at no hand dis-

---

[5] Τί οὖν ἡμῖν ὀβελίσκον καταπιὼν περιπατεῖς; ἤθελον ἵνα με καὶ οἱ ἀπαντῶντες θαυμάζωσι, καὶ ἐπακολουθοῦντες ἐπικραυγάζωσιν, ὦ μεγάλου φιλοσόφου.—Arrian. Epict. c. 21. l. i.   [6] Alter alteri satis amplum theatrum sumus; satis unus, satis nullus.—Sen.

parage them, or lessen the report, or make an objection; and think not the advancement of thy brother is a lessening of thy worth. But this act is also to extend further.

14. Be content that he should be employed, and thou laid by as unprofitable; his sentence approved, thine rejected; he be preferred, and thou fixed in a low employment.

15. Never compare thyself with others, unless it be to advance them and to depress thyself. To which purpose, we must be sure, in some sense or other, to think ourselves the worst in every company where we come: one is more learned than I am, another is more prudent, a third more honourable, a fourth more chaste, or he is more charitable, or less proud. For the humble man observes their good, and reflects only upon his own vileness; or considers the many evils of himself certainly known to himself, and the ill of others but by uncertain report; or he considers that the evils done by another are out of much infirmity or ignorance, but his own sins are against a clearer light, and if the other had so great helps, he would have done more good and less evil; or he remembers, that his old sins before his conversion were greater in the nature of the thing, or in certain circumstances, than the sins of other men. So St. Paul reckoned himself the chiefest of sinners, because formerly he had acted the chiefest sin of persecuting the church of God. But this rule is to be used with this caution, that though it be good always to think meanest of ourselves, yet it is not ever safe to speak it, because those circumstances and considerations which determine thy thoughts are not known to others as to thyself; and it may concern others that they hear thee give God thanks for the graces he hath given thee. But if thou preservest thy thoughts and opinions of thyself truly humble, you may with more safety give God thanks in public for that good which cannot or ought not to be concealed.

16. Be not always ready to excuse every oversight, or indiscretion, or ill action, but if thou beest guilty of it confess it plainly; for virtue scorns a lie for its cover, but to hide a sin with it is like a crust of leprosy drawn upon an ulcer. If thou beest not guilty, (unless it be scandalous,) be not over-earnest to remove it, but rather use it as an argument to chastise all greatness of fancy and opinion in thyself; and accustom thyself to bear reproof patiently and contentedly.

and the harsh words of thy enemies, as knowing that the
anger of an enemy is a better monitor, and represents our
faults, or admonishes us of our duty, with more heartiness
than the kindness does, or precious balms, of a friend.

17. Give God thanks for every weakness, deformity, and
imperfection, and accept it as a favour and grace of God, and
an instrument to resist pride, and nurse humility; ever remembering, that when God, by giving thee a crooked back,
hath also made thy spirit stoop or less vain, thou art more
ready to enter the narrow gate of heaven, than by being
straight, and standing upright, and thinking highly. Thus
the apostles rejoiced in their infirmities, not moral, but natural
and accidental, in their being beaten and whipped like slaves,
in their nakedness and poverty.

18. Upbraid no man's weakness to him to discomfort him,
neither report it to disparage him, neither delight to remember it to lessen him, or to set thyself above him. Be sure
never to praise thyself, or to dispraise any man else, unless
God's glory or some holy end do hallow it. And it was noted
to the praise of Cyrus, that, amongst his equals in age,[7] he
would never play at any sport, or use any exercise, in which
he knew himself more excellent than they; but in such in
which he was unskilful he would make his challenges, lest he
should shame them by his victory, and that himself might
learn something of their skill, and do them civilities.

19. Besides the foregoing parts and actions, humility
teaches us to submit ourselves and all our faculties to God,
"to believe all things, to do all things, to suffer all things,"
which his will enjoins us; to be content in every state or
change, knowing we have deserved worse than the worst we
feel, and (as Anytus said to Alcibiades) he hath taken but
half when he might have taken all: to adore his goodness, to
fear his greatness, to worship his eternal and infinite excellences, and to submit ourselves to all our superiors, in all
things, according to godliness, and to be meek and gentle in
our conversation towards others.[8]

[7] Ama l' amico tuo con il difetto suo. In colloquiis, pueri invisi aliis
non fient, si non omnino in disputationibus victoriam semper obtinere la-
borent. Non tantùm egregium est scire vincere, sed etiam posse vinci
pulchrum est, ubi victoria est damnosa.—Plut. de Ed·ac. Lib.

[8] Nihil ita dignum est odio, ut eorum mores, qui compellantibus se
difficiles præbent.—Plut.

Now, although, according to the nature of every grace, this begins as a gift, and is increased like a habit, that is, best by its own acts; yet, besides the former acts and offices of humility, there are certain other exercises and considerations, which are good helps and instruments for the procuring and increasing this grace, and the curing of pride.

Means and Exercises for obtaining and increasing the Grace of Humility.

1. Make confession of thy sins often to God; and consider what all that evil amounts to, which you then charge upon yourself. Look not upon them as scattered in the course of a long life, now an intemperate anger, then too full a meal; now idle talking, and another time impatience; but unite them into one continued representation, and remember, that he whose life seems fair, by reason that his faults are scattered at large distances in the several parts of his life, yet, if all his errors and follies were articled against him, the man would seem vicious and miserable; and possibly this exercise, really applied upon thy spirit, may be useful.

2. Remember that we usually disparage others upon slight grounds and little instances, and towards them one fly is enough to spoil a whole box of ointment; and if a man be highly commended, we think him sufficiently lessened if we clap one sin or folly or infirmity into his account. Let us, therefore, be just to ourselves, since we are so severe to others, and consider that whatsoever good any one can think or say of us, we can tell him of hundreds of base, and unworthy, and foolish actions, any one of which were enough (we hope) to destroy another's reputation; therefore, let so many be sufficient to destroy our over-high thoughts of ourselves.

3. When our neighbour is cried up by public fame and popular noises, that we may disparage and lessen him, we cry out that the people is a herd of unlearned and ignorant persons, ill judges, loud trumpets, but which never give certain sound: let us use the same art to humble ourselves, and never take delight and pleasure in public reports and acclamations of assemblies, and please ourselves with their judgment,[9] of whom, in other the like cases, we affirm that they are mad.

[9] Οὐχ οὗτοί εἰσι, περὶ ὧν εἰωθὸς λέγειν ὅτι μαίνονται; τί οὖν ὑπὸ τῶν μαινομένων θέλεις θαυμάζεσθαι;—Arrian.

4. We change our opinion of others by their kindness or unkindness towards us. If he be my patron and bounteous, he is wise, he is noble; his faults are but warts, his virtues are mountainous: but if he proves unkind, or rejects our importunate suit, then he is ill-natured, covetous, and his free meal is called gluttony; that which before we called civility is now very drunkenness, and all he speaks is flat, and dull, and ignorant as a swine. This, indeed, is unjust towards others; but a good instrument if we turn the edge of it upon ourselves. We use ourselves ill, abusing ourselves with false principles, cheating ourselves with lies and pretences, stealing the choice and election from our wills, placing voluntary ignorance in our understandings, denying the desires of the spirit, setting up a faction against every noble and just desire, the least of which, because we should resent up to reviling the injurious person, it is but reason we should, at least, not flatter ourselves with fond and too kind opinions.

5. Every day call to mind some one of thy foulest sins, or the most shameful of thy disgraces, or the indiscreetest of thy actions, or any thing that did then most trouble thee, and apply it to the present swelling of thy spirit and opinion, and it may help to allay it.

6. Pray often for his grace with all humility of gesture and passion of desire, and in thy devotion interpose many acts of humility, by way of confession and address to God, and reflection upon thyself.

7. Avoid great offices and employments, and the noises of worldly honour.[10] For in those states, many times so many ceremonies and circumstances will seem necessary, as will destroy the sobriety of thy thoughts. If the number of thy servants be fewer, and their observances less, and their reverences less solemn, possibly they will seem less than thy dignity; and if they be so much and so many, it is likely they will be too big for thy spirit. And here be thou very careful, lest thou be abused by a pretence, that thou wouldest use thy great dignity as an opportunity of doing great good. For supposing it might be good for others, yet it is not good for thee; they may have encouragement in noble things from thee, and, by the same instrument, thou mayest thyself be tempted to

[10] Fabis abstine, dixit Pythagoras. Olim nam magistratus per suffragia fabis lata creabantur.—Plut.

pride and vanity. And certain it is, God is as much glorified by thy example of humility in a low or temperate condition as by thy bounty in a great and dangerous.

8. Make no reflex acts upon thy own humility, nor upon
any other grace with which God hath enriched thy soul. For,
since God oftentimes hides from his saints and servants the
sight of those excellent things by which they shine to others,
(though the dark side of the lantern be toward themselves,)
that he may secure the grace of humility, it is good that thou
do so thyself: and if thou beholdest a grace of God in thee,
remember to give him thanks for it, that thou mayest not
boast in that which is none of thy own; and consider how
thou hast sullied it by handling it with dirty fingers, with thy
own imperfections, and with mixture of unhandsome circumstances. Spiritual pride is very dangerous, not only by reason
it spoils so many graces, by which we drew nigh unto the
kingdom of God, but also because it so frequently creeps upon
the spirit of holy persons. For it is no wonder for a beggar to
call himself poor, or a drunkard to confess that he is no sober
person; but for a holy person to be humble, for one whom all
men esteem a saint to fear lest himself become a devil, and to
observe his own danger, and to discern his own infirmities,
and make discovery of his bad adherences, is as hard as for a
prince to submit himself to be guided by tutors, and make
himself subject to discipline, like the meanest of his servants.

9. Often meditate upon the effects of pride on one side,
and humility on the other. First, That pride is like a canker,
and destroys the beauty of the fairest flowers, the most excellent gifts and graces; but humility crowns them all. Secondly,
That pride is a great hinderance to the perceiving the things
of God,[11] and humility is an excellent preparative and instrument of spiritual wisdom. Thirdly, That pride hinders the
acceptation of our prayers, but "humility pierceth the clouds,
and will not depart till the Most High shall regard." Fourthly,
That humility is but a speaking truth, and all pride is a lie.
Fifthly, That humility is the most certain way to real honour,
and pride is ever affronted or despised. Sixthly, That pride
turned Lucifer into a devil, and humility exalted the Son of
God above every name, and placed him eternally at the right
hand of his Father. Seventhly, That "God resisteth tho

[11] Matt. xi. 25.

G

proud," [12] professing open defiance and hostility against such
persons, but "giveth grace to the humble;" grace and pardon,
remedy and relief against misery and oppression, content in
all conditions, tranquillity of spirit, patience in afflictions, love
abroad, peace at home, and utter freedom from contention,
and the sin of censuring others, and the trouble of being censured themselves. For the humble man will not "judge his
brother for the mote in his eye," being more troubled at "the
beam in his own eye;" and is patient and glad to be reproved,
because himself hath cast the first stone at himself, and therefore wonders not that others are of his mind.

10. Remember that the blessed Saviour of the world hath
done more to prescribe, and transmit, and secure this grace,
than any other; [13] his whole life being a great continued example of humility, a vast descent from the glorious bosom of
his Father, to the womb of a poor maiden, to the form of a
servant, to the miseries of a sinner, to a life of labour, to a state
of poverty, to a death of malefactors, to the grave of death,
and the intolerable calamities which we deserved; and it
were a good design, and yet but reasonable, that we should
be as humble in the midst of our greatest imperfections and
basest sins, as Christ was in the midst of his fulness of the
Spirit, great wisdom, perfect life, and most admirable virtues.

11. Drive away all flatterers from thy company, and at no
hand endure them; for he that endures himself so to be abused
by another is not only a fool for entertaining the mockery, but
loves to have his own opinion of himself to be heightened and
cherished.

12. Never change thy employment for the sudden coming
of another to thee; but if modesty permits, or discretion, appear to him that visits thee the same that thou wert to God
and thyself in thy privacy. But if thou wert walking or
sleeping, or in any other innocent employment or retirement,
snatch not up a book to seem studious, nor fall on thy knees
to seem devout, nor alter any thing to make him believe thee
better employed than thou wert.

13. To the same purpose it is of great use, that he who
would preserve his humility should choose some spiritual
person to whom he shall oblige himself to discover his very
thoughts and fancies, every act of his, and all his intercourse

[12] James iv. 6.   [13] John xiii. 15.

with others, in which there may be danger; that by such an openness of spirit he may expose every blast of vain-glory, every idle thought, to be chastened and lessened by the rod of spiritual discipline; and he that shall find himself tied to confess every proud thought, every vanity of his spirit, will also perceive they must not dwell with him, nor find any kindness from him; and, besides this, the nature of pride is so shameful and unhandsome, that the very discovery of it is a huge mortification and means of suppressing it. A man would be ashamed to be told that he inquires after the faults of his last oration or action on purpose to be commended; and, therefore, when the man shall tell his spiritual guide the same shameful story of himself, it is very likely he will be humbled, and heartily ashamed of it.

14. Let every man suppose what opinion he should have of one that should spend his time in playing with drum-sticks and cockle-shells, and that should wrangle all day long with a little boy for pins, or should study hard and labour to cozen a child of his gauds; and who would run into a river, deep and dangerous, with a great burden upon his back, even then when he were told of the danger, and earnestly importuned not to do it; and let him but change the instances and the person, and he shall find that he hath the same reason to think as bad of himself, who pursues trifles with earnestness, spending his time in vanity, and his " labour for that which profits not;" who, knowing the laws of God, the rewards of virtue, the cursed consequents of sin, that it is an evil spirit that tempts him to it, a devil, one that hates him, that longs extremely to ruin him; that it is his own destruction that he is then working; that the pleasures of his sin are base and brutish, unsatisfying in the enjoyment, soon over, shameful in their story, bitter in the memory, painful in the effect here, and intolerable hereafter and for ever: yet in despite of all this, he runs foolishly into his sin and his ruin, merely because he is a fool, and winks hard, and rushes violently like a horse into the battle, or like a madman to his death. He that can think great and good things of such a person, the next step may court the rack for an instrument of pleasure, and admire a swine for wisdom, and go for counsel to the prodigal and trifling grasshopper.

After the use of these and such like instruments and considerations, if you would try how your soul is grown, you shall know that humility, like the root of a goodly tree, is thrust very far into the ground by these goodly fruits which appear above ground.

Signs of Humility.

1. The humble man trusts not to his own discretion, but in matters of concernment relies rather upon the judgment of his friends, counsellors, or spiritual guides. 2. He does not pertinaciously pursue the choice of his own will, but in all things lets God choose for him, and his superiors, in those things which concern them. 3. He does not murmur against commands.[14] 4. He is not inquisitive into the reasonableness of indifferent and innocent commands, but believes their command to be reason enough in such cases to exact his obedience. 5. He lives according to a rule, and with compliance to public customs, without any affectation or singularity. 6. He is meek and indifferent in all accidents and chances. 7. He patiently bears injuries.[15] 8. He is always unsatisfied in his own conduct, resolutions, and counsels. 9. He is a great lover of good men, and a praiser of wise men, and a censurer of no man. 10. He is modest in his speech, and reserved in his laughter. 11. He fears when he hears himself commended, lest God make another judgment concerning his actions than men do. 12. He gives no pert or saucy answers when he is reproved, whether justly or unjustly. 13. He loves to sit down in private, and, if he may, he refuses the temptation of offices and new honours. 14. He is ingenuous, free, and open, in his actions and discourses. 15. He mends his fault, and gives thanks, when he is admonished. 16. He is ready to do good offices to the murderers of his fame, to his slanderers, backbiters, and detractors, as Christ washed the feet of Judas. 17. And is contented to be suspected of indiscretion, so before God he may be really innocent, and not offensive to his neighbour, nor wanting to his just and prudent interest.

Sect. V. *Of Modesty.*

Modesty is the appendage of sobriety, and is to chastity, to temperance, and to humility, as the fringes are to a garment. It is a grace of God, that moderates the over-activeness and

---

[14] Assai commanda, chi ubbidisce al saggio.
[15] Verum humilem patientia ostendit _ Hier.

curiosity of the mind, and orders the passions of the body and external actions, and is directly opposed to curiosity, to bold-- ness, to indecency. The practice of modesty consists in these following rules.

Acts and Duties of Modesty, as it is opposed to Curiosity.[1]

1. Inquire not into the secrets of God,[2] but be content to learn thy duty according to the quality of thy person or employment: that is, plainly, if thou beest not concerned in the conduct of others ; but if thou beest a teacher, learn it so as may best enable thee to discharge thy office. God's commandments were proclaimed to all the world ; but God's counsels are to himself and to his secret ones, when they are admitted within the veil.

2. Inquire not into the things which are too hard for thee, but learn modestly to know thy infirmities and abilities ;[3] and raise not thy mind up to inquire into mysteries of state, or the secrets of government, or difficulties theological, if thy employment really be, or thy understanding be judged to be, of a lower rank.

3. Let us not inquire into the affairs of others that concern us not, but be busied within ourselves and our own spheres ; ever remembering that to pry into the actions or interests of other men not under our charge, may minister to pride, to tyranny, to uncharitableness, to trouble, but can never consist with modesty ; unless where duty or the mere intentions of charity and relation do warrant it.

4. Never listen at the doors or windows :[4] for, besides that it contains in it danger and a snare, it is also an invading my neighbour's privacy, and a laying that open which he therefore enclosed, that it might not be open. Never ask what he carries covered so curiously ; for it is enough that it is covered curiously. Hither, also, is reducible that we never open letters without public authority, or reasonable presumed leave, or great necessity, or charity.

---

[1] Εὐσχημοσύνη. [2] Ecclus. iii. 21—23.
[3] Qui scrutator est majestatis, opprimetur à gloria.—Prov. xxv. Αὕτη ἀρχὴ τοῦ φιλοσοφεῖν, αἴσθησις τοῦ ἰδίου ἡγεμονικοῦ, πῶς ἔχει· μετὰ γὰρ τὸ γνῶναι ὅτι ἀσθενῶς, οὐκέτι ϑελήσει χρῆσθαι αὐτῷ πρὸς τὰ μέγιστα. Arrian. lib. i. cap. 26. Et plus sapere interdum vulgus, quòd, quantum opus est, sapiat. Lactant. [4] Eccles. vii. 21. Ne occhi in lettera, ne mano in tasca, ne orecchi in secreti altrui.

Every man hath in his own life sins enough, in his own mind trouble enough, in his own fortune evils enough, and in performance of his offices failings more than enough, to entertain his own inquiry; so that curiosity after the affairs of others cannot be without envy and an evil mind. What is it to me, if my neighbour's grandfather were a Syrian, or his grandmother illegitimate; or that another is indebted five thousand pounds, or whether his wife be expensive? But commonly curious persons, or (as the apostle's phrase is) "busy bodies," are not solicitous or inquisitive into the beauty and order of a well-governed family, or after the virtues of an excellent person; but if there be any thing for which men keep locks and bars, and porters, things that blush to see the light, and either are shameful in manners, or private in nature, these things are their care and their business. But if great things will satisfy our inquiry, the course of the sun and moon, the spots in their faces, the firmament of heaven, and the supposed orbs, the ebbing and flowing of the sea, are work enough for us: or if this be not, let him tell me whether the number of the stars be even or odd, and when they began to be so; since some ages have discovered new stars which the former knew not, but might have seen if they had been where now they are fixed. If these be too troublesome, search lower, and tell me why this turf this year brings forth a daisy, and the next year a plantain, why the apple bears his seed in his heart, and wheat bears it in his head: let him tell why a graft, taking nourishment from a crab-stock, shall have a fruit more noble than its nurse and parent: let him say why the best of oil is at the top, the best of wine in the middle, and the best of honey at the bottom, otherwise than it is in some liquors that are thinner, and in some that are thicker. But these things are not such as please busy-bodies; they must feed upon tragedies, and stories of misfortunes and crimes: and yet tell them ancient stories of the ravishment of chaste maidens, or the debauchment of nations, or the extreme poverty of learned persons, or the persecutions of the old saints, or the changes of government, and sad accidents happening in royal families among the Arsacidæ, the Cæsars, the Ptolemies, these were enough to scratch the itch of knowing sad stories; but unless you tell them something sad and new, something that is done within the bounds of their own knowledge or relation it seem tedious and unsatisfying ; which shows plainly, it is an evil spirit: envy and idleness married together, and begot curiosity. Therefore Plutarch rarely well compares curious and inquisitive ears to the execrable gates of cities, out of which only malefactors and hangmen and tragedies pass— nothing that is chaste or holy. If a physician should go from house to house unsent for, and inquire what woman hath a cancer in her bowels, or what man hath a fistula in his colic-gut, though he could pretend to cure it, he would be almost as unwelcome as the disease itself; and therefore it is inhuman to inquire after crimes and disasters without pretence of amending them, but only to discover them. We are not angry with searchers and publicans, when they look only on public merchandise; but when they break open trunks, and pierce vessels, and unrip packs, and open sealed letters.

Curiosity is the direct incontinency of the spirit; and adultery itself, in its principle, is many times nothing but a curious inquisition after, and envying of, another man's enclosed pleasures ; and there have been many who refused fairer objects that they might ravish an enclosed woman from her retirement and single possessor. But these inquisitions are seldom without danger, never without baseness; they are neither just, nor honest, nor delightful, and very often useless to the curious inquirer. For men stand upon their guards against them, as they secure their meat against harpies and cats, laying all their counsels and secrets out of their way ; or as men clap their garments close about them, when the searching and saucy winds would discover their nakedness ; as knowing that what men willingly hear they do willingly speak of. Knock, therefore, at the door before you enter upon your neighbour's privacy; and remember, that there is no difference between entering into his house, and looking into it.

Acts of Modesty as it is opposed to Boldness.[s]

1. Let us always bear about us such impressions of reverence and fear of God as to tremble at his voice, to express our apprehensions of his greatness in all great accidents, in popular judgments, loud thunders, tempests, earthquakes ; not only for fear of being smitten ourselves, or that we are concerned in the accident, but also that we may humble our-

[s] Αἰσχύνη.

selves before his Almightiness, and express that infinite distance between his infiniteness and our weaknesses, at such times especially when he gives such visible arguments of it. He that is merry and airy at shore when he sees a sad and a loud tempest on the sea, or dances briskly when God thunders from heaven, regards not when God speaks to all the world, but is possessed with a firm immodesty.

2. Be reverent, modest, and reserved in the presence of thy betters, giving to all according to their quality their titles of honour, keeping distance, speaking little, answering pertinently, not interposing without leave or reason, not answering to a question propounded to another; and ever present to thy superiors the fairest side of thy discourse, of thy temper, of thy ceremony, as being ashamed to serve excellent persons with unhandsome intercourse.

3. Never lie before a king or a great person, nor stand in a lie, when thou art accused; nor offer to justify what is indeed a fault, but modestly be ashamed of it, ask pardon, and make amends.[6]

4. Never boast of thy sin, but at least lay a veil upon thy nakedness and shame,[7] and put thine hand before thine eyes, that thou mayest have this beginning of repentance, to believe thy sin to be thy shame. For he that blushes not at his crime, but adds shamelessness to his shame, hath no instrument left to restore him to the hopes of virtue.

5. Be not confident and affirmative in an uncertain matter, but report things modestly and temperately, according to the degree of that persuasion which is, or ought to be, begotten in thee by the efficacy of the authority, or the reason inducing thee.

6. Pretend not to more knowledge than thou hast, but be content to seem ignorant where thou art so, lest thou beest either brought to shame, or retirest into shamelessness.[8]

Acts of Modesty as it is opposed to Indecency.[9]

1. In your prayers, in churches and places of religion, use

---

[6] Quem Deus tegit verecundiæ pallio, hujus maculas hominibus non ostendit.—Maimon. Can. Eth.

Πρῶτον ἀγαθῶν ἀναμάρτητον, δεύτερον δ' αἰσχύναι.—Meliss.

Obstare primum est velle, nec labi via;
Pudor est secundus, nôsse peccandi modum.—Senec. Hip. 140.

[7] A Chione saltem, vel ab Helide disce pudorem;
Abscondunt spurcas hæc monumenta lupas.—Mart. lib. i. Ep. 35

[8] Ecclus. iii. 25.   [9] Κοσμιότης, εὐταξίι or εὐπρέπεια.

reverent postures, great attention, grave ceremony, the lowest gestures of humility, remembering that we speak to God, in our reverence to whom we cannot possibly exceed; but that the expression of this reverence be according to law or custom, and the example of the most prudent and pious persons; that is, let it be the best in its kind to the best of essences.

2. In all public meetings, private addresses, in discourses, in journeys, use those forms of salutation, reverence, and decency, which the custom prescribes, and is usual amongst the most sober persons; giving honour to whom honour belongeth, taking place of none of thy betters, and in all cases of question concerning civil precedency, giving it to any one that will take it, if it be only thy own right that is in question.

3. Observe the proportion of affections in all meetings and to all persons: be not merry at a funeral, nor sad upon a festival; but rejoice with them that rejoice, and weep with them that weep.

4. Abstain from wanton and dissolute laughter, petulant and uncomely jests, loud talking, jeering, and all such actions, which in civil account are called indecencies and incivilities.

5. Towards your parents use all modesty of duty and humble carriage; towards them and all your kindred, be severe in the modesties of chastity; ever fearing lest the freedoms of natural kindness should enlarge into any neighbourhood of unhandsomeness. For all incestuous mixtures, and all circumstances and degrees towards it, are the highest violations of modesty in the world: for therefore incest is grown to be so high a crime, especially in the last periods of the world, because it breaks that reverence which the consent of all nations and the severity of human laws hath enjoined towards our parents and nearest kindred, in imitation of that law which God gave to the Jews in prosecution of modesty in this instance.

6. Be a curious observer of all those things which are of good report, and are parts of public honesty.[10] For public fame, and the sentence of prudent and public persons, is the measure of good and evil in things indifferent; and charity requires us to comply with those fancies and affections which are agreeable to nature, or the analogy of virtue, or public laws, or old customs. It is against modesty for a woman to marry a second husband as long as she bears a burden by the first;

[10] Philip. iv. 8.

or to admit a second love while her funeral tears are not wiped
from her cheeks. It is against public honesty to do some
lawful actions of privacy in public theatres, and therefore in
such cases retirement is a duty of modesty.[11]

7. Be grave, decent, and modest, in thy clothing and ornament: never let it be above thy condition, not always equal
to it, never light or amorous, never discovering a nakedness
through a thin veil, which thou pretendest to hide, never to
lay a snare for a soul; but remember what becomes a Christian, professing holiness, chastity, and the discipline of the
Holy Jesus: and the first effect of this let your servants feel
by your gentleness and aptness to be pleased with their usual
diligence, and ordinary conduct. For the man or woman that
is dressed with anger and impatience,[12] wears pride under
their robes, and immodesty above.

8. Hither, also, is to be reduced singular and affected walking, proud, nice, and ridiculous gestures of body, painting and
lascivious dressings: all which together God reproves by the
prophet: "The Lord saith, Because the daughters of Sion
are haughty, and walk with stretched-forth necks and wanton
eyes, walking and mincing as they go, and make a tinkling
with their feet; therefore the Lord will smite her with a scab
of the crown of the head, and will take away the bravery of
their tinkling ornaments."[13] And this duty of modesty, in
this instance, is expressly enjoined to all Christian women by
St. Paul: "That women adorn themselves in modest apparel,
with shamefacedness and sobriety, not with broidered hair, or
gold, or pearl, or costly array, but (which becometh women
professing godliness) with good works."[14]

9. As those meats are to be avoided which tempt our
stomachs beyond our hunger, so, also, should prudent persons
decline all such spectacles, relations, theatres, loud noises and
outcries, which concern us not, and are besides our natural or
moral interest. Our senses should not, like petulant and
wanton girls, wander into markets and theatres without just

[11] At meretrix abigit testem veloque seráque;
    Raraque Summœni fornice rima patet.—Mart. i. 53.
[12] Tuta sit ornatrix: odi quæ sauciat ora
    Unguibus, et raptâ brachia figit acu.
  Devovet, et tangit dominæ caput illa, simulque
    Plorat ad invisas sanguinolenta comas.—Ovid. A. A. iii. 239.
[13] Isa. iii. 16—18.   [14] 1 Tim. ii. 9.

employment; but when they are sent abroad by reason, return
quickly with their errand, and remain modestly at home under
their guide, till they be sent again.[15]

10. Let all persons be curious in observing modesty towards
themselves, in the handsome treating their own body, and such
as are in their power, whether living or dead. Against this
rule they offend who expose to others their own, or pry into
others' nakedness beyond the limits of necessity, or where a
leave is not made holy by a permission from God. It is also
said, that God was pleased to work a miracle about the body
of Epiphanius to reprove the immodest curiosity of an unconcerned person who pried too near, when charitable people
were composing it to the grave. In all these cases and particulars, although they seem little, yet our duty and concernment is not little. Concerning which I use the words of the
son of Sirach, "He that despiseth little things, shall perish
by little and little."

SECT. VI. *Of Contentedness in all Estates and Accidents.*

VIRTUES and discourses are, like friends, necessary in all fortunes; but those are the best, which are friends in our sadnesses, and support us in our sorrows and sad accidents: and
in this sense, no man that is virtuous can be friendless; nor
hath any man reason to complain of the Divine providence, or
accuse the public disorder of things, or his own infelicity,
since God hath appointed one remedy for all the evils in the
world, and that is a contented spirit: for this alone makes a
man pass through fire, and not be scorched; through seas,
and not be drowned; through hunger and nakedness, and
want nothing. For since all the evil in the world consists in
the disagreeing between the object and the appetite, as when
a man hath what he desires not, or desires what he hath not,
or desires amiss; he that composes his spirit to the present
accident, hath variety of instances for his virtue, but none to
trouble him, because his desires enlarge not beyond his present fortune: and a wise man is placed in the variety of
chances, like the nave or centre of a wheel, in the midst of all
the circumvolutions and changes of posture, without violence
or change, save that it turns gently in compliance with its
changed parts, and is indifferent which part is up, and which is

[15] Œdipum curiositas in extremas conjecit calamitates.—Plut.

down; for there is some virtue or other to be exercised, whatever happens, either patience or thanksgiving, love or fear, moderation or humility, charity or contentedness, and they are every one of them equally in order to his great end and immortal felicity: and beauty is not made by white or red, by black eyes and a round face, by a straight body and a smooth skin; but by a proportion to the fancy. No rules can make amiability; our minds and apprehensions make that: and so is our felicity; and we may be reconciled to poverty and a low fortune, if we suffer contentedness and the grace of God to make the proportions. For no man is poor that does not think himself so: but if, in a full fortune, with impatience he desires more, he proclaims his wants and his beggarly condition.[1] But because this grace of contentedness was the sum of all the old moral philosophy, and a great duty in Christianity, and of most universal use in the whole course of our lives, and the only instrument to ease the burdens of the world and the enmities of sad chances, it will not be amiss to press it by the proper arguments by which God hath bound it upon our spirits; it being fastened by reason and religion, by duty and interest, by necessity and conveniency, by example, and by the proposition of excellent rewards, no less than peace and felicity.

1. Contentedness in all estates is a duty of religion; it is the great reasonableness of complying with the Divine Providence, which governs all the world, and hath so ordered us in the administration of his great family. He were a strange fool that should be angry because dogs and sheep need no shoes, and yet himself is full of care to get some. God hath supplied those needs to them by natural provisions, and to thee by an artificial: for he hath given thee reason to learn a trade, or some means to make or buy them, so that it only differs in the manner of our provision: and which had you rather want, shoes or reason? and my patron, that hath given me a farm, is freer to me than if he gives a loaf ready baked. But, however, all these gifts come from him, and therefore it is fit he should dispense them as he pleases; and if we murmur here, we may, at the next melancholy, be troubled that God did not make us to be angels or stars. For if that which we

[1] N·n facta tibi est, si dissimules, injuria.

are or have do not content us, we may be troubled for every thing in the world which is beside our being or our possessions.

God is the master of the scenes; we must not choose which part we shall act; it concerns us only to be careful that we do it well, always saying, "If this please God, let it be as it is:"[2] and we, who pray that God's will may be done in earth as it is in heaven, must remember that the angels do whatsoever is commanded them, and go wherever they are sent, and refuse no circumstances; and if their employment be crossed by a higher decree, they sit down in peace, and rejoice in the event; and when the angel of Judea could not prevail in behalf of the people committed to his charge,[3] because the angel of Persia opposed it, he only told the story at the command of God, and was as content, and worshipped with as great an ecstasy in his proportion, as the prevailing spirit. Do thou so likewise: keep the station where God hath placed you, and you shall never long for things without, but sit at home, feasting upon the Divine Providence and thy own reason, by which we are taught that it is necessary and reasonable to submit to God.

For is not all the world God's family? Are not we his creatures? Are we not as clay in the hand of the potter? Do we not live upon his meat, and move by his strength, and do our work by his light? Are we any thing but what we are from him? And shall there be a mutiny among the flocks and herds, because their lord or their shepherd chooses their pastures, and suffers them not to wander into deserts and unknown ways? If we choose, we do it so foolishly that we cannot like it long, and most commonly not at all: but God, who can do what he pleases, is wise to choose safely for us, affectionate to comply with our needs, and powerful to execute all his wise decrees. Here, therefore, is the wisdom of the contented man, to let God choose for him; for when we have given up our wills to him, and stand in that station of the battle where our great General hath placed us, our spirits must needs rest while our conditions have for their security the power, the wisdom, and the charity of God.

2. Contentedness in all accidents brings great peace of spirit, and is the great and only instrument of temporal felicity. It removes the sting from the accident, and makes a

---

[2] Εἰ τοῦτο τῷ Θεῷ φίλον, τοῦτο γενέσθω.　　　　[3] Dan. x. 13.

man not to depend upon chance and the uncertain dispositions of men for his well-being, but only on God and his own spirit. We ourselves make our fortunes good or bad ;[4] and when God lets loose a tyrant upon us, or a sickness, or scorn, or a lessened fortune, if we fear to die, or know not to be patient, or are proud, or covetous, then the calamity sits heavy on us. But if we know how to manage a noble principle, and fear not death so much as a dishonest action, and think impatience a worse evil than a fever, and pride to be the biggest disgrace, and poverty to be infinitely desirable before the torments of covetousness; then we who now think vice to be so easy, and make it so familiar, and think the cure so impossible, shall quickly be of another mind, and reckon these accidents amongst things eligible.

But no man can be happy that hath great hopes and great fears of things without, and events depending upon other men, or upon the chances of fortune. The rewards of virtue are certain, and our provisions for our natural support are certain; or if we want meat till we die, then we die of that disease—and there are many worse than to die with an atrophy or consumption, or unapt and coarser nourishment. But he that suffers a transporting passion concerning things within the power of others, is free from sorrow and amazement no longer than his enemy shall give him leave; and it is ten to one but he shall be smitten then and there where it shall most trouble him; for so the adder teaches us where to strike, by her curious and fearful defending of her head. The old Stoics, when you told them of a sad story, would still answer, τὶ πρὸς με; "*What is that to me?*" Yes, for the tyrant hath sentenced you also to prison. Well, what is that? He will put a chain upon my leg; but he cannot bind my soul. No; but he will kill you. Then I will die. If presently, let me go, that I may presently be freer than himself: but if not till anon, or to-morrow, I will dine first, or sleep, or do what reason or nature calls for, as at other times. This, in Gentile philosophy, is the same with the discourse of St. Paul,[5] "I have learned, in whatsoever state I am, therewith to be content. I know both how to be abased, and I know how to abound: every where and in all things I am instructed,

---

[4] Ὁ Θεὸς τέθεικε, καὶ φῆσιν, εἴ τι ἀγαθὸν Θέλεις, παρὰ σεαυτοῦ λαβὶ —Arrian. Ep.   [5] Phil. iv. 11, 12; 1 Tim. vi. 6; Heb. xiii. 5.

both to be full and to be hungry; both to abound and suffer need."[6]

We are in the world like men playing at tables; the chance is not in our power, but to play it is; and when it is fallen we must manage it as we can: and let nothing trouble us, but when we do a base action, or speak like a fool, or think wickedly,—these things God hath put into our powers; but concerning those things which are wholly in the choice of another, they cannot fall under our deliberation, and therefore neither are they fit for our passions. My fear may make me miserable, but it cannot prevent what another hath in his power and purpose; and prosperities can only be enjoyed by them who fear not at all to lose them; since the amazement and passion concerning the future takes off all the pleasure of the present possession. Therefore, if thou hast lost thy land, do not also lose thy constancy; and if thou must die a little sooner, yet do not die impatiently. For no chance is evil to him that is content: and to a man nothing is miserable unless it be unreasonable.[7] No man can make another man to be his slave unless he hath first enslaved himself to life and death, to pleasure or pain, to hope or fear: command these passions, and you are freer than the Parthian kings.

Instruments or Exercises to procure Contentedness.

Upon the strength of these premises, we may reduce this virtue to practice by its proper instruments first, and then by some more special considerations or arguments of content.

1. When any thing happens to our displeasure, let us endeavour to take off its trouble by turning it into spiritual or artificial advantage, and handle it on that side in which it may be useful to the designs of reason; for there is nothing but hath a double handle, or at least we have two hands to apprehend it. When an enemy reproaches us, let us look on him as an impartial relater of our faults, for he will tell thee truer than thy fondest friend will; and thou mayest call them precious balms, though they break thy head, and forgive his anger, while thou makest use of the plainness of his declamation. "The ox, when he is weary, treads surest:" and if there be nothing else in the disgrace, but that it makes us to

---

[6] Chi ben e mal non può soffrire, a grand onor non può venire.
[7] Πᾶν τὸ εὔλογον, φορητόν.

walk warily, and tread sure for fear of our enemies, that is better than to be flattered into pride and carelessness. This is the charity of Christian philosophy, which expounds the sense of the Divine providence fairly, and reconciles us to it by a charitable construction: and we may as well refuse all physic, if we consider it only as unpleasant in the taste; and we may find fault with the rich valleys of Thasus, because they are circled by sharp mountains: but so, also, we may be in charity with every unpleasant accident, because, though it taste bitter, it is intended for health and medicine.

If, therefore, thou fallest from thy employment in public, take sanctuary in an honest retirement, being indifferent to thy gain abroad, or thy safety at home. If thou art out of favour with thy prince, secure the favour of the King of kings, and then there is no harm come to thee. And when Zeno Citiensis lost all his goods in a storm, he retired to the studies of philosophy, to his short cloak and a severe life, and gave thanks to fortune for his prosperous mischance. When the north wind blows hard, and it rains sadly, none but fools sit down in it and cry; wise people defend themselves against it with a warm garment, or a good fire and a dry roof. When a storm of a sad mischance beats upon our spirits, turn it into some advantage by observing where it can serve another end, either of religion or prudence, of more safety or less envy: it will turn into something that is good, if we list to make it so; at least it may make us weary of the world's vanity, and take off our confidence from uncertain riches, and make our spirits to dwell in those regions where content dwells essentially. If it does any good to our souls, it hath made more than sufficient recompence for all the temporal affliction. He that threw a stone at a dog, and hit his cruel step-mother, said, that although he intended it otherwise, yet the stone was not quite lost; and if we fail in the first design, if we bring it home to another equally to content us, or more to profit us, then we have put our conditions past the power of chance; and this was called, in the old Greek comedy, "a being revenged on fortune by becoming philosophers," and turning the chance into reason or religion: for so a wise man shall overrule his stars, and have a greater influence upon his own content than all the constellations and planets of the firmament.

2. Never compare thy condition with those above thee;

but, to secure thy content, look upon those thousands with
whom thou wouldest not, for any interest, change thy fortune
and condition. A soldier must not think himself unprosperous
if he be not successful as the son of Philip, or cannot grasp a
fortune as big as the Roman empire. Be content that thou
art not lessened as was Pyrrhus, or, if thou beest, that thou
art not routed like Crassus; and when that comes to thee, it
is a great prosperity that thou art not caged and made a
spectacle, like Bajazet, or thy eyes were not pulled out, like
Zedekiah's, or that thou wert not flayed alive, like Valentinian.
If thou admirest the greatness of Xerxes, look also on those
that digged the mountain Atho, or whose ears and noses were
cut off because the Hellespont carried away the bridge. It is
a fine thing (thou thinkest) to be carried on men's shoulders;
but give God thanks that thou art not forced to carry a rich
fool upon thy shoulders, as those poor men do whom thou beholdest. There are but a few kings in mankind; but many
thousands who are very miserable if compared to thee. However, it is a huge folly rather to grieve for the good of others
than to rejoice for that good which God hath given us of our
own.

And yet there is no wise or good man that would change
persons or conditions entirely with any man in the world. It
may be, he would have one man's wealth added to himself, or
the power of a second, or the learning of a third; but still he
would receive these into his own person because he loves that
best, and therefore esteems it best, and therefore overvalues
all that which he is, before all that which any other man in
the world can be. Would any man be Dives to have his
wealth, or Judas for his office, or Saul for his kingdom, or
Absalom for his beauty, or Achitophel for his policy? It is
likely he would wish all these, and yet he would be the same
person still. For every man hath desires of his own, and objects just fitted to them, without which he cannot be, unless he
were not himself. And let every man that loves himself so well
as to love himself before all the world, consider if he have not
something for which in the whole he values himself far more
than he can value any man else. There is, therefore, no reason
to take the finest feathers from all the winged nation to deck
that bird that thinks already she is more valuable than any of
the inhabitants of the air. Either change all or none. Cease

to love yourself best, or be content with that portion of being and blessing for which you love yourself so well.

3. It conduces much to our content, if we pass by those things which happen to our trouble, and consider that which is pleasing and prosperous, that, by the representation of the better, the worst may be blotted out; and, at the worst, you have enough to keep you alive, and to keep up and to improve your hopes of heaven. If I be overthrown in my suit at law, yet my house is left me still and my land; or I have a virtuous wife, or hopeful children, or kind friends, or good hopes. If I have lost one child, it may be I have two or three still left me. Or else reckon the blessings which already you have received, and therefore be pleased, in the change and variety of affairs, to receive evil from the hand of God as well as good. Antipater, of Tarsus, used this art to support his sorrows on his death-bed, and reckoned the good things of his past life, not forgetting to recount it as a blessing, an argument that God took care of him, that he had a prosperous journey from Cilicia to Athens. Or else please thyself with hopes of the future;[8] for we were not born with this sadness upon us, and it was a change that brought us into it, and a change may bring us out again. Harvest will come, and then every farmer is rich, at least for a month or two.[9] It may be thou art entered into the cloud, which will bring a gentle shower to refresh thy sorrows.

Now suppose thyself in as great a sadness as ever did load thy spirit, wouldst thou not bear it cheerfully and nobly if thou wert sure that within a certain space some strange excellent fortune would relieve thee, and enrich thee, and recompense thee, so as to overflow all thy hopes and thy desires and capacities? Now then, when a sadness lies heavy upon thee, remember that thou art a Christian designed to the inheritance of Jesus; and what dost thou think concerning thy great fortune, thy lot and portion of eternity? Dost thou think thou shalt be saved or damned? Indeed, if thou thinkest thou shalt perish, I cannot blame thee to be sad, till thy heart-strings crack; but then why art thou troubled at the loss of thy money? What should a damned man do with

---

[8] La speranza è il pan de poveri.
      Non si malè nunc, et olim sic erit.—Hor. ii. 10.
[9] Ἀεὶ γεωργὸς εἰς νέωτα πλούσιος.

money, which in so great a sadness it is impossible for him to enjoy? Did ever any man upon the rack afflict himself because he had received a cross answer from his mistress? or call for the particulars of a purchase upon the gallows? If thou dost really believe thou shalt be damned, I do not say it will cure the sadness of thy poverty, but it will swallow it up. But if thou believest thou shalt be saved, consider how great is that joy, how infinite is that change, how unspeakable is the glory, how excellent is the recompence, for all the sufferings in the world, if they were all laden upon the spirit? So that let thy condition be what it will, if thou considerest thy own present condition, and comparest it to thy future possibility, thou canst not feel the present smart of a cross fortune to any great degree, either because thou hast a far bigger sorrow, or a far bigger joy. Here thou art but a stranger travelling to thy country, where the glories of a kingdom are prepared for thee; it is therefore a huge folly to be much afflicted because thou hast a less convenient inn to lodge in by the way.

But these arts of looking forwards and backwards are more than enough to support the spirit of a Christian: there is no man but hath blessings enough in present possession to outweigh the evils of a great affliction. Tell the joints of thy body, and do not accuse the universal Providence for a lame leg, or the want of a finger, when all the rest is perfect, and you have a noble soul, a particle of divinity, the image of God himself; and by the want of a finger you may the better know how to estimate the remaining parts, and to account for every degree of the surviving blessings. Aristippus, in a great suit at law, lost a farm, and to a gentleman, who in civility pitied and deplored his loss, he answered, "I have two farms left still, and that is more than I have lost, and more than you have by one." If you miss an office for which you stood candidate, then, besides that you are quit of the cares and the envy of it, you still have all those excellences which rendered you capable to receive it, and they are better than the best office in the commonwealth. If your estate be lessened, you need the less to care who governs the province, whether he be rude or gentle. I am crossed in my journey, and yet I escaped robbers; and I consider that if I had been set upon by villains, I would have redeemed that evil by this which I now suffer, and have counted it a deliverance: or if I did fall

H 2

into the hands of thieves, yet they did not steal my land. Or, I am fallen into the hands of publicans and sequestrators, and they have taken all from me: what now? let me look about me. They have left me the sun and moon, fire and water, a loving wife, and many friends to pity me, and some to relieve me, and I can still discourse; and, unless I list, they have not taken away my merry countenance, and my cheerful spirit, and a good conscience: they still have left me the providence of God, and all the promises of the gospel, and my religion, and my hopes of heaven, and my charity to them too; and still I sleep and digest, I eat and drink, I read and meditate; I can walk in my neighbour's pleasant fields, and see the varieties of natural beauties, and delight in all that in which God delights—that is, in virtue and wisdom, in the whole creation, and in God himself. And he that hath so many causes of joy, and so great, is very much in love with sorrow and peevishness, who loses all these pleasures, and chooses to sit down upon his little handful of thorns. Such a person is fit to bear Nero company in his funeral sorrow for the loss of one of Poppea's hairs, or help to mourn for Lesbia's sparrow; and because he loves it, he deserves to starve in the midst of plenty, and to want comfort while he is encircled with blessings.

4. Enjoy the present, whatsoever it be, and be not solicitous for the future; for if you take your foot from the present standing, and thrust it forward towards to-morrow's event, you are in a restless condition: it is like refusing to quench your present thirst by fearing you shall want drink the next day.[10] If it be well to-day, it is madness to make the present miserable by fearing it may be ill to-morrow—when your belly is full of to-day's dinner, to fear you shall want the next day's supper; for it may be you shall not, and then to what purpose was this day's affliction? But if to-morrow you shall

---

[10] Quid sit futurum cras, fuge quærere; et
Quem fors dierum cunque dabit, lucro
    Appone.   Hor. l. i. Od. 9.
Prudens futuri temporis exitum
Caliginosâ nocte premit Deus,
    Ridetque, si mortalis ultra
        Fas trepidat: quod adest, memento
Componere æquus.   Hor. l. iii. Od. 29.
'Ἰ ὸ σήμερον μέλει μοι·
Τὸ δ' αὔριον τίς οἶδεν;   Anacr. Od. 15

want, your sorrow will come time enough, though you do not hasten it; let your trouble tarry till its own day comes. But if it chance to be ill to-day, do not increase it by the care of to-morrow. Enjoy the blessings of this day, if God sends them, and the evils of it bear patiently and sweetly; for this day is only ours: we are dead to yesterday, and we are not yet born to the morrow. He, therefore, that enjoys the present, if it be good, enjoys as much as is possible; and if only that day's trouble leans upon him, it is singular and finite. "Sufficient to the day (said Christ) is the evil thereof:" sufficient, but not intolerable. But if we look abroad, and bring into one day's thoughts the evil of many, certain and uncertain, what will be, and what will never be, our load will be as intolerable as it is unreasonable. To reprove this instrument of discontent, the ancients feigned that in hell stood a man twisting a rope of hay; and still he twisted on, suffering an ass to eat up all that was finished: so miserable is he who thrusts his passions forwards towards future events, and suffers all that he may enjoy to be lost and devoured by folly and inconsideration, thinking nothing fit to be enjoyed but that which is not or cannot be had. Just so, many young persons are loth to die, and therefore desire to live to old age, and when they are come thither, are troubled that they are come to that state of life, to which, before they were come, they were hugely afraid they should never come.

5. Let us prepare our minds against changes, always expecting them, that we be not surprised when they come: for nothing is so great an enemy to tranquillity and a contented spirit as the amazement and confusions of unreadiness and inconsideration; and when our fortunes are violently changed, our spirits are unchanged if they always stood in the suburbs and expectation of sorrows. "O death, how bitter art thou to a man that is at rest in his possessions!" And to the rich man who had promised to himself ease and fulness for many years, it was a sad arrest that his soul was surprised the first night: but the apostles, who every day knocked at the gate of death, and looked upon it continually, went to their martyrdom in peace and evenness.

6. Let us often frame to ourselves, and represent to our considerations, the images of those blessings we have, just as we usually understand them when we want them. Consider how

desirable health is to a sick man, or liberty to a prisoner; and if but a fit of the toothache seizes us with violence, all those troubles which in our health afflicted us disband instantly, and seem inconsiderable. He that in his health is troubled that he is in debt, and spends sleepless nights, and refuses meat because of his infelicity, let him fall into a fit of the stone or a high fever, he despises the arrest of all his first troubles, and is as a man unconcerned. Remember, then, that God hath given thee a blessing, the want of which is infinitely more trouble than thy present debt, or poverty, or loss; and therefore is now more to be valued in the possession, and ought to outweigh thy trouble. The very privative blessings, the blessings of immunity, safeguard, liberty, and integrity, which we commonly enjoy, deserve the thanksgiving of a whole life. If God should send a cancer upon thy face, or a wolf into thy side, if he should spread a crust of leprosy upon thy skin, what wouldest thou give to be but as now thou art? Wouldest thou not, on that condition, be as poor as I am, or as the meanest of thy brethren? Would you not choose your present loss and affliction as a thing extremely eligible, and a redemption to thee, if thou mightest exchange the other for this? Thou art quit from a thousand calamities, every one of which, if it were upon thee, would make thee insensible of thy present sorrow: and therefore let thy joy (which should be as great for thy freedom from them, as is thy sadness when thou feelest any of them) do the same cure upon thy discontent. For if we be not extremely foolish or vain, thankless or senseless, a great joy is more apt to cure sorrow and discontent than a great trouble is. I have known an affectionate wife, when she hath been in fear of parting with her beloved husband, heartily desire of God his life or society upon any conditions that were not sinful; and choose to beg with him rather than to feast without him; and the same person hath, upon that consideration, borne poverty nobly, when God hath heard her prayer in the other matter. What wise man in the world is there who does not prefer a small fortune with peace before a great one with contention, and war, and violence? And then he is no longer wise if he alters his opinion when he hath his wish.

7. If you will secure a contented spirit, you must measure your desires by your fôrtune and condition, not your fortunes

by your desires—that is, be governed by your needs, not by your fancy; by nature, not by evil customs and ambitious principles.[11] He that would shoot an arrow out of a plough, or hunt a hare with an elephant, is not unfortunate for missing the mark or prey; but he is foolish for choosing such unapt instruments: and so is he that runs after his content with appetites not springing from natural needs, but from artificial, fantastical, and violent necessities. These are not to be satisfied; or if they were, a man hath chosen an evil instrument towards his content: nature did not intend rest to a man by filling of such desires. Is that beast better that hath two or three mountains to graze on, than a little bee that feeds on dew or manna, and lives upon what falls every morning from the storehouses of heaven, clouds and providence? Can a man quench his thirst better out of a river than a full urn, or drink better from the fountain which is finely paved with marble, than when it swells over the green turf?[12] Pride and artificial gluttonies do but adulterate nature, making our diet healthless, our appetites impatient and unsatisfiable, and the taste mixed, fantastical, and meretricious. But that which we miscall poverty is indeed nature: and its proportions are the just measures of a man, and the best instruments of content. But when we create needs that God or nature never made, we have erected to ourselves an infinite stock of trouble that can have no period. Sempronius complained of want of clothes, and was much troubled for a new suit, being ashamed to appear in the theatre with his gown a little threadbare: but when he got it, and gave his old clothes to Codrus, the poor man was ravished with joy, and went and gave God thanks for his new purchase; and Codrus was made richly fine and

[11] Assai basta per chi non è ingordo.
[12] ———— Quantò præstantius esset
Numen aquæ, viridi si margine clauderet undas
Herba, nec ingenuum violarent marmora tophum.

Juv. iii. 20.

———— me pascunt olivæ,
Me cichorea levesque malvæ.
Frui paratis et valido mihi,
Latoë, dones.   Horat. l. i. Od. 31.
Amabo levem cupressum,
Omissis Cretæ pascuis:
Terræ mihi datum est parùm;
Careo interim doloribus.   Pindar. Frag. 43.

cheerfully warm by that which Sempronius was ashamed to
wear: and yet their natural needs were both alike; the difference only was, that Sempronius had some artificial and fantastical necessities superinduced, which Codrus had not, and
was harder to be relieved, and could not have joy at so cheap
a rate, because he only lived according to nature, the other
by pride and ill customs, and measures taken by other men's
eyes and tongues, and artificial needs. He that propounds to
his fancy things greater than himself or his needs, and is discontent and troubled when he fails of such purchases, ought
not to accuse providence, or blame his fortune, but his folly.
God and nature made no more needs than they mean to satisfy;
and he that will make more must look for satisfaction where
he can.

8. In all troubles and sadder accidents, let us take sanctuary in religion, and by innocence cast out anchors for our
souls, to keep them from shipwreck, though they be not kept
from storm.[13] For what philosophy shall comfort a villain
that is haled to the rack for murdering his prince, or that is
broken upon the wheel for sacrilege? His cup is full of pure
and unmingled sorrow: his body is rent with torment, his name
with ignominy, his soul with shame and sorrow, which are to
last eternally.   But when a man suffers in a good cause, or is
afflicted, and yet walks not perversely with his God, then
"Anytus and Melitus may kill me, but they cannot hurt me;"
then St. Paul's character is engraved in the forehead of our
fortune:[14] "We are troubled on every side, but not distressed;
perplexed, but not in despair; persecuted, but not forsaken;
cast down, but not destroyed.   And who is he that will harm
you, if ye be followers of that which is good?"[15]   For, indeed, every thing in the world is indifferent but sin; and all
the scorchings of the sun are very tolerable in respect of the
burnings of a fever or a calenture.   The greatest evils are
from within us; and from ourselves, also, we must look for
our greatest good; for God is the fountain of it, but reaches
it to us by our own hands; and when all things look sadly
round about us, then only we shall find how excellent a fortune it is to have God to our friend; and, of all friendships,
that only is created to support us in our needs; for it is sin

[13] Vacare culpâ in calamitatibus maximum solatium.
[14] 2 Cor. iv. 8, 9.   [15] 1 Pet. iii. 13; iv. 15, 16.

that turns an ague into a fever, and a fever to the plague, fear into despair, anger into rage, and loss into madness, and sorrow to amazement and confusion. But if either we were innocent, or else by the sadness are made penitent, we are put to school, or into the theatre, either to learn how, or else actually to combat for a crown; the accident may serve an end of mercy, but is not a messenger of wrath.

Let us not therefore be governed by external, and present, and seeming things; nor let us make the same judgment of things that common and weak understandings do; nor make other men, and they not the wisest, to be judges of our felicity, so that we be happy or miserable as they please to think us: but let reason, and experience, and religion, and hope relying upon the Divine promises, be the measure of our judgment. No wise man did ever describe felicity without virtue;[16] and no good man did ever think virtue could depend upon the variety of a good or bad fortune. It is no evil to be poor, but to be vicious and impatient.

Means to obtain Content by way of consideration.

To these exercises and spiritual instruments if we add the following considerations concerning the nature and circum stances of human chance, we may better secure our peace. For as to children, who are afraid of vain images, we use to persuade confidence by making them to handle and look nearer such things, that, when in such a familiarity they perceive them innocent, they may overcome their fears : so must timorous, fantastical, sad, and discontented persons be treated ; they must be made to consider, and on all sides to look upon the accident, and to take all its dimensions, and consider its consequences, and to behold the purposes of God, and the common mistakes of men, and their evil sentences they usually pass upon them. For then we shall perceive that, like colts, or unmanaged horses, we start at dead bones and lifeless blocks, things that are inactive as they are innocent. But if we secure our hopes and our fears, and make them moderate and within government, we may the sooner overcome the evil of the accident; for nothing that we feel is so bad as what we fear.

[16] Beatitudo pendet à rectis consiliis in affectionem animi constantem desinentibus.—Plut.

1. Consider that the universal providence of God hath so ordered it, that the good things of nature and fortune are divided, that we may know how to bear our own, and relieve each other's wants and imperfections. It is not for a man, but for a God, to have all excellences and all felicities.[17] He supports my poverty with his wealth; I counsel and instruct him with my learning and experience. He hath many friends, I many children; he hath no heir, I have no inheritance; and any one great blessing, together with the common portions of nature and necessity, is a fair fortune, if it be but health or strength, or the swiftness of Ahimaaz. For it is an unreasonable discontent to be troubled that I have not so good cocks, or dogs, or horses, as my neighbour, being more troubled that I want one thing that I need not, than thankful for having received all that I need. Nero had this disease, that he was not content with the fortune of the whole empire, but put the fiddlers to death for being more skilful in the trade than he was; and Dionysius the elder was so angry at Philoxenus for singing, and with Plato for disputing, better than he did, that he sold Plato a slave into Ægina, and condemned the other to the quarries.

This consideration is to be enlarged by adding to it, that there are some instances of fortune and a fair condition that cannot stand with some others; but if you desire this, you must lose that, and unless you be content with one, you lose the comfort of both. If you covet learning, you must have leisure and a retired life; if to be a politician, you must go abroad and get experience, and do all businesses, and keep all company, and have no leisure at all. If you will be rich, you must be frugal; if you will be popular, you must be bountiful; if a philosopher, you must despise riches. The Greek that designed to make the most exquisite picture that could be imagined, fancied the eye of Chione, and the hair of Pægnium, and Tarsia's lip, Philenium's chin, and the forehead of Delphia, and set all these upon Milphidippa's neck, and thought that he should outdo both art and nature. But when he came to view the proportions, he found that what was excellent in Tarsia, did not agree with the other excellency of Philenium;

[17] Non te ad omnia læta genuit, O Agamemnon, Atreus. Opus est te gaudere et mœrere: mortalis enim natus es, et ut haud velis: superi sic constituerunt.

and although, singly, they were rare pieces, yet in the whole they made a most ugly face. The dispersed excellences and blessings of many men, if given to one, would not make a handsome, but a monstrous fortune. Use, therefore, that faculty which nature hath given thee, and thy education hath made actual, and thy calling hath made a duty. But if thou desirest to be a saint, refuse not his persecution; if thou wouldest be famous as Epaminondas or Fabricius, accept also of their poverty; for that added lustre to their persons, and envy to their fortune, and their virtue without it could not have been so excellent. Let Euphorion sleep quietly with his old rich wife; and let Medius drink on with Alexander; and remember thou canst not have the riches of the first, unless you have the old wife too; nor the favour which the second had with his prince, unless you buy it at his price;[18] that is, lay thy sobriety down at first, and thy health a little after; and then their condition, though it look splendidly, yet, when you handle it on all sides, it will prick your fingers.

2. Consider how many excellent personages in all ages have suffered as great or greater calamities than this which now tempts thee to impatience. Agis was the most noble of the Greeks, and yet his wife bore a child by Alcibiades; and Philip was prince of Ituræa, and yet his wife ran away with his brother Herod into Galilee; and certainly, in a great fortune, that was a great calamity. But these are but single instances. Almost all the ages of the world have noted that their most eminent scholars were most eminently poor, some by choice, but most by chance, and an inevitable decree of Providence; and in the whole sex of women God hath decreed the sharpest pains of child-birth, to show that there is no state exempt from sorrow, and yet that the weakest persons have strength more than enough to bear the greatest evil: and the greatest queens, and the mothers of saints and apostles, have no charter of exemption from this sad sentence. But the Lord of men and angels was also the king of sufferings; and if thy coarse robe trouble thee, remember the swaddling-clothes of Jesus; if thy bed be uneasy, yet it is not worse than his manger; and it is no sadness to have a thin table, if thou callest to mind that the King of heaven and earth was fed with a little

[18] Prandet Aristoteles, quando Philippo lubet; Diogenes, quando Diogeni.

breast-milk; and yet, besides this, he suffered all the sorrows which we deserved. We, therefore, have great reason to sit down upon our hearths, and warm ourselves at our own fires, and feed upon content at home; for it were a strange pride to expect to be more gently treated by the Divine Providence than the best and wisest men, than apostles and saints, nay, the Son of the eternal God, the heir of both the worlds.

This consideration may be enlarged by surveying all the states and families of the world: and he[19] that at once saw Ægina and Megara, Piræus and Corinth, lie gasping in their ruins, and almost buried in their own heaps, had reason to blame Cicero for mourning impatiently the death of one woman. In the most beauteous and splendid fortune there are many cares and proper interruptions and allays: in the fortune of a prince there is not the coarse robe of beggary, but there are infinite cares; and the judge sits upon the tribunal with great ceremony and ostentation of fortune, and yet, at his house or in his breast there is something that causes him to sigh deeply. Pittacus[20] was a wise and valiant man, but his wife overthrew the table when he had invited his friends; upon which the good man, to excuse her incivility, and his own misfortune, said that "every man had one evil, and he was most happy that had but that alone." And if nothing else happens, yet sicknesses so often do embitter the fortune and content of a family, that a physician in a few years, and with the practice upon a very few families, gets experience enough to administer to almost all diseases. And when thy little misfortune troubles thee, remember that thou hast known the best of kings and the best of men put to death publicly by his own subjects.

3. There are many accidents which are esteemed great calamities, and yet we have reason enough to bear them well and unconcernedly; for they neither touch our bodies nor our souls—our health and our virtue remain entire, our life and our reputation. It may be I am slighted, or I have re-

[19] Servius Sulpicius.

[20] Hic in foro beatus esse creditur,
  Cùm foribus apertis sit suis miserrimus;
  Imperat mulier, jubet omnia, semper litigat.
  Multa adferunt illi dolorem, nihil mihi.

  Ferre quam sortem patiuntur omnes,
    Nemo recusat.

ceived ill language; but my head aches not for it, neither hath it broke my thigh, nor taken away my virtue, unless I lose my charity or my patience. Inquire, therefore, what you are the worse, either in your soul or in your body, for what hath happened; for upon this very stock many evils will disappear, since the body and the soul make up the whole man.[21] And when the daughter of Stilpo proved a wanton, he said it was none of his sin, and therefore there was no reason it should be his misery. And if an enemy hath taken all that from a prince whereby he was a king, he may refresh himself by considering all that is left him whereby he is a man.

4. Consider that sad accidents and a state of affliction is a school of virtue; it reduces our spirits to soberness, and our counsels to moderation; it corrects levity, and interrupts the confidence of sinning. "It is good for me (said David) that I have been afflicted, for thereby have I learned thy law."[22] And, "I know, O Lord, that thou of very faithfulness hast caused me to be troubled." For God, who in mercy and wisdom governs the world, would never have suffered so many sadnesses, and have sent them especially to the most virtuous and the wisest men, but that he intends they should be the seminary of comfort, the nursery of virtue, the exercise of wisdom, the trial of patience, the venturing for a crown, and the gate of glory.

5. Consider that afflictions are oftentimes the occasions of great temporal advantages; and we must not look upon them as they sit down heavily upon us, but as they serve some of God's ends, and the purposes of universal providence. And when a prince fights justly, and yet unprosperously, if he could see all those reasons for which God hath so ordered it, he would think it the most reasonable thing in the world, and that it would be very ill to have it otherwise. If a man could have opened one of the pages of the Divine counsel, and could have seen the event of Joseph's being sold to the merchants

---

[21] Si natus es tu, Trophime, solus omnium
Hac lege, partu cum te mater edidit,
Ut semper eant tibi res arbitrio tuo,—
Felicitatem hanc si quis promisit deûm,
Irascereris jure : nam mala is fide
Et, &c.   Plutarch. Xyl. t. ii. p. 103.
[22] Psal. cxix. part 10, ver. 3.

of Amalek, he might, with much reason, have dried up the young man's tears: and when God's purposes are opened in the events of things, as it was in the case of Joseph, when he sustained his father's family and became lord of Egypt, then we see what ill judgment we made of things, and that we were passionate as children, and transported with sense and mistaken interest. The case of Themistocles was almost like that of Joseph; for, being banished into Egypt, he also grew in favour with the king, and told his wife, " he had been un-done, unless. he had been undone." For God esteems it one of his glories, that he brings good out of evil; and therefore it were but reason we should trust God to govern his own world as he pleases; and that we should patiently wait till the change cometh, or the reason be discovered.

And this consideration is also of great use to them who envy at the prosperity of the wicked, and the success of per-secutors, and the baits of fishes, and the bread of dogs. God fails not to sow blessings in the long furrows which the ploughers plough upon the back of the church; and this suc-cess which troubles us will be a great glory to God, and a great benefit to his saints and servants, and a great ruin to the persecutors, who shall have but the fortune of Thera-menes, one of the thirty tyrants of Athens, who escaped when his house fell upon him, and was shortly after put to death with torments by his colleagues in the tyranny.

To which, also, may be added, that the great evils which happen to the best and wisest men are one of the great argu-ments upon the strength of which we can expect felicity to our souls and the joys of another world. And certainly they are then very tolerable and eligible, when with so great ad-vantages they minister to the faith and hope of a Christian. But if we consider what unspeakable tortures are provided for the wicked to all eternity, we should not be troubled to see them prosperous here, but rather wonder that their portion in this life is not bigger, and that ever they should be sick, or crossed, or affronted, or troubled with the contradiction and disease of their own vices, since, if they were fortunate be-yond their own ambition, it could not make them recompence for one hour's torment in hell, which yet they shall have for their eternal portion.

After all these considerations deriving from sense and ex-

perience, grace and reason, there are two remedies still remaining, and they are necessity and time.

6. For it is but reasonable to bear that accident patiently
which God sends, since impatience does but entangle us, like
the fluttering of a bird in a net, but cannot at all ease our
trouble, or prevent the accident:[23] it must be run through,
and therefore it were better we compose ourselves to a patient
than to a troubled and miserable suffering.

7. But, however, if you will not otherwise be cured, time
at last will do it alone; and then consider, do you mean to
mourn always, or but for a time? If always, you are miserable and foolish. If for a time, then why will you not apply
those reasons to your grief at first with which you will cure
it at last? or if you will not cure it with reason, see how little
of a man there is in you, that you suffer time to do more with
you than reason or religion! You suffer yourself to be cured,
just as a beast or a tree is; let it alone, and the thing will
heal itself: but this is neither honourable to thy person, nor
of reputation to thy religion. However, be content to bear
thy calamity, because thou art sure, in a little time, it will sit
down gentle and easy, for to a mortal man no evil is immortal. And here let the worst thing happen that can, it will
end in death, and we commonly think that to be near enough.

8. Lastly, of those things which are reckoned amongst
evils, some are better than their contraries; and to a good
man the very worst is tolerable.

Poverty or a low Fortune.

1. Poverty is better than riches, and a mean fortune to be
chosen before a great and splendid one. It is indeed despised, and makes men contemptible; it exposes a man to the
insolence of evil persons, and leaves a man defenceless; it is
always suspected; its stories are accounted lies, and all its
counsels follies; it puts a man from all employment; it makes
a man's discourses tedious, and his society troublesome. This
is the worst of it; and yet all this, and far worse than this,
the apostles suffered for being Christians; and Christianity
itself may be esteemed an affliction as well as poverty, if this
be all that can be said against it; for the apostles and the
most eminent Christians were really poor, and were used

[23] Nemo recusat ferre, quod necesse est pati.

contemptuously : and yet, that poverty is despised may be an
argument to commend it, if it be despised by none but persons
vicious and ignorant.[24] However, certain it is that a great
fortune is a great vanity, and riches is nothing but danger,
trouble, and temptation ; like a garment that is too long, and
bears a train; not so useful to one, but it is troublesome to
two—to him that bears the one part upon his shoulders, and
to him that bears the other part in his hand. But poverty is
the sister of a good mind, the parent of sober counsels, and
the nurse of all virtue.

For what is that you admire in the fortune of a great king ?
Is it that he always goes in a great company? You may
thrust yourself into the same crowd, or go often to church,
and then you have as great a company as he hath ; and that
may upon as good grounds please you as him, that is, justly
neither: for so impertinent and useless pomp, and the other
circumstances of his distance, are not made for him, but for
his subjects, that they may learn to separate him from common usages, and be taught to be governed.[25] But if you look
upon them as fine things in themselves, you may quickly alter
your opinion when you shall consider that they cannot cure
the toothache, nor make one wise, or fill the belly, or give one
night's sleep (though they help to break many)—not satisfying any appetite of nature, or reason, or religion ; but they are
states of greatness which only make it possible for a man to
be made extremely miserable. And it was long ago observed by the Greek tragedians, and from them by Arrianus,[26]
saying, that "all our tragedies are of kings and princes, and
rich or ambitious personages ; but you never see a poor man
have a part, unless it be as a chorus, or to fill up the scenes, to
dance or to be derided ; but the kings and the great generals.
First," says he, "they begin with joy, στέψατε δώματα, crown
the houses, but about the third or fourth act they cry out, O
Citheron ! why didst thou spare my life to reserve me for

---

[24] Alta fortuna alto travaglio apporta.   [25] Da autorità la ceremonia
al' atto.

[26] Οὐδεὶς δὲ πένης τραγῳδίαν συμπληροῖ, εἰ μὴ χορευτής.
  Bis sex dierum mensurâ consero ego agros,
  Berecynthia arva.
  Animusque meus sursùm usque evectus ad polum
  Decidit humi, et me sic videtur alloqui :
  Disce haud nimis magni facere mortalia.—Tantal. in Tragœd

this more sad calamity?" And this is really true in the great accidents of the world; for a great estate hath great crosses, and a mean fortune hath but small ones. It may be the poor man loses a cow, for if his child dies he is quit of his biggest care; but such an accident in a rich and splendid family doubles upon the spirits of the parents. Or, it may be the poor man is troubled to pay his rent, and that is his biggest trouble; but it is a bigger care to secure a great fortune in a troubled estate, or with equal greatness, or with the circumstances of honour and the niceness of reputation, to defend a law-suit; and that which will secure a common man's whole estate is not enough to defend a great man's honour.

And therefore it was not without mystery observed among the ancients, that they who made gods of gold and silver, of hope and fear, peace and fortune, garlic and onions, beasts and serpents, and a quartan ague, yet never deified money;[27] meaning, that however wealth was admired by common or abused understandings, yet from riches, that is, from that proportion of good things which is beyond the necessities of nature, no moment could be added to a man's real content or happiness. Corn from Sardinia, herds of Calabrian cattle, meadows through which pleasant Liris glides, silks from Tyrus, and golden chalices to drown my health in, are nothing but instruments of vanity or sin; and suppose a disease in the soul of him that longs for them or admires them. And this I have otherwhere represented more largely; to which I here add, that riches have very great dangers to their souls, not only who covet them, but to all that have them.[28] For if a great personage undertakes an action passionately and upon great interest, let him manage it indiscreetly, let the whole design be unjust, let it be acted with all the malice and impotency in the world, he shall have enough to flatter him, but not enough to reprove him. He had need be a bold man that shall tell his patron he is going to hell; and that prince had need be a good man that shall suffer such a monitor; and though it be a strange kind of civility, and an evil dutifulness, in friends and relatives, to suffer him to perish without re-

[27]   —— funesta Pecunia, templo
Nondum habitas, nullas nummorum ereximus aras,
Ut colitur Pax atque Fides.   Juv. i. 113.
[28] Chap. iv. Sect. 8.—Title, *Of Covetousness*

5

proof or medicine, rather than to seem unmannerly to a great sinner, yet it is none of their least infelicities that their wealth and greatness shall put them into sin, and yet put them past reproof. I need not instance in the habitual intemperance of rich tables, nor the evil accidents and effects of fulness, pride and lust, wantonness and softness of disposition, huge talking and an imperious spirit, despite of religion, and contempt of poor persons: at the best, "it is a great temptation for a man to have in his power whatsoever he can have in his sensual desires;"[29] and therefore riches is a blessing like to a present made of a whole vintage to a man in a hectic fever; he will be much tempted to drink of it, and if he does, he is inflamed, and may chance to die with the kindness.

Now, besides what hath been already noted in the state of poverty, there is nothing to be accounted for but the fear of wanting necessaries; of which if a man could be secured that he might live free from care, all the other parts of it might be reckoned amongst the advantages of wise and sober persons, rather than objections against that state of fortune.

But, concerning this, I consider that there must needs be great security to all Christians, since Christ not only made express promises that we should have sufficient for this life, but also took great pains and used many arguments to create confidence in us; and such they were, which by their own strength were sufficient, though you abate the authority of the speaker. The Son of God told us, his Father takes care of us; he that knew all his Father's counsels, and his whole kindness towards mankind, told us so. How great is that truth, how certain, how necessary, which Christ himself proved by arguments! The excellent words and most comfortable sentences which are our bills of exchange, upon the credit of which we lay our cares down and receive provisions for our need, are these: "Take no thought for your life, what ye shall eat, or what ye shall drink, nor yet for your body, what ye shall put on. Is not the life more than meat, and the body than raiment? Behold the fowls of the air, for they sow not, neither do they reap, nor gather into barns, yet your heavenly Father feedeth them. Are ye not much better than they? Which of you, by taking thought, can add one cubit to his stature? And why take ye thought for raiment? Consider the lilies of

[29] James ii. 5—7.

the field, how they grow; they toil not, neither do they spin; and yet I say unto you, that even Solomon in all his glory was not arrayed like one of these. Therefore if God so clothe the grass of the field, which to-day is, and to-morrow is cast into the oven, shall he not much more clothe you, O ye of little faith? Therefore take no thought, saying, What shall we eat. or what shall we drink, or wherewithal shall we be clothed? (for after all these things do the Gentiles seek;) for your heavenly Father knoweth that ye have need of all these things. But seek ye first the kingdom of God and his righteousness, and all these things shall be added unto you. Take therefore no thought for the morrow, for the morrow shall take thought for the things of itself: sufficient to the day is the evil thereof."[30] The same discourse is repeated by St. Luke;[31] and accordingly our duty is urged, and our confidence abetted, by the disciples of our Lord, in divers places of Holy Scripture. So St. Paul—"Be careful for nothing; but in every thing by prayer and supplication, with thanksgiving, let your requests be made known unto God."[32] And again, "Charge them that are rich in this world, that they be not high-minded, nor trust in uncertain riches, but in the living God, who giveth us richly all things to enjoy."[33] And yet again, "Let your conversation be without covetousness, and be content with such things as ye have; for he hath said, I will never leave thee, nor forsake thee: so that we may boldly say, The Lord is my helper."[34] And all this is by St. Peter summed up in our duty thus: "Cast all your care upon him, for he careth for you." Which words he seems to have borrowed out of the fifty-fifth Psalm, ver. 22, where David saith the same thing almost in the same words. To which I only add the observation made by him, and the argument of experience: "I have been young, and now am old, and yet saw I never the righteous forsaken, nor his seed begging their bread." And now, after all this, a fearless confidence in God, and concerning a provision of necessaries, is so reasonable, that it is become a duty; and he is scarce a Christian whose faith is so little as to be jealous of God and suspicious concerning meat and clothes: that man hath nothing in him of the nobleness or confidence of charity.

[30] Matt. vi. 25, &c.   [31] Luke xii. 22—31.   [32] Phil. iv. 6.
[33] 1 Tim. vi. 17.   [34] Heb. xiii. 5, 6.

I 2

Does not God provide for all the birds, and beasts, and fishes? Do not the sparrows fly from their bush, and every morning find meat where they laid it not? Do not the young ravens call to God, and he feeds them? And were it reasonable that the sons of the family should fear the Father would give meat to the chickens and the servants, his sheep and his dogs, but give none to them? He were a very ill father that should do so; or he were a very foolish son that should think so of a good father. But, besides the reasonableness of this faith and this hope, we have infinite experience of it. How innocent, how careless, how secure, is infancy, and yet how certainly provided for! We have lived at God's charges all the days of our life, and have (as the Italian proverb says) sat down to meat at the sound of a bell; and hitherto he hath not failed us; we have no reason to suspect him for the future; we do not use to serve men so; and less time of tria creates great confidences in us towards them, who for twenty years together never broke their word with us: and God hath so ordered it, that a man shall have had the experience of many years' provision before he shall understand how to doubt; that he may be provided for an answer against the temptation shall come, and the mercies felt in his childhood may make him fearless when he is a man. Add to this, that God hath given us his Holy Spirit; he hath promised heaven to us; he hath given us his Son; and we are taught from Scripture to make this inference from hence, "How should not he with him give us all things else?"

The Charge of many Children.

We have a title to be provided for as we are God's creatures, another title as we are his children, another because God hath promised; and every of our children hath the same title; and therefore it is a huge folly and infidelity to be troubled and full of care because we have many children. Every child we have to feed is a new revenue, a new title to God's care and providence; so that many children are a great wealth; and if it be said they are chargeable, it is no more than all wealth and great revenues are. For what difference is it? Titius keeps ten ploughs, Cornelia hath ten children: he hath land enough to employ and to feed all his hinds; she, blessings and promises, and the provisions and the truth of God, to maintain all her children. His hinds and horses eat up all his corn, and her children are sufficiently maintained with her little. They bring in and eat up, and she indeed eats up, but they also bring in from the store-houses of heaven and the granaries of God; and my children are not so much mine as they are God's: he feeds them in the womb, by ways secret and insensible, and would not work a perpetual miracle to bring them forth, and then to starve them.

Violent Necessities.

But some men are highly tempted, and are brought to a strait, that, without a miracle, they cannot be relieved: what shall they do? It may be their pride or vanity hath brought the necessity upon them, and it is not a need of God's making; and if it be not, they must cure it themselves, by lessening their desires and moderating their appetites: and yet, if it be innocent, though unnecessary, God does usually relieve such necessities; and he does not only upon our prayers grant us more than he promised of temporal things, but also he gives many times more than we ask. This is no object for our faith, but ground enough for a temporal and prudent hope; and if we fail in the particular, God will turn it to a bigger mercy if we submit to his dispensation, and adore him in the denial. But if it be a matter of necessity, let not any man, by way of impatience, cry out that God will not work a miracle; for God, by miracle, did give meat and drink to his people in the wilderness, of which he had made no particular promise in any covenant; and if all natural means fail, it is certain that God will rather work a miracle than break his word; he can do that—he cannot do this. Only we must remember that our portion of temporal things is but food and raiment. God hath not promised us coaches and horses, rich houses and jewels, Tyrian silks and Persian carpets; neither hath he promised to minister to our needs in such circumstances as we shall appoint, but such as himself shall choose. God will enable either thee to pay thy debt, (if thou beggest it of him,) or else he will pay it for thee; that is, take thy desire as a discharge of thy duty, and pay it to thy creditor in blessings, or in some secret of his providence. It may be hath laid up the corn that shall feed thee in the granary of thy brother, or will clothe thee with his wool. He enabled St. Peter to **pay** his gabel by the ministry of a fish, and Elias to be waited on by a crow, who was both his minister and his steward for provisions; and his holy Son rode in triumph upon an ass that grazed in another man's pastures. And if God gives to him the dominion, and reserves the use to thee, thou hast the better half of the two; but the charitable man serves God and serves thy need, and both join to provide for thee, and God blesses both. But if he takes away the flesh-pots from thee, he can also alter the appetite, and he hath given thee power and commandment to restrain it; and if he lessens the revenue, he will also shrink the necessity; or if he gives but a very little, he will make it go a great way; or if he sends thee but a coarse diet, he will bless it and make it healthful, and can cure all the anguish of thy poverty by giving thee patience and the grace of contentedness. For the grace of God secures you of provisions, and yet the grace of God feeds and supports the spirit in the want of provisions; and if a thin table be apt to enfeeble the spirits of one used to feed better, yet the cheerfulness of a spirit that is blessed will make a thin table become a delicacy, if the man was as well taught as he was fed, and learned his duty when he received the blessing. Poverty, therefore, is in some senses eligible, and to be preferred before riches; but in all senses it is very tolerable.

Death of Children, or nearest Relatives and Friends.

There are some persons, who have been noted for excellent in their lives and passions, rarely innocent, and yet hugely penitent for indiscretions and harmless infirmities; such as was Paulina, one of the ghostly children of St. Jerome; and yet, when any of her children died, she was arrested with a sorrow so great as brought her to the margent of her grave. And the more tender our spirits are made by religion, the more easy we are to let in grief, if the cause be innocent, and be but in any sense twisted with piety and due affections; to cure which, we may consider that all the world must die, and therefore to be impatient at the death of a person concerning whom it was certain and known that he must die, is to mourn because thy friend or child was not born an angel; and when thou hast a while made thyself miserable by an importunate and useless grief, it may be thou shalt die thyself, and leave others to their choice whether they will mourn for thee or no; but by that time it will appear how impertinent that grief was which served no end of life, and ended in thy own funeral. But what great matter is it if sparks fly upward, or a stone falls into a pit; if that which was combustible be burned, or that which was liquid be melted, or that which is mortal do die? It is no more than a man does every day; for every night death hath gotten possession of that day, and we shall never live that day over again; and when the last day is come, there are no more days left for us to die. And what is sleeping and waking, but living and dying? what is spring and autumn, youth and old age, morning and evening, but real images of life and death, and really the same to many considerable effects and changes?

Untimely Death.

But it is not mere dying that is pretended by some as the cause of their impatient mourning; but that the child died young, before he knew good and evil, his right hand from his left, and so lost all his portion of this world, and they know not of what excellency his portion in the next shall be. If he died young, he lost but little, for he understood but little, and had not capacities of great pleasures or great cares; but yet he died innocent, and before the sweetness of his soul was deflowered and ravished from him by the flames and follies of a froward age; he went out from the dining-room before he had fallen into error by the intemperance of his meat, or the deluge of drink; and he hath obtained this favour of God, that his soul had suffered a less imprisonment, and her load was sooner taken off, that he might, with lesser delays, go and converse with immortal spirits—and the babe is taken into paradise before he knows good and evil (for that knowledge threw our great father out, and this ignorance returns the child thither). But (as concerning thy own particular) remove thy thoughts back to those days in which thy child was not born, and you are now but as then you was, and there is no difference, but that you had a son born; and if you reckon that for evil, you are unthankful for the blessing; if it be good, it is better that you had the blessing for awhile, than not at all; and yet, if he had never been born, this sorrow had not been at all.[35] But be no more displeased at God

[35] Iidem si puer parvulus occidat, æquo animo ferendum putant; si

for giving you a blessing for awhile, than you would have been if he had not given it at all; and reckon that intervening blessing for a gain, but account it not an evil; and if it be a good, turn it not into sorrow and sadness. But if we have great reason to complain of the calamities and evils of our life, then we have the less reason to grieve that those whom we love have so small portion of evil assigned to them. And it is no small advantage that our children dying young receive; for their condition of a blessed immortality is rendered to them secure by being snatched from the dangers of an evil choice, and carried to their little cells of felicity, where they can weep no more. And this the wisest of the Gentiles understood well, when they forbade any offerings or libations to be made for dead infants, as was usual for their other dead; as believing they were entered into a secure possession, to which they went with no other condition but that they passed into it through the way of mortality, and, for a few months, wore an uneasy garment. And let weeping parents say if they do not think that the evils their little babes have suffered are sufficient. If they be, why are they troubled that they were taken from those many and greater, which in succeeding years are great enough to try all the reason and religion which art, and nature, and the grace of God have produced in us, to enable us for such sad contentions? And, possibly, we may doubt concerning men and women, but we cannot suspect that to infants death can be such an evil, but that it brings to them much more good than it takes from them in this life.

Death unseasonable.

But others can well bear the death of infants; but when they have spent some years of childhood or youth, and are entered into arts and society, when they are hopeful and provided for, when the parents are to reap the comfort of all their fears and cares, then it breaks the spirit to lose them. This is true in many; but this is not love to the dead, but to themselves; for they miss what they had flattered themselves into by hope and opinion; and if it were kindness to the dead, they may consider, that since we hope he is gone to God and to

vero in cunis, ne querendum quidem; atqui ab hoc acerbius exegit natura quod dederat. At id quidem ipsum in cæteris rebus melius putatur, ali quam partem quàm nullam attingere.—Senec.

rest, it is an ill expression of our love to them that we weep for their good fortune. For that life is not best which is longest : and when they are descended into the grave it shall not be inquired how long they have lived, but how well : and yet this shortening of their days is an evil wholly depending upon opinion.[36] For if men did naturally live but twenty years, then we should be satisfied if they died about sixteen or eighteen; and yet eighteen years now are as long as eighteen years would be then : and if a man were but of a day's life, it is well if he lasts till evensong, and then says his compline an hour before the time : and we are pleased, and call not that death immature, if he lives till seventy ; and yet this age is as short of the old periods before and since the flood, as this youth's age (for whom you mourn) is of the present fulness. Suppose, therefore, a decree passed upon this person, (as there have been many upon all mankind,) and God hath set him a shorter period ; and then we may as well bear the immature death of the young man as the death of the oldest men ; for they also are immature and unseasonable in respect of the old periods of many generations. And why are we troubled that he had arts and sciences before he died? or are we troubled that he does not live to make use of them? The first is cause of joy, for they are excellent in order to certain ends ; and the second cannot be cause of sorrow, because he hath no need to use them, as the case now stands, being provided for with the provisions of an angel and the manner of eternity. However, the sons and the parents, friends and relatives, are in the world like hours and minutes to a day. The hour comes, and must pass ; and some stay by minutes, and they also pass, and shall never return again. But let it be considered, that from the time in which a man is conceived, from that time forward to eternity he shall never cease to be ; and let him die young or old, still he hath an immortal soul, and hath laid down his body only for a time, as that which was the instrument of his trouble and sorrow, and the scene of sicknesses and disease. But he is in a more noble manner of being after death than he can be here ; and the child may with more reason be allowed to cry for leaving his mother's womb for this world, than a man can for changing this world for another.

[36] Juvenis relinquit vitam, quem Dii diligunt.—Menand. Clerc. v. 46

Sudden Death, or Violent.

Others are yet troubled at the manner of their child's or friend's death. He was drowned, or lost his head, or died of the plague; and this is a new spring of sorrow. But no man can give a sensible account how it shall be worse for a child to die with drowning in half an hour, than to endure a fever of one-and-twenty days. And if my friend lost his head, so he did not lose his constancy and his religion, he died with huge advantage.

Being Childless.

But by this means I am left without an heir. Well, suppose that: thou hast no heir, and I have no inheritance; and there are many kings and emperors that have died childless, many royal lines are extinguished, and Augustus Cæsar was forced to adopt his wife's son to inherit all the Roman greatness. And there are many wise persons that never married: and we read no where that any of the children of the apostles did survive their fathers; and all that inherit any thing of Christ's kingdom come to it by adoption, not by natural inheritance: and to die without a natural heir is no intolerable evil, since it was sanctified in the person of Jesus, who died a virgin.

Evil or unfortunate Children.

And by this means we are freed from the greater sorrows of having a fool, a swine, or a goat, to rule after us in our families; and yet even this condition admits of comfort.[37] For all the wild Americans are supposed to be the sons of Dodonaim; and the sons of Jacob are now the most scattered and despised people in the whole world. The son of Solomon was but a silly, weak man; and the son of Hezekiah was wicked: and all the fools and barbarous people, all the thieves and pirates, all the slaves and miserable men and women of the world, are the sons and daughters of Noah; and we must not look to be exempted from that portion of sorrow which God gave to Noah and Adam, to Abraham, to Isaac, and to Jacob. I pray God send us into the lot of Abraham. But if any thing happens worse to us, it is enough for us that we bear it evenly.[38]

[37] Κρείσσον υἱὸν κακὸν εἶναι, ἤ σε κακοδαίμονα.—Epict. c. 16.
[38] Σοὶ δ' ἀρκείτω τὸ εὐσταθεῖν.

Our own Death.

And how if you were to die yourself? You know you must. Only be ready for it by the preparations of a good life;[39] and then it is the greatest good that ever happened to thee; else there is nothing that can comfort you. But if you have served God in a holy life, send away the women and the weepers; tell them it is as much intemperance to weep too much, as to laugh too much; and when thou art alone, or with fitting company, die as thou shouldest, but do not die impatiently, and like a fox catched in a trap. For if you fear death, you shall never the more avoid it, but you make it miserable. Fannius, that killed himself for fear of death, died as certainly as Portia, that ate burning coals, or Cato, that cut his own throat. To die is necessary and natural, and it may be honourable; but to die poorly, and basely, and sinfully, that alone is it that can make a man unfortunate.[40] No man can be a slave, but he that fears pain, or fears to die. To such a man nothing but chance and peaceable times can secure his duty, and he depends upon things without for his felicity; and so is well but during the pleasure of his enemy, or a thief, or a tyrant, or it may be of a dog or a wild bull.

Prayers for the several Graces and Parts of Christian Sobriety.

A Prayer against Sensuality.

O eternal Father, thou that sittest in heaven invested with essential glories and Divine perfections, fill my soul with so deep a sense of the excellences of spiritual and heavenly things, that, my affections being weaned from the pleasures of the world and the false allurements of sin, I may, with great severity, and the prudence of a holy discipline and strict desires, with clear resolutions and a free spirit, have my conversation in heaven and heavenly employments; that being, in affections as in my condition, a pilgrim and a stranger here, I may covet after and labour for an abiding city, and at last may enter into and for ever dwell in the celestial Jerusalem, which is the mother of us all, through Jesus Christ, our Lord. Amen.

[39] Ad fines cùm perveneris, ne revertito.—Pythag.
[40] Οὐ κατθανεῖν γάρ, κ. τ. λ.—Eurip. Priestley's edit. vol. vii. p. 714.

For Temperance.

O Almighty God and gracious Father of men and angels, who openest thy hand and fillest all things with plenty, and hast provided for thy servant sufficient to satisfy all my needs; teach me to use thy creatures soberly and temperately, that I may not, with loads of meat or drink, make the temptations of my enemy to prevail upon me, or my spirit unapt for the performance of my duty, or my body healthless, or my affections sensual and unholy. O my God, never suffer that the blessings which thou givest me may either minister to sin or sickness, but to health and holiness and thanksgiving; that in the strength of thy provisions I may cheerfully and actively and diligently serve thee; that I may worthily feast at thy table here, and be accounted worthy, through thy grace, to be admitted to thy table hereafter, at the eternal supper of the Lamb, to sing an hallelujah to God the Father, the Son, and the Holy Ghost, for ever and ever. Amen.

For Chastity; to be said especially by unmarried Persons.

Almighty God, our most holy and eternal Father, who art of pure eyes, and canst behold no uncleanness; let thy gracious and holy Spirit descend upon thy servant, and reprove the spirit of fornication and uncleanness, and cast him out; that my body may be a holy temple, and my soul a sanctuary to entertain the Prince of purities, the holy and eternal Spirit of God. O, let no impure thoughts pollute that soul which God hath sanctified; no unclean words pollute that tongue which God hath commanded to be an organ of his praises; no unholy and unchaste action rend the veil of that temple where the holy Jesus hath been pleased to enter, and hath chosen for his habitation: but seal up all my senses from all vain objects, and let them be entirely possessed with religion, and fortified with prudence, watchfulness, and mortification; that I, possessing my vessel in holiness, may lay it down with a holy hope, and receive it again in a joyful resurrecction, through Jesus Christ our Lord. Amen.

A Prayer for the Love of God, to be said by Virgins and Widows, professed or resolved so to live: and may be used by any one.

O holy and purest Jesus, who wert pleased to espouse

every holy soul, and join it to thee with a holy union and mysterious instruments of religious society and communications: O, fill my soul with religion, and desires holy as the thoughts of cherubim, passionate beyond the love of women; that I may love thee as much as ever any creature loved thee, even with all my soul and all my faculties, and all the degrees of every faculty; let me know no loves but those of duty and charity, obedience and devotion; that I may for ever run after thee, who art the King of virgins, and with whom whole kingdoms are in love, and for whose sake queens have died, and at whose feet kings with joy have laid their crowns and sceptres. My soul is thine, O dearest Jesu; thou art my Lord, and hast bound up my eyes and heart from all stranger affections; give me for my dowry, purity and humility, modesty and devotion, charity and patience, and at last bring me into the bride-chamber to partake of the felicities, and to lie in the bosom, of the Bridegroom to eternal ages, O holy and sweetest Saviour Jesus. Amen.

A Prayer to be said by Married Persons in behalf of themselves and each other.

O eternal and gracious Father, who hast consecrated the holy estate of marriage to become mysterious, and to represent the union of Christ and his church, let thy Holy Spirit so guide me in the doing the duties of this state, that it may not become a sin unto me; nor that liberty, which thou hast hallowed by the holy Jesus, become an occasion of licentiousness by my own weakness and sensuality; and do thou forgive all those irregularities and too sensual applications which may have, in any degree, discomposed my spirit and the severity of a Christian. Let me, in all accidents and circumstances, be severe in my duty towards thee, affectionate and dear to my wife, (or *husband*,) a guide and good example to my family, and in all quietness, sobriety, prudence, and peace, a follower of those holy pairs, who have served thee with godliness and a good testimony. And the blessings of the eternal God, blessings of the right hand and of the left, be upon the body and soul of thy servant my wife, (or *husband*,) and abide upon her (or *him*) till the end of a holy and happy life; and grant that both of us may live together for ever in the embraces of the holy and eternal Jesus, our Lord and Saviour. Amen.

A Prayer for the Grace of Humility.

O holy and most gracious Master and Saviour Jesus, who by thy example and by thy precept, by the practice of a whole life and frequent discourses, didst command us to be meek and humble, in imitation of thy incomparable sweetness and great humility; be pleased to give me the grace, as thou hast given me the commandment; enable me to do whatsoever thou commandest, and command whatsoever thou pleasest. O, mortify in me all proud thoughts and vain opinions of myself; let me return to thee the acknowledgment and the fruits of all those good things thou hast given me, that, by confessing I am wholly in debt to thee for them, I may not boast myself for what I have received, and for what I am highly accountable; and for what is my own teach me to be ashamed and humbled, it being nothing but sin and misery, weakness and uncleanness. Let me go before my brethren in nothing but in striving to do them honour and thee glory, never to seek my own praise, never to delight in it when it is offered; that, despising myself, I may be accepted by thee in the honours with which thou shalt crown thy humble and despised servants, for Jesus' sake, in the kingdom of eternal glory. Amen.

Acts of Humility and Modesty by way of Prayer and Meditation.

I.

Lord, I know that my spirit is light and thorny, my body is brutish and exposed to sickness; I am constant to folly, and inconstant in holy purposes. My labours are vain and fruitless; my fortune full of change and trouble, seldom pleasing, never perfect; my wisdom is folly; being ignorant even of the parts and passions of my own body: and what am I, O Lord, before thee, but a miserable person, hugely in debt, not able to pay?

II.

Lord, I am nothing, and I have nothing of myself: I am less than the least of all thy mercies.

III.

What was I before my birth? First, nothing, and then uncleanness. What during my childhood? Weakness and folly. What in my youth? Folly still, and passion, lust, and wildness. What in my whole life? A great sinner, a deceived and an abused person. Lord, pity me; for it is thy goodness that I am kept from confusion and amazement, when I consider the misery and shame of my person, and the defilements of my nature.

IV.

Lord, what am I? And, Lord, what art thou? "What is man, that thou art mindful of him? and the son of man, that thou so regardest him?"

V.

"How can man be justified with God? Or how can he be clean that is born of a woman? Behold, even to the moon, and it shineth not; yea, the stars are not pure in his sight: how much less man, that is a worm, and the son of man, which is a worm!"[41]

A Prayer for a contented Spirit, and the Grace of Moderation and Patience.

O Almighty God, Father and Lord of all the creatures, who hast disposed all things and all chances so as may best glorify thy wisdom, and serve the ends of thy justice, and magnify thy mercy by secret and undiscernible ways, bringing good out of evil; I most humbly beseech thee to give me wisdom from above, that I may adore thee and admire thy ways and footsteps, which are in the great deep and not to be searched out: teach me to submit to thy providence in all things, to be content in all changes of person and condition, to be temperate in prosperity, and to read my duty in the lines of thy mercy; and in adversity to be meek, patient, and resigned; and to look through the cloud, that I may wait for the consolation of the Lord and the day of redemption; in the mean time doing my duty with an unwearied diligence, and an undisturbed resolution, having no fondness for the vanities or possessions of this world, but laying up my hopes in heaven and the rewards of holy living, and being strengthened with the spirit of the inner man, through Jesus Christ our Lord. Amen.

[41] Job **xxv** 4, &c.

CHAP. III. OF CHRISTIAN JUSTICE.

JUSTICE is, by the Christian religion, enjoined in all its parts by these two propositions in Scripture: "Whatsoever ye would that men should do to you, even so do to them." This is the measure of commutative justice, or of that justice which supposes exchange of things profitable for things profitable: that as I supply your need you may supply mine; as I do a benefit to you I may receive one by you. And, because every man may be injured by another, therefore his security shall depend upon mine: if he will not let me be safe, he shall not be safe himself; (only the manner of his being punished is, upon great reason, both by God and all the world, taken from particulars, and committed to a public disinterested person, who will do justice, without passion, both to him and to me;) if he refuses to do me advantage, he shall receive none when his needs require it. And thus God gave necessities to man, that all men might need; and several abilities to several persons, that each man might help to supply the public needs, and, by joining to fill up all wants, they may be knit together by justice, as the parts of the world are by nature. And he hath made all obnoxious to injuries, and made every little thing strong enough to do us hurt by some instrument or other; and hath given us all a sufficient stock of self-love and desire of self-preservation, to be as the chain to tie together all the parts of society, and to restrain us from doing violence lest we be violently dealt withal ourselves.

The other part of justice is commonly called distributive, and is commanded in this rule, " Render to all their dues: tribute to whom tribute is due; custom to whom custom; fear to whom fear; honour to whom honour. Owe no man any thing, but to love one another."[1] This justice is distinguished from the first: because the obligation depends not upon contract or express bargain, but passes upon us by virtue of some command of God or of our superior, by nature or by grace, by piety or religion, by trust or by office, according to that commandment—" As every man hath received the gift, so let him minister the same one to another, as good stewards of the manifold grace of God."[2] And, as the first

[1] Rom. xiii. 7.   [2] 1 Pet. iv. 10.

considers an equality of persons in respect of the contract or particular necessity, this supposes a difference of persons, and no particular bargains, but such necessary intercourses as by the laws of God or man are introduced. But I shall reduce all the particulars of both kinds to these four heads : 1. Obedience ; 2. Provision ; 3. Negotiation ; 4. Restitution.

Sect. I. *Of Obedience to our Superiors.*

Our superiors are set over us in affairs of the world, or the affairs of the soul and things pertaining to religion, and are called accordingly ecclesiastical or civil. Towards whom our duty is thus generally described in the New Testament. For temporal or civil governors the commands are these: "Render to Cæsar the things that are Cæsar's ;" and, "Let every soul be subject to the higher powers: for there is no power but of God; the powers that be are ordained of God: whosoever, therefore, resisteth the power resisteth the ordinance of God; and they that resist shall receive to themselves damnation:"[1] and, "Put them in mind to be subject to principalities and powers, and to obey magistrates:"[2] and, "Submit yourselves to every ordinance of man, for the Lord's sake : whether it be to the king, as supreme ; or unto governors, as unto them that are sent by him for the punishment of evil-doers, and the praise of them that do well."[3]

For spiritual or ecclesiastical governors, thus we are commanded : "Obey them that have the rule over you, and submit yourselves ; for they watch for your souls, as they that must give an account :"[4] and, "Hold such in reputation :"[5] and, "To this end did I write, that I might know the proof of you, whether ye be obedient in all things,"[6] said St. Paul to the church of Corinth. Our duty is reducible to practice by the following rules.

Acts and Duties of Obedience to all our Superiors.

1. We must obey all human laws appointed and constituted by lawful authority, that is, of the supreme power, according to the constitution of the place in which we live ; all laws, I mean, which are not against the law of God.

2. In obedience to human laws, we must observe the letter of the law where we can, without doing violence to the reason

[1] Rom. xiii. 1. [2] Titus iii. 1. [3] 1 Pet. ii. 13.
[4] Heb. xiii. 17. [5] Phil. ii. 29. [6] 2 Cor. ii. 9.

K

of the law and the intention of the lawgiver ; but where they cross each other the charity of the law is to be preferred before its discipline, and the reason of it before the letter.

3. If the general reason of the law ceases in our particular, and a contrary reason rises upon us, we are to procure dispensation, or leave to omit the observation of it in such circumstances, if there be any persons or office appointed for granting it ; but if there be none, or if it is not easily to be had, or not without an inconvenience greater than the good of the observation of the law in our particular, we are dispensed withal in the nature of the thing, without further process or trouble.

4. As long as the law is obligatory, so long our obedience is due ; and he that begins a contrary custom without reason, sins : but he that breaks the law, when the custom is entered and fixed, is excused ; because it is supposed the legislative power consents, when, by not punishing, it suffers disobedience to grow to a custom.[7]

5. Obedience to human laws must be for conscience' sake ; that is, because in such obedience public order, and charity, and benefit, are concerned, and because the law of God commands us ; therefore we must make a conscience in keeping the just laws of superiors : and, although the matter before the making of the law was indifferent, yet now the obedience is not indifferent ;[8] but, next to the laws of God, we are to obey the laws of all our superiors, who, the more public they are, the first they are to be in the order of obedience.

6. Submit to the punishment and censure of the laws, and seek not to reverse their judgment by opposing, but by submitting, or flying, or silence, to pass through it or by it, as we can ; and although from inferior judges we may appeal where the law permits us, yet we must sit down and rest in the judgment of the supreme ; and if we be wronged, let us complain to God of the injury, not of the persons ; and he will deliver thy soul from unrighteous judges.

7. Do not believe thou hast kept the law, when thou hast suffered the punishment. For although patiently to submit to the power of the sword be a part of obedience, yet this is

---

[7] Mores leges perduxerunt jam in potestatem suam. Leges mori serviunt.—Ernesti, vol. ii. p. 421.   [8] Ἐξ ἀρχῆς μὲν οὐδὲν διαφέρει· ὅταν δὲ Ͻῶνται, διαφέρει.—Arist. Eth. 5. cap. 7.

such a part as supposes another left undone; and the law punishes, not because she is as well pleased in taking vengeance as in being obeyed; but, because she is pleased, she uses punishment as a means to secure obedience for the future, or in others. Therefore, although in such cases the law is satisfied, and the injury and the injustice are paid for, yet the sins of irreligion, and scandal, and disobedience to God, must still be so accounted for, as to crave pardon and be washed off by repentance.

8. Human laws are not to be broken with scandal, nor at all without reason; for he that does it causelessly is a despiser of the law, and undervalues the authority. For human laws differ from Divine laws principally in this: 1. That the positive commands of a man may be broken upon smaller and more reasons than the positive commands of God; we may, upon a smaller reason, omit to keep any of the fasting-days of the church than omit to give alms to the poor: only this, the reason must bear weight according to the gravity and concernment of the law; a law, in a small matter, may be omitted for a small reason; in a great matter, not without a greater reason. And, 2. The negative precepts of men may cease by many instruments, by contrary customs, by public disrelish, by long omission: but the negative precepts of God never can cease, but when they are expressly abrogated by the same authority. But what those reasons are that can dispense with the command of a man, a man may be his own judge, and sometimes take his proportions from his own reason and necessity, sometimes from public fame, and the practice of pious and severe persons, and from popular customs; in which a man shall walk most safely when he does not walk alone, but a spiritual man takes him by the hand.

9. We must not be too forward in procuring dispensations, nor use them any longer than the reason continues for which we first procured them: for to be dispensed withal is an argument of natural infirmity, if it be necessary; but if it be not, it signifies an undisciplined and unmortified spirit.

10. We must not be too busy in examining the prudence and unreasonableness of human laws: for, although we are not bound to believe them all to be the wisest, yet if, by inquiring into the lawfulness of them, or by any other instrument, we find them to fail of that wisdom with which some

others are ordained, yet we must never make use of it to disparage the person of the lawgiver, or to countenance any man's disobedience, much less our own.

11. Pay that reverence to the person of thy prince, of his ministers, of thy parents and spiritual guides, which, by the customs of the place thou livest in, are usually paid to such persons in their several degrees: that is, that the highest reverence be paid to the highest person, and so still in proportion; and that this reverence be expressed in all the circumstances and manners of the city and nation.

12. Lift not up thy hand against thy prince or parent, upon what pretence soever; but bear all personal affronts and inconveniences at their hands, and seek no remedy but by patience and piety, yielding and praying, or absenting thyself.

13. Speak not evil of the ruler of thy people, neither curse thy father or mother, nor revile thy spiritual guides, nor discover and lay naked their infirmities; but treat them with reverence and religion, and preserve their authority sacred by esteeming their persons venerable.

14. Pay tribute and customs to princes according to the laws, and maintenance to thy parents according to their necessity, and honourable support to the clergy according to the dignity of the work, and the customs of the place.

15. Remember always, that duty to our superiors is not an act of commutative justice, but of distributive; that is, although kings and parents and spiritual guides are to pay a great duty to their inferiors, the duty of their several charges and government, yet the good government of a king and of parents are actions of religion, as they relate to God, and of piety, as they relate to their people and families. And, although we usually call them just princes who administer their laws exactly to the people, because the actions are in the manner of justice, yet, in propriety of speech, they are rather to be called pious and religious. For as he is not called a just father that educates his children well, but pious; so that prince who defends and well rules his people is religious, and does that duty for which alone he is answerable to God. The consequence of which is this, so far as concerns our duty: if the prince or parent fail of their duty, we must not fail of ours; for we are answerable to them and to God too, as being accountable to

al our superiors, and so are they to theirs: they are above us, and God is above them.

Remedies against Disobedience, and Means to endear our Obedience; by way of consideration.

1. Consider, that all authority descends from God, and our superiors bear the image of the Divine power, which God imprints on them as on an image of clay, or a coin upon a less perfect metal, which whoso defaces shall not be answerable for the loss or spoil of the materials, but the defacing the king's image; and in the same measure will God require it at our hands, if we despise his authority, upon whomsoever he hath imprinted it. "He that despiseth you, despiseth me." And Dathan and Abiram were said to be "gathered together against the Lord." And this was St. Paul's argument for our obedience: "The powers that be are ordained of God."

2. There is very great peace and immunity from sin in resigning our wills up to the command of others: for, provided that our duty to God be secured, their commands are warrants to us in all things else; and the case of conscience is determined, if the command be evident and pressing: and it is certain, the action that is but indifferent and without reward, if done only upon our own choice, is an action of duty and of religion, and rewardable by the grace and favour of God, if done in obedience to the command of our superiors. For, since naturally we desire what is forbidden us, (and sometimes there is no other evil in the thing but that it is forbidden us,) God hath in grace enjoined and proportionably accepts obedience, as being directly opposed to the former irregularity; and it is acceptable, although there be no other good in the thing that is commanded us but that it is commanded.

3. By obedience we are made a society and a republic, and distinguished from herds of beasts, and heaps of flies, who do what they list, and are incapable of laws, and obey none: and therefore are killed and destroyed, though never punished, and they never can have a reward.

4. By obedience we are rendered capable of all the blessings of government, signified by St. Paul in these words: "He is the minister of God to thee for good;"[9] and by St. Peter in these, "Governors are sent by him for the punish-

* Rom. xiii. 4.

ment of evil-doers, and for the praise of them that do well."[10]
And he that ever felt, or saw, or can understand, the miseries
of confusion in public affairs, or amazement in a heap of sad,
tumultuous, and indefinite thoughts, may from thence judge
of the admirable effects of order, and the beauty of government.   What health is to the body, and peace is to the spirit,
that is government to the societies of men ; the greatest blessing which they can receive in that temporal capacity.

5. No man shall ever be fit to govern others that knows
not first how to obey.   For if the spirit of a subject be rebellious, in a prince it will be tyrannical and intolerable ; and
of so ill example, that, as it will encourage the disobedience
of others, so it will render it unreasonable for him to exact of
others what in the like case he refused to pay.

6. There is no sin in the world which God hath punished
with so great severity and high detestation as this of disobedience.   For the crime of idolatry God sent the sword amongst
his people ; but it was never heard that the earth opened and
swallowed up any but rebels against their prince.

7. Obedience is better than the particular actions of religion ; and he serves God better that follows his prince in
lawful services than he that refuses his command upon pretence he must go say his prayers.   But rebellion is compared
to that sin which of all sin seems the most unnatural and
damned impiety,—" Rebellion is as the sin of witchcraft."

8. Obedience is a complicated act of virtue, and many
graces are exercised in one act of obedience.   It is an act of
humility, of mortification and self-denial, of charity to God, of
care of the public, of order and charity to ourselves and all
our society, and a great instance of a victory over the most
refractory and unruly passions.

9. To be a subject is a greater temporal felicity than to be
a king : for all eminent governments, according to their height,
have a great burden, huge care, infinite business,[11] little rest,
innumerable fears ; and all that he enjoys above another is, that
he does enjoy the things of the world with other circumstances
and a bigger noise; and if others go at his single command,
it is also certain he must suffer inconvenience at the needs

---

[10] 1 Pet. ii. 14.

[11] Οὐ χρὴ παννύχιον εὕδειν βουληφόρον ἄνδρα,
Ὁι λαοί τ' ἐπιτετράφαται, καὶ τόσσα μέμηλε.—Homer, Il β'. 24

and disturbances of all his people: and the evils of one man
and of one family are not enough for him to bear, unless also
he be almost crushed with the evils of mankind.   He, therefore, is an ungrateful person that will press the scales down
with a voluntary load, and, by disobedience, put more thorns
into the crown or mitre of his superior.   Much better is the
advice of St. Paul; "Obey them that have the rule over you,
as they that must give an account for your souls ; that they
may do it with joy and not with grief: for (besides that it is
unpleasant to them) it is unprofitable for you."

10. The angels are ministering spirits, and perpetually execute the will and commandment of God: and all the wise
men and all the good men of the world are obedient to their
governors ; and the eternal Son of God esteemed it his "meat
and drink to do the will of his Father," and for his obedience
alone obtained the greatest glory: and no man ever came to
perfection but by obedience ; and thousands of saints have
chosen such institutions and manners of living, in which they
might not choose their own work, nor follow their own will,
nor please themselves, but be accountable to others, and subject to discipline, and obedient to command ; as knowing this
to be the highway of the cross, the way that the King of sufferings and humility did choose, and so became the King of glory.

11. No man ever perished who followed first the will of
God, and then the will of his superiors : but thousands have
been damned merely for following their own will, and relying
upon their own judgments, and choosing their own work, and
doing their own fancies.   For if we begin with ourselves,
whatsoever seems good in our eyes is most commonly dis-
pleasing in the eyes of God.

12. The sin of rebellion, though it be a spiritual sin, and
imitable by devils, yet it is of that disorder, unreasonableness,
and impossibility, amongst intelligent spirits, that they never
murmured or mutinied in their lower stations against their
superiors.   Nay, the good angels of an inferior order durst
not revile a devil of a higher order.   This consideration,
which I reckon to be most pressing in the discourses of reason, and obliging next to the necessity of a Divine precept,
we learn from St. Jude, 8, 9, "Likewise also these filthy
dreamers despise dominion, and speak evil of dignities.   And
yet Michael the archangel, when, contending with the devil,

he disputed about the body of Moses, durst not bring against him a railing accusation."

But because our superiors rule by their example, by their word or law, and by the rod, therefore in proportion there are several degrees and parts of obedience, of several excellences and degrees towards perfection.

Degrees of Obedience.

1. The first is the obedience of the outward work ; and this is all that human laws of themselves regard ; for lecause man cannot judge the heart, therefore it prescribes nothing to it: the public end is served, not by good wishes, but by real and actual performances ; and if a man obeys against his will, he is not punishable by the laws.

2. The obedience of the will: and this is also necessary in our obedience to human laws, not because man requires it for himself, but because God commands it towards man : and of it, although man cannot, yet God will demand an account. For we are to do it as to the Lord, and not to men ; and therefore we must do it willingly. But by this means our obedience in private is secured against secret arts and subterfuges: and when we can avoid the punishment, yet we shall not decline our duty, but serve man for God's sake, that is, cheerfully, promptly, vigorously ; for these are the proper parts of willingness and choice.

3. The understanding must yield obedience in general, though not in the particular instance ; that is, we must be firmly persuaded of the excellency of the obedience, though we be not bound, in all cases, to think the particular law to be most prudent. But, in this, our rule is plain enough. Our understanding ought to be inquisitive, whether the civil constitution agree with our duty to God ; but we are bound to inquire no further: and therefore beyond this, although he who, having no obligation to it, (as counsellors have,) inquires not at all into the wisdom or reasonableness of the law, be not always the wisest man, yet he is ever the best subject. For when he hath given up his understanding to his prince and prelate, provided that his duty to God be secured by a precedent search, be hath also, with the best and with all the instruments in the world, secured his obedience to man.

SECT. II. *Of Provision, or that part of Justice which is due from Superiors to Inferiors.*

As God hath imprinted his authority in several parts upon several estates of men, as princes, parents, spiritual guides; so he hath also delegated and committed parts of his care and providence unto them, that they may be instrumental in the conveying such blessings which God knows we need, and which he intends should be the effects of government. For since God governs all the world as a king, provides for us as a father, and is the great guide and conductor of our spirits as the head of the church, and the great shepherd and bishop of our souls, they who have portions of these dignities have also their share of the administration: the sum of all which is usually signified in these two words, *governing* and *feeding*, and is particularly recited in these following rules.

Duties of Kings, and all the Supreme Power, as Lawgivers.

1. Princes of the people, and all that have legislative power, must provide useful and good laws for the defence of property, for the encouragement of labour, for the safeguard of their persons, for determining controversies, for reward of noble actions and excellent arts and rare inventions, for promoting trade, and enriching their people.

2. In the making laws, princes must have regard to the public dispositions, to the affections and disaffections of the people, and must not introduce a law with public scandal and displeasure; but consider the public benefit, and the present capacity of affairs, and general inclinations of men's minds.[1] For he that enforces a law upon a people against their first and public apprehensions, tempts them to disobedience, and makes laws to become snares and hooks to catch the people, and to enrich the treasury with the spoils, and tears, and curses of the commonalty, and to multiply their mutiny and their sin.

3. Princes must provide, that the laws be duly executed: for a good law, without execution, is like an unperformed promise: and therefore they must be severe exactors of accounts from their delegates and ministers of justice.

4. The severity of laws must be tempered with dispensations, pardons, and remissions, according as the case shall alter,

[1] Omittenda potiùs prævalida et adulta vitia, quàm hoc adsequi, ut palàm fiat, quibus flagitiis impares simus.—Tacit.

and new necessities be introduced, or some singular accident shall happen, in which the law would be unreasonable or intolerable, as to that particular.[2] And thus the people, with their importunity, prevailed against Saul in the case of Jonathan, and obtained his pardon for breaking the law which his father made, because his necessity forced him to taste honey; and his breaking the law, in that case, did promote that service whose promotion was intended by the law.

5. Princes must be fathers of the people, and provide such instances of gentleness, ease, wealth, and advantages, as may make mutual confidence between them; and must fix their security under God in the love of the people; which, therefore, they must, with all arts of sweetness, remission, popularity, nobleness, and sincerity, endeavour to secure to themselves.

6. Princes must not multiply public oaths without great, eminent, and violent necessity; lest the security of the king become a snare to the people, and they become false, when they see themselves suspected, or impatient, when they are violently held fast: but the greater and more useful caution is upon things than upon persons; and if security of kings can be obtained otherwise, it is better that oaths should be the last refuge, and when nothing else can be sufficient.

7. Let not the people be tempted with arguments to disobey, by the imposition of great and unnecessary taxes; for that lost to the son of Solomon the dominion of the ten tribes of Israel.[3]

8. Princes must, in a special manner, be guardians of pupils and widows, not suffering their persons to be oppressed, or their estates imbeciled, or in any sense be exposed to the rapine of covetous persons; but be provided for by just laws, and provident judges, and good guardians, ever having an ear ready open to their just complaints, and a heart full of pity, and one hand to support them, and the other to avenge them.

9. Princes must provide, that the laws may be so administered that they be truly and really an ease to the people, not an instrument of vexation: and therefore must be careful, that the shortest and most equal ways of trials be appointed, fees moderated, and intricacies and windings as much cut off as may be, lest injured persons be forced to perish under the op-

---

[2] Ἐπιείκειά ἐστιν ἐπανόρθωμα νόμου, ᾗ ἐλλείπει διὰ τὸ καθόλου.—Eth. 5. c. 10.   [3] L' avaritia de' re, peste de' regni.

pression or under the law, in the injury or in the suit. Laws are like princes, those best and most beloved who are most easy of access.

10. Places of judicature ought, at no hand, to be sold by pious princes, who remember themselves to be fathers of the people. For they that buy the office will sell the act;[4] and they that, at any rate, will be judges, will not, at any easy rate, do justice; and their bribery is less punishable, when bribery opened the door by which they entered.

11. Ancient privileges, favours, customs, and acts of grace, indulged by former kings to their people, must not, without high reason and great necessities, be revoked by their successors, nor forfeitures be exacted violently, nor penal laws urged rigorously, nor in light cases; nor laws be multiplied without great need; nor vicious persons, which are publicly and deservedly hated, be kept in defiance of popular desires; nor any thing that may unnecessarily make the yoke heavy and the affection light, that may increase murmurs and lessen charity; always remembering that the interest of the prince and the people is so infolded in a mutual embrace, that they cannot be untwisted without pulling a limb off, or dissolving the bands and conjunction of the whole body.

12. All princes must esteem themselves as much bound by their word, by their grants, and by their promises, as the meanest of their subjects are by the restraint and penalty of laws:[5] and, although they are superior to the people, yet they are not superior to their own voluntary concessions and engagements, their promises and oaths, when once they are passed from them.

The Duty of Superiors as they are Judges.

1. Princes in judgment and their delegate judges must judge the causes of all persons uprightly and impartially, without any personal consideration of the power of the mighty, or the bribe of the rich, or the needs of the poor. For, although the poor must fare no worse for his poverty, yet, in justice, he must fare no better for it; and, although the rich must be no more regarded, yet he must not be less. And to this purpose

[4] Chi compra il magistrato, forza è, che vendra la giustitia.
[5] Nulla lex (civilis) sibi soli conscientiam justitiæ suæ debet, sed eis à quibus obsequium expectat.—Tertul. Apologet.

the tutor of Cyrus instructed him, when, in a controversy, where a great boy would have taken a large coat from a little boy, because his own was too little for him, and the other's was too big, he adjudged the great coat to the great boy: his tutor answered, "Sir, if you were made a judge of decency or fitness you had judged well in giving the biggest to the biggest; but when you are appointed judge, not whom the coat did fit, but whose it was, you should have considered the title and the possession, who did the violence, and who made it, or who bought it." And so it must be in judgments between the rich and the poor: it is not to be considered what the poor man needs, but what is his own.

2. A prince may not, much less may inferior judges, deny justice, when it is legally and competently demanded: and if the prince will use his prerogative in pardoning an offender, against whom justice is required, he must be careful to give satisfaction to the injured person, or his relatives, by some other instrument; and be watchful to take away the scandal, that is, lest such indulgence might make persons more bold to do injury: and if he spares the life, let him change the punishment into that which may make the offender, if not suffer justice, yet do justice, and more real advantage to the injured person.

These rules concern princes and their delegates in the making or administering laws, in the appointing rules of justice, and doing acts of judgment. The duty of parents to their children and nephews is briefly described by St. Paul.

The Duty of Parents to their Children.

1. "Fathers, provoke not your children to wrath;"[6] that is, be tender-bowelled, pitiful, and gentle, complying with all the infirmities of the children, and, in their several ages, proportioning to them several usages, according to their needs and their capacities.

2. "Bring them up in the nurture and admonition of the Lord:" that is, secure their religion; season their younger years with prudent and pious principles; make them in love with virtue; and make them habitually so, before they come to choose or to discern good from evil, that their choice may be with less difficulty and danger. For while they are under discipline, they suck in all that they are first taught, and be-

* Ephes vi. 4.

lieve it infinitely. Provide for them wise, learned, and virtuous tutors, and good company and discipline, seasonable
baptism, catechism, and confirmation.[7] For it is great folly
to heap up much wealth for our children, and not to take care
concerning the children for whom we get it. It is as if a man
should take more care about his shoe than about his foot.

3. Parents must show piety at home ;[8] that is, they must
give good example and reverend deportment in the face of
their children ; and all those instances of charity, which usually endear each other—sweetness of conversation, affability,
frequent admonitions, all significations of love and tenderness,
care and watchfulness—must be expressed towards children,
that they may look upon their parents as their friends and
patrons, their defence and sanctuary, their treasure and their
guide. Hither is to be reduced the nursing of children, which
is the first and most natural and necessary instance of piety
which mothers can show to their babes ; a duty from which
nothing will excuse, but a disability, sickness, danger, or public necessity.

4. Parents must provide for their own,[9] according to their
condition, education, and employment; called, by St. Paul, "a
laying up for the children," that is, an enabling them, by
competent portions, or good trades, arts, or learning, to defend
themselves against the chances of the world, that they may
not be exposed to temptation, to beggary, or unworthy arts.
And, although this must be done without covetousness, without impatient and greedy desires of making them rich ; yet it
must be done with much care and great affection, with all
reasonable provision, and according to our power : and if we
can, without sin, improve our estates for them, that, also, is
part of the duty we owe to God for them. And this rule is
to extend to all that descend from us, although we have been
overtaken in a fault, and have unlawful issue ; they, also, become part of our care, yet so as not to injure the production
of the lawful bed.

5. This duty is to extend to a provision of conditions and
an estate of life.[10] Parents must, according to their power

[7] Potior mihi ratio vivendi honestè, quàm et optimè dicendi videtur.—
Quintil. lib. i. cap. 2. [8] Heb. xii. 9. Crates apud Plutarch. de Liber.
Educand. 1 Tim. v. 4. [9] 1 Tim. v. 8.
[10] Νυμφευμάτων μὲν τῶν ἐμῶν πατὴρ ἐμὸς
Μέριμναν ἕξει, κοὐκ ἐμὸν κρίνειν τάδε.—Eurip. Androm. 988.

and reason, provide husbands or wives for their children.[11]
In which they must secure piety and religion,[12] and the affection and love of the interested persons ; and, after these, let
them make what provisions they can for other conveniences or
advantages: ever remembering that they can do no injury
more afflictive to the children than to join them with cords of
a disagreeing affection ; it is like tying a wolf and a lamb, or
planting the vine in a garden of coleworts. Let them be persuaded with reasonable inducements to make them willing,
and to choose according to the parent's wish ; but at no hand
let them be forced. Better to sit up all night than to go to
bed with a dragon.

Rules for Married Persons.

1. Husbands must give to their wives love,[13] maintenance,

Me tibi Tyndareus vitâ gravis auctor et annis
    Tradidit: arbitrium neptis habebat avus.—Ov. in Ep. Herm.

[11] Liberi sine consensu parentum contrahere non debent. Androma-
cha, apud Euripidem, cum petita fuit ad nuptias, respondit, patris sui esse
sponsalium suorum curam habere : et Achilles, apud Homerum, regis
filiam sine patris sui consensu noluit ducere. Il. i. 393. Ἢν γὰρ δή με
σόωσι θεοὶ, καί οἴκαδ᾽ ἵκωμαι, Πηλεὺς θήν μοι ἔπειτα γυναῖκα γαμέσσεται
αὐτός. Et Justinianus Imp. ait, naturali simul et civili rationi congruere,
ne filii ducant uxores citra parentum authoritatem. Simo Terentianus
parat abdicationem, quia Pamphilus clam ipso duxisset uxorem. Istius-
modi sponsalia fiunt irrita, nisi velint parentes : at si subsequuta est
copula, nè temere rescindantur connubia, multæ suadent cautiones et pe-
ricula. Liberi, autem, quamdiu secundùm leges patrias sui juris non sunt,
clandestinas nuptias si ineant, peccant contra quintum præceptum, et jus
naturale secundarium. Propriè enim loquendo parentes non habent
ἐξουσίαν, sive potestatem, sed authoritatem ; habent jus jubendi aut pro-
hibendi, sed non irritum faciendi. Atque etiam ista authoritas exercenda
est secundùm æquum et bonum ; scil. ut nè morosus et difficilis sit pater.
Mater enim vix habet aliquod juris præter suasionis, et amoris, et grati-
tudinis. Si autem pater filiam non collocâsset ante 25 annos, filia nubere
poterat cui voluerat, ex jure Romanorum. Patrum enim authoritas major aut minor est ex legibus patriis, et solet extendi ad certam ætatem, et
tum exspirat quoad matrimonium ; et est major in filias quàm filios.—
Num. 30.   [12] Eosdem quos maritus nôsse deos et colere solos uxor
debet; supervacaneis autem religionibus et alienis superstitionibus fores
occludere. Nulli enim deûm grata sunt sacra, quæ mulier clanculùm et
furtim facit.—Plutarch. Conjug. Præcept. Gen. 24. Vocemus puellam, et
quæramus os ejus.—The Duty of Husbands, &c. See Chap. ii. Sect. 3.
   [13] Σοὶ δὲ θεοὶ τόσα δοῖεν⸺
      Ἄνδρα τε καὶ οἶκον, καὶ ὁμοφροσύνην ὀπάσειαν
      Ἐσθλήν· οὐ μὲν γὰρ τοῦ γε κρεῖσσον καὶ ἄρειον,
      Ἢ ὅθ᾽ ὁμοφρονέοντε νοήμασιν οἶκον ἔχητον
      Ἀνὴρ ἠδὲ γυνή· πόλλ᾽ ἄλγεα δυσμενέεσσι,
      Χάρματα δ᾽ εὐμενέτῃσι· μάλιστα δέ τ᾽ ἔκλυον αὐτοί.—Odyss. ζ´. 180

duty, and the sweetnesses of conversation ; and wives [14] must pay to them all they have or can, with the interest of obedience and reverence : and they must be complicated in affections and interest, that there be no distinction between them of mine and thine. And if the title be the man's or the woman's, yet the use must be common; only the wisdom of the man is to regulate all extravagances and indiscretions. In other things no question is to be made ; and their goods should be as their children, not to be divided, but of one possession and provision : whatsoever is otherwise is not marriage, but merchandise. And upon this ground I suppose it was, that St. Basil commended that woman who took part of her husband's goods to do good works withal ;[15] for supposing him to be unwilling, and that the work was his duty or hers alone, or both theirs in conjunction, or of great advantage to either of their souls, and no violence to the support of their families, she had right to all that: and Abigail, of her own right, made a costly present to David, when her husband Nabal had refused it. The husband must [16] rule over his wife, as the soul does over the body, obnoxious to the same sufferings, and bound by the same affections, and doing or suffering by the permissions and interest of each other : that, (as the old philosopher said,) as the humours of the body are mingled with each other in the whole substances, so marriage may be a mixture of interests, of bodies, of minds, of friends, a conjunction [17] of the whole life, and the noblest of friendships. But if, after all the fair deportments and innocent chaste compliances, the husband be morose and ungentle, let the wife discourse thus :[18] "If, while I do my duty, my husband

---

[14] Ἔνεστ' ἀληθὲς φίλτρον εὐγνώμων τρόπος·
Τούτῳ κατακρατεῖν ἀνδρὸς εἴωθεν γυνή.—Menan.
Ἢ μοῦνοι φιλέουσ' ἀλόχους μερόπων ἀνθρώπων
Ἀτρεῖδαι; ἐπεί, ὅστις ἀνὴρ ἀγαθὸς καὶ ἐχέφρων,
Τὴν αὐτοῦ φιλέει καὶ κήδεται· ὡς καὶ ἐγὼ τὴν
Ἐκ θυμοῦ φιλέον, δουρικτητήν περ ἐοῦσαν.—Homer. Il. i. 340.

[15] Κλέψασα καλὰ κλέμματα ἄνευ ἀνδρὸς τὰς εὐποιίας ἐποίησε.

[16] Lætum esse debet et officiosum mariti imperium.—Plut.

Namque es ei pater et frater, venerandaque mater: nec minus facit ad dignitatem viri, si mulier eum suum præceptorem, philosophum, magistrumque appellet.—Plutarch.

[17] Convictio est quasi quædam intensio benevolentiæ.

[18] Οὐ χρυσός, οὐ τυραννίς, οὐ πλούτου χλιδὴ
Τοσοῦτον εἶχε διαφόρους τὰς ἡδονὰς,

neglects me, what will he do if I neglect him?" And if she thinks to be separated by reason of her husband's unchaste life, let her consider, that then the man will be incurably ruined, and her rivals could wish nothing more than that they might possess him alone.

The Duty of Masters of Families.

1. The same care is to extend to all of our family, in their proportions, as to our children; for as, by St. Paul's economy, the heir differs nothing from a servant while he is in minority, so a servant should differ nothing from a child, in the substantial part of the care: and the difference is only in degrees. Servants and masters are of the same kindred, of the same nature, and heirs of the same promises, and therefore, 1. must be provided of necessaries, for their support and and maintenance. 2. They must be used with mercy. 3. Their work must be tolerable and merciful. 4. Their restraints must be reasonable. 5. Their recreations fitting and healthful. 6. Their religion and the interest of souls taken care of. 7. And masters must correct their servants with gentleness, prudence, and mercy; not for every slight fault, not always, not with upbraiding and disgraceful language, but with such only as may express and reprove the fault, and amend the person. But in all these things measures are to be taken by the contract made, by the laws and customs of the place, by the sentence of prudent and merciful men, and by the cautions and remembrances given us by God; such as is that written by St. Paul, " as knowing that we also have a Master in heaven." The master must not be a lion in his house, lest his power be obeyed and his person hated; his eye be waited on, and his business be neglected in secret. No servant will do his duty, unless he make a conscience, or love his master: if he does it not for God's sake or his master's, he will not need to do it always for his own.

The Duty of Guardians or Tutors.

Tutors and guardians are in the place of parents: and what they are in fiction of law, they must remember as an

Ὡς ἀνδρὸς ἐσθλοῦ καὶ γυναικὸς εὐσεβοῦς
Γνώμη δικαία, καὶ φρονοῦσα τ' ἀνδρικά.

Inferior matrona suo sit, Prisce, marito;
Non aliter fiunt fœmina virque pares.

argument to engage them to do in reality of duty. They must do all the duty of parents, excepting those obligations which are merely natural.

¶ The duty of ministers and spiritual guides to the people is of so great burden, so various rules, so intricate and busy caution, that it requires a distinct tractate by itself.

Sect. III. *Of Negotiation, or Civil Contracts.*

This part of justice is such as depends upon the laws of man directly, and upon the laws of God only by consequence and indirect reason; and from civil laws or private agreements it is to take its estimate and measures: and, although our duty is plain and easy, requiring of us honesty in contracts, sincerity in affirming, simplicity in bargaining, and faithfulness in performing, yet it may be helped by the addition of these following rules and considerations.

Rules and Measures of Justice in Bargaining.

1. In making contracts, use not many words: for all the business of a bargain is summed up in few sentences; and he that speaks least means fairest, as having fewer opportunities to deceive.

2. Lie not at all, neither in a little thing nor in a great, neither in the substance nor in the circumstance, neither in word nor deed; that is, pretend not what is false, cover not what is true: and let the measure of your affirmation or denial be the understanding of your contractor; for he that deceives the buyer or the seller by speaking what is true in a sense not intended or understood by the other, is a liar and a thief. For in bargains you are to avoid not only what is false, but that also which deceives.

3. In prices of bargaining concerning uncertain merchandises, you may buy as cheap, ordinarily, as you can ; and sell as dear as you can: so it be, 1. without violence ; and, 2. when you contract on equal terms with persons in all senses (as to the matter and skill of bargaining) equal to yourself, that is, merchants with merchants, wise men with wise men, rich with rich ; and, 3. when there is no deceit, and no necessity, and no monopoly : for in these cases, viz. when the contractors are equal, and no advantage on either side, both parties are voluntary, and therefore there can be no injustice or wrong

to either. But then add also this consideration, that the public be not oppressed by unreasonable and unjust rates; for
which the following rules are the best measure.

4. Let your prices be according to that measure of good
and evil which is established in the fame and common accounts
of the wisest and most merciful men, skilled in that manufacture or commodity; and the gain such which, without scandal, is allowed to persons in all the same circumstances.

5. Let no prices be heightened by the necessity or unskilfulness of the contractor: for the first is direct uncharitableness to the person, and injustice in the thing, because the
man's necessity could not naturally enter into the consideration of the value of the commodity; and the other is deceit
and oppression: much less must any man make necessities;
as by engrossing a commodity, by monopoly, by detaining
corn, or the like indirect arts; for such persons are unjust to
all single persons, with whom, in such cases, they contract,
and oppressors of the public.

6. In intercourse with others, do not do all which you may
lawfully do, but keep something within thy power; and, because there is a latitude of gain in buying and selling, take
not thou the utmost penny that is lawful, or which thou
thinkest so: for, although it be lawful, yet it is not safe; and
he that gains all that he can gain lawfully this year, possibly,
next year, will be tempted to gain something unlawfully.

7. He that sells dearer, by reason he sells not for ready
money, must increase his price no higher than to make himself
recompence for the loss which, according to the rules of trade,
he sustained by his forbearance, according to common com-
putation, reckoning in, also, the hazard, which he is prudently,
warily, and charitably to estimate. But although this be the
measure of his justice, yet, because it happens either to their
friends, or to necessitous and poor persons, they are, in these
cases, to consider the rules of friendship and neighbourhood,
and the obligations of charity, lest justice turn into unmercifulness.

8. No man is to be raised in his price or rents in regard
of any accident, advantage, or disadvantage, of his person.[19]
A prince must be used conscionably, as well as a common
person; and a beggar be treated justly, as well as a prince;

[19] Mercanzia non vuol nè amici nè parenti.

with this only difference, that to poor persons the utmost measure and extent of justice is unmerciful, which to a rich person is innocent, because it is just, and he needs not thy mercy and remission.

9. Let no man, for his own poverty, become more oppressing and cruel in his bargain, but quietly, modestly, diligently, and patiently recommend his estate to God, and follow its interest, and leave the success to him: for such courses will more probably advance his trade; they will certainly procure him a blessing and a recompence; and, if they cure not his poverty, they will take away the evil of it; and there is nothing else in it that can trouble him.

10. Detain not the wages of the hireling; for every degree of detention of it beyond the time is injustice and uncharitableness, and grinds his face, till tears and blood come out; but pay him exactly according to covenant, or according to his needs.

11. Religiously keep all promises and covenants, though made to your disadvantage, though afterwards you perceive you might have been better; and let not any precedent act of yours be altered by any after-accident. Let nothing make you break your promise, unless it be unlawful or impossible: that is, either out of your natural, or out of your civil power, yourself being under the power of another; or that it be intolerably inconvenient to yourself, and of no advantage to another; or that you have leave expressed, or reasonably presumed.[20]

12. Let no man take wages or fees for a work that he cannot do, or cannot with probability undertake, or in some sense profitably, and with ease, or with advantage, manage. Physicians must not meddle with desperate diseases, and known to be incurable, without declaring their sense beforehand; that if the patient please, he may entertain him at adventure, or to do him some little ease. Advocates must deal plainly with their clients, and tell them the true state and danger of their case, and must not pretend confidence in an evil cause; but when he hath so cleared his own innocence, if the client will

[20] Surgam ad sponsalia, quia promisi, quamvis non concoxerim: sed non, si febricitavero: subest enim tacita exceptio, si potero, si debebo. Effice ut idem status sit, cùm exigitur, qui fuit, cùm promitterem. Destituere levitas non erit, si aliquid intervenit novi Eadem mihi omnia præsta: et idem sum.—Seneca, De Benefic. li iv. cap. 39. Rubis. vol iv. p. 197

have collateral and legal advantages obtained by his industry, he may engage his endeavour, provided he do no injury to the right cause, or any man's person.

13. Let no man appropriate to his own use what God, by a special mercy, or the republic, hath made common;[21] for that is both against justice and charity too: and, by miraculous accidents, God hath declared his displeasure against such enclosure. When the kings of Naples enclosed the gardens of Œnotria, where the best manna of Calabria descends, that no man might gather it without paying tribute, the manna ceased till the tribute was taken off, and then it came again: and so when, after the third trial, the princes found they could not have that in proper which God made to be common, they left it as free as God gave it. The like happened in Epire. when Lysimachus laid an impost upon the Tragasæan salt, it vanished till Lysimachus left it public.[22] And when the procurators of King Antigonus imposed a rate upon the sick people that came to Edepsum to drink the waters, which were lately sprung, and were very healthful, instantly the waters dried up, and the hope of gain perished.

The sum of all is in these words of St. Paul, "Let no man go beyond and defraud his brother in any matter; because the Lord is the avenger of all such."[23] And our blessed Saviour, in the enumerating the duties of justice, besides the commandment of "Do not steal," adds, "Defraud not,"[24] forbidding (as a distinct explication of the old law) the tacit and secret theft of abusing our brother in civil contracts. And it needs no other arguments to enforce this caution, but only that the Lord hath undertaken to avenge all such persons. And, as he always does it in the great day of recompences, so very often he does it here, by making the unclean portion of injustice to be as a cankerworm eating up all the other increase: it procures beggary, and a declining estate, or a caitiff cursed spirit, an ill name, the curse of the injured and oppressed person, and a fool or a prodigal to be his heir.

Sect. IV.　Of Restitution.

RESTITUTION is that part of justice to which a man is obliged by a precedent contract or a foregoing fault, by his own act

---

[21] Brassavol. in exam. simpl.　　[22] Cælius Rhod. l. ix. c. 12. Athenæ. Deipnos. l. iii.　　[23] 1 Thess. iv. 6.　　[24] Lev. xix. 13; 1 Cor. vi. 8; Mark x. 19.

or another man's, either with or without his will. He that
borrows is bound to pay, and much more he that steals or
cheats.[1] For if he that borrows, and pays not when he is able,
be an unjust person and a robber, because he possesses another
man's goods, to the right owner's prejudice, then he that took
them at first without leave, is the same thing in every instant
of his possession, which the debtor is after the time in which
he should, and could, have made payment. For, in all sins,
we are to distinguish the transient or passing act from the remaining effect or evil. The act of stealing was soon over, and
cannot be undone; and for it the sinner is only answerable to
God, or his vicegerent: and he is, in a particular manner, appointed to expiate it by suffering punishment, and repenting,
and asking pardon, and judging and condemning himself, doing acts of justice and charity, in opposition and contradiction
to that evil action. But because, in the case of stealing, there
is an injury done to our neighbour, and the evil still remains
after the action is past; therefore for this we are accountable
to our neighbour, and we are to take the evil off from him,
which we brought upon him;[2] or else he is an injured person,
a sufferer all the while: and that any man should be the worse
for me, and my direct act, and by my intention, is against the
rule of equity, of justice, and of charity; I do not that to
others which I would have done to myself; for I grow richer
upon the ruins of his fortune. Upon this ground, it is a determined rule in divinity, "Our sin can never be pardoned till
we have restored what we unjustly took, or wrongfully detain:" restored it (I mean) actually, or in purpose and desire,
which we must really perform when we can. And this doctrine, besides its evident and apparent reasonableness, is derived from the express words of Scripture, reckoning restitution to be a part of repentance, necessary in order to the
remission of our sins. "If the wicked restore the pledge,
give again that he had robbed, &c., he shall surely live, he
shall not die."[3] The practice of this part of justice is to be
directed by the following rules.

Rules of making Restitution.

1. Whosoever is an effective real cause of doing his neighbour wrong, by what instrument soever he does it, (whether

[1] Chi non vuol rendere, fa mal a prendere. [2] Si tuâ culpâ datum
est damnum, jure super his satisfacere te oportet [3] Ezek. xxxiii. 15

by commanding or encouraging it, by counselling or com-
mending it,[4] by acting it, or not hindering it when he might
and ought,[5] by concealing it, or receiving it,) is bound to
make restitution to his neighbour ; if, without him, the injury
had not been done, but by him, or his assistance, it was. For,
by the same reason that every one of these is guilty of the sin,
and is cause of the injury, by the same they are bound to make
reparation ; because by him his neighbour is made worse, and
therefore is to be put into that state from whence he was
forced. And suppose that thou hast persuaded an injury to
be done to thy neighbour, which others would have persuaded,
if thou hadst not, yet thou art still obliged, because thou really
didst cause the injury ; just as they had been obliged, if they
had done it : and thou art not at all the less bound, by having
persons as ill-inclined as thou wert.

2. He that commanded the injury to be done is first bound ;
then he that did it ; and, after these, they also are obliged who
did so assist, as without them the thing would not have been
done. If satisfaction be made by any of the former, the latter
is tied to repentance, but no restitution : but if the injured
person be not righted, every one of them is wholly guilty of
the injustice ; and therefore bound to restitution, singly and
entirely.

3. Whosoever intends a little injury to his neighbour, and
acts it, and by it a greater evil accidentally comes, he is obliged
to make an entire reparation of all the injury of that which he
intended, and of that which he intended not, but yet acted by
his own instrument going further than he at first purposed it.[6]
He that set fire on a plane-tree to spite his neighbour, and the
plane-tree set fire on his neighbour's house, is bound to pay
for all the loss, because it did all arise from his own ill intention. It is like murder committed by a drunken person, in-

---

[4] Ὁ γὰρ ἐπαινέσας τὸν δεδρακότα, οὐδέν τι ἧσσον τῶν πεπραγμένων,
αὐτουργὸς γίνεται.—Totilas apud Procop. Goth. 3.   Qui laudat servum
fugitivum, tenetur.   Non enim oportet laudando augeri malum.—Ulpian.
in lib. i. cap. de Servo corrupto.   [5] Ὁ ἐμπρησμένος τοῦ ἀνάψαν-
τος ἀλλὰ καὶ τοῦ καταβῆσαι δυναμένου, δρᾶσαι δὲ τοιοῦτον ὅλως μὴ βου-
ληθέντος.—Nicet. Choniat. in Michael. Comnen.   Sic Syri ab Amphic-
tyonibus judicio damnati, quia piraticam non prohibuerunt, cùm poterant.
    [6] Etiamsi partem damni dare noluisti, in totum quasi prudens dederis,
tenendus es.   Ex toto enim noluisse debet qui imprudentiâ defenditur.
—Sen. Contr. Involuntarium ortum ex voluntario censetur pro voluntario.
—Strabo.

voluntary in some of the effect, but voluntary in the other parts of it, and in all the cause; and therefore the guilty person is answerable for all of it. And when Ariarathes, the Cappadocian king, had but in wantonness stopped the mouth of the river Melanus, although he intended no evil, yet Euphrates being swelled by that means, and bearing away some of the strand of Cappadocia, did great spoil to the Phrygians and Galatians; he therefore, by the Roman senate, was condemned in three hundred talents, towards reparation of the damage. Much rather, therefore, when the lesser part of the evil was directly intended.

4. He that hinders a charitable person from giving alms to a poor man, is tied to restitution if he hindered him by fraud or violence, because it was a right which the poor man had, when the good man had designed and resolved it, and the fraud or violence hinders the effect, but not the purpose; and therefore he who used the deceit or the force is injurious, and did damage to the poor man. But if the alms were hindered only by entreaty, the hinderer is not tied to restitution, because entreaty took not liberty away from the giver, but left him still master of his own act, and he had power to alter his purpose, and so long there was no injustice done.[7] The same is the case of a testator giving a legacy, either by kindness, or by promise, and common right. He that hinders the charitable legacy by fraud or violence, or the due legacy by entreaty, is equally obliged to restitution. The reason of the latter part of this case is, because he that entreats or persuades to a sin, is as guilty as he that acts it; and if, without his persuasion, the sin and the injury would not be acted, he is in his kind the entire cause, and therefore obliged to repair the injury as much as the person that does the wrong immediately.

5. He that refuses to do any part of his duty (to which he is otherwise obliged) without a bribe, is bound to restore that money, because he took it in his neighbour's wrong, and not as a salary for his labour, or a reward for his wisdom, (for his stipend hath paid all that,) or he hath obliged himself to do it by his voluntary undertaking.

6. He that takes any thing from his neighbour which was justly forfeited, but yet takes it not as a minister of justice,

[7] Πλεονεκτεῖ οὐδὲν ὁ οὐ βοηθήσας χρήμασι δι' ἀνελευθερίαν.—Eth. l. v. c 4.

but to satisfy his own revenge or avarice, is tied to repentance, but not to restitution.   For my neighbour is not the worse for my act, for thither the law and his own demerits bore him; but because I took the forfeiture indirectly, I am answerable to God for my unhandsome, unjust, or uncharitable circumstances.   Thus Philip of Macedon was reproved by Aristides for destroying the Phocenses, because, although they deserved it, yet he did it not in prosecution of the law of nations, but to enlarge his own dominions.

7. The heir of an obliged person is not bound to make restitution, if the obligation passed only by a personal act ; but if it passed from his person to his estate, then the estate passes with all its burden.   If the father, by persuading his neighbour to do injustice, be bound to restore, the action is extinguished by the death of the father, because it was only the father's sin that bound him, which cannot directly bind the son ; therefore the son is free.   And this is so in all personal actions, unless where the civil law interposes and alters the case.
¶ These rules concern the persons that are obliged to make restitution ; the other circumstances of it are thus described.

8. He that by fact, or word, or sign, either fraudulently or violently does hurt to his neighbour's body, life, goods, good name, friends, or soul, is bound to make restitution in the several instances, according as they are capable to be made.   In all these instances we must separate entreaty and enticements from deceit or violence.   If I persuade my neighbour to commit adultery, I still leave him or her in their own power ; and though I am answerable to God for my sin, yet not to my neighbour. For I made her to be willing ; yet she was willing,[8] that is, the same at last as I was at first.   But if I have used fraud, and made her to believe a lie,[9] upon which confidence she did the act, and without it she would not, (as if I tell a woman her husband is dead, or intended to kill her, or is himself an adulterous man,) or if I use violence, that is, either force her or threaten her with death, or a grievous wound, or any thing that takes her from the liberty of her choice, I am bound to restitution ; that is, to restore her to a right understanding of things and to a full liberty, by taking from her the deceit or the violence.

[8] Δι' ἀλλότριον ἔργον πταίει οὐδείς.—Epict.
[9] Πᾶσα ψυχὴ ἄκουσα στερεῖται τῆς ἀληθείας.—Plato. Non licet suffurari mentem vel Samaritani.—R. Maimon. Can. Eth.

9. An adulterous person is tied to restitution of the injury,
so far as it is reparable, and can be made to the wronged person; that is, to make provision for the children begotten in
unlawful embraces, that they may do no injury to the legitimate by receiving a common portion; and if the injured person
do account of it, he must satisfy him with money for the wrong
done to his bed. He is not tied to offer this, because it is no
proper exchange, but he is bound to pay it if it be reasonably
demanded; for every man hath justice done him when himself
is satisfied, though by a word, or an action, or a penny.

10. He that hath killed a man is bound to restitution, by
allowing such a maintenance to the children and near relatives
of the deceased as they have lost by his death, considering and
allowing for all circumstances of the man's age, and health,
and probability of living. And thus Hercules is said to have
made expiation for the death of Iphitus, whom he slew, by
paying a mulct to his children.[10]

11. He that hath really lessened the fame of his neighbour
by fraud or violence, is bound to restore it by its proper instruments; such as are confession of his fault, giving testimony of his innocence or worth, doing him honour, or (if that
will do it, and both parties agree) by money, which answers
all things.[11]

12. He that hath wounded his neighbour is tied to the expenses of the surgeon and other incidences, and to repair whatever loss he sustains by his disability to work or trade; and
the same is in the case of false imprisonment, in which cases
only the real effect and remaining detriment are to be mended
and repaired, for the action itself is to be punished or repented
of, and enters not into the question of restitution. But in
these and all other cases, the injured person is to be restored
to that perfect and good condition from which he was removed
by my fraud or violence, so far as is possible. Thus a ravisher
must repair the temporal detriment or injury done to the maid,
and give her a dowry, or marry her if she desire it. For this
restores her into that capacity of being a good wife, which by
the injury was lost, as far as it can be done.

13. He that robbeth his neighbour of his goods, or detains

10 Ὁ γὰρ ἡ γυνὴ, ἢ οἱ παῖδες, ἢ οἱ συγγενεῖς τοῦ φονευθέντος ἔλαβον,
τρόπον τινὰ ἐκείνῳ δίδοται.—Mich. Ephes. ad 5. Eth.
11 Sic Vivianus resipuit de injustâ accusatione: apud Cassiodo. iv. 41.

any thing violently or fraudulently, is bound, not only to restore the principal, but all its fruits and emoluments, which would have accrued to the right owner, during the time of their being detained.   By proportion to these rules we may judge of the obligation that lies upon all sorts of injurious persons: the sacrilegious, the detainers of tithes, cheaters of men's inheritances, unjust judges, false witnesses, and accusers; those that do fraudulently or violently bring men to sin, that force men to drink, that laugh at and disgrace virtue, that persuade servants to run away, or commend such purposes; violent persecutors of religion in any instance; and all of the same nature.

14. He that hath wronged so many, or in that manner, (as in the way of daily trade,) that he knows not in what measure he hath done it, or who they are, must redeem his fault by alms and largesses to the poor, according to the value of his wrongful dealing, as near as he can proportion it.   Better it is to go begging to heaven, than to go to hell laden with the spoils of rapine and injustice.

15. The order of paying the debts of contract or restitution is, in some instances, set down by the civil laws of a kingdom, in which cases their rule is to be observed.   In destitution or want of such rules, we are, 1. to observe the necessity of the creditor; 2. then the time of the delay; and, 3. the special obligations of friendship or kindness; and according to these, in their several degrees, make our restitution, if we be not able to do all that we should; but, if we be, the best rule is to do it as soon as we can, taking our accounts in this, as in our human actions, according to prudence, and civil or natural conveniences or possibilities, only securing these two things: 1. that the duty be not wholly omitted; and, 2. that it be not deferred at all out of covetousness, or any other principle that is vicious.   Remember that the same day in which Zaccheus made restitution to all whom he had injured, the same day Christ himself pronounced that salvation was come to his house.[12]

16. But besides the obligation arising from contract or default, there is one of another sort, which comes from kindness, and the acts of charity and friendship.[13]   He that does me a favour hath bound me to make him a return of thankfulness. The obligation comes not by covenant, not by his own express

[12] Luke xix. 9.   [13] Gratitude.

intention, but by the nature of the thing, and is a duty spring
ing up within the spirit of the obliged person, to whom it is
more natural to love his friend, and to do good for good, than
to return evil for evil, because a man may forgive an injury,
but he must never forget a good turn. For every thing that
is excellent, and every thing that is profitable, whatsoever is
good in itself, or good to me, cannot but be beloved ; and what
we love we naturally cherish and do good to.   He, therefore,
that refuses to do good to them whom he is bound to love, or
to love that which did him good, is unnatural and monstrous
in his affections, and thinks all the world born to minister to
him with a greediness worse than that of the sea, which, although it receives all rivers into itself, yet it furnishes the
clouds and springs with a return of all they need.

Our duty to benefactors is to esteem and love their persons,
to make them proportionable returns of service, or duty, or
profit, according as we can, or as they need, or as opportunity presents itself, and according to the greatnesses of their
kindness ; and to pray to God to make them recompence for
all the good they have done to us; which last office is also
requisite to be done for our creditors, who, in charity, have
relieved our wants.

*Prayers to be said in relation to the several Obligations and
Offices of Justice.*

*A Prayer for the Grace of Obedience, to be said by
all Persons under Command.*

O eternal God, great Ruler of men and angels, who hast
constituted all things in a wonderful order, making all the
creatures subject to man, and one man to another, and all to
thee, the last link of this admirable chain being fastened to
the foot of thy throne ; teach me to obey all those whom thou
hast set over me, reverencing their persons, submitting indifferently to all their lawful commands, cheerfully undergoing
those burdens which the public wisdom and necessity shall
impose upon me, at no hand murmuring against government,
lest the spirit of pride and mutiny, of murmur and disorder,
enter into me, and consign me to the portion of the disobedient and rebellious, of the despisers of dominion, and revilers
of dignity.   Grant this, O holy God, for his sake, who, for

his obedience to the Father, hath obtained the glorification of eternal ages, our Lord and Saviour Jesus Christ. Amen.

Prayers for Kings and all Magistrates, for our Parents spiritual and natural, are in the following Litanies, at the end of the fourth chapter.

A Prayer to be said by Subjects when the Land is invaded and overrun by barbarous or wicked People, enemies of the Religion or the Government.

I.

O eternal God, thou alone rulest in the kingdoms of men; thou art the great God of battles and recompences; and by thy glorious wisdom, by thy almighty power, and by thy secret providence, dost determine the events of war, and the issues of human counsels, and the returns of peace and victory: now, at last, be pleased to let the light of thy countenance, and the effects of a glorious mercy and a gracious pardon, return to this land. Thou seest how great evils we suffer under the power and tyranny of war, and although we submit to and adore thy justice in our sufferings, yet be pleased to pity our misery, to hear our complaints, and to provide us of remedy against our present calamities; let not the defenders of a righteous cause go away ashamed, nor our counsels be for ever confounded, nor our parties defeated, nor religion suppressed, nor learning discountenanced, and we be spoiled of all the exterior ornaments, instruments, and advantages of piety, which thou hast been pleased formerly to minister to our infirmities, for the interests of learning and religion. Amen.

II.

We confess, dear God, that we have deserved to be totally extinct and separate from the communion of saints and the comforts of religion, to be made servants to ignorant, unjust, and inferior persons, or to suffer any other calamity which thou shalt allot us as the instrument of thy anger, whom we have so often provoked to wrath and jealousy. Lord, we humbly lie down under the burden of thy rod, begging of thee to remember our infirmities, and no more to remember our sins, to support us with thy staff, to lift us up with thy hand, to refresh us with thy gracious eye; and if a sad cloud of tempo ral infelicities must still encircle us, open unto us the window of heaven, that, with an eye of faith and hope, we may see beyond the cloud, looking upon those mercies which, in thy secret providence and admirable wisdom, thou designest to all thy servants from such unlikely and sad beginnings. Teach us diligently to do all our duty, and cheerfully to submit to all thy will; and, at last, be gracious to thy people that call upon thee, that put their trust in thee, that have laid up all their hopes in the bosom of God, that, besides thee, have no helper. Amen.

III.

Place a guard of angels about the person of the king, and immure him with the defence of thy right hand, that no unhallowed arm may do violence to him. Support him with aids from heaven in all his battles, trials, and dangers, that he may, in every instant of his temptation, become dearer to thee; and do thou return to him with mercy and deliverance. Give unto him the hearts of all his people, and put into his hand a prevailing rod of iron, a sceptre of power, and a sword of justice; and enable him to defend and comfort the churches under his protection.

IV.

Bless all his friends, relatives, confederates, and lieges; direct their counsels, unite their hearts, strengthen their hands, bless their actions. Give unto them holiness of intention, that they may, with much candour and ingenuity, pursue the cause of God and the king. Sanctify all the means and instruments of their purposes, that they may not with cruelty, injustice, or oppression, proceed towards the end of their just desires; and do thou crown all their endeavours with a prosperous event, that all may co-operate to, and actually produce, those great mercies which we beg of thee—honour and safety to our sovereign, defence of his just rights, peace to his people, establishment and promotion to religion, advantages and encouragement to learning and holy living, deliverance to all the oppressed, comfort to all thy faithful people, and, from all these, glory to thy holy name. Grant this, O King of kings, for his sake, by whom thou hast consigned us to all thy mercies and promises, and to whom thou hast given all power in heaven and earth, our Lord and Saviour Jesus Christ. Amen.

A Prayer to be said by Kings or Magistrates, for themselves and their People.

O my God and King, thou rulest in the kingdoms of men ; by thee kings reign, and princes decree justice : thou hast appointed me under thyself [*and under my prince* [14]] to govern this portion of thy church, according to the laws of religion and the commonwealth. O Lord, I am but an infirm man, and know not how to decree certain sentences without erring in judgment; but do thou give to thy servant an understanding heart to judge this people, that I may discern between good and evil. Cause me to walk before thee and all the people in truth and righteousness, and in sincerity of heart, that I may not regard the person of the mighty, nor be afraid of his terror, nor despise the person of the poor, and reject his petition ; but that, doing justice to all men, I and my people may receive mercy of thee, peace and plenty in our days, and mutual love, duty, and correspondence ; that there be no leading into captivity, no complaining in our streets, but we may see the church in prosperity all our days, and religion established and increasing. Do thou establish the house of thy servant, and bring me to a participation of the glories of thy kingdom, for his sake who is my Lord and King, the holy and ever blessed Saviour of the world, our Redeemer, Jesus. Amen.

A Prayer to be said by Parents for their Children.

O almighty and most merciful Father, who hast promised children as a reward to the righteous, and hast given them to me as a testimony of thy mercy, and an engagement of my duty; be pleased to be a Father unto them, and give them healthful bodies, understanding souls, and sanctified spirits, that they may be thy servants and thy children all their days. Let a great mercy and providence lead them through the dangers, and temptations, and ignorances of their youth, that they may never run into folly and the evils of an unbridled appetite. So order the accidents of their lives, that, by good education, careful tutors, holy example, innocent company, prudent counsels, and thy restraining grace, their duty to thee may be secured in the midst of a crooked and untoward generation ; and if it seem good in thy eyes, let me be enabled to provide conveniently for the support of their per-

[14] These words to be added by a delegate or inferior.

sons, that they may not be destitute and miserable in my death; or if thou shalt call me off from this world by a more timely summons, let their portion be thy care, mercy, and providence over their bodies and souls; and may they never live vicious lives, nor die violent or untimely deaths; but let them glorify thee here with a free obedience, and the duties of a whole life; that when they have served thee in their generations, and have profited the Christian commonwealth, they may be coheirs with Jesus in the glories of thy eternal kingdom, through the same our Lord Jesus Christ. Amen.

A Prayer to be said by Masters of Families, Curates, Tutors, or other obliged Persons, for their Charges.

O almighty God, merciful and gracious, have mercy upon my family [or *pupils*, or *parishioners*, &c.] and all committed to my charge; sanctify them with thy grace, preserve them with thy providence, guard them from all evil by the custody of angels, direct them in the ways of peace and holy religion by my ministry and the conduct of thy most Holy Spirit, and consign them all, with the participation of thy blessings and graces in this world, with healthful bodies, with good understandings and sanctified spirits, to a full fruition of thy glories hereafter, through Jesus Christ our Lord.

A Prayer to be said by Merchants, Tradesmen, and Handicraftsmen.

O eternal God, thou fountain of justice, mercy, and benediction, who, by my education and other effects of thy providence, hast called me to this profession, that, by my industry, I may, in my small proportion, work together for the good of myself and others; I humbly beg thy grace to guide me in my intention, and in the transaction of my affairs, that I may be diligent, just, and faithful; and give me thy favour, that this my labour may be accepted by thee as a part of my necessary duty; and give me thy blessing to assist and prosper me in my calling to such measures as thou shalt, in mercy, choose for me; and be pleased to let the Holy Spirit be for ever present with me, that I may never be given to covetousness and sordid appetites, to lying and falsehood, or any other base, indirect, and beggarly arts: but give me prudence, honesty, and Christian sincerity, that my trade may be sanctified by my religion, my labour by my intention and thy bless-

ing, that, when I have done my portion of work thou hast allotted me, and improved the talent thou hast intrusted to me,
and served the commonwealth in my capacity, I may receive
the mighty price of my high calling, which I expect and beg,
in the portion and inheritance of the ever blessed Saviour and
Redeemer, Jesus. Amen.

A Prayer to be said by Debtors, and all Persons obliged whether by Crime or Contract.

O almighty God, who art rich unto all, the treasury and
fountain of all good, of all justice, and all mercy, and all
bounty, to whom we owe all that we are and all that we have,
being thy debtors by reason of our sins and by thy own gracious contract made with us in Jesus Christ; teach me, in the
first place, to perform all my obligations to thee, both of duty
and thankfulness; and, next, enable me to pay my duty to all
my friends, and my debts to all my creditors, that none be made
miserable or lessened in his estate by his kindness to me, or
traffic with me. Forgive me all those sins and irregular actions
by which I entered into debt further than my necessity required, or by which such necessity was brought upon me; but
let them not suffer by occasion of my sin. Lord, reward all
their kindness into their bosoms, and make them recompence
where I cannot, and make me very willing in all that I can, and
able for all that I am obliged to; or, if it seem good in thine
eyes to afflict me by the continuance of this condition, yet make
it up by some means to them, that the prayer of thy servant
may obtain of thee, at least, to pay my debt in blessings. Amen.

II.

Lord, sanctify and forgive all that I have tempted to evil
by my discourse or my example, instruct them in the right
way whom I have led to error, and let me never run further
on the score of sin; but do thou blot out all the evils I have
done by the sponge of thy passion, and the blood of thy cross,
and give me a deep and an excellent repentance, and a free
and a gracious pardon, that thou mayest answer for me, O
Lord, and enable me to stand upright in judgment; for in thee,
O Lord, have I trusted, let me never be confounded. Pity
me and instruct me, guide me and support me, pardon me and
save me, for my sweet Saviour Jesus Christ's sake. Amen.

A Prayer for Patron and Benefactors.

O almighty God, thou fountain of all good, of all excellency both to men and angels, extend thine abundant favour and loving-kindness to my patron, to all my friends and benefactors; reward them and make them plentiful recompence for all the good which from thy merciful providence they have conveyed unto me. Let the light of thy countenance shine upon them, and let them never come into any affliction or sadness, but such as may be an instrument of thy glory and their eternal comfort. Forgive them all their sins; let thy divinest Spirit preserve them from all deeds of darkness; let thy ministering angels guard their persons from the violence of the spirits of darkness. And thou, who knowest every degree of their necessity by thy infinite wisdom, give supply to all their needs by thy glorious mercy, preserving their persons, sanctifying their hearts, and leading them in the ways of righteousness, by the waters of comfort, to the land of eternal rest and glory, through Jesus Christ our Lord. Amen.

CHAP. IV. OF CHRISTIAN RELIGION.

RELIGION, in a large sense, doth signify the whole duty of man, comprehending in it justice, charity, and sobriety; because all these being commanded by God, they become a part of that honour and worship which we are bound to pay to him. And thus the word is used in St. James, "Pure religion and undefiled before God and the Father is this, to visit the fatherless and widows in their affliction, and to keep himself unspotted from the world."[1] But, in a more restrained sense, it is taken for that part of duty which particularly relates to God in our worshippings and adoration of him, in confessing his excellences, loving his person, admiring his goodness, believing his word, and doing all that which may, in a proper and direct manner, do him honour. It contains the duties of the first table only, and so it is called godliness,[2] and is by St. Paul distinguished from justice and sobriety. In this sense I am now to explicate the parts of it.

[1] James i. 27. [2] Tit. ii. 12.

x

Of the internal Actions of Religion.

Those I call the internal actions of religion, in which the
soul only is employed, and ministers to God in the special
actions of faith, hope, and charity. Faith believes the revelations of God; hope expects his promises; and charity loves
his excellences and mercies. Faith gives our understanding
to God; hope gives up all the passions and affections to heaven and heavenly things; and charity gives the will to the
service of God. Faith is opposed to infidelity, hope to despair, charity to enmity and hostility: and these three sanctify
the whole man, and make our duty to God and obedience to
his commandments to be chosen, reasonable, and delightful,
and therefore to be entire, persevering, and universal.

Sect. I. *Of Faith.*

The Acts and Offices of Faith are,

1. To believe every thing which God hath revealed to us;[1]
and, when once we are convinced that God hath spoken it, to
make no further inquiry, but humbly to submit; ever remembering that there are some things which our understanding cannot fathom, nor search out their depth.

2. To believe nothing concerning God but what is honourable and excellent, as knowing that belief to be no honouring
of God which entertains of him any dishonourable thoughts.
Faith is the parent of charity; and whatsoever faith entertains must be apt to produce love to God: but he that believes God to be cruel or unmerciful, or a rejoicer in the unavoidable damnation of the greatest part of mankind, or that
he speaks one thing and privately means another, thinks evil
thoughts concerning God, and such as for which we should
hate a man, and therefore are great enemies of faith, being
apt to destroy charity. Our faith concerning God must be as
himself hath revealed and described his own excellences; and,
in our discourses, we must remove from him all imperfection,
and attribute to him all excellency.

3. To give ourselves wholly up to Christ, in heart and desire, to become disciples of his doctrine with choice, (besides
conviction,) being in the presence of God but as idiots, that is,

[1] Demus Deum aliquid posse quod nos fateamur investigare non posse.
—St. Aug. l. xxi. c. 7. de Civitat.

without any principles of our own to hinder the truth of God; but sucking in greedily all that God hath taught us, believing it infinitely, and loving to believe it. For this is an act of love, reflected upon faith; or an act of faith, leaning upon love.

4. To believe all God's promises, and that whatsoever is promised in Scripture shall, on God's part, be as surely performed as if we had it in possession. This act makes us to rely upon God with the same confidence as we did on our parents when we were children, when we made no doubt but whatsoever we needed we should have it, if it were in their power.

5. To believe, also, the conditions of the promise, or that part of the revelation which concerns our duty. Many are apt to believe the article of remission of sins, but they believe it without the condition of repentance, or the fruits of holy life; and that is to believe the article otherwise than God intended it. For the covenant of the gospel is the great object of faith, and that supposes our duty to answer his grace; that God will be our God, so long as we are his people. The other is not faith, but flattery.

6. To profess publicly the doctrine of Jesus Christ, openly owning whatsoever he hath revealed and commanded, not being ashamed of the word of God, or of any practices enjoined by it; and this without complying with any man's interest, not regarding favour, nor being moved with good words, not fearing disgrace, or loss, or inconvenience, or death itself.

7. To pray without doubting, without weariness, without faintness; entertaining no jealousies or suspicions of God, but being confident of God's hearing us, and of his returns to us, whatsoever the manner or the instance be, that, if we do our duty, it will be gracious and merciful.

These acts of faith are in several degrees in the servants of Jesus; some have it but as a grain of mustard-seed; some grow up to a plant; some have the fulness of faith: but the least faith that is must be a persuasion so strong as to make us undertake the doing of all that duty which Christ built upon the foundation of believing. But we shall best discern the truth of our faith by these following signs. St. Jerome reckons three.[2]

Signs of true Faith.

1. An earnest and vehement prayer: for it is impossible

[2] Dial. adver. Lucif.

we should heartily believe the things of God and the glories of the gospel, and not most importunately desire them. For every thing is desired according to our belief of its excellency and possibility.

2. To do nothing for vain-glory, but wholly for the interests of religion and these articles we believe; valuing not at all the rumours of men, but the praise of God, to whom, by faith, we have given up all our intellectual faculties.

3. To be content with God for our judge, for our patron, for our Lord, for our friend; desiring God to be all in all to us, as we are, in our understanding and affections, wholly his.

Add to these:

4. To be a stranger upon earth in our affections, and to have all our thoughts and principal desires fixed upon the matters of faith, the things of heaven. For, if a man were adopted heir to Cæsar, he would (if he believed it real and effective) despise the present, and wholly be at court in his father's eye; and his desires would outrun his swiftest speed, and all his thoughts would spend themselves in creating ideas and little fantastic images of his future condition. Now, God hath made us heirs of his kingdom, and co-heirs with Jesus: if we believed this, we would think, and affect, and study accordingly. But he that rejoices in gain, and his heart dwells in the world, and is espoused to a fair estate, and transported with a light momentary joy, and is afflicted with losses, and amazed with temporal persecutions, and esteems disgrace or poverty in a good cause to be intolerable—this man either hath no inheritance in heaven, or believes none; and believes not that he is adopted to be the son of God, the heir of eternal glory.

5. St. James's sign is the best: "Show me thy faith by thy works." Faith makes the merchant diligent and venturous, and that makes him rich. Ferdinando of Arragon believed the story told him by Columbus, and therefore he furnished him with ships, and got the West Indies by his faith in the undertaker. But Henry the Seventh of England believed him not; and therefore trusted him not with shipping, and lost all the purchase of that faith. It is told us by Christ, "He that forgives shall be forgiven:" if we believe this, it is certain we shall forgive our enemies; for none of us

all but need and desire to be forgiven. No man can possibly despise, or refuse to desire, such excellent glories as are revealed to them that are servants of Christ; and yet we do nothing that is commanded us as a condition to obtain them. No man could work a day's labour without faith; but because he believes he shall have his wages at the day's or week's end, he does his duty. But he only believes who does that thing which other men, in like cases, do when they do believe. He that believes money gotten with danger is better than poverty with safety, will venture for it in unknown lands or seas; and so will he that believes it better to get to heaven with labour, than to go to hell with pleasure.

6. He that believes, does not make haste, but waits patiently till the times of refreshment come, and dares trust God for the morrow, and is no more solicitous for the next year than he is for that which is past; and it is certain that man wants faith who dares be more confident of being supplied when he hath money in his purse, than when he hath it only in bills of exchange from God; or that relies more upon his own industry than upon God's providence when his own industry fails him. If you dare trust to God when the case, to human reason, seems impossible, and trust to God then also out of choice, not because you have nothing else to trust to, but because he is the only support of a just confidence, then you give a good testimony of your faith.

7. True faith is confident, and will venture all the world upon the strength of its persuasion. Will you lay your life on it, your estate, your reputation, that the doctrine of Jesus Christ is true in every article? Then you have true faith. But he that fears men more than God, believes men more than he believes in God.

8. Faith, if it be true, living, and justifying, cannot be separated from a good life; it works miracles, makes a drunkard become sober, a lascivious person become chaste, a covetous man become liberal; "it overcomes the world," it "works righteousness,"[3] and makes us diligently to do, and cheerfully to suffer, whatsoever God hath placed in our way to heaven.

The Means and Instruments to obtain Faith are,

1. A humble, willing, and docile mind, or desire to be instructed in the way of God; for persuasion enters like a sun-

[3] 2 Cor. xiii. 5; Rom. viii. 10.

beam, gently, and without violence; and open but the window,
and draw the curtain, and the Sun of righteousness will enlighten your darkness.

2. Remove all prejudice and love to every thing which may
be contradicted by faith. "How can ye believe (said Christ)
that receive praise one of another?" An unchaste man cannot easily be brought to believe that, without purity, he shall
never see God. He that loves riches can hardly believe the
doctrine of poverty and renunciation of the world; and alms
and martyrdom, and the doctrine of the cross, is folly to him
that loves his ease and pleasures. He that hath within him
any principle contrary to the doctrines of faith cannot easily
become a disciple.

3. Prayer, which is instrumental to every thing, hath a
particular promise in this thing. "He that lacks wisdom, let
him ask it of God:" and, "If you give good things to your
children, how much more shall your heavenly Father give his
Spirit to them that ask him!"

4. The consideration of the Divine omnipotence and infinite
wisdom, and our own ignorance, are great instruments of curing
all doubting, and silencing the murmurs of infidelity.[4]

5. Avoid all curiosity of inquiry into particulars and circumstances and mysteries: for true faith is full of ingenuity
and hearty simplicity, free from suspicion, wise and confident,
trusting upon generals, without watching and prying into
unnecessary or indiscernible particulars. No man carries his
bed into his field, to watch how his corn grows, but believes
upon the general order of Providence and nature; and at harvest finds himself not deceived.

6. In time of temptation be not busy to dispute, but rely
upon the conclusion, and throw yourself upon God; and contend not with him but in prayer, and in the presence, and with
the help, of a prudent untempted guide; and be sure to esteem
all changes of belief which offer themselves in the time of your
greatest weakness (contrary to the persuasions of your best understanding) to be temptations, and reject them accordingly.

7. It is a prudent course that, in our health and best advantages, we lay up particular arguments and instruments of persuasion and confidence, to be brought forth and used in the
great day of expense; and that especially in such things in

[4] In rebus miris summa credendi ratio est omnipotentia Creatoris.—
St. Aug.

which we use to be most tempted, and in which we are least confident, and which are most necessary, and which commonly the devil uses to assault us withal in the days of our visitation.

8. The wisdom of the church of God is very remarkable in appointing festivals or holy days, whose solemnity and offices have no other special business but to record the article of the day; such as Trinity Sunday, Ascension, Easter, Christmas-day ; and to those persons who can only believe, not prove or dispute, there is no better instrument to cause the remembrance and plain notion, and to endear the affection and hearty assent to the article, than the proclaiming and recommending it by the festivity and joy of a holy day.

SECT. II. *Of the Hope of a Christian.*

FAITH differs from hope in the extension of its object, and in the intention of degree. St. Austin thus accounts their differences.[1] Faith is of all things revealed, good and bad, rewards and punishments, of things past, present, and to come, of things that concern us, of things that concern us not; but hope hath for its object things only that are good, and fit to be hoped for, future, and concerning ourselves ; and because these things are offered to us upon conditions of which we may so fail as we may change our will, therefore our certainty is less than the adherences of faith; which (because faith relies only upon one proposition, that is, the truth of the word of God) cannot be made uncertain in themselves, though the object of our hope may become uncertain to us, and to our possession. For it is infallibly certain that there is heaven for all the godly, and for me amongst them all, if I do my duty. But that I shall enter into heaven is the object of my hope, not of my faith; and is so sure as it is certain I shall persevere in the ways of God.

The Acts of Hope are,

1. To rely upon God with a confident expectation of his promises: ever esteeming that every promise of God is a magazine of all that grace and relief which we can need in that instance for which the promise is made. Every degree of hope is a degree of confidence.

2. To esteem all the danger of an action, and the possibili-

---

[1] Enchirid. c. 8.

ties of miscarriage, and every cross accident that can intervene, to be no defect on God's part, but either a mercy on his part or a fault on ours; for then we shall be sure to trust in God when we see him to be our confidence, and ourselves the cause of all mischances. The hope of a Christian is prudent and religious.

3. To rejoice in the midst of a misfortune or seeming sadness, knowing that this may work for good, and will, if we be not wanting to our souls. This is a direct act of hope, to look through the cloud, and look for a beam of the light from God; and this is called in Scripture "rejoicing in tribulation, when the God of hope fills us with all joy in believing." Every degree of hope brings a degree of joy.

4. To desire, to pray, and to long for the great object of our hope, the mighty price of our high calling; and to desire the other things of this life as they are promised; that is, so far as they are made necessary and useful to us, in order to God's glory and the great end of souls. Hope and fasting are said to be the two wings of prayer. Fasting is but as the wing of a bird; but hope is like the wing of an angel, soaring up to heaven, and bears our prayers to the throne of grace. Without hope, it is impossible to pray; but hope makes our prayers reasonable, passionate, and religious; for it relies upon God's promise, or experience, or providence, and story. Prayer is always in proportion to our hope, zealous and affectionate.

5. Perseverance is the perfection of the duty of hope, and its last act; and so long as our hope continues, so long we go on in duty and diligence; but he that is to raise a castle in an hour, sits down and does nothing towards it; and Herod, the sophister, left off to teach his son, when he saw that twenty-four pages, appointed to wait on him, and called by the several letters of the alphabet, could not make him to understand his letters perfectly.

Rules to govern our Hope.

1. Let your hope be moderate; proportioned to your state, person, and condition, whether it be for gifts or graces, or temporal favours. It is an ambitious hope for persons, whose diligence is like them that are least in the kingdom of heaven, to believe themselves endeared to God as the greatest saints; or that they shall have a throne equal to St. Paul, or the blessed

Virgin Mary. A stammerer cannot, with moderation, hope for the gift of tongues; or a peasant to become learned as Origen; or if a beggar desires, or hopes, to become a king, or asks for a thousand pound a-year, we call him impudent, not passionate, much less reasonable. Hope that God will crown your endeavours with equal measures of that reward which he indeed freely gives, but yet gives according to our proportions. Hope for good success according to, or not much beyond, the efficacy of the causes and the instrument; and let the husbandman hope for a good harvest, not for a rich kingdom, or a victorious army.

2. Let your hope be well founded, relying upon just confidences; that is, upon God, according to his revelations and promises. For it is possible for a man to have a vain hope upon God; and, in matters of religion, it is presumption to hope that God's mercies will be poured forth upon lazy persons, that do nothing towards holy and strict walking, nothing (I say) but trust and long for an event besides and against all disposition of the means. Every false principle in religion is a reed of Egypt, false and dangerous. Rely not in temporal things upon uncertain prophecies and astrology, not upon our own wit and industry, not upon gold or friends, not upon armies and princes; expect not health from physicians, that cannot cure their own breath, much less their mortality: use all lawful instruments, but expect nothing from them above their natural or ordinary efficacy, and, in the use of them, from God expect a blessing. A hope that is easy and credulous is an arm of flesh, an ill supporter without a bone.[2]

3. Let your hope be without vanity, or garishness of spirit; but sober, grave, and silent, fixed in the heart, not borne upon the lip, apt to support our spirits within, but not to provoke envy abroad.

4. Let your hope be of things possible, safe, and useful.[3] He that hopes for an opportunity of acting his revenge, or lust, or rapine, watches to do himself a mischief. All evils of ourselves or brethren are objects of our fear, not hope; and, when it is truly understood, things useless and unsafe can no more be wished for than things impossible can be obtained.

5. Let your hope be patient, without tediousness of spirit, or hastiness of prefixing time. Make no limits or prescriptions

[1] Jer. xvii. 5. [3] Di cosi fuori di credenza, Non vuoler far speranza.

to God; but let your prayers and endeavours go on still with a constant attendance on the periods of God's providence. The men of Bethulia resolved to wait upon God but five days longer; but deliverance stayed seven days, and yet came at last. And take not every accident for an argument of despair ; but go on still in hoping ; and begin again to work if any ill accident have interrupted you.

Means of Hope, and Remedies against Despair.

The means to cure despair, and to continue or increase hope, are, partly by consideration, partly by exercise.

1. Apply your mind to the cure of all the proper causes of despair : and they are, weakness of spirit or violence of passion. He that greedily covets is impatient of delay, and desperate in contrary accidents; and he that is little of heart is also little of hope, and apt to sorrow and suspicion.[4]

2. Despise the things of the world, and be indifferent to all changes and events of Providence : and for the things of God, the promises are certain to be performed in kind; and where there is less variety of chance, there is less possibility of being mocked;[5] but he that creates to himself thousands of little hopes, uncertain in the promise, fallible in the event, and depending upon ten thousand circumstances, (as are all the things of this world,) shall often fail in his expectations, and be used to arguments of distrust in such hopes.

3. So long as your hopes are regular and reasonable, though in temporal affairs, such as are deliverance from enemies, escaping a storm or shipwreck, recovery from a sickness, ability to to pay your debts, &c., remember that there are some things ordinary, and some things extraordinary, to prevent despair. In ordinary, remember, 1. that the very hoping in God is an endearment of him, and a means to obtain the blessing; "I will deliver him, because he hath put his trust in me." 2. There

---

[4] Μικρόψυχοι μακρόλυποι.

[5] 'Ελπὶς καὶ σὺ Τύχη, μέγα χαίρετε· τὴν ὁδὸν εὗρον.
Οὐκέτι γὰρ σφετέροις ἐπιτέρπομαι· ἔῤῥετε ἄμφω·
Οὔνεκεν ἐν μερόπεσσι πολυπλανέες μάλα ἐστέ·
"Οσσα γὰρ ἀτρεκέως οὐκ ἔσσεται, ὕμμες ἐν ἡμῖν
Φάσματα, ὡς ἐν ὕπνῳ, ἐμβάλλετε, οἷά τ' ἐόντα·
Παίζοιτε, στροφέοιτε, ὅσους ἐμεῦ ὕστερον ὄντας
Εὕροιτ' οὐ νοέοντας ὅπερ θέμις ἐστὶ νοῆσαι.
Pallad. Brunck. Anthol. t. ii. p. 437.

are in God all those glorious attributes and excellences which in the nature of things can possibly create or confirm hope. God is, 1. strong; 2. wise; 3. true; 4. loving. There cannot be added another capacity to create a confidence; for upon these premises we cannot fail of receiving what is fit for us. 3. God hath obliged himself by promise that we shall have the good of every thing we desire; for even losses and denials shall work for the good of them that fear God. And, if we will trust the truth of God for performance of the general, we may well trust his wisdom to choose for us the particular. But the extraordinaries of God are apt to supply the defect of all natural and human possibilities. 1. God hath, in many instances, given extraordinary virtue to the active causes and instruments—to a jaw-bone, to kill a multitude; to three hundred men, to destroy a great army; to Jonathan and his armour-bearer, to rout a whole garrison. 2. He hath given excellent sufferance and vigorousness to the sufferers, arming them with strange courage, heroical fortitude, invincible resolution, and glorious patience: and thus he lays no more upon us than we are able to bear; for when he increases our sufferings, he lessens them by increasing our patience. 3. His providence is extra-regular, and produces strange things beyond common rules; and he that led Israel through a sea, and made a rock pour forth waters, and the heavens to give them bread and flesh, and whole armies to be destroyed with fantastic noises, and the fortune of all France to be recovered and entirely revolved by the arms and conduct of a girl, against the torrent of the English fortune and chivalry, can do what he please, and still retain the same affections to his people, and the same providence over mankind as ever. And it is impossible for that man to despair who remembers that his helper is omnipotent, and can do what he please.[6] Let us rest there a while; he can if he please: and he is infinitely loving, willing enough: and he is infinitely wise, choosing better for us than we can do for ourselves. This, in all ages and chances, hath supported the afflicted people of God, and carried them on dry ground through a Red Sea. God invites and cherishes the hopes of men by all the variety of his providence.

4. If your case be brought to the last extremity, and that

* Heb. ii. 18.

you are at the pit's brink, even the very margin of the grave,
yet then despair not; at least put it off a little longer: and
remember that whatsoever final accident takes away all hope
from you, if you stay a little longer, and, in the mean while,
bear it sweetly, it will also take away all despair too. For,
when you enter into the regions of death, you rest from all
your labours and your fears.

5. Let them who are tempted to despair of their salvation
consider how much Christ suffered to redeem us from sin and
its eternal punishment; and he that considers this must needs
believe that the desires which God had to save us were not
less than infinite, and therefore not easily to be satisfied
without it.

6. Let no man despair of God's mercies to forgive him, unless he be sure that his sins are greater than God's mercies.
If they be not, we have much reason to hope that the stronger
ingredient will prevail, so long as we are in the time and state
of repentance, and within the possibilities and latitude of the
covenant; and as long as any promise can but reflect upon
him with an oblique beam of comfort. Possibly the man may
err in his judgment of circumstances; and therefore let him
fear: but, because it is not certain he is mistaken, let him
not despair.

7. Consider that God, who knows all the events of men,
and what their final condition shall be, who shall be saved and
who will perish; yet he treateth them as his own, calls them
to be his own, offers fair conditions as to his own, gives them
blessings, arguments of mercy, and instances of fear, to call
them off from death, and to call them home to life; and, in
all this, shows no despair of happiness to them; and therefore
much less should any man despair for himself, since he never
was able to read the scrolls of the eternal predestination.

8. Remember that despair belongs only to passionate fools
or villains, such as were Achitophel and Judas, or else to
devils and damned persons; and as the hope of salvation is a
good disposition towards it, so is despair a certain consignation to eternal ruin. A man may be damned for despairing
to be saved. Despair is the proper passion of damnation.
"God hath placed truth and felicity in heaven, curiosity and
repentance upon earth, but misery and despair are the portions of hell." [7]

        [7] Ven. Bede

9. Gather together into your spirit and its treasure-house, the memory, not only all the promises of God, but also the remembrances of experience and the former senses of the Divine favours, that from thence you may argue from times past to the present, and enlarge to the future and to greater blessings. For although the conjectures and expectations of hope are not like the conclusions of faith, yet they are a helmet against the scorchings of despair in temporal things, and an anchor of the soul, sure and stedfast, against the fluctuations of the spirit in matters of the soul. St. Bernard reckons divers principles of hope by enumerating the instances of the Divine mercy; and we may by them reduce this rule to practice, in the following manner: 1. God hath preserved me from many sins; his mercies are infinite; I hope he will still preserve me from more, and for ever. 2. I have sinned, and God smote me not; his mercies are still over the penitent: I hope he will deliver me from all the evils I have deserved. He hath forgiven me many sins of malice, and therefore surely he will pity my infirmities. .3. God visited my heart, and changed it; he loves the work of his own hands, and so my heart is now become; I hope he will love this too. 4. When I repented, he received me graciously; and therefore I hope, if I do my endeavour, he will totally forgive me. 5. He helped my slow and beginning endeavours; and therefore I hope he will lead me to perfection. 6. When he had given me something first, then he gave me more: I hope, therefore, he will keep me from falling, and give me the grace of perseverance. 7. He hath chosen me to be a disciple of Christ's institution; he hath elected me to his kingdom of grace; and therefore I hope, also, to the kingdom of his glory. 8. He died for me when I was his enemy; and therefore I hope he will save me when he hath reconciled me to him and is become my friend. 9. "God hath given us his Son: how should not he with him give us all things else?" All these St. Bernard reduces to these three heads, as the instruments of all our hopes: 1. The charity of God adopting us; 2. The truth of his promises;. 3. The power of his performance: which if any truly weighs, no infirmity or accident can break his hopes into indiscernible fragments, but some good planks will remain after the greatest storm and shipwreck. This was St. Paul's instrument: "Experience begets hope, and hope maketh not ashamed."

10. Do thou take care only of thy duty, of the means and proper instruments of thy purpose, and leave the end to God: lay that up with him, and he will take care of all that is intrusted to him: and this, being an act of confidence in God, is also a means of security to thee.

11. By special arts of spiritual prudence and arguments, secure the confident belief of the resurrection; and thou canst not but hope for every thing else which you may reasonably expect or lawfully desire upon the stock of the Divine mercies and promises.

12. If a despair seizes you in a particular temporal instance, let it not defile thy spirit with impure mixture, or mingle in spiritual considerations; but rather let it make thee fortify thy soul in matters of religion, that, by being thrown out of your earthly dwelling and confidence, you may retire into the strengths of grace, and hope the more strongly in that by how much you are the more defeated in this, that despair of a fortune or a success may become the necessity of all virtue.

Sect. III. *Of Charity, or the Love of God.*

Love is the greatest thing that God can give us; for himself is love: and it is the greatest thing we can give to God; for it will also give ourselves, and carry with it all that is ours. The apostle calls it the band of perfection: it is the old, and it is the new, and it is the great commandment, and it is all the commandments; for it is the fulfilling of the law. It does the work of all other graces without any instrument but its own immediate virtue. For, as the love to sin makes a man sin against all his own reason, and all the discourses of wisdom, and all the advices of his friends, and without temptation, and without opportunity, so does the love of God; it makes a man chaste without the laborious arts of fasting and exterior disciplines, temperate in the midst of feasts, and is active enough to choose it without any intermedial appetites, and reaches at glory through the very heart of grace, without any other arms but those of love. It is a grace that loves God for himself, and our neighbours for God. The consideration of God's goodness and bounty, the experience of those profitable and excellent emanations from him, may be, and most commonly are, the first motive of our love; but when we are once entered, and have tasted the goodness of God, we love the spring for its own excellency, passing from passion to reason, from thanking to adoring, from sense to spirit, from considering ourselves to an union with God: and this is the image and little representation of heaven; it is beatitude in picture, or rather the infancy and beginnings of glory.

We need no incentives by way of special enumeration to move us to the love of God; for we cannot love any thing for any reason, real or imaginary, but that excellence is infinitely more eminent in God. There can but two things create love—perfection and usefulness: to which answer on our part, 1. Admiration; and, 2. Desire; and both these are centred in love. For the entertainment of the first, there is in God an infinite nature, immensity or vastness without extension or limit, immutability, eternity, omnipotence, omniscience, holiness, dominion, providence, bounty, mercy, justice, perfection in himself, and the end to which all things and all actions must be directed, and will at last arrive. The consideration of which may be heightened, if we consider our distance from all these glories; our smallness and limited nature, our nothing, our inconstancy, our age like a span, our weakness and ignorance, our poverty, our inadvertency and inconsideration, our disabilities and disaffections to do good, our harsh natures and unmerciful inclinations, our universal iniquity, and our necessities and dependencies, not only on God originally and essentially, but even our need of the meanest of God's creatures, and our being obnoxious to the weakest and most contemptible. But, for the entertainment of the second, we may consider that in him is a torrent of pleasure for the voluptuous; he is the fountain of honour for the ambitious, an inexhaustible treasure for the covetous. Our vices are in love with fantastic pleasures and images of perfection, which are truly and really to be found no where but in God. And therefore our virtues have such proper objects that it is but reasonable they should all turn into love; for certain it is that this love will turn all into virtue. For in the scrutinies for righteousness and judgment, when it is inquired whether such a person be a good man or no, the meaning is not, What does he believe? or what does he hope? but what he loves.[1]

The Acts of Love to God are,

1. Love does all things which may please the beloved per-

---

[1] St. Aug. l. ii. Confes c. 6.

son; it performs all his commandments: and this is one of the greatest instances and arguments of our love that God requires of us—"this is love, that we keep his commandments." Love is obedient.

2. It does all the intimations and secret significations of his pleasure whom we love; and this is an argument of a great degree of it. The first instance is, it makes the love accepted: but this gives a greatness and singularity to it. The first is the least, and less than it cannot do our duty; but, without this second, we cannot come to perfection. Great love is also pliant and inquisitive in the instances of its expression.

3. Love gives away all things, that so he may advance the interest of the beloved person: it relieves all that he would have relieved, and spends itself in such real significations as it is enabled withal. He never loved God that will quit any thing of his religion to save his money. Love is always liberal and communicative.

4. It suffers all things that are imposed by its beloved, or that can happen for his sake, or that intervene in his service, cheerfully, sweetly, willingly; expecting that God should turn them into good, and instruments of felicity. "Charity hopeth all things, endureth all things."[2] Love is patient and content with any thing, so it be together with its beloved.

5. Love is also impatient of any thing that may displease the beloved person, hating all sin as the enemy of its friend; for love contracts all the same relations, and marries the same friendships and the same hatreds; and all affection to a sin is perfectly inconsistent with the love of God. Love is not divided between God and God's enemy: we must love God with all our heart; that is, give him a whole and undivided affection, having love for nothing else but such things which he allows, and which he commands or loves himself.

6. Love endeavours for ever to be present, to converse with, to enjoy, to be united with its object; loves to be talking of him, reciting his praises, telling his stories, repeating his words, imitating his gestures, transcribing his copy in every thing; and every degree of union and every degree of likeness is a degree of love; and it can endure any thing but the displeasure and the absence of its beloved. For we are not to use God and religion as men use perfumes, with which they are delighted when they have them, but can very well be without

[2] 1 Cor. xiii.

them. True charity is restless till it enjoys God in such instances in which it wants him: it is like hunger and thirst,
it must be fed, or it cannot be answered:[3] and nothing can supply the presence, or make recompence for the absence of God,
or of the effects of his favour and the light of his countenance.

7. True love in all accidents looks upon the beloved person,
and observes his countenance, and how he approves or disap-
proves, and accordingly looks sad or cheerful. He that loves
God is not displeased at those accidents which God chooses;
nor murmurs at those changes which he makes in his family;
nor envies at those gifts he bestows; but chooses as he likes,
and is ruled by his judgment, and is perfectly of his persuasion;
loving to learn where God is the teacher, and being content to
be ignorant or silent where he is not pleased to open himself.

8. Love is curious of little things, of circumstances and
measures, and little accidents; not allowing to itself any infirmity which it strives not to master, aiming at what it cannot
yet reach, desiring to be of an angelical purity, and of a perfect
innocence, and a seraphical fervour, and fears every image of
offence; is as much afflicted at an idle word as some at an act
of adultery, and will not allow to itself so much anger as will
disturb a child, nor endure the impurity of a dream.[4] And
this is the curiosity and niceness of divine love; this is the
fear of God, and is the daughter and production of Love.

The Measures and Rules of Divine Love.

But, because this passion is pure as the brightest and
smoothest mirror, and, therefore, is apt to be sullied with
every impurer breath, we must be careful that our love to
God be governed by these measures.

1. That our love to God be sweet, even, and full of tranquillity; having in it no violences or transportations, but
going on in a course of holy actions and duties, which are
proportionable to our condition and present state; not to
satisfy all the desire, but all the probabilities and measures of
our strength. A new beginner in religion hath passionate
and violent desires; but they must not be the measure of his
actions: but he must consider his strength, his late sickness

---

[3] Amoris ut morsum qui verè senserit. [4] Plutarchus citans car-
men de suo Apolline, adjicit ex Herodoto quasi de suo, De eo os meum
continens esto.

and state of death, the proper temptations of his condition, and stand at first upon his defence; not go to storm a strong fort, or attack a potent enemy, or do heroical actions, and fitter for giants in religion. Indiscreet violences and untimely forwardness are the rocks of religion, against which tender spirits often suffer shipwreck.

2. Let our love be prudent and without illusion: that is, that it express itself in such instances which God hath chosen, or which we choose ourselves by proportion to his rules and measures. Love turns into doting when religion turns into superstition. No degree of love can be imprudent, but the expressions may: we cannot love God too much, but we may proclaim it in indecent manners.

3. Let our love be firm, constant, and inseparable; not coming and returning like the tide, but descending like a never-failing river, ever running into the ocean of Divine excellency, passing on in the channels of duty and a constant obedience, and never ceasing to be what it is, till it comes to be what it desires to be; still being a river till it be turned into sea and vastness, even the immensity of a blessed eternity.

Although the consideration of the Divine excellences and mercies be infinitely sufficient to produce in us love to God (who is invisible, and yet not distant from us, but we feel him in his blessings, he dwells in our hearts by faith, we feed on him in the sacrament, and are made all one with him in the incarnation and glorifications of Jesus); yet, that we may the better enkindle and increase our love to God, the following advices are not useless.

Helps to increase our Love to God, by way of Exercise.

1. Cut off all earthly and sensual loves, for they pollute and unhallow the pure and spiritual love. Every degree of inordinate affection to the things of this world, and every act of love to a sin, is a perfect enemy to the love of God; and it is a great shame to take any part of our affection from the eternal God, to bestow it upon his creature in defiance of the Creator; or to give it to the devil, our open enemy, in disparagement of him, who is the fountain of all excellences and celestial amities.

2. Lay fetters and restraints upon the imaginative and fantastic part; because our fancy, being an imperfect and higher

faculty, is usually pleased with the entertainment of shadows and gauds; and, because the things of the world fill it with such beauties and fantastic imagery, the fancy presents such objects as are amiable to the affections and elective powers. Persons of fancy, such as are women and children, have always the most violent loves; but, therefore, if we be careful with what representments we fill our fancy, we may the sooner rectify our love. To this purpose it is good that we transplant the instruments of fancy into religion; and for this reason music was brought into churches, and ornaments, and perfumes, and comely garments, and solemnities, and decent ceremonies, that the busy and less discerning fancy, being bribed with its proper objects, may be instrumental to a more celestial and spiritual love.

3. Remove solicitude or worldly cares, and multitudes of secular businesses; for, if these take up the intention and actual application of our thoughts and our employments, they will also possess our passions; which, if they be filled with one object, though ignoble, cannot attend another, though more excellent. We always contract a friendship and relation with those with whom we converse; our very country is dear to us for our being in it; and the neighbours of the same village, and those that buy and sell with us, have seized upon some portions of our love; and, therefore, if we dwell in the affairs of the world we shall also grow in love with them; and all our love or all our hatred, all our hopes or all our fears, which the eternal God would willingly secure to himself, and esteem amongst his treasures and precious things, shall be spent upon trifles and vanities.

4. Do not only choose the things of God, but secure your inclinations and aptnesses for God and for religion. For it will be a hard thing for a man to do such a personal violence to his first desires as to choose whatsoever he hath no mind to. A man will many times satisfy the importunity and daily solicitations of his first longings; and, therefore, there is nothing can secure our loves to God, but stopping the natural fountains and making religion to grow near the first desires of the soul.

5. Converse with God by frequent prayer. In particular desire that your desires may be right, and love to have your affections regular and holy. To which purpose make very frequent addresses to God by ejaculations and communions

and an assiduous daily devotion; discover to him all your
wants; complain to him of all your affronts; do as Hezekiah
did, lay your misfortunes and your ill news before him, spread
them before the Lord; call to him for health, run to him for
counsel, beg of him for pardon; and it is as natural to love
him to whom we make such addresses, and of whom we have
such dependencies, as it is for children to love their parents.

6. Consider the immensity and vastness of the Divine love
to us, expressed in all the emanations of his providence: 1. In
his creation; 2. In his conservation of us. For it is not my
prince, or my patron, or my friend, that supports me, or relieves my needs; but God, who made the corn that my friend
sends me; who created the grapes, and supported him, who
hath as many dependencies, and as many natural necessities,
and as perfect disabilities, as myself. God, indeed, made him
the instrument of his providence to me, as he hath made his
own land or his own cattle to him—with this only difference,
that God, by his ministration to me, intends to do him a favour
and a reward, which to natural instruments he does not. 3.
In giving his Son; 4. In forgiving our sins; 5. In adopting
us to glory; and ten thousand times ten thousand little accidents and instances happening in the doing every of these:—
and it is not possible but for so great love we should give
love again; for God, we should give man; for felicity, we
should part with our misery. Nay, so great is the love of the
holy Jesus, God incarnate, that he would leave all his triumph-
ant glories, and die once more for man, if it were necessary
for procuring felicity to him.[5]

In the use of these instruments, love will grow in several
knots and steps, like the sugar-canes of India, according to a
thousand varieties in the persons loving; and it will be great
or less, in several persons, and in the same, according to his
growth in Christianity. But, in general discoursing, there are
but two states of love; and those are, labour of love, and the
zeal of love: the first is duty; the second is perfection.

The two States of Love to God.

1. The least love that is must be obedient, pure, simple, and
communicative; that is, it must exclude all affection to sin, and
all inordinate affection to the world, and must be expressive,

[5] Sic Jesus dixit S. Carpo apud Dionysium epist. ad Demophilum.

according to our power, in the instances of duty, and must be love for love's sake; and of this love martyrdom is the highest instance—that is, a readiness of mind rather to suffer any evil than to do any. Of this our blessed Saviour affirmed that no man had greater love than this; that is, this is the highest point of duty, the greatest love that God requires of man. And yet he that is the most imperfect must have this love, also, in preparation of mind, and must differ from another in nothing, except in the degrees of promptness and alacrity. And, in this sense, he that loves God truly, though but with a beginning and tender love, yet he loves God with all his heart, that is, with that degree of love which is the highest point of our duty and of God's charge upon us; and he that loves God with all his heart may yet increase with the increase of God; just as there are degrees of love to God among the saints, and yet each of them love him with all their powers and capacities.

2. But the greater state of love is the zeal of love, which runs out into excrescences and suckers, like a fruitful and pleasant tree; or bursting into gums, and producing fruits, not of a monstrous, but of an extraordinary and heroical, greatness. Concerning which these cautions are to be observed:

Cautions and Rules concerning Zeal.

1. If zeal be in the beginnings of our spiritual birth, or be short, sudden, and transient, or be a consequent of a man's natural temper, or come upon any cause but after a long growth of a temperate and well-regulated love—it is to be suspected for passion and frowardness, rather than the vertical point of love.[6]

2. That zeal only is good which, in a fervent love, hath temperate expressions. For, let the affection boil as high as it can, yet if it boil over into irregular and strange actions, it will have but few, but will need many, excuses. Elijah was zealous for the Lord of hosts; and yet he was so transported with it, that he could not receive answer from God till by music he was recomposed and tamed; and Moses broke both the tables of the law by being passionately zealous against them that brake the first.

3. Zeal must spend its greatest heat principally in those

* Καλὸν δὲ τὸ ζηλοῦσθαι ἐν τῷ καλῷ πάντοτε.—Gal. iv. 18

things that concern ourselves; but with great care and restraint in those that concern others.

4. Remember that zeal, being an excrescence of Divine love, must in no sense contradict any action of love. Love to God includes love to our neighbour; and therefore no pretence of zeal[7] for God's glory must make us uncharitable to our brother; for that is just so pleasing to God as hatred is an act of love.

5. That zeal that concerns others can spend itself in nothing but arts, and actions, and charitable instruments, for their good; and when it concerns the good of many that one should suffer, it must be done by persons of a competent authority, and in great necessity, in seldom instances, according to the law of God or man; but never by private right, or for trifling accidents, or in mistaken propositions. The Zelots, in the old law, had authority to transfix and stab some certain persons, but God gave them warrant; it was in the case of idolatry, or such notorious huge crimes, the danger of which was insupportable, and the cognisance of which was infallible; and yet that warrant expired with the synagogue.

6. Zeal in the instances of our own duty and personal deportment, is more safe than in matters of counsel, and actions besides our just duty, and tending towards perfection. Though in these instances there is not a direct sin, even where the zeal is less wary, yet there is much trouble and some danger; as, if it be spent in the too forward vows of chastity, and restraints of natural and innocent liberties.

7. Zeal may be let loose in the instances of internal, personal, and spiritual actions, that are matters of direct duty; as in prayers, and acts of adoration, and thanksgiving, and frequent addresses, provided that no indirect act pass upon them to defile them; such as complacency, and opinions of sanctity, censuring others, scruples and opinions of necessity, unnecessary fears, superstitious numberings of times and hours: but let the zeal be as forward as it will, as devout as it will, as seraphical as it will, in the direct address and intercourse with God, there is no danger, no transgression. Do all the parts of your duty as earnestly as if the salvation of all the world, and the whole glory of God, and the confusion of all devils, and all that you hope or desire, did depend upon every one action.[8]

[7] Phil. iii. 6.   [8] Lavora, come se tu avessi a campar ogni hora Adora, come se tu avessi a morir allora.

8. Let zeal be seated in the will and choice, and regulated with prudence and sober understanding, not in the fancies and affections;[9] for *these* will make it full of noise and empty of profit; but *that* will make it deep and smooth, material and devout.

The sum is this: that zeal is not a direct duty, no where commanded for itself, and is nothing but a forwardness and circumstance of another duty, and therefore is then only acceptable when it advances the love of God and our neighbours, whose circumstance it is.[10]   That zeal is only safe, only acceptable, which increases charity directly; and because love to our neighbour and obedience to God are the two great portions of charity, we must never account our zeal to be good but as it advances both these, if it be in a matter that relates to both; or severally, if it relates severally.   St. Paul's zeal was expressed in preaching without any offerings or stipend, in travelling, in spending and being spent for his flock, in suffering, in being willing to be accursed for love of the people of God and his countrymen.   Let our zeal be as great as his was, so it be in affections to others, but not at all in angers against them: in the first there is no danger; in the second there is no safety.   In brief, let your zeal (if it must be expressed in anger) be always more severe against thyself than against others.[11]

¶ The other part of love to God is love to our neighbour, for which I have reserved the paragraph of alms.

Of the external Actions of Religion.

Religion teaches us to present to God our bodies as well as our souls, for God is the Lord of both ; and if the body serves the soul in actions natural, and civil, and intellectual, it must not be eased in the only offices of religion, unless the body shall expect no portion of the rewards of religion, such as are resurrection, reunion, and glorification.   Our bodies are to God a living sacrifice; and to present them to God is holy and acceptable.[12]

The actions of the body as it serves to religion, and as it is distinguished from sobriety and justice, either relate to the word of God, or to prayer, or to repentance, and make these

* Rom. x. 2.   [10] Tit. ii. 14; Rev. iii. 16.   [11] 2 Cor. vii. 11.
[12] Rom. xii. 1.

kinds of external actions of religion : 1. Reading and hearing
the word of God; 2. Fasting and corporal austerities, called
by St. Paul bodily exercise ; 3. Feasting, or keeping days of
public joy and thanksgiving.

SECT. IV. *Of reading or hearing the Word of God.*

READING and hearing the word of God are but the several
circumstances of the same duty ; instrumental especially to
faith, but consequently to all other graces of the Spirit. It is
all one to us whether by the eye or by the ear the Spirit
conveys his precepts to us. If we hear St. Paul saying to us,
that "whoremongers and adulterers God will judge," or read
it in one of his epistles, in either of them we are equally and
sufficiently instructed. The Scriptures read are the same
thing to us which the same doctrine was when it was preached
by the disciples of our blessed Lord ; and we are to learn of
either with the same dispositions. There are many that cannot read the word, and they must take it in by the ear ; and
they that can read find the same word of God by the eye.
It is necessary that all men learn it in some way or other,
and it is sufficient in order to their practice that they learn it
any way. The word of God is all those commandments and
revelations, those promises and threatenings, the stories and
sermons, recorded in the Bible : nothing else is the word of
God that we know of by any certain instrument. The good
books and spiritual discourses, the sermons or homilies, written or spoken by men, are but the word of men, or rather ex-
plications of, and exhortations according to, the word of God ;
but of themselves they are not the word of God. In a sermon, the text only is in a proper sense to be called God's word ;
and yet good sermons are of great use and convenience for the
advantages of religion. He that preaches an hour together
against drunkenness, with the tongue of men or angels, hath
spoke no other word of God but this, "Be not drunk with
wine, wherein is excess ;" and he that writes that sermon in
a book, and publishes that book, hath preached to all that read
it a louder sermon than could be spoken in a church. This
I say to this purpose, that we may separate truth from error,
popular opinions from substantial truths. For God preaches
to us in the Scripture, and by his secret assistances and spiritual thoughts and holy motions : good men preach to us when

they, by popular arguments and human arts and compliances, expound and press any of those doctrines which God hath preached unto us in his holy word. But,

1. The Holy Ghost is certainly the best preacher in the world, and the words of Scripture the best sermons.

2. All the doctrine of salvation is plainly set down there, that the most unlearned person, by hearing it read, may understand all his duty. What can be plainer spoken than this, "Thou shalt not kill; Be not drunk with wine; Husbands, love your wives; Whatsoever ye would that men should do to you, do ye so to them"? The wit of man cannot more plainly tell us our duty, or more fully, than the Holy Ghost hath done already.

3. Good sermons and good books are of excellent use; but yet they can serve no other end but that we practise the plain doctrines of Scripture.

4. What Abraham, in the parable, said concerning the brethren of the rich man, is here very proper; "They have Moses and the prophets, let them hear them; but if they refuse to hear these, neither will they believe though one should arise from the dead to preach unto them." [1]

5. Reading the Holy Scriptures is a duty expressly commanded us,[2] and is called in Scripture "preaching:" all other preaching is the effect of human skill and industry; and although of great benefit, yet it is but an ecclesiastical ordinance; the law of God concerning preaching being expressed in the matter of reading the Scriptures, and hearing that word of God which is, and as it is, there described.

But this duty is reduced to practice in the following rules

Rules for hearing or reading the Word of God.

1. Set apart some portion of thy time, according to the opportunities of thy calling and necessary employment, for the reading of Holy Scripture; and, if it be possible, every day read or hear some of it read: you are sure that book teaches all truth, commands all holiness, and promises all happiness.

2. When it is in your power to choose, accustom yourself to such portions which are most plain and certain duty, and which contain the story of the life and death of our blessed

[1] Luke xvi. 29, 31.   [2] Deut. xxxi. 11; Luke xxiv. 45; Matt xxii. 29; Acts xv. 21; 2 Tim. iii. 16; Rev. i. 3.

Saviour. Read the Gospels, the Psalms of David, and especially those portions of Scripture which, by the wisdom of the
church, are appointed to be publicly read upon Sundays and
holidays, viz. the Epistles and Gospels. In the choice of any
other portions, you may advise with a spiritual guide, that
you may spend your time with most profit.

3. Fail not diligently to attend to the reading of Holy Scriptures upon those days wherein it is most publicly and solemnly
read in churches: for at such times, besides the learning our
duty, we obtain a blessing along with it; it becoming to us,
upon those days, a part of the solemn Divine worship.

4. When the word of God is read or preached to you, be
sure you be of a ready heart and mind, free from worldly cares
and thoughts, diligent to hear, careful to mark, studious to
remember, and desirous to practise all that is commanded, and
to live according to it: do not hear for any other end but to
become better in your life and to be instructed in every good
work, and to increase in the love and service of God.

5. Beg of God, by prayer, that he would give you the spirit
of obedience and profit, and that he would, by his Spirit, write
the word in your heart, and that you describe it in your life.
To which purpose serve yourself of some affectionate ejaculations to that purpose before and after this duty.

*Concerning Spiritual Books and Ordinary Sermons, take in
these Advices also.*

6. Let not a prejudice to any man's person hinder thee from
receiving good by his doctrine, if it be according to godliness;
but (if occasion offer it, or especially if duty present it to thee
—that is, if it be preached in that assembly where thou art
bound to be present) accept the word preached as a message
from God, and the minister as his angel in that ministration.

7. Consider and remark the doctrine that is represented to
thee in any discourse; and if the preacher adds accidental advantages, any thing to comply with thy weakness, or to put
thy spirit into action or holy resolution, remember it and make
use of it. But if the preacher be a weak person, yet the text
is the doctrine thou art to remember, that contains all thy
duty; it is worth thy attendance to hear that spoken often
and renewed upon thy thoughts: and though thou beest a
learned man, yet the same thing which thou knowest already,

if spoken by another, may be made active by that application. I can better be comforted by my own considerations if another hand applies them than if I do it myself; because the word of God does not work as a natural agent, but as a Divine instrument; it does not prevail by the force of deduction and artificial discoursings only, but chiefly by way of blessing in the ordinance and in the ministry of an appointed person. At least, obey the public order, and reverence the constitution, and give good example of humility, charity, and obedience.

8. When Scriptures are read, you are only to inquire, with diligence and modesty, into the meaning of the Spirit: but if homilies or sermons be made upon the words of Scripture, you are to consider, whether all that be spoken be conformable to the Scriptures: for, although you may practise for human reasons, and human arguments, ministered from the preacher's art; yet you must practise nothing but the command of God, nothing but the doctrine of Scripture, that is, the text.

9. Use the advice of some spiritual or other prudent men for the choice of such spiritual books, which may be of use and benefit for the edification of thy spirit in the ways of holy living; and esteem that time well accounted; for that is prudently and affectionately employed in hearing or reading good books and pious discourses; ever remembering, that God, by hearing us speak to him in prayer, obliges us to hear him speak to us in his word, by what instrument soever it be conveyed.

SECT. V. *Of Fasting.*

FASTING, if it be considered in itself, without relation to spiritual ends, is a duty no where enjoined or counselled. But Christianity hath to do with it as it may be made an instrument of the Spirit, by subduing the lusts of the flesh, or removing any hinderances of religion. And it hath been practised by all ages of the church, and advised in order to three ministries; 1. To prayer; 2. To mortification of bodily lusts; 3. To repentance: and it is to be practised according to the following measures.

Rules for Christian Fasting.

1. Fasting, in order to prayer, is to be measured by the proportions of the times of prayer; that is, it ought to be a

total fast from all things, during the solemnity, unless a probable necessity intervene. Thus the Jews ate nothing upon
the sabbath days till their great offices were performed; that
is, about the sixth hour: and St. Peter used it as an argument,
that the apostles in Pentecost were not drunk, because it was
but the third hour of the day; of such a day in which it was
not lawful to eat or drink till the sixth hour: and the Jews
were offended at the disciples for plucking the ears of corn
on the sabbath, early in the morning, because it was before
the time in which, by their customs, they esteemed it lawful
to break their fast. In imitation of this custom, and in prosecution of the reason of it, the Christian church hath religiously observed fasting before the holy communion; and the
more devout persons (though without any obligation at all)
refused to eat or drink till they had finished their morning
devotions: and further yet, upon days of public humiliation,
which are designed to be spent wholly in devotion, and for
the averting God's judgments, (if they were imminent,) fasting
is commanded together with prayer: commanded (I say) by
the church to this end—that the spirit might be clearer and
more angelical, when it is quitted in some proportions from
the loads of flesh.

2. Fasting, when it is in order to prayer, must be a total
abstinence from all meat, or else an abatement of the quan-
tity: for the help which fasting does to prayer cannot be
served by changing flesh into fish, or milk-meats into dry
diet; but by turning much into little, or little into none at all,
during the time of solemn and extraordinary prayer.

3. Fasting, as it is instrumental to prayer, must be attended with other aids of the like virtue and efficacy; such as
are removing for the time all worldly cares and secular businesses; and therefore our blessed Saviour enfolds these parts
within the same caution; "Take heed, lest your hearts be
overcharged with surfeiting, and drunkenness, and the cares
of this world, and that day overtake you unawares." To
which add alms; for upon the wings of fasting and alms holy
prayer infallibly mounts up to heaven.[1]

4. When fasting is intended to serve the duty of repentance, it is then best chosen when it is short, sharp, and afflictive; that is, either a total abstinence from all nourishment.

[1] Jejunium sine eleemosyna, lampas sine oleo.—St. Aug.

according as we shall appoint or be appointed, during such a
time as is separate for the solemnity and attendance upon the
employment; or, if we shall extend our severity beyond the
solemn days, and keep our anger against our sin, as we are
to keep our sorrow, that is, always in a readiness, and often
to be called upon; then, to refuse a pleasant morsel, to abstain from the bread of our desires, and only to take wholesome and less pleasing nourishment, vexing our appetite by
the refusing a lawful satisfaction, since, in its petulancy and
luxury, it preyed upon an unlawful.

5. Fasting designed for repentance must be ever joined
with an extreme care that we fast from sin; for there is no
greater folly or indecency in the world than to commit that
for which I am now judging and condemning myself. This
is the best fast; and the other may serve to promote the interest of this, by increasing the disaffection to it, and multiplying arguments against it.

6. He that fasts for repentance must, during that solemnity,
abstain from all bodily delights, and the sensuality of all his
senses and his appetites: for a man must not, when he mourns
in his fast, be merry in his sport; weep at dinner, and laugh
all day after; have a silence in his kitchen, and music in his
chamber; judge the stomach, and feast the other senses. I
deny not but a man may, in a single instance, punish a particular sin with a proper instrument. If a man have offended
in his palate, he may choose to fast only; if he have sinned in
softness and in his touch, he may choose to lie hard, or work
hard, and use sharp inflictions; but although this discipline
be proper and particular, yet because the sorrow is of the
whole man, no sense must rejoice, or be with any study or
purpose feasted and entertained softly. This rule is intended
to relate to the solemn days appointed for repentance publicly
or privately; besides which, in the whole course of our life,
even in the midst of our most festival and freer joys, we may
sprinkle some single instances and acts of self-condemning, or
punishing; as to refuse a pleasant morsel or a delicious draught
with a tacit remembrance of the sin that now returns to displease my spirit. And, though these actions be single, there
is no indecency in them; because a man may abate of his ordinary liberty and bold freedom with great prudence, so he
does it without singularity in himself or trouble to others.

but he may not abate of his solemn sorrow: that may be caution; but this would be softness, effeminacy, and indecency.

7. When fasting is an act of mortification, that is, is intended to subdue a bodily lust, as the spirit of fornication, or the fondness of strong and impatient appetites, it must not be a sudden, sharp, and violent fast, but a state of fasting, a diet of fasting, a daily lessening our portion of meat and drink, and a choosing such a coarse diet,[2] which may make the least preparation for the lusts of the body. He that fasts three days without food will weaken other parts more than the ministers of fornication; and when the meals return as usually, they also will be served as soon as any. In the mean time, they will be supplied and made active by the accidental heat that comes with such violent fastings; for this is a kind of aërial devil—the prince that rules in the air is the devil of fornication; and he will be as tempting with the windiness of a violent fast as with the flesh of an ordinary meal.[3] But a daily subtraction of the nourishment will introduce a less busy habit of body; and that will prove the more effectual remedy.

8. Fasting alone will not cure this devil, though it helps much towards it; but it must not therefore be neglected, but assisted by all the proper instruments of remedy against this unclean spirit; and what it is unable to do alone, in company with other instruments, and God's blessing upon them, it may effect.

9. All fasting, for whatsoever end it be undertaken, must be done without any opinion of the necessity of the thing itself, without censuring others, with all humility, in order to the proper end; and just as a man takes physic, of which no man hath reason to be proud, and no man thinks it necessary, but because he is in sickness, or in danger and disposition to it.

10. All fasts ordained by lawful authority are to be observed in order to the same purposes to which they are enjoined, and to be accompanied with actions of the same nature, just as it is in private fasts; for there is no other difference, but that in public our superiors choose for us what in private we do for ourselves.

[2] Digiuna assai chi mal mangia.
[3] Chi digiuna, ed altro ben non fa,
   Sparagna il pane, ed al inferno va.—See chap. ii. sect. ii. 2.

11. Fasts ordained by lawful authority are not to be neglected; because alone they cannot do the thing in order to which they were enjoined. It may be, one day of humiliation will not obtain the blessing, or alone kill the lust; yet it must not be despised if it can do any thing towards it. An act of fasting is an act of self-denial; and, though it do not produce the habit, yet it is a good act.

12. When the principal end why a fast is publicly prescribed is obtained by some other instrument, in a particular person— as if the spirit of fornication be cured by the rite of marriage, or by a gift of chastity—yet that person so eased is not freed from the fasts of the church by that alone, if those fasts can prudently serve any other end of religion, as that of prayer, or repentance, or mortification of some other appetite: for when it is instrumental to any end of the Spirit, it is freed from superstition; and then we must have some other reason to quit us from the obligation, or that alone will not do it.

13. When the fast publicly commanded, by reason of some indisposition in the particular person, cannot operate to the end of the commandment, yet the avoiding offence, and the complying with public order, is reason enough to make the obedience to be necessary. For he that is otherwise disobliged, as when the reason of the law ceases as to his particular, yet remains still obliged if he cannot do otherwise without scandal: but this is an obligation of charity, not of justice.

14. All fasting is to be used with prudence and charity: for there is no end to which fasting serves but may be obtained by other instruments; and, therefore, it must at no hand be made an instrument of scruple; or become an enemy to our health; or be imposed upon persons that are sick or aged, or to whom it is, in any sense, uncharitable, such as are wearied travellers; or to whom, in the whole kind of it, it is useless, such as are women with child, poor people, and little children. But in these cases the church hath made provision and inserted caution into her laws; and they are to be reduced to practice according to custom, and the sentence of prudent persons, with great latitude, and without niceness and curiosity: having this in our first care, that we secure our virtue; and, next, that we secure our health, that we may the better exercise the labours of virtue; lest, out of too much austerity,

we bring ourselves to that condition that it be necessary to be indulgent to softness, ease, and extreme tenderness.[4]

15. Let not intemperance be the prologue or the epilogue to your fast; lest the fast be so far from taking off any thing of the sin, that it be an occasion to increase it: and, therefore, when the fast is done, be careful that no supervening act of gluttony or excessive drinking unhallow the religion of the past day; but eat temperately according to the proportion of other meals, lest gluttony keep either of the gates to abstinence.[5]

The Benefits of Fasting.

He that undertakes to enumerate the benefits of fasting may, in the next page, also reckon all the benefits of physic; for fasting is not to be commended as a duty, but as an instrument; and in that sense no man can reprove it, or undervalue it, but he that knows neither spiritual arts nor spiritual necessities. But by the doctors of the church it is called the nourishment of prayer, the restraint of lust, the wings of the soul, the diet of angels, the instrument of humility and self-denial, the purification of the spirit; and the paleness and meagreness of visage, which is consequent to the daily fast of great mortifiers, is by St. Basil said to be the mark in the forehead which the angel observed when he signed the saints in the forehead to escape the wrath of God. "The soul that is greatly vexed, which goeth stooping and feeble, and the eyes that fail, and the hungry soul, shall give thee praise and righteousness, O Lord!"[6]

Sect. VI. *Of keeping Festivals, and Days holy to the Lord; particularly the Lord's Day.*

True natural religion, that which was common to all nations and ages, did principally rely upon four great propositions: 1. That there is one God; 2. That God is nothing of those things which we see; 3. That God takes care of all things below, and governs all the world; 4. That he is the great Creator of all things, without himself: and according to these were framed the four first precepts of the decalogue. In the first, the unity of the Godhead is expressly affirmed; in the second, his invisibility and immateriality; in the third, is

---

[4] S. Basil. Monast. Constit. cap. 5. Cassian. Col. 21. cap. 22. Ne per causam necessitatis eò impingamus, ut voluptatibus serviamus.

[5] Ἀμυνόμενοι τὴν ἡμέραν.—Naz.   [6] Baruch ii. 18.

affirmed God's government and providence, by avenging them
that swear falsely by his name ; by which also his omniscience is declared: in the fourth commandment, he proclaims
himself the Maker of heaven and earth; for, in memory of
God's rest from the work of six days, the seventh was hallowed into a sabbath ; and the keeping it was confessing God
to be the great Maker of heaven and earth ; and consequently
to this, it also was a confession of his goodness, his omnipotence, and his wisdom: all which were written with a sunbeam in the great book of the creature.

So long as the law of the sabbath was bound upon God's
people, so long God would have that to be the solemn manner
of confessing these attributes ; but when, the priesthood being
changed, there was a change also of the law, the great duty
remained unalterable in changed circumstances.   We are
eternally bound to confess God Almighty to be the Maker of
heaven and earth: but the manner of confessing it is changed
from a rest, or a doing nothing, to a speaking something ; from
a day to a symbol ; from a ceremony to a substance ; from a
Jewish rite to a Christian duty: we profess it in our creed,
we confess it in our lives ; we describe it by every line of our
life, by every action of duty, by faith, and trust, and obedience : and we do also, upon great reason, comply with the
Jewish manner of confessing the creation, so far as it is instrumental to a real duty.   We keep one day in seven, and so
confess the manner and circumstance of the creation ; and we
rest also, that we may tend holy duties: so imitating God's
rest better than the Jew in Synesius, who lay upon his face
from evening to evening, and could not, by stripes or wounds,
be raised up to steer the ship in a great storm.   God's rest
was not a natural cessation ; he who could not labour could
not be said to rest: but God's rest is to be understood to be a
beholding and a rejoicing in his work finished ; and therefore
we truly represent God's rest when we confess and rejoice in
God's works and God's glory.

This the Christian church does upon every day; but
especially upon the Lord's day, which she hath set apart for
this and all other offices of religion, being determined to this
day by the resurrection of her dearest Lord, it being the first
day of joy the church ever had.   And now, upon the Lord's
day, we are not tied to the rest of the sabbath, but to all the

o

work of the sabbath; and we are to abstain from bodily labour, not because it is a direct duty to us, as it was to the
Jews, but because it is necessary, in order to our duty, that
we attend to the offices of religion.

The observation of the Lord's day differs nothing from the
observation of the sabbath in the matter of religion, but in the
manner. They differ in the ceremony and external rite: rest,
with them, was the principal; with us, it is the accessory.
They differ in the office or forms of worship; for they were
then to worship God as a Creator and a gentle Father; we are
to add to that, our Redeemer, and all his other excellences
and mercies. And, though we have more natural and proper
reason to keep the Lord's day than the sabbath, yet the Jews
had a Divine commandment for their day, which we have not
for ours: but we have many commandments to do all that
honour to God which was intended in the fourth commandment; and the apostles appointed the first day of the week for
doing it in solemn assemblies. And the manner of worshipping God, and doing him solemn honour and service upon
this day, we may best observe in the following measures.

Rules for keeping the Lord's Day and other Christian Festivals.

1. When you go about to distinguish festival days from
common, do it not by lessening the devotions of ordinary days,
that the common devotion may seem bigger upon festivals;
but, on every day, keep your ordinary devotions entire, and
enlarge upon the holy day.

2. Upon the Lord's day we must abstain from all servile and
laborious works, except such which are matters of necessity,
of common life, or of great charity; for these are permitted by
that authority which hath separated the day for holy uses.
The sabbath of the Jews, though consisting principally in
rest, and established by God, did yield to these. The labour
of love and the labours of religion were not against the reason
and the spirit of the commandment, for which the letter was
decreed, and to which it ought to minister. And, therefore,
much more is it so on the Lord's day, where the letter is wholly
turned into spirit, and there is no commandment of God but
of spiritual and holy actions. The priests might kill their
beasts, and dress them for sacrifice; and Christ, though born
under the law, might heal a sick man; and the sick man might

carry his bed to witness his recovery, and confess the mercy, and leap and dance to God for joy; and an ox might be led to water, and an ass be haled out of a ditch; and a man may take physic, and he may eat meat, and therefore there were of necessity some to prepare and administer it: and the performing these labours did not consist in minutes and just determining stages; but they had, even then, a reasonable latitude; so only as to exclude unnecessary labour, or such as did not minister to charity or religion. And, therefore, this is to be enlarged in the gospel, whose sabbath or rest is but a circumstance, and accessory to the principal and spiritual duties. Upon the Christian sabbath necessity is to be served first; then charity; and then religion—for this is to give place to charity, in great instances, and the second to the first, in all; and in all cases God is to be worshipped in spirit and in truth.

3. The Lord's day, being the remembrance of a great blessing, must be a day of joy, festivity, spiritual rejoicing, and thanksgiving: and therefore it is a proper work of the day to let your devotions spend themselves in singing or reading psalms; in recounting the great works of God; in remembering his mercies; in worshipping his excellences; in celebrating his attributes; in admiring his person; in sending portions of pleasant meat to them for whom nothing is provided; and in all the arts and instruments of advancing God's glory, and the reputation of religion: in which it were a great decency that the memorial of the resurrection should be inserted, that the particular religion of the day be not swallowed up in the general. And of this we may the more easily serve ourselves, by rising seasonably in the morning to private devotion, and by retiring at the leisures and spaces of the day not employed in public offices.

4. Fail not to be present at the public hours and places of prayer, entering early and cheerfully, attending reverently and devoutly, abiding patiently during the whole office, piously assisting at the prayers, and gladly also hearing the sermon; and, at no hand, omitting to receive the holy communion, when it is offered, (unless some great reason excuse it,) this being the great solemnity of thanksgiving, and a proper work of the day.

5. After the solemnities are past, and in the intervals between the morning and evening devotion, (as you shall find opportunity,) visit sick persons, reconcile differences, do offices

o 2

of neighbourhood, inquire into the needs of the poor, especially housekeepers, relieve them, as they shall need, and as you are able; for then we truly rejoice in God, when we make our neighbours, the poor members of Christ, rejoice together with us.

6. Whatsoever you are to do yourself, as necessary, you are to take care that others also, who are under your charge, do in their station and manner. Let your servants be called to church, and all your family that can be spared from necessary and great household ministries; those that cannot, let them go by turns, and be supplied otherwise, as well as they may; and provide, on these days especially, that they be instructed in the articles of faith and necessary parts of their duty.

7. Those who labour hard in the week must be eased upon the Lord's day; such ease being a great charity and alms: but, at no hand, must they be permitted to use any unlawful games, any thing forbidden by the laws, any thing that is scandalous, or any thing that is dangerous and apt to mingle sin with it; no games prompting to wantonness, to drunkenness, to quarrelling, to ridiculous and superstitious customs; but let their refreshments be innocent, and charitable, and of good report, and not exclusive of the duties of religion.

8. Beyond these bounds, because neither God nor man hath passed any obligation upon us, we must preserve our Christian liberty, and not suffer ourselves to be entangled with a yoke of bondage; for even a good action may become a snare to us, if we make it an occasion of scruple by a pretence of necessity, binding loads upon the conscience, not with the bands of God, but of men, and of fancy, or of opinion, or of tyranny. Whatsoever is laid upon us by the hands of man must be acted and accounted of by the measures of a man: but our best measure is this; he keeps the Lord's day best that keeps it with most religion and with most charity.

9. What the church hath done in the article of the resurrection, she hath in some measure done in the other articles of the nativity, of the ascension, and of the descent of the Holy Ghost at Pentecost: and so great blessings deserve an anniversary solemnity; since he is a very unthankful person that does not often record them in the whole year, and esteem them the ground of his hopes, the object of his faith, the comfort of his troubles, and the great effluxes of the Divine mercy, greater than all the victories over our temporal enemies, for which all

glad persons usually give thanks. And if, with great reason, the memory of the resurrection does return solemnly every week, it is but reason the other should return once a year. To which I add, that the commemoration of the articles of our Creed in solemn days and offices is a very excellent instrument to convey and imprint the sense and memory of it upon the spirits of the most ignorant persons. For, as a picture may with more fancy convey a story to a man than a plain narrative either in word or writing, so a real representment, and an office of remembrance, and a day to declare it, is far more impressive than a picture, or any other art of making and fixing imagery.

10. The memories of the saints are precious to God, and therefore they ought also to be so to us; and such persons who serve God by holy living, industrious preaching, and religious dying, ought to have their names preserved in honour, and God be glorified in them, and their holy doctrines and lives published and imitated: and we, by so doing, give testimony to the article of the communion of saints. But, in these cases as every church is to be sparing in the number of days, so also should she be temperate in her injunctions, not imposing them but upon voluntary and unbusied persons, without snare or burden. But the holy day is best kept by giving God thanks for the excellent persons, apostles, or martyrs, we then remember, and by imitating their lives: this all may do; and they that can also keep the solemnity must do that too, when it is publicly enjoined.

The mixed Actions of Religion are, 1. Prayer, 2. Alms, 3. Repentance, 4. Receiving the blessed Sacrament.

Sect. VII. *Of Prayer.*

THERE is no greater argument in the world of our spiritual danger and unwillingness to religion, than the backwardness which most men have always, and all men have sometimes, to say their prayers—so weary of their length, so glad when they are done, so witty to excuse and frustrate an opportunity; and yet all is nothing but a desiring of God to give us the greatest and the best things we can need, and which can make us happy: it is a work so easy, so honourable, and to so great purpose, that in all the instances of religion and providence (except only the incarnation of his Son,) God hath not given

us a greater argument of his willingness to have us saved, and
of our unwillingness to accept it, his goodness and our grace-
lessness, his infinite condescension and our carelessness and
folly, than by rewarding so easy a duty with so great blessings.

Motives to Prayer.

I cannot say any thing beyond this very consideration and
its appendages to invite Christian people to pray often. But
we may consider that, 1. It is a duty commanded by God and
his holy Son. 2. It is an act of grace and highest honour,
that we, dust and ashes, are admitted to speak to the eternal
God, to run to him as to a father, to lay open our wants, to
complain of our burdens, to explicate our scruples, to beg
remedy and ease, support and counsel, health and safety, deliverance and salvation. And, 3. God hath invited us to it
by many gracious promises of hearing us. 4. He hath appointed his most glorious Son to be the precedent of prayer,
and to make continual intercession for us to the throne of
grace. 5. He hath appointed an angel to present the prayers
of his servants. And, 6. Christ unites them to his own, and
sanctifies them, and makes them effective and prevalent: and,
7. hath put it into the hands of men to rescind, or alter, all
the decrees of God, which are of one kind, (that is, conditional,
and concerning ourselves and our final estate, and many instances of our intermedial or temporal,) by the power of
prayers. 8. And the prayers of men have saved cities and
kingdoms from ruin: prayer hath raised dead men to life,
hath stopped the violence of fire, shut the mouths of wild
beasts, hath altered the course of nature, caused rain in Egypt,
and drought in the sea: it made the sun to go from west to
east, and the moon to stand still, and rocks and mountains to
walk; and it cures diseases without physic, and makes physic
to do the work of nature, and nature to do the work of grace,
and grace to do the work of God; and it does miracles of accident and event: and yet prayer, that does all this, is, of itself,
nothing but an ascent of the mind to God, a desiring things
fit to be desired, and an expression of this desire to God as
we can, and as becomes us. And our unwillingness to pray
is nothing else but a not desiring what we ought passionately
to long for; or, if we do desire it, it is a choosing rather to
miss our satisfaction and felicity than to ask for it.

There is no more to be said in this affair, but that we reduce it to practice, according to the following rules :—

Rules for the Practice of Prayer.

1. We must be careful that we never ask any thing of God that is sinful, or that directly ministers to sin ; for that is to ask God to dishonour himself, and to undo us. We had need consider what we pray ; for before it returns in blessing it must be joined with Christ's intercession, and presented to God. Let us principally ask of God power and assistance to do our duty, to glorify God, to do good works, to live a good life, to die in the fear and favour of God and eternal life : these things God delights to give, and commands that we shall ask, and we may with confidence expect to be answered graciously ; for these things are promised without any reservation of a secret condition : if we ask them, and do our duty towards the obtaining them, we are sure never to miss them.

2. We may lawfully pray to God for the gifts of the Spirit that minister to holy ends ; such as are the gift of preaching, the spirit of prayer, good expression, a ready and unloosed tongue, good understanding, learning, opportunities to publish them, &c., with these only restraints: 1. That we cannot be so confident of the event of those prayers as of the former. 2. That we must be curious to secure our intention in these desires, that we may not ask them to serve our own ends, but only for God's glory ; and then we shall have them, or a blessing for desiring them. In order to such purposes our intentions in the first desires cannot be amiss ; because they are able to sanctify other things, and therefore cannot be unhallowed themselves. 3. We must submit to God's will. desiring him to choose our employment, and to furnish our persons as he shall see expedient.

3. Whatsoever we may lawfully desire of temporal things, we may lawfully ask of God in prayer, and we may expect them, as they are promised. 1. Whatsoever is necessary to our life and being is promised to us : and therefore we may, with certainty, expect food and raiment ; food to keep us alive, clothing to keep us from nakedness and shame : so long as our life is permitted to us, so long all things necessary to our life shall be ministered. We may be secure of maintenance,

but not secure of our life; for that is promised, not this: only concerning food and raiment we are not to make accounts by the measure of our desires, but by the measure of our needs. 2. Whatsoever is convenient for us, pleasant, and modestly delectable, we may pray for, so we do it, 1. With submission to God's will. 2. Without impatient desires. 3. That it be not a trifle and inconsiderable, but a matter so grave and concerning, as to be a fit matter to be treated on between God and our souls. 4. That we ask it not to spend upon our lusts, but for ends of justice, or charity, or religion, and that they be employed with sobriety.

4. He that would pray with effect must live with care and piety.[1] For although God gives to sinners and evil persons the common blessings of life and chance, yet either they want the comfort and blessing of those blessings, or they become occasions of sadder accidents to them, or serve to upbraid them in their ingratitude or irreligion: and, in all cases, they are not the effects of prayer, or the fruits of promise, or instances of a father's love; for they cannot be expected with confidence, or received without danger, or used without a curse and mischief in their company. But as all sin is an impediment to prayer, so some have a special indisposition towards acceptation; such are uncharitableness and wrath, hypocrisy in the present action, pride and lust: because these, by defiling the body or the spirit, or by contradicting some necessary ingredient in prayer, (such as are mercy, humility, purity, and sincerity,) do defile the prayer, and make it a direct sin, in the circumstances or formality of the action.

5. All prayer must be made with faith and hope; that is, we must certainly believe[2] we shall receive the grace which God hath commanded us to ask; and we must hope for such things, which he hath permitted us to ask, and our hope shall not be vain, though we miss what is not absolutely promised; because we shall at least have an equal blessing in the denial as in the grant. And, therefore, the former conditions must first be secured: that is, that we ask things necessary, or at least good and innocent and profitable, and that our persons be gracious in the eyes of God: or else, what God hath pro-

---

[1] 1 John iii. 22; John ix. 31; Isa. i. 15; lviii. 5; Mal. iii. 10; 1 Tim. ii. 8; Psal. xxxiv. 15; lxvi. 18.　　　　[2] Mark xi. 24; James i. 6, 7.

mised to our natural needs he may, in many degrees, deny to our personal incapacity; but the thing being secured, and the person disposed, there can be no fault at all; for whatsoever else remains is on God's part, and that cannot possibly fail. But because the things which are not commanded cannot possibly be secured, (for we are not sure they are good in all circumstances,) we can but hope for such things, even after we have secured our good intentions. We are sure of a blessing, but in what instance we are not yet assured.

6. Our prayers must be fervent, intense, earnest, and importunate, when we pray for things of high concernment and necessity. "Continuing instant in prayer; striving in prayer; labouring fervently in prayer; night and day praying exceedingly; praying always with all prayer:" so St. Paul calls it.[3] "Watching unto prayer:" so St. Peter.[4] "Praying earnestly:" so St. James.[5] And this is not at all to be abated in matters spiritual and of duty: for, according as our desires are, so are our prayers; and as our prayers are, so shall be the grace; and as that is, so shall be the measure of glory. But this admits of degrees according to the perfection or imperfection of our state of life; but it hath no other measures, but ought to be as great as it can; the bigger the better: we must make no positive restraints upon ourselves. In other things we are to use a bridle; and as we must limit our desires with submission to God's will, so also we must limit the importunity of our prayers by the moderation and term of our desires. Pray for it as earnestly as you may desire it.

7. Our desires must be lasting, and our prayers frequent, assiduous, and continual; not asking for a blessing once, and then leaving it, but daily renewing our suits, and exercising our hope, and faith, and patience, and long-suffering, and religion, and resignation, and self-denial, in all the degrees we shall be put to. This circumstance of duty our blessed Saviour taught, saying, that "men ought always to pray, and not to faint."[6] Always to pray, signifies the frequent doing of the duty in general; but, because we cannot always ask several things, and we also have frequent need of the same things, and those are such as concern our great interest, the precept comes home to this very circumstance; and St. Paul

[3] Rom. xii. 12; xv. 30; Col. iv. 12; 1 Thess. iii. 10; Eph. vi. 18.
[4] 1 Pet. iv. 7. [5] James v. 16. [6] Luke xviii. 1; xxi. 36.

calls it " praying without ceasing ;"[7] and himself in his own case gave a precedent—" For this cause I besought the Lord thrice." And so did our blessed Lord: he went thrice to God on the same errand, with the same words, in a short space—about half a night; for his time to solicit his suit was but short. And the Philippians were remembered by the apostle, their spiritual father, " always in every prayer of his."[8] And thus we must always pray for the pardon of our sins, for the assistance of God's grace, for charity, for life eternal, never giving over till we die; and thus also we pray for supply of great temporal needs in their several proportions ; in all cases being curious we do not give over out of weariness or impatience ; for God oftentimes defers to grant our suit, because he loves to hear us beg it, and hath a design to give us more than we ask, even a satisfaction of our desires, and a blessing for the very importunity.

8. Let the words of our prayers be pertinent, grave, material, not studiously many, but according to our need, sufficient to express our wants, and to signify our importunity. God hears us not the sooner for our many words, but much the sooner for an earnest desire; to which let apt and sufficient words minister, be they few or many, according as it happens. A long prayer and a short differ not in their capacities of being accepted, for both of them take their value according to the fervency of spirit, and the charity of the prayer. That prayer which is short by reason of an impatient spirit, or dulness, or despite of holy things, or indifferency of desires, is very often criminal, always imperfect : and that prayer which is long out of ostentation, or superstition, or a trifling spirit, is as criminal and imperfect as the other in their several instances. This rule relates to private prayer. In public, our devotion is to be measured by the appointed office, and we are to support our spirit with spiritual arts, that our private spirit may be a part of the public spirit, and be adopted into the society and blessings of the communion of saints.

9. In all forms of prayer mingle petition with thanksgiving, that you may endear the present prayer and the future blessing, by returning praise and thanks for what we have already received. This is St. Paul's advice—" Be careful for nothing ; but in every thing by prayer and supplication with thanksgiving let your requests be made known unto God."[9]

[7] 1 Thess. v. 17.   [8] Phil. i. 4.   [9] Phil. iv. 6.

10. Whatever we beg of God, let us also work for it, if the thing be matter of duty, or a consequent to industry; for God loves to bless labour and to reward it, but not to support idleness.[10] And therefore our blessed Saviour in his sermons joins watchfulness with prayer, for God's graces are but assistances, not new creations of the whole habit, in every instant or period of our life. Read Scriptures, and then pray to God for understanding. Pray against temptation; but you must also resist the devil, and then he will flee from you. Ask of God competency of living; but you must also work with your hands the things that are honest, that ye may have to supply in time of need. We can but do our endeavour, and pray for blessing, and then leave the success with God; and beyond this we cannot deliberate, we cannot take care—but, so far, we must.

11. To this purpose let every man study his prayers and read his duty in his petitions. For the body of our prayer is the sum of our duty; and as we must ask of God whatsoever we need, so we must labour for all that we ask. Because it is our duty, therefore we must pray for God's grace; but because God's grace is necessary, and without it we can do nothing, we are sufficiently taught, that in the proper matter of our religious prayers is the just matter of our duty; and if we shall turn our prayers into precepts, we shall the easier turn our hearty desires into effective practices.

12. In all our prayers we must be careful to attend our present work,[11] having a present mind, not wandering upon impertinent things, not distant from our words, much less contrary to them; and if our thoughts do at any time wander, and divert upon other objects, bring them back again with prudent and severe arts—by all means striving to obtain a diligent, a sober, an untroubled, and a composed spirit.

13. Let your posture and gesture of body in prayers be reverent, grave, and humble: according to public order, or the best examples, if it be in public: if it be in private, either stand or kneel, or lie flat upon the ground on your face, in your ordinary and more solemn prayers; but in extraordinary, casual, and ejaculatory prayers, the reverence and devotion of

---

[10] Εἶτα λέγομεν· Κύριε ὁ Θεὸς, πῶς μὴ ἀγωνιῶ; μωρὲ, χεῖρας οὐκ ἔχεις; οὐκ ἐποίησέ σοι αὐτὰς ὁ Θεὸς; εὔχου νῦν καθήμενος, ὅπως αἱ μύξαι σου μὴ ῥέωσιν· ἀπόμυξαι μᾶλλον.—Arrian, l. ii. c. 16.

[11] Inter sacra et vota, verbis etiam profanis abstinere.—Tacit.

the soul, and the lifting up the eyes and hands to God with any other posture not indecent, is usual and commendable; for we may pray in bed, on horseback, "every where,"[12] and at all times, and in all circumstances; and it is well if we do so: and some servants have not opportunity to pray so often as they would, unless they supply the appetites of religion by such accidental devotions.

14. " Let prayers, and supplications, and giving of thanks be made for all men; for kings, and all that are in authority; for this is good and acceptable in the sight of God our Saviour."[13]   We, who must love our neighbours as ourselves, must also pray for them as for ourselves, with this only difference, that we may enlarge in our temporal desires for kings, and pray for secular prosperity to them with more importunity than for ourselves; because they need more to enable their duty and government, and for the interests of religion and justice.   This part of prayer is by the apostle called *intercession;* in which, with special care, we are to remember our relatives, our family, our charge, our benefactors, our creditors, not forgetting to beg pardon and charity for our enemies, and protection against them.

15. Rely not on a single prayer in matters of great concernment; but make it as public as you can, by obtaining of others to pray for you—this being the great blessing of the communion of saints, that a prayer united is strong, like a well-ordered army; and God loves to be tied fast with such cords of love, and constrained by a holy violence.

16. Every time that is not seized upon by some other duty is seasonable enough for prayer; but let it be performed as a solemn duty morning and evening, that God may begin and end all our business, that " the outgoing of the morning and evening may praise him,"—for so we bless God, and God blesses us.   And yet fail not to find or make opportunities to worship God at some other times of the day, at least by ejaculations and short addresses, more or less, longer or shorter, solemnly or without solemnity, privately or publicly, as you can, or are permitted; always remembering, that as every sin is a degree of danger and unsafety, so every pious prayer and well-employed opportunity is a degree of return to hope and pardon.

[12] 1 Tim. ii. 8.   [13] 1 Tim. ii. 1—3

Cautions for making Vows.

17. A vow to God is an act of prayer, and a great degree and instance of opportunity, and an increase of duty by some new uncommanded instance, or some more eminent degree of duty, or frequency of action, or earnestness of spirit in the same. And because it hath pleased God, in all ages of the world, to admit of intercourse with his servants in the matters of vows, it is not ill advice that we make vows to God in such cases in which we have great need or great danger. But let it be done according to these rules and by these cautions.

1. That the matter of the vow be lawful. 2. That it be useful in order to religion or charity. 3. That it be grave, not trifling or impertinent; but great in our proportion of duty towards the blessing. 4. That it be an uncommanded instance; that is, that it be of something, or in some manner, or in some degree, to which formerly we were not obliged, or which we might have omitted without sin. 5. That it be done with prudence; that is, that it be safe in all the circumstances of person, lest we beg a blessing and fall into a snare. 6. That every vow of a new action be also accompanied with a new degree and enforcement of our essential and unalterable duty—such as was Jacob's vow, that (besides the payment of a tithe) God should be his God; that so he might strengthen his duty to him, first in essentials and precepts, and then in additionals and accidentals. For it is but an ill tree that spends more in leaves, and suckers, and gums, than in fruit; and that thankfulness and religion is best that first secures duty and then enlarges in counsels. Therefore let every great prayer, and great need, and great danger, draw us nearer to God by the approach of a pious purpose to live more strictly; and let every mercy of God answering that prayer produce a real performance of it. 7. Let not young beginners in religion enlarge their hearts and straiten their liberty by vows of long continuance; nor, indeed, any one else, without a great experience of himself and of all accidental dangers.[14] Vows of single actions are safest, and proportionable to those single blessings

[14] Angustum annulum non gesta, dixit Pythag., id est, vitæ genus liberum sectare, nec vinculo temetipsum obstringe.—Plutarch. Sic Novatus novitios suos compulit ad jurandum, nè unquam ad Catholicos episcopos redirent.—Euseb. l. ii. Eccl. Hist.

ever begged in such cases of sudden and transient importuni-
ties. 8. Let no action which is matter of question and dispute in religion ever become the matter of a vow. He vows
foolishly that promises to God to live and die in such an
opinion in an article not necessary nor certain; or that, upon
confidence of his present guide, binds himself for ever to the
profession of what he may afterwards more reasonably contradict, or may find not to be useful, or not profitable, but of
some danger or of no necessity.

If we observe the former rules we shall pray piously and
effectually; but because even this duty hath in it some special
temptations, it is necessary that we be armed by special remedies against them. The dangers are, 1. Wandering thoughts;
2. Tediousness of spirit. Against the first these advices are
profitable.

Remedies against Wandering Thoughts in Prayer.

If we feel our spirits apt to wander in our prayers, and to
retire into the world, or to things unprofitable, or vain and
impertinent;

1. Use prayer to be assisted in prayer; pray for the spirit
of supplication, for a sober, fixed, and recollected spirit; and
when to this you add a moral industry to be steady in your
thoughts, whatsoever wanderings after this do return irreme-
diably are a misery of nature and an imperfection, but no sin,
while it is not cherished and indulged to.

2. In private it is not amiss to attempt the cure by reducing your prayers into collects and short forms of prayer,
making voluntary interruptions; and beginning again, that
the want of spirit and breath may be supplied by the short
stages and periods.

3. When you have observed any considerable wanderings
of your thoughts, bind yourself to repeat that prayer again
with actual attention, or else revolve the full sense of it in
your spirit, and repeat it in all the effect and desires of it;
and, possibly, the tempter may be driven away with his own
art, and may cease to interpose his trifles when he perceives
they do but vex the person into carefulness and piety; and
yet he loses nothing of his devotion, but doubles the earnestness of his care.

4. If this be not seasonable or opportune, or apt to any

man's circumstances, yet be sure, with actual attention, to say a hearty Amen to the whole prayer with one united desire, earnestly begging the graces mentioned in the prayer; for that desire does the great work of the prayer, and secures the blessing, if the wandering thoughts were against our will, and disclaimed by contending against them.

5. Avoid multiplicity of businesses of the world; and in those that are unavoidable, labour for an evenness and tranquillity of spirit, that you may be untroubled and smooth in all tempests of fortune; for so we shall better tend religion when we are not torn in pieces with the cares of the world, and seized upon with low affections, passions, and interest.

6. It helps much to attention and actual advertisement in our prayers, if we say our prayers silently, without the voice, only by the spirit. For, in mental prayer, if our thoughts wander we only stand still; when our mind returns we go on again—there is none of the prayer lost, as it is if our mouths speak and our hearts wander.

7. To incite you to the use of these, or any other counsels you shall meet with, remember that it is a great indecency to desire of God to hear those prayers a great part whereof we do not hear ourselves. If they be not worthy of our attention they are far more unworthy of God's.

Signs of Tediousness of Spirit in our Prayers and all Actions of Religion.

The second temptation in our prayer is a tediousness of spirit or a weariness of the employment; like that of the Jews, who complained that they were weary of the new moons, and their souls loathed the frequent return of their sabbaths: so do very many Christians, who first pray without fervour and earnestness of spirit; and, secondly, meditate but seldom, and that without fruit, or sense, or affection; or, thirdly, who seldom examine their consciences, and when they do it, they do it but sleepily, slightly, without compunction, or hearty purpose, or fruits of amendment. 4. They enlarge themselves in the thoughts and fruition of temporal things, running for comfort to them only in any sadness and misfortune. 5. They love not to frequent the sacraments, nor any the instruments of religion, as sermons, confessions, prayers in public, fastings; but love ease and a loose undisciplined life. 6. They obey not their superiors, but follow their own judgment when their judgment follows their affections, and their affections follow sense and worldly pleasures. 7. They neglect, or dissemble, or defer, or do not attend to the motions and inclinations to virtue which the Spirit of God puts into their soul. 8. They repent them of their vows and holy purposes, not because they discover any indiscretion in them, or intolerable inconvenience, but because they have within them labour, (as the case now stands,) to them displeasure. 9. They content themselves with the first degrees and necessary parts of virtue; and when they are arrived thither, they sit down as if they were come to the mountain of the Lord, and care not to proceed on toward perfection. 10. They inquire into all cases in which it may be lawful to omit a duty; and, though they will not do less than they are bound to, yet they will do no more than needs must; for they do out of fear and self-love, not out of the love of God, or the spirit of holiness and zeal. The event of which will be this : he that will do no more than needs must, will soon be brought to omit something of his duty, and will be apt to believe less to be necessary than is.

Remedies against Tediousness of Spirit.

The remedies against this temptation are these.

1. Order your private devotions so that they become not arguments and causes of tediousness by their indiscreet length, but reduce your words into a narrow compass, still keeping all the matter; and what is cut off in the length of your prayers supply in the earnestness of your spirit; for so nothing is lost, while the words are changed into matter, and length of time into fervency of devotion. The forms are made not the less perfect, and the spirit is more, and the scruple is removed.

2. It is not imprudent, if we provide variety of forms of prayer to the same purposes, that the change, by consulting with the appetites of fancy, may better entertain the spirit; and, possibly, we may be pleased to recite a hymn when a collect seems flat to us and unpleasant; and we are willing to sing rather than to say, or to sing this rather than that: we .are certain that variety is delightful; and whether that be natural to us, or an imperfection, yet if it be complied with, it may remove some part of the temptation.

3. Break your office and devotion into fragments, and make frequent returnings by ejaculation and abrupt intercourses with God; for so no length can oppress your tenderness and sickliness of spirit: and, by often praying in such manner and in all circumstances, we shall habituate our souls to prayer by making it the business of many lesser portions of our time: and by thrusting in between all our other employ- ments, it will make every thing relish of religion, and by degrees turn all into its nature.

4. Learn to abstract your thoughts and desires from plea- sures and things of the world; for nothing is a direct cure to this evil but cutting off all other loves and adherences. Order your affairs so that religion may be propounded to you as a reward, and prayer as your defence, and holy actions as your security, and charity and good works as your treasure. Con- sider that all things else are satisfactions but to the brutish part of a man; and that these are the refreshments and re- lishes of that noble part of us by which we are better than beasts; and whatsoever other instrument, exercise, or con- sideration, is of use to take our loves from the world, the same is apt to place them upon God.

5. Do not seek for deliciousness and sensible consolations in the actions of religion, but only regard the duty and the conscience of it; for although in the beginning of religion most frequently, and at some other times irregularly, God complies with our infirmity, and encourages our duty with little overflowings of spiritual joy, and sensible pleasure, and delicacies in prayer, so as we seem to feel some little beam of heaven and great refreshments from the spirit of consolation, yet this is not always safe for us to have, neither safe for us to expect and look for; and when we do, it is apt to make us cool in our inquiries and waitings upon Christ when we want them: it is a running after him, not for the miracles but for the loaves; not for the wonderful things of God, and the de- sires of pleasing him, but for the pleasures of pleasing our- selves. And as we must not judge our devotion to be barren or unfruitful when we want the overflowings of joy running over, so neither must we cease for want of them. If our spirits can serve God choosingly and greedily out of pure con- science of our duty, it is better in itself and more safe to us.

6. Let him use to soften his spirit with frequent meditation

P

upon sad and dolorous objects, as of death, the terrors of the day of judgment, fearful judgments upon sinners, strange horrid accidents, fear of God's wrath, the pains of hell, the unspeakable amazements of the damned, the intolerable load of sad eternity: for whatsoever creates fear, or makes the spirit to dwell in a religious sadness, is apt to entender the spirit and make it devout and pliant to any part of duty; for a great fear, when it is ill managed, is the parent of superstition; but a discreet and well-guided fear produces religion.

7. Pray often, and you shall pray oftener; and when you are accustomed to a frequent devotion, it will so insensibly unite to your nature and affections, that it will become trouble to omit your usual or appointed prayers; and what you obtain at first by doing violence to your inclinations, at last will not be left without as great unwillingness as that by which at first it entered. This rule relies not only upon reason derived from the nature of habits, which turn into a second nature, and make their actions easy, frequent, and delightful: but it relies upon a reason depending upon the nature and constitution of grace, whose productions are of the same nature with the parent, and increases itself, naturally growing from grains to huge trees, from minutes to vast proportions, and from moments to eternity. But be sure not to omit your usual prayers without great reason, though without sin it may be done; because after you have omitted something, in a little while you will be past the scruple of that, and begin to be tempted to leave out more. Keep yourself up to your usual forms—you may enlarge when you will; but do not contract or lessen them without a very probable reason.

8. Let a man frequently and seriously, by imagination, place himself upon his death-bed, and consider what great joys he shall have for the remembrance of every day well spent, and what then he would give that he had so spent all his days. He may guess at it by proportions; for it is certain he shall have a joyful and prosperous night who hath spent his day holily; and he resigns his soul with peace into the hands of God, who hath lived in the peace of God and the works of religion in his life-time. This consideration is of a real event; it is of a thing that will certainly come to pass. "It is appointed for all men once to die; and after death" comes "judgment;" the apprehension of which is dreadful, and the prs

sence of it is intolerable; unless, by religion and sanctity, we
are disposed for so venerable an appearance.

9. To this may be useful that we consider the easiness of
Christ's yoke,[15] the excellences and sweetnesses that are in
religion, the peace of conscience, the joy of the Holy Ghost,
the rejoicing in God, the simplicity and pleasure of virtue,
the intricacy, trouble, and business of sin; the blessings and
health, and reward of that; the curses, the sicknesses, and
sad consequences of this; and that, if we are weary of the labours of religion, we must eternally sit still and do nothing;
for whatsoever we do contrary to it is infinitely more full of
labour, care, difficulty, and vexation.

10. Consider this also, that tediousness of spirit is the beginning of the most dangerous condition and estate in the
whole world. For it is a great disposition to the sin against
the Holy Ghost: it is apt to bring a man to backsliding and
the state of unregeneration; to make him return to his vomit
and his sink; and either to make the man impatient, or his
condition scrupulous, unsatisfied, irksome, and desperate: and
it is better that he had never known the way of godliness,
than, after the knowledge of it, that he should fall away.
There is not in the world a greater sign that the spirit of re-
probation is beginning upon a man, than when he is habitually
and constantly, or very frequently, weary, and slights or
loathes holy offices.

11. The last remedy that preserves the hope of such a
man, and can reduce him to the state of zeal and the love of
God, is a pungent, sad, and a heavy affliction; not desperate,
but recreated with some intervals of kindness, or little comforts, or entertained with hopes of deliverance; which condition, if a man shall fall into, by the grace of God he is likely
to recover; but, if this help him not, it is infinite odds but he
will quench the Spirit.

Sect. VIII. *Of Alms.*

LOVE is as communicative as fire, as busy and as active, and
it hath four twin daughters, extreme like each other; and
but that the doctors of the school have done, as Thamar's
midwife did, who bound a scarlet thread, something to dis-

[15] See the Great Exemplar, Part iii. Disc. xiv., of the Easiness of
Christian Religion.

tinguish them, it would be very hard to call them asunder
Their names are, 1. Mercy; 2. Beneficence, or well-doing,
3. Liberality; and, 4. Alms; which, by a special privilege,
hath obtained to be called after the mother's name, and is
commonly called Charity. The first, or eldest, is seated in the
affection: and it is that which all the other must attend; for
mercy without alms is acceptable when the person is disabled
to express outwardly what he heartily desires. But alms
without mercy are like prayers without devotion, or religion
without humility. 2. Beneficence, or well-doing, is a promptness and nobleness of mind, making us to do offices of courtesy
and humanity to all sorts of persons in their need, or out of
their need. 3. Liberality is a disposition of mind opposite to
covetousness; and consists in the despite and neglect of money
upon just occasions, and relates to our friends, children, kindred, servants, and other relatives. 4. But alms is a relieving
the poor and needy.—The first and the last only are duties of
Christianity. The second and third are circumstances and
adjuncts of these duties; for liberality increases the degree of
alms, making our gift greater; and beneficence extends it to
more persons and orders of men, spreading it wider. The
former makes us sometimes to give more than we are able;
and the latter gives to more than need by the necessity of beggars, and serves the needs and conveniences of persons, and
supplies circumstances; whereas, properly, alms are doles and
largesses to the necessitous and calamitous people, supplying
the necessities of nature, and giving remedies to their miseries.

Mercy and alms are the body and soul of that charity which
we must pay to our neighbour's need; and it is a precept
which God therefore enjoined to the world, that the great in-
equality which he was pleased to suffer in the possessions and
accidents of men might be reduced to some temper and evenness, and the most miserable person might be reconciled to
some sense and participation of felicity.

Works of Mercy, or the several Kinds of corporal Alms.

The works of mercy are so many as the affections of mercy
have objects, or as the world hath kinds of misery. Men want
meat, or drink, or clothes, or a house, or liberty, or attendance,
or a grave. In proportion to these, seven works are usually
assigned to mercy, and there are seven kinds of corporal alms

reckoned: 1. To feed the hungry;[1] 2. To give drink to the thirsty; 3. Or clothes to the naked; 4. To redeem captives; 5. To visit the sick; 6. To entertain strangers; 7. To bury the dead.[2] But many more may be added. Such as are, 8. To give physic to sick persons; 9. To bring cold and starved people to warmth and to the fire—for sometimes clothing will not do it, or this may be done when we cannot do the other. 10. To lead the blind in right ways; 11. To lend money; 12. To forgive debts; 13. To remit forfeitures; 14. To mend highways and bridges; 15. To reduce or guide wandering travellers; 16. To ease their labours by accommodating their work with apt instruments, or their journey with beasts of carriage; 17. To deliver the poor from their oppressors; 18. To die for my brother;[3] 19. To pay maidens' dowries, and to procure for them honest and chaste marriages.

Works of Spiritual Alms and Mercy are—

1. To teach the ignorant; 2. To counsel doubting persons; 3. To admonish sinners diligently, prudently, seasonably, and charitably; to which also may be reduced, provoking and encouraging to good works;[4] 4. To comfort the afflicted; 5. To pardon offenders; 6. To suffer and support the weak;[5] 7. To pray for all estates of men, and for relief to all their necessities. To which may be added, 8. To punish or correct refractoriness; 9. To be gentle and charitable in censuring the actions of others; 10. To establish the scrupulous, wavering, and inconstant spirits; 11. To confirm the strong; 12. Not to give scandal; 13. To quit a man of his fear; 14. To redeem maidens from prostitution and publication of their bodies.[6]

To both these kinds a third also may be added of a mixed nature, partly corporal, and partly spiritual: such are, 1. Reconciling enemies;[7] 2. Erecting public schools of learning; 3. Maintaining lectures of divinity; 4. Erecting colleges of religion and retirement from the noises and more frequent temptations of the world; 5. Finding employment for un-

---

[1] Matt. xxv. 35.   [2] Matt. xxvi. 12; 2 Sam. ii. 5.

[3] Nobilis hæc esset pietatis rixa duobus;
Quòd pro fratre mori vellet uterque prior.—Mart.

[4] Heb. x. 24.   [5] 1 Thess. v. 14.

[6] Puella prosternit se ad pedes: Miserere virginitatis meæ, nè prostituas hoc corpus sub tam turpi titulo.—Hist. Apol. Tya.   [7] Laudi ductum apud vet., αἴψά τε καὶ μέγα νεῖκος ἔπιε ρέπαυσε.

busied persons, and putting children to honest trades. For the particulars of mercy or alms cannot be narrower than men's needs are ; and the old method of alms is too narrow to comprise them all ; and yet the kinds are too many to be discoursed of particularly ; only our blessed Saviour, in the precept of alms, uses the instances of relieving the poor, and forgiveness of injuries; and by proportion to these, the rest, whose duty is plain, simple, easy, and necessary, may be determined. But alms in general are to be disposed of according to the following rules :—

Rules for giving Alms.

1. Let no man do alms of that which is none of his own ;[8] for of that he is to make restitution ; that is due to the owners, not to the poor: for every man hath need of his own, and that is first to be provided for ; and then you must think of the needs of the poor. He that gives the poor what is not his own, makes himself a thief, and the poor to be the receivers. This is not to be understood as if it were unlawful for a man that is not able to pay his debts to give smaller alms to the poor. He may not give such portions as can in any sense more disable him to do justice ;[9] but such which if they were saved could not advance the other duty, may retire to this, and do here what they may, since, in the other duty, they cannot do what they should. But, generally, cheaters and robbers cannot give alms of what they have cheated and robbed, unless they cannot tell the persons whom they have injured, or the proportions ; and, in such cases, they are to give those unknown portions to the poor by way of restitution, for it is no alms ; only God is the supreme Lord to whom those escheats devolve, and the poor are his receivers.

2. Of money unjustly taken, and yet voluntarily parted with, we may, and are bound, to give alms ; such as is money given and taken for false witness, bribes, simoniacal contracts ; because the receiver hath no right to keep it, nor the giver any right to recall it; it is unjust money, and yet payable to none but the supreme Lord, (who is the person injured,) and to his delegates, that is, the poor. To which I insert these cautions : 1. If the person injured by the unjust sentence of

[8] S. Greg. vii. l. 110. Epist.   [9] Præbeant misericordiâ, ut conservetur justitia.—St. Aug. Prov. iii. 9.

& bribed judge, or by false witness, be poor, he is the proper object and bosom to whom the restitution is to be made. 2. In the case of simony[10] the church, to whom the simony was injurious, is the lap into which the restitution is to be poured; and if it be poor and out of repair, the alms, or restitution, (shall I call it?) are to be paid to it.

3. There is some sort of gain that hath in it no injustice, properly so called; but it is unlawful and filthy lucre; such as is money taken for work done unlawfully upon the Lord's day; hire taken for disfiguring oneself, and for being professed jesters; the wages of such as make unjust bargains, and of harlots. Of this money there is some preparation to be made before it be given in alms: the money is infected with the plague, and must pass through the fire or the water before it be fit for alms; the person must repent and leave the crime, and then minister to the poor.

4. He that gives alms must do it in mercy; that is, out of a true sense of the calamity of his brother, first feeling it in himself in some proportion, and then endeavouring to ease himself and the other of their common calamity.[11] Against this rule they offend who give alms out of custom, or to upbraid the poverty of the other, or to make him mercenary and obliged, or with any unhandsome circumstances.

5. He that gives alms must do it with a single eye and heart; that is, without designs to get the praise of men; and if he secures that, he may either give them publicly or privately: for Christ intended only to provide against pride and hypocrisy when he bade alms to be given in secret: it being otherwise one of his commandments, "that our light should shine before men:" this is more excellent; that is more safe.

6. To this also appertains that he who hath done a good turn should so forget it as not to speak of it;[12] but he that boasts it, or upbraids it, hath paid himself, and lost the nobleness of the charity.

7. Give alms with a cheerful heart and countenance; "not grudgingly or of necessity, for God loveth a cheerful giver;"[13] and therefore give quickly when the power is in thy hand, and the need is in thy neighbour, and thy neighbour at the door. He gives twice that relieves speedily.

[10] Decret. ep. tit. de Simonia. sensu vestiatur. l. iii. C. de Pactis. ~~~et, qui accepit.—Senec.

[11] Donum nudum est, nisi consensu
[12] Qui dedit beneficium, taceat;
[13] 2 Cor. ix. 7.

8. According to thy ability give to all men that need ;[14] and in equal needs, give first to good men rather than to bad men: and if the needs be unequal, do so too, provided that the need of the poorest be not violent or extreme; but, if an evil man be in extreme necessity, he is to be relieved rather than a good man who can tarry longer, and may subsist without it; and if he be a good man, he will desire it should be so, because himself is bound to save the life of his brother with doing some inconvenience to himself; and no difference of virtue or vice can make the ease of one beggar equal with the life of another.

9. Give no alms to vicious persons, if such alms will support their sin: as if they will continue in idleness; " if they will not work, neither let them eat ;"[15] or if they will spend it in drunkenness,[16] or wantonness : such persons, when they are reduced to very great want, must be relieved in such proportions as may not relieve their dying lust, but may refresh their faint or dying bodies.

10. The best objects of charity are, poor housekeepers that labour hard, and are burdened with many children ; or gentlemen fallen into sad poverty, especially if by innocent misfortune (and if their crimes brought them into it, yet they are to be relieved according to the former rule) ; persecuted persons; widows, and fatherless children, putting them to honest trades or schools of learning. And search into the needs of numerous and meaner families,[17] for there are many persons that have nothing left them but misery and modesty ; and towards such we must add two circumstances of charity : 1. To inquire them out; 2. To convey our relief to them so as we do not make them ashamed.

11. Give, looking for nothing again; that is, without consideration of future advantages : give to children, to old men, to the unthankful, and the dying, and to those you shall never see again ; for else your alms or courtesy is not charity, but traffic and merchandise ; and be sure that you omit not to relieve the needs of your enemy and the injurious ; for so, pos-

---

[14] Luke vi. 30; Gal. vi. 10.   [15] 2 Thess. iii. 10.   A cavallo chi non porta sella, biada non si crivella.

[16] De mendico malè meretur, qui ei dat quod edat aut quod bibat :
Nam et illud quod dat perdit, et illi producit vitam ad miseriam.

Trin.

[17] Beatus qui intelligit super egenum et pauperem.—Psal.   A donari è tenere ingegno bisogna avere.

sibly, you may win him to yourself; but do you intend the winning him to God.

12. Trust not your alms to intermedial, uncertain, and under dispensers: by which rule is not only intended the securing your alms in the right channel, but the humility of your person, and that which the apostle calls "the labour of love." And if you converse in hospitals and alms-houses, and minister with your own hand what your heart hath first decreed, you will find your heart endeared and made familiar with the needs and with the persons of the poor, those excellent images of Christ.

13. Whatsoever is superfluous in thy estate is to be dispensed in alms.[18] "He that hath two coats must give to him that hath none;" that is, he that hath beyond his need must give that which is beyond it. Only among needs, we are to reckon not only what will support our life, but also what will maintain the decency of our estate and person, not only in present needs, but in all future necessities, and very probable contingencies, but no further; we are not obliged beyond this, unless we see very great, public, and calamitous necessities. But yet, if we do extend beyond our measures, and give more than we are able, we have the Philippians and many holy persons for our precedent; we have St. Paul for our encouragement; we have Christ for our counsellor; we have God for our rewarder; and a great treasure in heaven for our recompence and restitution. But I propound it to the consideration of all Christian people, that they be not nice and curious, fond and indulgent to themselves in taking accounts of their personal conveniences; and that they make their proportions moderate and easy, according to the order and manner of Christianity; and the consequent will be this, that the poor will more plentifully be relieved, themselves will be more able to do it, and the duty will be less chargeable, and the owners of estates charged with fewer accounts in the spending them. It cannot be denied, but in the expenses of all liberal and great personages, many things might be spared: some superfluous servants, some idle meetings, some unnecessary and imprudent feasts, some garments too costly, some unnecessary law-suits, some vain journeys; and when we are tempted

[18] ————— Præmonstro tibi
Ut ita te aliorum miserescat, nè tui alios misereat.—Trinummus.

to such needless expenses, if we shall descend to moderation, and lay aside the surplusage, we shall find it with more
profit to be laid out upon the poor members of Christ than
upon our own with vanity.   But this is only intended to be an
advice in the manner of doing alms; for I am not ignorant
that great variety of clothes always have been permitted to
princes and nobility, and others in their proportion; and they
usually give those clothes as rewards to servants, and other
persons needful enough, and then they may serve their own
fancy, and their duty too; but it is but reason and religion to
be careful that they be given to such only where duty, or prudent liberality, or alms determine them; but, in no sense, let
them do it so as to minister to vanity, to luxury, to prodigality.
The like also is to be observed in other instances; and if we
once give our minds to the study and arts of alms, we shall find
ways enough to make this duty easy, profitable, and useful.

1. He that plays at any game must resolve beforehand to be
indifferent to win or lose; but if he gives to the poor all that
he wins, it is better than to keep it to himself; but it were
better yet that he lay by so much as he is willing to lose, and
let the game alone, and, by giving so much alms, traffic for
eternity.   That is one way.

2. Another is keeping the fasting-days of the church, which,
if our condition be such as to be able to cast our accounts, and
make abatements for our wanting so many meals in the whole
year, (which by the old appointment did amount to one hundred and fifty-three, and since most of them are fallen into
desuetude, we may make up as many of them as we please by
voluntary fasts,) we may, from hence, find a considerable relief
for the poor.   But if we be not willing sometimes to fast, that
our brother may eat, we should ill die for him.   St. Martin
had given all that he had in the world to the poor save one
coat; and that also he divided between two beggars.   A father
in the mount of Nitria was reduced at last to the inventory of
one Testament, and that book also was tempted from him by
the needs of one whom he thought poorer than himself.
Greater yet: St. Paulinus sold himself to slavery to redeem a
young man for whose captivity his mother wept sadly; and it
is said that St. Katherine sucked the envenomed wounds of a
villain who had injured her most impudently.   And I shall
tell you of a greater charity than all these put together: Christ

gave himself to shame and death to redeem his enemies from bondage, and death, and hell.

3. Learn of the frugal man, and only avoid sordid actions, and turn good husband, and change your arts of getting into providence for the poor, and we shall soon become rich in good works: and why should we not do as much for charity, as for covetousness; for heaven, as for the fading world; for God and the holy Jesus, as for the needless superfluities of back and belly?

14. In giving alms to beggars and persons of that low rank, it is better to give little to each, that we may give to the more; so extending our alms to many persons: but in charities of religion, as building hospitals, colleges, and houses for devotion, and supplying the accidental wants of decayed persons, fallen from great plenty to great necessity, it is better to unite our alms than to disperse them; to make a noble relief or maintenance to one, and to restore him to comfort, than to support only his natural needs, and keep him alive only, unrescued from sad discomforts.

15. The precept of alms or charity binds not indefinitely to all the instances and kinds of charity : for he that delights to feed the poor, and spends all his portion that way, is not bound to enter into prisons and redeem captives; but we are obliged by the presence of circumstances, and the special disposition of Providence, and the pitiableness of an object, to this or that particular act of charity. The eye is the sense of mercy, and the bowels are its organ ; and that enkindles pity, and pity produces alms: when the eye sees what it never saw, the heart will think what it never thought; but when we have an object present to our eye, then we must pity; for there the providence of God hath fitted our charity with circumstances. He that is in thy sight, or in thy neighbourhood, is fallen into the lot of thy charity.

16. If thou hast no money,[19] yet thou must have mercy, and art bound to pity the poor, and pray for them, and throw thy holy desires and devotions into the treasure of the church ; and if thou dost what thou art able, be it little or great, corporal or spiritual, the charity of alms or the charity of prayers, a cup of wine or a cup of water, if it be but love to the brethren,[20]

[19] Luke xii. 2 ; Acts iii. 6.   Chi ti da un' ossa, non ti verrebbe morto.
[20] 1 Pet. i. 22.

or a desire to help all or any of Christ's poor, it shall be accepted according to that a man hath, not according to that he
hath not.[21] For love is all this, and all the other commandments ; and it will express itself where it can ; and where it
cannot, yet it is love still ; and it is also sorrow that it cannot.

Motives to Charity.

The motives to this duty are such, as Holy Scripture hath
propounded to us by way of consideration and proposition of
its excellences and consequent reward. 1. There is no one
duty which our blessed Saviour did recommend to his disciples
with so repeated an injunction as this of charity and alms.[22]
To which add the words spoken by our Lord, " It is better to
give than to receive." And when we consider how great a
blessing it is that we beg not from door to door, it is a ready
instance of our thankfulness to God, for his sake to relieve them
that do. 2. This duty is that alone whereby the future day
of judgment shall be transacted. For nothing but charity and
alms is that whereby Christ shall declare the justice and mercy
of the eternal sentence. Martyrdom itself is not there expressed, and no otherwise involved, but as it is the greatest
charity. 3. Christ made himself the greatest and daily example
of alms or charity. He went up and down doing good, preaching the gospel, and healing all diseases: and God the Father
is imitable by us in nothing but in purity and mercy. 4. Alms
given to the poor redound to the emolument of the giver both
temporal and eternal.[23] 5. They are instrumental to the remission of sins; our forgiveness and mercy to others cing
made the very rule and proportion of our confidence and hope,
and our prayer to be forgiven ourselves.[24] 6. It is a treasure
in heaven ; it procures friends when we die. It is reckoned
as done to Christ, whatsoever we do to our poor brother ; and,
therefore, when a poor man begs for Christ's sake, if he have
reason to ask for Christ's sake, give it him if thou canst. Now
every man hath title to ask for Christ's sake whose need is
great, and himself unable to cure it, and if the man be a Christian. Whatsoever charity Christ will reward, all that is given
for Christ's sake, and therefore it may be asked in his name ;
but every man that uses that sacred name for an endearment

[21] 2 Cor. viii. 12.   [22] Matt. vi. 4; xxv. 45; Luke xi. 41; xii. 33.
[23] Phil. iv. 17.   [24] Acts x. 4 : Heb. xiii. 16; Dan. iv. 27.

hath not a title to it, neither he nor his need. 7. It is one of the wings of prayer, by which it flies to the throne of grace. 8. It crowns all the works of piety.[25] 9. It causes thanksgiving to God on our behalf : 10. And the bowels of the poor bless us, and they pray for us. 11. And that portion of our estate out of which a tenth, or a fifth, or a twentieth, or some offering to God for religion and the poor goes forth, certainly returns with a great blessing upon all the rest. It is like the effusion of oil by the Sidonian woman ; as long as she pours into empty vessels it could never cease running ; or like the widow's barrel of meal, it consumed not as long as she fed the prophet. 12. The sum of all is contained in the words of our blessed Saviour : " Give alms of such things as you have, and behold all things are clean unto you." 13. To which may be added, that charity or mercy is the peculiar character of God's elect, and a sign of predestination, which advantage we are taught by St. Paul : " Put on, therefore, as the elect of God, holy and beloved, bowels of mercy, kindness, &c. Forbearing one another, and forgiving one another, if any man have a quarrel against any."[26] The result of all which we may read in the words of St. Chrysostom : " To know the art of alms is greater than to be crowned with the diadem of kings. And yet to convert one soul is greater than to pour out ten thousand talents into the baskets of the poor."

But because giving alms is an act of the virtue of mercifulness, our endeavour must be, by proper arts, to mortify the parents of unmercifulness, which are, 1. Envy; 2. Anger ; 3. Covetousness: in which we may be helped by the following rules or instruments :—

Remedies against Unmercifulness and Uncharitableness.

1. *Against Envy, by way of consideration.*

Against envy I shall use the same argument I would use to persuade a man from the fever or the dropsy. 1. Because it is a disease ; it is so far from having pleasure in it or a temptation to it, that it is full of pain, a great instrument of vexation : it eats the flesh and dries up the marrow, and makes hollow eyes and lean cheeks and a pale face. 2. It is nothing but a direct resolution never to enter into heaven by the way

---

[24] Nunquam memini me legisse malâ morte mortuum, qui libenter opera charitatis exercuit.—St. Hieron. Ep. ad Nepot.   [26] Coloss. iii. 12.

cf noble pleasure taken in the good of others.   3. It is most
contrary to God.   4. And a just contrary state to the felicities
and actions of heaven, where every star increases the light of
the other, and the multitudes of guests at the supper of the
Lamb makes the eternal meal more festival.   5. It is perfectly
the state of hell and the passion of devils; for they do nothing
but despair in themselves,[27] and envy others' quiet or safety,
and yet cannot rejoice either in their good or in their evil, although they endeavour to hinder that and procure this with
all the devices and arts of malice and of a great understanding.
6. Envy can serve no end in the world: it cannot please any
thing, nor do any thing, nor hinder any thing, but the content and felicity of him that hath it.   7. Envy can never pretend to justice, as hatred and uncharitableness sometimes may:
for there may be causes of hatred, and I may have wrong
done me, and then hatred hath some pretence, though no just
argument.   But no man is unjust or injurious for being prosperous or wise.   8. And therefore many men profess to hate
another, but no man owns envy, as being an enmity and displeasure for no cause, but goodness or felicity: envious men
being like cantharides and caterpillars, that delight most to
devour ripe and most excellent fruits.[28] 2. It is of all crimes
the basest: for malice and anger are appeased with benefits,
but envy is exasperated, as envying to fortunate persons both
their power and their will to do good, and never leaves murmuring till the envied person be levelled, and then only the
vulture leaves to eat the liver.   For if his neighbour be made
miserable, the envious man is apt to be troubled; like him
that is so long unbuilding the turrets, till all the roof is low
or flat, or that the stones fall upon the lower buildings and
do a mischief, that the man repents of.

2. Remedies against Anger, by way of exercise.

The next enemy to mercifulness and the grace of alms is
anger; against which there are proper instruments both in
prudence and religion.

1. Prayer is the great remedy against anger: for it must
suppose it, in some degree, removed before we pray, and then

---

[27] Nemo alienæ virtuti invidet, qui satis confidit suæ.—Cic. contra M.
Anton.   [28] Homerus, Thersitis malos mores describens, malitiæ summam apposuit, Pelidæ imprimis erat a que inimicus Ulyssi.

it is the more likely it will be finished when the prayer is done. We must lay aside the act of anger as a preparatory to prayer; and the curing the habit will be the effect and blessing of prayer: so that if a man, to cure his anger, resolves to address himself to God by prayer, it is first necessary that, by his own observation and diligence, he lay the anger aside before his prayer can be fit to be presented; and when we so pray, and so endeavour, we have all the blessings of prayer which God hath promised to it to be our security for success.

2. If anger arises in thy breast, instantly seal up thy lips and let it not go forth;[29] for, like fire when it wants vent, it will suppress itself. It is good, in a fever, to have a tender and a smooth tongue; but it is better that it be so in anger: for if it be rough and distempered, there it is an ill sign, but here it is an ill cause. Angry passion is a fire, and angry words are like breath to fan them together; they are like steel and flint sending out fire by mutual collision. Some men will discourse themselves into passion; and if their neighbour be enkindled too, together they flame with rage and violence.

3. Humility is the most excellent natural cure for anger in the world; for he that, by daily considering his own infirmities and failings, makes the error of his neighbour or servant to be his own case, and remembers that he daily needs God's pardon and his brother's charity, will not be apt to rage at the levities, or misfortunes, or indiscretions of another, greater than which he considers that he is very frequently and more inexcusably guilty of.

4. Consider the example of the ever blessed Jesus, who suffered all the contradictions of sinners, and received all affronts and reproaches of malicious, rash, and foolish persons, and yet in all of them was as dispassionate and gentle as the morning sun in autumn; and in this also he propounded himself imitable by us. For if innocence itself did suffer so great injuries and disgraces, it is no great matter for us quietly to receive all the calamities of fortune, and indiscretion of servants, and mistakes of friends, and unkindnesses of kindred, and rudenesses of enemies, since we have deserved these and worse, even hell itself.

[29] Ira cùm pectus rapida occupavit,
Futiles linguæ jubeo cavere
Vana latratus jaculantis.—Sappho.
Turbatus sum, et non sum locutus.—Psal. xxxix.

5. If we be tempted to anger in the actions of government
and discipline to our inferiors, (in which case anger is permitted so far as it is prudently instrumental to government, and
only is a sin when it is excessive and unreasonable, and ap'
to disturb our own discourse, or to express itself in impruden
words or violent actions,) let us propound to ourselves the example of God the Father, who, at the same time and with
the same tranquillity, decreed heaven and hell, the joys of
blessed angels and souls, and the torments of devils and accursed spirits; and at the day of judgment, when all the
world shall burn under his feet, God shall not be at all inflamed or shaken in his essential seat and centre of tranquillity and joy.   And if at first the cause seems reasonable, yet
defer to execute thy anger till thou mayest better judge. For,
as Phocion told the Athenians, who upon the first news of
the death of Alexander were ready to revolt, "Stay a while,
for if the king be not dead, your haste will ruin you; but if
he be dead, your stay cannot prejudice your affairs, for he
will be dead to-morrow as well as to-day:" so if thy servant
or inferior deserve punishment, staying till to-morrow will
not make him innocent; but it may possibly preserve thee so,
by preventing thy striking a guiltless person, or being furious for a trifle.

6. Remove from thyself all provocations and incentives to
anger; especially, 1. Games of chance and great wager. Patroclus killed his friend,[30] the son of Amphidamas, in his rage
and sudden fury, rising upon a cross game at tables.   Such
also are petty curiosities, and worldly business and carefulness about it; but manage thyself with indifferency or contempt of those external things, and do not spend a passion
upon them, for it is more than they are worth.   But they
that desire but few things, can be crossed but in a few.[31] 2. In
not heaping up, with an ambitious or curious prodigality, any
very curious or choice utensils, seals, jewels, glasses, precious
stones; because those very many accidents which happen in
the spoiling or loss of these rarities, are, in event, an irresistible
cause of violent anger. 3. Do not entertain nor suffer tale-
bearers; for they abuse our ears first, and then our credulity,

[30] Ἥματι τῷ, ὅτε, παῖδα κατέκτανον Ἀμφιδάμαντος,
    Νήπιος, οὐκ ἐθέλων, ἀμφ' ἀστραγάλοισι χολωθείς.—Iliad. ψ'. 87.
[31] Qui pauca requirunt, non multis excidunt.—Plut.

and then steal our patience, and, it may be, for a lie; and, if it be true, the matter is not considerable; or if it be, yet it is pardonable. And we may always escape with patience at one of these outlets; either, 1. By not hearing slanders; or, 2. By not believing them; or, 3. By not regarding the thing; or, 4. By forgiving the person. 4. To this purpose also it may serve well, if we choose (as much as we can) to live with peaceable persons, for that prevents the occasions of confusion; and if we live with prudent persons, they will not easily occasion our disturbance. But because these things are not in many men's power, therefore I propound this rather as a felicity than a remedy or a duty, and an art of prevention than of cure.

7. Be not inquisitive into the affairs of other men, nor the faults of thy servants, nor the mistakes of thy friends; but what is offered to you, use according to the former rules; but do not thou go out to gather sticks to kindle a fire to burn thine own house. And add this: "If my friend said or did well in that for which I am angry, I am in the fault, not he; but if he did amiss, he is in the misery, not I: for either he was deceived, or he was malicious; and either of them both is all one with a miserable person; and that is an object of pity, not of anger."

8. Use all reasonable discourses to excuse the faults of others; considering that there are many circumstances of time, of person, of accident, of inadvertency, of infrequency, of aptness to amend, of sorrow for doing it; and it is well that we take any good in exchange; for the evil is done or suffered.

9. Upon the arising of anger, instantly enter into a deep consideration of the joys of heaven, or the pains of hell; for "fear and joy are naturally apt to appease this violence."[32]

10. In contentions be always passive, never active; upon the defensive, not the assaulting part; and then also give a gentle answer, receiving the furies and indiscretions of the other, like a stone into a bed of moss and soft compliance, and you shall find it sit down quietly; whereas anger and violence make the contention loud and long, and injurious to both the parties.

11. In the actions of religion, be careful to temper all thy instances with meekness, and the proper instruments of it;

[32] Homer

Q

and if thou beest apt to be angry, neither fast violently, nor
entertain the too-forward heats of zeal, but secure thy duty
with constant and regular actions, and a good temper of body,
with convenient refreshments and recreations.

12. If anger rises suddenly and violently, first restrain it
with consideration; and then let it end in a hearty player for
him that did the real or seeming injury. The former of the
two stops its growth, and the latter quite kills it; and makes
amends for its monstrous and involuntary birth.

Remedies against Anger, by way of consideration.

1. Consider, that anger is a professed enemy to counsel;
it is a direct storm, in which no man can be heard to speak or
call from without: for if you counsel gently, you are despised;
if you urge it and be vehement, you provoke it more. Be
careful, therefore, to lay up beforehand a great stock of reason
and prudent consideration,[33] that, like a besieged town, you
may be provided for, and be defensible from within, since you
are not likely to be relieved from without. Anger is not to
be suppressed but by something that is as inward as itself and
more habitual. To which purpose add, that, 2. Of all passions
it endeavours most to make reason useless. 3. That it is a
universal poison, of an infinite object; for no man was ever so
amorous as to love a toad, none so envious as to repine at the
condition of the miserable, no man so timorous as to fear a
dead bee; but anger is troubled at every thing, and every
man, and every accident: and therefore, unless it be suppressed, it will make a man's condition restless. 4. If it proceeds from a great cause, it turns to fury; if from a small
cause, it is peevishness; and so is always either terrible or
ridiculous.[34] 5. It makes a man's body monstrous, deformed,
and contemptible; the voice horrid; the eyes cruel; the face
pale or fiery; the gait fierce; the speech clamorous and loud.
6. It is neither manly nor ingenuous. 7. It proceeds from
softness of spirit and pusillanimity; which makes that women
are more angry than men, sick persons more than the healthful, old men more than young, unprosperous and calamitous

---

[33] Καὶ μανθάνω μὲν, οἷα δρᾶν μέλλω κακά·

Θυμὸς δὲ κρείσσων τῶν ἐμῶν βουλευμάτων.—Medea, Porson. 1074.

[34] Ὁ Θυμὸς φόνων αἴτιον, συμφορᾶς σύμμαχον, βλάβης σύνεργον καὶ
ἀτιμίας, χρημάτων ἀπώλεια, ἔτι δὲ καὶ φθορᾶς ἀρχηγόν.—Aristot.

people than the blessed and fortunate. 8. It is a passion fitter for flies and insects than for persons professing nobleness and bounty. 9. It is troublesome not only to those that suffer it, but to them that behold it ; there being no greater incivility of entertainment, than for the cook's fault,[35] or the negligence of the servants, to be cruel or outrageous, or unpleasant in the presence of the guests. 10. It makes marriage to be a necessary and unavoidable trouble ; friendships, and societies, and familiarities, to be intolerable. 11. It multiplies the evils of drunkenness, and makes the levities of wine to run into madness. 12. It makes innocent jesting to be the beginning of tragedies. 13. It turns friendship into hatred ; it makes a man lose himself, and his reason, and his argument, in disputation. It turns the desires of knowledge into an itch of wrangling. It adds insolency to power. It turns justice into cruelty, and judgment into oppression. It changes discipline into tediousness and hatred of liberal institution. It makes a prosperous man to be envied, and the unfortunate to be unpitied. It is a confluence of all the irregular passions ; there is in it envy and sorrow, fear and scorn, pride and prejudice, rashness and inconsideration, rejoicing in evil and a desire to inflict it, self-love, impatience, and curiosity. And, lastly, though it be very troublesome to others, yet it is most troublesome to him that hath it.

In the use of these arguments and the former exercises, be diligent to observe lest, in your desires to suppress anger, you be passionate and angry at yourself for being angry ; like physicians[36] who give a bitter potion when they intend to eject the bitterness of choler ; for this will provoke the person and increase the passion. But placidly and quietly set upon the mortification of it, and attempt it first for a day, resolving that day not at all to be angry, and to be watchful and observant ; for a day is no great trouble : but then, after one day's watchfulness, it will be as easy to watch two days as at first it was to watch one day, and so you may increase till it becomes easy and habitual.

Only observe, that such an anger alone is criminal which is against charity to myself or my neighbour ; but anger against sin is a holy zeal, and an effect of love to God and my brother

---

[35] Dicere quid cœnâ possis ingratius istâ ?
[36] Amaram amaro bilem pharmaco qui eluunt

for whose int rest I am passionate, like a concerned person ;
and if I take care that my anger makes no reflection of scorn
or cruelty upon the offender, or of pride and violence, or trans-
portation to myself, anger becomes charity and duty.   And
when one commended Charilaus the king of Sparta for a gentle,
a good, and a meek prince, his colleague said well, " How can
he be good, who is not an enemy even to vicious persons ?[37]

3. *Remedies against Covetousness, the third Enemy of Mercy.*

Covetousness is also an enemy to alms, though not to all the
effects of mercifulness: but this is to be cured by the proper
motives to charity before mentioned, and by the proper rules
of justice, which being secured, the arts of getting money are
not easily made criminal.   To which also we may add :

1. Covetousness makes a man miserable,[38] because riches
are not means to make a man happy ; and unless felicity were
to be bought with money, he is a vain person who admires
heaps of gold and rich possessions.   For what Hippomachus
said to some persons, who commended a tall man as fit to be
a champion in the Olympic games, " It is true," said he, "if
the crown hang so high that the longest arm could reach it;"
the same we may say concerning riches ; they were excellent
things, if the richest man were certainly the wisest and the
best : but as they are, they are nothing to be wondered at,
because they contribute nothing towards felicity ; which appears, because some men choose to be miserable that they
may be rich, rather than be happy with the expense of money
and doing noble things.

2. Riches are useless and unprofitable ; for, beyond our
needs and conveniences, nature knows no use of riches : and
they say, that the princes of Italy, when they sup alone, eat
out of a single dish, and drink in a plain glass, and the wife
eats without purple ; for nothing is more frugal than the back
and belly, if they be used as they should ; but when they would
entertain the eyes of strangers, when they are vain, and would
make a noise, then riches come forth to set forth the spectacle,
and furnish out the comedy of wealth, of vanity.[39]   No man

[37] Plutar. de Odio et Invidiâ.
[38] Quid refert igitur quantis jumenta fatiget
Porticibus, quantâ nemorum vectetur in umbrâ,
Jugera quot vicina foro, quas emerit ædes ?
Nemo malus felix.   Juv. Sat.
[39] Plutarch.

cat , with all the wealth in the world, buy so much skill as to be a good lutenist; he must go the same way that poor people do, he must learn and take pains: much less can he buy constancy, or chastity, or courage; nay, not so much as the contempt of riches: and by possessing more than we need, we cannot obtain so much power over our souls as not to require more. And certainly riches must deliver me from no evil, if the possession of them cannot take away the longing for them. If any man be thirsty, drink cools him; if he be hungry, eating meat satisfies him; and when a man is cold and calls for a warm cloak, he is pleased if you give it him ; but you trouble him if you load him with six or eight cloaks. Nature rests, and sits still, when she hath her portion; but that which exceeds it is a trouble and a burden : and, therefore, in true philosophy, no man is rich but he that is poor according to the common account: for when God hath satisfied those needs which he made, that is, all that is natural, whatsoever is beyond it is thirst and a disease; and, unless it be sent back again in charity or religion, can serve no end but vice or vanity: it can increase the appetite to represent the man poorer, and full of a new and artificial, unnatural need ; but it never satisfies the need it makes, or makes the man richer. No wealth can satisfy the covetous desire of wealth.

3. Riches are troublesome; but the satisfaction of those appetites which God and nature hath made, are cheap and easy; for who ever paid use-money for bread, and onions, and water to keep him alive?[40] But when we covet after houses of the frame and design of Italy, or long for jewels, or for my next neighbour's field, or horses from Barbary, or the richest perfumes of Arabia, or Galatian mules, or fat eunuchs for our slaves from Tunis, or rich coaches from Naples, then we can never be satisfied till we have the best thing that is fancied, and all that can be had, and all that can be desired, and that we can lust no more ; but before we come to the one half of our first wild desires, we are the bondmen of usurers, and of our worse tyrant appetites, and the tortures of envy and impatience. But I consider that those who drink on still when their thirst is quenched, or eat after they have well dined, are forced to vomit not only their superfluity, but even that

[40] Ergo solicitæ tu causa, pecunia, vitæ es:
Per te immaturum mortis adimus iter.—Propert. 3. 7. 2.

which at first was necessary: so those that covet more than
they can temperately use, are oftentimes forced to part even
with that patrimony which would have supported their persons in freedom and honour, and have satisfied all their reasonable desires.

4. Contentedness is therefore health, because covetousness
is a direct sickness: and it was well said of Aristippus, (as
Plutarch reports him,) if any man, after much eating and
drinking, be still unsatisfied, he hath no need of more meat or
more drink, but of a physician; he more needs to be purged
than to be filled: and, therefore, since covetousness cannot be
satisfied, it must be cured by emptiness and evacuation. The
man is without remedy, unless he be reduced to the scantling
of nature, and the measures of his personal necessity. Give
to a poor man a house, and a few cows, pay his little debt, and
set him on work, and he is provided for, and quiet: but when
a man enlarges beyond a fair possession, and desires another
lordship, you spite him if you let him have it; for, by that,
he is one degree the further off from rest in his desires and
satisfaction; and now he sees himself in a bigger capacity to
a larger fortune; and he shall never find his period, till you
begin to take away something of what he hath; for then he
will begin to be glad to keep that which is left: but reduce
him to nature's measures, and there he shall be sure to find
rest: for there no man can desire beyond his bellyful; and,
when he wants that, any one friend or charitable man can cure
his poverty, but all the world cannot satisfy his covetousness.

5. Covetousness is the most fantastical and contradictory
disease in the whole world: it must therefore be incurable,
because it strives against its own cure. No man therefore
abstains from meat, because he is hungry; nor from wine, because he loves it and needs it: but the covetous man does so,
for he desires it passionately, because he says he needs it, and
when he hath it he will need it still, because he dares not use
it. He gets clothes, because he cannot be without them; but
when he hath them, then he can; as if he needed corn for his
granary, and clothes for his wardrobe, more than for his back
and belly. For covetousness pretends to heap much together
for fear of want; and yet, after all his pains and purchase, he
suffers that really, which, at first, he feared vainly; and by
not using what he gets, he makes that suffering to be actual,

present, and necessary, which, in his lowest condition, was but future, contingent, and possible. It stirs up the desire, and takes away the pleasure of being satisfied. It increases the appetite, and will not content it: it swells the principal to no purpose, and lessens the use to all purposes; disturbing the order of nature, and the designs of God; making money not to be the instrument of exchange or charity, nor corn to feed himself or the poor, nor wool to clothe himself or his brother, nor wine to refresh the sadness of the afflicted, nor his oil to make his own countenance cheerful; but all these to look upon, and to tell over, and to take accounts by, and make himself considerable, and wondered at by fools; that while he lives he may be called rich, and when he dies may be accounted miserable; and, like the dish-makers of China, may leave a greater heap of dirt for his nephews, while he himself hath a new lot fallen to him in the portion of Dives. But thus the ass carried wood and sweet herbs to the baths, but was never washed or perfumed himself: he heaped up sweets for others, while himself was filthy with smoke and ashes. And yet it is considerable; if the man can be content to feed hardly, and labour extremely, and watch carefully, and suffer affronts and disgrace, that he may get money more than he uses in his temperate and just needs, with how much ease might this man be happy! and with how great uneasiness and trouble does he make himself miserable! For he takes pains to get content, and when he might have it he lets it go. He might better be content with a virtuous and quiet poverty, than with an artificial, troublesome, and vicious. The same diet and a less labour would, at first, make him happy, and, for ever after, rewardable.

6. The sum of all is that which the apostle says, "Covetousness is idolatry;" that is, it is an admiring money for itself, not for its use; it relies upon money, and loves it more than it loves God and religion: and it is "the root of all evil;" it teaches men to be cruel and crafty, industrious in evil, full of care and malice; it devours young heirs, and grinds the face of the poor, and undoes those who specially belong to God's protection, helpless, craftless, and innocent people; it inquires into our parents' age, and longs for the death of our friends; it makes friendship an art of rapine, and changes a partner into a vulture, and a companion into a thief; and, after all this, it is for no good to itself; for it dares not spend those

heaps of treasure which it snatched: and men hate serpents
and basilisks worse than lions and bears; for these kill because
they need the prey, but they sting to death and eat not.[41] And
if they pretend all this care and heap for their heirs, (like the
mice of Africa, hiding the golden ore in their bowels, and refusing to give back the indigested gold till their guts be out,)
they may remember that what was unnecessary for themselves
is as unnecessary for their sons; and why cannot they be without it as well as their fathers who did not use it?   And it
often happens that to the sons it becomes an instrument to
serve some lust or other; that, as the gold was useless to their
fathers, so may the sons be to the public, fools or prodigals,
loads to their country, and the curse and punishment of their
father's avarice: and yet all that wealth is short of one blessing; but it is a load, coming with a curse, and descending
from the family of a long-derived sin.   However, the father
transmits it to the son, and it may be the son to one more; till
a tyrant, or an oppressor, or a war, or change of government,
or the usurer, or folly, or an expensive vice, makes holes in
the bottom of the bag, and the wealth runs out like water,
and flies away like a bird from the hand of a child.

7. Add to these the consideration of the advantages of poverty:[42] that it is a state freer from temptation, secure in
dangers, but of one trouble, safe under the Divine Providence,
cared for in heaven by a daily ministration, and for whose
support God makes every day a new decree; a state, of which
Christ was pleased to make open profession, and many wise
men daily make vows: that a rich man is but like a pool, to
whom the poor run, and first trouble it, and then draw it dry:
that he enjoys no more of it than according to the few and
limited needs of a man; he cannot eat like a wolf or an elephant; that variety of dainty fare ministers but to sin and
sicknesses: that the poor man feasts oftener than the rich,[43]

---

[41] Ἡ φιλοχρημοσύνη μήτηρ κακότητος ἁπάσης.
  Χρυσὸς ἀεὶ δόλος ἐστὶ καὶ ἄργυρος ἀνθρώποισιν.
  Χρυσὲ, κακῶν ἀρχηγὲ, βιοφθόρε, πάντα χαλέπτων,
  Εἴθέ σε μὴ θνητοῖσι γενέσθαι πῆμα ποθεινόν·
  Σοῦ γὰρ ἕκητι μάχαι τε, λεηλασίαι τε, φόνοι τε,
  Ἐχθρὰ δὲ τέκνα γονεῦσιν, ἀδελφειοί τε συναίμοις.—Phocylid 38.
[42] Provocet ut segnes animos, rerumque remotas
  Ingeniosa vias paulatim exploret egestas.—Claudian, 36. 3?.
[43] —————————————Sed olim
  Prodigio par est in nobilitate senectus.—Juven. Sat.

because every little enlargement is a feast to the poor, but he that feasts every day feasts no day, there being nothing left to which he may, beyond his ordinary, extend his appetite : that the rich man sleeps not so soundly as the poor labourer; that his fears are more, and his needs are greater (for who is poorer, he that needs 5*l.* or he that needs 5000*l.?*); the poor man hath enough to fill his belly, and the rich hath not enough to fill his eye ; that the poor man's wants are easy to be relieved by a common charity, but the needs of rich men cannot be supplied but by princes ; and they are left to the temptation of great vices to make reparation of their needs ; and the ambitious labours of men to get great estates is but like the selling of a fountain to buy a fever, a parting with content to buy necessity, a purchase of an unhandsome condition at the price of infelicity; that princes, and they that enjoy most of the world, have most of it but in title, and supreme rights, and reserved privileges, peppercorns, homages, trifling services, and acknowledgments, the real use descending to others, to more substantial purposes. These considerations may be useful to the curing of covetousness; that, the grace of mercifulness enlarging the heart of a man, his hand may not be contracted, but reached out to the poor in alms.

Sect. IX. *Of Repentance.*

REPENTANCE, of all things in the world, makes the greatest change: it changes things in heaven and earth ; for it changes the whole man from sin to grace, from vicious habits to holy customs, from unchaste bodies to angelical souls, from swine to philosophers, from drunkenness to sober counsels : and God himself, "with whom is no variableness or shadow of change," is pleased, by descending to our weak understandings, to say that he changes also upon man's repentance, that he alters his decrees, revokes his sentence, cancels the bills of accusation, throws the records of shame and sorrow from the court of heaven, and lifts up the sinner from the grave to life, from his

Hortulus hîc, puteusque brevis, nec reste movendus,
In tenues plantas facili diffunditur haustu.
Vive bidentis amans, et culti villicus horti ;
Unde epulum possis centum dare Pythagoreis.
Est aliquid, quocunque loco, quocunque recessu,
Unius sese dominum fecisse lacertæ.—Juven. Sat. iii. 226.

prison to a throne, from hell and the guilt of eternal torture
to heaven, and to a title to never-ceasing felicities. If we be
bound on earth, we shall be bound in heaven ; if we be absolved here, we shall be loosed there ; if we repent, God will
repent, and not send the evil upon us which we had deserved.

But repentance is a conjugation and society of many duties ;
and it contains in it all the parts of a holy life, from the time
of our return to the day of our death inclusively ; and it hath
in it some things specially relating to the sins of our former
days, which are now to be abolished by special arts, and have
obliged us to special labours, and brought in many new necessities, and put us into a very great deal of danger.   And because it is a duty consisting of so many parts and so much
employment, it also requires much time, and leaves a man in
the same degree of hope of pardon, as is his restitution to the
state of righteousness and holy living, for which we covenanted in baptism.   For we must know, that there is but one repentance in a man's whole life, if repentance be taken in the
proper and strict evangelical covenant sense, and not after the
ordinary understanding of the word : that is, we are but once
to change our whole state of life, from the power of the devil
and his entire possession, from the state of sin and death, from
the body of corruption, to the life of grace, to the possession
of Jesus, to the kingdom of the gospel : and this is done in
the baptism of water, or in the baptism of the Spirit, when
the first rite comes to be verified by God's grace coming upon
us, and by our obedience to the heavenly calling, we working
together with God.   After this change, if ever we fall into
the contrary state, and be wholly estranged from God and
religion, and profess ourselves servants of unrighteousness,
God hath made no more covenant of restitution to us ; there
is no place left for any more repentance, or entire change of
condition, or new birth ; a man can be regenerated but once :
and such are voluntary malicious apostates, witches, obstinate
impenitent persons, and the like.   But if we be overtaken by
infirmity, or enter into the marches or borders of this estate,
and commit a grievous sin, or ten, or twenty, so we be not in
the entire possession of the devil, we are, for the present, in
a damnable condition if we die ; but if we live, we are in a
recoverable condition ; for so we may repent often.   We repent or rise from death but once, but from sickness many

times; and by the grace of God we shall be pardoned if so we repent. But our hopes of pardon are just as is the repentance; which, if it be timely, hearty, industrious, and effective, God accepts; not by weighing grains or scruples, but by estimating the great proportions of our life. A hearty endeavour and an effectual general change shall get the pardon; the unavoidable infirmities, and past evils, and present imperfections, and short interruptions, against which we watch, and pray, and strive, being put upon the accounts of the cross, and paid for by the holy Jesus. This is the state and condition of repentance; its parts and actions must be valued according to the following rules:—

Acts and Parts of Repentance.

1. He that repents truly is greatly sorrowful for his past sins: not with a superficial sigh or tear, but a pungent afflictive sorrow; such a sorrow as hates the sin so much, that the man would choose to die rather than act it any more. This sorrow is called in Scripture "a weeping sorely; a weeping with bitterness of heart; a weeping day and night; a sorrow of heart; a breaking of the spirit; mourning like a dove, and chattering like a swallow;"[1] and we may read the degree and manner of it by the lamentations and sad accents of the prophet Jeremy, when he wept for the sins of the nation; by the heart-breaking of David, when he mourned for his murder and adultery; and the bitter weeping of St. Peter, after the shameful denying of his Master. The expression of this sorrow differs according to the temper of the body, the sex, the age, and circumstance of action, and the motive of sorrow, and by many accidental tendernesses, or masculine hardnesses; and the repentance is not to be estimated by the tears, but by the grief; and the grief is to be valued not by the sensitive trouble, but by the cordial hatred of the sin, and ready actual dereliction of it, and a resolution and real resisting its consequent temptations. Some people can shed tears for nothing, some for any thing; but the proper and true effects of a godly sorrow are, fear of the Divine judgments, apprehension of God's displeasure, watchings and strivings against sin, patiently enduring the cross of sorrow, (which God sends as their punishment,) in accusation of ourselves, in perpetually

[1] Jer. xiii. 17; Joel ii. 13; Ezek. xxvii. 31; James iv. 9.

begging pardon, in mean and base opinions of ourselves, and in all the natural productions from these, according to our temper and constitution. For if we be apt to weep in other accidents, it is ill if we weep not also in the sorrows of repentance; not that weeping is of itself a duty, but that the sorrow, if it be as great, will be still expressed in as great a manner.

2. Our sorrow for sins must retain the proportion of our sins, though not the equality. We have no particular measures of sins; we know not which is greater, of sacrilege or superstition, idolatry or covetousness, rebellion or witchcraft; and therefore God ties us not to nice measures of sorrow, but only that we keep the general rules of proportion; that is, that a great sin have a great grief, a smaller crime being to be washed off with a lesser shower.

3. Our sorrow for sins is then best accounted of for its degree, when it, together with all the penal and afflictive duties of repentance, shall have equalled or exceeded the pleasure we had in commission of the sin.[2]

4. True repentance is a punishing duty, and acts its sorrow; and judges and condemns the sin by voluntary submitting to such sadnesses as God sends on us, or (to prevent the judgment of God) by judging ourselves, and punishing our bodies and our spirits by such instruments of piety as are troublesome to the body: such as are fasting, watching, long prayers, troublesome postures in our prayers, expensive alms, and all outward acts of humiliation. For he that must judge himself must condemn himself if he be guilty; and if he be condemned, he must be punished; and if he be so judged, it will help to prevent the judgment of the Lord, St. Paul instructing us in this particular.[3] But I before intimated that the punishing actions of repentance are only actions of sorrow, and therefore are to make up the proportions of it. For our grief may be so full of trouble as to outweigh all the burdens of fasts and bodily afflictions, and then the other are the less necessary; and when they are used, the benefit of them is to obtain of God a remission or a lessening of such temporal judgments which God hath decreed against the sins, as it was in the case of Ahab; but the sinner is not, by any thing of this, reconciled to the eternal favour of God; for, as yet, this is but the introduction to repentance.

[2] Hugo de St. Victor.   [3] 1 Cor. xi. 31.

5. Every true penitent is obliged to confess his sins, and to humble himself before God for ever. Confession of sins hath a special promise : "If we confess our sins, he is faithful and just to forgive us our sins ;"[4] meaning that God hath bound himself to forgive us if we duly confess our sins, and do all that for which confession was appointed; that is, be ashamed of them, and own them no more. For confession of our sins to God can signify nothing of itself in its direct nature : he sees us when we act them, and keeps a record of them ; and we forget them, unless he reminds us of them by his grace. So "that to confess them to God does not punish us or make us ashamed : but confession to him, if it proceeds from shame and sorrow, and is an act of humility and self-condemnation," and is a laying open our wounds for cure, then it is a duty God delights in. In all which circumstances, because we may very much be helped if we take in the assistance of a spiritual guide, therefore the church of God, in all ages, hath commended, and, in most ages, enjoined, that we confess our sins,[5] and discover the state and condition of our souls to such a person, whom we or our superiors judge fit to help us in such needs. For so, "if we confess our sins one to another," as St. James advises, we shall obtain the prayers of the holy man whom God and the church have appointed solemnly to pray for us ; and when he knows our needs, he can best minister comfort or reproof, oil or caustics ; he can more opportunely recommend your particular state to God ; he can determine your cases of conscience, and judge better for you than you do for yourself ; and the shame of opening such ulcers may restrain your forwardness to contract them ; and all these circumstances of advantage will do very much towards the forgiveness. And this course was taken by the new converts in the days of the apostles : "For many that believed came and confessed and showed their deeds."[6] And it were well if this duty were practised prudently and innocently, in order to public discipline, or private comfort and instruction ; but that it be done to God is a duty, not directly for itself, but for its adjuncts and the duties that go with it, or before it, or after it : which duties, because they are all to be helped and guided

[4] 1 John i. 9.   [5] Ἀναγκαῖον τοῖς πεπιστευμένοις τὴν οἰκονομίαν τῶν μυστηρίων τοῦ Θεοῦ ἐξομολογεῖσθαι τὰ ἁμαρτήματα.—St. Basil. reg. brev. 228. Concil. Laod. c. 2. Concil. Quin.sext. c. 102. Tertul. de Pœnit
[6] Acts xix. 18.

by our pastors and curates of souls, he is careful of his eternal interest, that will not lose the advantage of using a private guide and judge. "He that hideth his sins shall not prosper;" *Non dirigetur*, saith the vulgar Latin, "he shall want a guide:" "but who confesseth and forsaketh them shall have mercy."[7] And to this purpose Climacus reports, that divers holy persons in that age did use to carry table-books with them, and in them described an account of all their determinate thoughts, purposes, words, and actions, in which they had suffered infirmity; that by communicating the estate of their souls, they might be instructed and guided, or corrected or encouraged.

6. True repentance must reduce to act all its holy purposes, and enter into and run through the state of holy living,[8] which is contrary to that state of darkness in which in times past we walked.[9] For to resolve to do it, and yet not to do it, is to break our resolution and our faith, to mock God, to falsify and evacuate all the preceding acts of repentance, and to make our pardon hopeless, and our hope fruitless. He that resolves to live well when a danger is upon him, or a violent fear, or when the appetites of lust are newly satisfied, or newly served, and yet when the temptation comes again, sins again, and then is sorrowful, and resolves once more against it, and yet falls when the temptation returns, is a vain man, but no true penitent, nor in the state of grace; and if he chance to die in one of these good moods, is very far from salvation; for if it be necessary that we resolve to live well, it is necessary we should do so. For resolution is an imperfect act, a term of relation, and signifies nothing but in order to the actions; it is as a faculty is to the act, as spring is to the harvest, as eggs are to birds, as a relative to its correspondent, nothing without it. No man, therefore, can be in the state of grace and actual favour by resolutions and holy purposes; these are but the gate and portal towards pardon: a holy life is the only perfection of repentance, and the firm ground upon which we can cast the anchor of hope in the mercies of God, through Jesus Christ.

[7] Prov. xxviii. 13.   [8] Rom. vi. 3, 4, 7; viii. 10; xi. 22, 27; xiii. 13, 14; Gal. v. 6, 24; vi. 15; 1 Cor. vii. 19; 2 Cor. xiii. 5; Col. i. 21—23; Heb. xii. 1, 14, 16; x. 16, 22; 1 Pet. i. 15; 2 Pet. i. 4, 9, 10; iii. 11; 1 John i. 6; iii. 8, 9; v. 16.   [9] Nequam illud verbum, Bene vult, nisi qui bene facit.—Trinummus, act. ii. scen. iii. 38.

7. No man is to reckon his pardon immediately upon his returns from sin to the beginnings of good life, but is to begin his hopes and degrees of confidence according as sin dies in him, and grace lives; as the habits of sin lessen, and righteousness grows; according as sin returns but seldom in smaller instances and without choice, and by surprise without deliberation, and is highly disrelished, and presently dashed against the rock Christ Jesus, by a holy sorrow and renewed care, and more strict watchfulness. For a holy life being the condition of the covenant on our part, as we return to God, so God returns to us, and our state returns to the probabilities of pardon.

8. Every man is to work out his salvation with fear and trembling; and after the commission of sins his fears must multiply; because every new sin and every great declining from the ways of God is still a degree of new danger, and hath increased God's anger, and hath made him more uneasy to grant pardon: and when he does grant it, it is upon harder terms both for doing and suffering: that is, we must do more for pardon; and, it may be, suffer much more. For we must know that God pardons our sins by parts; as our duty increases, and our care is more prudent and active, so God's anger decreases: and yet, it may be, the last sin you committed made God unalterably resolve to send upon you some sad judgment. Of the particulars in all cases we are uncertain; and therefore we have reason always to mourn for our sins that have so provoked God, and made our condition so full of danger that, it may be, no prayers, or tears, or duty, can alter his sentence concerning some sad judgment upon us. Thus God irrevocably decreed to punish the Israelites for idolatry, although Moses prayed for them, and God forgave them in some degree; that is, so that he would not cut them off from being a people; yet he would not forgive them so, but he would visit that their sin upon them; and he did so.

9. A true penitent must, all the days of his life,[10] pray for pardon, and never think the work completed till he dies; not by any act of his own, by no act of the church, by no forgiveness by the party injured, by no restitution. These are all instruments of great use and efficacy, and the means by which it is to be done at length; but still the sin lies at the door,

[10] Dand m interstitium pœnitentiæ.—Tacit.

ready to return upon us in judgment and damnation, if we
return to it in choice or action.   And whether God hath forgiven us or no, we know not,[11] and how far we know not;
and all that we have done, is not of sufficient worth to obtain
pardon : therefore still pray, and still be sorrowful for ever
having done it, and for ever watch against it; and then those
beginnings of pardon, which are working all the way, will at
last be perfected in the day of the Lord.

10. Defer not at all to repent ; much less mayest thou put
it off to thy death-bed.   It is not an easy thing to root out the
habits of sin[12] which a man's whole life hath gathered and
confirmed.   We find work enough to mortify one beloved
lust, in our very best advantage of strength and time, and before it is so deeply rooted, as it must needs be supposed to be
at the end of a wicked life: and, therefore, it will prove impossible, when the work is so great and the strength so little,
when sin is so strong and grace so weak: for they always
keep the same proportion of increase and decrease, and as sin
grows grace decays: so that the more need we have of grace,
the less at that time we shall have; because the greatness of
our sins, which makes the need, hath lessened the grace of
God, which should help us, into nothing.   To which add this
consideration; that on a man's death-bed the day of repentance is past; for repentance being the renewing of a holy life,
a living the life of grace, it is a contradiction to say that a
man can live a holy life upon his death-bed; especially if we
consider, that for a sinner to live a holy life must first suppose him to have overcome all his evil habits, and then to
have made a purchase of the contrary graces, by the labours
of great prudence, watchfulness, self-denial, and severity.[13]
"Nothing that is excellent can be wrought suddenly."[14]

11. After the beginnings of thy recovery, be infinitely fearful of a relapse ; and therefore, upon the stock of thy sad experience, observe where thy failings were, and by especial arts
fortify that faculty, and arm against that temptation.   For if
all those arguments which God uses to us to preserve our innocence, and thy late danger, and thy fears, and the goodness

---

[11] I peccati et i debbiti son sempre più di quel che si crede.

[12] Τί οὖν πρὸς ἔθος ἐστὶν εὑρίσκειν βοήθημα; τὸ ἐναντίον ἔθος.—Arrian

[13] Mortem venientem nemo hilaris excipit, nisi qui se ad illam diu com-
posuerat.   [14] Οὐδὲν τῶν μεγάλων ἄφνω γίνεται.—Arrian.

cf God making thee once to escape, and the shame of thy fall, and the sense of thy own weaknesses, will not make thee watchful against a fall, especially knowing how much it costs a man to be restored, it will be infinitely more dangerous if ever thou fallest again; not only for fear God should no more accept thee to pardon, but even thy own hopes will be made more desperate, and thy impatience greater, and thy shame turn to impudence, and thy own will be more estranged, violent, and refractory, and thy latter end will be worse than thy beginning. To which add this consideration: that thy sin, which was formerly in a good way of being pardoned, will not only return upon thee with all its own loads, but with the baseness of unthankfulness, and thou wilt be set as far back from heaven as ever; and all thy former labours, and fears, and watchings, and agonies, will be reckoned for nothing, but as arguments to upbraid thy folly, who, when thou hadst set one foot in heaven, didst pull that back, and carry both to hell.

Motives to Repentance.

I shall use no other arguments to move a sinner to repentance, but to tell him, unless he does he shall certainly perish; and if he does repent timely and entirely, that is, live a holy life, he shall be forgiven and be saved. But yet I desire, that this consideration be enlarged with some great circumstances; and let us remember,

1. That to admit mankind to repentance and pardon, was a favour greater than ever God gave to the angels and devils; for they were never admitted to the condition of second thoughts: Christ never groaned one groan for them; he never suffered one stripe, nor one affront, nor shed one drop of blood, to restore them to hopes of blessedness after their first failings. But this he did for us; he paid the score of our sins, only that we might be admitted to repent, and that this repentance might be effectual to the great purposes of felicity and salvation.

2. Consider, that as it cost Christ many millions of prayers and groans and sighs, so he is now at this instant, and hath been for these sixteen hundred years, night and day, incessantly praying for grace to us, that we may repent; and for pardon when we do; and for degrees of pardon beyond the capacities of our infirmities, and the merit of our sorrows and

amendment: and this prayer he will continue till his second coming; for "he ever liveth to make intercession for us." [15] And that we may know what it is in behalf of which he intercedes, St. Paul tells us his design; "We are ambassadors for Christ, as though he did beseech you by us; we pray you in Christ's stead to be reconciled to God." [16]   And what Christ prays us to do, he prays to God that we may do: that which he desires of us as his servants, he desires of God, who is the fountain of the grace and powers unto us, and without whose assistance we can do nothing.

3. That ever we should repent, was so costly a purchase, and so great a concernment, and so high a favour, and the event is esteemed by God himself so great an excellency, that our blessed Saviour tells us, "there shall be joy in heaven over one sinner that repenteth;" [17] meaning, that when Christ shall be glorified, and at the right hand of his Father make intercession for us, praying for our repentance, the conversion and repentance of every sinner is part of Christ's glorification, it is the answering of his prayers, it is a portion of his reward, in which he does essentially glory by the joys of his glorified humanity. This is the joy of our Lord himself directly, not of the angels, save only by reflection: the joy (said our blessed Saviour) shall be in the presence of the angels; they shall see the glory of the Lord, the answering of his prayers, the satisfaction of his desires, and the reward of his sufferings, in the repentance and consequent pardon of a sinner. For therefore he once suffered, and for that reason he rejoices for ever. And therefore, when a penitent sinner comes to receive the effect and full consummation of his pardon, it is called "an entering into the joy of our Lord;" that is, a partaking of that joy which Christ received at our conversion and enjoyed ever since.

4. Add to this, that the rewards of heaven are so great and glorious, and Christ's burden is so light, his yoke is so easy, that it is a shameless impudence to expect so great glories at a less rate than so little a service, at a lower rate than a holy life. It cost the heart-blood of the Son of God to obtain heaven for us upon that condition; and who shall die again to get heaven for us upon easier terms? What would you do,

---

[15] Heb. vii. 25.   [16] 2 Cor. v. 20.   [17] Luke xv. 7

if God should command you to kill your eldest son, or to work in the mines for a thousand years together, or to fast all thy life-time with bread and water? were not heaven a very great bargain even after all this? And when God requires nothing of us but to live soberly, justly, and godly, (which things themselves are to a man a very great felicity, and necessary to our present well-being,) shall we think this to be an intolerable burden, and that heaven is too little a purchase at that price; and that God, in mere justice, will take a death-bed sigh or groan, and a few unprofitable tears and promises, in exchange for all our duty?

If these motives, joined together with our own interest, (even as much as felicity, and the sight of God, and the avoiding the intolerable pains of hell, and many intermedial judgments, come to,) will not move us to leave, 1. the filthiness, and, 2. the trouble, and, 3. the uneasiness, and, 4. the unreasonableness of sin, and turn to God—there is no more to be said; we must perish in our folly.

SECT. X.   *Of Preparation to, and the Manner how to receive, the holy Sacrament of the Lord's Supper.*

THE celebration of the holy sacrament is the great mysteriousness of the Christian religion, and succeeds to the most solemn rite of natural and Judaical religion, the law of sacrificing. For God spared mankind, and took the sacrifice of beasts, together with our solemn prayers, for an instrument of expiation. But these could not purify the soul from sin, but were typical of the sacrifice of something that could. But nothing could do this, but either the offering of all that sinned, that every man should be the *anathema* or *devoted thing*; or else by some one of the same capacity, who by some superadded excellency might in his own personal sufferings have a value great enough to satisfy for all the whole kind of sinning persons. This the Son of God, Jesus Christ, God and man, undertook, and finished by a sacrifice of himself upon the altar of the cross.

2. This sacrifice, because it was perfect, could be but one, and that once: but because the needs of the world should last as long as the world itself, it was necessary that there should be a perpetual ministry established, whereby this one sufficient sacrifice should be made eternally effectual to the several

R 2

new arising needs of all the world, who should desire it, or in
any sense be capable of it.

3. To this end Christ was made a priest for ever: he was
initiated or consecrated on the cross, and there began his
priesthood, which was to last till his coming to judgment. It
began on earth, but was to last and be officiated in heaven,
where he sits perpetually representing and exhibiting to the
Father that great effective sacrifice which he offered on the
cross, to eternal and never-failing purposes.

4. As Christ is pleased to represent to his Father that great
sacrifice as a means of atonement and expiation for all .man-
kind, and with special purposes and intendment for all the
elect, all that serve him in holiness; so he hath appointed
that the same ministry shall be done upon earth too, in our
manner, and according to our proportion; and therefore hath
constituted and separated an order of men who, by " showing
forth the Lord's death" by sacramental representation, may
pray unto God after the same manner that our Lord and High
Priest does; that is, offer to God and represent in this solemn
prayer and sacrament, Christ as already offered ; so sending
up a gracious instrument, whereby our prayers may, for his
sake and in the same manner of intercession, be offered up to
God in our behalf, and for all them for whom we pray, to all
those purposes for which Christ died.

5. As the ministers of the sacrament do, in a sacramental
manner, present to God the sacrifice of the cross, by being
imitators of Christ's intercession ; so the people are sacrificers
too in their manner : for besides that, by saying *Amen*, they
join in the act of him that ministers, and make it also to be
their own ; so, when they eat and drink the consecrated and
blessed elements worthily, they receive Christ within them,
and therefore may also offer him to God, while, in their sacrifice of obedience and thanksgiving, they present themselves to
God with Christ, whom they have spiritually received, that is,
themselves, with that which will make them gracious and
acceptable.   The offering their bodies, and souls, and services
to God in him, and by him, and with him, who is his Father's
well-beloved, and in whom he is well pleased, cannot but be
accepted to all the purposes of blessing, grace, and glory.[1]

[1] Nôsti tempora tu Jovis sereni,
   Cùm fulget placidus, suoque vultu.
   Quo nil supplicibus solet negare.—Martial. ep. l. v. 6.

6. This is the sum of the greatest mystery of our religion : it is the copy of the passion, and the ministration of the great mystery of our redemption ; and therefore, whatsoever entitles us to the general privileges of Christ's passion, all that is ne- cessary by way of disposition to the celebration of the sacra- ment of his passion ; because this celebration is our manner of applying or using it.   The particulars of which preparation are represented in the following rules.

1. No man must dare to approach to the holy sacrament of the Lord's supper, if he be in a state of any one sin,[2] that is, unless he have entered into the state of repentance, that is, of sorrow and amendment ; lest it be said concerning him, as it was concerning Judas, "the hand of him that betrayeth me is with me on the table :" and he that receiveth Christ into an impure soul or body, first turns his most excellent nourish- ment into poison, and then feeds upon it.

2. Every communicant must first have examined himself ; that is, tried the condition and state of his soul, searched out the secret ulcers, inquired out its weaknesses and indiscretions, and all those aptnesses where it is exposed to temptation ; that by finding out its diseases he may find a cure, and by discover- ing its aptnesses he may secure his present purposes of future amendment, and may be armed against dangers and tempta- tions.

3. This examination must be a man's own act and inquisi- tion into his life : but then also it should lead a man on to run to those whom the great Physician of our souls, Christ Jesus, hath appointed to minister physic to our diseases ; that in all dangers and great accidents we may be assisted for comfort and remedy, for medicine and caution.

4. In this affair let no man deceive himself, and against such a time which public authority hath appointed for us to receive the sacrament, weep for his sins by way of solemnity and ceremony, and still retain the affection : but he that comes to this feast must have on the wedding-garment, that is, he must have put on Jesus Christ, and he must have put off the old man with his affections and lusts ; and he must be wholly conformed to Christ in the image of his mind.   For then we have put on Christ when our souls are clothed with his righteousness, when every faculty of our soul is proportioned and vested ac-

[2] Vasa pura ad rem divinam.—Plaut. in Cap. act. iv. sc. 1.

cording to the pattern of Christ's life. And, therefore, a man
must not leap from his last night's surfeit and bath, and then
communicate: but when he hath begun the work of God
effectually, and made some progress in repentance, and hath
walked some stages and periods in the ways of godliness, then
let him come to him that is to minister it, and having made
known the state of his soul, he is to be admitted: but to receive it into an unhallowed soul and body is to receive the
dust of the tabernacle in the waters of jealousy; it will make
the belly to swell, and the thigh to rot; it will not convey
Christ to us, but the devil will enter and dwell there, till with
it he returns to his dwelling of torment. Remember always,
that after a great sin, or after a habit of sins, a man is not
soon made clean; and no unclean thing must come to this
feast. It is not the preparation of two or three days that can
render a person capable of this banquet: for in this feast, all
Christ, and Christ's passion, and all his graces, the blessings
and effects of his sufferings, are conveyed. Nothing can fit us
for this but what can unite us to Christ, and obtain of him to
present our needs to his heavenly Father; this sacrament can
no otherwise be celebrated but upon the same terms on which
we may hope for pardon and heaven itself.

5. When we have this general and indispensably necessary
preparation, we are to make our souls more adorned and trimmed up with circumstances of pious actions and special devotions, setting apart some portion of our time immediately before
the day of solemnity, according as our great occasions will
permit: and this time is specially to be spent in actions of repentance, confession of our sins, renewing our purposes of holy
living, praying for pardon of our failings, and for those graces
which may prevent the like sadnesses for the time to come,
meditation upon the passion, upon the infinite love of God, expressed in so great mysterious manners of redemption ; and
indefinitely in all acts of virtue which may build our souls
up into a temple fit for the reception of Christ himself, and the
inhabitation of the Holy Spirit.

6. The celebration of the holy sacrament, being the most
solemn prayer, joined with the most effectual instrument of its
acceptance, must suppose us in the love of God and in charity
with all the world; and therefore we must, before every communion especially, remember what differences or jealousies are

between us and any one else, and recompose all disunions, and cause right understandings between each other; offering to satisfy whom we have injured, and to forgive them who have injured us, without thoughts of resuming the quarrel when the solemnity is over; for that is but to rake the embers in light and fantastic ashes: it must be quenched, and a holy flame enkindled—no fires must be at all, but the fires of love and zeal; and the altar of incense will send up a sweet perfume, and make atonement for us.

7. When the day of the feast is come, lay aside all cares and impertinences of the world, and remember that this is thy soul's day, a day of traffic and intercourse with heaven. Arise early in the morning. 1. Give God thanks for the approach of so great a blessing. 2. Confess thine own unworthiness to admit so Divine a guest. 3. Then remember and deplore thy sins, which have made thee so unworthy. 4. Then confess God's goodness, and take sanctuary there, and upon him place thy hopes; 5. And invite him to thee with renewed acts of love, of holy desire, of hatred of his enemy, sin. 6. Make oblation of thyself wholly to be disposed by him, to the obedience of him, to his providence and possession, and pray him to enter and dwell there for ever. And after this, with joy and holy fear, and the forwardness of love, address thyself to the receiving of him, to whom, and by whom, and for whom, all faith, and all hope, and all love, in the whole catholic church, both in heaven and earth, is designed; him, whom kings and queens, and whole kingdoms, are in love with, and count it the greatest honour in the world that their crowns and sceptres are laid at his holy feet.

8. When the holy man stands at the table of blessing, and ministers the rite of consecration, then do as the angels do, who behold, and love, and wonder that the Son of God should become food to the souls of his servants; that he, who cannot suffer any change or lessening, should be broken into pieces, and enter into the body to support and nourish the spirit, and yet at the same time remain in heaven, while he descends to thee upon earth; that he who hath essential felicity should become miserable and die for thee, and then give himself to thee for ever to redeem thee from sin and misery; that by his wounds he should procure health to thee, by his affronts he should entitle thee to glory, by his death he should bring thee

to life, and by becoming a man he should make thee partaker
of the Divine nature.   These are such glories that, although
they are made so obvious that each eye may behold them, yet
they are also so deep that no thought can fathom them : but
so it hath pleased him to make these mysteries to be sensible,
because the excellency and depth of the mercy is not intelli-
gible; that while we are ravished and comprehended within
the infiniteness of so vast and mysterious a mercy, yet we may
be as sure of it as of that thing we see and feel, and smell and
taste; but yet it is so great that we cannot understand it.

9. These holy mysteries are offered to our senses, but not
to be placed under our feet; they are sensible, but not common ; and, therefore, as the weakness of the elements adds
wonder to the excellency of the sacrament, so let our reverence
and venerable usages of them add honour to the elements,
and acknowledge the glory of the mystery, and the Divinity
of the mercy.   Let us receive the consecrated elements with
all devotion and humility of body and spirit; and do this
honour to it, that it be the first food we eat, and the first be-
verage we drink that day, unless it be in case of sickness, or
other great necessity ; and that your body and soul both be
prepared to its reception with abstinence from secular pleasures, that you may better have attended fastings and preparatory prayers.   For if ever it be seasonable to observe the
counsel of St. Paul, that married persons by consent should
abstain for a time, that they may attend to solemn religion, it
is now.[3]   It was not by St. Paul, nor the after-ages of the
church, called a duty so to do, but it is most reasonable that
the more solemn actions of religion should be attended to, without the mixture of any thing that may discompose the mind
and make it more secular or less religious.

10. In the act of receiving, exercise acts of faith with much
confidence and resignation, believing it not to be common
bread and wine, but holy in their use, holy in their signification, holy in their change, and holy in their effect: and believe,
if thou art a worthy communicant, thou dost as verily receive
Christ's body and blood to all effects and purposes of the Spirit,
as thou dost receive the blessed elements into thy mouth—that
thou puttest thy finger to his hand, and thy hand into his side,

---

[3] Discedite ab aris, Queis tulit hesternâ gaudia nocte Venus.—Tibul.
ii. 1. 12.

and thy lips to his fontinel of blood, sucking life from his heart;[4] and yet, if thou dost communicate unworthily, thou eatest and drinkest Christ to thy danger, and death, and destruction. Dispute not concerning the secret of the mystery, and the nicety of the manner, of Christ's presence; it is sufficient to thee that Christ shall be present to thy soul as an instrument of grace, as a pledge of the resurrection, as the earnest of glory and immortality, and a means of many intermedial blessings, even all such as are necessary for thee, and are in order to thy salvation. And to make all this good to thee, there is nothing necessary on thy part but a holy life, and a true belief of all the sayings of Christ; amongst which, indefinitely assent to the words of institution, and believe that Christ, in the holy sacrament, gives thee his body and his blood. He that believes not this is not a Christian. He that believes so much needs not to inquire further, nor to entangle his faith by disbelieving his sense.

11. Fail not, this solemnity, according to the custom of pious and devout people, to make an offering to God for the uses of religion and the poor, according to thy ability. For when Christ feasts his body, let us also feast our fellow members, who have right to the same promises, and are partakers of the same sacrament, and partners of the same hope, and cared for under the same Providence, and descended from the same common parents, and whose Father God is, and Christ is their elder Brother. If thou chancest to communicate where this holy custom is not observed publicly, supply that want by thy private charity; but offer it to God at his holy table, at least by thy private designing it there.

12. When you have received, pray and give thanks. Pray for all estates of men; for they also have an interest in the body of Christ, whereof they are members: and you, in conjunction with Christ, (whom then you have received,) are more fit to pray for them in that advantage, and in the celebration of that holy sacrifice, which then is sacramentally represented to God. Give thanks for the passion of our dearest Lord: remember all its parts, and all the instruments of your redemption; and beg of God, that by a holy perseverance in well-doing you may from shadows pass on to substances, from eat-

[4] Cruci hæremus, sanguinem sugimus, et inter ipsa Redemptoris nostri vulnera, figimus linguam.—Cyprian, de Cœnâ Dom.

ing his body to seeing his face, from the typical, sacramental, and transient, to the real and eternal supper of the Lamb.

13. After the solemnity is done, let Christ dwell in your hearts by faith, and love, and obedience, and conformity to his life and death: as you have taken Christ into you, so put Christ on you, and conform every faculty of your soul and body to his holy image and perfection. Remember, that now Christ is all one with you; and, therefore, when you are to do an action, consider how Christ did, or would do the like; and do you imitate his example, and transcribe his copy, and understand all his commandments, and choose all that he propounded, and desire his promises, and fear his threatenings, and marry his loves and hatreds, and contract his friendships; for then you do every day communicate; especially when Christ thus dwells in you, and you in Christ, growing up towards a perfect man in Christ Jesus.

14. Do not instantly, upon your return from church, return also to the world, and secular thoughts and employments; but let the remaining parts of that day be like a post-communion, or an after-office, entertaining your blessed Lord with all the caresses and sweetness of love and colloquies, and intercourses of duty and affection, acquainting him with all your needs, and revealing to him all your secrets, and opening all your infirmities; and as the affairs of your person or employment call you off, so retire again with often ejaculations and acts of entertainment to your beloved guest.

The Effects and Benefits of Worthy Communicating.

When I said that the sacrifice of the cross, which Christ offered for all the sins and all the needs of the world, is represented to God by the minister in the sacrament, and offered up in prayer and sacramental memory, after the manner that Christ himself intercedes for us in heaven, (so far as his glorious priesthood is imitable by his ministers on earth,) I must of necessity also mean, that all the benefits of that sacrifice are then conveyed to all that communicate worthily. But if we descend to particulars, then and there the church is nourished in her faith, strengthened in her hope, enlarged in her bowels with an increasing charity; there all the members of Christ are joined with each other, and all to Christ their head; and we again renew the covenant with God in Jesus

Christ, and God seals his part, and we promise for ours, and Christ unites both, and the Holy Ghost signs both in the collation of those graces which we then pray for, and exercise and receive all at once.   There our bodies are nourished with the signs, and our souls with the mystery: our bodies receive into them the seed of an immortal nature, and our souls are joined with him who is the first-fruits of the resurrection and never can die.   And if we desire any thing else and need it. here it is to be prayed for, here to be hoped for, here to be received.   Long life and health, and recovery from sickness, and competent support and maintenance, and peace and deliverance from our enemies, and content, and patience, and joy, and sanctified riches, or a cheerful poverty, and liberty, and whatsoever else is a blessing, was purchased for us by Christ in his death and resurrection, and in his intercession in heaven.   And this sacrament being that to our particulars which the great mysteries are in themselves and by design to all the world, if we receive worthily, we shall receive any of these blessings, according as God shall choose for us ; and he will not only choose with more wisdom, but also with more affection, than we can for ourselves.

After all this, it is advised by the guides of souls, wise men and pious, that all persons should communicate very often, even as often as they can, without excuses or delays; every thing that puts us from so holy an employment, when we are moved to it, being either a sin or an imperfection, an infirmity or indevotion, and an inactiveness of spirit.   All Christian people must come.   They, indeed, that are in a state of sin must not come so, but yet they must come.   First, they must quit their state of death, and then partake of the bread of life. They that are at enmity with their neighbours must come— that is no excuse for their not coming ; only they must not bring their enmity along with them, but leave it, and then come.   They that have a variety of secular employments must come ;[5] only they must leave their secular thoughts and affections behind them, and then come and converse with God. If any man be well grown in grace, he must needs come, because he is excellently disposed to so holy a feast: but he that is but in the infancy of piety had need to come, that so he may grow in grace.   The strong must come lest they become

<hr>

* L'Evêque de Geneve, Introd. à la Vie Devoté.

weak; and the weak that they may become strong. The sick must come to be cured; the healthful to be preserved. They that have leisure must come, because they have no excuse; they that have no leisure must come hither, that by so excellent religion they may sanctify their business. The penitent sinners must come, that they may be justified; and they that are justified, that they may be justified still. They that have fears and great reverence to these mysteries, and think no preparation to be sufficient, must receive, that they may learn how to receive the more worthily; and they that have a less degree of reverence must come often to have it heightened: that as those creatures that live amongst the snows of the mountains turn white with their food and conversation with such perpetual whitenesses, so our souls may be transformed into the similitude and union with Christ by our perpetual feeding on him, and conversation, not only in his courts, but in his very heart, and most secret affections, and incomparable purities.

Prayers for all sorts of Men and all Necessities; relating to the several parts of the Virtue of Religion.

A Prayer for the Graces of Faith, Hope, Charity.

O Lord God of infinite mercy, of infinite excellency, who hast sent thy holy Son into the world to redeem us from an intolerable misery, and to teach us a holy religion, and to forgive us an infinite debt; give me thy Holy Spirit, that my understanding and all my faculties may be so resigned to the discipline and doctrine of my Lord, that I may be prepared in mind and will to die for the testimony of Jesus, and to suffer any affliction or calamity that shall offer to hinder my duty or tempt me to shame, or sin, or apostacy; and let my faith be the parent of a good life, a strong shield to repel the fiery darts of the devil, and the author of a holy hope, of modest desires, of confidence in God, and of a never-failing charity to thee, my God, and to all the world; that I may never have my portion with the unbelievers, or uncharitable and desperate persons; but may be supported by the strengths of faith in all temptations, and may be refreshed with the comforts of a holy hope in all my sorrows, and may bear the burden of the Lord, and the infirmities of my neighbour, by the support of charity; that the yoke of Jesus may become easy to me, and my love may do all the miracles of grace, till from grace it swell to glory, from earth to heaven, from duty to reward, from the imperfections of a beginning and still growing love, it may arrive to the consummation of an eternal and never-ceasing charity, through Jesus Christ the Son of thy love, the anchor of our hope, and the author and finisher of our faith : to whom, with thee, O Lord God, Father of heaven and earth, and with thy Holy Spirit, be all glory, and love, and obedience, and dominion, now and for ever. Amen.

Acts of Love by way of Prayer and Ejaculation ; to be used in private.

O God, thou art my God, early will I seek thee: my soul thirsteth for thee, my flesh longeth for thee in a dry and thirsty land, where no water is ; to see thy power and thy glory so as I have seen thee in the sanctuary. Because thy loving-kindness is better than life, my lips shall praise thee. Psal. lxiii. 1, &c.

I am ready, not only to be bound, but to die for the name of the Lord Jesus. Acts xxi. 13.

How amiable are thy tabernacles, thou Lord of hosts! My soul longeth, yea, even fainteth for the courts of the Lord ; my heart and my flesh crieth out for the living God. Blessed are they that dwell in thy house; they will still be praising thee. Psal. lxxxiv. 1, 2, 4.

O blessed Jesu, thou art worthy of all adoration, and all honour, and all love : thou art the Wonderful, the Counsellor, the mighty God, the everlasting Father, the Prince of Peace ; of thy government and peace there shall be no end ; thou art the brightness of thy Father's glory, the express image of his person, the appointed heir of all things. Thou upholdest all things by the word of thy power; thou didst by thyself purge our sins ; thou art set on the right hand of the Majesty on high ; thou art made better than the angels ; thou hast by inheritance obtained a more excellent name than they. Thou, O dearest Jesus, art the head of the church, the beginning and the first-born from the dead : in all things thou hast the pre-eminence, and it pleased the Father that in thee should all fulness dwell. Kingdoms are in love with thee : kings lay their crowns and sceptres at thy feet; and queens are thy handmaids, and wash the feet of thy servants.

A Prayer to be said in any Affliction, as Death of Children, of Husband or Wife, in great Poverty, in Imprisonment, in a sad and disconsolate Spirit, and in Temptations to Despair.

O eternal God, Father of mercies, and God of all comfort, with much mercy look upon the sadnesses and sorrows of thy servant. My sins lie heavy upon me, and press me sore, and there is no health in my bones by reason of thy displeasure and my sin. The waters are gone over me, and I stick fast in the deep mire, and my miseries are without comfort, because they are punishments of my sin : and I am so evil and unworthy a person, that, though I have great desires, yet I have no dispositions or worthiness toward receiving comfort. My sins have caused my sorrow, and my sorrow does not cure my sins : and unless for thy own sake, and merely because thou art good, thou shalt pity me and relieve me, I am as much without remedy as now I am without comfort. Lord, pity me! Lord, let thy grace refresh my spirit! Let thy comforts support me, thy mercy pardon me, and never let my portion be amongst hopeless and accursed spirits ; for thou art good and gracious, and I throw myself upon thy mercy. Let me never let my hold go, and do thou with me what seems good in thy own eyes. I cannot suffer more than I have deserved ; and yet I can need no relief so great as thy mercy is ; for thou art infinitely more merciful than I can be miserable ; and thy mercy, which is above all thy own works, must needs be far above all my sin and all my misery. Dearest Jesus, let me trust in thee for ever, and let me never be confounded. Amen.

Ejaculations and short Meditations to be used in time of Sickness and Sorrow, or Danger of Death.

Hear my prayer, O Lord, and let my cry come unto thee.[6] Hide not thy face from me in the time of my trouble, incline thine ear unto me when I call : O hear me, and that right soon. For my days are consumed like smoke, and my bones are burnt up as it were with a fire-brand. My heart is smitten down and withered like grass, so that I forget to eat my bread : and that because of thine indignation and wrath ; for thou hast taken me up and cast me down : thine arrows stick

* Psal. cii. 2—4, 10.

fast in me, and thine hand presseth me sore.[7]   There is no health in my flesh because of thy displeasure; neither is there any rest in my bones by reason of my sin.   My wickednesses are gone over my head, and are a sore burden, too heavy for me to bear.   But I will confess my wickedness, and be sorry for my sin.   O Lord, rebuke me not in thine indignation, neither chasten me in thy displeasure.[8]   Lord, be merciful unto me, heal my soul, for I have sinned against thee.[9]

Have mercy upon me, O God, after thy great goodness, according to the multitude of thy mercies do away mine offences.[10] O remember not the sins and offences of my youth; but according to thy mercy think thou upon me, O Lord, for thy goodness.[11]   Wash me throughly from my wickedness; and cleanse me from my sin.   Make me a clean heart, O God, and renew a right spirit within me.[12]   Cast me not away from thy presence, from thy all-hallowing and life-giving presence: and take not thy Holy Spirit, thy sanctifying, thy guiding, thy comforting, thy supporting, and confirming Spirit, from me.

O God, thou art my God for ever and ever: thou shalt be my guide unto death.[13]   Lord, comfort me now that I lie sick upon my bed: make thou my bed in all my sickness.[14] O deliver my soul from the place of hell; and do thou receive me.[15]   My heart is disquieted within me, and the fear of death is fallen upon me.[16]   Behold, thou hast made my days as it were a span long, and my age is even as nothing in respect of thee; and verily every man living is altogether vanity.[17] When thou with rebukes dost chasten man for sin, thou makest his beauty to consume away, like a moth fretting a garment: every man therefore is but vanity.   And now, Lord, what is my hope? truly my hope is even in thee.   Hear my prayer, O Lord, and with thine ears consider my calling: hold not thy peace at my tears.   Take this plague away from me: I am consumed by the means of thy heavy hand.   I am a stranger with thee and a sojourner, as all my fathers were. O spare me a little, that I may recover my strength, before I go hence and be no more seen.   My soul cleaveth unto the dust: O quicken me according to thy word.[18]   And when the

[7] Psal. xxxviii. 2—4, 18.   [8] Psal. vi. 1.   [9] Psal. xli. 4.
[10] Psal. li. 1.   [11] Psal. xxv. 7.   [12] Psal. li. 2, 10, 11.
[13] Psal. xlviii. 13.   [14] Psal. xli. 3.   [15] Psal. xlix. 15.
[16] Psal. lv. 4.   [17] Psal. xxxix. 5.   [18] Psal. cxix. 25.

snares of death compass me round about, let not the pains of hell take hold upon me.[19]

An Act of Faith concerning the Resurrection and the Day of Judgment, to be said by Sick Persons, or meditated.

I know that my Redeemer liveth, and that he shall stand at the latter day upon the earth: and though after my skin worms destroy this body, yet in my flesh shall I see God; whom I shall see for myself, and mine eyes shall behold, though my reins be consumed within me.   Job xix. 25, &c.

God shall come, and shall not keep silence; there shall go before him a consuming fire, and a mighty tempest shall be stirred up round about him: he shall call the heaven from above, and the earth, that he may judge his people.[20]   O blessed Jesu, thou art my judge and thou art my advocate: have mercy upon me in the hour of my death, and in the day of judgment.   See John v. 28, and 1 Thess. iv. 15.

Short Prayers to be said by Sick Persons.

O holy Jesus, thou art a merciful high priest, and touched with the sense of our infirmities; thou knowest the sharpness of my sickness and the weakness of my person.   The clouds are gathered about me, and thou hast covered me with thy storm: my understanding hath not such apprehension of things as formerly.   Lord, let thy mercy support me, thy Spirit guide me, and lead me through the valley of this death safely; that I may pass it patiently, holily, with perfect resignation; and let me rejoice in the Lord, in the hopes of pardon, in the expectation of glory, in the sense of thy mercies, in the refreshments of thy Spirit, in a victory over all temptations.

Thou hast promised to be with us in tribulation.   Lord, my soul is troubled, and my body is weak, and my hope is in thee, and my enemies are busy and mighty; now make good thy holy promise.   Now, O holy Jesus, now let thy hand of grace be upon me: restrain my ghostly enemies, and give me all sorts of spiritual assistances.   Lord, remember thy servant in the day when thou bindest up thy jewels.

O take from me all tediousness of spirit, all impatience and unquietness: let me possess my soul in patience, and resign my soul and body into thy hands, as into the hands of a faithful Creator and a blessed Redeemer.

[20] Psal. l. 3, 4.

O holy Jesu, thou didst die for us ; by thy sad, pungent, and intolerable pains, which thou enduredst for me, have pity on me, and ease my pain, or increase my patience. Lay on me no more than thou shalt enable me to bear. I have deserved it all, and more, and infinitely more. Lord, I am weak and ignorant, timorous and inconstant ; and I fear lest something should happen that may discompose the state of my soul, that may displease thee : do what thou wilt with me, so thou dost but preserve me in thy fear and favour. Thou knowest that it is my great fear, but let thy Spirit secure that nothing may be able to separate me from the love of God in Jesus Christ : then smite me here that thou mayest spare me for ever ; and yet, O Lord, smite me friendly, for thou knowest my infirmities. Into thy hands I commend my spirit; for thou hast redeemed me, O Lord, thou God of truth. Come, Holy Spirit, help me in this conflict. Come, Lord Jesus, come quickly.

[Let the sick man often meditate upon these following promises and gracious words of God.]

My help cometh of the Lord, who preserveth them that are true of heart. Psal. vii. 11.

And all they that know thy name will put their trust in thee : for thou, Lord, hast never failed them that seek thee. Psal. ix. 10.

O how plentiful is thy goodness, which thou hast laid up for them that fear thee, and that thou hast prepared for them that put their trust in thee, even before the sons of men ! Psal. xxxi. 21.

Behold, the eye of the Lord is upon them that fear him, and upon them that put their trust in his mercy, to deliver their souls from death. Psal. xxxiii. 17.

The Lord is nigh unto them that are of a contrite heart ; and will save such as are of an humble spirit. Psal. xxxiv. 18.

Thou, Lord, shalt save both man and beast : how excellent is thy mercy, O God ! and the children of men shall put their trust under the shadow of thy wings. Psal. xxxvi. 7.

They shall be satisfied with the plenteousness of thy house ; and thou shalt give them to drink of thy pleasures, as out of the rivers. Ver. 8.

For with thee is the well of life ; and in thy light we shall see light. Ver. 9.

Commit thy way unto the Lord, and put thy trust in him, and he shall bring it to pass. Psal. xxxvii. 5.

But the salvation of the righteous cometh of the Lord, who is also their strength in the time of trouble. Ver. 40.

So that a man shall say, Verily there is a reward for the righteous: doubtless there is a God that judgeth the earth. Psal. lviii. 10.

Blessed is the man whom thou choosest and receivest unto thee: he shall dwell in thy court, and shall be satisfied with the pleasures of thy house, even of thy holy temple. Psal. lxv. 4.

They that sow in tears shall reap in joy. Psal. cxxvi. 6.

It is written, I will never leave thee nor forsake thee. Heb. xiii. 5.

The prayer of faith shall save the sick; and the Lord shall raise him up: and if he have committed sins, they shall be forgiven him. James v. 15.

Come, and let us return unto the Lord; for he hath torn, and he will heal us; he hath smitten, and he will bind us up. Hos. vi. 1.

If we sin, we have an advocate with the Father, Jesus Christ the righteous; and he is the propitiation for our sins. 1 John ii. 1, 2.

If we confess our sins, he is faithful and righteous to forgive us our sins, and to cleanse us from all unrighteousness. 1 John i. 9.

He that forgives shall be forgiven. Luke vi. 37.

And this is the confidence that we have in him, that if we ask any thing according to his will, he heareth us. 1 John v. 14.

And ye know that he was manifested to take away our sins. 1 John iii. 5.

If ye, being evil, know how to give good things to your children, how much more shall your Father which is in heaven give good things to them that ask him? Matt. vii. 11.

This is a faithful saying, and worthy of all acceptation, that Jesus Christ came into the world to save sinners. 1 Tim. i. 15.

He that hath given us his Son, how should he not, with him, give us all things else? Rom. viii. 32.

Acts of Hope, to be used by Sick Persons after a pious Life.

I am persuaded, that neither death, nor life, nor angels, nor principalities, nor powers, nor things present, nor things to come, nor height, nor depth, nor any other creature, shall be able to separate me from the love of God, which is in Christ Jesus our Lord. Rom. viii. 38, 39.

I have fought a good fight: I have finished my course: I have kept the faith. Henceforth there is laid up for me a crown of righteousness, which the Lord, the righteous Judge, shall give me at that day; and not to me only, but unto all them also that love his appearing. 2 Tim. iv. 7, 8.

Blessed be God, even the Father of our Lord Jesus Christ, the Father of mercies and the God of all comforts, who comforts us in all our tribulation. 2 Cor. i. 3, 4.

A Prayer to be said in behalf of a Sick or Dying Person.

O Lord God, there is no number of thy days nor of thy mercies, and the sins and sorrows of thy servant also are multiplied. Lord, look upon him with much mercy and pity, forgive him all his sins, comfort his sorrows, ease his pain, satisfy his doubts, relieve his fears, instruct his ignorances, strengthen his understanding, take from him all disorders of spirit, weakness and abuse of fancy. Restrain the malice and power of the spirits of darkness: and suffer him to be injured neither by his ghostly enemies nor his own infirmities; and let a holy and a just peace, the peace of God, be within his conscience.

Lord, preserve his senses till the last of his time, strengthen his faith, confirm his hope, and give him a never-ceasing charity to thee, our God, and to all the world: stir up in him a great and proportionable contrition for all the evils he hath done, and give him a just measure of patience for all he suffers: give him prudence, memory, and consideration, rightly to state the accounts of his soul; and do thou remind him of all his duty, that, when it shall please thee that his soul goes out from the prison of his body, it may be received by angels, and preserved from the surprise of evil spirits, and from the horrors and amazements of new and strange regions, and be laid up in the bosom of our Lord, till, at the day of thy second coming, it shall be reunited to the body, which is now to be laid down in weakness and dishonour; but we humbly beg may then be raised up with glory and power for ever to live, and to behold the face of God in the glories of the Lord Jesus, who is our hope, our resurrection, and our life, the light of our eyes and the joy of our souls, our blessed and ever-glorious Redeemer. Amen.

s 2

[Hither the sick person may draw in, and use the acts of several virtues respersed in the several parts of this book, the several litanies, viz. of repentance, of the passion and the single prayers, according to his present needs.]

A Prayer to be said in a Storm at Sea.

O my God, thou didst create the earth and the sea for thy glory and the use of man, and dost daily show wonders in the deep: look upon the danger and fear of thy servant. My sins have taken hold upon me, and without the supporting arm of thy mercy I cannot look up; but my trust is in thee. Do thou, O Lord, rebuke the sea, and make it calm, for to thee the winds and the sea obey; let not the waters swallow me up, but let thy Spirit, the spirit of gentleness and mercy, move upon the waters. Be thou reconciled unto thy servants, and then the face of the waters will be smooth. I fear that my sins make me, like Jonas, the cause of the tempest. Cast out all my sins, and throw not thy servants away from thy presence, and from the land of the living, into the depth, where all things are forgotten. But if it be thy will that we shall go down into the waters, Lord, receive my soul into thy holy hands, and preserve it in mercy and safety till the day of restitution of all things; and be pleased to unite my death to the death of thy Son, and to accept of it so united as a punishment for all my sins, that thou mayest forget all thine anger, and blot my sins out of thy book, and write my soul there, for Jesus Christ's sake, our dearest Lord and most mighty Redeemer. Amen.

Then make an Act of Resignation thus:

To God pertain the issues of life and death. It is the Lord, let him do what seemeth good in his own eyes. Thy will be done in earth as it is in heaven.

Recite Psalms cvii. and cxxx.

A Form of a Vow to be made in this or the like Danger.

If the Lord will be gracious and hear the prayer of his servant, and bring me safe to shore, then I will praise him secretly and publicly, and pay unto the uses of charity [or religion] [then name the sum you design for holy uses]. O my God, my goods are nothing unto thee: I will also be thy servant all the days of my life, and remember this mercy and my present purposes, and live more to God's glory and with a stricter duty. And do thou please to accept this vow as an instance of my importunity, and the greatness of my needs; and be thou graciously moved to pity and deliver me. Amen.

[*This form also may be used in praying for a blessing on an enterprise, and may be instanced in actions of devotion as well as of charity.*]

A Prayer before a Journey.

O almighty God, who fillest all things with thy presence, and art a God afar off as well as near at hand; thou didst send thy angel to bless Jacob in his journey, and didst lead the children of Israel through the Red Sea, making it a wall on the right hand and on the left; be pleased to let thy angel go out before me and guide me in my journey, preserving me from dangers of robbers, from violence of enemies, and sudden and sad accidents, from falls and errors. And prosper my journey to thy glory, and to all my innocent purposes; and preserve me from all sin, that I may return in peace and holiness, with thy favour and thy blessing, and may serve thee in thankfulness and obedience all the days of my pilgrimage; and at last bring me to thy country, to the celestial Jerusalem, there to dwell in thy house, and to sing praises to thee for ever. Amen.

Ad Sect. 4.] *A Prayer to be said before the hearing or reading the Word of God.*

O holy and eternal Jesus, who hast begotten us by thy word, renewed us by thy Spirit, fed us by thy sacraments, and by the daily ministry of thy word, still go on to build us up to life eternal. Let thy most Holy Spirit be present with me and rest upon me in the reading or hearing thy sacred word, that I may do it humbly, reverently, without prejudice, with a mind ready and desirous to learn and to obey; that I may be readily furnished and instructed to every good work, and may practise all thy holy laws and commandments, to the glory of thy holy name, O holy and eternal Jesus. Amen.

Ad Sect. 5, 9, 10.] *A Form of Confession of Sins and Repentance, to be used upon Fasting Days, or Days of Humiliation, especially in Lent, and before the Holy Sacrament.*

" Have mercy upon me, O God, after thy great goodness;

according to the multitude of thy mercies do away mine offences : for I will confess my wickedness, and be sorry for my sin." O my dearest Lord, I am not worthy to be accounted amongst the meanest of thy servants, not worthy to be sustained by the least fragments of thy mercy, but to be shut out of thy presence for ever with dogs and unbelievers.—But for thy name's sake, O Lord, be merciful unto my sin, for it is great.

I am the vilest of sinners, and the worst of men ; proud and vain-glorious, impatient of scorn or of just reproof; not enduring to be slighted, and yet extremely deserving it ; I have been cozened by the colours of humility, and when I have truly called myself vicious I could not endure any man else should say so or think so. I have been disobedient to my superiors, churlish and ungentle in my behaviour, unchristian and unmanly.—But for thy name's sake, &c.

O just and dear God, how can I expect pity or pardon, who am so angry and peevish, with and without cause, envious at good, rejoicing in the evil of my neighbours, negligent of my charge, idle and useless, timorous and base, jealous and impudent, ambitious and hard-hearted, soft, unmortified, and effeminate in my life, undevout in my prayers, without fancy or affection, without attendance to them or perseverance in them ; but passionate and curious in pleasing my appetite of meat, and drink, and pleasures, making matter both for sin and sickness; and I have reaped the cursed fruits of such improvidence, entertaining indecent and impure thoughts ; and I have brought them forth in indecent and impure actions, and the spirit of uncleanness hath entered in and unhallowed the temple which thou didst consecrate for the habitation of thy Spirit of love and holiness.—But for thy name's sake, O Lord, be merciful unto my sin, for it is great.

Thou hast given me a whole life to serve thee in, and to advance my hopes of heaven; and this precious time I have thrown away upon my sins and vanities, being improvident of my time and of my talent, and of thy grace and my own advantages, resisting thy Spirit and quenching him. I have been a great lover of myself, and yet used many ways to destroy myself. I have pursued my temporal ends with greediness and indirect means. I am revengeful and unthankful, forgetting benefits, but not so soon forgetting injuries, curious and murmuring, a great breaker of promises. I have not loved my neighbour's good, nor advanced it in all things, where I could.   I have been unlike thee in all things.   I am unmerci ful and unjust; a sottish admirer of things below, and careless of heaven and the ways that lead thither.

But for thy name's sake, O Lord, be merciful unto my sin, for it is great.

All my senses have been windows to let sin in, and death by sin.   Mine eyes have been adulterous and covetous; mine ears open to slander and detraction; my tongue and palate loose and wanton, intemperate and of foul language, talkative and lying, rash and malicious, false and flattering, irreligious and irreverent, detracting and censorious; my hands have been injurious and unclean, my passions violent and rebellious, my desires impatient and unreasonable; all my members and all my faculties have been servants of sin; and my very best actions have more matter of pity than of confidence, being imperfect in my best, and intolerable in most.—But for thy name's sake, O Lord, &c.

Unto this and a far bigger heap of sin I have added also the faults of others to my own score, by neglecting to hinder them to sin in all that I could and ought; but I also have encouraged them in sin, have taken off their fears, and hardened their consciences, and tempted them directly, and prevailed in it to my own ruin and theirs, unless thy glorious and unspeakable mercy hath prevented so intolerable a calamity.

Lord, I have abused thy mercy, despised thy judgments, turned thy grace into wantonness.   I have been unthankful for thy infinite loving-kindness.   I have sinned and repented, and then sinned again and resolved against it, and presently broke it; and then I tied myself up with vows, and then was tempted, and then I yielded by little and little, till I was willingly lost again, and my vows fell off like cords of vanity.

Miserable man that I am! who shall deliver me from this body of sin?

And yet, O Lord, I have another heap of sins to be unloaded. My secret sins, O Lord, are innumerable; sins I noted not; sins that I willingly neglected; sins that I acted upon wilful ignorance and voluntary mispersuasion; sins that I have forgot; and sins which a diligent and a watchful spirit might have prevented, but I would not.   Lord, I am confounded with the multitude of them, and the horror of their remembrance, though

I consider them nakedly in their direct appearance, without the deformity of their unhandsome and aggravating circumstances: but, so dressed, they are a sight too ugly, an instance of amazement, infinite in degrees, and insufferable in their load.

And yet thou hast spared me all this while, and hast not thrown me into hell, where I have deserved to have been long since, and even now to have been shut up to an eternity of torments with insupportable amazement, fearing the revelation of thy day.

Miserable man that I am! who shall deliver me from this body of sin?

Thou shalt answer for me, O Lord my God. Thou that prayest for me shalt be my judge.

The Prayer.

Thou hast prepared for me a more healthful sorrow: O deny not thy servant when he begs sorrow of thee. Give me a deep contrition for my sins, a hearty detestation and loathing of them, hating them worse than death with torments. Give me grace entirely, presently, and for ever, to forsake them ; to walk with care and prudence, with fear and watchfulness, all my days ; to do all my duty with diligence and charity, with zeal and a never-fainting spirit; to redeem the time, to trust upon thy mercies, to make use of all the instruments of grace, to work out my salvation with fear and trembling: that thou mayest have the glory of pardoning all my sins, and I may reap the fruit of all thy mercies and all thy graces, of thy patience and long-suffering, even to live a holy life here, and to reign with thee for ever, through Jesus Christ our Lord. Amen.

Ad Sect. 6.] *Special Devotions to be used upon the Lord's Day, and the great Festivals of Christians.*

In the morning recite the following form of thanksgiving, upon the special festivals, adding the commemoration of the special blessings according to the following prayers ; adding such prayers as you shall choose out of the foregoing devotions.

Besides the ordinary and public duties of the day, if you retire into your closet to read and meditate, after you have performed that duty, say the Song of St. Ambrose, (commonly called the *Te Deum*,) or, We praise thee, &c. ; then add the prayers for particular graces, which are at the end of the former chapter, such and as many of them as shall fit your present needs and affections, ending with the Lord's Prayer. This form of devotion may, for variety, be indifferently used at other times.

A form of thanksgiving, with a recital of public and private blessings, to be used upon Easter-day, Whit-Sunday, Ascension-day, and all Sundays of the year : but the middle part of it may be reserved for the more solemn festivals, and the other used upon the ordinary, as every man's affections or leisure shall determine.

[1.] *Ex Liturgia S. Basilii magna ex parte.*

O eternal Essence, Lord God, Father Almighty, Maker of all things in heaven and earth; it is a good thing to give thanks to thee, O Lord, and to pay to thee all reverence, worship, and devotion, from a clean and prepared heart, and with an humble spirit to present a living and reasonable sacrifice to thy holiness and majesty; for thou hast given unto us the knowledge of thy truth; and who is able to declare thy greatness, and to recount all thy marvellous works which thou hast done in all the generations of the world?

O great Lord and Governor of all things, Lord and Creator of all things visible and invisible, who sittest upon the throne of thy glory, and beholdest the secret of the lowest abyss and darkness, thou art without beginning, uncircumscribed, incomprehensible, unalterable, and seated for ever unmovable in thy own essential happiness and tranquillity; thou art the Father of our Lord Jesus Christ, who is

Our dearest and most gracious Saviour, our hope, the wisdom of the Father, the image of thy goodness, the Word eternal, and the brightness of thy person, the power of God from eternal ages, the true light that lighteneth every man that cometh into the world, the redemption of man, and the sanctification of our spirits.

By whom the Holy Ghost descended upon the church, the Holy Spirit of truth, the seal of adoption; the earnest of the inheritance of the saints; the first-fruits of everlasting felicity; the life-giving power; the fountain of sanctification; the comfort of the church, the ease of the afflicted, the support of the weak, the wealth of the poor, the teacher of the doubtful, scrupulous, and ignorant; the anchor of the fearful; the infinite reward of all faithful souls, by whom all reasonable and understanding creatures serve thee, and send up a never-ceasing and a never-rejected sacrifice of prayer, and praises, and adoration.

All angels and archangels, all thrones and dominions, all principalities and powers, the cherubim with many eyes, and the seraphim covered with wings from the terror and amazement of thy brightest glory; these, and all the powers of heaven, do perpetually sing praises and never-ceasing hymns and eternal anthems to the glory of the eternal God, the Almighty Father of men and angels.

Holy is our God; holy is the Almighty; holy is the Immortal; holy, holy, holy, Lord God of sabaoth, heaven and earth are full of the majesty of thy glory. Amen. With these holy and blessed spirits I also, thy servant, O thou great lover of souls, though I be unworthy to offer praise to such a majesty; yet, out of my bounden duty, humbly offer up my heart and voice to join in this blessed choir, and confess the glories of the Lord. For thou art holy, and of thy greatness there is no end; and in thy justice and goodness thou hast measured out to us all thy works.

Thou madest man out of the earth, and didst form him after thine own image; thou didst place him in a garden of pleasure, and gavest him laws of righteousness to be to him a seed of immortality.

" Oh that men would therefore praise the Lord for his goodness, and declare the wonders that he hath done for the children of men."

For when man sinned and listened to the whispers of a tempting spirit, and refused to hear the voice of God, thou didst throw him out from paradise, and sentest him to till the earth; but yet leftest not his condition without remedy, but didst provide for him the salvation of a new birth, and by the blood of thy Son didst redeem and pay the price to thine own justice for thine own creature, lest the work of thine own hands should perish.

" Oh that men would therefore praise the Lord," &c.

For thou, O Lord, in every age didst send testimonies from heaven, blessings, and prophets, and fruitful seasons, and preachers of righteousness, and miracles of power and mercy; thou spakest by thy prophets and saidst, "I will help by one that is mighty;" and, in the fulness of time, spakest to us by

thy Son, by whom thou didst make both the worlds, who, by
the word of his power, sustains all things in heaven and earth;
who thought it no robbery to be equal to the Father; who,
being before all time, was pleased to be born in time to converse with men, to be incarnate of a holy virgin; he emptied
himself of all his glories, took on him the form of a servant,
in all things being made like unto us, in a soul of passions
and discourses, in a body of humility and sorrow, but in all
things innocent, and in all things afflicted; and suffered death
for us, that we by him might live, and be partakers of his
nature and his glories, of his body and of his Spirit, of the
blessings of earth, and of immortal felicities in heaven.

"Oh that men would therefore praise the Lord," &c.

For thou, O holy and immortal God, O sweetest Saviour
Jesus, wert made under the law to condemn sin in the flesh:
thou, who knewest no sin, wert made sin for us; thou gavest
to us righteous commandments, and madest known to us all
thy Father's will; thou didst redeem us from our vain conversation, and from the vanity of idols, false principles, and
foolish confidences, and broughtest us to the knowledge of the
true and only God and our Father, and hast made us to thyself a peculiar people of thy own purchase, a royal priesthood,
a holy nation; thou hast washed our souls in the laver of re-
generation, the sacrament of baptism; thou hast reconciled
us by thy death, justified us by thy resurrection, sanctified us
by thy Spirit, sending him upon thy church in visible forms,
and giving him in powers and miracles and mighty signs, and
continuing this incomparable favour in gifts and sanctifying
graces, and promising that he shall abide with us for ever;
thou hast fed us with thine own broken body, and given drink
to our souls out of thine own heart, and hast ascended up on
high, and hast overcome all the powers of death and hell, and
redeemed us from the miseries of a sad eternity; and sittest
at the right hand of God, making intercession for us with a
never-ceasing charity.

"Oh that men would therefore praise the Lord," &c.

The grave could not hold thee long, O holy and eternal
Jesus; thy body could not see corruption, neither could thy
soul be left in hell; thou wert free among the dead, and thou
brakest the iron gates of death, and the bars and chains of the
lower prisons. Thou broughtest comfort to the souls of the

patriarchs, who waited for thy coming, who longed for the redemption of man, and the revelation of thy day. Abraham, Isaac, and Jacob, saw thy day and rejoiced ; and when thou didst arise from thy bed of darkness, and leftest the grave-clothes behind thee, and didst put on a robe of glory, (over which for forty days thou didst wear a veil,) and then enteredst into a cloud, and then into glory, then the powers of hell were confounded, then death lost its power and was swallowed up into victory ; and though death is not quite destroyed, yet it is made harmless and without a sting, and the condition of human nature is made an entrance to eternal glory ; and art become the Prince of life, the first-fruits of the resurrection, the first-born from the dead, having made the way plain before our faces, that we may also arise again in the resurrection of the last day, when thou shalt come again unto us, to render to every man according to his works.

" Oh that men would therefore praise the Lord," &c.

O give thanks unto the Lord ; for he is gracious, and his mercy endureth for ever.

O all ye angels of the Lord, praise ye the Lord ; praise him and magnify him for ever.

O ye spirits and souls of the righteous, praise ye the Lord ; praise him and magnify him for ever.

And now, O Lord God, what shall I render to thy Divine Majesty for all the benefits thou hast done unto thy servant in my personal capacity ?

Thou art my Creator and my Father, my Protector and my Guardian ; thou hast brought me from my mother's womb ; thou hast told all my joints, and in thy book were all my members written ; thou hast given me a comely body, Christian and careful parents, holy education ; thou hast been my guide and my teacher all my days ; thou hast given me ready faculties, an unloosed tongue, a cheerful spirit, straight limbs, a good reputation, and liberty of person, a quiet life, and a tender conscience, [a loving wife or husband, and hopeful children]. Thou wert my hope from my youth, through thee have I been holden up ever since I was born. Thou hast clothed me and fed me, given me friends and blessed them ; given me many days of comfort and health, free from those sad infirmities with which many of thy saints and dearest servants are afflicted. Thou hast sent thy angel to snatch me from the violence of fire and water, to prevent precipices, fracture of bones, to rescue me from thunder and lightning, plague and pestilential diseases, murder and robbery, violence of chance and enemies, and all the spirits of darkness; and in the days of sorrow thou hast refreshed me; in the destitution of provisions thou hast taken care of me, and thou hast said unto me, " I will never leave thee, nor forsake thee."

" I will give thanks unto the Lord with my whole heart, secretly among the faithful, and in the congregation."

Thou, O my dearest Lord and Father, hast taken care of my soul, hast pitied my miseries, sustained my infirmities, relieved and instructed my ignorances: and though I have broken thy righteous laws and commandments, run passionately after vanities, and was in love with death, and was dead in sin, and was exposed to thousands of temptations, and fell foully, and continued in it, and loved to have it so, and hated to be reformed; yet thou didst call me with the checks of conscience, with daily sermons and precepts of holiness, with fear and shame, with benefits and the admonitions of thy most Holy Spirit, by the counsel of my friends, by the example of good persons, with holy books and thousands of excellent arts, and wouldst not suffer me to perish in my folly, but didst force me to attend to thy gracious calling, and hast put me into a state of repentance, and possibilities of pardon, being infinitely desirous I should live, and recover, and make use of thy grace, and partake of thy glories.

" I will give thanks unto the Lord with my whole heart, secretly among the faithful, and in the congregation. For salvation belongeth unto the Lord, and thy blessing is upon thy servant. But as for me, I will come into thy house in the multitude of thy mercies, and in thy fear will I worship towards thy holy temple. For of thee, and in thee, and through and for thee, are all things. Blessed be the name of God, from generation to generation." Amen.

A short Form of Thanksgiving to be said upon any special Deliverance, as from Childbirth, from Sickness, from Battle, or imminent Danger at Sea or Land, &c.

· O most merciful and gracious God, thou fountain of all mercy and blessing, thou hast opened the hand of thy mercy to fill me with blessings and the sweet effects of thy loving-kindness; thou feedest us like a shepherd, thou governest us as a king, thou bearest us in thy arms like a nurse, thou dost cover us under the shadow of thy wings and shelter us like a hen; thou (O dearest Lord!) wakest for us as a watchman, thou providest for us like a husband, thou lovest us as a friend, and thinkest on us perpetually as a careful mother on her helpless babe, and art exceeding merciful to all that fear thee. And now, O Lord, thou hast added this great blessing of deliverance from my late danger [*here name the blessing*]; it was thy hand and the help of thy mercy that relieved me; the waters of affliction had drowned me, and the stream had gone over my soul, if the Spirit of the Lord had not moved upon these waters. Thou, O Lord, didst revoke thy angry sentence which I had deserved, and which was gone out against me. Unto thee, O Lord, I ascribe the praise and honour of my redemption. I will be glad and rejoice in thy mercy, for thou hast considered my trouble, and hast known my soul in adversity. As thou hast spread thy hand upon me for a covering, so also enlarge my heart with thankfulness, and fill my mouth with praises, that my duty and returns to thee may be great as my needs of mercy are; and let thy gracious favours and loving-kindness endure for ever and ever upon thy servant; and grant that what thou hast sown in mercy may spring up in duty; and let thy grace so strengthen my purposes, that I may sin no more, lest thy threatening return upon me in anger, and thy anger break me into pieces, but let me walk in the light of thy favour, and in the paths of thy commandments; that I, living here to the glory of thy name, may at last enter into the glory of my Lord, to spend a whole eternity in giving praise to thy exalted and ever-glorious name. Amen.

"We praise thee, O God, we acknowledge thee to be the Lord. All the earth doth worship thee, the Father everlasting. To thee all angels cry aloud, the heavens and all the powers therein. To thee cherubim and seraphim continually do cry, Holy, holy, holy, Lord God of sabaoth; heaven and earth are full of the majesty of thy glory. The glorious company of the apostles praise thee. The goodly fellowship of the prophets praise thee. The noble army of martyrs praise thee. The holy church throughout all the world doth acknowledge thee, the Father, of an infinite majesty; thine honourable, true, and only Son; also the Holy Ghost the Comforter. Thou art the King of glory, O Christ; thou art the everlasting Son of the Father.   When thou tookest upon thee to deliver man, thou didst not abhor the virgin's womb.   When thou hadst overcome the sharpness of death, thou didst open the kingdom of heaven to all believers.   Thou sittest at the right hand of God in the glory of the Father.   We believe that thou shalt come to be our judge.   We, therefore, pray thee, help thy servants, whom thou hast redeemed with thy precious blood.   Make them to be numbered with thy saints in glory everlasting.   O Lord, save thy people, and bless thine heritage.   Govern them, and lift them up for ever.   Day by day we magnify thee, and we worship thy name ever world without end.   Vouchsafe, O Lord, to keep us this day without sin.   O Lord, have mercy upon us, have mercy upon us.   O Lord, let thy mercy lighten upon us, as our trust is in thee.   O Lord, in thee have I trusted: let me never be confounded." Amen.

A Prayer of Thanksgiving after the receiving of some great Blessing, as the Birth of an Heir, the Success of an honest Design, a Victory, a good Harvest, &c.

O Lord God, Father of mercies, the fountain of comfort and blessing, of life and peace, of plenty and pardon, who fillest heaven with thy glory, and earth with thy goodness; I give thee the most earnest, most humble, and most enlarged returns of my glad and thankful heart, for thou hast refreshed me with thy comforts, and enlarged me with thy blessing; thou hast made my flesh and my bones to rejoice; for, besides the blessings of all mankind, the blessings of nature, and the blessings of grace, the support of every minute, and the comforts of every day, thou hast opened thy bosom, and at this time hast poured out an excellent expression of thy loving-kindness [*here name the blessing*].   What am I, O Lord, and what is my father's house; what is the life and what are the capacities of thy servant, that thou shouldst do this unto me; that the great God of men and angels should make a special decree in heaven for me, and send out an angel of blessing, and instead of condemning and ruining me, as I miserably have deserved, to distinguish me from many my equals and my betters, by this and many other special acts of grace and favour?

Praised be the Lord daily, even the Lord that helpeth us, and poureth his benefits upon us.   He is our God, even the God of whom cometh salvation; God is the Lord, by whom we escape death.   Thou hast brought me to great honour, and comforted me on every side.

Thou, Lord, hast made me glad through thy works; I will rejoice in giving praise for the operation of thy hands.

O give thanks unto the Lord, and call upon his name; tell the people what things he hath done.

As for me, I will give great thanks unto the Lord, and praise him among the multitude.

Blessed be the Lord God, even the Lord God of Israel, which only doeth wondrous and gracious things.

And blessed be the name of his Majesty for ever; and all the earth shall be filled with his majesty.   Amen.   Amen.

Glory be to the Father, &c.

As it was in the beginning, &c.

A Prayer to be said on the Feast of Christmas, or the Birth of our blessed Saviour Jesus; the same, also, may be said upon the Feast of the Annunciation and Purification of the B. Virgin Mary.

O holy and almighty God, Father of mercies, Father of our Lord Jesus Christ, the Son of thy love and eternal mercies, I adore, and praise, and glorify thy infinite and unspeakable love and wisdom, who hast sent thy Son from the bosom of felicities to take upon him our nature, and our misery, and our guilt, and hast made the Son of God to become the Son of man, that we might become the sons of God, and partakers of the Divine nature; since thou hast so exalted human nature, be pleased also to sanctify my person, that, by a conformity to the humility, and laws, and sufferings of my dearest Saviour, I may be united to his Spirit, and be made all one with the most holy Jesus.   Amen.

O holy and eternal Jesus, who didst pity mankind lying in his blood, and sin, and misery, and didst choose our sadnesses and sorrows, that thou mightest make us to partake of thy felicities; let thine eyes pity me, thy hands support me, thy holy feet tread down all the difficulties in my way to heaven; let me dwell in thy heart, be instructed with thy wisdom, moved by thy affections, choose with thy will, and be clothed with thy righteousness; that, in the day of judgment, I may be found having on thy garments, sealed with thy impression; and that, bearing upon every faculty and member the character of my elder Brother, I may not be cast out with strangers and unbelievers. Amen.

O holy and ever-blessed Spirit, who didst overshadow the holy virgin-mother of our Lord, and caused her to conceive by a miraculous and mysterious manner; be pleased to overshadow my soul, and enlighten my spirit, that I may conceive the holy Jesus in my heart, and may bear him in my mind, and may grow up to the fulness of the stature of Christ, to be a perfect man in Christ Jesus. Amen.

To God, the Father of our Lord Jesus Christ, to the eternal Son, that was incarnate and born of a virgin, to the Spirit of the Father and the Son, be all honour and glory, worship and adoration, now and for ever. Amen.

[The same form of prayer may be used upon our own birthday, or day of our baptism; adding the following prayer.]

A Prayer to be said upon our Birth-day, or Day of Baptism.

O blessed and eternal God, I give thee praise and glory for thy great mercy to me, in causing me to be born of Christian parents, and didst not allot to me a portion with misbelievers and heathen that have not known thee. Thou didst not suffer me to be strangled at the gate of the womb, but thy hand sustained and brought me to the light of the world, and the illumination of baptism, with thy grace preventing my election, and by an artificial necessity and holy prevention engaging me to the profession and practices of Christianity. Lord, since that I have broken the promises made in my behalf, and which I confirmed by my after-act: I went back from them by an evil life; and yet thou hast still continued to me life and time of repentance; and didst not cut me off in the beginning of my days, and the progress of my sins. O dearest God, pardon the errors and ignorances, the vices and vanities, of my youth, and the faults of my more forward years, and let me never more stain the whiteness of my baptismal robe; and now that by thy grace I still persist in the purposes of obedience, and do give up my name to Christ, and glory to be a disciple of thy institution, and a servant of Jesus, let me never fail of thy grace; let no root of bitterness spring up, and disorder my purposes, and defile my spirit. O let my years be so many degrees of nearer approach to thee; and forsake me not, O God, in my old age, when I am gray-headed; and when my strength faileth me, be thou my strength and my guide unto death; that I may reckon my years, and apply my heart unto wisdom; and at last, after spending a holy and a blessed life, I may be brought unto a glorious eternity, through Jesus Christ our Lord. Amen.

[Then add the form of thanksgiving formerly described.]

A Prayer to be said upon the Days of the Memory of Apostles, Martyrs, &c.

O eternal God, to whom do live the spirits of them that depart hence in the Lord, and in whom the souls of them that be elected, after they be delivered from the burden of the flesh, be in peace and rest from their labours, and their works follow them, and their memory is blessed; I bless and magnify thy holy and ever-glorious name, for the great grace and blessing manifested to thy apostles and martyrs, and other holy persons, who have glorified thy name in the days of their flesh, and have served the interest of religion and of thy service: and this day we have thy servant [*name the apostle or martyr*, &c.] in remembrance, whom thou hast led through the troubles and temptations of this world, and now hast lodged in the bosom of a certain hope and great beatitude, until the day of restitution of all things. Blessed be the mercy and eternal goodness of God; and the memory of all thy saints is blessed. Teach me to practise their doctrine, to imitate their lives, following their example, and being united as a part of the same mystical body by the band of the same faith, and a holy hope, and a never-ceasing charity. And may it please thee, of thy gracious goodness, shortly to accomplish the number of thine elect, and to hasten thy kingdom, that we, with thy servant and all others departed in the true faith and fear of thy holy name, may have our perfect consummation and bliss, in body and soul, in thy eternal and everlasting kingdom. Amen.

A Form of Prayer recording all the parts and mysteries of Christ's Passion, being a short history of it: to be used especially in the Week of the Passion, and before the receiving the blessed Sacrament.

All praise, honour, and glory be to the holy and eternal

Jesus.   I adore thee, O blessed Redeemer, eternal God, the light of the Gentiles, and the glory of Israel; for thou hast done and suffered for me more than I could wish; more than I could think of; even all that a lost and a miserable perishing sinner could possibly need.

Thou wert afflicted with thirst and hunger, with heat and cold, with labours and sorrows, with hard journeys and restless nights; and when thou wert contriving all the mysterious and admirable ways of paying our scores, thou didst suffer thyself to be designed to slaughter by those for whom, in love, thou wert ready to die.

"What is man, that thou art mindful of him; and the son of man, that thou thus visitest him?"

Blessed be thy name, O holy Jesus; for thou wentest about doing good, working miracles of mercy, healing the sick, comforting the distressed, instructing the ignorant, raising the dead, enlightening the blind, strengthening the lame, straightening the crooked, relieving the poor, preaching the gospel, and reconciling sinners by the mightiness of thy power, by the wisdom of thy Spirit, by the word of God, and the merits of thy passion, thy healthful and bitter passion.

"Lord, what is man, that thou art mindful of him," &c.

Blessed be thy name, O holy Jesus, who wert content to be conspired against by the Jews, to be sold by thy servant for a vile price, and to wash the feet of him that took money for thy life, and to give to him and to all thy apostles thy most holy body and blood, to become a sacrifice for their sins, even for their betraying and denying thee; and for all my sins, even for my crucifying thee afresh, and for such sins, which I am ashamed to think, but that the greatness of my sins magnify the infiniteness of thy mercies, who didst so great things for so vile a person.

"Lord, what is man," &c.

Blessed be thy name, O holy Jesus, who, being to depart the world, didst comfort thy apostles, pouring out into their ears and hearts treasures of admirable discourses; who didst recommend them to thy Father with a mighty charity, and then didst enter into the garden set with nothing but briers and sorrows, where thou didst suffer a most unspeakable agony, until the sweat strained through thy pure skin like drops of blood, and there didst sigh and groan, and fall flat upon the earth, and pray, and submit to the intolerable burden of thy Father's wrath, which I had deserved, and thou sufferedst.

"Lord, what is man," &c.

Blessed be thy name, O holy Jesus, who hast sanctified to us all our natural infirmities and passions, by vouchsafing to be in fear and trembling, and sore amazement, by being bound and imprisoned, by being harassed and dragged with cords of violence and rude hands, by being drenched in the brook in the way, by being sought after like a thief, and used like a sinner, who wert the most holy and the most innocent, cleaner than an angel, and brighter than the morning star.

"Lord, what is man," &c.

Blessed be thy name, O holy Jesus, and blessed be thy loving-kindness and pity, by which thou didst neglect thy own sorrows, and go to comfort the sadness of thy disciples, quickening their dulness, encouraging their duty, arming their weakness with excellent precepts against the day of trial. Blessed be that humility and sorrow of thine, who, being Lord of the angels, yet wouldest need and receive comfort from thy servant the angel; who didst offer thyself to thy persecutors, and madest them able to seize thee; and didst receive the traitor's kiss, and sufferedst a veil to be thrown over thy holy face that thy enemies might not presently be confounded by so bright a lustre; and wouldst do a miracle to cure a wound of one of thy spiteful enemies; and didst reprove a zealous servant in behalf of a malicious adversary; and then didst go like a lamb to the slaughter, without noise, or violence, or resistance, when thou couldst have commanded millions of angels for thy guard and rescue.

"Lord, what is man," &c.

Blessed be thy name, O holy Jesus, and blessed be that holy sorrow thou didst suffer, when thy disciples fled, and thou wert left alone in the hands of cruel men, who, like evening wolves, thirsted for a draught of thy best blood: and thou wert led to the house of Annas, and there asked insnaring questions, and smitten on the face by him whose ear thou hadst but lately healed; and from thence wert dragged to the house of Caiaphas; and there all night didst endure spittings, affronts, scorn contumelies, blows, and intolerable insolences, and all this for man, who was thy enemy, and the cause of all thy sorrows.

"Lord, what is man " &c.

Blessed be thy name, O holy Jesus, and blessed be thy mercy, who, when thy servant Peter denied thee, and forsook thee, and forswore thee, didst look back upon him, and by that gracious and chiding look didst call him back to himself and thee; who wert accused before the high priest, and railed upon, and examined to evil purposes, and with designs of blood; who wert declared guilty of death for speaking a most necessary and most profitable truth ; who wert sent to Pilate and found innocent, and sent to Herod and still found innocent, and wert arrayed in white, both to declare thy innocence, and yet to deride thy person, and wert sent back to Pilate, and examined again, and yet nothing but innocence found in thee, and malice round about thee to devour thy life, which yet thou wert more desirous to lay down for them than they were to take it from thee.

"Lord, what is man," &c.

Blessed be thy name, O holy Jesus, and blessed be that patience and charity, by which for our sakes thou wert content to be smitten with canes, and have that holy face, which angels with joy and wonder do behold, be spit upon and be despised, when compared with Barabbas, and scourged most rudely with unhallowed hands, till the pavement was purpled with that holy blood, and condemned to a sad and shameful, a public and painful death, and arrayed in scarlet, and crowned with thorns and stripped naked, and then clothed, and loaden with the cross, and tormented with a tablet stuck with nails at the fringes of thy garment, and bound hard with cords, and dragged most vilely and most piteously till the load was too great, and did sink thy tender and virginal body to the earth ; and yet didst comfort the weeping women, and didst more pity thy persecutors than thyself, and wert grieved for the miseries of Jerusalem to come forty years after, more than for thy present passion.

"Lord, what is man," &c.

Blessed be thy name, O holy Jesus, and blessed be that incomparable sweetness and holy sorrow which thou sufferedst, when thy holy hands and feet were nailed upon the cross, and the cross, being set in a hollowness of the earth, did in the fall rend the wounds wider, and there naked and bleeding, sick and faint, wounded and despised, didst hang upon the weight of thy wounds three long hours, praying for thy persecutors, satis-

fying thy Father's wrath, reconciling the penitent thief, providing for thy holy and afflicted mother, tasting vinegar and
gall; and when the fulness of thy suffering was accomplished,
didst give thy soul into the hands of God, and didst descend
to the regions of longing souls, who waited for the revelation
of this thy day in their prisons of hope: and then thy body
was transfixed with a spear, and issued forth two sacraments,
water and blood, and thy body was composed to burial, and
dwelt in darkness three days and three nights.

"Lord, what is man, that thou art mindful of him, and the
son of man, that thou thus visitest him?"

The Prayer.

Thus, O blessed Jesu, thou didst finish thy holy passion with
pain and anguish so great, that nothing could be greater than
it, except thyself and thy own infinite mercy: and all this for
man, even for me, than whom nothing could be more miserable,
thyself only excepted, who becamest so by undertaking our
guilt and our punishment. And now, Lord, who hast done
so much for me, be pleased only to make it effectual to me,
that it may not be useless and lost as to my particular, lest I
become eternally miserable, and lost to all hopes and possibilities of comfort. All this deserves more love than I have to
give: but, Lord, do thou turn me all into love, and all my
love into obedience, and let my obedience be without interruption, and then I hope thou wilt accept such a return as I can
make. Make me to be something that thou delightest in, and
thou shalt have all that I am or have from thee, even whatsoever thou makest fit for thyself. Teach me to live wholly for
my Saviour Jesus, and to be ready to die for Jesus, and to be
conformable to his life and sufferings, and to be united to him
by inseparable unions, and to own no passions but what may
be servants to Jesus and disciples of his institution. O sweetest
Saviour, clothe my soul with thy holy robe; hide my sins in
thy wounds, and bury them in thy grave; and let me rise in
the life of grace, and abide and grow in it, till I arrive at the
kingdom of glory. Amen. " Our Father," &c.

Ad Sect. 7, 8, 10.]   *A Form of Prayer or Intercession for
all Estates of People in the Christian Church. The parts
of which may be added to any other forms; and the whole*

office, entirely as it lies, is proper to be said in our prepara-
tion to the Holy Sacrament, or on the day of celebration.

1. *For ourselves.*

O thou gracious Father of mercy, Father of our Lord Jesus
Christ, have mercy upon thy servants, who bow our heads,
and our knees, and our hearts to thee : pardon and forgive us
all our sins : give us the grace of holy repentance, and a strict
obedience to thy holy word : strengthen us in the inner man
with the power of the Holy Ghost for all the parts and duties
of our calling and holy living : preserve us for ever in the
unity of the holy catholic church, and in the integrity of the
Christian faith, and in the love of God and of our neighbours,
and in hope of life eternal. Amen.

2. *For the whole Catholic Church.*

O holy Jesus, King of the saints, and Prince of the catholic
church, preserve thy spouse, whom thou hast purchased with
thy right hand, and redeemed and cleansed with thy blood ;
the whole catholic church, from one end of the earth to the
other ; she is founded upon a rock, but planted in the sea. O,
preserve her safe from schism, heresy, and sacrilege ! Unite
all her members with the bands of faith, hope, and charity,
and an external communion, when it shall seem good in thine
eyes. Let the daily sacrifice of prayer and sacramental thanksgiving never cease, but be for ever presented to thee, and for
ever united to the intercession of her dearest Lord, and for
ever prevail for the obtaining for every of its members grace
and blessing, pardon and salvation. Amen.

3. *For all Christian Kings, Princes, and Governors.*

O King of kings, and Prince of all the rulers of the earth,
give thy grace and Spirit to all Christian princes, the spirit of
wisdom and counsel, the spirit of government and godly fear.
Grant unto them to live in peace and honour, that their people
may love and fear them, and they may love and fear God.
Speak good unto their hearts concerning the church, that they
may be nursing fathers to it, fathers to the fatherless, judges
and avengers of the cause of widows : that they may be compassionate to the wants of the poor, and the groans of the oppressed ; that they may not vex or kill the Lord's people with
unjust or ambitious wars, but may feed the flock of God, and
may inquire after and do all things which may promote peace.

public honesty, and holy religion : so administering things present that they may not fail of the everlasting glories of the world to come, where all thy faithful people shall reign kings for ever. Amen.

4. *For all the Orders of them that minister about Holy Things.*

O thou great Shepherd and Bishop of our souls, holy and eternal Jesus, give unto thy servants the ministers of the mysteries of Christian religion the spirit of prudence and sanctity, faith and charity, confidence and zeal, diligence and watchfulness, that they may declare thy will unto the people faithfully, and dispense thy sacraments rightly, and intercede with thee graciously and acceptably for thy servants.   Grant, O Lord, that by a holy life and true belief, by well doing and patient suffering, (when thou shalt call them to it,) they may glorify thee, the great lover of souls, and, after a plentiful conversion of sinners from the error of their ways, they may shine like the stars in glory.   Amen.

Give unto thy servants, the bishops, a discerning spirit, that they may lay hands suddenly on no man, but may depute such persons to the ministries of religion who may adorn the gospel of God, and whose lips may preserve knowledge, and such who by their good preaching and holy living may advance the service of the Lord Jesus.   Amen.

5. *For our nearest Relatives, as Husband, Wife, Children, Family, &c.*

O God of infinite mercy, let thy loving mercy and compassion descend upon the head of thy servants [*my wife, or husband, children, and family*]: be pleased to give them health of body and of spirit, a competent portion of temporals, so as may with comfort support them in their journey to heaven : preserve them from all evil and sad accidents, defend them in all assaults of their enemies, direct their persons and their actions, sanctify their hearts, and words, and purposes ; that we all may, by the bands of obedience and charity, be united to our Lord Jesus, and, always feeling thee our merciful and gracious Father, may become a holy family, discharging our whole duty in all our relations ; that we in this life being thy children by adoption and grace, may be admitted into thy holy family hereafter, for ever to sing praises to thee in the church of the firstborn, in the family of thy redeemed ones.   Amen.

6. *For our Parents, our Kindred in the Flesh, our Friends and Benefactors.*

O God, merciful and gracious, who hast made [*my parents*] my friends and my benefactors ministers of thy mercy, and instruments of providence to thy servant, I humbly beg a blessing to descend upon the heads of [*name the persons or the relations*]. Depute thy holy angels to guard their persons, thy Holy Spirit to guide their souls, thy providence to minister to their necessities ; and let thy grace and mercy preserve them from the bitter pains of eternal death, and bring them to everlasting life, through Jesus Christ. Amen.

7. *For all that lie under the Rod of War, Famine, Pestilence: to be said in the Time of Plague, or War, &c.*

O Lord God almighty, thou art our Father, we are thy children ; thou art our Redeemer, we thy people, purchased with the price of thy most precious blood : be pleased to moderate thy anger towards thy servants ; let not thy whole displeasure arise, lest we be consumed and brought to nothing. Let health and peace be within our dwellings ; let righteousness and holiness dwell for ever in our hearts, and be expressed in all our actions, and the light of thy countenance be upon us in all our sufferings, that we may delight in the service and in the mercies of God for ever. Amen.

O gracious Father and merciful God, if it be thy will, say unto the destroying angel, "It is enough ;" and though we are not better than our brethren who are smitten with the rod of God, but much worse, yet may it please thee, even because thou art good, and because we are timorous and sinful, not yet fitted for our appearance, to set thy mark upon our foreheads, that thy angel, the minister of thy justice, may pass over us, and hurt us not ; let thy hand cover thy servants and hide us in the clefts of the rock, in the wounds of the holy Jesus, from the present anger, that is gone out against us ; that though we walk through the valley of the shadow of death, we may fear no evil, and suffer none ; and those whom thou hast smitten with thy rod, support with thy staff, and visit them with thy mercies and salvation, through Jesus Christ. Amen.

8. *For all Women with Child, and for unborn Children.*

O Lord God, who art the Father of them that trust in thee.

and showest mercy to a thousand generations of them that fear thee; have mercy upon all women great with child; be pleased to give them a joyful and a safe deliverance: and let thy grace preserve the fruit of their wombs, and conduct them to the holy sacrament of baptism; that they, being regenerated by thy Spirit, and adopted into thy family, and the portion and duty of sons, may live to the glory of God, to the comfort of their parents and friends, to the edification of the Christian commonwealth, and the salvation of their own souls, through Jesus Christ. Amen.

9. *For all Estates of Men and Women in the Christian Church.*

O holy God, King eternal, out of the infinite storehouses of thy grace and mercy, give unto all virgins chastity and a religious spirit; to all persons dedicated to thee and to religion, continence and meekness, and active zeal, and an unwearied spirit; to all married pairs, faith and holiness; to widows and fatherless, and all that are oppressed, thy patronage, comfort, and defence; to all Christian women, simplicity and modesty, humility and chastity, patience and charity; give unto the poor, to all that are robbed and spoiled of their goods, a competent support, and a contented spirit, and a treasure in heaven hereafter; give unto prisoners and captives, to them that toil in the mines, and row in the galleys, strength of body and of spirit, liberty and redemption, comfort and restitution; to all that travel by land, thy angel for their guide, and a holy and prosperous return; to all that travel by sea, freedom from pirates and shipwreck, and bring them to the haven where they would be; to distressed and scrupulous consciences, to melancholy and disconsolate persons, to all that are afflicted with evil and unclean spirits, give a light from heaven, great grace, and proportionable comforts and timely deliverance; give them patience and resignation; let their sorrows be changed into grace and comfort, and let the storm waft them certainly to the regions of rest and glory.

Lord God of mercy, give to thy martyrs, confessors, and all thy persecuted, constancy and prudence, boldness and hope, a full faith, and a never-failing charity. To all who are condemned to death, do thou minister comfort, a strong, a quiet, and a resigned spirit; take from them the fear of death, and all remaining affections to sin, and all imperfections of duty and cause them to die full of grace, full of hope. And give to all faithful, and particularly to them who have recommended themselves to the prayers of thy unworthy servant, a supply of all their needs temporal and spiritual, and according to their several states and necessities, rest and peace, pardon and refreshment; and show us all a mercy in the day of judgment. Amen.

Give, O Lord, to the magistrates, equity, sincerity, courage, and prudence, that they may protect the good, defend religion, and punish the wrong-doers. Give to the nobility, wisdom, valour, and loyalty; to merchants, justice and faithfulness; to all artificers and labourers, truth and honesty; to our enemies, forgiveness and brotherly kindness.

Preserve to us the heavens and the air in healthful influence and disposition, the earth in plenty, the kingdom in peace and good government, our marriages in peace, and sweetness, and innocence of society, thy people from famine and pestilence, our houses from burning and robbery, our persons from being burnt alive, from banishment and prison, from widowhood and destitution, from violence of pains and passions, from tempests and earthquakes, from inundation of waters, from rebellion or invasion, from impatience and inordinate cares, from tediousness of spirit and despair, from murder, and all violent, accursed, and unusual deaths, from the surprise of sudden and violent accidents, from passionate and unreasonable fears; from all thy wrath, and from all our sins, good Lord, deliver and preserve thy servants for ever. Amen.

Repress the violence of all implacable, warring, and tyrant nations; bring home unto thy fold all that are gone astray; call into the church all strangers; increase the number and holiness of thine own people; bring infants to ripeness of age and reason; confirm all baptized people with thy grace and with thy Spirit; instruct the novices and new Christians; let a great grace and merciful providence bring youthful persons safely and holily through the indiscretions, and passions, and temptations of their younger years; and to those whom thou hast or shalt permit to live to the age of a man, give competent strength and wisdom; take from them covetousness and churlishness, pride and impatience; fill them full of devotion and charity, repentance and sobriety, holy thoughts and longing desires after heaven and heavenly things; give them a holy and a blessed death, and to us all a joyful resurrection, through Jesus Christ, our Lord. Amen.

Ad Sect. 10.] *The Manner of using these Devotions by way of Preparation to the receiving the blessed Sacrament of the Lord's Supper.*

The just preparation to this holy feast, consisting principally in a holy life, and, consequently, in the repetition of the acts of all virtues, and especially of faith, repentance, charity, and thanksgiving ; to the exercise of these four graces, let the person that intends to communicate, in the times set apart for his preparation and devotion, for the exercise of his faith recite the prayer or litany of the passion ; for the exercise of repentance, the form of confession of sins with the prayer annexed ; and for the graces of thanksgiving and charity, let him use the special forms of prayer above described.   Or if a less time can be allotted for preparatory devotion, the two first will be the more proper, as containing in them all the personal duty of the communicant.   To which, upon the morning of that holy solemnity, let him add,

A Prayer of Preparation or Address to the Holy Sacrament.

An Act of Love.

O most gracious and eternal God, the helper of the helpless, the comforter of the comfortless, the hope of the afflicted, the bread of the hungry, the drink of the thirsty, and the Saviour of all them that wait upon thee ; I bless and glorify thy name, and adore thy goodness, and delight in thy love, that thou hast once more given me the opportunity of receiving the greatest favour which I can receive in this world, even the body and blood of my dearest Saviour.   O take from me all affection to sin or vanity ; let not my affections dwell below, but soar upwards to the element of love, to the seat of God, to the regions of glory, and the inheritance of Jesus : that I may hunger and thirst for the bread of life, and the wine of elect souls, and may know no loves but the love of God, and the most merciful Jesus.   Amen.

An Act of Desire.

O blessed Jesus, thou hast used many arts to save me, thou hast given thy life to redeem me, thy Holy, Spirit to sanctify me, thyself for my example, thy word for my rule, thy grace for my guide, the fruit of thy body hanging on the tree of the cross for the sin of my soul ; and, after all this, thou hast sent thy apostles and ministers of salvation to call me, to importune me, to constrain me to holiness, and peace, and felicity. O now come, Lord Jesus, come quickly; my heart is desirous of thy presence and thirsty of thy grace, and would fain entertain thee, not as a guest, but as an inhabitant, as the Lord of all my faculties. Enter in and take possession, and dwell with me for ever; that I also may dwell in the heart of my dearest Lord, which was opened for me with a spear and love.

An Act of Contrition.

Lord, thou shalt find my heart full of cares and worldly desires, cheated with love of riches, and neglect of holy things, proud and unmortified, false and crafty to deceive itself, intricated and entangled with difficult cases of conscience, with knots which my own wildness and inconsideration and impatience have tied and shuffled together. O my dearest Lord, if thou canst behold such an impure seat, behold the place to which thou art invited is full of passion and prejudice, evil principles and evil habits, peevish and disobedient, lustful and intemperate, and full of sad remembrances, that I have often provoked to jealousy and to anger thee my God, my dearest Saviour, him that died for me, him that suffered torments for me, that is infinitely good to me, and infinitely good and perfect in himself. This, O dearest Saviour, is a sad truth, and I am heartily ashamed, and truly sorrowful for it, and do deeply hate all my sins, and am full of indignation against myself for so unworthy, so careless, so continued, so great a folly; and humbly beg of thee to increase my sorrow, and my care, and my hatred against sin; and make my love to thee swell up to a great grace, and then to glory and immensity.

An Act of Faith.

This indeed is my condition: but I know, O blessed Jesus, that thou didst take upon thee my nature that thou mightest suffer for my sins, and thou didst suffer to deliver me from them and from thy Father's wrath; and I was delivered from this wrath, that I might serve thee in holiness and righteousness all my days. Lord, I am as sure thou didst the great work of redemption for me and all mankind, as that I am alive. This is my hope, the strength of my spirit, my joy, and my confidence; and do thou never let the spirit of unbelief enter into me and take me from this rock. Here I will dwell, for I have a delight therein; here I will live, and here I desire to die.

The Petition.

Therefore, O blessed Jesu, who art my Saviour and my God, whose body is my food, and thy righteousness is my robe, thou art the priest and the sacrifice, the master of the feast and the feast itself, the physician of my soul, the light of my eyes, the purifier of my stains: enter into my heart, and cast out from thence all impurities, all the remains of the old man; and grant I may partake of this holy sacrament with much reverence, and holy relish, and great effect, receiving hence the communication of thy holy body and blood, for the establishment of an unreprovable faith, of an unfeigned love, for the fulness of wisdom, for the healing my soul, for the blessing and preservation of my body, for the taking out the sting of temporal death, and for the assurance of a holy resurrection; for the ejection of all evil from within me, and the fulfilling all thy righteous commandments; and to procure for me a mercy and a fair reception at the day of judgment, through thy mercies, O holy and ever-blessed Saviour Jesus.   Amen.

[Here also may be added the prayer after receiving the cup.]

Ejaculations to be said before or at the receiving the Holy Sacrament.

Like as the hart desireth the water-brooks, so longeth my soul after thee, O God. My soul is athirst for God, yea, even for the living God: when shall I come before the presence of God? Psal. xlii. 1, 2.

O Lord my God, great are thy wondrous works which thou hast done; like as be also thy thoughts, which are to us-ward: and yet there is no man that ordereth them unto thee. Psal. xl. 6.

O send out thy light and thy truth, that they may lead me, and bring me unto thy holy hill, and to thy dwelling; and that I may go unto the altar of God, even unto the God of my joy and gladness; and with my heart will I give thanks to thee, O God my God. Psal. xliii. 3, 4.

I will wash my hands in innocence, O Lord, and so will I go to thine altar: that I may show the voice of thanksgiving, and tell of all thy wondrous works. Psal. xxvi. 6, 7.

Examine me, O Lord, and prove me, try thou my reins and
my heart. For thy loving-kindness is now and ever before
my eyes: and I will walk in thy truth. Ver. 2, 3.

Thou shalt prepare a table before me against them that
trouble me: thou hast anointed my head with oil, and my cup
shall be full. But thy loving-kindness and mercy shall follow me all the days of my life, and I will dwell in the house of
the Lord for ever. Psal. xxiii. 5, 6.

This is the bread that cometh down from heaven, that a
man may eat thereof and not die. John vi. 50.

Whoso eateth my flesh, and drinketh my blood, dwelleth in
me and I in him, and hath eternal life abiding in him; and I
will raise him up at the last day. Ver. 54, 56.

Lord, whither shall we go but to thee? thou hast the words
of eternal life. John vi. 68.

If any man thirst, let him come unto me and drink. John
vii. 37.

The bread which we break, is it not the communication of
the body of Christ? and the cup which we drink, is it not the
communication of the blood of Christ? 1 Cor. x. 16.

What are those wounds in thy hands? They are those
with which I was wounded in the house of my friends. Zech.
xiii. 6.

Immediately before the receiving, say,

Lord, I am not worthy that thou shouldest enter under my
roof. But do thou speak the word only, and thy servant shall
be healed. Matt. viii. 8.

Lord, open thou my lips, and my mouth shall show thy
praise. O God, make speed to save me: O Lord, make haste
to help me.

Come, Lord Jesus, come quickly.

After receiving the consecrated and blessed Bread, say,

O taste and see how gracious the Lord is: blessed is the
man that trusteth in him. The beasts do lack and suffer hunger; but they which seek the Lord shall want no manner of
thing that is good. Lord, what am I, that my Saviour should
become my food; that the Son of God should be the meat of
worms, of dust and ashes, of a sinner, of him that was his
enemy? But this thou hast done to me, because thou art infinitely good and wonderfully gracious, and lovest to bless

every one of us, in turning us from the evil of our ways.
Enter into me, blessed Jesus: let no root of bitterness spring
up in my heart; but be thou Lord of all my faculties.   O let
me feed on thee by faith, and grow up by the increase of God
to a perfect man in Christ Jesus.   Amen.   Lord, I believe:
help mine unbelief.

Glory be to God the Father, Son, &c.

After the receiving the Cup of Blessing.

It is finished.   Blessed be the mercies of God revealed to
us in Jesus Christ.   O blessed and eternal High Priest, let
the sacrifice of the cross, which thou didst once offer for the
sins of the whole world, and which thou dost now and always
represent in heaven to thy Father by thy never-ceasing intercession, and which this day hath been exhibited on thy holy
table sacramentally, obtain mercy and peace, faith and charity,
safety and establishment to thy holy church, which thou hast
founded upon a rock, the rock of a holy faith; and let not
the gates of hell prevail against her, nor the enemy of mankind take any soul out of thy hand, whom thou hast purchased with thy blood, and sanctified by thy Spirit.   Preserve
all thy people from heresy and division of spirit, from scandal
and the spirit of delusion, from sacrilege and hurtful persecutions.   Thou, O blessed Jesus, didst die for us; keep me
for ever in holy living, from sin and sinful shame, in the communion of thy church, and thy church in safety and grace,
in truth and peace, unto thy second coming.   Amen.

Dearest Jesu, since thou art pleased to enter into me, O be
jealous of thy house and the place where thine honour dwelleth: suffer no unclean spirit or unholy thought to come near
thy dwelling, lest it defile the ground where thy holy feet
have trod.   O teach me so to walk, that I may never disre-
pute the honour of my religion, nor stain the holy robe which
thou hast now put upon my soul, nor break my holy vows,
which I have made, and thou hast sealed, nor lose my right
of inheritance, my privilege of being co-heir with Jesus, into
the hope of which I have now further entered: but be thou
pleased to love me with the love of a father, and a brother, and
a husband, and a lord ; and make me to serve thee in the communion of saints, in receiving the sacrament, in the practice
of all holy virtues, in the imitation of thy life, and conformity

to thy sufferings: that I, having now put on the Lord Jesus, may marry his loves and his enmities, may desire his glory, and may obey his laws, and be united to his Spirit, and in the day of the Lord I may be found having on the wedding garment, and bearing in my body and soul the marks of the Lord Jesus, that I may enter into the joy of my Lord, and partake of his glories for ever and ever.   Amen.

Ejaculations to be used any time that Day after the Solemnity is ended.

Lord, if I had lived innocently, I could not have deserved to receive the crumbs that fall from thy table.   How great is thy mercy, who hast feasted me with the bread of virgins, with the wine of angels, with manna from heaven!

O when I shall pass from this dark glass, from this veil of sacraments, to the vision of thy eternal charity; from eating thy body, to beholding thy face in thy eternal kingdom?

Let not my sins crucify the Lord of life again: let it never be said concerning me, "The hand of him that betrayeth me is with me on the table."

Oh that I might love thee as well as ever any creature loved thee!   Let me think nothing but thee, desire nothing but thee, enjoy nothing but thee.

O Jesus, be a Jesus unto me.   Thou art all things unto me.   Let nothing ever please me but what savours of thee and thy miraculous sweetness.

Blessed be the mercies of our Lord, who of God is made unto me wisdom, and righteousness, and sanctification, and redemption.

"He that glorieth, let him glory in the Lord."   **Amen.**

THE END OF HOLY LIVING.

THE

RULE AND EXERCISES

OF

HOLY DYING, &c.

TO THE RIGHT HONOURABLE

AND NOBLEST LORD,

RICHARD, EARL OF CARBERY, &c., &c.

My Lord,

I am treating your Lordship as a Roman gentleman did St. Augustine and his mother; I shall entertain you in a charnel-house, and carry your meditations awhile into the chambers of death, where you shall find the rooms dressed up with melancholic arts, and fit to converse with your most retired thoughts, which begin with a sigh, and proceed in a deep consideration, and end in a holy resolution. The sight that St. Augustine most noted in that house of sorrow was the body of Cæsar, clothed with all the dishonours of corruption that you can suppose in a six months' burial. But I know, that, without pointing, your first thoughts will remember the change of a greater beauty, which is now dressing for the brightest immortality, and from her bed of darkness calls to you to dress your soul for that change which shall mingle your bones with that beloved dust, and carry your soul to the same quire, where you may both sit and sing for ever. My Lord, it is your dear Lady's anniversary, and she deserved the biggest honour, and the longest memory, and the fairest monument, and the most solemn mourning: and in order to it, give me leave, my Lord, to cover her hearse with these following sheets. This book was intended first to minister to her piety; and she desired all good people should partake of the advantages which are here recorded: she knew how to live rarely well, and she desired to know how to die; and God taught her by an experiment. But since her work is done, and God supplied her with provisions of his own, before I could minister to her, and perfect what she desired, it is necessary to present to your Lordship those bundles of cypress which were intended to dress her closet, but come now to dress her hearse. My Lord, both your Lordship

u 2

and myself have lately seen and felt such sorrows of death, and such
sad departure of dearest friends, that it is more than high time we
should think ourselves nearly concerned in the accidents. Death
hath come so near to you, as to fetch a portion from your very
heart; and now you cannot choose but dig your own grave, and
place your coffin in your eye, when the angel hath dressed your
scene of sorrow and meditation with so particular and so near an
object : and, therefore, as it is my duty, I am come to minister to
your pious thoughts, and to direct your sorrows, that they may turn
into virtues and advantages.

And since I know your Lordship to be so constant and regular in
your devotions, and so tender in the matter of justice, so ready in
the expressions of charity, and so apprehensive of religion; and that
you are a person whose work of grace is apt, and must every day
grow toward those degrees where, when you arrive, you shall triumph over imperfection, and choose nothing but what may please
God ; I could not by any compendium conduct and assist your pious
purposes so well as by that which is the great argument and the great
instrument of Holy Living, the consideration and exercises of death.

My Lord, it is a great art to die well, and to be learned by men in
health, by them that can discourse and consider, by those whose
understanding and acts of reason are not abated with fear or pains :
and as the greatest part of death is passed by the preceding years of
our life, so also in those years are the greatest preparations to it;
and he that prepares not for death before his last sickness, is like
him that begins to study philosophy when he is going to dispute
publicly in the faculty. All that a sick and dying man can do is
but to exercise those virtues which he before acquired, and to perfect that repentance which was begun more early. And of this, my
Lord, my book, I think, is a good testimony; not only because it
represents the vanity of a late and sick-bed repentance, but because
it contains in it so many precepts and meditations, so many propositions and various duties, such forms of exercise, and the degrees
and difficulties of so many graces, which are necessary preparatives
to a holy death, that the very learning the duties requires study and
skill, time and understanding, in the ways of godliness; and it were
very vain to say so much is necessary, and not to suppose more
time to learn them, more skill to practise them, more opportunities
to desire them, more abilities both of body and mind, than can be
supposed in a sick, amazed, timorous, and weak person; whose natural acts are disabled, whose senses are weak, whose discerning
faculties are lessened, whose principles are made intricate and entangled, upon whose eyes sits a cloud, and the heart is broken with
sickness, and the liver pierced through with sorrows and the strokes
of death. And, therefore, my Lord, it is intended by the necessity
of affairs that the precepts of dying well be part of the studies of
them that live in health, and the days of discourse and understand-

ing : which, in this case, hath another degree of necessity superadded ; because, in other notices, an imperfect study may be supplied by a frequent exercise and renewed experience; here, if we practise imperfectly once, we shall never recover the error, for we die but once; and, therefore, it will be necessary that our skill be more exact, since it is not to be mended by trial, but the actions must be for ever left imperfect, unless the habit be contracted with study and contemplation beforehand.

And, indeed, I were vain if I should intend this book to be read and studied by dying persons; and they were vainer that should need to be instructed in those graces, which they are then to exercise and to finish. For a sick bed is only a school of severe exercise, in which the spirit of a man is tried and his graces are rehearsed; and the assistances which I have, in the following pages, given to those virtues which are proper to the state of sickness, are such as suppose a man in the state of grace; or they confirm a good man, or they support the weak, or add degrees, or minister comfort, or prevent an evil, or cure the little mischiefs which are incident to tempted persons in their weakness. That is the sum of the present design, as it relates to dying persons. And, therefore, I have not inserted any advices proper to old age, but such as are common to it and the state of sickness, for I suppose very old age to be a longer sickness; it is labour and sorrow when it goes beyond the common period of nature; but if it be on this side that period, and be healthful, in the same degree it is so I reckon it in the accounts of life, and therefore it can have no distinct consideration. But I do not think it is a station of advantage to begin the change of an evil life in; it is a middle state between life and death-bed; and, therefore, although it hath more of hopes than this, and less than that, yet as it partakes of either state, so it is to be regulated by the advices of that state, and judged by its sentences.

Only this : I desire that all old persons would sadly consider that their advantages in that state are very few, but their inconveniences are not few; their bodies are without strength, their prejudices long and mighty, their vices (if they have lived wicked) are habitual, the occasions of the virtues not many, the possibilities of some (in the matter of which they stand very guilty) are past, and shall never return again (such are chastity and many parts of self-denial); that they have some temptations proper to their age, as peevishness and pride, covetousness and talking, wilfulness and unwillingness to learn:[1] and they think they are protected by age from learning anew, or repenting the old, and do not leave, but change their vices;[2]

---

[1] Vel quia nil rectum, nisi quod placuit sibi, ducunt;
Vel quia turpe putant parere minoribus, et, quæ
Imberbes didicere, senes perdenda fateri.—Hor. Ep. ii. 84.

[2] Tenellis adhuc infantiæ suæ persuasionibus in senectute puerascunt.— Mamertus.

and, after all this, either the day of their repentance is past, as we see it true in very many, or it is expiring and towards the sunset, as it is in all; and, therefore, although in these to recover is very possible, yet we may also remember that, in the matter of virtue and repentance, possibility is a great way off from performance; and how few do repent of whom it is only possible that they may! and that many things more are required to reduce their possibility to act; a great grace, an assiduous ministry, an effective calling, mighty assistances, excellent counsel, great industry, a watchful diligence, a well-disposed mind, passionate desires, deep apprehensions of danger, quick perceptions of duty, and time, and God's good blessing, and effectual impression, and seconding all this, that to will and to do may, by him, be wrought to great purposes, and with great speed.

And, therefore, it will not be amiss, but it is hugely necessary, that these persons who have lost their time and their blessed opportunities should have the diligence of youth, and the zeal of new converts, and take account of every hour that is left them, and pray perpetually, and be advised prudently, and study the interest of their souls carefully, with diligence, and with fear; and their old age, which, in effect, is nothing but a continual death-bed, dressed with some more order and advantages, may be a state of hope, and labour, and acceptance; through the infinite mercies of God, in Jesus Christ.

But concerning sinners really under the arrest of death, God hath made no death-bed covenant, the Scripture hath recorded no promises, given no instructions; and, therefore, I had none to give, but only the same which are to be given to all men that are alive, because they are so, and because it is uncertain when they shall be otherwise. But, then, this advice I also am to insert, that they are the smallest number of Christian men who can be divided by the characters of a certain holiness or an open villany; and between these there are many degrees of latitude, and most are of the middle sort, concerning which we are tied to make the judgments of charity, and possibly God may do so too. But, however, all they are such to whom the rules of Holy Dying are useful and applicable, and therefore no separation is to be made in this world. But where the case is not evident, men are to be permitted to the unerring judgment of God; where it is evident, we can rejoice or mourn for them that die.

In the church of Rome they reckon otherwise concerning sick and dying Christians than I have done. For they make profession, that from death to life, from sin to grace, a man may very certainly be changed, though the operation begin not before his last hour; and half this they do upon his death-bed, and the other half when he is in his grave; and they take away the eternal punishment in an instant, by a school-distinction, or the hand of the priest; and the temporal punishment shall stick longer, even then, when the man is no more measured with time, having nothing to do with any thing of or under the sun; but that they pretend to take away too, when

the man is dead; and, God knows, the poor man for all this pays
them both in hell. The distinction of temporal and eternal is a just
measure of pain when it refers to this life and another: but to
dream of a punishment temporal, when all his time is done, and to
think of repentance when the time of grace is past, are great errors,
the one in philosophy, and both in divinity, and are a huge folly in
their pretence, and infinite danger if they are believed: being a certain destruction of the necessity of holy living, when men dare trust
them, and live at the rate of such doctrines. The secret of these is
soon discovered: for, by such means, though a holy life be not necessary, yet a priest is; as if God did not appoint the priest to minister to holy living, but to excuse it; so making the holy calling not
only to live upon the sins of the people, but upon their ruin, and
the advantages of their function to spring from their eternal dangers.
It is an evil craft to serve a temporal end upon the death of souls;
that is an interest not to be handled but with nobleness and ingenuity, fear and caution, diligence and prudence, with great skill
and great honesty, with reverence, and trembling, and severity; a
soul is worth all that, and the need we have requires all that; and,
therefore, those doctrines that go less than all this are not friendly,
because they are not safe.

I know no other difference in the visitation and treating of sick
persons than what depends upon the article of late repentance; for
all churches agree in the same essential propositions, and assist the
sick by the same internal ministries. As for external, I mean unction, used in the church of Rome, since it is used when the man is
above half dead, when he can exercise no act of understanding, it
must needs be nothing; for no rational man can think that any ceremony can make a spiritual change, without a spiritual act of him that
is to be changed; nor work by way of nature, or by charm, but
morally, and after the manner of reasonable creatures; and, therefore, I do not think that ministry at all fit to be reckoned among the
advantages of sick persons. The fathers of the Council of Trent first
disputed, and after their manner at last agreed, that extreme unction
was instituted by Christ. But, afterwards, being admonished by one
of their theologues that the apostles ministered unction to infirm
people before they were priests, (the priestly order, according to their
doctrine, being collated in the institution of the last supper,) for
fear that it should be thought that this unction might be administered by him that was no priest, they blotted out the word *instituted*,
and put in its stead *insinuated*, this sacrament, and that it was published by St. James. So it is in their doctrine; and yet in their
anathematisms they curse all them that shall deny it to have been
instituted by Christ. I shall lay no more prejudice against it, or the
weak arts of them that maintain it, but add this only, that there
being but two places of Scripture pretended for this ceremony, some
chief men of their own side have proclaimed these two invalid as to

the institution of it: for Suarez says, that the unction used by the apostles, in Mark vi. 13, is not the same with what is used in the church
of Rome; and that it cannot be plainly gathered from the Epistle of
St. James, Cajetan affirms, and that it did belong to the miraculous
gift of healing, not to a sacrament. The sick man's exercise of grace
formerly acquired, his perfecting repentance begun in the days of
health, the prayers and counsels of the holy man that ministers, the
giving the holy sacrament, the ministry and assistance of angels, and
the mercies of God, the peace of conscience, and the peace of the
church, are all the assistances and preparatives that can help to dress
his lamp. But if a man shall go to buy oil when the bridegroom
comes, if his lamp be not first furnished and then trimmed, that in
this life, this upon his death-bed, his station shall be without-doors,
his portion with unbelievers; and the unction of the dying man
shall no more strengthen his soul than it cures his body; and the
prayers for him after his death shall be of the same force, as if they
should pray that he should return to life again the next day, and
live as long as Lazarus in his return. But I consider that it is not
well that men should pretend any thing will do a man good when he
dies; and yet the same ministries, and ten times more assistances, are
found for forty or fifty years together to be ineffectual. Can extreme unction at last cure what the holy sacrament of the eucharist,
all his life-time, could not do? Can prayers for a dead man do him
more good than when he was alive? If all his days the man be-
longed to death and the dominion of sin, and from thence could not
be recovered by sermons, and counsels, and perpetual precepts, and
frequent sacraments, by confessions and absolutions, by prayers and
advocations, by external ministries and internal acts, it is but too
certain that his lamp cannot then be furnished: his extreme unction
is only then of use when it is made by the oil that burned in his
lamp in all the days of his expectation and waiting for the coming
of the Bridegroom.

Neither can any supply be made in this case by their practice of
praying for the dead; though they pretend for this the fairest precedents of the church and of the whole world.[3] The heathens, they
say, did it, and the Jews did it, and the Christians did it; some were
baptized for the dead in the days of the apostles, and very many
were communicated for the dead for many ages after. It is true
they were so, and did so; the heathens prayed for an easy grave,[4] and
a perpetual spring, that saffron would rise from their beds of grass.
The Jews prayed that the souls of their dead might be in the garden
of Eden, that they might have their part in Paradise, and in the

[3] Tertul. de Monog. S. Cyprian. lib. i. ep. 9. S. Athan. q. 33. S. Cyril.
Myst. Cat. 5. Epiphan. Hæres. 75. Aug. de Hæres. cap. 33. Concil. Carth.
3. cap. 29.
[4] Di, majorum umbris tenuem et sine pondere terram,
   Spirantesque crocos, et in urnâ perpetuum ver.—Juven. Sat. vii. 208.

world to come; and that they might hear the peace of the fathers of their generation sleeping in Hebron. And the Christians prayed for a joyful resurrection, for mercy at the day of judgment, for hastening of the coming of Christ, and the kingdom of God; and they named all sorts of persons in their prayers, all, I mean, but wicked persons, all but them that lived evil lives: they named apostles, saints, and martyrs. And all this is so nothing to their purpose, or so much against it, that the prayers for the dead, used in the church of Rome, are most plainly condemned, because they are against the doctrines and practices of all the world, in other forms, to other purposes, relying upon distinct doctrines, until new opinions began to arise, about St. Augustine's time, and changed the face of the proposition. Concerning prayer for the dead, the church hath received no commandment from the Lord; and therefore concerning it we can have no rules nor proportions but from those imperfect revelations of the state of departed souls, and the measures of charity, which can relate only to the imperfection of their present condition, and the terrors of the day of judgment; but to think that any suppletory to an evil life can be taken from such devotions, after the sinners are dead, may encourage a bad man to sin, but cannot relieve him when he hath.

But of all things in the world, methinks, men should be most careful not to abuse dying people; not only because their condition is pitiable, but because they shall soon be discovered, and, in the secret region of souls, there shall be an evil report concerning those men who have deceived them: and if we believe we shall go to that place where such reports are made, we may fear the shame and the amazement of being accounted impostors in the presence of angels, and all the wise and holy men of the world. To be erring and innocent, is hugely pitiable, and incident to mortality; that we cannot help; but to deceive or to destroy so great an interest as is that of a soul, or to lessen its advantages, by giving it trifling and false confidences, is injurious and intolerable. And therefore it were very well if all the churches of the world would be extremely curious concerning their offices and ministries of the visitation of the sick: that their ministers they send be holy and prudent; that their instruction be severe and safe; that their sentences be merciful and reasonable; that their offices be sufficient and devout; that their attendances be frequent and long; that their deputations be special and peculiar; that the doctrines upon which they ground their offices be true, material, and holy; that their ceremonies be few, and their advices wary; that their separation be full of caution, their judgments not remiss, their remissions not loose and dissolute; and that all the whole ministration be made by persons of experience and charity. For it is a sad thing to see our dead go out of our hands: they live incuriously, and die without regard; and the last scene of their life, which should be dressed with all spiritual advantages, is abused by flattery and easy propositions, and let go with carelessness and folly.

My Lord, I have endeavoured to cure some part of the evil as well as I could, being willing to relieve the needs of indigent people in such ways as I can; and, therefore, have described the duties which every sick man may do alone, and such in which he can be assisted by the minister; and am the more confident that these my endeavours will be the better entertained, because they are the first entire body of directions for sick and dying people that I remember to have been published in the church of England. In the church of Rome there have been many; but they are dressed with such doctrines, which are sometimes useless, sometimes hurtful, and their whole design of assistance, which they commonly yield, is at the best imperfect, and the representment is too careless and loose for so severe an employment. So that, in this affair, I was almost forced to walk alone; only that I drew the rules and advices from the fountains of Scripture, and the purest channels of the primitive church, and was helped by some experience in the cure of souls. I shall measure the success of my labours, not by popular noises or the sentences of curious persons, but by the advantage which good people may receive. My work here is not to please the speculative part of men, but to minister to practice, to preach to the weary, to comfort the sick, to assist the penitent, to reprove the confident, to strengthen weak hands and feeble knees, having scarce any other possibilities left me of doing alms, or exercising that charity by which we shall be judged at doomsday. It is enough for me to be an under builder in the house of God, and I glory in the employment; I labour in the foundations; and therefore the work needs no apology for being plain, so it be strong and well laid. But, my Lord, as mean as it is, I must give God thanks for the desires and the strength; and, next to him, to you, for that opportunity and little portion of leisure which I had to do it in: for I must acknowledge it publicly, (and, besides my prayers, it is all the recompence I can make you,) my being quiet I owe to your interest, much of my support to your bounty, and many other collateral comforts I derive from your favour and nobleness. My Lord, because I much honour you, and because I would do honour to myself, I have written your name in the entrance of my book: I am sure you will entertain it, because the design related to your dear Lady, and because it may minister to your spirit in the day of visitation; when God shall call for you to receive your reward for your charity and your noble piety, by which you have not only endeared very many persons, but in great degrees have obliged me to be,

My noblest Lord,

Your Lordship's most thankful and most humble servant,

JER. TAYLOR

CHAPTER I.

SECT. I. *Consideration of the Vanity and Shortness of Man's Life.*

A MAN is a bubble, (said the Greek proverb,)[1] which Lucian represents with advantages and its proper circumstances, to this purpose; saying, that all the world is a storm, and men rise up in their several generations, like bubbles descending *à Jove pluvio*, from God and the dew of heaven, from a tear and a drop of rain, from nature and Providence; and some of these instantly sink into the deluge of their first parent, and are hidden in a sheet of water, having had no other business in the world but to be born, that they might be able to die; others float up and down two or three turns, and suddenly disappear, and give their place to others: and they that live longest upon the face of the waters, are in perpetual motion, restless and uneasy; and, being crushed with the great drop of a cloud, sink into flatness and a froth; the change not being great, it being hardly possible it should be more a nothing than it was before. So is every man: he is born in vanity and sin; he comes into the world like morning mushrooms, soon thrusting up their heads into the air, and conversing with their kindred of the same production, and as soon they turn into dust and forgetfulness—some of them without any other interest in the affairs of the world, but that they made their parents a little glad and very sorrowful: others ride longer in the storm; it may be until seven years of vanity be expired, and then peradventure the sun shines hot upon their heads. and they fall into the shades below, into the cover of death and darkness of the grave to hide them. But if the bubble stands the shock of a bigger drop, and outlives the chances of a child, of a careless nurse, of drowning in a pail of water, of being overlaid by a sleepy servant, or such little accidents, then the young man dances like a bubble, empty and gay, and shines like a dove's neck, or the image of a rainbow, which hath no substance, and whose very imagery and colours are

[1] Πομφόλυξ ὁ ἄνθρωπος.

fantastical; and so he dances out the gaiety of his youth, and
is all the while in a storm, and endures only because he is not
knocked on the head by a drop of bigger rain, or crushed by
the pressure of a load of indigested meat, or quenched by the
disorder of an ill-placed humour: and to preserve a man alive
in the midst of so many chances and hostilities, is as great a
miracle as to create him; to preserve him from rushing into
nothing, and at first to draw him up from nothing, were equally
the issues of an almighty power. And therefore the wise men
of the world have contended who shall best fit man's condition
with words signifying his vanity and short abode. Homer
calls a man, "a leaf," the smallest, the weakest piece of a
short-lived, unsteady plant. Pindar calls him, "the dream
of a shadow:" another "the dream of the shadow of smoke."
But St. James spake by a more excellent Spirit, saying, "Our
life is but a vapour,"[2] viz. drawn from the earth by a celestial
influence; made of smoke, or the lighter parts of water, tossed
with every wind, moved by the motion of a superior body,
without virtue in itself, lifted up on high, or left below, according as it pleases the sun, its foster-father. But it is lighter
yet. It is but "appearing;"[3] a fantastic vapour, an apparition,
nothing real; it is not so much as a mist, not the matter of a
shower, nor substantial enough to make a cloud; but it is like
Cassiopeia's chair, or Pelops' shoulder, or the circles of heaven, φαινόμενα, than which you cannot have a word that can
signify a verier nothing. And yet the expression is one degree more made diminutive: a *vapour*, and *fantastical*, or a
mere appearance, and this but for a little while neither;[4] the
very dream, the phantasm, disappears in a small time, "like
the shadow that departed; or, like a tale that is told; or as a
dream when one awaketh." A man is so vain, so unfixed, so
perishing a creature, that he cannot long last in the scene of
fancy; a man goes off, and is forgotten, like the dream of a
distracted person. The sum of all is this: that thou art a
man, than whom there is not in the world any greater instance
of heights and declensions, of lights and shadows, of misery
and folly, of laughter and tears, of groans and death.[5]

And because this consideration is of great usefulness and

[2] James iv. 14, ἀτμίς.   [3] Φαινομένη.   [4] Πρὸς ὀλίγον.
[5] Τὸ δὲ κεφάλαιον τῶν λόγων· ἄνθρωπος εἶ, οὐ μεταβολὴν θᾶττον
πρὸς ὕψος, καὶ πάλιν τα- ινότητα, ζῶον οὐδὲν λαμβάνει.

great necessity to many purposes of wisdom and the spirit, all
the succession of time, all the changes in nature, all the varieties of light and darkness, the thousand thousands of accidents in the world, and every contingency to every man, and
to every creature, doth preach our funeral sermon, and calls
us to look and see how the old sexton, Time, throws up the
earth, and digs a grave, where we must lay our sins or our
sorrows, and sow our bodies, till they rise again in a fair or
an intolerable eternity.   Every revolution which the sun
makes about the world divides between life and death; and
death possesses both those portions by the next morrow; and
we are dead to all those months which we have already lived,
and we shall never live them over again: and still God
makes little periods of our age.[6]   First we change our world,
when we come from the womb to feel the warmth of the sun.
Then we sleep and enter into the image of death, in which
state we are unconcerned in all the changes of the world: and
if our mothers or our nurses die, or a wild boar destroy our
vineyards, or our king be sick, we regard it not, but, during
that state, are as disinterested as if our eyes were closed with
the clay that weeps in the bowels of the earth.   At the end
of seven years our teeth fall and die before us, representing a
formal prologue to the tragedy; and still, every seven years
it is odds but we shall finish the last scene: and when nature,
or chance, or vice, takes our body in pieces, weakening some
parts and loosing others, we taste the grave and the solemnities of our own funerals, first, in those parts that ministered
to vice; and, next, in them that served for ornament; and in
a short time, even they that served for necessity become useless and entangled like the wheels of a broken clock.   Bald-
ness is but a dressing to our funerals,[7] the proper ornament of
mourning, and of a person entered very far into the regions
and possession of death: and we have many more of the same
signification—gray hairs, rotten teeth, dim eyes, trembling
joints, short breath, stiff limbs, wrinkled skin, short memory,
decayed appetite.   Every day's necessity calls for a repara-

[6] Nihil sibi quisquam de futuro debet promittere. Id quoque, quod
tenemur, per manus exit, et ipsam quam premimus, horam casus incidit.
Volvitur tempus ratâ quidem lege, sed per obscurum —Seneca.
[7] Ut mortem citiùs venire credas,
Scito jam capitis perisse partem.

tion of that portion which death fed on all night, when we
lay in his lap, and slept in his outer chambers. The very
spirits of a man prey upon the daily portion of bread and flesh,
and every meal is a rescue from one death, and lays up for
another ; and while we think a thought, we die ; and the clock
strikes, and reckons on our portion of eternity : we form our
words with the breath of our nostrils—we have the less to
live upon for every word we speak.

Thus nature calls us to meditate of death by those things
which are the instruments of acting it ; and God, by all the
variety of his providence, makes us see death every where, in
all variety of circumstances, and dressed up for all the fancies,
and the expectation of every single person. Nature hath
given us one harvest every year, but death hath two : and
the spring and the autumn send throngs of men and women
to charnel-houses ; and all the summer long men are recover-
ing from their evils of the spring, till the dog-days come, and
then the Sirian star makes the summer deadly ; and the fruits
of autumn are laid up for all the year's provision, and the
man that gathers them eats and surfeits, and dies and needs
them not, and himself is laid up for eternity ; and he that
escapes till winter only stays for another opportunity, which
the distempers of that quarter minister to him with great variety. Thus, death reigns in all the portions of our time.
The autumn with its fruits provides disorders for us, and the
winter's cold turns them into sharp diseases, and the spring
brings flowers to strew our hearse, and the summer gives
green turf and brambles to bind upon our graves. Calentures
and surfeit, cold and agues, are the four quarters of the year,
and all minister to death ; and you can go no whither, but you
tread upon a dead man's bones.

The wild fellow, in Petronius, that escaped upon a broken
table from the furies of a shipwreck, as he was sunning himself upon the rocky shore, espied a man, rolled upon his float-
ing bed of waves, ballasted with sand in the folds of his garment, and carried by his civil enemy, the sea, towards the
shore to find a grave : and it cast him into some sad thoughts ;[1]

* Navigationes longas, et, pererratis littoribus alienis, seros in patriam
reditus proponimus, militiam, et castrensium laborum tarda manu pretia
procurationes, officiorumque per officia processus, cùm interim ad latus
mors est ; quæ quoniam nunquam cogitatur nisi aliena, nobis subinde in

that, peradventure, this man's wife, in some part of the continent, safe and warm, looks next month for the good man's return; or, it may be, his son knows nothing of the tempest; or his father thinks of that affectionate kiss, which still is warm upon the good old man's cheek, ever since he took a kind farewell; and he weeps with joy to think how blessed he shall be when his beloved boy returns into the circle of his father's arms. These are the thoughts of mortals, this is the end and sum of all their designs; a dark night and an ill guide, a boisterous sea and a broken cable, a hard rock and a rough wind, dashed to pieces the fortune of a whole family; and they that shall weep loudest for the accident are not yet entered into the storm, and yet have suffered shipwreck. Then, looking upon the carcass, he knew it, and found it to be the master of the ship, who, the day before, cast up the accounts of his patrimony and his trade, and named the day when he thought to be at home: see how the man swims who was so angry two days since; his passions are becalmed with the storm, his accounts cast up, his cares at an end, his voyage done, and his gains are the strange events of death, which, whether they be good or evil, the men that are alive seldom trouble themselves concerning the interest of the dead.

But seas alone do not break our vessel in pieces: every where we may be shipwrecked. A valiant general, when he is to reap the harvest of his crowns and triumphs, fights unprosperously, or falls into a fever with joy and wine, and changes his laurel into cypress, his triumphal chariot to a hearse; dying the night before he was appointed to perish in the drunkenness of his festival joys. It was a sad arrest of the loosenesses and wilder feasts of the French court, when their king (Henry II.) was killed really by the sportive image of a fight. And many brides have died under the hands of paranymphs and maidens, dressing them for uneasy joy, the new and undiscerned chains of marriage, according to the saying of Bensirah, the wise Jew, " The bride went into her chamber, and knew not what should befall her there." Some have been paying their vows, and giving thanks for a prosperous return to their own house, and the roof hath descended upon their heads, and· turned their loud religion into the deeper

geruntur mortalitatis exempla, non diutiùs quàm miramur hæsura.—
Seneca.

silence ot a grave. And how many teeming moth rs have rejoiced over their swelling wombs, and pleased themselves in becoming the channels of blessing to a family ; and the mid-wife hath quickly bound their heads and feet, and carried them forth to burial ! Or else the birth-day of an heir hath seen the coffin of the father brought into the house, and the divided mother hath been forced to travail twice, with a pain-ful birth and a sadder death.[9]

There is no state, no accident, no circumstance of our life, but it hath been soured by some sad instance of a dying friend : a friendly meeting often ends in some sad mischance, and makes an eternal parting ; and when the poet Æschylus was sitting under the walls of his house, an eagle, hovering over his bald head, mistook it for a stone, and let fall his oyster, hoping there to break the shell, but pierced the poor man's skull.

Death meets us every where, and is procured by every in-strument, and in all chances, and enters in at many doors ; by violence and secret influence, by the aspect of a star and the stink of a mist, by the emissions of a cloud and the meeting of a vapour, by the fall of a chariot and the stumbling at a stone, by a full meal or an empty stomach, by watching at the wine or by watching at prayers, by the sun or the moon, by a heat or a cold, by sleepless nights or sleeping days, by water frozen into the hardness and sharpness of a dagger,[10] or water thawed into the floods of a river, by a hair or a raisin, by violent motion or sitting still, by severity or dis-solution, by God's mercy or God's anger ; by every thing in providence and every thing in manners, by every thing in nature and every thing in chance.[11] *Eripitur persona, manet res;* we take pains to heap up things useful to our life, and get our death in the purchase ; and the person is snatched away, and the goods remain. And all this is the law and

[9] Quia lex eadem manet omnes,
  Gemitum dare sorte sub unâ,
  Cognataque funera nobis
  Aliena in morte dolere.—Prud. Hymn. Exequiis Defunctor.
[10] Aut ubi mors non est, si jugulatis, aquæ ?—Martial.
[11] ——————— Currit mortalibus ævum,
  Nec nasci bis posse datur ; fugit hora, rapitque
  Tartareus torrens, ac secum ferre sub umbras,
  Si qua animo placuere, negat.—Sil. Ital. l. xv. 64.

constitution of nature; it is a punishment to our sins, the unalterable event of Providence, and the decree of Heaven. The chains that confine us to this condition are strong as destiny, and immutable as the eternal laws of God.

I have conversed with some men who rejoiced in the death or calamity of others, and accounted it as a judgment upon them for being on the other side, and against them in the contention: but within the revolution of a few months, the same man met with a more uneasy and unhandsome death; which, when I saw, I wept, and was afraid; for I knew that it must be so with all men; for we also die,[12] and end our quarrels and contentions by passing to a final sentence.

SECT. II. *The Consideration reduced to Practice.*

IT will be very material to our best and noblest purposes, if we represent this scene of change and sorrow a little more dressed up in circumstances; for so we shall be more apt to practise those rules, the doctrine of which is consequent to this consideration. It is a mighty change that is made by the death of every person, and it is visible to us who are alive. Reckon but from the sprightfulness of youth and the fair cheeks and full eyes of childhood, from the vigorousness and strong flexure of the joints of five-and-twenty, to the hollowness and dead paleness, to the loathsomeness and horror of a three days' burial, and we shall perceive the distance to be very great and very strange. But so have I seen a rose newly springing from the clefts of its hood, and, at first, it was fair as the morning, and full with the dew of heaven, as a lamb's fleece; but when a ruder breath had forced open its virgin modesty, and dismantled its too youthful and unripe retirements, it began to put on darkness, and to decline to softness and the symptoms of a sickly age: it bowed the head and broke its stalk; and, at night, having lost some of its leaves and all its beauty, it fell into the portion of weeds and outworn faces. The same is the portion of every man and every woman: the heritage of worms and serpents, rottenness and cold dishonour, and our beauty so changed that our acquaintance quickly knew us not; and that change mingled with so much horror, or else meets so with our fears and weak dis-

Τέθναθι· κῆρα δ' ἐγὼ τότε δέξομαι, ὅπποτέ κεν δὴ
Ζεὺς ἐθέλῃ τελέσαι.—Il. χ'. 365.

x

coursings, that they who, six hours ago, tended upon us, either with charitable or ambitious services, cannot, without some regret, stay in the room alone where the body lies stripped of its life and honour. I have read of a fair young German gentleman, who, living, often refused to be pictured, but put off the importunity of his friends' desire by giving way, that, after a few days' burial, they might send a painter to his vault, and, if they saw cause for it, draw the image of his death unto the life. They did so, and found his face half eaten, and his midriff and backbone full of serpents; and so he stands pictured among his armed ancestors. So does the fairest beauty change,[1] and it will be as bad for you and me; and then what servants shall we have to wait upon us in the grave? what friends to visit us? what officious people to cleanse away the moist and unwholesome cloud reflected upon our faces from the sides of the weeping vaults, which are the longest weepers for our funeral?

This discourse will be useful, if we consider and practise by the following rules and considerations respectively.

1. All the rich and all the covetous men in the world will perceive, and all the world will perceive for them, that it is but an ill recompence for all their cares, that, by this time, all that shall be left will be this,[2] that the neighbours shall say, "He died a rich man;" and yet his wealth will not profit him in the grave, but hugely swell the sad accounts of doomsday. And he that kills the Lord's people with unjust or ambitious wars, for an unrewarding interest, shall have this character,[3] that he threw away all the days of his life, that one year might be reckoned with his name, and computed by his reign or consul-ship: and many men, by great labours and affronts, many in-dignities and crimes, labour only for a pompous epitaph, and a loud title upon their marble; whilst those, into whose posses-sions their heirs or kindred are entered, are forgotten, and lie unregarded as their ashes, and without concernment or rela-

---

[1] Anceps forma bonum mortalibus,
   Exigui donum breve temporis;
   Ut fulgor, teneris qui radiat genis,
   Momento rapitur, nullaque non dies
   Formosi spolium corporis abstulit.—Senec. Hipp. 770.

[2] Rape, congere, aufer, posside; relinquendum est.—Martial.

[3] Annos omnes prodegit, ut ex eo annus unus numeretur, et per mille indignitates laboravit in titulum sepulchri.—Sen.

tion, as the turf upon the face of their grave.[4]   A man may read a sermon, the best and most passionate that ever man preached, if he shall but enter into the sepulchres of kings.[5] In the same Escurial where the Spanish princes live in greatness and power, and decree war or peace, they have wisely placed a cemetery, where their ashes and their glory shall sleep till time shall be no more; and where our kings have been crowned their ancestors lie interred, and they must walk over their grandsire's head to take his crown.   There is an acre sown with royal seed, the copy of the greatest change, from rich to naked, from ceiled roofs to arched coffins, from living like gods to die like men.   There is enough to cool the flames of lust, to abate the heights of pride, to appease the itch of covetous desires, to sully and dash out the dissembling colours of a lustful, artificial, and imaginary beauty.   There the warlike and the peaceful, the fortunate and the miserable, the beloved and the despised princes mingle their dust, and pay down their symbol of mortality, and tell all the world that, when we die, our ashes shall be equal to kings', and our accounts easier, and our pains or our crowns shall be less.   To my apprehension, it is a sad record which is left by Athenæus concerning Ninus, the great Assyrian monarch, whose life and death are summed up in these words: " Ninus, the Assyrian, had an ocean of gold, and other riches, more than the sand in the Caspian Sea; he never saw the stars, and perhaps he never desired it; he never stirred up the holy fire among the Magi, nor touched his god with the sacred rod according to the laws; he never offered sacrifice, nor worshipped the deity, nor administered justice, nor spake to his people, nor numbered them; but he was most valiant to eat and drink, and having mingled his wines, he threw the rest upon the stones.   This man is dead; behold his sepulchre;

[4] Jam eorum præbendas alii possident, et nescio utrum de iis cogitant. Gerson.

[5] —— —— Me veterum frequens
Memphis Pyramidum docet,
Me pressæ tumulo lacryma gloriæ,
Me projecta jacentium
Passim per populos busta Quiritium,
Et vilis Zephyro jocus
Jactati cineres et procerum rogi,
Fumantúmque cadavera
Regnorum tacito, Rufe, silentio
Mæstum multa monent.—Cas. l. ii. Od. 27.

x 2

and now hear where Ninus is.   Sometimes I was Ninus, and
drew the breath of a living man; but now am nothing but
clay.   I have nothing but what I did eat, and what I served
to myself in lust; that was and is all my portion.   The wealth
with which I was esteemed blessed, my enemies, meeting together, shall bear away, as the mad Thyades carry a raw goat.
I am gone to hell; and when I went thither I neither carried
gold, nor horse, nor silver chariot.   I that wore a mitre am
now a little heap of dust." I know not any thing that can
better represent the evil condition of a wicked man, or a changing greatness.[6]   From the greatest secular dignity to dust and
ashes his nature bears him; and from thence to hell his sins
carry him, and there he shall be for ever under the dominion
of chains and devils, wrath and an intolerable calamity.   This
is the reward of an unsanctified condition, and a greatness ill-
gotten or ill-administered.

2.   Let no man extend his thoughts, or let his hopes wander
towards future and far-distant events and accidental contingencies.   This day is mine and yours, but ye know not what
shall be on the morrow;[7] and every morning creeps out of a
dark cloud, leaving behind it an ignorance and silence deep as
midnight and undiscerned as are the phantasms that make a
chrisom-child to smile; so that we cannot discern what comes
hereafter,[8] unless we had a light from heaven brighter than
the vision of an angel, even the spirit of prophecy.   Without
revelation we cannot tell whether we shall eat to-morrow, or
whether a squinancy shall choke us: and it is written in the
unrevealed folds of Divine predestination, that many who are
this day alive shall to-morrow be laid upon the cold earth, and
the women shall weep over their shroud, and dress them for
their funeral.   St. James, in his Epistle, notes the folly of some
men, his contemporaries, who were so impatient of the event
of to-morrow, or the accidents of next year, or the good or
evils of old age, that they would consult astrologers and witches,

---

[6] 'Αθανασίας δ' οὐκ ἔστιν, οὐδ' ἂν συναγάγῃς
Τὰ Ταντάλου τάλαντ' ἐκεῖνα λεγόμενα.
'Αλλ' ἂν ἀποθανῇς, ταῦτα καταλείψεις τισίν.—Menand. Clerc. p. 214.

[7] Τὸ σήμερον μέλει μοι,
Τὸ δ' αὔριόν τις οἶδε;—Anacr. Od. 15.

[8] Quid sit futurum cras, fuge quærere, et
Quem sors dierum cunque dabit, lucro
Appone   Horat. l. ix. 15.

oracles and devils, what should befall them the next calends—
what should be the event of such a voyage—what God had
written in his book concerning the success of battles, the election of emperors, the heirs of families, the price of merchandise, the return of the Tyrian fleet, the rate of Sidonian carpets : and as they were taught by the crafty and lying demons,
so they would expect the issue : and oftentimes, by disposing
their affairs in order towards such events, really did produce
some little accidents according to their expectation ; and that
made them trust the oracles in greater things, and in all.
Against this he opposes his counsel, that we should not search
after forbidden records,[9] much less by uncertain significations :
for whatsoever is disposed to happen by the order of natural
causes or civil counsels, may be rescinded by a peculiar decree
of Providence, or be prevented by the death of the interested
persons ; who, while their hopes are full, and their causes con-
joined, and the work brought forward, and the sickle put into
the harvest, and the first-fruits offered and ready to be eaten,
even then, if they put forth their hand to an event that stands
but at the door, at that door their body may be carried forth
to burial before the expectation shall enter into fruition. When
Richilda, the widow of Albert, earl of Ebersberg, had feasted
the emperor Henry III., and petitioned in behalf of her nephew, Welpho, for some lands formerly possessed by the earl
her husband, just as the emperor held out his hand to signify
his consent, the chamber-floor suddenly fell under them, and
Richilda falling upon the edge of a bathing-vessel, was bruised
to death, and stayed not to see her nephew sleep in those lands
which the emperor was reaching forth to her, and placed at
the door of restitution.

3. As our hopes must be confined, so must our designs :[10] let
us not project long designs, crafty plots, and diggings so deep

---

[9]   —————— Nec Babylonios
Tentâris numeros, ut meliùs, quicquid erit, pati,
Seu plures hyemes, seu tribuit Jupiter ultimam.—Horat. l. ii. 2.
Incertam frustra, mortales, funeris horam
    Quæritis, et quâ sit mors aditura viâ.—Propert. ii. 27. 1.
Pœna minor certam subitò perferre ruinam ;
    Quod timeas gravius sustinuisse diu.—Catul. Eleg. i. 29.
[10] Certa amittimus, dum incerta petimus; atque hoc evenit,
In labore atque in dolore, ut mors obrepat interim.
                                Plaut. Pseud. act. ii. scen. 3.

that the intrigues of a design shall never be unfolded till our
grandchildren have forgotten our virtues or our vices.   The
work of our soul is cut short, facile, sweet, and plain, and fitted
to the small portions of our shorter life : and as we must not
trouble our inquiry, so neither must we intricate our labour
and purposes with what we shall never enjoy.   This rule does
not forbid us to plant orchards, which shall feed our nephews
with their fruit ; for by such provisions they do something
towards an imaginary immortality, and do charity to their
relatives ; but such projects are reproved which discompose our
present duty by long and future designs ;[11] such which, by
casting our labours to events at distance, make us less to remember our death standing at the door.   It is fit for a man to
work for his day's wages, or to contrive for the hire of a week,
or to lay a train to make provisions for such a time as is within
our eye, and in our duty, and within the usual periods of man's
life ; for whatsoever is made necessary is also made prudent :
but while we plot and busy ourselves in the toils of an ambitious war, or the levies of a great estate, night enters in upon
us, and tells all the world how like fools we lived, and how
deceived and miserably we died.   Seneca tells of Senecio Cornelius, a man crafty in getting, and tenacious in holding, a
great estate, and one who was as diligent in the care of his body
as of his money, curious of his health as of his possessions, that
he all day long attended upon his sick and dying friend ; but
when he went away, was quickly comforted, supped merrily,
went to bed cheerfully, and on a sudden being surprised by a
squinancy, scarce drew his breath until the morning, but by
that time died, being snatched from the torrent of his fortune,
and the swelling tide of wealth, and a likely hope bigger than
the necessities of ten men.   This accident was much noted
then in Rome, because it happened in so great a fortune, and
in the midst of wealthy designs ; and presently it made wise
men to consider how imprudent a person he is who disposes
of ten years to come, when he is not lord of to-morrow.

4. Though we must not look so far off, and pry abroad, yet
we must be busy near at hand ; we must, with all arts of the

[11] Quid brevi fortes jaculamur ævo
Multa ?   Horat. ii. 16.
    Jam te premet nox, fabulæque Manes,
Et domus exilis Plutonia.—Horat. i. 4.

spirit, seize upon the present,[12] because it passes from us while we speak, and because in it all our certainty does consist. We must take our waters as out of a torrent and sudden shower, which will quickly cease dropping from above, and quickly cease running in our channels here below : this instant will never return again, and yet, it may be, this instant will declare or secure the fortune of a whole eternity. The old Greeks and Romans taught us the prudence of this rule ; but Christianity teaches us the religion of it. They so seized upon the present, that they would lose nothing of the day's pleasure.[13] "Let us eat and drink, for to-morrow we shall die ;" that was their philosophy ; and at their solemn feasts they would talk of death to heighten the present drinking, and that they might warm their veins with a fuller chalice, as knowing the drink that was poured upon their graves would be cold and without relish. "Break the beds, drink your wine, crown your head with roses, and besmear your curled locks with nard ; for God bids you to remember death :" so the epigrammatist speaks the sense of their drunken principles.[14] Something towards this signification is that of Solomon, "There is nothing better for a man than that he should eat and drink, and that he should make his soul enjoy good in his labour ; for that is his portion ; for who shall bring him to see that which shall be after him?"[15] But, although he concludes all this to be vanity, yet because it was the best thing that was then commonly known, that they should seize upon the present with a temperate use of permitted pleasures,[16] I had reason to say that Christianity taught us to turn this into religion. For he that by a present and constant holiness secures the present, and makes it useful to his noblest purposes, he turns his condition into his best advantage, by making his unavoidable fate become his necessary religion.

[12] Ille enim ex futuro suspenditur, cui irritum est præsens.—Sen.
[13] Ætate fruere ; mobili cursu fugit.—Seneca.
[14] Martial. l. ii. Epig. 59.   [15] Eccles. ii. 24 ; iii. 22.
[16] Amici, dum vivimus, vivamus.

> Πίνε, λέγει το γλύμμα, καὶ ἐσθίε, καὶ περίκεισο
> Ἄνθεα· τοιοῦτοι γιγνόμεθ' ἐξαπίνης.
> Hoc etiam faciunt, ubi discubuere, tenentque
> Pocula sæpe homines, et inumbrant ora coronis ;
> Ex animo ut dicant, " brevis est hic fructus homullis ;
> Jam fuerit ; neque pòst unquam revocare licebit ! "
>
> Lucret. lib. iii. 925.

To the purpose of this rule is that collect of Tuscan hieroglyphics which we have from Gabriel Simeon: " Our life is
very short, beauty is a cozenage, money is false and fugitive;
empire is odious, and hated by them that have it not, and un
easy to them that have; victory is always uncertain, and
peace, most commonly, is but a fraudulent bargain ; old age
is miserable, death is the period, and is a happy one, if it be
not sorrowed by the sins of our life: but nothing continues
but the effects of that wisdom which employs the present time
in the acts of a holy religion and a peaceable conscience."
For they make us to live even beyond our funerals, embalmed
in the spices and odours of a good name, and entombed in the
grave of the holy Jesus, where we shall be dressed for a
blessed resurrection to the state of angels and beatified spirits.

5. Since we stay not here, being people but of a day's
abode, and our age is like that of a fly and contemporary with
a gourd, we must look some where else for an abiding city, a
place in another country to fix our house in, whose walls and
foundation is God, where we must find rest, or else be restless for ever. For whatsoever ease we can have or fancy here,
is shortly to be changed into sadness or tediousness; [17] it goes
away too soon, like the periods of our life, or stays too long,
like the sorrows of a sinner ; its own weariness, or a contrary
disturbance, is its load ; or it is eased by its revolution into
vanity and forgetfulness: and where either there is sorrow, or
an end of joy, there can be no true felicity; which, because
it must be had by some instrument, and in some period of our
duration, we must carry up our affections to the mansions
prepared for us above, where eternity is the measure, felicity
is the state, angels are the company, the Lamb is the light,
and God is the portion and inheritance.

SECT. III. *Rules and Spiritual Arts of lengthening our Days,
and to take off the objection of a Short Life.*

IN the accounts of a man's life, we do not reckon that portion
of days in which we are shut up in the prison of the womb;
we tell our years from the day of our birth; and the same

[17] —————— Quis sapiens bono
Confidat fragili ? dum licet utere :
Tempus te tacitum subruet, horâque
Semper præteritâ deterior subit.—Senec. Hippol. 775.

PREPARATORY TO DEATH. 313

reason that makes our reckoning to stay so long, says also, that then it begins too soon. For then we are beholden to others to make the account for us; for we know not of a long time whether we are alive or no, having but some little approaches and symptoms of a life. To feed, and sleep, and move a little, and imperfectly, is the state of an unborn child; and when he is born he does no more for a good while; and what is it that shall make him to be esteemed to live the life of a man? and when shall that account begin? For we should be loth to have the accounts of our age taken by the measures of a beast; and fools and distracted persons are reckoned as civilly dead; they are no parts of the commonwealth, not subject to laws, but secured by them in charity, and kept from violence as a man keeps his ox: and a third part of our life is spent before we enter into a higher order, into the state of a man.

2. Neither must we think that the life of a man begins when he can feed himself, or walk alone, when he can fight, or beget his like; for so he is contemporary with a camel or a cow; but he is first a man when he comes to a certain steady use of reason, according to his proportion: and when that is, all the world of men cannot tell precisely. Some are called at age at fourteen; some at one-and-twenty; some never; but all men late enough; for the life of a man comes upon him slowly and insensibly. But as, when the sun approaches towards the gates of the morning, he first opens a little eye of heaven, and sends away the spirits of darkness, and gives light to a cock, and calls up the lark to matins, and by and by gilds the fringes of a cloud, and peeps over the eastern hills, thrusting out his golden horns, like those which decked the brows of Moses when he was forced to wear a veil because himself had seen the face of God; and still, while a man tells the story, the sun gets up higher, till he shows a fair face and a full light, and then he shines one whole day, under a cloud often, and sometimes weeping great and little showers, and sets quickly; so is a man's reason and his life. He first begins to perceive himself to see or taste, making little reflections upon his actions of sense, and can discourse of flies and dogs, shells and play, horses and liberty; but when he is strong enough to enter into arts and little institutions, he is at first entertained with trifles and impertinent things. not

because he needs them, but because his understanding is no bigger, and little images of things are laid before him, like a cock-boat to a whale, only to play withal ; but before a man comes to be wise, he is half dead with gouts and consumptions, with catarrhs and aches, with sore eyes and a worn-out body. So that, if we must not reckon the life of a man but by the accounts of his reason, he is long before his soul be dressed ; and he is not to be called a man without a wise and an adorned soul, a soul at least furnished with what is necessary towards his well-being : but by that time his soul is thus furnished his body is decayed ; and then you can hardly reckon him to be alive, when his body is possessed by so many degrees of death.

3. But there is yet another arrest. At first he wants strength of body, and then he wants the use of reason ; and when that is come, it is ten to one but he stops by the impediments of vice, and wants the strength of the spirit ; and we know that body, and soul, and spirit, are the constituent parts of every Christian man. And now let us consider what that thing is which we call years of discretion. The young man is past his tutors, and arrived at the bondage of a caitiff spirit ; he is run from discipline, and is let loose to passion ; the man by this time hath wit enough to choose his vice, to act his lust, to court his mistress, to talk confidently, and ignorantly, and perpetually, to despise his betters, to deny nothing to his appetite, to do things that, when he is indeed a man, he must for ever be ashamed of ; for this is all the discretion that most men show in the first stage of their manhood ; they can discern good from evil ; and they prove their skill by leaving all that is good, and wallowing in the evils of folly and an unbridled appetite. And, by this time, the young man hath contracted vicious habits; and is a beast in manners, and therefore it will not be fitting to reckon the beginning of his life ; he is a fool in his understanding, and that is a sad death ; and he is dead in trespasses and sins, and that is sadder ; so that he hath no life but a natural, the life of a beast or a tree ; in all other capacities he is dead ; he neither hath the intellectual nor the spiritual life, neither the life of a man nor of a Christian ; and this sad truth lasts too long. For old age seizes upon most men while they still retain the minds of boys and vicious youth, doing actions from principles of great folly,

and a mighty ignorance, admiring things useless and hurtful, and filling up all the dimensions of their abode with businesses of empty affairs, being at leisure to attend no virtue: they cannot pray because they are busy, and because they are passionate; they cannot communicate because they have quarrels and intrigues of perplexed causes, complicated hostilities, and things of the world, and therefore they cannot attend to the things of God; little considering that they must find a time to die in; when death comes they must be at leisure for that. Such men are like sailors loosing from a port, and tossed immediately with a perpetual tempest lasting till their cordage crack, and either they sink or return back again to the same place; they did not make a voyage, though they were long at sea. The business and impertinent affairs of most men steal all their time, and they are restless in a foolish motion: but this is not the progress of a man; he is no further advanced in the course of a life, though he reckon many years;[1] for still his soul is childish and trifling like an untaught boy.

If the parts of this sad complaint find their remedy, we have by the same instruments also cured the evils and the vanity of a short life. Therefore,

1. Be infinitely curious you do not set back your life in the accounts of God by the intermingling of criminal actions, or the contracting vicious habits. There are some vices which carry a sword in their hand, and cut a man off before his time. There is a sword of the Lord, and there is a sword of a man, and there is a sword of the devil. Every vice of our own managing in the matter of carnality, of lust or rage, ambition or revenge, is a sword of Satan put into the hands of a man: these are the destroying angels; sin is the Apollyon, the destroyer that is gone out, not from the Lord, but from the tempter: and we hug the poison, and twist willingly with the vipers, till they bring us into the regions of an irrecoverable sorrow. We use to reckon persons as good as dead if they have lost their limbs and their teeth, and are confined to a hospital, and converse with none but surgeons and physicians, mourners and divines, those *pollinctores*, the dressers of bodies and souls to funeral; but it is worse when the soul, the principle of life, is employed wholly in the offices of death: and

---

[1] Bis jam consul trigesimus instat,
Et numerat paucos vix uia vita dies.—Mart. i. 16.

that man was worse than dead of whom Seneca tells, that, being a rich fool, when he was lifted up from the baths and set into a soft couch, asked his slaves, *An ego jam sedeo?* Do I now sit? The beast was so drowned in sensuality and the death of his soul, that whether he did sit or no, he was to believe another. Idleness and every vice are as much of death as a long disease is, or the expense of ten years; and "she that lives in pleasure is dead while she liveth" (saith the apostle); and it is the style of the Spirit concerning wicked persons, "they are dead in trespasses and sins." For, as every sensual pleasure and every day of idleness and useless living lops off a little branch from our short life; so every deadly sin and every habitual vice does quite destroy us: but innocence leaves us in our natural portions and perfect period; we lose nothing of our life if we lose nothing of our soul's health; and, therefore, he that would live a full age must avoid a sin as he would decline the regions of death and the dishonours of the grave.

2. If we would have our life lengthened,[2] let us begin betimes to live in the accounts of reason and sober counsels, of religion and the spirit, and then we shall have no reason to complain that our abode on earth is so short; many men find it long enough, and indeed it is so to all senses. But when we spend in waste what God hath given us in plenty, when we sacrifice our youth to folly, our manhood to lust and rage, our old age to covetousness and irreligion, not beginning to live till we are to die, designing that time to virtue which indeed is infirm to every thing and profitable to nothing; then we make our lives short, and lust runs away with all the vigorous and healthful part of it, and pride and animosity steal the manly portion, and craftiness and interest possess old age: *velut ex pleno et abundanti perdimus*, we spend as if we had too much time, and knew not what to do with it: we fear every thing, like weak and silly mortals, and desire strangely and greedily, as if we were immortal: we complain our life is short, and yet we throw away much of it, and are weary of many of its parts: we complain the day is long, and the night is long, and we want company, and seek out arts to drive the

[2] Ædepol, proinde ut bene vivitur, diu vivitur.—Plaut. Trinum.
Non accepimus brevem vitam, sed fecimus; nec inopes ejus, sed prodigi sumus.—Seneca.

time away, and then weep because it is gone too soon. But so the treasure of the capitol is but a small estate when Cæsar comes to finger it, and to pay with it all his legions; and the revenue of all Egypt and the eastern provinces was but a little sum when they were to support the luxury of Mark Antony, and feed the riot of Cleopatra; but a thousand crowns is a vast proportion to be spent in the cottage of a frugal person, or to feed a hermit. Just so is our life: it is too short to serve the ambition of a haughty prince, or a usurping rebel; too little time to purchase great wealth, to satisfy the pride of a vain-glorious fool, to trample upon all the enemies of our just or unjust interest: but for the obtaining virtue, for the purchase of sobriety and modesty, for the actions of religion, God gave us time sufficient, if we make the "outgoings of the morning and evening," that is, our infancy and old age, to be taken into the computations of a man. Which we may see in the following particulars.

1. If our childhood, being first consecrated by a forward baptism, it be seconded by a holy education and a complying obedience; if our youth be chaste and temperate, modest and industrious, proceeding through a prudent and sober manhood to a religious old age; then we have lived our whole duration,[3] and shall never die, but be changed, in a just time, to the preparations of a better and an immortal life.

2. If, besides the ordinary returns of our prayers and periodical and festival solemnities, and our seldom communions, we would allow to religion and the studies of wisdom those great shares that are trifled away upon vain sorrow, foolish mirth, troublesome ambition, busy covetousness, watchful lust, and impertinent amours, and balls, and revellings, and banquets,—all that which was spent viciously, and all that time that lay fallow and without employment,—our life would quickly amount to a great sum. Tostatus Abulensis was a very painful person, and a great clerk, and in the days of his manhood he wrote so many books, and they not ill ones, that the world computed a sheet for every day of his life; I sup-

[3] Sed potes, Publi, geminare magnâ
　　　　Secula famâ.
Quem sui raptum gemuere cives,
Hic diu vixit. Sibi quisque famam
Scribat hæredem : rapiunt avaræ
　　　　Cætera Lunæ.—Casim. i. 2.

pose they meant after he came to the use of reason and the
state of a man: and John Scotus died about the two-and-
thirtieth year of his age; and yet, besides his public disputations, his daily lectures of divinity in public and private, the
books that he wrote, being lately collected and printed at
Lyons, do equal the number of volumes of any two the most
voluminous fathers of the Latin church. Every man is not
enabled to such employments, but every man is called and enabled to the works of a sober and a religious life; and there
are many saints of God that can reckon as many volumes of
religion and mountains of piety as those others did of good
books. St. Ambrose (and I think, from his example, St.
Augustine) divided every day into three *tertias* of employment: eight hours he spent in the necessities of nature and
recreation; eight hours in charity and doing assistance to
others, despatching their businesses, reconciling their enmities,
reproving their vices, correcting their errors, instructing their
ignorances, transacting the affairs of his diocese; and the
other eight hours he spent in study and prayer. If we were
thus minute and curious in the spending our time, it is impossible but our life would seem very long. For so have I seen
an amorous person tell the minutes of his absence from his
fancied joy, and while he told the sands of his hour-glass, or
the throbs and little beatings of his watch, by dividing an hour
into so many members, he spun out its length by number, and
so translated a day into the tediousness of a month. And if
we tell our days by canonical hours of prayer, our weeks by a
constant revolution of fasting-days or days of special devotion,
and over all these draw a black cypress, a veil of penitential
sorrow and severe mortification, we shall soon answer the
calumny and objection of a short life. He that governs the
day and divides the hours hastens from the eyes and observation of a merry sinner; but loves to stand still, and behold,
and tell the sighs, and number the groans and sadly delicious
accents, of a grieved penitent. It is a vast work that any man
may do if he never be idle: and it is a huge way that a man
may go in virtue if he never goes out of his way by a vicious
habit or a great crime: and he that perpetually reads good
books, if his parts be answerable, will have a huge stock of
knowledge. It is so in all things else. Strive not to forget
your time, and suffer none of it to pass undiscerned; and then

measure your life, and tell me how you find the measure of its abode. However, the time we live is worth the money we pay for it ; and therefore it is not to be thrown away.

3. When vicious men are dying, and scared with the affrighting truths of an evil conscience, they would give all the world for a year, for a month: nay, we read of some that called out with amazement, *inducias usque ad mane*, truce but till the morning ; and if that year or some few months were given, those men think they could do miracles in it. And let us awhile suppose what Dives would have done if he had been loosed from the pains of hell, and permitted to live on earth one year. Would all the pleasures of the world have kept him one hour from the temple ? would he not perpetually have been under the hands of priests, or at the feet of the doctors, or by Moses' chair, or attending as near the altar as he could get, or relieving poor Lazarus, or praying to God, and crucifying all his sin ? I have read of a melancholy person, who saw hell but in a dream or vision, and the amazement was such, that he would have chosen ten times to die rather than feel again so much of that horror: and such a person cannot be fancied but that he would spend a year in such holiness that the religion of a few months would equal the devotion of many years, even of a good man. Let us but compute the proportions. If we should spend all our years of reason so as such a person would spend that one, can it be thought that life would be short and trifling in which he had performed such a religion, served God with so much holiness, mortified sin with so great a labour, purchased virtue at such a rate and so rare an industry ? It must needs be that such a man must die when he ought to die, and be like ripe and pleasant fruit falling from a fair tree, and gathered into baskets for the planter's use. He that hath done all his business, and is begotten to a glorious hope by the seed of an immortal Spirit, can never die too soon, nor live too long.[4]

Xerxes wept sadly when he saw his army of 2,300,000 men, because he considered that within a hundred years all the youth of that army should be dust and ashes: and yet, as Seneca well observes of him, he was the man that should bring them to their graves ; and he consumed all that army in two years for whom he feared and wept the death after a hundred. Just

[4] Huic neque defungi visum est, nec vivere pulchrum :
Cura fuit rectè vivere, sicque mori.

so we do all. We complain that within thirty or forty years, a little more or a great deal less, we shall descend again into the bowels of our mother, and that our life is too short for any great employment; and yet we throw away five-and-thirty years of our forty, and the remaining five we divide between art and nature, civility and customs, necessity and convenience, prudent counsels and religion: but the portion of the last is little and contemptible, and yet that little is all that we can prudently account of our lives. We bring that fate and that death near us of whose approach we are so sadly apprehensive.

4. In taking the accounts of your life, do not reckon by great distances, and by the periods of pleasure, or the satisfaction of your hopes, or the sating your desires; but let every intermedial day and hour pass with observation. He that reckons he hath lived but so many harvests, thinks they come not often enough, and that they go away too soon :[5] some lose the day by longing for the night, and the night in waiting for the day. Hope and fantastic expectations spend much of our lives; and while with passion we look for a coronation, or the death of an enemy, or a day of joy, passing from fancy to possession without any intermedial notices, we throw away a precious year, and use it but as the burden of our time, fit to be pared off and thrown away, that we may come at those little pleasures which first steal our hearts, and then steal our life.

5. A strict course of piety is the way to prolong our lives in the natural sense, and to add good portions to the number of our years; and sin is sometimes by natural causality, very often by the anger of God and the Divine judgment, a cause of sudden and untimely death. Concerning which I shall add nothing, (to what I have some where else said of this article,[6]) but only the observation of Epiphanius;[7] that for three thousand three hundred and thirty-two years, even to the twentieth age, there was not one example of a son that died before his father; but the course of nature was kept, that he who was first born in the descending line did first die, (I speak of natural death, and therefore Abel cannot be opposed to this ob-

---

[5] In spe viventibus proximum quodque tempus elabitur, subitque aviditas temporis, et miserrimus, atque miserrima omnia efficiens, metus mortis.——Ex hac autem indigentia timor nascitur, et cupiditas futuri exedens animum.—Seneca.

[6] Life of Christ, part iii. Disc. 14.   [7] Lib. i. tom. i. Panar. sect. vi.

servation,) till that Terah, the father of Abraham, taught the
people a new religion, to make images of clay and worship
them; and concerning him it was first remarked, that "Haran
died before his father Terah in the land of his nativity:" God,
by an unheard-of judgment and a rare accident, punishing his
newly-invented crime by the untimely death of his son.

6. But if I shall describe a living man, a man that hath that
life that distinguishes him from a fool or a bird, that which
gives him a capacity next to angels, we shall find that even a
good man lives not long, because it is long before he is born
to this life, and longer yet before he hath a man's growth.
" He that can look upon death, and see its face with the same
countenance with which he hears its story;[8] that can endure
all the labours of his life with his soul supporting his body ;
that can equally despise riches when he hath them and when he
hath them not; that is not sadder if they lie in his neighbour's
trunks, nor more brag if they shine round about his own walls :
he that is neither moved with good fortune coming to him nor
going from him; that can look upon another man's lands evenly
and pleasedly, as if they were his own, and yet look upon his
own, and use them too, just as if they were another man's ; that
neither spends his goods prodigally and like a fool, nor yet
keeps them avariciously and like a wretch; that weighs not
benefits by weight and number, but by the mind and circumstances of him that gives them ; that never thinks his charity
expensive if a worthy person be the receiver; he that does
nothing for opinion sake, but every thing for conscience, being
as curious of his thoughts as of his actings in markets and theatres, and is as much in awe of himself as of a whole assembly ;
he that knows God looks on, and contrives his secret affairs as
in the presence of God and his holy angels; that eats and
drinks because he needs it, not that he may serve a lust or load
his belly; he that is bountiful and cheerful to his friends, and
charitable and apt to forgive his enemies ; that loves his country,
and obeys his prince, and desires and endeavours nothing more
than that he may do honour to God :"—this person may reckon
his life to be the life of a man, and compute his months, not
by the course of the sun, but the zodiac and circle of his virtues ; because these are such things which fools and children,
and birds and beasts, cannot have ; these are therefore, the

* Seneca de Vitâ Beatâ, cap. 20.

Y

actions of life, because they are the seeds of immortality. That day in which we have done some excellent thing we may as truly reckon to be added to our life as were the fifteen years to the days of Hezekiah.

SECT. IV. *Consideration of the Miseries of Man's Life.*

As our life is very short, so it is very miserable; and therefore it is well it is short. God, in pity to mankind, lest his burden should be insupportable, and his nature an intolerable load, hath reduced our state of misery to an abbreviature; and the greater our misery is, the less while it is like to last: the sorrows of a man's spirit being like ponderous weights, which, by the greatness of their burden, make a swifter motion, and descend into the grave to rest and ease our wearied limbs; for then only we shall sleep quietly when those fetters are knocked off, which not only bound our souls in prison, but also ate the flesh, till the very bones opened the secret garments of their cartilages, discovering their nakedness and sorrow.

1. Here is no place to sit down in, but you must rise as soon as you are set, for we have gnats in our chambers, and worms in our gardens,[1] and spiders and flies in the palaces of the greatest kings. How few men in the world are prosperous ! What an infinite number of slaves and beggars, of persecuted and oppressed people, fill all corners of the earth with groans, and heaven itself with weeping, prayers, and sad remembrances! How many provinces and kingdoms are afflicted by a violent war, or made desolate by popular diseases ! Some whole countries are remarked with fatal evils or periodical sicknesses. Grand Cairo in Egypt feels the plague every three years returning like a quartan ague, and destroying many thousands of persons. All the inhabitants of Arabia the desert are in a continual fear of being buried in huge heaps of sand, and therefore dwell in tents, and ambulatory houses, or retire to unfruitful mountains, to prolong an uneasy and wilder life. And all the countries round about the Adriatic Sea feel such violent convulsions by tempests and intolerable earthquakes, that sometimes whole cities find a tomb, and every man sinks with his own house made ready to become his monument, and his bed is crushed into the disorders of a grave. Was not all the

---

[1] Nulla requies in terris; surgite, postquam sederitis; hic est locus pulicum et culicum.

world drowned at one deluge and breach of the Divine anger?
And shall not all the world again be destroyed by fire?[2]
Are there not many thousands that die every night, and that
groan and weep sadly every day? But what shall we think
of that great evil which for the sins of men God hath suffered
to possess the greatest part of mankind? Most of the men
that are now alive, or that have been living for many ages,
are Jews, heathens, or Turks: and God was pleased to suffer
a base epileptic person, a villain and a vicious, to set up a religion which hath filled all the nearer parts of Asia, and much
of Africa, and some part of Europe; so that the greatest number of men and women born in so many kingdoms and provinces are infallibly made Mahometans, strangers and enemies
to Christ, by whom alone we can be saved. This consideration is extremely sad, when we remember how universal and
how great an evil it is; that so many millions of sons and
daughters are born to enter into the possession of devils to eternal ages. These evils are the miseries of great parts of mankind, and we cannot easily consider more particularly the evils
which happen to us, being the inseparable affections or inci-
dents to the whole nature of man.

2. We find that all the women in the world are either born
for barrenness or the pains of childbirth, and yet this is one
of our greatest blessings; but such, indeed, are the blessings
of this world, we cannot be well with nor without many things.
Perfumes make our heads ache, roses prick our fingers, and in
our very blood, where our life dwells, is the scene under which
nature acts many sharp fevers and heavy sicknesses. It were
too sad if I should tell how many persons are afflicted with
evil spirits, with spectres and illusions of the night; and that
huge multitudes of men and women live upon man's flesh, nay,
worse yet, upon the sins of men, upon the sins of their sons
and of their daughters, and they pay their souls down for the
bread they eat, buying this day's meal with the price of the
last night's sin.

3. Or if you please in charity to visit a hospital, which is
indeed a map of the whole world, there you shall see the effects
of Adam's sin, and the ruins of human nature; bodies laid up
in heaps like the bones of a destroyed town, *homines precarii*

---

[2] Ἔσται καὶ Σάμος ἄμμος, ἐσεῖται Δῆλος ἄδηλος,
Καὶ Ῥώμη ῥύμη.—Sibyll. Orac.

spiritus et male hærentis, men whose souls seem to be borrowed, and are kept there by art and the force of medicine,
whose miseries are so great, that few people have charity or
humanity enough to visit them, fewer have the heart to dress
them, and we pity them in civility or with a transient prayer,
but we do not feel their sorrows by the mercies of a religious
pity: and therefore, as we leave their sorrows in many degrees
unrelieved and uneased, so we contract by our unmercifulness
a guilt by which ourselves become liable to the same calamities. Those many that need pity, and those infinities of people that refuse to pity, are miserable upon a several charge,
but yet they almost make up all mankind.

4. All wicked men are in love with that which entangles
them in huge varieties of troubles ; they are slaves to the worst
of masters, to sin and to the devil, to a passion and to an imperious woman. Good men are for ever persecuted, and God
chastises every son whom he receives ; and whatsoever is easy
is trifling and worth nothing ; and whatsoever is excellent is
not to be obtained without labour and sorrow; and the conditions and states of men that are free from great cares, are
such as have in them nothing rich and orderly, and those that
have, are stuck full of thorns and trouble. Kings are full of
care: and learned men in all ages have been observed to be
very poor,[3] *honestas miserias accusant*, they complain of their
honest miseries.

5. But these evils are notorious and confessed ; even they
also whose felicity men stare at and admire, besides their splendour and the sharpness of their light, will with their appendant
sorrows wring a tear from the most resolved eye : for not only
the winter quarter is full of storms and cold and darkness,
but the beauteous spring hath blasts and sharp frosts ; the
fruitful teeming summer is melted with heat, and burnt with
the kisses of the sun her friend, and choked with dust ; and
the rich autumn is full of sickness ; and we are weary of that

---

[3] Vilis adulator picto jacet ebrius ostro,
    Et qui solicitat nuptas, ad præmia peccat.
    Sola pruinosis horret facundia pannis,
    Atque inopi linguâ desertas invocat artes.
                            Petron. c. 83. p. 249. ed. Ant
    Hinc et jocus apud Aristophanem in Avibus, 934.
    Σὺ μέντοι σπολάδα καὶ χιτῶν' ἔχεις·
    'Απόδυθι, καὶ δὸς τῷ ποιητῇ τῷ σοφῷ.

which we enjoy, because sorrow is its biggest portion : and when we remember, that upon the fairest face is placed one of the worst sinks of the body, the nose, we may use it not only as a mortification to the pride of beauty, but as an allay to the fairest outside of condition which any of the sons and daughters of Adam do possess. For look upon kings and conquerors ; I will not tell that many of them fall into the condition of servants,[4] and their subjects rule over them, and stand upon the ruins of their families, and that to such persons the sorrow is bigger than usually happens in smaller fortunes : but let us suppose them still conquerors, and see what a goodly purchase they get by all their pains, and amazing fears, and continual dangers. They carry their arms beyond Ister, and pass the Euphrates, and bind the Germans with the bounds of the river Rhine : I speak in the style of the Roman greatness : for now-a-days the biggest fortune swells not beyond the limits of a petty province or two, and a hill confines the progress of their prosperity, or a river checks it ; but whatsoever tempts the pride and vanity of ambitious persons is not so big as the smallest star which we see scattered in disorder and unregarded upon the pavement and floor of heaven. And if we would suppose the pismires had but our understandings, they also would have the method of a man's greatness, and divide their little molehills into provinces and exarchates : and if they also grew as vicious and as miserable, one of their princes would lead an army out, and kill his neighbour ants, that he might reign over the next handful of a turf. But then, if we consider at what price and with what felicity all this is purchased, the sting of the painted snake will quickly appear, and the fairest of their fortunes will properly enter into this account of human infelicities.

We may guess at it by the constitution of Augustus's fortune, who struggled for his power, first, with the Roman citizens, then with Brutus and Cassius, and all the fortune of the republic ; then with his colleague, Mark Antony ; then with his kindred and nearest relatives ; and after he was wearied with slaughter of the Romans, before he could sit down and rest in his imperial chair, he was forced to carry armies into

---

[4] Vilis servus habet regni bona, cellaque capti
Deridet festam Romuleamque casam.—Petron. Frag. 21.
Omnia, crede mihi, etiam felicibus dubia sunt.—Seneca.

Macedonia, Galatia, beyond Euphrates, Rhine, and Danubius:
and when he dwelt at home in greatness and within the circles
of a mighty power, he hardly escaped the sword of the Eg-
natii, of Lepidus, Cæpio, and Muræna: and after he had entirely reduced the felicity and grandeur into his own family,
his daughter, his only child, conspired with many of the young
nobility, and, being joined with adulterous complications, as
with an impious sacrament,[5] they affrighted and destroyed the
fortune of the old man, and wrought him more sorrow than
all the troubles that were hatched in the baths and beds of
Egypt between Antony and Cleopatra.[6] This was the great
est fortune that the world had then or ever since, and therefore we cannot expect it to be better in a less prosperity.

6. The prosperity of this world is so infinitely soured with
the overflowing of evils, that he is counted the most happy
who hath the fewest; all conditions being evil and miserable,
they are only distinguished by the number of calamities. The
collector of the Roman and foreign examples, when he had
reckoned two-and-twenty instances of great fortunes, every
one of which had been allayed with great variety of evils; in
all his reading or experience, he could tell but of two who had
been famed for an entire prosperity—Quintus Metellus, and
Gyges the king of Lydia : and yet concerning the one of them
he tells, that his felicity was so inconsiderable (and yet it was
the bigger of the two) that the oracle said, that Aglaus So-
phidius, the poor Arcadian shepherd, was more happy than
he, that is, he had fewer troubles ; for so, indeed, we are to
reckon the pleasures of this life ; the limit of our joy is the
absence of some degree of sorrow,[7] and he that hath the least
of this is the most prosperous person. But then we must look
for prosperity, not in palaces or courts of princes, not in the
tents of conquerors, or in the gaieties of fortunate and prevailing sinners ; but something rather in the cottages of honest, innocent, and contented persons, whose mind is no bigger
than their fortune, nor their virtue less than their security.
As for others, whose fortune looks bigger, and allures fools to
follow it, like the wandering fires of the night, till they run
into rivers, or are broken upon rocks with staring and run-

---

[5] Et adulterio velut sacramento adacti.—Tacit.

[6] Plusque et iterum timenda cum Antonio mulier.

[7] Ὅσος τοῦ μεγέθους τῶν ἡδονῶν, ἡ παντὸς τοῦ ἀλγεινοῦ ὑπεξαίρεσις.

ning after them, they are all in the condition of Marius, than whose condition nothing was more constant, and nothing more mutable: if we reckon them amongst the happy, they are the most happy men; if we reckon them amongst the miserable, they are the most miserable.[8] For just as is a man's condition, great or little, so is the state of his misery; all have their share; but kings and princes, great generals and consuls, rich men and mighty, as they have the biggest business and the biggest charge, and are answerable to God for the greatest accounts, so they have the biggest trouble; that the uneasiness of their appendage may divide the good and evil of the world, making the poor man's fortune as eligible as the greatest; and also restraining the vanity of man's spirit, which a great fortune is apt to swell from a vapour to a bubble; but God in mercy hath mingled wormwood with their wine, and so restrained the drunkenness and follies of prosperity.

7. Man never hath one day to himself of entire peace from the things of the world, but either something troubles him, or nothing satisfies him, or his very fulness swells him, and makes him breathe short upon his bed. Men's joys are troublesome; and, besides that the fear of losing them takes away the present pleasure, (and a man hath need of another felicity to preserve this,) they are also wavering and full of trepidation, not only from their inconstant nature, but from their weak foundation: they arise from vanity, and they dwell upon ice, and they converse with the wind, and they have the wings of a bird, and are serious but as the resolutions of a child, commenced by chance, and managed by folly, and proceed by inadvertency, and end in vanity and forgetfulness. So that, as Livius Drusus said of himself, he never had any play-days or days of quiet when he was a boy;[9] for he was troublesome and busy, a restless and unquiet man; the same may every man observe to be true of himself; he is always restless and uneasy, he dwells upon the waters, and leans upon thorns, and lays his head upon a sharp stone.

SECT. V. *The Consideration reduced to Practice.*

1. THE effect of this consideration is this, that the sadnesses

---

[8] Quem si inter miseros posueris, miserrimus; inter felices, felicissimus reperietur.

[9] Uni sibi nec puero unquam ferias contigisse. Seditiosus et foro gravis.

of this life help to sweeten the bitter cup of death. For let our life be never so long, if our strength were great as that of oxen and camels, if our sinews were strong as the cordage at the foot of an oak, if we were as fighting and prosperous people as Siccius Dentatus, who was on the prevailing side in a hundred and twenty battles, who had three hundred and twelve public rewards assigned him by his generals and princes for his valour and conduct in sieges and sharp encounters, and, besides all this, had his share in nine triumphs; yet still the period shall be that all this shall end in death, and the people shall talk of us awhile, good or bad, according as we deserve, or as they please; and once it shall come to pass, that concerning every one of us it shall be told in the neighbourhood that we are dead. This we are apt to think a sad story, but therefore let us help it with a sadder; for we therefore need not be much troubled that we shall die, because we are not here in ease, nor do we dwell in a fair condition; but our days are full of sorrow and anguish, dishonoured and made unhappy with many sins, with a frail and a foolish spirit, entangled with difficult cases of conscience, insnared with passions, amazed with fears, full of cares, divided with curiosities and contradictory interests, made airy and impertinent with vanities, abused with ignorance and prodigious errors, made ridiculous with a thousand weaknesses, worn away with labours, loaden with diseases, daily vexed with dangers and temptations, and in love with misery; we are weakened with delights, afflicted with want, with the evils of myself and of all my family, and with the sadnesses of all my friends, and of all good men, even of the whole church; and, therefore, methinks we need not be troubled that God is pleased to put an end to all these troubles, and to let them sit down in a natural period, which, if we please, may be to us the beginning of a better life. When the prince of Persia wept because his army should all die in the revolution of an age, Artabanus told him that they should all meet with evils so many and so great that every man of them should wish himself dead long before that. Indeed it were a sad thing to be cut of the stone, and we that are in health tremble to think of it; but the man that is wearied with the disease, looks upon that sharpness as upon his cure and remedy; and as none need to have a tooth drawn, so none could well endure it but he that felt the pain of it in his head: so is our life so

full of evils, that therefore death is no evil to them that have
felt the smart of this, or hope for the joys of a better.

2. But as it helps to ease a certain sorrow, as a fire draws
out fire, and a nail drives forth a nail, so it instructs us in a
present duty, that is, that we should not be so fond of a perpetual storm, nor dote upon the transient gauds and gilded
thorns of this world. They are not worth a passion, nor worth
a sigh or a groan, not of the price of one night's watching ; and
therefore they are mistaken and miserable persons who, since
Adam planted thorns round about Paradise, are more in love
with that hedge than all the fruits of the garden, sottish admirers of things that hurt them, of sweet poisons, gilded dag-
gers, and silken halters. Tell them they have lost a bounteous
friend, a rich purchase, a fair farm, a wealthy donative, and
you dissolve their patience ; it is an evil bigger than their spirit
can bear ; it brings sickness and death ; they can neither eat
nor sleep with such a sorrow. But if you represent to them
the evils of a vicious habit, and the dangers of a state of sin, if
you tell them they have displeased God, and interrupted their
hopes of heaven, it may be they will be so civil as to hear it
patiently, and to treat you kindly, and first to commend, and
then forget your story, because they prefer this world with
all its sorrows before the pure unmingled felicities of heaven.
But it is strange that any man should be so passionately in
love with the thorns which grow on his own ground that he
should wear them for armlets, and knit them in his shirt, and
prefer them before a kingdom and immortality. No man loves
this world the better for his being poor ; but men that love it
because they have great possessions, love it because it is troublesome and chargeable, full of noise and temptation, because
it is unsafe and ungoverned, flattered and abused : and he that
considers the troubles of an over-long garment and of a crammed stomach, a trailing gown, and a loaden table, may justly
understand that all that for which men are so passionate is
their hurt and their objection—that which a temperate man
would avoid and a wise man cannot love.

He that is no fool, but can consider wisely, if he be in love
with this world, we need not despair but that a witty man
might reconcile him with tortures, and make him think charitably of the rack, and be brought to dwell with vipers and dragons, and entertain his guests with the shrieks of mandrakes,

cats, and screech-owls, with the filing of iron, and the harshness of rending of silk, or to admire the harmony that is made
by a herd of evening wolves, when they miss their draught of
blood in their midnight revels.   The groans of a man in a fit
of the stone are worse than all these, and the distractions of a
troubled conscience are worse than those groans ; and yet a
careless merry sinner is worse than all that.   But if we could,
from one of the battlements of heaven, espy how many men and
women at this time lie fainting and dying for want of bread,
how many young men are hewn down by the sword of war,
how many poor orphans are now weeping over the graves of
their father, by whose life they were enabled to eat ; if we
could but hear how many mariners and passengers are at this
present in a storm, and shriek out because their keel dashes
against a rock, or bulges under them, how many people there
are that weep with want, and are mad with oppression, or are
desperate by too quick a sense of a constant infelicity ; in all
reason we should be glad to be out of the noise and participation of so many evils.   This is a place of sorrows and tears, of
great evils and a constant calamity ; let us remove from hence,
at least in affections and preparation of mind.

CHAP. II.   A GENERAL PREPARATION TOWARDS A HOLY AND BLESSED DEATH, BY WAY OF EXERCISE.

Sect. I. *Three Precepts preparatory to a Holy Death, to be practised in our whole Life.*

1. He that would die well must always look for death, every
day knocking at the gates of the grave ; and then the gates of
the grave shall never prevail upon him to do him mischief.[1]
This was the advice of all the wise and good men of the world,
who, especially in the days and periods of their joy in festival
egressions, chose to throw some ashes into their chalices, some
sober remembrances of their fatal period.[2]   Such was the black
shirt of Saladine ; the tombstone presented to the emperor of

---

[1] Propera vivere, et singulos dies singulas vitas puta.   Nihil interest
inter diem et seculum.

[2] Si sapis, utaris totis, Coline, diebus ;
      Extremumque tibi semper adesse putes.—Martial.

Constantinople on his coronation-day; the bishop of Rome's
two reeds with flax and a wax-taper; the Egyptian skeleton
served up at feasts; and Trimalcion's banquet in Petronius, in
which was brought in the image of a dead man's bones of silver, with spondyles exactly returning to every of the guests,[3]
and saying to every one, that you and you must die, and look
not one upon another, for every one is equally concerned in
this sad representment. These in fantastic semblances declare
a severe counsel and useful meditation; and it is not easy for
a man to be gay in his imagination, or to be drunk with joy or
wine, pride or revenge, who considers sadly, that he must, ere
long, dwell in a house of darkness and dishonour, and his body
must be the inheritance of worms, and his soul must be what
he pleases, even as a man makes it here by his living good or
bad. I have read of a young hermit, who, being passionately
in love with a young lady, could not, by all the arts of religion and mortification, suppress the trouble of that fancy,
till at last, being told that she was dead, and had been buried
about fourteen days, he went secretly to her vault, and with
the skirt of his mantle wiped the moisture from the carcass,
and still at the return of his temptation laid it before him,
saying, Behold, this is the beauty of the woman thou didst so
much desire: and so the man found his cure. And if we
make death as present to us, our own death, dwelling and
dressed in all its pomp of fancy and proper circumstances—if
any thing will quench the heats of lust or the desires of money,
or the greedy, passionate affections of this world, this must do
it. But withal, the frequent use of this meditation, by curing
our present inordinations, will make death safe and friendly,
and by its very custom will make, that the king of terrors shall
come to us without his affrighting dresses; and that we shall
sit down in the grave as we compose ourselves to sleep, and do
the duties of nature and choice. The old people that lived
near the Riphæan mountains[4] were taught to converse with

[3] Heu, heu, nos miseros! quàm totus homuncio nil est!
Sic erimus cuncti, postquam nos auferet Orcus:
Ergo vivamus, dum licet esse, bene.
[4] —— Certè populi quos despicit Arctos
Felices errore suo, quos ille timorum
Maximus haud urget, lethi metus. Inde ruendi
In ferrum mens prona viris, animæque capaces
Mortis, et ignavum redituræ parcere vitæ. Lucan. i. 4:8.

death, and to handle it on all sides, and to discourse of it as of
a thing that will certainly come, and ought so to do.   Thence
their minds and resolutions became capable of death, and they
thought it a dishonourable thing with greediness to keep a
life that must go from us, to lay aside its thorns, and to return
again, circled with a glory and a diadem.

2. "He that would die well must, all the days of his life,
lay up against the day of death,"[5] not only by the general
provisions of holiness and a pious life indefinitely, but provisions proper to the necessities of that great day of expense,
in which a man is to throw his last cast for an eternity of
joys or sorrows, ever remembering that this alone, well performed, is not enough to pass us into paradise, but that alone,
done foolishly, is enough to send us to hell, and the want of
either a holy life or death makes a man to fall short of the
mighty price of our high calling.   In order to this rule we are
to consider what special graces we shall then need to exercise,
and by the proper arts of the spirit, by a heap of proportioned
arguments, by prayers, and a great treasure of devotion laid
up in heaven, provide beforehand a reserve of strength and
mercy.[6] Men, in the course of their lives, walk lazily and
incuriously, as if they had both their feet in one shoe; and
when they are passively resolved to the time of their dissolution, they have no mercies in store, no patience, no faith, no
charity to God or despite of the world, being without gust or
appetite for the land of their inheritance, which Christ with
so much pain and blood had purchased for them.   When we
come to die indeed, we shall be very much put to it to stand
firm upon the two feet of a Christian, faith and patience.
When we ourselves are to use the articles, to turn our former
discourses into present practice, and to feel what we never
felt before, we shall find it to be quite another thing to be
willing presently to quit this life and all our present possessions for the hopes of a thing which we were never suffered
to see, and such a thing of which we may fail so many ways,
and of which, if we fail any way, we are miserable for ever.
Then we shall find how much we have need to have secured
the Spirit of God and the grace of faith by an habitual, perfect, unmovable resolution.   The same, also, is the case of

* Qui quotidiè vitæ suæ manum imposuit, non indiget tempore.—Senec.
* Insere nunc, Meliboee, pyros, pone ordine vites.

patience, which will be assaulted with sharp pains, disturbed fancies, great fears, want of a present mind, natural weaknesses, frauds of the devil, and a thousand accidents and imperfections. It concerns us, therefore, highly, in the whole course of our lives, not only to accustom ourselves to a patient suffering of injuries and affronts, of persecutions and losses, of cross accidents and unnecessary circumstances; but, also, by representing death as present to us, to consider with what arguments then to fortify our patience, and by assiduous and fervent prayer to God all our life long to call upon him to give us patience and great assistances, a strong faith and a confirmed hope, the Spirit of God and his holy angels assistants at that time, to resist and to subdue the devil's temptations and assaults; and so to fortify our heart that it break not into intolerable sorrows and impatience, and end in wretchedness and infidelity. But this is to be the work of our life, and not to be done at once; but, as God gives us time, by succession, by parts and little periods. For it is very remarkable, that God who giveth plenteously to all creatures, he hath scattered the firmament with stars, as a man sows corn in his fields, in a multitude bigger than the capacities of human order; he hath made so much variety of creatures, and gives us great choice of meats and drinks, although any one of both kinds would have served our needs, and so in all instances of nature; yet in the distribution of our time God seems to be straight-handed, and gives it to us, not as nature gives us rivers, enough to drown us, but drop by drop, minute after minute, so that we never can have two minutes together, but he takes away one when he gives us another. This should teach us to value our time, since God so values it, and, by his so small distribution of it, tells us it is the most precious thing we have. Since, therefore, in the day of our death we can have still but the same little portion of this precious time, let us, in every minute of our life, I mean in every discernible portion, lay up such a stock of reason and good works, that they may convey a value to the imperfect and shorter actions of our death-bed, while God rewards the piety of our lives by his gracious acceptation and benediction upon the actions preparatory to our death-bed.

3. He that desires to die well and happily, above all things must be careful that he do not live a soft, a delicate, and

voluptuous life; but a life severe, holy, and under the discipline of the cross, under the conduct of prudence and observation, a life of warfare and sober counsels, labour and watchfulness.   No man wants cause of tears and a daily sorrow
Let every man consider what he feels, and acknowledge
his misery; let him confess his sin, and chastise it; let
him bear his cross patiently, and his persecutions nobly, and
his repentances willingly and constantly; let him pity the
evils of all the world, and bear his share of the calamities of
his brother; let him long and sigh for the joys of heaven; let
him tremble and fear, because he hath deserved the pains of
hell; let him commute his eternal fear with a temporal suffering, preventing God's judgment by passing one of his own;
let him groan for the labours of his pilgrimage and the dangers of his warfare: and by that time he hath summed up al
these labours, and duties, and contingencies, all the proper
causes, instruments, and acts of sorrow, he will find that for
a secular joy and wantonness of spirit there are not left many
void spaces of his life.   It was St. James's advice,[7] "Be afflicted, and mourn, and weep; let your laughter be turned
into mourning, and your joy into weeping:" and Bonaven-
ture, in the Life of Christ, reports that the holy virgin-mother
said to St. Elizabeth, that grace does not descend into the
soul of a man but by prayer and affliction.[8]   Certain it is,
that a mourning spirit and an afflicted body are great instruments of reconciling God to a sinner, and they always dwell
at the gates of atonement and restitution.   But besides this,
a delicate and prosperous life is hugely contrary to the hopes
of a blessed eternity.   "Woe be to them that are at ease in
Sion;"[9] so it was said of old; and our blessed Lord said, "Woe
be to you that laugh, for ye shall weep;[10] but blessed are
they that mourn, for they shall be comforted."[11]   Here or
hereafter we must have our portion of sorrows.   "He that
now goeth on his way weeping, and beareth forth good seed
with him, shall doubtless come again with joy, and bring his
sheaves with him."[12]   And certainly he that sadly considers
the portion of Dives, and remembers that the account which
Abraham gave him for the unavoidableness of his torment

---

[7] Chap. iv. 9.   [8] Neque enim Deus ullâ re perinde atque corporis ærumnâ conciliatur.—Naz. Orat. 18.   [9] Amos vi. 1
[10] Luke vi. 25.   [11] Matt. v. 4.   [12] Psal. cxxvi. 6.

was, because he had his good things in this life, must, in all reason, with trembling run from a course of banquets and faring deliciously every day, as being a dangerous estate, and a consignation to an evil greater than all danger, the pains and torments of unhappy souls. If, either by patience or repentance, by compassion or persecution, by choice or by conformity, by severity or discipline, we allay the festival follies of a soft life, and profess under the cross of Christ, we shall more willingly and more safely enter into our grave ; but the death-bed of a voluptuous man upbraids his little and cozening prosperities, and exacts pains made sharper by the passing from soft beds, and a softer mind.[13] He that would die holily and happily, must in this world love tears, humility, solitude, and repentance.

SECT. II. *Of daily Examination of our Actions in the whole course of our Health, preparatory to our Death-bed.*

HE that will die well and happily must dress his soul by a diligent and frequent scrutiny ; he must perfectly understand and watch the state of his soul ; he must set his house in order, before he be fit to die. And for this there is great reason, and great necessity.

Reasons for a daily Examination.

1. For if we consider the disorders of every day, the multitude of impertinent words, the great portions of time spent in vanity, the daily omissions of duty, the coldness of our prayers, the indifference of our spirit in holy things, the uncertainty of our secret purposes, our infinite deceptions and hypocrisies, sometimes not known, very often not observed by ourselves, our want of charity, our not knowing in how many degrees of action and purpose every virtue is to be exercised, the secret adherences of pride, and too-forward complacency in our best actions, our failings in all our relations, the niceties of difference between some virtues and some vices, the secret indiscernible passages from lawful to unlawful in the first instances of change, the perpetual mistakings of permissions for duty, and licentious practices for permissions, our daily abusing the liberty that God gives us, our unsuspected sins in the

[13] —— Sed longi pœnas fortuna favoris
Exigit à misero, quæ tanto pondere famæ
Res premit adversas, fatisque prioribus urget.—Lucan. l. viii.

managing a course of life certainly lawful, our little greedi-
nesses in eating, our surprises in the proportions of our drink-
ings, our too-great freedoms and fondnesses in lawful loves,
our aptness for things sensual, and our deadness and tediousness of spirit in spiritual employments ; besides infinite variety
of cases of conscience that do occur in the life of every man,
and in all intercourses of every life, and that the productions
of sin are numerous and increasing, like the families of the
northern people, or the genealogies of the first patriarchs of
the world ; from all this we shall find that the computations
of a man's life are busy as the tables of sines and tangents,
and intricate as the accounts of eastern merchants ; and,
therefore, it were but reason we should sum up our accounts
at the foot of every page, I mean that we call ourselves to
scrutiny every night, when we compose ourselves to the little
images of death.

2. For if we make but one general account, and never
reckon till we die, either we shall only reckon by great sums,
and remember nothing but clamorous and crying sins, and
never consider concerning particulars, or forget very many ;
or if we could consider all that we ought, we must needs be
confounded with the multitude and variety. But if we observe
all the little passages of our life, and reduce them into the
order of accounts and accusations, we shall find them multiply
so fast, that it will not only appear to be an ease to the accounts of our death-bed, but, by the instrument of shame, will
restrain the inundation of evils ; it being a thing intolerable
to human modesty to see sins increase so fast, and virtues
grow up so slow ; to see every day stained with the spots of
leprosy, or sprinkled with the marks of a lesser evil.

3. It is not intended we should take accounts of our lives
only to be thought religious, but that we may see our evil and
amend it, that we dash our sins against the stones, that we may
go to God, and to a spiritual guide, and search for remedies,
and apply them. And, indeed, no man can well observe his
own growth in grace, but by accounting seldomer returns of
sin, and a more frequent victory over temptations ; concerning
which every man makes his observations, according as he makes
his inquiries and search after himself. In order to this it was
that St. Paul wrote, before receiving the holy sacrament, " Let
a man examine himself, and so let him eat." This precept was

given in those days when they communicated every day; and, therefore, a daily examination also was intended.

4. And it will appear highly fitting, if we remember that, at the day of judgment, not only the greatest lines of life, but every branch and circumstance of every action, every word and thought, shall be called to scrutiny and severe judgment; insomuch that it was a great truth which one said, "Woe be to the most innocent life, if God should search into it without mixtures of mercy!" And, therefore, we are here to follow St. Paul's advice, "Judge yourselves, and you shall not be judged of the Lord." The way to prevent God's anger is to be angry with ourselves; and, by examining our actions, and condemning the criminal, by being assessors in God's tribunal, at least we shall obtain the favour of the court. As, therefore, every night we must make our bed the memorial of our grave, so let our evening thoughts be an image of the day of judgment.

5. This advice was so reasonable and proper an instrument of virtue, that it was taught even to the scholars of Pythagoras by their master:[1] "Let not sleep seize upon the regions of your senses before you have three times recalled the conversation and accidents of the day." Examine what you have committed against the Divine law, what you have omitted of your duty, and in what you have made use of the Divine grace to the purposes of virtue and religion; joining the judge, reason, to the legislative mind or conscience, that God may reign there as a lawgiver and a judge. Then Christ's kingdom is set up in our hearts: then we always live in the eye of our Judge, and live by the measures of reason, religion, and sober counsels.

The benefits we shall receive by practising this advice, in order to a blessed death, will also add to the account of reason and fair inducements.

The Benefits of this Exercise.

1. By a daily examination of our actions we shall the easier cure a great sin, and prevent its arrival to become habitual. For to examine we suppose to be a relative duty, and instrumental to something else. We examine ourselves, that we may find out our failings and cure them; and, therefore, if we use our remedy when the wound is fresh and bleeding, we shall find the cure more certain and less painful. For so a

[1] Hierocl.

z

taper, when its crown of flame is newly blown off, retains a nature so symbolical to light, that it will with greediness rekindle and snatch a ray from the neighbour fire. So is the soul of man when it is newly fallen into sin; although God be angry with it, and the state of God's favour and its own graciousness is interrupted, yet the habit is not naturally changed; and still God leaves some roots of virtue standing, and the man is modest, or apt to be made ashamed, and he is not grown a bold sinner; but if he sleeps on it, and returns again to the same sin, and by degrees grows in love with it, and gets the custom, and the strangeness of it is taken away, then it is his master, and is swelled into a heap, and is abetted by use and corroborated by newly entertained principles, and is insinuated into his nature, and hath possessed his affections, and tainted the will and the understanding; and by this time a man is in the state of a decaying merchant, his accounts are so great and so intricate, and so much in arrear, that to examine it will be but to represent the particulars of his calamity: therefore, they think it better to pull the napkin before their eyes, than to stare upon the circumstances of their death.

2. A daily or frequent examination of the parts of our life will interrupt the proceeding and hinder the journey of little sins into a heap. For many days do not pass the best persons in which they have not many idle words or vainer thoughts to sully the fair whiteness of their souls; some indiscreet passions or trifling purposes, some impertinent discontents or unhandsome usages of their own persons or their dearest relations. And though God is not extreme to mark what is done amiss, and therefore puts these upon the accounts of his mercy, and the title of the cross; yet in two cases these little sins combine and cluster; and we know that grapes were once in so great a bunch, that one cluster was the load of two men; that is, 1. When either we are in love with small sins; or, 2. When they proceed from a careless and incurious spirit into frequency and continuance. For so the smallest atoms that dance in all the little cells of the world are so trifling and immaterial, that they cannot trouble an eye, nor vex the tenderest part of a wound where a barbed arrow dwelt; yet when, by their infinite numbers, (as Melissa and Parmenides affirm,) they danced first into order, then into little bodies, at last they made the matter of the world: so are the little indiscretions of our life;

they are always inconsiderable if they be considered, and contemptible if they be not despised, and God does not regard them, if we do. We may easily keep them asunder by our daily or nightly thoughts, and prayers, and severe sentences ; but even the least sand can check the tumultuous pride, and become a limit to the sea, when it is in a heap and in united multitudes; but if the wind scatter and divide them, the little drops and the vainer froth of the water begin to invade the strand. Our sighs can scatter such little offences; but then be sure to breathe such accents frequently, lest they knot and combine, and grow big as the shore, and we perish in sand, in trifling instances. "He that despiseth little things, shall perish by little and little:" so said the son of Sirach.[2]

3. A frequent examination of our actions will intenerate and soften our consciences, so that they shall be impatient of any rudeness or heavier load ; and he that is used to shrink, when he is pressed with a branch of twining osier,[3] will not willingly stand in the ruins of a house when the beam dashes upon the pavement. And provided that our nice and tender spirit be not vexed into scruple, nor the scruple turn into unreasonable fears, nor the fears into superstition ; he that, by any arts, can make his spirit tender and apt for religious impressions, hath made the fairest seat for religion, and the unaptest and uneasiest entertainment for sin and eternal death, in the whole world.

4. A frequent examination of the smallest parts of our lives is the best instrument to make our repentance particular, and a fit remedy to all the members of the whole body of sin. For our examination, put off to our death-bed, of necessity brings us into this condition, that very many thousands of our sins must be (or not be at all) washed off with a general repentance, which the more general and indefinite it is, it is ever so much the worse. And if he that repents the longest and the oftenest, and upon the most instances, is still, during his whole life, but an imperfect penitent, and there are very many reserves left to be wiped off by God's mercies, and to be eased by collateral assistances, or to be groaned for at the terrible day of judgment ; it will be but a sad story to consider that the sins of a whole life, or of very great portions of it, shall be put upon the

---

[2] Ecclus. xix. 1.   [3] Qui levi comminatione pellitur, non opus est ut fortitudine et armis invadatur.—Seneca.

remedy of one examination, and the advices of one discourse
and the activities of a decayed body, and a weak and an amazed
spirit. Let us do the best we can, we shall find that the mere
sins of ignorance and unavoidable forgetfulness will be enough
to be intrusted to such a bank ; and that if a general repent
ance will serve towards their expiation, it will be an infinite
mercy : but we have nothing to warrant our confidence, if we
shall think it to be enough on our death-bed to confess the
notorious actions of our lives, and to say, " The Lord be merciful unto me for the infinite transgressions of my life, which
I have wilfully or carelessly forgot ;" for very many of which
the repentance, the distinct, particular, circumstantiate repentance, of a whole life would have been too little if we could
have done more.

5. After the enumeration of these advantages, I shall not
need to add, that if we decline or refuse to call ourselves frequently to account, and to use daily advices concerning the
state of our souls, it is a very ill sign that our souls are not
right with God, or that they do not dwell in religion. But
this I shall say, that they who do use this exercise frequently
will make their conscience much at ease, by casting out a daily
load of humour and surfeit, the matter of diseases and the instruments of death. " He that does not frequently search his
conscience, is a house without a window," and like a wild un-
tutored son of a fond and undiscerning widow.

But if this exercise seem too great a trouble, and that by
such advices religion will seem a burden, I have two things to
oppose against it.

1. One is, that we had better bear the burden of the Lord
than the burden of a base and polluted conscience. Religion
cannot be so great a trouble as a guilty soul ; and whatsoever
trouble can be fancied in this or any other action of religion,
it is only to inexperienced persons. It may be a trouble at
first, just as is every change and every new accident : but if
you do it frequently, and accustom your spirit to it, as the custom will make it easy,[4] so the advantages will make it delec
table ; that will make it facile as nature, these will make it a
pleasant and eligible as reward.

2. The other thing I have to say is this, that to examine our
lives will be no trouble, if we do not intricate it with busi

---

[4] Elige vitam optimam, consuetudo faciet jucundissimam.—Sen.

nesses of the world and the labyrinths of care and impertinent affairs.[5] A man had need have a quiet and disentangled life who comes to search into all his actions, and to make judgment concerning his errors and his needs, his remedies and his hopes. They that have great intrigues of the world have a yoke upon their necks, and cannot look back: and he that covets many things greedily, and snatches at high things ambitiously, that despises his neighbour proudly, and bears his crosses peevishly, or his prosperity impotently and passionately; he that is prodigal of his precious time, and is tenacious and retentive of evil purposes, is not a man disposed to this exercise: he hath reason to be afraid of his own memory, and to dash his glass in pieces, because it must needs represent to his own eyes an intolerable deformity. He therefore that resolves to live well, whatsoever it costs him; he that will go to heaven at any rate, shall best tend this duty by neglecting the affairs of the world in all things where prudently he may. But if we do otherwise, we shall find that the accounts of our death-bed and the examination made by a disturbed understanding will be very empty of comfort and full of inconveniences.

6. For hence it comes that men die so timorously and uncomfortably, as if they were forced out of their lives by the violence of an executioner. Then, without much examination, they remember how wickedly they have lived, without religion, against the laws of the covenant of grace, without God in the world; then they see sin goes off like an amazed, wounded, affrighted person from a lost battle, without honour, without a veil, with nothing but shame and sad remembrances: then they can consider, that if they had lived virtuously, all the trouble and objection of that would now be past, and all that had remained should be peace and joy, and all that good which dwells within the house of God and eternal life. But now they find they have done amiss and dealt wickedly, they have no bank of good works, but a huge treasure of wrath, and they are going to a strange place, and what shall be their lot is uncertain; (so they say, when they would comfort and flatter themselves;) but in truth of religion their portion is sad and intolerable, without hope and without refreshment, and they must use little silly arts to make them go off from

---

[5] Securæ et quietæ mentis est in omnes vitæ partes discurrere; occupa-torum animi velut sub jugo sunt, respicere non possunt.—Seneca.

their stage of sins with some handsome circumstances of opinion: they will in civility be abused, that they may die quietly, and go decently to their execution, and leave their friends indifferently contented, and apt to be comforted; and by that time they are gone awhile they see that they deceived themselves all their days, and were by others deceived at last.

Let us make it our own case: we shall come to that state and period of condition in which we shall be infinitely comforted if we have lived well; or else be amazed and go off trembling, because we are guilty of heaps of unrepented and unforsaken sins. It may happen, we shall not then understand it so, because most men of late ages have been abused with false principles, and they are taught (or they are willing to believe) that a little thing is enough to save them, and that heaven is so cheap a purchase that it will fall upon them whether they will or no. The misery of it is, they will not suffer themselves to be confuted till it be too late to recant their error. In the interim, they are impatient to be examined, as a leper is of a comb; and are greedy of the world, as children of raw fruit; and they hate a severe reproof as they do thorns in their bed; and they love to lay aside religion, as a drunken person does to forget his sorrow; and all the way they dream of fine things, and their dreams prove contrary, and become the hieroglyphics of an eternal sorrow. The daughter of Polycrates dreamed that her father was lifted up, and that Jupiter washed him, and the sun anointed him; but it proved to him but a sad prosperity; for after a long life of constant prosperous successes he was surprised by his enemies, and hanged up till the dew of heaven wet his cheeks, and the sun melted his grease. Such is the condition of those persons who, living either in the despite or in the neglect of religion, lie wallowing in the drunkenness of prosperity or worldly cares: they think themselves to be exalted, till the evil day overtakes them; and then they can expound their dream of life to end in a sad and hopeless death. I remember that Cleomenes was called a god by the Egyptians, because when he was hanged a serpent grew out of his body, and wrapped itself about his head: till the philosophers of Egypt said it was natural that from the marrow of some bodies such productions should arise. And, indeed, it represents the condition of some men, who being dead are esteemed saints and beatified persons, when their head is encircled with dragons and is entered into the possession of the devil, that old serpent and deceiver. For, indeed, their life was secretly so corrupted, that such serpents fed upon the ruins of the spirit and the decays of grace and reason. To be cozened in making judgments concerning our final condition is extremely easy; but if we be cozened we are infinitely miserable.

SECT. III. *Of exercising Charity during our whole Life.*

HE that would die well and happily must in his life-time, according to all his capacities, exercise charity;[1] and because religion is the life of the soul, and charity is the life of religion, the same which gives life to the better part of man, which never dies, may obtain of God a mercy to the inferior part of a man in the day of its dissolution.

1. Charity is the great channel through which God passes all his mercy upon mankind. For we receive absolution of our sins in proportion to our forgiving our brother. This is the rule of our hopes, and the measure of our desire in this world; and in the day of death and judgment the great sentence upon mankind shall be transacted according to our alms, which is the other part of charity. Certain it is, that God cannot, will not, never did, reject a charitable man in his greatest needs and in his most passionate prayers;[2] for God himself is love, and every degree of charity that dwells in us is the participation of the Divine nature; and, therefore, when upon our death-bed a cloud covers our head, and we are enwrapped with sorrow; when we feel the weight of a sickness, and do not feel the refreshing visitations of God's loving-kindness; when we have many things to trouble us, and looking round about us, we see no comforter; then call to mind what injuries you have forgiven, how apt you were to pardon all affronts and real persecutions, how you embraced peace when it was offered you, how you followed after peace when it ran from you: and when you are weary of one side, turn upon the other, and remember the alms that, by the grace of God and his assistances, you have done, and look up to God, and with the eye

---

[1] Respice quid prodest praesentis temporis aevum;
    Omne quod est, nihil est, praeter amare Deum.
[2] Quod expendi habui,   Quod negavi punior,
    Quod donavi habeo;   Quod servavi perdidi.

of faith behold him coming in the cloud, and pronouncing the sentence of doomsday according to his mercies and thy charity.

2. Charity, with its twin daughters, alms and forgiveness, is especially effectual for the procuring God's mercies in the day and manner of our death. "Alms deliver from death," said old Tobias;[3] and "alms make an atonement for sins," said the son of Sirach;[4] and so said Daniel,[5] and so say all the wise men of the world. And in this sense, also, is that of St. Peter,[6] "Love covers a multitude of sins;" and St. Clement, in his Constitutions,[7] gives this counsel, "If you have any thing in your hands, give it, that it may work to the remission of thy sins; for by faith and alms sins are purged." The same also is the counsel of Salvian, who wonders that men, who are guilty of great and many sins, will not work out their pardon by alms and mercy. But this also must be added out of the words of Lactantius, who makes this rule complete and useful; "But think not, because sins are taken away by alms, that by thy money thou mayest purchase a licence to sin; for sins are abolished if because thou hast sinned thou givest to God," that is, to God's poor servants, and his indigent, necessitous creatures: but if thou sinnest upon confidence of giving, thy sins are not abolished. For God desires infinitely that men should be purged from their sins, and therefore commands us to repent; but to repent is nothing else but to profess and affirm (that is, to purpose, and to make good that purpose) that they will sin no more.[8]

Now, alms are therefore effective to the abolition and pardon of our sins, because they are preparatory to, and impetratory of, the grace of repentance, and are fruits of repentance; and therefore St. Chrysostom affirms,[9] that repentance without alms is dead, and without wings, and can never soar upwards to the element of love. But because they are a part of repentance, and hugely pleasing to Almighty God, therefore they deliver us from the evils of an unhappy and accursed death; for so Christ delivered his disciples from the sea when he appeased the storm, though they still sailed in the channel: and this

---

[3] Tob. iv. 10; xii. 9.   [4] Ecclus. iii. 30.   [5] Dan. iv. 27.
[6] 1 Pet. iv. 8; Isa. i. 17.   [7] Lib. vii. cap. 13. Ἐὰν ἔχεις δια τῶν χειρῶν σου, δὸς, ἵνα ἐργάσῃ εἰς λύτρωσιν ἁμαρτιῶν σου ἐλεημοσύναις γὰρ καὶ πίστεσιν ἀποκαθαίρονται ἁμαρτίαι.

[8] Agere autem pœnitentiam nihil aliud est quàm profiteri et affirmare se non ulteriùs peccaturum.   Orat. ii. de Pœnitentiâ.

St. Jerome verifies with all his reading and experience, saying, " I do not remember to have read that ever any charitable person died an evil death."[10]   And although a long experience hath observed God's mercies to descend upon charitable people, like the dew upon Gideon's fleece, when all the world was dry; yet for this also we have a promise, which is not only an argument of a certain number of years, (as experience is,) but a security for eternal ages.   " Make ye friends of the mammon of unrighteousness, that when ye fail they may receive you into everlasting habitations."   When faith fails, and chastity is useless, and temperance shall be no more, then charity shall bear you upon wings of cherubim to the eternal mountain of the Lord.   " I have been a lover of mankind, and a friend, and merciful; and now I expect to communicate in that great kindness which he shows that is the great God and Father of men and mercies," said Cyrus the Persian, on his death-bed.[11]

I do not mean this should only be a death-bed charity, any more than a death-bed repentance ; but it ought to be the charity of our life and healthful years, a parting with portions of our goods then,[12] when we can keep them: we must not first kindle our lights when we are to descend into our houses of darkness, or bring a glaring torch suddenly to a dark room that will amaze the eye, and not delight it or instruct the body ; but if our tapers have, in their constant course, descended into their grave, crowned all the way with light, then let the death-bed charity be doubled, and the light burn brightest when it is to deck our hearse.   But concerning this I shall afterwards give account.

SECT. IV. *General Considerations to enforce the former Practices.*

THESE are the general instruments of preparation in order to a holy death; it will concern us all to use them diligently and speedily ; for we must be long in doing that which must be done but once :[1] and therefore we must begin betimes, and lose

[10] Nunquam memini me legisse, malâ morte mortuum, qui libenter opera charitatis exercuit.—Ad Nepot.   [11] Ἐγὼ φιλάνθρωπος ἐγενόμην, καὶ νῦν ἡδέως ἄν μοι δοκῶ κοινωνῆσαι τοῦ εὐεργετοῦντος ἀνθρώπους.

[12] Da dum tempus habes; tibi propria sit manus hæres;
  Auferet hoc nemo, quod dabis ipse Deo.

[1] Quod sæpe fieri non potest, fiat diu.—Seneca.

no time; especially since it is so great a venture, and upon it depends so great a state. Seneca said well, " There is no science or art in the world so hard as to live and die well; the professors of other arts are vulgar and many ;"[2] but he that knows how to do this business is certainly instructed to eternity. But then let me remember this, that a wise person will also put most upon the greatest interest. Common prudence will teach us this. No man will hire a general to cut wood, or shake hay with a sceptre, or spend his soul and all his faculties upon the purchase of a cockle-shell; but he will fit instruments to the dignity and exigence of the design : and, therefore, since heaven is so glorious a state, and so certainly designed for us if we please, let us spend all that we have, all our passions and affections, all our study and industry, all our desires and stratagems, all our witty and ingenious faculties,[3] towards the arriving thither; whither if we do come, every minute will infinitely pay for all the troubles of our whole life ; if we do not, we shall have the reward of fools, an unpitied and an upbraided misery.[4]

To this purpose I shall represent the state of dying and dead men in the devout words of some of the fathers of the church, whose sense I shall exactly keep, but change their order ; that, by placing some of their dispersed meditations into a chain or sequel of discourse, I may with their precious stones make a union, and compose them into a jewel; for though the meditation is plain and easy, yet it is affectionate and material, and true and necessary.

The Circumstances of a Dying Man's Sorrow and Danger.

When the sentence of death is decreed and begins to be put in execution, it is sorrow enough to see or feel respectively the sad accents of the agony and last contentions of the soul, and the reluctances and unwillingnesses of the body : the forehead washed with a new and stranger baptism, besmeared with a cold sweat, tenacious and clammy, apt to make it cleave to the roof of his coffin ; the nose cold and undiscerning, not pleased

[2] Nullius rei quàm vivere difficilior est scientia : professores aliarum artium vulgò multique sunt.—Seneca.
[3] Nunc ratio nulla est restandi, nulla facultas,
      Æternas quoniam pœnas in morte timendum.—Lucret. i. 112.
[4] Virtutem videant, intabescantque relictâ.

with perfumes, nor suffering violence with a cloud of unwholesome smoke ;[5] the eyes dim as a sullied mirror, or the face of
heaven when God shows his anger in a prodigious storm ; the
feet cold, the hands stiff, the physicians despairing, our friends
weeping, the rooms dressed with darkness and sorrow, and
the exterior parts betraying what are the violences which the
soul and spirit suffer ;[6] the nobler part, like the lord of the
house, being assaulted by exterior rudenesses, and driven from
all the outworks, at last, faint and weary with short and frequent breathings, interrupted with the longer accents of sighs,
without moisture but the excrescences of a spilt humour
when the pitcher is broken at the cistern, it retires to its last
fort, the heart, whither it is pursued, and stormed, and beaten
out, as when the barbarous Thracian sacked the glory of the
Grecian empire.   Then calamity is great, and sorrow rules in
all the capacities of man: then the mourners weep, because it
is civil, or because they need thee, or because they fear: but
who suffers for thee with a compassion sharp as is thy pain?
Then the noise is like the faint echo of a distant valley, and
few hear, and they will not regard thee, who seemest like a
person void of understanding, and of a departing interest.
Vere tremendum est mortis sacramentum.   But these accidents are common to all that die ; and when a special providence shall distinguish them, they shall die with easy circumstances ; but as no piety can secure it, so must no confidence
expect it, but wait for the time, and accept the manner of the
dissolution.   But that which distinguishes them is this:
    He that hath lived a wicked life, if his conscience be alarm-
ed, and that he does not die like a wolf or a tiger, without
sense or remorse of all his wildness and his injury, his beastly nature, and desert and untilled manners—if he have but
sense of what he is going to suffer, or what he may expect to
be his portion—then we may imagine the terror of their
abused fancies, how they see affrighting shapes, and, because
they fear them, they feel the gripes of devils, urging the unwilling souls from the kinder and fast embraces of the body,
calling to the grave and hastening to judgment, exhibiting
great bills of uncancelled crimes, awaking and amazing the
conscience, breaking all their hope in pieces, and making faith
useless and terrible, because the malice was great, and the

[5] Nilus   [6] St. Basil.

charity was none at all.   Then they look for some to have
pity on them, but there is no man.[7]   No man dares to be
their pledge: no man can redeem their soul, which now feels
what it never feared.   Then the tremblings and the sorrow,
the memory of the past sin, and the fear of future pains, and
the sense of an angry God, and the presence of some devils,
consign him to the eternal company of all the damned and accursed spirits.[8]   Then they want an angel for their guide,
and the Holy Spirit for their comforter, and a good conscience
for their testimony, and Christ for their advocate; and they
die and are left in prisons of earth or air, in secret and undiscerned regions, to weep and tremble, and infinitely to fear
the coming of the day of Christ; at which time they shall be
brought forth to change their condition into a worse, where
they shall for ever feel more than we can believe or understand.

But when a good man dies, one that hath lived innocently,
or made joy in heaven at his timely and effective repentance,
and in whose behalf the holy Jesus hath interceded prosperously, and for whose interest the Spirit makes interpellations
with groans and sighs unutterable, and in whose defence
the angels drive away the devils on his death-bed, because
his sins are pardoned, and because he resisted the devil in his
life-time, and fought successfully, and persevered unto the
end; then the joys break forth through the clouds of sickness,
and the conscience stands upright, and confesses the glories of
God, and owns so much integrity, that it can hope for pardon,
and obtain it too; then the sorrows of the sickness, and the
flames of the fever, or the faintness of the consumption, do
but untie the soul from its chain, and let it go forth, first into
liberty, and then to glory: for it is but for a little while that
the face of the sky was black, like the preparations of the
night, but quickly the cloud was torn and rent, the violence
of thunder parted it into little portions, that the sun might
look forth with a watery eye, and then shine without a tear.
But it is an infinite refreshment to remember all the comforts
of his prayers, the frequent victory over his temptation, the
mortification of his lust, the noblest sacrifice to God, in which
he most delights, that we have given him our wills, and killed
our appetites for the interests of his services: then all the
trouble of that is gone; and what remains is a portion in the

---

    [7] S. Chrysostomus.   [8] Ephraem Syrus.

inheritance of Jesus, of which he now talks no more, as a thing at distance, but is entering into the possession. When the veil is rent,[9] and the prison-doors are open at the presence of God's angel, the soul goes forth full of hope, sometimes with evidence, but always with certainty in the thing, and instantly it passes into the throngs of spirits, where angels meet it singing, and the devils flock with malicious and vile purposes, desiring to lead it away with them into their houses of sorrow: there they see things which they never saw, and hear voices which they never heard. There the devils charge them with many sins, and the angels remember that themselves rejoiced when they were repented of. Then the devils aggravate and describe all the circumstances of the sin, and add calumnies; and the angels bear the sword forward still, because their Lord doth answer for them. Then the devils rage and gnash their teeth;[10] they see the soul chaste and pure, and they are ashamed; they see it penitent, and they despair; they perceive that the tongue was refrained and sanctified, and then hold their peace. Then the soul passes forth and rejoices, passing by the devils in scorn and triumph, being securely carried into the bosom of the Lord, where they shall rest till their crowns are finished, and their mansions are prepared; and then they shall feast and sing, rejoice and worship, for ever and ever.[11] Fearful and formidable to unholy persons is the first meeting with spirits in their separation. But the victory which holy souls receive by the mercies of Jesus Christ, and the conduct of angels, is a joy that we must not understand till we feel it; and yet such which by an early and a persevering piety we may secure; but let us inquire after it no further, because it is secret.

CHAP. III. OF THE STATE OF SICKNESS, AND THE TEMPTATIONS INCIDENT TO IT, WITH THEIR PROPER REMEDIES.

SECT. I. *Of the State of Sickness.*

ADAM's sin brought death into the world, and man did die the same day in which he sinned, according as God had

---

[9] S. Martyrius, S. Eustratius Martyr.   [10] S. Chrysostomus.
[11] Μεγίστη τῶν ἀρετῶν θεοσέβεια, δι' ἧς ἀθανατίζεται ἡ ψυχή.—Phil

threatened.   He did not die as death is taken for a separation
of soul and body ; that is not death properly, but the ending
of the last act of death ; just as a man is said to be born when
he ceases any longer to be borne in his mother's womb : but
whereas to man was intended a life long and happy, without
sickness, sorrow, or infelicity, and this life should be lived
here or in a better place, and the passage from one to the other
should have been easy, safe, and pleasant, now that man sinned he fell from that state to a contrary.

If Adam had stood, he should not always have lived in this
world; for this world was not a place capable of giving a
dwelling to all those myriads of men and women which should
have been born in all the generations of infinite and eternal
ages ; for so it must have been if man had not died at all, nor
yet have removed hence at all.   Neither is it likely that man's
innocence should have lost to him all possibility of going
thither, where the duration is better, measured by a better
time, subject to fewer changes, and which is now the reward
of a returning virtue, which in all natural senses is less than
innocence, save that it is heightened by Christ to an equality
of acceptation with the state of innocence : but so it must have
been, that his innocence should have been punished with an
eternal confinement to this state, which in all reason is the
less perfect, the state of a traveller, not of one possessed of
his inheritance.   It is therefore certain man should have
changed his abode: for so did Enoch, and so did Elias, and
so shall all the world that shall be alive at the day of judgment; they shall not die, but they shall change their place
and their abode, their duration and their state, and all this
without death.

That death therefore which God threatened to Adam,
and which passed upon his posterity, is not the going out of
this world, but the manner of going.   If he had stayed in innocence, he should have gone from hence placidly and fairly,
without vexatious and afflictive circumstances ; he should not
have died by sickness, misfortune, defect, or unwillingness :
but when he fell, then he began to die—the same day (so said
God); and that must needs be true : and therefore it must
mean that upon that very day he fell into an evil and dangerous condition, a state of change and affliction ;[1] then death

> Prima quæ vitam dedit hora carpit.—Hercul. Fur.
> Nascentes morimur, finisque ab origine pendet.—Manil.

began, that is, the man began to die by a natural diminution and aptness to disease and misery. His first state was and should have been (so long as it lasted) a happy duration; his second was a daily and miserable change: and this was the dying properly.

This appears in the great instance of damnation, which, in the style of Scripture, is called eternal death; not because it kills or ends the duration—it hath not so much good in it— but because it is a perpetual infelicity. Change or separation of soul and body is but accidental to death; death may be with or without either: but the formality, the curse, and the sting of death, that is, misery, sorrow, fear, diminution, defect, anguish, dishonour, and whatsoever is miserable and afflictive in nature, that is death. Death is not an action, but a whole state and condition; and this was first brought in upon us by the offence of one man.

But this went no further than thus to subject us to temporal infelicity. If it had proceeded so far as was supposed, man had been much more miserable, for man had more than one original sin in this sense; and though this death entered first upon us by Adam's fault, yet it came nearer unto us, and increased upon us by the sins of more of our forefathers; for Adam's sin left us in strength enough to contend with human calamities for almost a thousand years together. But the sins of his children, our forefathers, took off from us half the strength about the time of the flood; and then from five hundred to two hundred and fifty, and from thence to one hundred and twenty, and from thence to threescore and ten; so often halving it till it is almost come to nothing. But by the sins of men in the several generations of the world, death, that is, misery and disease, is hastened so upon us that we are of a contemptible age; and because we are to die by suffering evils, and by the daily lessening of our strength and health, this death is so long a doing, that it makes so great a part of our short life useless and unserviceable, that we have not time enough to get the perfection of a single manufacture, but ten or twelve generations of the world must go to the making up of one wise man, or one excellent art; and in the succession of those ages there happen so many changes and interruptions, so many wars and violences, that seven years' fighting sets a whole kingdom back in learning and virtue to which they were creeping, it may be, a whole age.

And thus also we do evil to our posterity, as Adam did to
his, and Cham did to his, and Eli to his, and all they to theirs
who by sins caused God to shorten the life and multiply the
evils of mankind; and for this reason it is the world grows
worse and worse, because so many original sins are multiplied,
and so many evils from parents descend upon the succeeding
generations of men, that they derive nothing from us but
original misery.

But he who restored the law of nature, did also restore us to
the condition of nature, which, being violated by the introduction of death, Christ then repaired when he suffered and over-
came death for us; that is, he hath taken away the unhappiness
of sickness, and the sting of death, and the dishonours of the
grave, of dissolution and weakness, of decay and change, and
hath turned them into acts of favour, into instances of comfort, into opportunities of virtue; Christ hath now knit them
into rosaries and coronets; he hath put them into promises
and rewards; he hath made them part of the portion of his
elect: they are instruments, and earnests, and securities, and
passages, to the greatest perfection of human nature and the
Divine promises. So that it is possible for us now to be reconciled to sickness; it came in by sin, and therefore is cured
when it is turned into virtue; and although it may have in it
the uneasiness of labour, yet it will not be uneasy as sin, or
the restlessness of a discomposed conscience. If, therefore,
we can well manage our state of sickness, that we may not
fall by pain as we usually do by pleasure, we need not fear;
for no evil shall happen to us.

Sect. II. *Of the First Temptation proper to the State of Sickness, Impatience.*

Men that are in health are severe exactors of patience at the
hands of them that are sick; and they usually judge it not by
terms of relation between God and the suffering man, but between him and the friends that stand by the bed-side. It will
be therefore necessary that we truly understand to what duties and actions the patience of a sick man ought to extend.

1. Sighs and groans, sorrow and prayers, humble complaints and dolorous[1] expressions, are the sad accents of a
sick man's language; for it is not to be expected that a sick

[1] Ejulatu, questu, gemitu, fremitibus,
Resonando multùm flebiles voces refert.—Cic. Tusc. ii. 13.

man should act a part of patience with a countenance like an orator, or grave like a dramatic person; it were well if all men could bear an exterior decency in their sickness, and regulate their voice, their face, their discourse, and all their circumstances, by the measures and proportions of comeliness and satisfaction to all the standers-by. But this would better please them than assist him; the sick man would do more good to others than he would receive to himself.

2. Therefore silence and still composures, and not complaining, are no parts of a sick man's duty; they are not necessary parts of patience.[2] We find that David roared for the very disquietness of his sickness; and he lay chattering like a swallow, and his throat was dry with calling for help upon his God. That's the proper voice of sickness; and certain it is that the proper voices of sickness are expressly vocal and petitory in the ears of God, and call for pity in the same accent as the cries and oppressions of widows and orphans do for vengeance upon their persecutors, though they say no collect against them. For there is the voice of man, and there is the voice of the disease, and God hears both; and the louder the disease speaks, there is the greater need of mercy and pity, and therefore God will the sooner hear it. Abel's blood had a voice and cried to God; and humility hath a voice, and cries so loud to God that it pierces the clouds; and so hath every sorrow and every sickness; and when a man cries out and complains but according to the sorrows of his pain,[3] it cannot be any part of a culpable impatience, but an argument for pity.

3. Some men's senses are so subtile, and their perceptions so quick and full of relish, and their spirits so active, that the same load is double upon them to what it is to another person; and therefore comparing the expressions of the one to the silence of the other, a different judgment cannot be made concerning their patience. Some natures are querulous, and melancholy, and soft, and nice, and tender, and weeping, and expressive; others are sullen, dull, without apprehension, apt to tolerate and carry burdens; and the crucifixion of our blessed Saviour falling upon a delicate and virgin body, of

---

[2] Concedendum est gementi.
[3] —— Flagrantior æquo
Non debet dolor esse viri, nec vulnere major.—Juv. Sat. xiii. 11.

curious temper, and strict, equal composition, was naturally
more full of torment than that of the ruder thieves, whose
proportions were coarser and uneven.

4. In this case it was no imprudent advice which Cicero
gave:[4] nothing in the world is more amiable than an even
temper in our whole life, and in every action ; but this evenness cannot be kept unless every man follows his own nature,
without striving to imitate the circumstances of another. And
what is so in the thing itself ought to be so in our judgments
concerning the things. We must not call any one impatient
if he be not silent in a fever, as if he were asleep, or as if he
were dull, as Herod's son of Athens.

5. Nature in some cases hath made cryings out and exclamations to be an entertainment of the spirit, and an abatement or diversion of the pain. For so did the old champions
when they threw their fatal nets that they might load their
enemy with the snares and weights of death ; they groaned
aloud, and sent forth the anguish of their spirit into the eyes
and heart of the man that stood against them,[5] so it is in the
endurance of some sharp pains, the complaints and shriekings,
the sharp groans and the tender accents, send forth the afflicted spirits, and force a way that they may ease their oppression and their load; that, when they have spent some of their
sorrows by a sally forth, they may return better able to fortify the heart. Nothing of this is a certain sign, much less
an action or part of impatience ; and when our blessed Saviour
suffered his last and sharpest pang of sorrow, he cried out
with a loud voice, and resolved to die, and did so.

Sect. III. *Constituent or Integral Parts of Patience.*

1. THAT we may secure our patience, we must take care that
our complaints be without despair. Despair sins against the
reputation of God's goodness, and the efficacy of all our old
experience. By despair we destroy the greatest comfort of
our sorrows, and turn our sickness into the state of devils and
perishing souls. No affliction is greater than despair; for
that is it which makes hell-fire, and turns a natural evil into

[4] Omnino si quicquam est decorum, nihil est profectò magis quàm
æquabilitas universæ vitæ, tum singularum actionum ; quam autem con-
servare non possis, si aliorum naturam imitans omittas tuam.—1. Offic. 88.
[5] Quia profundendà voce omne corpus intenditur, venitque plaga ve-
hementior.—Cic. Pro Muren. 48.

an intolerable; it hinders prayers, and fills up the intervals of sickness with a worse torture: it makes all spiritual arts useless, and the office of spiritual comforters and guides to be impertinent.

Against this, hope is to be opposed; and its proper acts, as it relates to the virtue and exercise of patience, are, 1. Praying to God for help and remedy; 2. Sending for the guides of souls; 3. Using all holy exercises and acts of grace proper to that state, which whoso does hath not the impatience of despair: every man that is patient hath hope in God in the day of his sorrows.

2. Our complaints in sickness must be without murmur. Murmur sins against God's providence and government; by it we grow rude, and, like the falling angels, displeased at God's supremacy; and nothing is more unreasonable—it talks against God, for whose glory all speech was made; it is proud and fantastic, hath better opinions of a sinner than of the Divine justice, and would rather accuse God than himself.

Against this is opposed that part of patience which resigns the man into the hands of God, saying with old Eli, "It is the Lord, let him do what he will;" and, "Thy will be done in earth as it is in heaven;" and so by admiring God's justice and wisdom, does also dispose the sick person for receiving God's mercy, and secures him the rather in the grace of God. The proper acts of this part of patience are, 1. To confess our sins and our own demerits; 2. It increases and exercises humility; 3. It loves to sing praises to God, even from the lowest abyss of human misery.

3. Our complaints in sickness must be without peevishness. This sins against civility and that necessary decency which must be used towards the ministers and assistants. By peevishness we increase our own sorrows, and are troublesome to them that stand there to ease ours. It hath in it harshness of nature and ungentleness, wilfulness and fantastic opinions, morosity and incivility.

Against it are opposed obedience, tractability, easiness of persuasion, aptness to take counsel. The acts of this part of patience are, 1. To obey our physicians; 2. To treat our persons with respect to our present necessities; 3. Not to be ungentle and uneasy to the ministers and nurses that attend us.[*]

* Vide chap. iv. sect. 1.

2 A 2

but to take their diligent and kind offices as sweetly as we can. and to bear their indiscretions or unhandsome accidents contentedly and without disquietness within, or evil language or angry words without; 4. Not to use unlawful means for our recovery.

If we secure these particulars, we are not lightly to be judged of by noises and postures, by colours and images of things, by paleness, or tossings from side to side. For it were a hard thing that those persons who are loaden with the greatest of human calamities should be strictly tied to ceremonies and forms of things. He is patient that calls upon God; that hopes for health or heaven; that believes God is wise and just in sending him afflictions; that confesses his sins, and accuses himself and justifies God; that expects God will turn this into good; that is civil to his physicians and his servants; that converses with the guides of souls, the ministers of religion: and in all things submits to God's will, and would use no indirect means for his recovery; but had rather be sick and die than enter at all into God's displeasure.

SECT. IV. *Remedies against Impatience, by way of Consideration.*

As it happens concerning death, so it is in sickness, which is death's handmaid. It hath the fate to suffer calumny and reproach, and hath a name worse than its nature.

1. For there is no sickness so great but children endure it, and have natural strengths to bear them out quite through the calamity, what period soever nature hath allotted it. Indeed they make no reflections upon their sufferings, and complain of sickness with an uneasy sigh or a natural groan, but consider not what the sorrows of sickness mean; and so bear it by a direct sufferance, and as a pillar bears the weight of a roof. But then why cannot we bear it so too? For this which we call a reflection upon, or a considering of, our sickness, is nothing but a perfect instrument of trouble, and consequently a temptation to impatience. It serves no end of nature; it may be avoided, and we may consider it only as an expression of God's anger, and an emissary or procurator of repentance. But all other considering it,[1] except where it

[1] Prætulerim . . . delirus inersque videri,
    Dum mea delectent mala me, vel denique fallant,
    Quàm sapere et ringi.   Horat. lib. ii. ep. 2.

serves the purposes of medicine and art, is nothing but, under
the colour of reason, an unreasonable device to heighten the
sickness and increase the torment. But then as children want
this act of reflex perception or reasonable sense, whereby their
sickness becomes less pungent and dolorous, so also do they
want the helps of reason, whereby they should be able to support it. For certain it is, reason was as well given us to
harden our spirits, and stiffen them in passions and sad accidents, as to make us bending and apt for action; and if in
men God hath heightened the faculties of apprehension, he
hath increased the auxiliaries of reasonable strengths; that
God's rod and God's staff might go together, and the beam
of God's countenance may as well refresh us with its light as
scorch us with its heat. For poor children that endure so
much have not inward supports and refreshments to bear them
through it; they never heard the sayings of old men, nor
have been taught the principles of severe philosophy, nor are
assisted with the results of a long experience, nor know they
how to turn a sickness into virtue, and a fever into a reward;
nor have they any sense of favours, the remembrance of which
may alleviate their burden; and yet nature hath in them teeth
and nails enough to scratch and fight against the sickness, and
by such aids as God is pleased to give them they wade through
the storm and murmur not. And besides this, yet, although
infants have not such brisk perceptions upon the stock of
reason, they have a more tender feeling upon the accounts of
sense, and their flesh is as uneasy by their natural softness and
weak shoulders as ours by our too forward apprehensions.
Therefore, bear up;[2] either you, or I, or some man wiser, and
many a woman weaker than us both, or the very children,
have endured worse evil than this that is upon thee now.

2. That sorrow is hugely tolerable which gives its smart but
by instants and smallest proportions of time. No man at once
feels the sickness of a week or of a whole day, but the smart
of an instant; and still every portion of a minute feels but its
proper share; and the last groan ended all the sorrow of its
peculiar burden. And what minute can that be which can
pretend to be intolerable? and the next minute is but the

[2] Στῆθος δὲ πλήξας, κραδίην ἠνίπαπε μύθῳ·
Τέτλαθι δή, κραδίη· καὶ κύντερον ἄλλο πότ' ἔτλης.
Ulysses apud Hom. Od. ν. 17.

same as the last, and the pain flows like the drops of a river,
or the little shreds of time; and if we do but take care of the
present minute, it cannot seem a great charge or a great burden; but that care will secure our duty, if we still but secure
the present minute.

3. If we consider how much men can suffer if they list, and
how much they do suffer for great and little causes, and that
no causes are greater than the proper causes of patience in
sickness, (that is, necessity and religion,) we cannot, without
huge shame to our nature, to our persons, and to our manners,
complain of this tax and impost of nature. This experience
added something to the old philosophy. When the gladiators
were exposed naked to each other's short swords, and were
to cut each other's souls away in portions of flesh, as if their
forms had been as divisible as the life of worms, they did not
sigh or groan—it was a shame to decline the blow but according to the just measures of art. The women that saw the
wound[3] shriek out; and he that receives it holds his peace.
He did not only stand bravely, but would also fall so; and,
when he was down, scorned to shrink his head when the insolent conqueror came to lift it from the shoulders: and yet this
man, in his first design, only aimed at liberty, and the reputation of a good fencer; and when he sunk down he saw he
could only receive the honour of a bold man, the noise of
which he shall never hear when his ashes are crammed in his
narrow urn. And what can we complain of the weakness of
our strengths, or the pressure of diseases, when we see a poor
soldier stand in a breach almost starved with cold and hunger,
and his cold apt to be relieved only by the heats of anger, a
fever, or a fired musket, and his hunger slackened by a greater
pain and a huge fear? This man shall stand in his arms and
wounds, *patiens luminis atque solis*, pale and faint, weary and
watchful; and at night shall have a bullet pulled out of his
flesh, and shivers from his bones, and endure his mouth to be
sewed up from a violent rent to its own dimensions; and all
this for a man whom he never saw, or, if he did, was not
noted by him; but one that shall condemn him to the gallows
if he runs from all this misery. It is seldom that God sends

---

[3] Spectatores vociferantur, ictus tacet.—Quis mediocris gladiator in-
gemuit? Quis vultum mutavit unquam? Quis non modò stetit, verùm
etiam decubuit turpiter?—Tusc. Q. lib. ii. 16.

such calamities upon men as men bring upon themselves and suffer willingly. But that which is most considerable is, that any passion and violence upon the spirit of man makes him able to suffer huge calamities with a certain constancy and an unwearied patience. Scipio Africanus was wont to commend that saying in Xenophon, That the same labours of warfare were easier far to a general than to a common soldier; because he was supported by the huge appetites of honour, which made his hard marches nothing but stepping forward and reaching at a triumph. Did not the lady of Sabinus, for others' interest, bear twins privately and without groaning? Are not the labours and cares, the spare diet and the waking nights, of covetous and adulterous, of ambitious and revengeful persons, greater sorrows and of more smart than a fever, or the short pains of child-birth? What will not tender women suffer to hide their shame! And if vice and passion, lust and inferior appetites, can supply to the tenderest persons strengths more than enough for the sufferance of the greatest natural violences, can we suppose that honesty and religion and the grace of God are more nice, tender, and effeminate?

4. Sickness is the more tolerable, because it cures very many evils, and takes away the sense of all the cross fortunes which amaze the spirits of some men, and transport them certainly beyond all the limits of patience. Here all losses and disgraces, domestic cares and public evils, the apprehensions of pity and a sociable calamity, the fears of want and the troubles of ambition, lie down and rest upon the sick man's pillow. One fit of the stone takes away from the fancies of men all relations to the world and secular interests: at least, they are made dull and flat, without sharpness and an edge.

And he that shall observe the infinite variety of troubles which afflict some busy persons and almost all men in very busy times, will think it not much amiss, that those huge numbers were reduced to certainty, to method and an order; and there is no better compendium for this than that they be reduced to one. And a sick man seems so unconcerned in the things of the world, that although this separation be done with violence, yet it is no otherwise than all noble contentions are, and all honours are purchased, and all virtues are acquired, and all vices mortified, and all appetites chastised, and all rewards obtained; there is infallibly to all these a difficulty and

a sharpness annexed, without which there could be no proportion between a work and a reward. To this add that sickness
does not take off the sense of secular troubles and worldly cares
from us, by employing all the perceptions and apprehensions
of men; by filling all faculties with sorrow, and leaving no
room for the lesser instances of troubles, as little rivers are
swallowed up in the sea; but sickness is a messenger of God,
sent with purposes of abstraction and separation, with a secret
power and a proper efficacy to draw us off from unprofitable
and useless sorrows: and this is effected partly by reason that
it represents the uselessness of the things of this world, and
that there is a portion of this life in which honours and things
of the world cannot serve us to many purposes; partly by preparing us to death, and telling us that a man shall descend
thither, whence this world cannot redeem us, and where the
goods of this world cannot serve us.

5. And yet, after all this, sickness leaves in us appetites so
strong, and apprehensions so sensible, and delights so many,
and good things in so great a degree, that a healthless body
and a sad disease do seldom make men weary of this world,
but still they would fain find an excuse to live.[4] The gout, the
stone, and the tooth-ache, the sciatica, sore eyes, and an aching
head, are evils indeed; but such which, rather than die, most
men are willing to suffer; and Mæcenas added also a wish rather to be crucified than to die; and though his wish was low,
timorous, and base, yet we find the same desires in most men,
dressed up with better circumstances. It was a cruel mercy
in Tamerlane, who commanded all the leprous persons to be
put to death, as we knock some beasts quickly on their head to
put them out of pain, and lest they should live miserably; the
poor men would rather have endured another leprosy, and have
more willingly taken two diseases than one death. Therefore
Cæsar wondered that the old crazed soldier begged leave he
might kill himself, and asked him, "Dost thou think, then, to
be more alive than now thou art?" We do not die suddenly,
but we descend to death by steps and slow passages; and therefore men (so long as they are sick) are unwilling to proceed
and go forward in the finishing that sad employment. Be-

---

[4] Debilem facito manu, debilem pede, coxâ, lubricos quate dentes; vita
dum superest, bene est. Hanc mihi, vel acutam, si das, sustineo crucem.
—Sen. Ep. x. 1.

tween a disease and death there are many degrees, and all those are like the reserves of evil things, the declining of every one of which is justly reckoned amongst those good things which alleviate the sickness and make it tolerable. Never account that sickness intolerable in which thou hadst rather remain than die: and yet if thou hadst rather die than suffer it, the worst of it that can be said is this, that this sickness is worse than death; that is, it is worse than that which is the best of all evils, and the end of all troubles; and then you have said no great harm against it.

6. Remember that thou art under a supervening necessity. Nothing is intolerable that is necessary; and therefore when men are to suffer a sharp incision, or what they are pleased to call intolerable, tie the man down to it, and he endures it.[5] Now God hath bound this sickness upon thee by the condition of nature; for every flower must wither and droop; it is also bound upon thee by special providence and with a design to try thee, and with purposes to reward and to crown thee. These cords thou canst not break; and therefore lie thou down gently, and suffer the hand of God to do what he please, that at least thou mayest swallow an advantage which the care and severe mercies of God force down thy throat.

7. Remember that all men have passed this way;[6] the bravest, the wisest, and the best men have been subject to sickness and sad diseases; and it is esteemed a prodigy that a man should live to a long age, and not be sick; and it is recorded for a wonder concerning Xenophilus the musician, that he lived to one hundred and six years of age in a perfect and continual health. No story tells the like of a prince, or a great or a wise person;[7] unless we have a mind to believe the tales concerning Nestor and the Euboean sibyl, or reckon Cyrus of Persia, or Masinissa the Mauritanian, to be rivals of old age, or that Argantonius the Tartessian king did really outstrip that age, according as his story tells, reporting him to have reigned eighty years,[8] and to have lived one hundred and twenty. Old age and healthful bodies are seldom made the appendages to great

---

[5] Improbæque Tigres indulgent patientiam flagello. Impiger et fortis virtute coactus.

[6]   Cerno equidem gemmâ constratos morte Philippos,
      Thessaliæque rogos, et funera gentis Iberæ.

[7] Rara est in nobilitate senectus.   [8] Cicero de Senect.

fortunes; and under so great and so universal precedents,[9] so common fate of men, he that will not suffer his portion deserves to be something else than a man, but nothing that is better.

8. We find in story that many Gentiles, who walked by no light but that of reason, opinion, and human examples, did bear their sickness nobly, and with great contempt of pain, and with huge interests of virtue. When Pompey came from Syria, and called at Rhodes, to see Posidonius the philosopher, he found him hugely afflicted with the gout, and expressed his sorrow that he could not hear his lectures, from which by this pain he must needs be hindered. Posidonius told him, "But you may hear me for all this;" and he discoursed excellently in the midst of his tortures, even then when the torches were put to his feet,[10] "That nothing was good but what was honest;" and therefore "nothing could be an evil if it were not criminal;" and summed up his lectures with this saying, "O pain, in vain dost thou attempt me; for I will never confess thee to be an evil, as long as I can honestly bear thee." And when Pompey himself was desperately sick at Naples, the Neapolitans wore crowns and triumphed, and the men of Puteoli came to congratulate his sickness, not because they loved him not, but because it was the custom of their country to have better opinions of sickness than we have. The boys of Sparta would, at their altars, endure whipping till their very entrails saw the light through their torn flesh; and some of them to death, without crying or complaint. Cæsar would drink his portions of rhubarb rudely mixed, and unfitly allayed, with little sippings, and tasting the horror of the medicine, spreading the loathsomeness of his physic so, that all the parts of his tongue and palate might have an entire share; and when C. Marius suffered the veins of his leg to be cut out for the curing his gout, and yet shrunk not, he declared not only the rudeness of their physic, but the strength of a man's spirit, if it be contracted and united by the aids of reason or religion, by resolution or any accidental harshness, against a violent disease.

9. All impatience, howsoever expressed, is perfectly useless to all purposes of ease, but hugely effective to the multiplying the trouble; and the impatience and vexation is another, but the sharper disease of the two: it does mischief by itself, and

[9] Ferre quam sortem patiuntur omnes, nemo recusat.
[10] Tusc. l. ii. Cùm faces doloris admoverentur.

mischief by the disease. For men grieve themselves as much as they please;[11] and when, by impatience, they put themselves into the retinue of sorrows, they become solemn mourners. For so have I seen the rays of the sun or moon dash upon a brazen vessel, whose lips kissed the face of those waters that lodged within its bosom; but being turned back, and sent off with its smooth pretences or rougher waftings, it wandered about the room, and beat upon the roof, and still doubled its heat and motion. So is a sickness and a sorrow, entertained by an unquiet and a discontented man, turned back either with anger or with excuses; but then the pain passes from the stomach to the liver, and from the liver to the heart, and from the heart to the head, and from feeling to consideration, from thence to sorrow, and at last ends in impatience and useless murmur; and all the way the man was impotent and weak, but the sickness was doubled, and grew imperious and tyrannical over the soul and body. Masurius Sabinus tells that the image of the goddess Angerona was, with a muffler upon her mouth, placed upon the altar of Volupia, to represent that those persons who bear their sicknesses and sorrows without murmurs[12] shall certainly pass from sorrow to pleasure, and the ease and honours of felicity; but they that with spite and indignation bite the burning coal, or shake the yoke upon their necks, gall their spirits, and fret the skin, and hurt nothing but themselves.

10. Remember that this sickness is but for a short time: if it be sharp, it will not last long; if it be long, it will be easy and very tolerable. And although St. Eadsine, archbishop of Canterbury, had twelve years of sickness, yet all that while he ruled his church prudently, gave example of many virtues, and after his death was enrolled in the calendar of saints who had finished their course prosperously.

---

[11] Tantum doluerunt, quantum doloribus se inseruerunt.—St. August.
—Virg. l. viii. v. 4.

> Ceu rore seges viret,
> Sic crescunt riguis tristia fletibus;
> Urget lacryma lacrymam,
> Fœcundusque sui se numerat dolor.
> Quem fortuna semel virum
> Udo degenerem lumine viderit,
> Illum sæpe ferit.——

[12] —— Levius fit patientiâ
> Quicquid corrigere est nefas.—Horat.

Nothing is more unreasonable than to entangle our spirits in
wildness and amazement, like a partridge fluttering in a net,
which she breaks not, though she breaks her wings.

SECT. V. *Remedies against Impatience, by way of Exercise.*

1. THE fittest instrument of esteeming sickness easily tolerable is, to remember that which indeed makes it so; and that
is, that God doth minister proper aids and supports to every
of his servants whom he visits with his rod. He knows our
needs, he pities our sorrows, he relieves our miseries, he supports our weakness, he bids us ask for help, and he promises
to give us all that, and he usually gives us more : and indeed
it is observable, that no story tells of any godly man who,
living in the fear of God, fell into a violent and unpardoned
impatience in his natural sickness, if he used those means
which God and his holy church have appointed. We see
almost all men bear their last sickness with sorrows indeed,
but without violent passions ; and unless they fear death violently, they suffer the sickness with some indifferency ; and
it is a rare thing to see a man who enjoys his reason in his
sickness to express the proper signs of a direct and solemn
impatience. For when God lays a sickness upon us, he seizes
commonly on a man's spirits, which are the instruments of
action and business ; and when they are secured from being
tumultuous, the sufferance is much the easier ; and, therefore,
sickness secures all that which can do the man mischief; it
makes him tame and passive, apt for suffering, and confines
him to an inactive condition. To which, if we add, that God
then commonly produces fear, and all those passions which
naturally tend to humility and poverty of spirit, we shall soon
perceive by what instruments God verifies his promises to us,
(which is the great security for our patience, and the easiness
of our condition,) that God will lay no more upon us than he will
make us able to bear, but, together with the affliction, he will
find a way to escape.[1] Nay, if any thing can be more than this,
we have two or three promises in which we may safely lodge
ourselves, and roll from off our thorns, and find ease and rest ·
God hath promised to be with us in our trouble, and to be with
us in our prayers, and to be with us in our hope and confidence.[2]

[1] 1 Cor. x. 13.   [2] Psal. ix. 9 ; Matt. vii. 7 ; James v. 13 ; Psal.
xxxi. 19, 24 ; xxxiv. 22.

2. Prevent the violence and trouble of thy spirit by an act of thanksgiving; for which in the worst of sicknesses thou canst not want cause, especially if thou rememberest that this pain is not an eternal pain. Bless God for that: but take heed also, lest you so order your affairs that you pass from hence to an eternal sorrow. If that be hard, this will be intolerable: but as for the present evil, a few days will end it.

3. Remember that thou art a man and a Christian: as the covenant of nature hath made it necessary, so the covenant of grace hath made it to be chosen by thee, to be a suffering person: either you must renounce your religion, or submit to the impositions of God and thy portion of sufferings. So that here we see our advantages, and let us use them accordingly. The barbarous and warlike nations of old could fight well and willingly, but could not bear sickness manfully. The Greeks were cowardly in their fights, as most wise men are: but because they were learned and well taught, they bore their sickness with patience and severity. The Cimbrians and Celtiberians rejoice in battle, like giants; but in their diseases they weep like women. These, according to their institution and designs, had unequal courages and accidental fortitude. But since our religion hath made a covenant of sufferings, and the great business of our lives is sufferings, and most of the virtues of a Christian are passive graces, and all the promises of the gospel are passed upon us through Christ's cross, we have a necessity upon us to have an equal courage in all the variety of our sufferings; for without a universal fortitude we can do nothing of our duty.

4. Resolve to do as much as you can; for certain it is, we can suffer very much if we list; and many men have afflicted themselves unreasonably by not being skilful to consider how much their strength and state could permit; and our flesh is nice and imperious, crafty to persuade reason that she hath more necessities than indeed belong to her, and that she demands nothing superfluous. Suffer as much in obedience to God as you can suffer for necessity or passion, fear or desire. And if you can for one thing, you can for another; and there is nothing wanting but the mind. Never say, I can do no more, I cannot endure this; for God would not have sent it if he had not known thee strong enough to abide it; only he that knows thee well already would also take this occasion to

make thee know thyself; but it will be fit that you pray to
God to give you a discerning spirit, that you may rightly
distinguish just necessity from the flattery and fondness of
flesh and blood.

5. Propound to your eyes and heart the example of the
holy Jesus upon the cross; he endured more for thee than
thou canst either for thyself or him: and remember, that if
we be put to suffer, and do suffer, in a good cause, or in a
good manner, so that in any sense our sufferings be conformable to his sufferings, or can be capable of being united to his,
we shall reign together with him. The high-way of the cross,
which the King of sufferings hath trodden before us, is the
way to ease, to a kingdom, and to felicity.

6. The very suffering is a title to an excellent inheritance:
for God chastens every son whom he receives; and if we be
not chastised, we are bastards, and not sons. And be confident, that although God often sends pardon without correction,
yet he never sends correction without pardon, unless it be thy
fault: and therefore take every or any affliction as an earnest
penny of thy pardon: and, upon condition there may be peace
with God, let any thing be welcome that he can send as its
instrument or condition. Suffer therefore God to choose his
own circumstances of adopting thee, and be content to be under discipline, when the reward of that is to become the son
of God: and by such inflictions he hews and breaks thy body,
first dressing it to funeral, and then preparing it for immortality. And if this be the effect or the design of God's love to
thee, let it be occasion of thy love to him: and remember, that
the truth of love is hardly known but by somewhat that puts
us to pain.

7. Use this as a punishment for thy sins; and so God intends it most commonly; that is certain: if therefore thou
submittest to it, thou approvest of the Divine judgment; and
no man can have cause to complain of any thing but himself,
if either he believes God to be just or himself to be a sinner;
if he either thinks he hath deserved hell, or that this little may
be a means to prevent the greater and bring him to heaven.

8. It may be, that this may be the last instance and the
last opportunity that ever God will give thee to exercise any
virtue, to do him any service, or thyself any advantage: be
careful that thou losest not this; for to eternal ages this never
shall return again.

9. Or if thou, peradventure, shalt be restored to health, be careful that in the day of thy thanksgiving thou mayest not be ashamed of thyself for having behaved thyself poorly and weakly upon thy bed. It will be a sensible and excellent comfort to thee, and double upon thy spirit, if, when thou shalt worship God for restoring thee, thou shalt also remember that thou didst do him service in thy suffering, and tell that God was hugely gracious to thee in giving thee the opportunity of a virtue at so easy a rate as a sickness from which thou didst recover.

10. Few men are so sick but they believe that they may recover; and we shall seldom see a man lie down with a perfect persuasion that it is his last hour; for many men have been sicker, and yet have recovered; but whether thou dost or no, thou hast a virtue to exercise which may be a handmaid to thy patience. Epaphroditus was sick, sick unto death; and yet God had mercy upon him: and he hath done so to thousands to whom he found it useful in the great order of things and the events of universal providence. If, therefore, thou desirest to recover, here is cause enough of hope; and hope is designed in the arts of God and of the Spirit to support patience. But if thou recoverest not, yet there is something that is matter of joy naturally, and very much spiritually, if thou belongest to God; and joy is as certain a support to patience as hope: and it is no small cause of being pleased, when we remember that, if we recover not, our sickness shall the sooner sit down in rest and joy. For recovery by death, as it is easier and better than the recovery by a sickly health, so it is not so long in doing; it suffers not the tediousness of a creeping restitution, nor the inconvenience of surgeons and physicians, watchfulness and care, keepings in and suffering trouble, fears of relapse, and the little relics of a storm.

11. While we hear, or use, or think of these remedies, part of the sickness is gone away, and all of it is passing. And if by such instruments we stand armed and ready dressed beforehand, we shall avoid the mischiefs of amazements and surprise;[3] while the accidents of sickness are such as were expected, and against which we stood in readiness, with our spirits contracted, instructed, and put upon the defensive.

---

[3] Nulla mihi nova nunc facies inopinave surgit;
Omnia præcepi atque animo mecum ante peregi.—Virgil. lib. vi.

12. But our patience will be the better secured if we consider that it is not violently tempted by the usual arrests of sickness; for patience is with reason demanded while the sickness is tolerable, that is, so long as the evil is not too great; but if it be also eligible, and have in it some degrees of good, our patience will have in it the less difficulty and the greater necessity. This, therefore, will be a new stock of consideration: sickness is in many degrees eligible to many men and to many purposes.

SECT. VI. *Advantages of Sickness.*

1. I CONSIDER one of the greatest felicities of heaven consists in an immunity from sin: then we shall love God without mixtures of malice; then we shall enjoy without envy; then we shall see fuller vessels running over with glory, and crowned with bigger circles; and this we shall behold without spilling from our eyes (those vessels of joy and grief) any sign of anger, trouble, or a repining spirit: our passions shall be pure, our charity without fear, our desire without lust, our possessions all our own; and all in the inheritance of Jesus, in the richest soil of God's eternal kingdom. Now half of this reason, which makes heaven so happy by being innocent, is also in the state of sickness, making the sorrows of old age smooth, and the groans of a sick heart apt to be joined to the music of angels: and, though they sound harsh to our untuned ears and discomposed organs, yet those accents must needs be in themselves excellent which God loves to hear, and esteems them as prayers, and arguments of pity, instruments of mercy and grace, and preparatives to glory.

In sickness, the soul begins to dress herself for immortality. And, first, she unties the strings of vanity that made her upper garment cleave to the world and sit uneasy; first she puts off the light and fantastic summer robe of lust and wanton appetite; and as soon as that cestus, that lascivious girdle, is thrown away, then the reins chasten us, and give us warning in the night; then that which called us formerly to serve the manliness of the body, and the childishness of the soul, keeps us waking, to divide the hours with the intervals of prayer, and to number the minutes with our penitential groans; then the flesh sits uneasily and dwells in sorrow; and then the spirit feels itself at ease, freed from the petulant solicitations of those

passions which in health were as busy and as restless as atoms
in the sun, always dancing, and always busy, and never sitting
down, till a sad night of grief and uneasiness draws the veil,
and lets them die alone in secret dishonour.

2. Next to this, the soul, by the help of sickness, knocks off
the fetters of pride and vainer complacencies. Then she
draws the curtains, and stops the light from coming in, and
takes the pictures down, those fantastic images of self-love[1]
and gay remembrances of vain opinion and popular noises.
Then the spirit stoops into the sobrieties of humble thoughts,
and feels corruption chiding the forwardness of fancy, and
allaying the vapours of conceit and factious opinions. For
humility is the soul's grave, into which she enters, not to die,
but to meditate and inter some of its troublesome appendages.
There she sees the dust, and feels the dishonours of the body,
and reads the register of all the sad adherences ; and then she
lays by all her vain reflections, beating upon her crystal and
pure mirror from the fancies of strength and beauty, and little
decayed prettinesses of the body. And when, in sickness, we
forget all our knotty discourses of philosophy, and a syllogism
makes our head ache, and we feel our many and loud talkings
served no lasting end of the soul, no purpose that now we
must abide by, and that the body is like to descend to the land
where all things are forgotten ; then she lays aside all her remembrances of applauses, all her ignorant confidences, and
cares only to know " Christ Jesus and him crucified," to know
him plainly, and with much heartiness and simplicity. And
I cannot think this to be a contemptible advantage. For ever
since man tempted himself by his impatient desires of knowing and being as God, man thinks it the finest thing in the
world to know much, and therefore is hugely apt to esteem
himself better than his brethren if he knows some little impertinences, and them imperfectly, and that with infinite uncertainty. But God hath been pleased, with a rare art, to
prevent the inconveniences apt to arise by this passionate
longing after knowledge ; even by giving to every man a sufficient opinion of his own understanding : and who is there in
the world that thinks himself to be a fool, or indeed not fit to
govern his brother ? There are but few men but they think

[1] Nunc festinatos nimiùm sibi sentit honores,
  Actaque lauriferæ damnat Syllana juventæ —Lucan. lib. viii.

they are wise enough, and every man believes his own opinion the soundest; and, if it were otherwise, men would burst themselves with envy, or else become irrecoverable slaves to the talking and disputing man. But when God intended this permission to be an antidote of envy, and a satisfaction and allay to the troublesome appetites of knowing, and made that this universal opinion, by making men in some proportions equal, should be a keeper-out or a great restraint to slavery and tyranny respectively; man (for so he uses to do) hath turned this into bitterness: for when nature had made so just a distribution of understanding that every man might think he had enough, he is not content with that, but will think he hath more than his brother ; and whereas it might well be employed in restraining slavery, he hath used it to break off the bands of all obedience, and it ends in pride and schisms, in heresies and tyrannies ; and it being a spiritual evil, it grows upon the soul with old age and flattery, with health and the supports of a prosperous fortune.   Now, besides the direct operations of the Spirit, and a powerful grace, there is in nature left to us no remedy for this evil but a sharp sickness, or an equal sorrow, and allay of fortune ; and then we are humble enough to ask counsel of a despised priest, and to think that even a common sentence, from the mouth of an appointed comforter, streams forth more refreshment than all our own wiser and more reputed discourses : then our understandings and our bodies,[2] peeping through their own breaches, see their shame and their dishonour, their dangerous follies and their huge deceptions; and they go into the clefts of the rock, and every little hand may cover them.

3. Next to these, as the soul is still undressing, she takes off the roughness of her great and little angers and animosities, and receives the oil of mercies and smooth forgiveness, fair interpretations and gentle answers, designs of reconcilement and Christian atonement in their places.   For so did the wrestlers in Olympus; they stripped themselves of all their garments, and then anointed their naked bodies with oil, smooth and vigorous; with contracted nerves and enlarged voice, they contended vehemently, till they obtained their victory or

---

[1] —Ubi jam validis quassatum est viribus ævi
     Corpus, et obtusis ceciderunt viribus artus,
     Claudicat ingenium, delirat linguaque mensque.—Lucr. l. iii.

their ease; and a crown of olive, or a huge pity, was the reward of their fierce contentions. Some wise men have said, that anger sticks to a man's nature as inseparably[3] as other vices do to the manners of fools, and that anger is never quite cured: but God, that hath found out remedies for all diseases, hath so ordered the circumstances of man, that in the worser sort of men anger and great indignation consume and shrivel into little peevishnesses and uneasy accents of sickness, and spend themselves in trifling instances; and in the better and more sanctified it goes off in prayers, and alms, and solemn reconcilement. And, however the temptations of this state, such, I mean, which are proper to it, are little and inconsiderable, the man is apt to chide a servant too bitterly, and to be discontented with his nurse, or not satisfied with his physician, and he rests uneasily, and (poor man!) nothing can please him; and indeed these little indecencies must be cured and stopped, lest they run into an inconvenience. But sickness is, in this particular, a little image of the state of blessed souls, or of Adam's early morning in Paradise, free from the troubles of lust, and violences of anger, and the intricacies of ambition, or the restlessness of covetousness. For though a man may carry all these along with him into his sickness, yet there he will not find them; and, in despite of all his own malice, his soul shall find some rest from labouring in the galleys and baser captivity of sin: and if we value those moments of being in the love of God and in the kingdom of grace, which certainly are the beginnings of felicity, we may also remember that the not sinning actually is one step of innocence; and, therefore, that state is not intolerable which, by a sensible trouble, makes it in most instances impossible to commit those great sins which make death, hell, and horrid damnations. And then let us but add this to it, that God sends sicknesses, but he never causes sin; that God is angry with a sinning person, but never with a man for being sick; that sin causes God to hate us, and sickness causes him to pity us; that all wise men in the world choose trouble rather than dishonour, affliction rather than baseness; and that sickness stops the torrent of sin, and interrupts its violence, and even to the worst men makes it to retreat many degrees. We may reckon sickness amongst good things, as we

[3] ——Quatenus excidi penitus vitium iræ,
Cætera item nequeunt stultis hærentia.—Hor. lib. i. Sat. 3.

reckon rhubarb and aloes, and childbirth and labour, and obe
dience and discipline; these are unpleasant, and yet safe; they
are troubles in order to blessings, or they are securities from
danger, or the hard choices of a less and a more tolerable evil.

4. Sickness is in some sense eligible, because it is the opportunity and the proper scene of exercising some virtues.[4]
It is that agony in which men are tried for a crown.   And if
we remember what glorious things are spoken of the grace of
faith, that it is the life of just men, the restitution of the dead
in trespasses and sins, the justification of a sinner, the support of the weak, the confidence of the strong, the magazine
of promises, and the title to very glorious rewards; we may
easily imagine that it must have in it a work and a difficulty in some proportion answerable to so great effects.   But
when we are bidden to believe strange propositions, we are
put upon it when we cannot judge, and those propositions
have possessed our discerning faculties, and have made a
party there, and are become domestic, before they come to be
disputed; and then the articles of faith are so few, and are made
so credible, and in their event and in their object are so useful
and gaining upon the affections, that he were a prodigy of man,
and would be so esteemed, that should, in all our present circumstances, disbelieve any point of faith: and all is well as
long as the sun shines, and the fair breath of heaven gently
wafts us to our own purposes.   But if you will try the excellency and feel the work of faith, place the man in a persecution, let him ride in a storm, let his bones be broken with sorrow, and his eyelids loosened with sickness, let his bread be
dipped in tears, and all the daughters of music be brought
low; let God commence a quarrel against him, and be bitter
in the accents of his anger or his discipline: then God tries
your faith.   Can you then trust his goodness, and believe him
to be a father, when you groan under his rod?   Can you rely
upon all the strange propositions of Scripture, and be content
to perish if they be not true?   Can you receive comfort in
the discourses of death and heaven, of immortality and the resurrection, of the death of Christ and conforming to his sufferings?   Truth is, there are but two great periods in which
faith demonstrates itself to be a powerful and mighty grace;

---

[4] Nolo quod cupio statim tenere,
  Nec victoria mî placet parata.—Petron.

and they are persecution and the approaches of death, for the passive part; and a temptation, for the active. In the days of pleasure and the night of pain, faith is to fight her *agonisticon*, to contend for mastery: and faith overcomes all alluring and fond temptations to sin, and faith overcomes all our weaknesses and faintings in our troubles. By the faith of the promises we learn to despise the world, choosing those objects which faith discovers; and, by expectation of the same promises, we are comforted in all our sorrows, and enabled to look through and see beyond the cloud: but the vigour of it is pressed and called forth when all our fine discourses come to be reduced to practice. For in our health and clearer days it is easy to talk of putting trust in God:[5] we readily trust him for life, when we are in health; for provisions, when we have fair revenues; and for deliverance, when we are newly escaped: but let us come to sit upon the margent of our grave, and let a tyrant lean hard upon our fortunes and dwell upon our wrong, let the storm arise, and the keels toss till the cordage crack, or that all our hopes bulge under us and descend into the hollowness of sad misfortunes; then can you believe, when you neither hear, nor see, nor feel any thing but objections? This is the proper work of sickness: faith is then brought into the theatre, and so exercised, that if it abides but to the end of the contention we may see the work of faith which God will hugely crown. The same I say of hope, and of charity, or the love of God, and of patience, which is a grace produced from the mixtures of all these: they are virtues which are greedy of danger; and no man was ever honoured by any wise or discerning person for dining upon Persian carpets, nor rewarded with a crown for being at ease.[6] It was the fire that did honour to Mutius Scævola; poverty made Fabricius famous; Rutilius was made excellent by banishment, Regulus by torments, Socrates by prison, Cato by his death; and God hath crowned the memory of Job with a wreath of glory because

[5] Mors ipsa beatior indè est,
Quod per cruciamina lethi
Via panditur ardua justis,
Et ad astra doloribus itur.—Prud. Hymn. in Exeq. Defunct.
[6] Virtutes avidæ periculi monstrant, quàm non pœniteat tanto pretio æstimâsse virtutem.—Senec. Non enim hilaritate, nec lasciviâ, nec risu, aut joco comite levitatis, sed sæpe etiam tristes firmitate et constantiâ sunt beati.—Cic. de Fin. l. xxii.

he sat upon his dunghill wisely and temperately ; and his potsherd and his groans, mingled with praises and justifications of God, pleased him like an anthem sung by angels in the morning of the resurrection. God could not choose but be pleased with the delicious accents of martyrs, when in their tortures they cried out nothing but " Holy Jesus" and "Blessed be God ;" and they also themselves who, with a hearty resignation to the Divine pleasure, can delight in God's severe dispensation, will have the transportations of cherubim when they enter into the joys of God. If God be delicious to his servants when he smites them, he will be nothing but ravishments and ecstasies to their spirits when he refreshes them with the overflowings of joy in the day of recompences. No man is more miserable than he that hath no adversity ; that man is not tried,[7] whether he be good or bad : and God never crowns those virtues which are only faculties and dispositions ; but every act of virtue is an ingredient into reward. And we see many children fairly planted, whose parts of nature were never dressed by art, nor called from the furrows of their first possibilities by discipline and institution ; and they dwell for ever in ignorance, and converse with beasts ; and yet if they had been dressed and exercised, might have stood at the chairs of princes, or spoken parables amongst the rulers of cities. Our virtues are but in the seed when the grace of God comes upon us first ; but this grace must be thrown into broken furrows, and must twice feel the cold, and twice feel the heat,[8] and be softened with storms and showers ; and then it will arise into fruitfulness and harvests. And what is there in the world to distinguish virtues from dishonours, or the valour of Cæsar from the softness of the Egyptian eunuchs, or that can make any thing rewardable, but the labour and the danger, the pain and the difficulty ? Virtue could not be any thing but sensuality if it were the entertainment of our senses and fond desires ; and Apicius had been the noblest of all the Romans, if feeding a great appetite and despising the severities of temperance had been the work and proper employment of a wise man. But otherwise do fathers, and other-

---

[7] Nihil infelicius eo cui nihil unquam contigit adversi. Non licuit illi se experiri.—Seneca.

[8] ———— Illa seges votis respondet avari
Agricolæ, bis quæ solem, bis frigora sensit.—Virg. Georg. 1.

wise do mothers handle their children. These soften them with kisses and imperfect noises, with the pap and breast-milk of soft endearments; they rescue them from tutors, and snatch them from discipline; they desire to keep them fat and warm,[9] and their feet dry, and their bellies full; and then the children govern, and cry, and prove fools and troublesome so long as the feminine republic does endure. But fathers, because they design to have their children wise and valiant, apt for counsel or for arms, send them to severe governments,[10] and tie them to study, to hard labour, and afflictive contingencies. They rejoice when the bold boy strikes a lion with his hunting-spear, and shrinks not when the beast comes to affright his early courage. Softness is for slaves and beasts,[11] for minstrels and useless persons, for such who cannot ascend higher than the state of a fair ox, or a servant entertained for vainer offices; but the man that designs his son for nobler employments, to honours and to triumphs, to consular dignities and presidencies of councils, loves to see him pale with study, or panting with labour, hardened with sufferance, or eminent by dangers. And so God dresses us for heaven. He loves to see us struggling with a disease, and resisting the devil, and contesting against the weaknesses of nature, and against hope to believe in hope, resigning ourselves to God's will, praying him to choose for us, and dying in all things but faith and its blessed consequences; *ut ad officium cum periculo simus prompti;* and the danger and the resistance shall endear the office. For so I have known the boisterous north wind pass through the yielding air,[12] which opened its bosom, and appeased its violence by entertaining it with easy compliance in all the regions of its reception; but when the same breath of heaven had been checked with the stiffness of a tower, or the united strength of a wood, it grew mighty, and dwelt there, and made the highest branches stoop and make a smooth path for it on the top of all its glories. So is sickness, and so is the grace of God: when sickness hath

---

[9] Languent per inertiam saginata, nec labore tantùm, sed mole et ipso sui onere deficiunt.—Seneca.

[10] Callum per injurias ducunt;
 Ut sit luminis atque aquæ cœlestis patiens latus.

[11] Modestiâ filiorum delectantur; vernularum licentiâ et canum, non puerorum.

[12] Ventus ut amittit vires, nisi robora densæ
 Occurrunt sylvæ, spatio diffusus inani.—Lucan.

made the difficulty, then God's grace hath made a triumph, and by doubling its power hath created new proportions of a reward; and then shows its biggest glory,[13] when it hath the greatest difficulty to master, the greatest weaknesses to support, the most busy temptations to contest with; for so God loves that his strength should be seen in our weakness and our danger. Happy is that state of life in which our services to God are the dearest and the most expensive.[14]

5. Sickness hath some degrees of eligibility, at least by an after-choice; because to all persons which are within the pos sibilities and state of pardon it becomes a great instrument of pardon of sins. For as God seldom rewards here and hereafter too, so it is not very often that he punishes in both states. In great and final sins he doth so; but we find it expressed only in the case of the sin against the Holy Ghost, " which shall never be forgiven in this world nor in the world to come;" that is, it shall be punished in both worlds, and the infelicities of this world shall but usher in the intolerable calamities of the next. But this is in a case of extremity, and in sins of an unpardonable malice: in those lesser stages of death, which are deviations from the rule, and not a destruction and perfect antimony to the whole institution, God very often smites with his rod of sickness that he may not for ever be slaying the soul with eternal death. " I will visit their offences with the rod, and their sin with scourges; nevertheless my loving-kindness will I not utterly take from him, nor suffer my truth to fail."[15] And there is in the New Testament a delivering over to Satan,[16] and a consequent buffeting, for the mortification of the flesh indeed, but that the soul may be saved in the day of the Lord. And to some persons the utmost process of God's anger reaches but to a sharp sickness, or, at most, but to a temporal death; and then the little momentary anger is spent, and expires in rest and a quiet grave. Origen, St. Augustine, and Cassian say, concerning Ananias and Sapphira,[17] that they were slain with a sudden death, that by such a judgment their

[13] Marcet sine adversario virtus.
[14] Lætius est, quoties magno sibi constat honestum.
[15] Psalm lxxxix. 32, 33.   [16] 1 Cor. v. 5; 1 Tim. i. 20.
[17] Digni erant in hoc seculo recipere peccatum suum ut mundiores exeant ab hac vitâ, mundati castigatione sibi illatâ per mortem communem, quoniam credentes erant in Christum.—Origen. St. August. l. iii. c. 1. Contr. Parmen. et Cassian. Collat. vi. c. 11.

sin might be punished, and their guilt expiated, and their persons reserved for mercy in the day of judgment. And God cuts off many of his children from the land of the living; and yet, when they are numbered among the dead, he finds them in the book of life, written among those that shall live to him for ever. And thus it happened to many new Christians, in the church of Corinth, for their little indecencies and disorders in the circumstances of receiving the holy sacrament. St. Paul says, that "many amongst them were sick, many were weak, and some were fallen asleep."[18] He expresses the Divine anger against those persons in no louder accents; which is according to the style of the New Testament, where all the great transactions of duty and reproof are generally made upon the stock of heaven, and hell is plainly a reserve, and a period set to the declaration of God's wrath. For God knows that the torments of hell are so horrid, so insupportable a calamity, that he is not easy and apt to cast those souls, which he hath taken so much care and hath been at so much expense to save, into the eternal never-dying flames of hell lightly, for smaller sins, or after a fairly begun repentance, and in the midst of holy desires to finish it; but God takes such penalties and exacts such fines of us, which we may pay, *salvo contenemento*, saving the main stake of all, even our precious souls. And therefore St. Augustine prayed to God in his penitential sorrows, " Here, O Lord, burn and cut my flesh, that thou mayest spare me for ever." For so said our blessed Saviour, " Every sacrifice must be seasoned with salt, and every sacrifice must be burnt with fire;" that is, we must abide in the state of grace; and if we have committed sins, we must expect to be put into the state of affliction; and yet the sacrifice will send up a right and untroubled cloud, and a sweet smell, to join with the incense of the altar, where the eternal Priest offers a never-ceasing sacrifice. And now I have said a thing against which there can be no exceptions, and of which no just reason can make abatement. For when sickness, which is the condition of our nature, is called for with purposes of redemption; when we are sent to death to secure eternal life; when God strikes us that he may spare us—it shows that we have done things which he essentially hates; and therefore we must be smitten with the rod of God; but in the midst of judgment God remembers mercy, and makes the rod to be

[18] 1 Cor. xi. 30.

medicinal, and like the rod of God in the hand of Aaron, to
shoot forth buds and leaves and almonds, hopes and mercies,
and eternal recompences, in the day of restitution.   This is so
great a good to us, if it be well conducted in all the channels
of its intention and design, that if we had put off the objections
of the flesh with abstractions, contempts, and separations, so
as we ought to do, it were as earnestly to be prayed for as any
gay blessing that crowns our cup with joy, and our heads with
garlands and forgetfulness.   But this was it which I said, that
this may, nay, that it ought to be chosen, at least by an after-
election; for so said St. Paul, "If we judge ourselves, we shall
not be condemned of the Lord:" that is, if we judge ourselves
worthy of the sickness, if we acknowledge and confess God's
justice in smiting us, if we take the rod of God in our own
hands, and are willing to imprint it in the flesh, we are workers
together with God in the infliction; and then the sickness,
beginning and being managed in the virtue of repentance, and
patience, and resignation, and charity, will end in peace, and
pardon, and justification, and consignation to glory.   That I
have spoken truth, I have brought God's Spirit speaking in
Scripture for a witness.   But, if this be true, there are not
many states of life that have advantages which can outweigh
this great instrument of security to our final condition.   Moses
died at the mouth of the Lord, said the story; he died with
the kisses of the Lord's mouth[19] (so the Chaldee paraphrase):
it was the greatest act of kindness that God did to his servant
Moses; he kissed him and he died.   But I have some things
to observe for the better finishing this consideration.

1. All these advantages and lessenings of evils in the state
of sickness are only upon the stock of virtue and religion.
There is nothing can make sickness in any sense eligible, or in
many senses tolerable, but only the grace of God;[20] that only
turns sickness into easiness and felicity, which also turns it
into virtue.   For whosoever goes about to comfort a vicious
person, when he lies sick upon his bed, can only discourse of
the necessities of nature, of the unavoidableness of the suffer-

---

[19] Deut. xxxiv. 5.
[20] Hæc clementia non paratur arte : sed nôrunt cui serviunt . eones.
      Si latus aut renes morbo tententur acuto,
      Quære fugam morbi.   Vis rectè vivere?   quis non?
      Si virtus hoc una potest dare, 'ortis omissis
      Hoc age deliciis.   Horat. l. i. ep. 6

ing, of the accidental vexations and increase of torments by impatience, of the fellowship of all the sons of Adam, and such other little considerations; which, indeed, if sadly reflected upon, and found to stand alone, teach him nothing but the degree of his calamity, and the evil of his condition, and teach him such a patience, and minister to him such a comfort, which can only make him to observe decent gestures in his sickness, and to converse with his friends and standers-by so as may do them comfort, and ease their funeral and civil complaints, but do him no true advantage; for all that may be spoken to a beast when he is crowned with hair-laces, and bound with fillets to the altar, to bleed to death to appease the anger of the Deity, and to ease the burden of his relatives. And indeed what comfort can he receive whose sickness, as it looks back, is an effect of God's indignation and fierce vengeance, and if it goes forward, and enters into the gates of the grave, is the beginning of a sorrow that shall never have an ending? But when the sickness is a messenger sent from a chastising Father; when it first turn into degrees of innocence, and then into virtues, and thence into pardon; this is no misery, but such a method of the Divine economy and dispensation as resolves to bring us to heaven without any new impositions, but merely upon the stock and charges of nature.

2. Let it be observed, that these advantages which spring from sickness are not in all instances of virtue, nor to all persons. Sickness is the proper scene for patience and resignation, for all the passive graces of a Christian, for faith and hope, and for some single acts of the love of God. But sickness is not a fit station for a penitent; and it can serve the ends of the grace of repentance but accidentally. Sickness may begin a repentance,[21] if God continues life, and if we co-operate with the Divine grace; or sickness may help to alleviate the wrath of God, and to facilitate the pardon, if all the other parts of this duty be performed in our healthful state, so that it may serve at the entrance in or at the going out. But sickness, at no hand, is a good stage to represent all the substantial parts of this duty: 1. it invites to it; 2. it makes it appear necessary; 3. it takes off the fancies of vanity; 4. it attempers the spirit; 5. it cures hypocrisy; 6. it tames the

[21] Nec tamen putaverant ad rem pertinere, ubi inciperent, quod placuerat ut fieret.

fumes of pride; 7. it is the school of patience; 8. and by taking us from off the brisker relishes of the world, it makes us
with more gust to taste the things of the Spirit: and all this
only when God fits the circumstances of the sickness so as to
consist with acts of reason, consideration, choice, and a present
and reflecting mind, which then God sends, when he means
that the sickness of the body should be the cure of the soul.
But let no man so rely upon it as, by design, to trust the beginning, the progress, and the consummation of our piety to
such an estate, which for ever leaves it imperfect; and though
to some persons it adds degrees, and ministers opportunities,
and exercises single acts with great advantage in passive
graces; yet it is never an entire or sufficient instrument for
the change of our condition from the state of death to the
liberty and life of the sons of God.

3. It were good, if we would transact the affairs of our souls
with nobleness and ingenuity, and that we would, by an early
and forward religion, prevent the necessary arts of the Divine
providence. It is true that God cures some by incision, by
fire and torments; but these are ever the more obstinate and
more unrelenting natures. God's providence is not so afflictive
and full of trouble,[22] as that it hath placed sickness and infirmity amongst things simply necessary; and, in most persons,
it is but a sickly and an effeminate virtue, which is imprinted
upon our spirits with fears, and the sorrows of a fever, or a
peevish consumption. It is but a miserable remedy to be beholden to a sickness for our health; and though it be better
to suffer the loss of a finger, than that the arm and the whole
body should putrify, yet even then also it is a trouble and an
evil to lose a finger. He that mends with sickness, pares the
nails of the beast when they have already torn off part of the
flesh; but he that would have a sickness become a clear and an
entire blessing, a thing indeed to be reckoned among the good
things of God and the evil things of the world, must lead a
holy life, and judge himself with an early sentence; and so
order the affairs of his soul, that in the usual method of God's
saving us, there may be nothing left to be done, but that such
virtues should be exercised which God intends to crown; and
then, as when the Athenians upon a day of battle, with longing

---

[22] Neque tam aversa unquam videbitur ab opere suo providentia, ut
debilitas inter optima inventa sit.

and uncertain souls, sitting in their common hall, expecting what would be the sentence of the day, at last received a messenger who only had breath enough left him to say, " We are conquerors," and so died,—so shall the sick person, who hath " fought a good fight, and kept the faith," and only waits for his dissolution and his sentence, breathe forth his spirit with the accents of a conqueror, and his sickness and his death shall only make the mercy and the virtue more illustrious.

But for the sickness itself: if all the calumnies were true concerning it with which it is aspersed, yet it is far to be preferred before the most pleasant sin, and before a great secular business and a temporal care; and some men wake as much in the foldings of the softest beds, as others on the cross; and sometimes the very weight of sorrow, and the weariness of a sickness, press the spirit into slumbers and the images of rest, when the intemperate or the lustful person rolls upon his uneasy thorns, and sleep is departed from his eyes. Certain it is, some sickness is a blessing. Indeed, blindness were a most accursed thing,[23] if no man were ever blind but he whose eyes were pulled out with tortures or burning basins: and if sickness were always a testimony of God's anger, and a violence to a man's whole condition, then it were a huge calamity: but because God sends it to his servants, to his children, to little infants, to apostles and saints, with designs of mercy to preserve their innocence, to overcome temptation, to try their virtue, to fit them for rewards; it is certain that sickness never is an evil but by our own faults, and if we will do our duty, we shall be sure to turn it into a blessing. If the sickness be great, it may end in death, and the greater it is,[24] the sooner; and if it be very little, it hath great intervals of rest: if it be between both, we may be masters of it, and by serving the ends of Providence serve also the perfective end of human nature, and enter into the possession of everlasting mercies.

The sum is this: He that is afraid of pain is afraid of his own nature; and if his fear be violent, it is a sign his patience is none at all, and an impatient person is not ready dressed for heaven. None but suffering, humble, and patient persons can go to heaven; and when God hath given us the whole

[23] Detestabilis erit cæcitas, si nemo oculos perdiderit nisi cui eruendi sunt. [24] Memineris ergò maximos dolores morte finiri, parvos multa habere intervalla requietis, mediocrium nos esse dominos.—Cicero.

stage of our life to exercise all the active virtues of religion, it is necessary in the state of virtues, that some portion and period of our lives be assigned to passive graces; for patience, for Christian fortitude, for resignation or conformity to the Divine will. But as the violent fear of sickness makes us impatient, so it will make our death without comfort and without religion; and we shall go off from our stage of actions and sufferings with an unhandsome exit, because we were willing to receive the kindness of God, when he expressed it as we listed; but we would not suffer him to be kind and gracious to us in his own method, nor were willing to exercise and improve our virtues at the charge of a sharp fever, or a lingering consumption. " Woe be to the man that hath lost patience; for what will he do when the Lord shall visit him?"[25]

SECT. VII. *The second Temptation proper to the state of Sickness, Fear of Death, with its Remedies.*

THERE is nothing which can make sickness unsanctified, but the same also will give us cause to fear death. If, therefore, we so order our affairs and spirits that we do not fear death, our sickness may easily become our advantage; and we can then receive counsel, and consider, and do those acts of virtue, which are, in that state, the proper services of God, and such which men in bondage and fear are not capable of doing, or of advices how they should, when they come to the appointed days of mourning. And, indeed, if men would but place their design of being happy in the nobleness, courage, and perfect resolutions of doing handsome things, and passing through our unavoidable necessities, in the contempt and despite of the things of this world, and in holy living and the perfective desires of our natures, the longings and pursuances after heaven; it is certain they could not be made miserable by chance and change, by sickness and death. But we are so softened and made effeminate with delicate thoughts, and meditations of ease, and brutish satisfactions, that if our death come before we have seized upon a great fortune, or enjoy the promises of the fortune-tellers, we esteem ourselves to be robbed of our goods, to be mocked, and miserable. Hence it comes that men are impatient of the thoughts of death; hence come those arts of protraction and delaying the significations of old age:

[25] Ecclus. ii. 4.

thinking to deceive the world, men cozen themselves,[1] and by representing themselves youthful, they certainly continue their vanity, till Proscrpina pull the peruke from their heads. We cannot deceive God and nature; for a coffin is a coffin, though it be covered with a pompous veil; and the minutes of our time strike on, and are counted by angels, till the period comes which must cause the passing-bell to give warning to all the neighbours that thou art dead, and they must be so: and nothing can excuse or retard this. And if our death could be put off a little longer, what advantage can it be, in thy accounts of nature or felicity? They that three thousand years agone died unwillingly, and stopped death two days, or stayed it a week, what is their gain? where is that week? And poor-spirited men use arts of protraction,[2] and make their persons pitiable, but their condition contemptible, being like the poor sinners at Noah's flood: the waters drove them out of their lower rooms; then they crept up to the roof, having lasted half a day longer, and then they knew not how to get down; some crept upon the top-branch of a tree, and some climbed up to a mountain, and stayed, it may be, three days longer; but all that while they endured a worse torment than death; they lived with amazement, and were distracted with the ruins of mankind, and the horror of a universal deluge.

Remedies against the Fear of Death, by way of Consideration.

1. God having in this world placed us in a sea, and troubled the sea with a continual storm, hath appointed the church for a ship, and religion to be the stern; but there is no haven or port but death. Death is that harbour, whither God hath designed every one, that there he may find rest from the troubles of the world. How many of the noblest Romans have taken death for sanctuary, and have esteemed it less than shame or a mean dishonour? And Cæsar was cruel to Domitius, cap-

---

[1] Mentiris juvenem tinctis, Lentine, capillis,
    Tam subitò corvus, qui modò cygnus eras.
  Non omnes fallis, scit te Proserpina canum;
    Personam capiti detrahet illa tuo.—Mart. lib. iii. ep. 43.

[2] Audit iter, numeratque dies, spatioque viarum
  Metitur vitam, torquetur morte futurâ.
  Τί γὰρ βροτῶν ἂν σὺν κακοῖς μεμιγμένων
  Θνήσκειν ὁ μέλλων τοῦ χρόνου κέρδος φέροι;—Soph.

Nihil est miserius dubitatione venientium, quorsum evadant, quantum sit illud quod restat, aut quale.—Senec. lib. xvii. ep. 102.

tain of Corfinium, when he had taken the town from him, that
he refused to sign his petition of death. Death would have
hid his head with honour, but that cruel mercy reserved him
to the shame of surviving his disgrace.[3] The Holy Scripture,
giving an account of the reasons of the Divine providence
taking godly men from this world, and shutting them up in a
hasty grave, says, that " they are taken away from the evils to
come ;" and concerning ourselves it is certain, if we had ten
years agone taken seizure of our portion of dust, death had
not taken us from good things, but from infinite evils, such
which the sun hath seldom seen. Did not Priamus weep
oftener than Troilus?[4] and happy had he been, if he had died
when his sons were living, and his kingdom safe, and houses
full, and his city unburnt. It was a long life that made him
miserable, and an early death only could have secured his fortune. And it hath happened many times, that persons of a
fair life and a clear reputation, of a good fortune and an honourable name, have been tempted in their age to folly and
vanity,[5] have fallen under the disgrace of dotage, or into an
unfortunate marriage, or have besotted themselves with drinking, or outlived their fortunes, or become tedious to their
friends, or are afflicted with lingering and vexatious diseases,
or lived to see their excellent parts buried, and cannot understand the wise discourses and productions of their younger
years. In all these cases, and infinite more, do not all the
world say, that it had been better this man had died sooner?[6]
But so have I known passionate women to shriek aloud when
their nearest relatives were dying, and that horrid shriek hath
stayed the spirit of the man awhile to wonder at the folly, and
represent the inconvenience ; and the dying person hath lived
one day longer full of pain, amazed with an indeterminate
spirit, distorted with convulsions, and only come again to act
one scene more of a new calamity, and to die with less decency.

---

[3] —— Heu, quanto melius vel cæde peractâ
    Parcere Romano potuit fortuna pudori !—Lucanus.
[4] Hæc omnia vidit inflammari, Jovis aram sanguine turpari.
[5]   —— Sic longius ævum
    Destruit ingentes animos, et vita superstes
    Imperio ; nisi summa dies cum fine bonorum
    Adfuit, et celeri prævertit tristia leto,
    Dedecori est fortuna prior.—Lucan. lib. viii. 30.
[6] Mors illi melius quàm tu consuluit quidem.
    —— Quisquamne secundis
    Tradere se fatis audet, nisi morte paratâ ?—Lucan. lib. viii

So also do very many men; with passion and a troubled interest they strive to continue their life longer; and, it may be, they escape this sickness, and live to fall into a disgrace; they escape the storm, and fall into the hands of pirates; and, instead of dying with liberty, they live like slaves, miserable and despised, servants to a little time, and sottish admirers of the breath of their own lungs. Paulus Æmilius did handsomely reprove the cowardice of the king of Macedon, who begged of him, for pity's sake, and humanity, that, having conquered him and taken his kingdom from him, he would be content with that, and not lead him in triumph a prisoner to Rome. Æmilius told him, he need not be beholden to him for that; himself might prevent that in despite of him. But the timorous king durst not die. But certainly every wise man will easily believe, that it had been better the Macedonian kings should have died in battle, than protract their life so long, till some of them came to be scriveners and joiners at Rome: or that the tyrant of Sicily better had perished in the Adriatic, than to be wafted to Corinth safely, and there turn schoolmaster. It is a sad calamity, that the fear of death shall so imbecile man's courage and understanding, that he dares not suffer the remedy of all his calamities; but that he lives to say, as Laberius did, "I have lived this one day longer than I should."[7] Either, therefore, let us be willing to die when God calls, or let us never more complain of the calamities of our life, which we feel so sharp and numerous. And when God sends his angel to us with the scroll of death, let us look on it as an act of mercy, to prevent many sins and many calamities of a longer life, and lay our heads down softly and go to sleep without wrangling like babies and froward children. For a man (at least) gets this by death, that his calamities are not immortal.[8]

But I do not only consider death by the advantages of comparison; but if we look on it in itself, it is no such formidable thing, if we view it on both sides and handle it, and consider all its appendages.

2. It is necessary, and therefore not intolerable: and nothing is to be esteemed evil, which God and nature have fixed with eternal sanctions.[9] It is a law of God, it is a punish-

---

[7] Nimirum hac die unâ plus vixi, mihi quàm vivendum fuit.

[8] Hoc homo morte lucratur, ne malum esset immortale.—Naz.

[9] Nihil in malis ducamus, quod sit à Diis immortalibus vel à Naturâ

ment of our sins, and it is the constitution of our nature. Two differing substances were joined together with the breath of God,[10] and when that breath is taken away, they part asunder, and return to their several principles; the soul to God our Father, the body to the earth our mother: and what in all this is evil? Surely nothing, but that we are men; nothing, but that we are not born immortal: but by declining this change with great passion, or receiving it with a huge natural fear, we accuse the Divine Providence of tyranny, and exclaim against our natural constitution, and are discontent that we are men.

3. It is a thing that is no great matter in itself, if we consider that we die daily, that it meets us in every accident, that every creature carries a dart along with it, and can kill us. And, therefore, when Lysimachus threatened Theodorus to kill him, he told him that was no great matter to do, and he could do no more than the cantharides could; a little fly could do as much.

4. It is a thing that every one suffers,[11] even persons of the lowest resolution, of the meanest virtue, of no breeding, of no discourse. Take away but the pomps of death, the disguises and solemn bugbears, the tinsel, and the actings by candle-light, and proper and fantastic ceremonies, the minstrels and the noise-makers, the women and the weepers, the swoonings and the shriekings, the nurses and the physicians, the dark room and the ministers, the kindred and the watchers; and then to die is easy, ready, and quitted from its troublesome circumstances. It is the same harmless thing, that a poor shepherd suffered yesterday, or a maid-servant to-day; and at the same time in which you die, in that very night a thousand creatures die with you,[12] some wise men, and many fools; and the wisdom of the first will not quit him, and the folly of the latter does not make him unable to die.

5. Of all the evils of the world which are reproached with an evil character, death is the most innocent of its accusation. For when it is present, it hurts nobody;[13] and when it is ab-

parente omnium, constitutum.   [10] Concretum fuit, discretum est: rediitque unde venerat; terra deorsum, spiritus sursum. Quid ex his omnibus iniquum est? Nihil.—EPICHAR.   [11] Natura dedit usuram vitæ tanquam pecuniæ; quid est ergo quod querare, si repetat, cùm vult? eadem enim lege acceperas.—Sen.   [12] Vitæ est avidus, quisquis non vult mundo secum pereunte mori.—Seneca.

[13] Τοὺς γὰρ Ͽανόντας οὐχ ὁρῶ λυπουμένους.

Par est moriri: neque est melius morte in malis
Rebus miseris.   Plaut. Rud

ærnt, it is indeed troublesome, but the trouble is owing to our fears, not to the affrighting and mistaken object: and besides this, if it were an evil, it is so transient, that it passes like the instant or undiscerned portion of the present time; and either it is past, or it is not yet;[14] for just when it is, no man hath reason to complain of so insensible, so sudden, so undiscerned a change.

6. It is so harmless a thing, that no good man was ever thought the more miserable for dying, but much the happier. When men saw the graves of Calatinus, of the Servilii, the Scipios, the Metelli, did ever any man amongst the wisest Romans think them unhappy? And when St. Paul fell under the sword of Nero, and St. Peter died upon the cross, and St. Stephen from a heap of stones was carried into an easier grave, they that made great lamentation over them, wept for their own interest, and after the manner of men; but the martyrs were accounted happy, and their days kept solemnly, and their memoirs preserved in never-dying honours. When St. Hilary, bishop of Poictiers in France, went into the East to reprove the Arian heresy, he heard that a young noble gentleman treated with his daughter Abra for marriage. The bishop wrote to his daughter, that she should not engage her promise, nor do countenance to that request, because he had provided for her a husband, fair, rich, wise, and noble, far beyond her present offer. The event of which was this: she obeyed; and when her father returned from his eastern triumph to his western charge, he prayed to God that his daughter might die quickly; and God heard his prayers, and Christ took her into his bosom, entertaining her with antepasts and caresses of holy love, till the day of the marriage-supper of the Lamb shall come. But when the bishop's wife observed this event, and understood of the good man her husband what was done, and why, she never let him alone, till he obtained the same favour for her; and she also, at the prayers of St. Hilary, went into a more early grave and a bed of joys.

7. It is a sottish and an unlearned thing to reckon the time of our life, as it is short or long, to be good or evil fortune; life in itself being neither good nor bad, but just as we make it; and therefore so is death.

---

[14] Aut fuit, aut veniet; nihil est præsentis in illâ:
Morsque minus pœnæ quàm mora mortis habet

8. But when we consider, death is not only better than a
miserable life, not only an easy and innocent thing in itself,
but also that it is a state of advantage, we shall have reason
not to double the sharpnesses of our sickness by our fear of
death.   Certain it is, death hath some good upon its proper
stock; praise, and a fair memory, a reverence and religion
towards them so great, that it is counted dishonest to speak
evil of the dead;[15] then they rest in peace, and are quiet from
their labours, and are designed to immortality.   Cleobis and
Biton, Trophonius and Agamedes, had an early death sent
them as a reward; to the former, for their piety to their
mother; to the latter, for building of a temple.   To this all
those arguments will minister, which relate the advantages of
the state of separation and resurrection.

SECT. VIII. *Remedies against Fear of Death, by way of
Exercise.*

1. HE that would willingly be fearless of death, must learn
to despise the world: he must neither love any thing passionately, nor be proud of any circumstance of his life. "O death,
how bitter is the remembrance of thee to a man that liveth
at rest in his possessions, to a man that hath nothing to vex
him, and that hath prosperity in all things; yea, unto him
that is yet able to receive meat!" said the son of Sirach. But
the parts of this exercise help each other. If a man be not
incorporated in all his passions to the things of this world, he
will less fear to be divorced from them by a supervening death;
and yet, because he must part with them all in death, it is but
reasonable he should not be passionate for so fugitive and
transient interest.   But if any man thinks well of himself for
being a handsome person, or if he be stronger and wiser than
his neighbours, he must remember[1] that what he boasts of
will decline into weakness and dishonour; but that very boast-

---

[15] Virtutem incolumem odimus,
        Sublatam ex oculis quærimus invidi.—Horat.
     Et laudas nullos nisi mortuos poetas.—Mart.
 [1] Εἰ δέ τις ὄλβον ἔχων μορφὰν παραμεύσεται ἄλλων,
     Ἐν τ' ἀέθλοισιν ἀριστεύων ἐπέδειξεν βίαν·
     Θνατὰ μεμνάσθω περιστέλλων μέλη,
     Καὶ τελευτὰν ἁπάντων γᾶν ἐπιεσσόμενος.—Pindar. Nem. 10
     Dic, homo, vas cinerum, quid confert flos facierum?
     Copia quid rerum; mors ultima meta dierum.

ing and complacency will make death keener and more un-welcome, because it comes to take him from his confidences and pleasures, making his beauty equal to those ladies that have slept some years in charnel-houses, and their strength not so stubborn as the breath of an infant, and their wisdom such which can be looked for in the land where all things are forgotten.

2. He that would not fear death must strengthen his spirits with the proper instruments of Christian fortitude. All men are resolved upon this, that to bear grief honestly and tem-perately, and to die willingly and nobly, is the duty of a good and valiant man;[2] and they that are not so, are vicious, and fools, and cowards. All men praise the valiant and honest; and that which the very heathen admired in their noblest ex-amples is especially patience and contempt of death. Zeno Eleates endured torments rather than discover his friends, or betray them to the danger of the tyrant; and Calanus, the barbarous and unlearned Indian, willingly suffered himself to be burnt alive; and all the women did so, to do honour to their husbands' funeral, and to represent and prove their af-fections great to their lords. The religion of a Christian does more command fortitude than ever did any institution; for we are commanded to be willing to die for Christ, to die for the brethren, to die rather than to give offence or scandal: the effect of which is this, that he that is instructed to do the neces-sary parts of his duty, is, by the same instrument, fortified against death; as he that does his duty need not fear death, so neither shall he; the parts of his duty are parts of his se-curity. It is certainly a great baseness and pusillanimity of spirit that makes death terrible, and extremely to be avoided.

3. Christian prudence is a great security against the fear of death. For if we be afraid of death, it is but reasonable to use all spiritual arts to take off the apprehension of the evil; but therefore we ought to remove our fear, because fear gives to death wings, and spurs, and darts. Death hastens to a fearful man; if therefore you would make death harmless and slow, to throw off fear is the way to do it; and prayer is the way to do that. If therefore you be afraid of death, consider

---

[2] Amittenda fortitudo est, aut sepeliendus dolor.—Cicero.
Fortem posce animum mortis terrore carentem,
Qui spatium vitæ extremum inter munera ponat.

you will have less need to fear it by how much the less you
do fear it : and so cure your direct fear by a reflex act of prudence and consideration.　Fannius had not died so soon[3] if
he had not feared death ; and when Cneius Carbo begged the
respite of a little time for a base employment of the soldiers
of Pompey, he got nothing, but that the baseness of his fear
dishonoured the dignity of his third consulship; and he chose
to die in a place where none but his meanest servants should
have seen him.　I remember a story of the wrestler Polyda-
mas, that running into a cave to avoid the storm, the water
at last swelled so high that it began to press that hollowness
to a ruin ; which when his fellows espied, they chose to enter
into the common fate of all men, and went abroad ; but Poly-
damas thought by his strength to support the earth, till its
intolerable weight crushed him into flatness and a grave.
Many men run for shelter to a place, and they only find a remedy for their fears by feeling the worst of evils ; fear itself
finds no sanctuary but the worst of sufferance ; and they that
fly from a battle are exposed to the mercy and fury of the
pursuers, who, if they faced about, were as well disposed to
give laws of life and death as to take them, and at worst can
but die nobly ; but now, even at the very best, they live shamefully, or die timorously.　Courage is the greatest security ;
for it does most commonly safeguard the man, but always
rescues the condition from an intolerable evil.

4. If thou wilt be fearless of death, endeavour to be in love
with the felicities of saints and angels, and be once persuaded
to believe that there is a condition of living better than this ;
that there are creatures more noble than we ; that above there
is a country better than ours ; that the inhabitants know more
and know better, and are in places of rest and desire ; and
first learn to value it, and then learn to purchase it, and death
cannot be a formidable thing, which lets us into so much joy
and so much felicity.　And, indeed, who would not think his
condition mended if he passed from conversing with dull mortals, with ignorant and foolish persons, with tyrants and
enemies of learning, to converse with Homer and Plato, with
Socrates and Cicero, with Plutarch and Fabricius ?　So the
heathens speculated, but we consider higher.　" The dead that
die in the Lord" shall converse with St. Paul, and all the

---

[3] Hostem cùm fugeret, se Fannius ipse peremit.—Mart.

college of the apostles, and all the saints and martyrs, with all
the good men whose memory we preserve in honour, with excellent kings and holy bishops, and with the great Shepherd
and Bishop of our souls, Jesus Christ, and with God himself.
For "Christ died for us, that, whether we wake or sleep, we
might live together with him." Then we shall be free from
lust and envy,[4] from fear and rage, from covetousness and
sorrow, from tears and cowardice; and these indeed, properly,
are the only evils that are contrary to felicity and wisdom.
Then we shall see strange things, and know new propositions,
and all things in another manner and to higher purposes.
Cleombrotus was so taken with this speculation, that, having
learned from Plato's Phædon the soul's abode, he had not patience to stay nature's dull leisure, but leaped from a wall to
his portion of immortality. And when Pomponius Atticus
resolved to die by famine, to ease the great pains of his gout,
in the abstinence of two days he found his foot at ease; but
when he began to feel the pleasures of an approaching death,
and the delicacies of that ease he was to inherit below, he
would not withdraw his foot, but went on and finished his
death; and so did Cleanthes. And every wise man will despise
the little evils of that state, which indeed is the daughter of
fear, but the mother of rest, and peace, and felicity.

5. If God should say to us, Cast thyself into the sea, (as
Christ did to St. Peter, or as God concerning Jonas,) I have
provided for thee a dolphin or a whale, or a port, a safety or a
deliverance, security or a reward, were we not incredulous
and pusillanimous persons if we should tremble to put such a
felicity into act, and ourselves into possession? The very duty
of resignation and the love of our own interest are good anti-
dotes against fear. In forty or fifty years we find evils enough,
and arguments enough, to make us weary of this life; and to
a good man there are very many more reasons to be afraid of
life than death, this having in it less of evil and more of advantage. And it was a rare wish of that Roman,[5] that death
might come only to wise and excellent persons, and not to

---

[4] Beati erimus cùm, corporibus relictis, et cupiditatum et æmulatio-
num erimus expertes, quodque nunc facimus, cùm laxati curis sumus, at
spectare aliquid velimus et visere.—Tuscul. Q.

[5] Mors, utinam pavidos vitâ subducere nolles,
    Sed virtus te sola daret.   Lucan

fools and cowards; that it might not be a sanctuary for the timorous, but the reward of the virtuous: and indeed they only can make advantage of it.

6. Make no excuses to make thy desires of life seem reasonable; neither cover thy fear with pretences, but suppress it rather with arts of severity and ingenuity. Some are not willing to submit to God's sentence and arrest of death till they have finished such a design,[6] or made an end of the paragraph of their book, or raised such portions for their children, or preached so many sermons, or built their house, or planted their orchard, or ordered their estate with such advantages. It is well for the modesty of these men that the excuse is ready; but if it were not, it is certain they would search one out: for an idle man is never ready to die, and is glad of any excuse; and a busied man hath always something unfinished, and he is ready for every thing but death. And I remember that Petronius brings in Eumolpus composing verses in a desperate storm; and being called upon to shift for himself when the ship dashed upon the rock, crying out to let him alone till he had finished and trimmed his verse, which was lame in the hinder leg: the man either had too strong a desire to end his verse, or too great a desire not to end his life. But we must know, God's times are not to be measured by our circumstances; and what I value, God regards not; or if it be valuable in the accounts of men, yet God will supply it with other contingencies of his providence; and if Epaphroditus had died, when he had his great sickness St. Paul speaks of, God would have secured the work of the gospel without him: and he could have spared Epaphroditus as well as St. Stephen, and St. Peter as well as St. James. Say no more; but, when God calls, lay aside thy papers; and first dress thy soul, and then dress thy hearse.

Blindness is odious, and widowhood is sad, and destitution is without comfort, and persecution is full of trouble, and famine is intolerable, and tears are the sad ease of a sadder heart: but these are evils of our life, not of our death. For the dead that die in the Lord are so far from wanting the commodities of this life, that they do not want life itself.

After all this, I do not say it is a sin to be afraid of death: we find the boldest spirit that discourses of it with confidence,

* Pendent opera interrupta, minæque murorum ingentes.

and dares undertake a danger as big as death, yet doth shrink
at the horror of it when it comes dressed in its proper circumstances. And Brutus, who was as bold a Roman to undertake
a noble action as any was since they first reckoned by consuls,
yet when Furius came to cut his throat, after his defeat by
Antony, he ran from it like a girl, and being admonished to
die constantly, he swore by his life that he would shortly endure death. But what do I speak of such imperfect persons?
Our blessed Lord was pleased to legitimate fear to us by his
agony and prayers in the garden. It is not a sin to be afraid,
but it is a great felicity to be without fear; which felicity our
dearest Saviour refused to have, because it was agreeable to
his purposes to suffer any thing that was contrary to felicity,
every thing but sin. But when men will by all means avoid
death, they are like those who, at any hand, resolve to be rich.[7]
The case may happen in which they will blaspheme, and dishonour Providence, or do a base action, or curse God and die;
but, in all cases, they die miserable and insnared, and in no
case do they die the less for it. Nature hath left us the key
of the churchyard, and custom hath brought cemeteries and
charnel-houses into cities and churches, places most frequented,
that we might not carry ourselves strangely in so certain,[8] so
expected, so ordinary, so unavoidable, an accident. All re-
luctancy or unwillingness to obey the Divine decree is but a
snare to ourselves, and a load to our spirits,[9] and is either
an entire cause or a great aggravation of the calamity. Who
did not scorn to look upon Xerxes when he caused three hundred stripes to be given to the sea, and sent a chartel of defiance against the mountain Athos? Who did not scorn the
proud vanity of Cyrus, when he took so goodly a revenge upon
the river Gyndes for his hard passage over it? or did not deride or pity the Thracians for shooting arrows against heaven
when it thunders? To be angry with God,[10] to quarrel with
the Divine providence, by repining against an unalterable, a
natural, an easy sentence, is an argument of a huge folly, and
the parent of a great trouble; a man is base and foolish to no
purpose;[11] he throws away a vice to his own misery, and to

[7] Ἀλλ' οἱ ἐξ ἅπαντος φεύγοντες τὸν θάνατον.　　[8] Quam pellunt
lacrymæ, fovent sortem: dura negant cedere mollibus.　　[9] Siccas
si videat genas, duræ cedet hebes sors patientiæ.　　[10] Νήπιοι, οἳ Ζηνὶ
μενεαίνομεν ἀφρονέοντες.—Iliad. ó.　　[11] Et cùm nihil imminuat
dolores, cur frustrà turpes esse volumus?— Seneca

no advantages of ease and pleasure. Fear keeps men in bondage all their life, saith St. Paul: and patience makes him his own man, and lord of his own interest and person. Therefore possess yourselves in patience, with reason and religion, and you shall die with ease.[12]

If all the parts of this discourse be true, if they be better than dreams, and unless virtue be nothing but words, as a grove is a heap of trees;[13] if they be not the phantasms of hypochondriacal persons, and designs upon the interests of men, and their persuasions to evil purposes; then there is no reason but that we should really desire death, and account it among the good things of God, and the sour and laborious felicities of man. St. Paul understood it well when he desired to be dissolved; he well enough knew his own advantages, and pursued them accordingly. But it is certain that he that is afraid of death, I mean with a violent and transporting fear, with a fear apt to discompose his duty or his patience, that man either loves this world too much, or dares not trust God for the next.

SECT. IX. *General Rules and Exercises whereby our Sickness may become safe and sanctified.*

1. TAKE care that the cause of thy sickness be such as may not sour it in the principal and original causes of it. It is a sad calamity to pass into the house of mourning through the gates of intemperance, by a drunken meeting, or the surfeits of a loathed and luxurious table; for then a man suffers the pain of his own folly, and he is like a fool smarting under the whip which his own viciousness twisted for his back: then a man pays the price of his sin, and hath a pure and an unmingled sorrow in his suffering; and it cannot be alleviated by any circumstances, for the whole affair is a mere process of death and sorrow. Sin is in the head, sickness is in the body, and death and an eternity of pains in the tail; and nothing can make this condition tolerable unless the miracles of the Divine mercy will be pleased to exchange the eternal anger for the temporal. True it is, that in all sufferings the cause of it makes it noble or ignoble, honour or shame, tolerable or intolerable.[1]

---

[12] Non levat miseros dolor.   [13] Virtutem verba putas, ut lucum ligna.   [1] Solatium est pro honesto dura tolerare, et ad causam patientiæ respicit.—1 Pet. ii. 19; Heb. xi. 36; Matt. v. 11

For when patience is assaulted by a ruder violence, by a blow from heaven or earth, from a gracious God or an unjust man, patience looks forth to the doors, which way she may escape. And if innocence or a cause of religion keep the first entrance, then, whether she escapes at the gates of life or death, there is a good to be received greater than the evils of a sickness; but if sin thrust in that sickness, and that hell stands at the door, then patience turns into fury, and, seeing it impossible to go forth with safety, rolls up and down with a circular and infinite revolution, makes its motion not from, but upon, its own centre; it doubles the pain,[2] and increases the sorrow, till by its weight it breaks the spirit and bursts into the agonies of infinite and eternal ages. If we had seen St. Polycarp burning to death, or St. Lawrence roasted upon his gridiron, or St. Ignatius exposed to lions, or St. Sebastian pierced with arrows, or St. Attalus carried about the theatre with scorn unto his death, for the cause of Jesus, for religion, for God, and a holy conscience—we should have been in love with flames, and have thought the gridiron fairer than the *spondæ*, the ribs of a marital bed; and we should have chosen to converse with those beasts, rather than those men that brought those beasts forth; and estimated the arrows to be the rays of light brighter than the moon; and that disgrace and mistaken pageantry were a solemnity richer and more magnificent than Mordecai's procession upon the king's horse and in the robes of majesty: for so did these holy men account them; they kissed their stakes, and hugged their deaths, and ran violently to torments, and counted whippings and secular disgraces to be the enamel of their persons, and the ointment of their heads, and the embalming their names, and securing them for immortality. But to see Sejanus torn in pieces by the people, or Nero crying or creeping timorously to his death, when he was condemned to die *more majorum;* to see Judas pale and trembling, full of anguish, sorrow, and despair; to observe the groanings and intolerable agonies of Herod and Antiochus—will tell and demonstrate the causes of patience and impatience to proceed from the causes of the suffering; and it is sin only that makes the cup bitter and deadly. When men, by vomiting, measure up the drink they took in,[3] and sick and sad do again taste

---

[2] Magis his quæ patitur, vexat causa patiendi.   [3] Hi quicquid diberint, vomitu remetientur tristes, et bilem suam regustantes.—Seneca.

their meat turned into choler by intemperance, the sin and its
punishment are mingled so that shame covers the face and sorrow puts a veil of darkness upon the heart; and we scarce
pity a vile person that is haled to execution for murder or for
treason, but we say he deserves it, and that every man is concerned in it that he should die. If lust brought the sickness
or the shame, if we truly suffer the rewards of our evil deeds,
we must thank ourselves; that is, we are fallen into an evil
condition, and are the sacrifice of the Divine justice. But if
we live holy lives, and if we enter well in, we are sure to pass
on safe, and to go forth with advantage, if we list ourselves.

2. To this relates that we should not counterfeit sickness;
for he that is to be careful of his passage into a sickness will
think himself concerned that he fall not into it through a trap-
door: for so it hath sometimes happened, that such counterfeiting to light and evil purposes hath ended in a real sufferance. Appian tells of a Roman gentleman who, to escape the
proscription of the triumvirate, fled, and, to secure his privacy,
counterfeited himself blind on one eye, and wore a plaister upon
it; till, beginning to be free from the malice of the three prevailing princes, he opened his hood, but could not open his
eye, but for ever lost the use of it, and with his eye paid for
his liberty and hypocrisy. And Cælius counterfeited the gout,[4]
and all its circumstances and pains, its dressings and arts of
remedy and complaint, till at last the gout really entered and
spoiled the pageantry. His arts of dissimulation were so witty,
that they put life and motion into the very image of the disease; he made the very picture to sigh and groan.

It is easy to tell upon the interest of what virtue such counterfeiting is to be reproved. But it will be harder to snatch
the politics of the world from following that which they call a
canonized and authentic precedent; and David's counterfeiting
himself mad before the king of Gath, to save his life and liberty,
will be sufficient to entice men to serve an end upon the stock
and charges of so small an irregularity, not in the matter of
manners, but in the rules and decencies of natural or civil deportment: I cannot certainly tell what degrees of excuse David's action might put on. This only; besides his present
necessity, the laws whose coercive or directive power David

---

[4] Tantum cura potest et ars doloris:
Desit fingere Cælius podagram.—Mart. l. vii. ep. 38

lived under had less of severity, and more of liberty, and towards enemies had so little of restraint and so great a power,
that what amongst them was a direct sin, if used to their brethren the sons of Jacob, was lawful and permitted to be acted
against enemies.   To which also I add this general caution,
that the actions of holy persons in Scripture are not always
good precedents to us Christians, who are to walk by a rule and
a greater strictness, with more simplicity and heartiness of pursuit.   And amongst them sanctity and holy living did, in very
many of its instances, increase in new particulars of duty ; and
the prophets reproved many things which the law forbade not,
and taught many duties which Moses prescribed not; and as
the time of Christ's approach came, so the sermons and revelations too were more evangelical, and like the patterns which
were fully to be exhibited by the Son of God.   Amongst which
it is certain that Christian simplicity and godly sincerity are to
be accounted; and counterfeiting of sickness is a huge enemy
to this: it is an upbraiding the Divine providence, a jesting
with fire, a playing with a thunderbolt, a making the decrees
of God to serve the vicious or secular ends of men ; it is a
tempting of a judgment, a false accusation of God, a forestall-
ing and antedating his anger; it is a cozening of men by making God a party in the fraud: and, therefore, if the cozenage
returns upon the man's own head, he enters like a fox into his
sickness, and perceives himself catched in a trap, or earthed in
the intolerable dangers of the grave.

3. Although we must be infinitely careful to prevent it, that
sin does not thrust us into a sickness ; yet, when we are in the
house of sorrow, we should do well to take physic against sin,
and suppose that it is the cause of the evil; if not by way of
natural causality and proper effect, yet by a moral influence,
and by a just demerit.   We can easily see when a man hath
got a surfeit; intemperance is as plain as the handwriting upon
the wall, and easier to be read ; but covetousness may cause a
fever as well as drunkenness, and pride can produce a falling-
sickness as well as long washings and dilutions of the brain,
and intemperate lust ; and we find it recorded in Scripture,
that the contemptuous and unprepared manner of receiving
of the holy sacraments caused sickness and death ; and sacrilege and vow-breach in Ananias and Sapphira, made them
to descend quick into their graves.   Therefore, when sick-

ness is upon us, let us cast about; and, if we can, let us find
out the cause of God's displeasure; that, it being removed, we
may return into the health and securities of God's loving-kindness.   Thus, in the three years' famine, David inquired of the
Lord what was the matter: and God answered, "It is for Saul
and his bloody house;" and then David expiated the guilt, and
the people were full again of food and blessing.   And when
Israel was smitten by the Amorites, Joshua cast about, and
found out the accursed thing, and cast it out; and the people
after that fought prosperously.   And what God in that case
said to Joshua he will also verify to us: " I will not be with
you any more, unless you destroy the accursed thing from
among you."[5]   But in pursuance of this we are to observe,
that although in case of loud and clamorous sins the discovery
is easy, and the remedy not difficult; yet, because Christianity
is a nice thing, and religion is as pure as the sun, and the soul
of man is apt to be troubled from more principles than the intricate and curiously composed body in its innumerable parts,
it will often happen that if we go to inquire into the particular
we shall never find it out; and we may suspect drunkenness
when it may be also a morose delectation in unclean thoughts,
or covetousness, or oppression, or a crafty invasion of my neighbour's rights, or my want of charity, or my judging unjustly
in my own cause, or my censuring my neighbours, or a secret
pride, or a base hypocrisy, or the pursuance of little ends with
violence and passion, that may have procured the present messenger of death.   Therefore, ask no more after any one, but
heartily endeavour to reform all: " Sin no more, lest a worse
thing happen:"[6] for a single search or accusation may be the
design of an imperfect repentance; but no man does heartily
return to God but he that decrees against every irregularity;
and then only we can be restored to health or life, when we
have taken away the causes of sickness and a cursed death.

4. He that means to have his sickness turn into safety and
life, into health and virtue, must make religion the employment of his sickness, and prayer the employment of his religion.   For there are certain compendiums or abbreviatures
and shortenings of religion, fitted to several states.   They that
first gave up their names to Christ, and that turned from Pa-

[5] Josh. vii. 12.
[6] Ὅρα κακῶς πράσσοντες, μὴ μείζω κακα κτησώμεθα.—Soph.

ganism to Christianity, had an abbreviature fitted for them; they were to renounce their false worshippings, and give up their belief, and vow their obedience unto Christ; and in the very profession of this they were forgiven in baptism. For God hastens to snatch them from the power of the devil, and therefore shortens the passage, and secures the estate. In the case of poverty, God hath reduced this duty of man to an abbreviature of those few graces which they can exercise; such as are patience, contentedness, truth, and diligence; and the rest he accepts in good will, and the charities of the soul, in prayers, and the actions of a cheap religion. And to most men charity is also an abbreviature. And as the love of God shortens the way to the purchase of all virtues, so the expression of this to the poor goes a huge way in the requisites and towards the consummation of an excellent religion. And martyrdom is another abbreviature; and so is every act of an excellent and heroical virtue. But when we are fallen into the state of sickness, and that our understanding is weak and troubled, our bodies sick and useless, our passions turned into fear, and the whole state into suffering, God, in compliance with man's infirmity, hath also turned our religion into such a duty which a sick man can do most passionately, and a sad man and a timorous can perform effectually, and a dying man can do to many purposes of pardon and mercy; and that is, prayer. For, although a sick man is bound to do many acts of virtue of several kinds, yet the most of them are to be done in the way of prayer. Prayer is not only the religion that is proper to a sick man's condition, but it is the manner of doing other graces, which is then left and in his power. For, thus, the sick man is to do his repentance and his mortifications, his temperance and his chastity, by a fiction of imagination, bringing the offers of the virtue to the spirit, and making an action of election: and so our prayers are a direct act of chastity, when they are made in the matter of that grace; just as repentance for our cruelty is an act of the grace of mercy; and repentance for uncleanness is an act of chastity, is a means of its purchase, an act in order to the habit. And though such acts of virtue, which are only in the way of prayer, are ineffective to the entire purchase, and of themselves cannot change the vice into virtue, yet they are good renewings of the grace, and the proper exercise of a habit already gotten.

The purpose of this discourse is, to represent the excellency
of prayer, and its proper advantages which it hath in the time
of sickness. For, besides that it moves God to pity, piercing
the clouds, and making the heavens, like a pricked eye, to
weep over us and refresh us with showers of pity ; it also doth
the work of the soul, and expresses the virtue of his whole
life in effigy, in pictures and lively representments, so preparing it for a never-ceasing crown, by renewing the actions
in the continuation of a never-ceasing, a never-hindered affection. Prayer speaks to God when the tongue is stiffened
with the approachings of death : prayer can dwell in the heart,
and be signified by the hand or eye, by a thought or a groan :
prayer, of all the actions of religion, is the last alive, and it
serves God without circumstances, and exercises material
graces by abstraction from matter, and separation, and makes
them to be spiritual ; and, therefore, best dresses our bodies
for funeral or recovery, for the mercies of restitution or the
mercies of the grave.

5. In every sickness, whether it will or will not be so in
nature and in the event, yet in thy spirit and preparations resolve upon it, and treat thyself accordingly, as if it were a
sickness unto death. For many men support their unequal
courages by flattery and false hopes ; and because sicker men
have recovered, believe that they shall do so ; but therefore
they neglect to adorn their souls, or set their house in order :
besides the temporal inconveniences that often happen by such
persuasions and putting off the evil day, such as are dying in-
testate, leaving estates entangled and some relatives unprovided for, they suffer infinitely in the interest and affairs of
their soul ; they die carelessly and surprised, their burdens on,
and their scruples unremoved, and their cases of conscience
not determined, and, like a sheep, without any care taken concerning their precious souls. Some men will never believe
that a villain will betray them, though they receive often advices from suspicious persons and likely accidents, till they
are entered into the snare ; and then they believe it when
they feel it, and when they cannot return ; but so the treason
entered, and the man was betrayed by his own folly, placing
the snare in the regions and advantages of opportunity. This
evil looks like boldness and a confident spirit, but it is the
greatest timorousness and cowardice in the world. They are

so fearful to die, that they dare not look upon it as possible; and think that the making of a will is a mortal sign, and sending for a spiritual man an irrecoverable disease: and they are so afraid lest they should think and believe now they must die, that they will not take care that it may not be evil in case they should. So did the eastern slaves drink wine, and wrapped their heads in a veil, that they might die without sense or sorrow, and wink hard that they might sleep the easier. In pursuance of this rule, let a man consider that whatsoever must be done in sickness ought to be done in health; only let him observe, that his sickness, as a good monitor, chastises his neglect of duty, and forces him to live as he always should; and then all these solemnities and dressings for death are nothing else but the part of a religious life, which he ought to have exercised all his days: and if those circumstances can affright him, let him please his fancy by this truth, that then he does but begin to live. But it will be a huge folly if he shall think that confession of his sins will kill him, or receiving the holy sacrament will hasten his agony, or the priest shall undo all the hopeful language and promises of his physician. Assure thyself thou canst not die the sooner; but, by such addresses, thou mayest die much the better.

6. Let the sick person be infinitely careful that he do not fall into a state of death upon a new account; that is, at no hand commit a deliberate sin, or retain any affection to the old; for, in both cases, he falls into the evils of a surprise, and the horrors of a sudden death; for a sudden death is but a sudden joy, if it takes a man in the state and exercises of virtue; and it is only then an evil when it finds a man unready. They were sad departures when Tigellinus, Cornelius Gallus the prætor, Lewis the son of Gonzaga duke of Mantua, Ladislaus king of Naples, Speusippus, Giachettus of Geneva, and one of the popes, died in the forbidden embraces of abused women; or if Job had cursed God, and so died; or when a man sits down in despair, and in the accusation and calumny of the Divine mercy: they make their night sad, and stormy, and eternal. When Herod began to sink with the shameful torment of his bowels, and felt the grave open under him, he imprisoned the nobles of his kingdom, and commanded his sister that they should be a sacrifice to his departing ghost. This

2 D

was an egress fit only for such persons who meant to dwell with devils to eternal ages: and that man is hugely in love with sin who cannot forbear in the week of the assizes, and when himself stood at the bar of scrutiny, and prepared for his final, never-to-be-reversed sentence. He dies suddenly to the worse sense and event of sudden death, who so manages his sickness that even that state shall not be innocent, but that he is surprised in the guilt of a new account. It is a sign of a reprobate spirit, and an habitual, prevailing, ruling sin, which exacts obedience when the judgment looks him in the face. At least, go to God with the innocence and fair deportment of thy person in the last scene of thy life, that when thy soul breaks into the state of separation, it may carry the relishes of religion and sobriety to the places of its abode and sentence.[7]

7. When these things are taken care for, let the sick man so order his affairs that he have but very little conversation with the world, but wholly (as he can) attend to religion, and antedate his conversation in heaven, always having intercourse with God, and still conversing with the holy Jesus, kissing his wounds, admiring his goodness, begging his mercy, feeding on him with faith, and drinking his blood: to which purpose it were very fit (if all circumstances be answerable) that the narrative of the passion of Christ be read or discoursed to him at length, or in brief, according to the style of the four Gospels. But in all things let his care and society be as little secular as is possible.

CHAP. IV. OF THE PRACTICE OF THE GRACES PROPER TO THE STATE OF SICKNESS, WHICH A SICK MAN MAY PRACTISE ALONE.

SECT. I. *Of the Practice of Patience.*

Now we suppose the man entering upon his scene of sorrows and passive graces. It may be he went yesterday to a wedding, merry and brisk, and there he felt his sentence that he

[7] Whoso him bethoft   From pit unto pain
    Inwardly and oft   That nere shall cease again,
    How hard it were to flit He would not do one sin
    From bed unto the pit,   All the world to win.
                 *Inscript. marmori in Eccles. paroch. de Feversham
                  in agro Cantiano.*

must return home and die (for men very commonly enter into
the snare singing, and consider not whither their fate leads
them): nor feared that then the angel was to strike his stroke,
till his knees kissed the earth, and his head trembled with the
weight of the rod which God put into the hand of an exter-
minating angel. But whatsoever the ingress was, when the
man feels his blood boil, or his bones weary, or his flesh diseased with a load of a dispersed and disordered humour, or his
head to ache, or his faculties discomposed, then he must consider
that all those discourses he hath heard concerning patience
and resignation, and conformity to Christ's sufferings, and the
melancholy lectures of the cross, must all of them now be reduced to practice, and pass from an ineffective contemplation
to such an exercise as will really try whether we were true
disciples of the cross, or only believed the doctrines of religion
when we were at ease, and that they never passed through the
ear to the heart, and dwelt not in our spirits. But every man
should consider God does nothing in vain; that he would not
to no purpose send us preachers and give us rules, and furnish
us with discourse, and lend us books and provide sermons, and
make examples, and promise his Spirit, and describe the
blessedness of holy sufferings, and prepare us with daily
alarms, if he did not really purpose to order our affairs so
that we should need all this, and use it all. There were no
such thing as the grace of patience if we were not to feel a
sickness or enter into a state of sufferings; whither, when we
are entered, we are to practise by the following rules :

The Practice and Acts of Patience, by way of Rule.

1. At the first address and presence of sickness, stand still
and arrest thy spirit, that it may, without amazement or affright, consider that this was that thou lookedst for and wert
always certain should happen; and that now thou art to enter into the actions of a new religion, the agony of a strange
constitution; but at no hand suffer thy spirits to be dispersed
with fear, or wildness of thought, but stay their looseness and
dispersion by a serious consideration of the present and future
employment. For so doth the Libyan lion, spying the fierce
huntsman; first beats himself with the strokes of his tail, and
curls up his spirits, making them strong with union and recollection, till, being struck with a Mauritanian spear, he rushes

forth into his defence and noblest contention; and either 'scapes into the secrets of his own dwelling, or else dies the bravest of the forest.   Every man, when shot with an arrow from God's quiver, must then draw in all the auxiliaries of reason, and know that then is the time to try his strength, and to reduce the words of his religion into action, and consider, that if he behaves himself weakly and timorously, he suffers never the less of sickness; but if he returns to health, he carries along with him the mark of a coward and a fool; and if he descends into his grave, he enters into the state of the faithless and unbelievers.   Let him set his heart firm upon this resolution: "I must bear it inevitably, and I will, by God's grace, do it nobly."

2. Bear in thy sickness all along the same thoughts, propositions, and discourses, concerning thy person, thy life and death, thy soul and religion, which thou hadst in the best days of thy health, and when thou didst discourse wisely concerning things spiritual.   For it is to be supposed (and if it be not yet done, let this rule remind thee of it and direct thee) that thou hast cast about in thy health and considered concerning thy change and the evil day, that thou must be sick and die, that thou must need a comforter, and that it was certain thou shouldst fall into a state in which all the cords of thy anchor should be stretched, and the very rock and foundation of faith should be attempted: and whatsoever fancies may disturb you, or whatsoever weaknesses may invade you, yet consider, when you were better able to judge and govern the accidents of your life, you concluded it necessary to trust in God and possess your souls with patience.   Think of things as they think that stand by you, and as you did when you stood by others; that it is a blessed thing to be patient; that a quietness of spirit hath a certain reward; that still there is infinite truth and reality in the promises of the gospel; that still thou art in the care of God, in the condition of a son, and working out thy salvation with labour and pain, with fear and trembling; that now the sun is under a cloud, but it still sends forth the same influence: and be sure to make no new principles upon the stock of a quick and an impatient sense, or too busy an apprehension: keep your old principles, and upon their stock discourse and practise on towards your conclusion.

3. Resolve to bear your sickness like a child, that is, without considering the evils and the pains, the sorrows and the danger; but go straightforward, and let thy thoughts cast about for nothing but how to make advantages of it by the instrument of religion. He that from a high tower looks down upon the precipice, and measures the space through which he must descend, and considers what a huge fall he shall have, shall feel more by the horror of it than by the last dash on the pavement; and he that tells his groans and numbers his sighs, and reckons one for every gripe of his belly or throb of his distempered pulse, will make an artificial sickness greater than the natural. And if thou beest ashamed that a child should bear an evil better than thou, then take his instrument and allay thy spirit with it; reflect not upon thy evil, but contrive as much as you can for duty, and in all the rest inconsideration will ease your pain.

4. If thou fearest thou shalt need, observe and draw together all such things as are apt to charm thy spirit and ease thy fancy in the sufferance. It is the counsel of Socrates: "It is (said he) a great danger, and you must, by discourse and arts of reasoning, enchant it into slumber and some rest."[1] It may be, thou wert moved much to see a person of honour to die untimely; or thou didst love the religion of that death-bed, and it was dressed up in circumstances fitted to thy needs, and hit thee on that part where thou wert most sensible; or some little saying in a sermon or passage of a book was chosen and singled out by a peculiar apprehension, and made consent lodge awhile in thy spirit, even then when thou didst place death in thy meditation, and didst view it in all its dress of fancy. Whatsoever that was which at any time did please thee in thy most passionate and fantastic part, let not that go, but bring it home at that time especially; because, when thou art in thy weakness, such little things will easier move thee than a more severe discourse and a better reason. For a sick man is like a scrupulous; his case is gone beyond the cure of arguments, and it is a trouble that can only be helped by chance, or a lucky saying: and Ludovico Corbinelli was moved at the death of Henry the Second more than if he had read the saddest elegy of all the unfortunate princes in Christendom, or all the sad sayings of Scripture, or the threnes of

[1] Καλὸς γὰρ ὁ κίνδυνος, καὶ χρὴ τὰ τοιαῦτα ὥσπερ ἐπᾴδειν ἑαυτῷ.

the funeral prophets. I deny not but this course is most proper to weak persons; but it is a state of weakness for which
we are now providing remedies and instruction: a strong
man will not need it; but when our sickness hath rendered
us weak in all senses, it is not good to refuse a remedy because it supposes us to be sick. But then, if to the catalogue
of weak persons we add all those who are ruled by fancy, we
shall find that many persons in their health, and more in their
sickness, are under the dominion of fancy, and apt to be
helped by those little things which themselves have found
fitted to their apprehension, and which no other man can
minister to their needs, unless by chance, or in a heap of
other things. But, therefore, every man should remember
by what instruments he was at any time much moved, and
try them upon his spirit in the day of his calamity.

5. Do not choose the kind of thy sickness, or the manner of
thy death, but let it be what God please, so it be no greater
than thy spirit or thy patience; and for that you are to rely
upon the promise of God, and to secure thyself by prayer and
industry; but in all things else let God be thy chooser, and
let it be thy work to submit indifferently and attend thy duty.
It is lawful to beg of God that thy sickness may not be sharp
or noisome, infectious or unusual, because these are circumstances of evil which are also proper instruments of temptation: and though it may well concern the prudence of thy religion to fear thyself, and keep thee from violent temptations,
who hast so often fallen into little ones, yet, even in these
things, be sure to keep some degrees of indifferency; that is,
if God will not be entreated to ease thee, or to change thy
trial, then be importunate that thy spirit and its interest be
secured, and let him do what seemeth good in his eyes. But
as in the degrees of sickness thou art to submit to God, so in
the kind of it (supposing equal degrees) thou art to be altogether incurious whether God call thee by a consumption or
an asthma, by a dropsy or a palsy, by a fever in thy humours,
or a fever in thy spirits; because all such nicety of choice is
nothing but a colour to a legitimate impatience, and to make
an excuse to murmur privately, and for circumstances, when
in the sum of affairs we durst not own impatience. I have
known some persons vehemently wish that they might die of
a consumption, and some of these had a plot upon heaven

and hoped by that means to secure it after a careless life; as
thinking a lingering sickness would certainly infer a lingering
and a protracted repentance; and by that means they thought
they should be safest: others of them dreamed it would be an
easier death, and have found themselves deceived, and their
patience hath been tired with a weary spirit and a useless
body, by often conversing with healthful persons and vigorous neighbours, by uneasiness of the flesh and the sharpness
of their bones, by want of spirits and a dying life; and, in
conclusion, have been directly debauched by peevishness and
a fretful sickness; and these men had better have left it to
the wisdom and goodness of God; for they both are infinite.

6. Be patient in the desires of religion; and take care that
the forwardness of exterior actions do not discompose thy spirit,
while thou fearest, that by less serving God in thy disability
thou runnest backward in the accounts of pardon and the favour of God. Be content that the time which was formerly
spent in prayer be now spent in vomiting, and carefulness, and
attendances; since God hath pleased it should be so, it does
not become us to think hard thoughts concerning it. Do not
think that God is only to be found in a great prayer, or a
solemn office: he is moved by a sigh, by a groan, by an act of
love; and therefore, when your pain is great and pungent,
lay all your strength upon it, to bear it patiently: when the
evil is something more tolerable, let your mind think some
pious, though short, meditation; let it not be very busy, and
full of attention; for that will be but a new temptation to your
patience, and render your religion tedious and hateful. But
record your desires, and present yourself to God by general
acts of will and understanding, and by habitual remembrances
of your former vigorousness, and by verification of the same
grace, rather than proper exercises. If you can do more, do
it; but if you cannot, let it not become a scruple to thee. We
must not think man is tied to the forms of health, or that he
who swoons and faints is obliged to his usual forms and hours
of prayer: if we cannot labour, yet let us love. Nothing can
hinder us from that but our own uncharitableness.

7. Be obedient to thy physician in those things that concern him, if he be a person fit to minister unto thee. God is
he only that needs no help,[2] and God hath created the phy-

[2] Iosi ceu vi Deo nullo est opus; apud Senecam. Scaliger rectè emen-

sician for thine: therefore use him temperately without violent
confidences, and sweetly without uncivil distrustings, or refusing his prescriptions upon humours or impotent fear. A
man may refuse to have his arm or leg cut off, or to suffer
the pains of Marius's incision; and if he believes that to die
is the less evil, he may compose himself to it without hazard-
ing his patience, or introducing that which he thinks a worse
evil; but that which in this article is to be reproved and
avoided is, that some men will choose to die out of fear of
death, and send for physicians, and do what themselves list,
and call for counsel and follow none. When there is reason
they should decline him, it is not to be accounted to the stock
of sin; but where there is no just cause, there is a direct impatience.

Hither is to be reduced, that we be not too confident of the
physician, or drain our hopes of recovery from the fountain
through so imperfect channels, laying the wells of God dry,
and digging to ourselves broken cisterns. Physicians are the
ministers of God's mercies and providence in the matter of
health and ease, of restitution or death; and when God shall
enable their judgments, and direct their counsels, and prosper
their medicines, they shall do thee good, for which you must
give God thanks, and to the physician the honour of a blessed
instrument. But this cannot always be done: and Lucius
Cornelius,[3] the lieutenant in Portugal under Fabius the consul, boasted in the inscription of his monument, that he had
lived a healthful and vegete age till his last sickness, but then
complained he was forsaken by his physician, and railed upon
Æsculapius for not accepting his vow and passionate desire
of preserving his life longer; and all the effect of that impatience and folly was, that it is recorded to following ages
that he died without reason and without religion. But it was
a sad sight to see the favour of all France confined to a physician and a barber, and the king (Louis XI.) to be so much
their servant, that he should acknowledge and own his life
from them, and all his ease to their gentle dressing of his gout

dat, Ipsi ceu Deo, &c. Ex Græco scilicet, Μόνος Θεὸς ἀνελλιπὴς καὶ
ἀνενδεής.   [3] L. Cornel. legatus sub Fabio consule vividam naturam et virilem animum servavi, quoad animam efflavi; et tandem de-
sertus ope medicorum et Æsculapii Dei ingrati, cui me voveram sodalem
perpetuo futurum, si fila aliquantulùm optata protulisset.—Vetus Inscrip-
tio in Lusitaniâ.

and friendly ministries: for the king thought himself undone and robbed if he should die: his portion here was fair; and he was loath to exchange his possession for the interest of a bigger hope.[4]

8. Treat thy nurses and servants sweetly, and as it becomes an obliged and necessitous person. Remember that thou art very troublesome to them; that they trouble not thee willingly: that they strive to do thee ease and benefit, that they wish it, and sigh and pray for it, and are glad if thou likest their attendance; that whatsoever is amiss is thy disease, and the uneasiness of thy head or thy side, thy distemper or thy disaffections; and it will be an unhandsome injustice to be troublesome to them because thou art so to thyself; to make them feel a part of thy sorrows, that thou mayest not bear them alone; evilly to requite their care by thy too curious and impatient wrangling and fretful spirit. That tenderness is vicious and unnatural that shrieks out under the weight of a gentle cataplasm; and he will ill comply with God's rod, that cannot endure his friend's greatest kindness; and he will be very angry (if he durst) with God's smiting him, that is peevish with his servants that go about to ease him.

9. Let not the smart of your sickness make you to call violently for death; you are not patient unless you be content to live;[5] God hath wisely ordered that we may be the better reconciled with death, because it is the period of many calamities; but wherever the general hath placed thee, stir not from thy station until thou beest called off, but abide so, that death may come to thee by the design of him who intends it to be thy advantage. God hath made sufferance to be thy work, and do not impatiently long for evening, lest at night thou findest the reward of him that was weary of his work; for he that is weary before his time is an unprofitable servant, and is either idle or diseased.

10. That which remains in the practice of this grace is, that the sick man should do acts of patience by way of prayer and ejaculations; in which he may serve himself of the following collection.

---

4   ——— Nunc omnibus anxius aris
    Illacrymat, signatque fores, et pectore tergit
    Limina; nunc frustrà vocat exorabile numen.—Papin. lib. v.

5 Ἀποκαρτερεῖν Græci vocant, cùm mors propter impatientiam petitur

SECT. II. *Acts of Patience by way of Prayer and Ejaculation.*

I WILL seek unto God, unto God will I commit my cause, which doth great things and unsearchable, marvellous things without number. Job v. 8, 9, 11, 16—20.

To set up on high those that be low, that those which mourn may be exalted to safety.

So the poor have hope, and iniquity stoppeth her mouth.

Behold, happy is the man whom God correcteth: therefore despise not thou the chastening of the Almighty.

For he maketh sore, and bindeth up; he woundeth, and his hands make whole.

He shall deliver thee in six troubles; yea, in seven there shall no evil touch thee.

Thou shalt come to thy grave in a just age, like as a shock of corn cometh in his season.

I remember thee upon my bed, and meditate upon thee in the night watches. Because thou hast been my help, therefore under the shadow of thy wings will I rejoice. My soul followeth hard after thee; for thy right hand hath upholden me. Psalm lxiii. 6—8.

God restoreth my soul: he leadeth me in the path of righteousness for his name's sake. Yea, though I walk through the valley of the shadow of death, I will fear no evil; for thou art with me; thy rod and thy staff, they comfort me. Psalm xxiii. 3, 4.

In the time of trouble he shall hide me in his pavilion; in the secret of his tabernacle shall he hide me; he shall set me up upon a rock. Psalm xxvii. 5.

The Lord hath looked down from the height of his sanctuary: from the heaven did the Lord behold the earth: to hear the groaning of his prisoners; to loose those that are appointed to death. Psalm cii. 19, 20.

I cried unto God with my voice, even unto God with my voice, and he gave ear unto me. In the day of my trouble I sought the Lord; my sore ran in the night, and ceased not: my soul refused to be comforted; I remembered God, and was troubled; I complained, and my spirit was overwhelmed. Thou holdest mine eyes waking; I am so troubled that I cannot speak. Will the Lord cast me off for ever? and will he be favourable no more? Is his promise clean gone for ever?

Doth his promise fail for evermore? Hath God forgotten to be gracious? Hath he in anger shut up his tender mercies? And I said, This is in my infirmity; but I will remember the years of the right hand of the Most High. Psalm lxxvii. 1—4, 7—10.

No temptation hath taken me but such as is common to man: but God is faithful, who will not suffer me to be tempted above what I am able; but will, with the temptation, also make a way to escape, that I may be able to bear it. 1 Cor. x. 13.

Whatsoever things were written aforetime were written for our learning; that we, through patience and comfort of the Scriptures, might have hope. Now the God of peace and consolation grant me to be so minded. Rom. xv. 4, 5.

It is the Lord; let him do what seemeth good in his eyes. 1 Sam. iii. 18.

Surely the word that the Lord hath spoken is very good, but thy servant is weak: O remember mine infirmities; and lift thy servant up that leaneth upon thy right hand.

There is given unto me a thorn in the flesh to buffet me. For this thing I besought the Lord thrice, that it might depart from me. And he said unto me, My grace is sufficient for thee; for my strength is made perfect in weakness. Most gladly, therefore, will I glory in my infirmities, that the power of Christ may rest upon me. For when I am weak, then am I strong. 2 Cor. xii. 7—10.

O Lord, thou hast pleaded the causes of my soul; thou hast redeemed my life. And I said, My strength and my hope is in the Lord; remembering my affliction and my misery, the wormwood and the gall. My soul hath them still in remembrance, and is humbled within me. This I recall to my mind, therefore I have hope.

It is the Lord's mercies that we are not consumed, because his compassions fail not. They are new every morning; great is thy faithfulness. The Lord is my portion, said my soul; therefore will I hope in him.

The Lord is good to them that wait for him; to the soul that seeketh him. It is good that a man should both hope and quietly wait for the salvation of the Lord. For the Lord will not cast off for ever. But though he cause grief, yet will he have compassion according to the multitude of his mercies. For he doth not afflict willingly, nor grieve the children of men. Lam. iii. 58, 18—26, 31—33, 39.

Wherefore doth a living man complain—a man for the punishment of his sins?   O that thou wouldest hide me in the grave [of Jesus], that thou wouldest keep me secret, until thy wrath be past: that thou wouldest appoint me a set time, and remember me!   Job xiv. 13.

Shall we receive good at the hand of God, and shall we not receive evil?   Job ii. 10.

The sick man may recite, or hear recited, the following Psalms in the intervals of his agony.

I.

O Lord, rebuke me not in thine anger, neither chasten me in thy hot displeasure.   Psalm vi.

Have mercy upon me, O Lord, for I am weak: O Lord, heal me, for my bones are vexed.

My soul is also sore vexed; but thou, O Lord, how long?

Return, O Lord, deliver my soul; O save me, for thy mercy's sake.

For in death no man remembereth thee: in the grave who shall give thee thanks?

I am weary with my groaning; all the night make I my bed to swim: I water my couch with my tears.

Mine eye is consumed because of grief; it waxeth old because of all my [sorrows].

Depart from me, all ye workers of iniquity; for the Lord hath heard the voice of my weeping.

The Lord hath heard my supplication; the Lord will receive my prayer.

Blessed be the Lord, who hath heard my prayer, and hath not turned his mercy from me.

II.

In the Lord put I my trust: how say ye to my soul, Flee as a bird to your mountain?   Psalm xi.

The Lord is in his holy temple; the Lord's throne is in heaven; his eyes behold, his eyelids try, the children of men.

Preserve me, O God; for in thee do I put my trust.   Psalm xvi. 1.

O my soul, thou hast said unto the Lord, Thou art my Lord; my goodness extendeth not to thee.

The Lord is the portion of mine inheritance and of my cup: thou maintainest my lot.

I will bless the Lord who hath given me counsel; my reins also instruct me in the night seasons.

I have set the Lord always before me; because he is at my right hand I shall not be moved.

Therefore my heart is glad, and my glory rejoiceth: my flesh also shall rest in hope.

Thou wilt show me the path of life; in thy presence is the fulness of joy, at thy right hand there are pleasures for evermore.

As for me, I will behold thy face in righteousness: I shall be satisfied when I awake with thy likeness.   Psalm xvii.

III.

Have mercy upon me, O Lord, for I am in trouble: mine eye is consumed with grief; yea, my soul and my belly.   Psalm xxxi.

For my life is spent with grief, and my years with sighing; my strength faileth because of mine iniquity, and my bones are consumed.

I am like a broken vessel.

But I trusted in thee, O Lord; I said, Thou art my God.

My times are in thy hand; make thy face to shine upon thy servant: save me, for thy mercy's sake.

When thou saidst, Seek ye my face, my heart said unto thee, Thy face, Lord, will I seek.   Psalm xxvii.

Hide not thy face from me; put not thy servant away in thine anger; thou hast been my help; leave me not, neither forsake me, O God of my salvation.

I had fainted unless I had believed to see the goodness of the Lord in the land of the living.

O how great is thy goodness which thou hast laid up for them that fear thee; which thou hast wrought for them that trust in thee before the sons of men!   Psalm xxxi.

Thou shalt hide them in the secret of thy presence from the pride of man; thou shalt keep them secretly in a pavilion from the strife of tongues, [*from the calumnies and aggravation of sins by devils*].

I said in my haste, I am cut off from before thine eyes; nevertheless thou heardest the voice of my supplication when I cried unto thee.

O love the Lord, all ye his saints; for the Lord preserveth the faithful, and plenteously rewardeth the proud doer.

Be of good courage, and he shall strengthen your heart, all ye that hope in the Lord.

The Prayer to be said in the Beginning of a Sickness.

O Almighty God, merciful and gracious, who in thy justice didst send sorrow and tears, sickness and death, into the world, as a punishment for man's sins, and hast comprehended all under sin, and this sad covenant of sufferings, not to destroy us, but that thou mightest have mercy upon all, making thy justice to minister to mercy, short afflictions to an eternal weight of glory; as thou hast turned my sins into sickness, so turn my sickness to the advantages of holiness and religion, of mercy and pardon, of faith and hope, of grace and glory. Thou hast now called me to the fellowship of sufferings: Lord, by the instrument of religion let my present condition be so sanctified that my sufferings may be united to the sufferings of my Lord, that so thou mayest pity me and assist me. Relieve my sorrow and support my spirit; direct my thoughts, and sanctify the accidents of my sickness; and that the punishment of my sin may be the school of virtue, in which, since thou hast now entered me, Lord, make me a holy proficient, that I may behave myself as a son under discipline, humbly and obediently, evenly and penitently; that I may come by this means nearer unto thee; that, if I shall go forth of this sickness by the gate of life and health, I may return to the world with great strengths of spirit, to run a new race of a stricter holiness and a more severe religion: or, if I pass from hence with the outlet of death, I may enter into the bosom of my Lord, and may feel the present joys of a certain hope of that sea of pleasures, in which all thy saints and servants shall be comprehended to eternal ages. Grant this for Jesus Christ's sake, our dearest Lord and Saviour. Amen.

An Act of Resignation to be said by a Sick Person in all the evil Accidents of his Sickness.

O eternal God, thou hast made me and sustained me; thou hast blessed me in all the days of my life, and hast taken care of me in all variety of accidents; and nothing happens to me in vain, nothing without thy providence; and I know thou smitest thy servants in mercy, and with designs of the greatest pity in the world: Lord, I humbly lie down under thy rod; do with me as thou pleasest; do thou choose for me not only the whole state and condition of being, but every little and great accident of it. Keep me safe by thy grace, and then use what instrument thou pleasest of bringing me to thee. Lord, I am not solicitous of the passage, so I may get to thee. Only, O Lord, remember my infirmities, and let thy servant rejoice in thee always, and feel, and confess, and glory in thy goodness. O, be thou as delightful to me in this my medicinal sickness as ever thou wert in any of the dangers of my prosperity; let me not peevishly refuse thy pardon at the rate of a severe discipline. I am thy servant and thy creature, thy purchased possession, and thy son; I am all thine; and because thou hast mercy in store for all that trust in thee, I cover mine eyes, and in silence wait for the time of my redemption. Amen.

A Prayer for the Grace of Patience.

Most merciful and gracious Father, who, in the redemption of lost mankind by the passion of thy most holy Son, hast established a covenant of sufferings, I bless and magnify thy name that thou hast adopted me into the inheritance of sons, and hast given me a portion of my elder Brother. Lord, the cross falls heavy and sits uneasy upon my shoulders; my spirit is willing, but my flesh is weak; I humbly beg of thee that I may now rejoice in this thy dispensation and effect of providence. I know and am persuaded that thou art then as gracious when thou smitest us for amendment or trial, as when thou relievest our wearied bodies in compliance with our infirmity. I rejoice, O Lord, in thy rare and mysterious mercy, who by sufferings hast turned our misery into advantages unspeakable: for so thou makest us like to thy Son, and givest us a gift that the angels never did receive: for they cannot die in conformity to, and imitation of, their Lord and ours: but, blessed be thy name, we can; and, dearest Lord, let it be so. Amen.

II.

Thou, who art the God of patience and consolation, strengthen me in the inner man, that I may bear the yoke and burden of the Lord without any uneasy and useless murmurs and ineffective unwillingness. Lord, I am unable to stand under the cross, unable of myself; but thou, O holy Jesus, who didst feel the burden of it, who didst sink under it, and wert pleased to admit a man to bear part of the load, when thou underwentest all for him, be thou pleased to ease this load by fortifying my spirit, that I may be strongest when I am weakest, and may be able to do and suffer every thing thou pleasest through Christ, who strengthens me. Lord, if thou wilt support me, I will for ever praise thee; if thou wilt suffer the load to press me yet more heavily, I will cry unto thee, and complain unto my God; and at last I will lie down and die, and by the mercies and intercession of the holy Jesus, and the conduct of thy blessed Spirit, and the ministry of angels, pass into those mansions where holy souls rest and weep no more. Lord, pity me; Lord, sanctify this my sickness; Lord, strengthen me; holy Jesus, save me and deliver me. Thou knowest how shamefully I have fallen with pleasure; in thy mercy and very pity, let me not fall with pain too. O let me never charge God foolishly, nor offend thee by my impatience and uneasy spirit, nor weaken the hands and hearts of those that charitably minister to my needs: but let me pass through the valley of tears and the valley of the shadow of death with safety and peace, with a meek spirit and a sense of the Divine mercies; and though thou breakest me in pieces, my hope is thou wilt gather me up in the gatherings of eternity. Grant this, eternal God, gracious Father, for the merits and intercession of our merciful High Priest, who once suffered for me, and for ever intercedes for me, our most gracious and ever-blessed Saviour Jesus.

A Prayer to be said when the Sick Man takes Physic.

O most blessed and eternal Jesus, thou who art the great Physician of our souls, and the Sun of righteousness arising with healing in thy wings, to thee is given by thy heavenly Father the government of all the world, and thou disposest every great and little accident to thy Father's honour, and to the good and comfort of them that love and serve thee; be pleased to bless the ministry of thy servant in order to my ease and health, direct his judgment, prosper the medicines, and dispose the chances of my sickness fortunately, that I may feel the blessing and loving-kindness of the Lord in the ease of my pain and the restitution of my health; that I, being restored to the society of the living, and to thy solemn assemblies, may praise thee and thy goodness secretly among the faithful, and in the congregation of thy redeemed ones here in the outer courts of the Lord, and hereafter in thy eternal temple for ever and ever. Amen.

SECT. III. *Of the Practice of the Grace of Faith in the Time of Sickness.*

NOW is the time in which faith appears most necessary and most difficult. It is the foundation of a good life, and the foundation of all our hopes; it is that without which we cannot live well, and without which we cannot die well; it is a grace that then we shall need to support our spirits, to sustain our hopes, to alleviate our sickness, to resist temptation, to prevent despair; upon the belief of the articles of our religion we can do the works of a holy life, but upon belief of the promises we can bear our sickness patiently, and die cheerfully. The sick man may practise it in the following instances.

1. Let the sick man be careful that he do not admit of any doubt concerning that which he believed and received from a common consent in his best health and days of election and religion. For if the devil can but prevail so far as to unfix and unrivet the resolution and confidence or fulness of assent, it is easy for him so to unwind the spirit, that from *why* to *whether or no*, from *whether or no* to *scarcely not*, from *scarcely not* to *absolutely not at all*, are steps of a descending and falling spirit; and whatsoever a man is made to doubt of by the weakness of his understanding in a sickness, it will be hard to get an instrument strong or subtle enough to reinforce and insure: for when the strengths are gone by which faith held, and it does not stand firm by the weight of its own bulk and great constitution, nor yet by the cordage of a tenacious root, then it is prepared for a ruin, which it cannot escape in the tempests of a sickness and the assaults of a devil. Discourse and argument, the line of tradition and a never-failing experience, the Spirit of God and the truth of miracles, the word of prophecy and the blood of martyrs, the excellency of the doctrine and the necessity of men, the riches of the promises and the wisdom of the revelations, the reasonableness and sublimity, the concordance and the usefulness, of the articles, and their compliance with all the needs of man and the government of com-

monwealths, are like the strings and branches of the roots by
which faith stands firm and unmovable in the spirit and understanding of a man.   But in sickness the understanding is
shaken, and the ground is removed in which the root did grap-
ple and support its trunk ;[1] and therefore, there is no way now
but that it be left to stand upon the old confidences, and by
the firmament of its own weight; it must be left to stand, because it always stood there before ; and as it stood all its life-
time in the ground of understanding, so it must now be supported with will and a fixed resolution.[2] But disputation
tempts it, and shakes it with trying, and overthrows it with
shaking. Above all things in the world, let the sick man fear
a proposition which his sickness hath put into him contrary to
the discourses of health and a sober, untroubled reason.

2. Let the sick man mingle the recital of his creed together
with his devotions, and in that let him account his faith ; not
in curiosity and factions, in the confessions of parties and interests :[3] for some over-forward zeals are so earnest to profess
their little and uncertain articles, and glory so to die in a particular and divided communion, that in the profession of their
faith they lose or discompose their charity.   Let it be enough
that we secure our interest of heaven, though we do not go
about to appropriate the mansions to our sect; for every good
man hopes to be saved, as he is a Christian, and not as he is a
Lutheran, or of another division.   However, those articles
upon which he can build the exercise of any virtue in his sickness, or upon the stock of which he can improve his present

---

[1] Non jam validis radicibus hærens, pondere fixa suo.   [2] Sanctius-
que ac reverentius visum de actis Deorum credere quàm scire.—Tacit.

[3] Fides tua te salvum faciet : non exercitatio Scripturarum. Fides in
regulâ posita est (scil. in Symbolo quod jam recitaverat); habes legem, c'.
salutem de observatione legis: exercitatio autem in curiositate consistit,
habens gloriam solam de peritiæ studio. Cedat curiositas fidei ; cedat
gloria saluti. — Tert. de Præscript.   S. Augustinus vocat symbolum
comprehensionem fidei vestræ atque perfectionem ; cordis signaculum,
et nostræ militiæ sacramentum.—Amb. lib. iii. de Veland. Virgin. Aug.
Serm. 115. Non per difficiles nos Deus ad beatam vitam quæstiones
vocat. In absoluto nobis et facili est æternitas; Jesum suscitatum à
mortuis per Deum credere, et ipsum esse Dominum confiteri.—St. Hilar.
lib. 10. de Trinit. Hæc est fides catholica, de symbolo suo dixit Atha-
nasius, vel quicunque auctor est St. Athanas. de Fide Niceâ.
Γὰρ ἐν αὐτῇ παρὰ τῶν πατέρων κατὰ τὰς θείας γραφὰς ὁμολογηθεῖσα
πίστις αὐτάρκης ἐστὶ πρὸς ἀνατροπὴν μὲν πάσης ἀσεβείας, σύστασιν δὲ
τῆς εὐσεβείας ἐν Χριστῷ. —Ep. ad Epict.

condition, are such as consist in the greatness and goodness, the veracity and mercy, of God through Jesus Christ; nothing of which can be concerned in the fond disputations which faction and interest hath too long maintained in Christendom.

3. Let the sick man's faith especially be active about the promises of grace, and the excellent things of the gospel; those which can comfort his sorrows and enable his patience; those upon the hopes of which he did the duties of his life, and for which he is not unwilling to die; such as the intercession and advocation of Christ, remission of sins, the resurrection, the mysterious arts and mercies of man's redemption, Christ's triumph over death and all the powers of hell, the covenant of grace, or the blessed issues of repentance; and, above all, the article of eternal life, upon the strength of which eleven thousand virgins went cheerfully together to their martyrdom, and twenty thousand Christians were burned by Dioclesian on a Christmas-day, and whole armies of Asian Christians offered themselves to the tribunals of Arius Antonius, and whole colleges of severe persons were instituted, who lived upon religion, whose dinner was the eucharist, whose supper was praise, and their nights were watches, and their days were labour; for the hope of which then men counted it gain to lose their estates, and gloried in their sufferings, and rejoiced in their persecutions, and were glad at their disgraces. This is the article that hath made all the martyrs of Christ confident and glorious; and if it does not more than sufficiently strengthen our spirits to the present suffering, it is because we understand it not, but have the appetites of beasts and fools. But if the sick man fixes his thoughts and sets his habitation to dwell here, he swells his hope, and masters his fears, and eases his sorrows, and overcomes his temptations.

4. Let the sick man endeavour to turn his faith of the articles into the love of them; and that will be an excellent instrument, not only to refresh his sorrows, but to confirm his faith in defiance of all temptations. For a sick man and a disturbed understanding are not competent and fit instruments to judge concerning the reasonableness of a proposition. But, therefore, let him consider and love it, because it is useful and necessary, profitable and gracious; and when he is once in love with it, and then also renews his love to it, when he feels the need of it, he is an interested person, and for his own

sake will never let it go, and pass into the shadows of doubting, or the utter darkness of infidelity. An act of love will
make him have a mind to it; and we easily believe what we
love, but very uneasily part with our belief, which we for so
great an interest have chosen and entertained with a great
affection.

5. Let the sick person be infinitely careful that his faith be
not tempted by any man, or any thing; and when it is in any
degree weakened, let him lay fast hold upon the conclusion,
upon the article itself, and by earnest prayer beg of God to
guide him in certainty and safety. For let him consider that
the article is better than all its contrary or contradictory, and
he is concerned that it be true, and concerned also that he do
believe it : but he can receive no good at all if Christ did not
die, if there be no resurrection, if his creed hath deceived him;
therefore all that he is to do is to secure his hold, which he
can do no way but by prayer and by his interest. And by
this argument or instrument it was that Socrates refreshed
the evil of his condition, when he was to drink his aconite.[4]
" If the soul be immortal, and perpetual rewards be laid up
for wise souls, then I lose nothing by my death : but if there
be not, then I lose nothing by my opinion ; for it supports my
spirit in my passage, and the evil of being deceived cannot
overtake me when I have no being." So it is with all that
are tempted in their faith. If those articles be not true, then
the men are nothing ; if they be true, then they are happy :
and if the articles fail, there can be no punishment for believing ; but if they be true, my not believing destroys all my portion in them, and possibility to receive the excellent things
which they contain. By faith we quench the fiery darts of
the devil ; but if our faith be quenched, wherewithal shall we
be able to endure the assault? Therefore seize upon the
article, and secure the great object, and the great instrument,
that is, the hopes of pardon and eternal life through Jesus
Christ ; and do this by all means, and by any instrument,
artificial or inartificial, by argument or by stratagem, by perfect resolution or by discourse, by the hand and ears of premises or the foot of the conclusion, by right or by wrong ; because we understand it, or because we love it, *super totam
materiam;* because I will, and because I ought ; because it is

[4] In Phædon.

safe to do so, and because it is not safe to do otherwise; because, if I do, I may receive a good; and because if I do not, I am miserable; either for that I shall have a portion of sorrows, or that I can have no portion of good things without it.

SECT. IV. *Acts of Faith, by way of Prayer and Ejaculation, to be said by Sick Men, in the Days of their Temptation.*

LORD, whither shall I go? Thou hast the words of eternal life. John vi. 68.

I believe in God the Father Almighty, and in Jesus Christ, his only Son, our Lord, &c.

And I believe in the Holy Ghost, &c.

Lord, I believe; help thou mine unbelief. Mark ix. 24.

I know and am persuaded by the Lord Jesus, that none of us liveth to himself, and no man dieth to himself: for whether we live, we live unto the Lord; and whether we die, we die unto the Lord: whether we live, therefore, or die, we are the Lord's. Rom. xiv. 14, 7, 8.

If God be for us, who can be against us? Rom. viii. 31—34.

He that spared not his own Son, but delivered him up for us all, how shall he not with him give us all things?

Who shall lay any thing to the charge of God's elect? It is God that justifieth. Who is he that condemneth? It is Christ that died; yea, rather, that is risen again, who is even at the right hand of God; who also maketh intercession for us.

If any man sin, we have an advocate with the Father, Jesus Christ the righteous; and he is the propitiation for our sins. 1 John ii. 1, 2.

This is a faithful saying, and worthy of all acceptation, that Jesus Christ came into the world to save sinners. 1 Tim. i. 15.

O grant that I may obtain mercy, that in me Jesus Christ may show forth all long-suffering, that I may believe in him to life everlasting.

I am bound to give thanks unto God alway, because God hath from the beginning chosen me to salvation, through sanctification of the Spirit, and belief of the truth, whereunto he called me by the gospel, to the obtaining of the glory of the Lord Jesus Christ. 2 Thess. ii. 13, 14, 16, 17.

Now our Lord Jesus Christ himself, and God even our Father, which hath loved us, and hath given us everlasting consolation, and good hope through grace, comfort my heart, and stablish me in every good word and work.

The Lord direct my heart into the love of God, and into the patient waiting for Christ.   2 Thess. iii. 5.

O that our God would count me worthy of this calling, and fulfil all the good pleasure of his goodness, and the work of faith with power; that the name of our Lord Jesus Christ may be glorified in me, and I in him, according to the grace of our God and the Lord Jesus Christ.   2 Thess. i. 11, 12.

Let us who are of the day be sober, putting on the breastplate of faith and love, and for a helmet the hope of salvation.   For God hath not appointed us to wrath, but to obtain salvation by our Lord Jesus Christ, who died for us, that whether we wake or sleep we should live together with him. Wherefore comfort yourselves together, and edify one another. 1 Thess. v. 8—10, 12.

There is no name under heaven whereby we can be saved, but only the name of the Lord Jesus.   Acts iv. 12.   And every soul which will not hear that prophet, shall be destroyed from among the people.   Acts iii. 23.

God forbid that I should glory save in the cross of Jesus Christ.   Gal. vi. 14.   I desire to know nothing but Jesus Christ and him crucified.   1 Cor. ii. 2.   For me to live is Christ, and to die is gain.   Phil. i. 21.

Cease ye from man, whose breath is in his nostrils; for wherein is he to be accounted of?   Isa. ii. 22.   But the just shall live by faith.   Hab. ii. 4.

Lord, I believe that thou art the Christ, the Son of God, John xi. 27; the Saviour of the world, John iv. 42; the resurrection and the life; and he that believeth in thee, though he were dead, yet shall he live, John xi. 25, 40.

Jesus said unto her, Said I not to thee, that if thou wouldest believe, thou shouldest see the glory of God?

O death, where is thy sting?   O grave, where is thy victory?   The sting of death is sin, and the strength of sin is the law.   But thanks be to God, who giveth us the victory through our Lord Jesus Christ.   Lord, make me stedfast and unmovable, always abounding in the work of the Lord; for I know that my labour is not in vain in the Lord.   1 Cor. xv. 55—58.

The Prayer for the Grace and Strengths of Faith.

O holy and eternal Jesus, who didst die for me and all mankind, abolishing our sin, reconciling us to God, adopting us into the portion of thine heritage, and establishing with us a covenant of faith and obedience, making our souls to rely upon spiritual strengths, by the supports of a holy belief, and the expectation of rare promises, and the infallible truths of God; O let me for ever dwell upon the rock, leaning upon thy arm, believing thy word, trusting in thy promises, waiting for thy mercies, and doing thy commandments; that the devil may not prevail upon me, and my own weaknesses may not abuse or unsettle my persuasions, nor my sins discompose my just confidence in thee and thy eternal mercies. Let me always be thy servant and thy disciple, and die in the communion of thy church, of all faithful people. Lord, I renounce whatsoever is against thy truth; and if secretly I have or do believe any false proposition, I do it in the simplicity of my heart and great weakness; and, if I could discover it, would dash it in pieces by a solemn disclaiming it; for thou art the way, the truth, and the life. And I know that whatsoever thou hast declared, that is the truth of God; and I do firmly adhere to the religion thou hast taught, and glory in nothing so much as that I am a Christian, that thy name is called upon me. O my God, though I die, yet will I put my trust in thee. In thee, O Lord, have I trusted; let me never be confounded. Amen.

SECT. V. *Of the Practice of the Grace of Repentance in the Time of Sickness.*

MEN generally do very much dread sudden death, and pray against it passionately: and certainly it hath in it great inconveniences accidentally to men's estates, to the settlement of families, to the culture and trimming of souls; and it robs a man of the blessings which may be consequent to sickness, and to the passive graces and holy contentions of a Christian, while he descends to his grave without an adversary or a trial;[1] and a good man may be taken at such a disadvantage, that a sudden death would be a great evil even to the most

[1] Descendisti ad Olympia, sed nemo præter te: coronam habes, victoriam non habes.

excellent person, if it strikes him in an unlucky circumstance. But these considerations are not the only ingredients into those men's discourse who pray violently against sudden deaths; for, possibly, if this were all, there may be in the condition of sudden death something to make recompence for the evils of the over-hasty accident.   For certainly it is a less temporal evil to fall by the rudeness of a sword than the violences of a fever, and the axe is a much less affliction than a strangury; and though a sickness tries our virtues, yet a sudden death is free from temptation; a sickness may be more glorious, and a sudden death more safe.   The deadest deaths are best, the shortest and least premeditate,[2] so Cæsar said; and Pliny called a short death the greatest fortune of a man's life.   For even good men have been forced to an indecency of deportment by the violences of pain:[3] and Cicero observes concerning Hercules, that he was broken in pieces with pain even then when he sought for immortality by his death, being tortured with a plague knit up in the lappet of his shirt.[4] And therefore as a sudden death certainly loses the rewards of a holy sickness, so it makes that a man shall not so much hazard and lose the rewards of a holy life.

But the secret of this affair is a worse matter; men live at that rate either of an habitual wickedness, or else a frequent repetition of single acts of killing and deadly sins, that a sudden death is the ruin of all their hopes, and a perfect consignation to an eternal sorrow.   But in this case also so is a lingering sickness: for our sickness may change us from life to health, from health to strength, from strength to the firmness and confirmation of habitual graces; but it cannot change a man from death to life, and begin and finish that process which sits not down but in the bosom of blessedness.   He that washes in the morning, when his bath is seasonable and healthful,[5] is not only made clean, but sprightly, and the blood is brisk and coloured like the first springing of the morning; but they that wash their dead cleanse the skin, and leave paleness upon the cheek, and stiffness in all the joints.   A repentance upon our

[2] Mitiùs ille perit subitâ qui mergitur undâ,
    Quàm sua qui liquidis brachia lassat aquis.—Ovid.
[3] Etiam innocentes mentiri cogit dolor.   [4] Ipse illigatus peste interimor textili.   [5] Lavor honestâ horâ et salubri, quæ mihi et calorem et sanguinem servet; rigere et pallere post lavacrum mortuus possum.—Tertul. Apol. c. 42.

death-bed is like washing the corpse: it is cleanly and civil; but makes no change deeper than the skin. But God knows, it is a custom so to wash them that are going to dwell with dust, and to be buried in the lap of their kindred earth,[6] but all their lives-time wallow in pollutions without any washing at all; or if they do, it is like that of the Dardani,[7] who washed but thrice all their life-time,—when they are are born, and when they marry, and when they die; when they are baptized, or against a solemnity, or for the day of their funeral; but these are but ceremonious washings, and never purify the soul if it be stained and hath sullied the whiteness of its baptismal robes.

God intended we should live a holy life; he contracted with us in Jesus Christ for a holy life; he made no abatements of the strictest sense of it,[8] but such as did necessarily comply with human infirmities or possibilities: that is, he understood it in the sense of repentance, which still is so to renew our duty, that it may be a holy life in the second sense; that is, some great portion of our life to be spent in living as Christians should. A resolving to repent upon our death-bed is the greatest mockery of God in the world, and the most perfect contradictory to all his excellent designs of mercy and holiness: for therefore he threatened us with hell if we did not, and he promised heaven if we did, live a holy life; and a late repentance promises heaven to us upon other conditions,[9] even when we have lived wickedly. It renders a man useless and intolerable to the world; taking off the great curb of religion, of fear and hope, and permitting all impiety with the greatest impunity and encouragement in the world. By this means we see so many παῖδας πολυχρονίους,[10] as Philo calls them, or, as the prophets, *pueros centum annorum*, children of almost a hundred years old, upon whose grave we may write the inscription which was upon the tomb of Similis in Xiphilin:[11]

[6] — Cognatâ fæce sepulti. [7] Δαρδανεῖς τοὺς ἀπὸ τῆς Ἰλλυρίδος ἀκούω τρὶς λούεσθαι μόνον παρὰ πάντα τὸν ἑαυτῶν βίον, ἐξ ὠδίνων, καὶ γαμοῦντας, καὶ ἀποθανόντας.—Ælian. lib. iv. Var. Hist. cap. 1.
[8] Vide Aug. lib. 5. Hom. iv. et Serm. 57, de Tempore. Faustum ad Paulinum, Ep. 1, in Biblioth. tom. 5. vet. edit. Concil. Arelat. i. c. 3. Carthag. 4. cap. 7, 8.
[9] —— Quis luce supremâ
Dimisisse meas serò non ingemit horas?—Sil. Ital. l. 15.
[10] Sic contra rerum naturæ munera nota, corvus maturis frugibus ova refert. [11] In Adrian. Σίμιλις μὲν ἐνταῦθα κεῖται, βιοῦς κατὰ ἔτη τόσα, ζήσας δὲ ἔτη ἑπτά

"Here he lies, who *was* so many years, but *lived* but seven." And the course of nature runs counter to the perfect designs of piety: and God, who gave us a life to live to him, is only served at our death when we die to all the world; and we undervalue the great promises made by the holy Jesus,[12] for which the piety, the strictest unerring piety of ten thousand ages, is not a proportionable exchange: yet we think it a hard bargain to get heaven, if we be forced to part with one lust, or live soberly twenty years: but, like Demetrius Afer, (who having lived a slave all his life-time, yet desiring to descend to his grave in freedom,[13] begged manumission of his lord,) we lived in the bondage of our sin all our days, and hope to die the Lord's freedmen. But, above all, this course of a delayed repentance must of necessity therefore be ineffective and certainly mortal, because it is an entire destruction of the very formality and essential constituent reason of religion: which I thus demonstrate.

When God made man, and propounded to him an immortal and a blessed state as the end of his hopes and the perfection of his condition, he did not give it him for nothing, but upon certain conditions; which, although they could add nothing to God, yet they were such things which man could value, and they were his best: and God had made appetites of pleasure in man, that in them the scene of his obedience should lie. For when God made instances of man's obedience, he, 1. either commanded such things to be done which man did naturally desire; or, 2. such things which contradict his natural desires; or, 3. such which were indifferent. Not the first and the last: for it could be no effect of love or duty towards God for a man to eat when he was impatiently hungry, and could not stay from eating; neither was it any contention of obedience or labour of love for a man to look eastward once a day, or turn his back when the north wind blew fierce and loud. Therefore, for the trial and instance of obedience, God made his laws so that they should lay restraint upon man's appetites, so that man might part with something of his own.

---

[12] Vide the Life of Christ, Disc. of Repentance; Rule of Holy Living chap. iv. Sect. of Repentance; and volume of Sermons, Serm. v. vi.

[13] Ne tamen ad Stygias famulus descenderet umbras,
   Ureret implicitum cùm scelerata lues,
   Cavimus ————

that he may give to God his will, and deny it to himself for the interest of his service: and chastity is the denial of a violent desire; and justice is parting with money that might help to enrich me; and meekness is a huge contradiction to pride and revenge; and the wandering of our eyes, and the greatness of our fancy, and our imaginative opinions, are to be lessened that we may serve God. There is no other way of serving God; we have nothing else to present unto him: we do not else give him any thing or part of ourselves; but when we for his sake part with what we naturally desire, and difficulty is essential to virtue, (and without choice there can be no reward, and in the satisfaction of our natural desires there is no election,) we run to them as beasts to the river or the crib. If, therefore, any man shall teach or practise such a religion that satisfies all our natural desires in the days of desires and passion, of lust and appetites, and only turns to God when his appetites are gone and his desires cease, this man hath overthrown the very being of virtues, and the essential constitution of religion: religion is no religion, and virtue is no act of choice, and reward comes by chance and without condition, if we only are religious when we cannot choose; if we part with our money when we cannot keep it; with our lust when we cannot act it; with our desires when they have left us. Death is a certain mortifier; but that mortification is deadly, not useful to the purposes of a spiritual life. When we are compelled to depart from our evil customs,[14] and leave to live that we may begin to live, then we die to die; that life is the prologue to death; and thenceforth we die eternally.

St. Cyril speaks of certain people that chose to worship the sun because he was a day god: for, believing that he was quenched every night in the sea, or that he had no influence upon them that light up candles, and lived by the light of fire, they were confident they might be atheists all night, and live as they list. Men who divide their little portion of time between religion and pleasures, between God and God's enemy, think that God is to rule but in his certain period of time, and that our life is the stage for passion and folly, and the day of death for the work of our life. But as to God both the day and night are alike, so are the first and last of our

[14] Cogimur à suetis animum suspendere rebus,
Atque ut vivamus, vivere desinimus.—Corn. Gall.

days: all are his due, and he will account severely with us for the follies of the first, and the evil of the last.   The evils and the pains are great which are reserved for those who defer their restitution to God's favour till their death.[15]   And therefore Antisthenes said well, "It is not the happy death, but the happy life, that makes man happy."   It is in piety as in fame and reputation: he secures a good name but loosely[16] that trusts his fame and celebrity only to his ashes; and it is more a civility than the basis of a firm reputation that men speak honour of their departed relatives; but if their life be virtuous, it forces honour from contempt, and snatches it from the hand of envy, and it shines through the crevices of detraction; and as it anointed the head of the living, so it embalms the body of the dead.[17]   From these premises it follows, that when we discourse of a sick man's repentance it is intended to be not a beginning, but the prosecution and consummation of the covenant of repentance which Christ stipulated with us in baptism, and which we needed all our life, and which we began long before this last arrest, and in which we are now to make further progress, that we may arrive to that integrity and fulness of duty, "that our sins may be blotted out, when the times of refreshing shall come from the presence of the Lord."[18]

SECT. VI. *Rules for the Practice of Repentance in Sickness.*

1. LET the sick man consider at what gate this sickness entered; and if he can discover the particular, let him instantly, passionately, and with great contrition, dash the crime in pieces, lest he descend into his grave in the midst of a sin, and thence remove into an ocean of eternal sorrow. But if he only suffers the common fate of man, and knows not the particular inlet, he is to be governed by the following measures.

2. Inquire into the repentance of thy former life particularly; whether it were of a great and perfect grief, and pro-

---

[15] Gnossius hæc Rhadamanthus habet durissima regna,
       Castigatque, auditque dolos, subigitque fateri
       Quæ quis apud superos furto lætatus inani
       Distulit in seram commissa piacula mortem.—Æneid. 6
[16] —— Cineri gloria sera venit.
[17] Tu mihi, quod rarum est, vivo sublime dedisti
       Nomen, ab exsequiis quod dare fama solet.
* Acts iii. 19.

ductive of fixed resolutions of holy living, and reductive of these to act; how many days and nights we have spent in sorrow or care, in habitual and actual pursuances of virtue; what instrument we have chosen and used for the eradication of sin; how we have judged ourselves, and how punished; and, in sum, whether we have by the grace of repentance changed our life from criminal to virtuous, from one habit to another; and whether we have paid for the pleasure of our sin by smart or sorrow, by the effusion of alms, or pernoctations or abodes in prayers, so as the spirit hath been served in our repentance as earnestly and as greatly as our appetites have been provided for in the days of our shame and folly.

3. Supply the imperfections of thy repentance by a general or universal sorrow for thy sins, not only since the last communion or absolution, but of thy whole life; for all sins, known and unknown, repented and unrepented, of ignorance or infirmity, which thou knowest, or which others have accused thee of; thy clamorous and thy whispering sins, the sins of scandal and the sins of a secret conscience, of the flesh and of the spirit: for it would be but a sad arrest to thy soul wandering in strange and unusual regions, to see a scroll of uncancelled sins represented and charged upon thee for want of care and notices, and that thy repentance shall become invalid because of its imperfections.

4. To this purpose it is usually advised by spiritual persons, that the sick man make an universal confession, or a renovation and repetition of all the particular confessions and accusations of his whole life; that now, at the foot of his account, he may represent the sum total to God and his conscience, and make provisions for their remedy and pardon according to his present possibilities.

5. Now is the time to make reflex acts of repentance: that as, by a general repentance, we supply the want of the just extension of parts, so by this we may supply the proper measures of the intention of degrees. In our health we can consider concerning our own acts, whether they be real or hypocritical, essential or imaginary, sincere or upon interest, integral or imperfect, commensurate or defective. And although it is a good caution of securities, after all our care and diligence still to suspect ourselves and our own deceptions, and for ever to beg of God pardon and acceptance in the

union of Christ's passion and intercession ; yet, in proper
speaking, reflex acts of repentance, being a suppletory after
the imperfection of the direct, are then most fit to be used
when we cannot proceed in and prosecute the direct actions.
To repent because we cannot repent, and to grieve because
we cannot grieve, was a device invented to serve the turn of
the mother of Peter Gratian; but it was used by her, and so
advised to be, in her sickness and last actions of repentance :
for in our perfect health and understanding, if we do not understand our first act we cannot discern our second ; and if
we be not sorry for our sins we cannot be sorry for want of
sorrows : it is a contradiction to say we can ; because want of
sorrow, to which we are obliged, is certainly a great sin ; and
if we can grieve for that, then also for the rest; if not for all,
then not for this. But in the days of weakness the case is
otherwise ; for then our actions are imperfect, our discourse
weak, our internal actions not discernible, our fears great, our
work to be abbreviated, and our defects to be supplied by
spiritual arts : and therefore it is proper and proportionate to
our state, and to our necessity, to beg of God pardon for the
imperfections of our repentance, acceptance of our weaker
sorrows, supplies out of the treasures of grace and mercy.
And thus repenting of the evil and unhandsome adherences
of our repentance, in the whole integrity of the duty it will
become a repentance not to be repented of.

6. Now is the time beyond which the sick man must at no
hand defer to make restitution of all his unjust possessions,[1]
or other men's rights, and satisfactions for all injuries and
violences, according to his obligation and possibilities : for
although many circumstances might impede the acting it in
our life-time, and it was permitted to be deferred in many
cases because by it justice was not hindered, and oftentimes
piety and equity were provided for; yet, because this is the
last scene of our life, he that does not act it so far as he can,
or put it into certain conditions and order of effecting, can
never do it again, and therefore then to defer it is to omit it,
and leaves the repentance defective in an integral and constituent part.

7. Let the sick man be diligent and watchful that the principle of his repentance be contrition, or sorrow for sins, com-

[1] Ou pendre, ou rendre, ou les peines d'enfer attendre.

menced upon the love of God.   For although sorrow for sins upon any motive may lead us to God by many intermedia. passages, and is the threshold of returning sinners; yet it is not good nor effective upon our death-bed; because repentance is not then to begin, but must then be finished and completed; and it is to be a supply and reparation of all the imperfections of that duty, and therefore it must by that time be arrived to contrition; that is, it must have grown from fear to love, from the passions of a servant to the affections of a son.   The reason of which (besides the precedent) is this, Because, when our repentance is in this state it supposes the man also in a state of grace, a well-grown Christian; for to hate sin out of the love of God is not the felicity of a new convert, or an infant grace (or if it be, that love also is in its infancy); but it supposes a good progress, and the man habitually virtuous, and tending to perfection: and therefore contrition, or repentance so qualified, is useful to great degrees of pardon, because the man is a gracious person, and that virtue is of good degree, and, consequently, a fit employment for him that shall work no more, but is to appear before his Judge to receive the hire of his day.   And if his repentance be contrition even before this state of sickness, let it be increased by spiritual arts and the proper exercises of charity.

Means of exciting Contrition, or Repentance of Sins, proceeding from the Love of God.

To which purpose the sick man may consider, and is to be reminded, (if he does not,) that there are in God all the motives and causes of amiability in the world: that God is so infinitely good: that there are some of the greatest and most excellent spirits of heaven, whose work, and whose felicity, and whose perfections, and whose nature it is, to flame and burn in the brightest and most excellent love: that to love God is the greatest glory of heaven: that in him there are such excellencies, that the smallest rays of them, communicated to our weaker understandings, are yet sufficient to cause ravishments, and transportations, and satisfactions, and joys unspeakable and full of glory: that all the wise Christians of the world know and feel such causes to love God: that they all profess themselves ready to die for the love of God, and the apostles and millions of the martyrs did die for him: and although it be harder to live in his love than to die for it, yet all the good people that ever gave their names to Christ did, for his love, endure the crucifying their lusts, the mortification of their appetites, the contradictions and death of their most passionate, natural desires: that kings and queens have quitted their diadems, and many married saints have turned their mutual vows into the love of Jesus, and married him only, keeping a virgin chastity in a married life, that they may more tenderly express their love to God: that all the good we have derives from God's love to us, and all the good we can hope for is the effect of his love, and can descend only upon them that love him: that by his love it is that we receive the Holy Jesus, and by his love we receive the Holy Spirit, and by his love we feel peace and joy within our spirits, and by his love we receive the mysterious sacrament. And what can be greater than that from the goodness and love of God we receive Jesus Christ, and the Holy Ghost, and adoption, and the inheritance of sons, and to be co-heirs with Jesus, and to have pardon of our sins, and a divine nature, and restraining grace, and the grace of sanctification, and rest and peace within us, and a certain expectation of glory? Who can choose but love him who, when we had provoked him exceedingly, sent his Son to die for us, that we might live with him; who does so desire to pardon us and save us, that he hath appointed his holy Son continually to intercede for us? that his love is so great, that he offers us great kindness, and entreats us to be happy, and makes many decrees in heaven concerning the interests of our soul, and the very provision and support of our persons, that he sends an angel to attend upon every of his servants, and to be their guard and their guide in all their dangers and hostilities: that for our sakes he restrains the devil, and puts his mightiness in fetters and restraints, and chastises his malice with decrees of grace and safety: that he it is who makes all the creatures serve us, and takes care of our sleeps, and preserves all plants and elements, all minerals and vegetables, all beasts and birds, all fishes and insects, for food to us, and for ornament, for physic and instruction, for variety and wonder, for delight and for religion: that as God is all good in himself, and all good to us, so sin is directly contrary to God, to reason, to religion, to safety, and pleasure, and felicity; that it is a great dishonour to a man's spirit to

have been made a fool by a weak temptation and an empty
lust; and to have rejected God, who is so rich, so wise, so
good, and so excellent, so delicious, and so profitable to us:
that all the repentance in the world of excellent men does end
in contrition, or a sorrow for sins, proceeding from the love of
God; because they that are in the state of grace do not fear
hell violently; and so long as they remain in God's favour,
although they suffer the infirmities of men, yet they are God's
portion; and therefore all the repentance of just and holy men,
which is certainly the best, is a repentance not for lower ends,
but because they are the friends of God, and they are full of
indignation that they have done an act against the honour of
their patron, and their dearest Lord and Father: that it is a
huge imperfection and a state of weakness to need to be moved
with fear or temporal respects; and they that are so, as yet
are either immerged in the affections of the world or of themselves; and those men that bear such a character, are not yet
esteemed laudable persons, or men of good natures, or the sons
of virtue: that no repentance can be lasting that relies upon
any thing but the love of God; for temporal motives may
cease, and contrary contingencies may arise, and fear of hell
may be expelled by natural or acquired hardnesses, and is
always the least when we have most need of it and most cause
for it; for the more habitual our sins are, the more cauterized
our conscience is, the less is the fear of hell, and yet our
danger is much the greater: that although fear of hell or other
temporal motives may be the first inlet to a repentance, yet
repentance, in that constitution and under those circumstances,
cannot obtain pardon, because there is in that no union with
God, no adhesion to Christ, no endearment of passion or of
spirit, no similitude or conformity to the great instrument of
our peace, our glorious Mediator: for as yet a man is turned
from his sin, but not converted to God; the first and last of
our returns to God being love, and nothing but love; for obedience is the first part of love, and fruition is the last; and
because he that does not love God cannot obey him, therefore
he that does not love him cannot enjoy him.

Now that this may be reduced to practice, the sick man may
be advertised, that in the actions of repentance he separate
low, temporal, sensual, and self-ends from his thoughts, and
so do his repentance that he may still reflect honour upon God;

2 F

that he confess his justice in punishing, that he acknowledge himself to have deserved the worst of evils ; that he heartily believe and profess, that if he perish finally, yet that God ought to be glorified by that sad event, and that he hath truly merited so intolerable a calamity : that he also be put to make acts of election and preference, professing that he would willingly endure all temporal evils, rather than be in the disfavour of God or in the state of sin ; for, by this last instance, he will be quitted from the suspicion of leaving sin for temporal respects, because he, by an act of imagination or feigned presence of the object to him, entertains the temporal evil that he may leave the sin : and, therefore, unless he be a hypocrite, does not leave the sin to be quit of the temporal evil. And as for the other motive, of leaving sin out of the fear of hell, because that is an evangelical motive conveyed to us by the Spirit of God, and is immediate to the love of God, if the schoolmen had pleased, they might have reckoned it as the handmaid, and of the retinue of contrition : but the more the considerations are sublimed above this, of the greater effect and the more immediate to pardon will be the repentance.

8. Let the sick persons do frequent actions of repentance, by way of prayer for all those sins which are spiritual, and in which no restitution or satisfaction material can be made, and whose contrary acts cannot in kind be exercised. For penitential prayers in some cases are the only instances of repentance that can be. An envious man, if he gives God hearty thanks for the advancement of his brother, hath done an act of mortification of his envy, as directly as corporal austerities are an act of chastity, and an enemy to uncleanness : and if I have seduced a person that is dead or absent, if I cannot restore him to sober counsels by my discourse and undeceiving him, I can only repent of that by way of prayer : and intemperance is no way to be rescinded or punished by a dying man but by hearty prayers. Prayers are a great help in all cases ; in some they are proper acts of virtue, and direct enemies to sin : but although alone and in long continuance they alone can cure some one or some few little habits, yet they can never alone change the state of the man : and therefore are intended to be a suppletory to the imperfections of other acts : and by that reason are the proper and most pertinent employment of a clinic or death-bed penitent.

9. In those sins whose proper cure is mortification corporal, the sick man is to supply that part of his repentance by a patient submission to the rod of sickness: for sickness does the work of penances, or sharp afflictions and dry diet, perfectly well: to which if we also put our wills, and make it our act by an after-election, by confessing the justice of God, by bearing it sweetly, by begging it may be medicinal, there is nothing wanting to the perfection of this part, but that God confirm our patience and hear our prayers. When the guilty man runs to punishment,[2] the injured person is prevented, and hath no whither to go but to forgiveness.

10. I have learned but of one suppletory more for the perfection and proper exercise of a sick man's repentance; but it is such a one as will go a great way in the abolition of our past sins and making our peace with God, even after a less severe life; and that is, that the sick man do some heroical actions in the matter of charity or religion, of justice or severity. There is a story of an infamous thief, who, having begged his pardon of the emperor Mauricius, was yet put into the hospital of St. Samson, where he so plentifully bewailed his sins in the last agonies of his death, that the physician who attended him found him unexpectedly dead, and over his face a handkerchief bathed in tears; and soon after, somebody or other pretended to a revelation of this man's beatitude. It was a rare grief that was noted in this man, which begot in that age a confidence of his being saved; and that confidence (as things then went) was quickly called a revelation. But it was a stranger severity which is related by Thomas Cantipratanus concerning a young gentleman condemned for robbery and violence, who had so deep a sense of his sin, that he was not content with a single death, but begged to be tormented, and cut in pieces joint by joint, with intermedial senses, that he might, by such a smart, signify a greater sorrow. Some have given great estates to the poor and to religion; some have built colleges for holy persons; many have suffered martyrdom; and though those that died under the conduct of the Maccabees, in defence of their country and religion, had pendants on their breasts consecrated to the idols of the Jamnenses; yet that they gave their lives in such a cause with so great a duty, (the biggest things they could

[2] Quid debent læsi facere, ubi rei ad pœnam confugiunt?

2 F 2

do or give,) it was esteemed to prevail hugely towards the pardon and acceptation of their persons. An heroic action of virtue is a huge compendium of religion: for if it be attained to by the usual measures and progress of a Christian from inclination to act, from act to habit, from habit to abode, from abode to reigning, from reigning to perfect possession, from possession to extraordinary emanations, that is, to heroic actions, then it must needs do the work of man, by being so great towards the work of God: but if a man comes thither *per saltum*, or on a sudden, (which is seldom seen,) then it supposes the man always well inclined, but abused by accident or hope, by confidence or ignorance; then it supposes the man for the present in a great fear of evil, and a passionate desire of pardon; it supposes his apprehensions great and his time little; and what the event of that will be no man can tell; but it is certain that to some purposes God will account for our religion on our death-bed, not by the measures of our time, but the eminency of affection (as said Celestine the First);[3] that is, supposing the man in the state of grace, or in the revealed possibility of salvation, then an heroical act hath the reward of a longer series of good actions in an even and ordinary course of virtue.

11. In what can remain for the perfecting of a sick man's repentance, he is to be helped by the ministries of a spiritual guide.

SECT. VII. *Acts of Repentance, by way of Prayer and Ejaculation, to be used especially by Old Men in their Age, and by all Men in their Sickness.*

LET us search and try our ways, and turn again to the Lord. Let us lift up our hearts with our hands unto God in the heavens. We have transgressed and rebelled; and thou hast not pardoned. Thou hast covered with anger and persecuted us; thou hast slain, thou hast not pitied. O cover not thyself with a cloud, but let our prayer pass through. Lam. iii. 40—44.

I have sinned: what shall I do unto thee, O thou preserver of men? Why hast thou set me as a mark against thee, so that I am a burden to myself? And why dost not thou par-

---

[3] Vera ad Deum conversio in ultimis positorum mente potiùs est æstimanda quàm tempore.—Cel. P. ep. ii. c. 9. Vera conversio scil. ab infidelitate ad fidem Christi per baptismum.

don my transgression, and take away mine iniquity? for now shall I sleep in the dust, and thou shalt seek me in the morning, but I shall not be. Job vii. 20, 21.

The Lord is righteous; for I have rebelled against his commandments. Hear, I pray, all ye people, behold my sorrow. Behold, O Lord, I am in distress: my bowels are troubled: my heart is turned within me; for I have grievously rebelled. Lam. i. 18, 40.

Thou, O Lord, remainest for ever; thy throne from generation to generation. Wherefore dost thou forget us for ever, and forsake us so long time? Turn thou us unto thee, O Lord, and so shall we be turned; renew our days as of old. O reject me not utterly, and be not exceeding wroth against thy servant. Lam. v. 19—22.

O remember not the sins of my youth, nor my transgressions; but according to thy mercies remember thou me, for thy goodness' sake, O Lord. Psalm xxv. 7. Do thou for me, O God the Lord, for thy name's sake; because thy mercy is good, deliver thou me. For I am poor and needy, and my heart is wounded within me. I am gone like the shadow that declineth; I am tossed up and down as the locust. Psalm cix. 21—23.

Then Zaccheus stood forth, and said, Behold, Lord, half of my goods I give to the poor; and if I have wronged any man I restore him fourfold. Luke xix. 8.

Hear my prayer, O Lord, and consider my desire. Psalm cxliii. 1. Let my prayer be set forth in thy sight as the incense, and let the lifting up of my hands be an evening sacrifice. Psalm cxli. 2. And enter not into judgment with thy servant; for in thy sight shall no man living be justified. Teach me to do the thing that pleaseth thee, for thou art my God; let thy loving Spirit lead me forth into the land of righteousness. Psalm cxliii. 2, 10.

I will speak of mercy and judgment; unto thee, O Lord, will I make my prayer. I will behave myself wisely in a perfect way. Oh when wilt thou come unto me? I will walk in my house with a perfect heart. I will set no wicked thing before mine eyes: I hate the work of them that turn aside; it shall not cleave to me. Psalm ci. 1—3.

Hide thy face from my sins, and blot out all mine iniquities. Create in me a clean heart, O God, and renew a right spirit within me.   Deliver me from blood-guiltiness, O God, from malice, envy, the follies of lust, and violences of passion, &c., thou God of my salvation; and my tongue shall sing aloud of thy righteousness.   Psalm li. 9, 10, 14.

The sacrifice of God is a broken heart: a broken and a contrite heart, O God, thou wilt not despise.   Ver. 17.

Lord, I have done amiss; I have been deceived; let so great a wrong as this be removed, and let it be so no more.

The Prayer for the Grace and Perfection of Repentance.

I.

O Almighty God, thou art the great Judge of all the world, the Father of our Lord Jesus Christ, the Father of mercies, the Father of men and angels; thou lovest not that a sinner should perish, but delightest in our conversion and salvation, and hast, in our Lord Jesus Christ, established the covenant of repentance, and promised pardon to all them that confess their sins and forsake them: O my God, be thou pleased to work in me what thou hast commanded should be in me. Lord, I am a dry tree, who neither have brought forth fruit unto thee and unto holiness, nor have wept out salutary tears, the instrument of life and restitution, but have behaved myself like an unconcerned person in the ruins and breaches of my soul; but, O God, thou art my God, early will I seek thee: my soul thirsteth for thee in a barren and thirsty land where no water is.[1] Lord, give me the grace of tears and pungent sorrow; let my heart be as a land of rivers of waters, and my head a fountain of tears; turn my sin into repentance, and let my repentance proceed to pardon and refreshment.

II.

Support me with thy graces, strengthen me with thy Spirit, soften my heart with the fire of thy love and the dew of heaven, with penitential showers; make my care prudent, and the remaining portion of my days like the perpetual watches of the night, full of caution and observance, strong and resolute, patient and severe.   I remember, O Lord, that I did sin with greediness and passion, with great desires and an unabated choice; O let me be as great in my repentance as ever I have been in my calamity and shame; let my hatred of sin

[1] Psal. lxiii 1.

be as great as my love to thee, and both as near to infinite as my proportion can receive.

III.

O Lord, I renounce all affection to sin, and would not buy my health nor redeem my life with doing any thing against the laws of my God, but would rather die than offend thee. O dearest Saviour, have pity upon thy servant; let me, by thy sentence, be doomed to perpetual penance during the abode of this life ; let every sigh be the expression of a repentance, and every groan an accent of spiritual life, and every stroke of my disease a punishment of my sin and an instrument of pardon ; that at my return to the land of innocence and pleasure, I may eat of the votive sacrifice of the supper of the Lamb, that was, from the beginning of the world, slain for the sins of every sorrowful and returning sinner. O grant me sorrow here and joy hereafter, through Jesus Christ, who is our hope, the resurrection of the dead, the justifier of a sinner, and the glory of all faithful souls. Amen.

A Prayer for Pardon of Sins, to be said frequently in time of Sickness, and in all the portions of Old Age.

I.

O eternal and most gracious Father, I humbly throw myself down at the foot of thy mercy-seat upon the confidence of thy essential mercy, and thy commandment that we should come boldly to the throne of grace, that we may find mercy in time of need. O my God, hear the prayers and cries of a sinner who calls earnestly for mercy. Lord, my needs are greater than all the degrees of my desire can be; unless thou hast pity upon me, I perish infinitely and intolerably ; and then there will be one voice fewer in the choir of singers who shall recite thy praises to eternal ages. But, O Lord, in mercy deliver my soul. O save me for thy mercy's sake.[2] For in the second death there is no remembrance of thee : in that grave, who shall give thee thanks ?

II.

O just and dear God, my sins are innumerable; they are upon my soul in multitudes ; they are a burden too heavy for

---

[2] Psal. vi. 4, 5.

me to bear; they already bring sorrow and sickness, shame
and displeasure, guilt and a decaying spirit, a sense of thy
present displeasure and fear of worse, of infinitely worse.
But it is to thee so essential, so delightful, so usual, so desired
by thee to show mercy, that although my sin be very great,
and my fear proportionable, yet thy mercy is infinitely greater
than all the world, and my hope and my comfort rise up in
proportions towards it, that I trust the devils shall never be
able to reprove it, nor my own weakness discompose it. Lord,
thou hast sent thy Son to die for the pardon of my sins ; thou
hast given me thy Holy Spirit as a seal of adoption to consign
the article of remission of sins : thou hast, for all my sins,
still continued to invite me to conditions of life by thy ministers the prophets; and thou hast, with variety of holy acts,
softened my spirit, and possessed my fancy, and instructed
my understanding, and bended and inclined my will, and directed or overruled my passions, in order to repentance and
pardon : and why should not thy servant beg passionately,
and humbly hope for, the effects of all these thy strange and
miraculous acts of loving-kindness ? Lord, I deserve it not,
but I hope thou wilt pardon all my sins : and I beg it of thee
for Jesus Christ's sake, whom thou hast made the great endearment of thy promises, and the foundation of our hopes,
and the mighty instrument whereby we can obtain of thee
whatsoever we need and can receive.

III.

O my God, how shall thy servant be disposed to receive
such a favour, which is so great that the ever-blessed Jesus
did die to purchase it for us ; so great that the fallen angels
never could hope, and never shall obtain it ? Lord, I do from
my soul forgive all that have sinned against me: O forgive
me my sins, as I forgive them that have sinned against me.
Lord, I confess my sins unto thee daily by the accusations and
secret acts of conscience ; and if we confess our sins, thou hast
called it a part of justice to forgive us our sins, and to cleanse
us from all unrighteousness. Lord, I put my trust in thee ;
and thou art ever gracious to them that put their trust in
thee. I call upon my God for mercy ; and thou art always
more ready to hear than we to pray. But all that I can do,
and all that I am, and all that I know of myself, is nothing but

sin, and infirmity, and misery : therefore I go forth of myself, and throw myself wholly into the arms of thy mercy, through Jesus Christ, and beg of thee for his death and passion's sake, by his resurrection and ascension, by all the parts of our redemption, and thy infinite mercy, in which thou pleasest thyself above all the works of the creation, to be pitiful and compassionate to thy servant in the abolition of all my sins : so shall I praise thy glories with a tongue not defiled with evil language, and a heart purged by thy grace, quitted by thy mercy, and absolved by thy sentence from generation to generation. Amen.

An Act of holy Resolution of Amendment of Life, in case of Recovery.

O most just and most merciful Lord God, who hast sent evil diseases, sorrow and fear, trouble and uneasiness, briers and thorns, into the world, and planted them in our houses, and round about our dwellings, to keep sin from our souls, or to drive it thence ; I humbly beg of thee that this my sickness may serve the ends of the spirit, and be a messenger of spiritual life, an instrument of reducing me to more religious and sober courses. I say, O Lord, that I am unready and unprepared in my accounts, having thrown away great portions of my time in vanity, and set myself hugely back in the accounts of eternity, and I had need live my life over again, and live it better ; but thy counsels are in the great deep, and thy footsteps in the water ; and I know not what thou wilt determine of me. If I die, I throw myself into the arms of the holy Jesus, whom I love above all things ; and if I perish, I know I have deserved it ; but thou wilt not reject him that loves thee. But if I recover, I will live, by thy grace and help, to do the work of God, and passionately pursue my interest of heaven, and serve thee in the labour of love with the charities of a holy zeal, and the diligence of a firm and humble obedience. Lord, I will dwell in thy temple and in thy service ; religion shall be my employment, and alms shall be my recreation, and patience shall be my rest, and to do thy will shall be my meat and drink, and to live shall be Christ, and then to die shall be gain.

" O spare me a little, that I may recover my strength before I go hence, and be no more seen." "Thy will be done on earth as it is in heaven." Amen.

SECT. VIII. *An Analysis or Resolution of the Decalogue, and the special Precepts of the Gospel, describing the Duties enjoined, and the Sins forbidden respectively; for the Assistance of Sick Men in making their Confessions to God and his Ministers, and the rendering their Repentance more particular and perfect.*

I. Comm. *Thou shalt have none other Gods but me.*

Duties commanded are, 1. To love God above all things. 2. To obey him and fear him. 3. To worship him with prayers, vows, thanksgivings, presenting to him our souls and bodies, and all such actions and expressions, which the consent of nations, or the laws and customs of the place where we live, have appropriated to God. 4. To design all to God's glory. 5. To inquire after his will. 6. To believe all his word. 7. To submit to his providence. 8. To proceed towards all our lawful ends by such means as himself hath appointed. 9. To speak and think honourably of God, and recite his praises, and confess his attributes and perfections.

They sin against this commandment, 1. Who love themselves or any of the creatures inordinately and intemperately. 2. They that despise or neglect any of the Divine precepts. 3. They that pray to unknown or false gods. 4. They that disbelieve or deny there is a God. 5. They that make vows to creatures. 6. Or say prayers to the honour of men, or women, or angels; as Paternosters to the honour of the Virgin Mary, or St. Peter, which is a taking a part of that honour which is due to God, and giving it to the creature; it is a religion paid to men and women out of God's proper portion, out of prayers directed to God immediately; and it is an act contrary to that religion, which makes God the last end of all things; for this, through our addresses to God, passes something to the creatures as if they stood beyond him; for by the intermedial worship paid to God, they ultimately do honour to the man or angel. 7. They that make consumptive oblations to the creatures; as the Collyridians who offered cakes, and those that burnt incense or candles to the Virgin Mary. 8. They that give themselves to the devil, or make contracts with him and use fantastic conversation with him.

9. They that consult witches and fortune-tellers 10. They that rely upon dreams and superstitious observances. 11. That use charms, spells, superstitious words and characters, verses of psalms, the consecrated elements, to cure diseases, to be shot-free, to recover stolen goods, or inquire into secrets. 12. That are wilfully ignorant of the laws of God, or love to be deceived in their persuasions that they may sin with confidence. 13. They that neglect to pray to God. 14. They that arrogate to themselves the glory of any action or power, and do not give the glory to God, as Herod. 15. They that doubt of or disbelieve any article of the Creed, or any proposition of Scripture, or put false glosses to serve secular or vicious ends, against their conscience, or with violence any way done to their reason. 16. They that violently or passionately pursue any temporal end with an eagerness greater than the thing is in prudent account. 17. They that make religion to serve ill ends, or do good to evil purposes, or evil to good purposes. 18. They that accuse God of injustice or unmercifulness, remissness or cruelty; such as are the presumptuous and the desperate. 19. All hypocrites and pretenders to religion, walking in forms and shadows, but denying the power of godliness. 20. All impatient persons; all that repine or murmur against the prosperities of the wicked, or the calamities of the godly, or their own afflictions. 21. All that blaspheme God, or speak dishonourable things of so sacred a Majesty. 22. They that tempt God, or rely upon his protection against his rules, and without his promise and besides reason, entering into danger, from which, without a miracle, they cannot be rescued. 23. They that are bold in the midst of judgment, and fearless in the midst of the Divine vengeance and the accents of his anger.

II. Comm. *Thou shalt not make to thyself any graven image, nor worship it.*

The moral duties of this commandment are, 1. To worship God with all bodily worship and external forms of address, according to the custom of the church we live in. 2. To believe God to be a spiritual and pure substance, without any visible form or shape. 3. To worship God in ways of his own appointing, or by his proportions, or measures of nature, and right reason, or public and holy customs

AN ANALYSIS OR EXPLICATION

They sin against this commandment, 1. That make any image or pictures of the Godhead, or fancy any likeness to him. 2. They that use images in their religion, designing or addressing any religious worship to them; for if this thing could be naturally tolerable, yet it is too near an intolerable for a jealous God to suffer. 3. They that deny to worship God with lowly reverence of their bodies, according as the church expresses her reverence to God externally. 4. They that invent or practise superstitious worshippings, invented by man against God's word, or without reason, or besides the public customs or forms of worshipping, either foolishly or ridiculously, without the purpose of order, decency, proportion to a wise or a religious end, in prosecution of some virtue or duty.

III. Comm. *Thou shalt not take God's name in vain.*

The duties of this commandment are, 1. To honour and revere the most holy name of God. 2. To invocate his name directly, or by consequence, in all solemn and permitted adjurations or public oaths. 3. To use all things and persons, upon whom his name is called or any ways imprinted, with a regardful and separate manner of usage, different from common, and far from contempt and scorn. 4. To swear in truth and judgment.

They sin against this commandment, 1. Who swear vainly and customarily, without just cause, without competent authority. 2. They that blaspheme or curse God. 3. They that speak of God without grave cause or solemn occasion. 4. They that forswear themselves, that is, they that do not perform their vows to God, or that swear, or call God to witness, to a lie. 5. They that swear rashly or maliciously to commit a sin or an act of revenge. 6. They that swear by any creature falsely, or any way but as it relates to God, and consequently invokes his testimony. 7. All curious inquirers into the secrets, and intruders into the mysteries and hidden things, of God. 8. They that curse God, or curse a creature by God. 9. They that profane churches, holy utensils, holy persons, holy customs, holy sacraments. 10. They that provoke others to swear voluntarily and by design, or incuriously or negligently, when they might avoid it. 11. They that swear to things uncertain and unknown.

IV. Comm. *Remember that thou keep holy the Sabbath day.*

The duties of this commandment are, 1. To set apart some portions of our time for the immediate offices of religion and glorification of God. 2. This is to be done according as God or his holy church hath appointed. 3. One day in seven is to be set apart. 4. The Christian day is to be subrogated into the place of the Jews' day: the resurrection of Christ and the redemption of man was a greater blessing than to create him. 5. God on that day to be worshipped and acknowledged as our Creator and as our Saviour. 6. The day to be spent in holy offices, in hearing Divine service, public prayers, frequenting the congregations, hearing the word of God read or expounded, reading good books, meditation, alms, reconciling enmities, remission of burdens and of offences, of debts and of work; friendly offices, neighbourhood, and provoking one another to good works; and to this end all servile works must be omitted, excepting necessary and charitable offices to men or beasts, to ourselves or others.

They sin against this commandment, 1. That do, or compel or entice others to do, servile works without the cases of necessity or charity, to be estimated according to common and prudent accounts. 2. They that refuse or neglect to come to the public assemblies of the church, to hear and assist at the Divine offices entirely. 3. They that spend the day in idleness, forbidden or vain recreations, or the actions of sin and folly. 4. They that buy and sell without the cases of permission. 5. They that travel unnecessary journeys. 6. They that act or assist in contentions or lawsuits, markets, fairs, &c. 7. They that on that day omit their private devotion, unless the whole day be spent in public. 8. They that by any cross or contradictory actions against the customs of the church, do purposely desecrate or unhallow and make the day common; as they that, in despite and contempt, fast upon the Lord's day, lest they may celebrate the festival after the manner of the Christians.

V. Comm. *Honour thy father and thy mother.*

The duties are, 1. To do honour and reverence to, and to love our natural parents. 2. To obey all their domestic commands, for in them the scene of their authority lies. 3. To give them maintenance and support in their needs. 4. To obey kings and all that are in authority. 5. To pay tribute and honours, custom and reverence. 6. To do reverence to the aged and all our betters. 7. To obey our masters, spiritual governors and guides, in those things which concern their several respective interest and authority.

They sin against this commandment, 1. That despise their parents' age or infirmity. 2. That are ashamed of their poverty and extraction. 3. That publish their vices, errors, and infirmities, to shame them. 4. That refuse and reject all or any of their lawful commands. 5. Children that marry without or against their consent, when it may be reasonably obtained. 6. That curse them from whom they receive so many blessings. 7. That grieve the souls of their parents by not complying in their desires, and observing their circumstances. 8. That hate their persons, that mock them or use uncomely jestings. 9. That discover their nakedness voluntarily. 10. That murmur against their injunctions, and obey them involuntarily. 11. All rebels against their kings, or the supreme power, where it is legally and justly invested. 12. That refuse to pay tributes and impositions imposed legally. 13. They that disobey their masters, murmur or repine against their commands, abuse or deride their persons, talk rudely, &c. 14. They that curse the king in their heart, or speak evil of the ruler of their people. 15. All that are uncivil and rude towards aged persons, mockers and scorners of them.[1]

VI. Comm. *Thou shalt do no murder.*

The duties are, 1. To preserve our own lives, the lives of our relatives, and all with whom we converse, (or who can need us, and we assist,) by prudent, reasonable, and wary defences, advocations, discoveries of snares, &c. 2. To preserve our health, and the integrity of our bodies and minds, and of others. 3. To preserve and follow peace with all men.

They sin against this commandment, 1. That destroy the life of a man or woman, himself, or any other. 2. That do violence to, or dismember, or hurt, any part of the body with

---

[1] Credebant hoc grande nefas et morte piandum,
Si juvenis vetulo non assurrexerat, et si
Barbato cuicunque puer.   Juven. Sat. 13.

evil intent.   3. That fight duels, or commence unjust wars.
4. They that willingly hasten their own or others' death.   5.
That by oppression or violence embitter the spirits of any, so
as to make their life sad and their death hasty.   6. They
that conceal the dangers of their neighbour, which they can
safely discover.   7. They that sow strife and contention
among neighbours.   8. They that refuse to rescue or preserve those whom they can, and are obliged to preserve.   9.
They that procure abortion.   10. They that threaten, or
keep men in fears, or hate them.

VII. Comm.   Thou shalt not commit adultery.

The duties are, 1. To preserve our bodies in the chastity of
a single life, or of marriage.   2. To keep all the parts of our
bodies in the care and severities of chastity, so that we be
restrained in our eyes as well as in our feet.

They sin against this commandment, 1. Who are adulterous,
incestuous, sodomitical, or commit fornication.   2. They that
commit folly alone, dishonouring their own bodies with softness and wantonness.   3. They that immoderately let loose
the reins of their bolder appetite, though within the protection
of marriage.   4. They that by wanton gestures, wandering
eyes, lascivious dressings, discovery of the nakedness of themselves or others, filthy discourse, high diet, amorous songs,
balls and revellings, tempt and betray themselves or others to
folly.   5. They that marry a woman divorced for adultery.
6. They that divorce their wives, except for adultery, and
marry another.

VIII. Comm.   Thou shalt not steal.

The duties are, 1. To give every man his due.   2. To permit every man to enjoy his own goods and estate quietly.

They sin against this commandment, 1. That injure any
man's estate by open violence or by secret robbery, by stealth
or cozenage, by arts of bargaining or vexatious lawsuits.   2.
That refuse or neglect to pay their debts when they are able.
3. That are forward to run into debt knowingly beyond their
power, without hopes or purposes of repayment.   4. Oppressors of the poor.   5. That exact usury of necessitous persons, or of any beyond the permissions of equity, as determined
by the laws   6. All sacrilegious persons, people that rob

God of his dues or of his possessions.   7. All that game, viz. at cards and dice, &c., to the prejudice and detriment of other men's estates.   8. They that embase coin and metals, and obtrude them for perfect and natural.   9. That break their promises to the detriment of a third person.   10. They that refuse to stand to their bargains.   11. They that by negligence imbecile other men's estates, spoiling or letting any thing perish which is intrusted to them.   12. That refuse to restore the pledge.

IX. Comm.   *Thou shalt not bear false witness.*

The duties are, 1. To give testimony to truth, when we are called to it by competent authority.   2. To preserve the good name of our neighbours.   3. To speak well of them that deserve it.

They sin against this commandment, 1. That speak false things in judgment, accusing their neighbour unjustly or denying his crime publicly when they are asked, and can be commanded lawfully to tell it.   2. Flatterers; and, 3. Slanderers; 4. Backbiters; and, 5. Detractors.   6. They that secretly raise jealousies and suspicion of their neighbours causelessly.

X. Comm.   *Thou shalt not covet.*

The duties are, 1. To be content with the portion God hath given us.   2. Not to be covetous of other men's goods.

They sin against this commandment, 1. That envy the prosperity of other men.   2. They that desire passionately to be possessed of what is their neighbour's.   3. They that with greediness pursue riches, honours, pleasures, and curiosities. 4. They that are too careful, troubled, distracted, or amazed, affrighted and afflicted, with being solicitous in the conduct of temporal blessings.

These are the general lines of duty by which we may discover our failings and be humbled, and confess accordingly: only the penitent person is to remember, that although these are the kinds of sins described after the sense of the Jewish church, which consisted principally in the external action or the deed done, and had no restraints upon the thoughts of men, save only in the tenth commandment, which was mixed, and did relate as much to action as to thought (as appears in the instances); yet upon us Christians there are many circumstances and degrees of obligation, which endear our duty with greater severity and observation : and the penitent is to account of himself and enumerate his sins, not only by external actions or the deed done, but by words and by thoughts ; and so to reckon, if he have done it directly or indirectly, if he have caused others to do it, by tempting or encouraging, by assisting or counselling, by not dissuading when he could and ought, by fortifying their hands or hearts, or not weakening their evil purposes : if he have designed or contrived its action, desired it or loved it, delighted in the thought, remembered the past sin with pleasure or without sorrow ; these are the by-ways of sin, and the crooked lanes, in which a man may wander and be lost, as certainly as in the broad high-ways of iniquity.

But besides this, our blessed Lord and his apostles have added divers other precepts ; some of which have been with some violence reduced to the decalogue, and others have not been noted at all in the catalogues of confession. I shall therefore describe them entirely, that the sick man may discover his failings, that, by the mercies of God in Jesus Christ, and by the instrument of repentance, he may be presented pure and spotless before the throne of God.

The Special Precepts of the Gospel.

1. Prayer, frequent, fervent, holy, and persevering.[1] 2. Faith.[2] 3. Repentance.[3] 4. Poverty of spirit, as opposed to ambition and high designs.[4] 5. And in it is humility, or sitting down in the lowest place, and in giving honour to go before another.[5] 6. Meekness, as it is opposed to waywardness, fretfulness, immoderate grieving, disdain, and scorn.[6] 7. Contempt of the world. 8. Prudence, or the advantageous conduct of religion.[7] 9. Simplicity, or sincerity in words and actions, pretences and substances.[7] 10. Hope.[8] 11. Hearing the word.[9] 12. Reading.[10] 13. Assembling together.[11] 14. Obeying them that have the rule over us in spiritual affairs.[12]

---

[1] 1 Thess. v. 17; Luke xviii. 1.   [2] Mark xvi. 16.   [3] Luke xiii. 3; Acts iii. 19.   [4] Matt. v. 3.   [5] Luke xiv. 10; John xiii. 14. [6] Matt. v. 5; Col. iii. 12.   [7] Matt. x. 16; 1 Thess. v. 8.   [8] Rom viii. 24.   [9] Luke xvi. 29; Mark iv. 24.   [10] 1 Tim. iv. 13 [11] Heb. x. 25.   [12] Heb. xiii. 17; Matt. xviii. 17.

15. Refusing to communicate with persons excommunicate; whither also may be reduced, to reject heretics.[14] 16. Charity:[15] viz. Love to God above all things;[16] brotherly kindness, or profitable love to our neighbours as ourselves, to be expressed in alms, forgiveness,[17] and to die for our brethren.[18] 17. To pluck out the right eye, or violently to rescind all occasions of sins, though dear to us as an eye.[19] 18. To reprove our erring brother.[20] 19. To be patient in afflictions:[21] and longanimity is referred hither, or long-sufferance;[22] which is the perfection and perseverance of patience, and is opposed to hastiness and weariness of spirit. 20. To be thankful to our benefactors; but above all, in all things to give thanks to God.[23] 21. To rejoice in the Lord always.[24] 22. Not to quench,[25] not to grieve,[26] not to resist the Spirit.[27] 23. To love our wives as Christ loved his church, and to reverence our husbands.[28] 24. To provide for our families.[29] 25. Not to be bitter to our children.[30] 26. To bring them up in the nurture and admonition of the Lord.[31] 27. Not to despise prophesying.[32] 28. To be gentle, and easy to be entreated.[33] 29. To give no scandal or offence.[34] 30. To follow after peace with all men, and to make peace.[35] 31. Not to go to law before the unbelievers.[36] 32. To do all things that are of good report, or the actions of public honesty,[37] abstaining from all appearances of evil.[38] 33. To convert souls, or turn sinners from the error of their ways.[39] 34. To confess Christ before all the world.[40] 35. To resist unto blood, if God calls us to it.[41] 36. To rejoice in tribulation for Christ's sake.[42] 37. To remember and show forth the Lord's death till his second coming,[43] by celebrating the Lord's supper.[44] 38. To believe all the New Testament.[45] 39. To add nothing to St. John's

---

[13] 2 Thess. iii. 6; 2 John 10.   [14] Titus iii. 10.   [15] Col. iii. 14; 1 Tim. i. 5; 2 Tim. ii. 22.   [16] Mark xii. 30.   [17] Matt. vi. 14. [18] 1 John iii. 16.   [19] Matt. xviii. 9.   [20] Matt. xviii. 15.   [21] James i. 4; Luke xxi. 19.   [22] Heb. xii. 3; Gal. vi. 9.   [23] Eph. v. 20; 2 Thess. i. 3; Luke vi. 32; 2 Tim. iii. 2.   [24] 1 Thess. v. 16; Phil. iii. 1, and iv. 4.   [25] 1 Thess. v. 19.   [26] Eph. iv. 30.   [27] Acts vii. 51.   [28] Eph. v. 33.   [29] 1 Tim. v. 8.   [30] Col. iii. 21. [31] Eph. vi. 4.   [32] 1 Thess. v. 20.   [33] 2 Tim. ii. 24.   [34] Matt. xviii. 7; 1 Cor. x. 32.   [35] Heb. xii. 14.   [36] 1 Cor. vi, 1.   [37] Phil iv. 8; 2 Cor. viii. 21.   [38] 1 Thess. v. 22.   [39] James v. 19, 20. [40] Matt. x. 32.   [41] Heb. xii. 4.   [42] Matt. v. 12; James i. 2. [43] Luke xxii. 19.   [44] 1 Cor. xi. 26.   [45] John xx. 30, 31; Acts iii. 23; Mark i. 1; Luke x. 16.

last book, that is, to pretend to no new revelations.[46]   40. To keep the customs of the church, her festivals and solemnities ; lest we be reproved, as the Corinthians were by St. Paul, " We have no such customs, nor the churches of God."[47]   41. To contend earnestly for the faith.[48]   Not to be contentious in matters not concerning the eternal interest of our souls : but in matters indifferent to have faith to ourselves.[49]   42. Not to make schisms or divisions in the body of the church.[50] 43. To call no man master upon earth, but to acknowledge Christ our master and lawgiver.[51]   44. Not to domineer over the Lord's heritage.[52]   45. To try all things, and keep that which is best.[53]   46. To be temperate in all things.[54]   47. To deny ourselves.[55]   48. To mortify our lusts and their instruments.[56]   49. To lend, looking for nothing again, nothing by way of increase, nothing by way of recompence.[57]   50. To watch and stand in readiness against the coming of the Lord.[58] 51. Not to be angry without cause.[59]   52. Not at all to revile.[60]   53. Not to swear.[61]   54. Not to respect persons.[62] 55. To lay hands suddenly on no man.[63]   [This especially pertains to bishops ; to whom also, and to all the ecclesiastical order, it is enjoined that they preach the word,[64] that they be instant in season and out of season, that they rebuke, reprove, exhort with all long-suffering and doctrine.]   56. To keep the Lord's day (derived into an obligation from a practice apostolical).   57. To do all things to the glory of God.[65]   58. To hunger and thirst after righteousness and its rewards.[66] 59. To avoid foolish questions.[67]   60. To pray for persecutors, and to do good to them that persecute us, and despitefully use us.[68]   61. To pray for all men.[69]   62. To maintain good works for necessary uses.[70]   63. To work with our hands, that we be not burdensome to others, avoiding idleness.[71]   64. To be perfect as our heavenly Father is perfect.[72]   65. To be liberal and frugal ; for he that will call us to account for our time,

[46] Rev. xxii. 18.   [47] 1 Cor. xi. 16.   [48] Jude 3.   [49] Rom. xiv. 13, 22.   [50] Rom. xvi. 17.   [51] Matt. xxiii. 8—10.   [52] 1 Pet. v. 3.   [53] 1 John iv. 1 ; 1 Thess. v. 21.   [54] 1 Cor. ix. 25 ; Tit. ii. 2.   [55] Matt. xvi. 24.   [56] Col. iii. 5 ; Rom. viii. 13.   [57] Luke vi. 35.   [58] Matt. xxiv. 42.   [59] Matt. v. 22.   [60] 1 Cor. vi. 10. [61] Matt. v. 34.   [62] James ii. 1.   [63] 1 Tim. v. 22.   [64] 2 Tim. iv. 2.   [65] 1 Cor. x. 31.   [66] Matt. v. 6.   [67] Tit. iii. 9 [68] Matt. v. 44 ; Rom. xii. 14.   [69] 1 Tim. ii. 1.   [70] Tit. iii. 14. [71] Eph. iv. 28.   [72] Matt. v. 48.

will also for the spending our money.[73]   66. Not to use uncomely jestings.[74]   67. Modesty; as opposed to boldness, to
curiosity, to indecency.[75]   68. To be swift to hear, slow to
speak.[76]   69. To worship the holy Jesus at the mention of his
holy name; as of old God was at the mention of Jehovah.[77]

These are the straight lines of Scripture, by which we may
also measure our obliquities, and discover crooked walking.
If the sick man hath not done these things, or if he have done
contrary to any of them in any particular, he hath cause enough
for his sorrow and matter for his confession; of which he
needs no other forms, but that he heartily deplore and plainly
enumerate his follies, as a man tells the sad stories of his own
calamity.

SECT. IX. *Of the Sick Man's Practice of Charity and Justice, by way of Rule.*

1. LET the sick man set his house in order before he die;
state his cases of conscience, reconcile the fractures of his family, reunite brethren, cause right understandings, and remove
jealousies; give good counsels for the future conduct of their
persons and estates, charm them into religion by the authority
and advantages of a dying person; because the last words of
a dying man are like the tooth of a wounded lion, making a
deeper impression in the agony than in the most vigorous
strength.[1]

2. Let the sick man discover every secret of art, or profit,
physic, or advantage to mankind, if he may do it without the
prejudice of a third person.[2]   Some persons are so uncharita-
bly envious, that they are willing that a secret receipt should
die with them, and be buried in their grave, like treasure in
the sepulchre of David.   But this, which is a design of charity, must therefore not be done to any man's prejudice; and
the mason of Herodotus, the king of Egypt, who kept secret
his notice of the king's treasure, and when he was dying told
his son, betrayed his trust then, when he should have kept it
most sacredly for his own interest.   In all other cases let thy

---

[73] 1 Pet. iii. 8; 2 Pet. i. 6, 7; 2 Cor. viii. 7; ix. 5.   [74] Eph. v. 4.
[75] 1 Tim. ii. 9.   [76] James i. 19.   [77] Phil. ii. 10.
[1] Magnifica verba mors prope admota excutit.
[2] Nam veræ voces tum demum pectore ab imo
    Ejiciuntur.   Lucret. iii. 57.

charity outlive thee, that thou mayest rejoice in the mansion
of rest, because, by thy means, many living persons are eased
or advantaged.

3. Let him make his will with great justice and piety, that
is, that the right heirs be not defrauded for collateral respects,
fancies, or indirect fondnesses; but the inheritances descend
in their legal and due channel; and in those things where we
have a liberty, that we take the opportunity of doing virtuously,
that is, of considering how God may be best served by our
donatives, or how the interest of any virtue may be promoted;
in which we are principally to regard the necessities of our
nearest kindred and relatives, servants and friends.

4. Let the will or testament be made with ingenuity, openness, and plain expression,[3] that he may not entail a lawsuit
upon his posterity and relatives, and make them lose their
charity, or entangle their estates, or make them poorer by the
gift. He hath done me no charity, but dies in my debt, that
makes me sue for a legacy.

5. It is proper for the state of sickness, and an excellent
aneling us to burial, that we give alms in this state, so bu-
rying treasure in our graves, that will not perish, but rise
again in the resurrection of the just. Let the dispensation of
our alms be as little intrusted to our executors as may be,
excepting the lasting and successive portions;[4] but, with our
own present care, let us exercise the charity and secure the
stewardship.[5] It was the custom amongst the old Greeks to
bury horses, clothes, arms, and whatsoever was dear to the
deceased person, supposing they might need them, and that
without clothes they should be found naked by their judges;
and all the friends did use to bring gifts,[6] by such liberality
thinking to promote the interest of their dead. But we may
offer our ἐντάφια ourselves best of all;[7] our doles and funeral
meals, if they be our own early provisions, will then spend the

---

[3] Δεῖ δὲ καὶ τὴν βασιλείαν μὲ ἤδη σαφηνίσαντα καταλιπεῖν, ὡς ἂν μὴ
ἀμφίλογος γενομένη, πράγματα ὑμῖν παράσχῃ.—Cyrus apud Xenoph. l.
viii. Institut.   [4] Lucian. de Luctu.
[5] Vide reg. 6, paulo infr. Herodot. Musa 5. Plin. lib. iv. cap. 11
Xiphilin. in Severo.
[6] Ἀλλὰ, κόραι, τῷ παιδὶ λεχῶϊα δῶρα φέρουσαι,
Θερμὰ κατὰ ψυχροῦ δάκρυα χεῖτε τάφου.—Nicarchus.
[7] Fallax sæpe fides, testataque vota peribunt:
Constitues tumulum, si sapis, ipse tuum.

better; and it is good so to carry our passing penny in our
hand, and, by reaching that hand to the poor, make a friend
in the everlasting habitations. He that gives with his own
hand shall be sure to find it, and the poor shall find it;[8] but
he that trusts executors with his charity, and the economy and
issues of his virtue, by which he must enter into his hopes of
heaven and pardon, shall find but an ill account when his executors complain he died poor. Think on this. To this purpose, wise and pious was the counsel of Salvian:[9] "Let a dying
man, who hath nothing else of which he may make an effective
oblation, offer up to God of his substance; let him offer it with
compunction and tears, with grief and mourning, as knowing
that all our oblations have their value not by the price, but by
the affection; and it is our faith that commendeth the money,
since God receives the money by the hands of the poor, but
at the same time gives, and does not take the blessing; because he receives nothing but his own, and man gives that
which is none of his own, that of which he is only a steward,
and shall be accountable for every shilling. Let it therefore
be offered humbly, as a creditor pays his debts; not magnifi-
cally, as a prince gives a donative; and let him remember that
such doles do not pay for the sin, but they ease the punishment: they are not proper instruments of redemption, but instances of supplication and advantages of prayer; and when we
have done well, remember that we have not paid our debt, but
shown our willingness to give a little of the vast sum we owe;
and he that gives plentifully according to the measure of his
estate, is still behind-hand according to the measure of his sins.
Let him pray to God that this late oblation may be accepted;
and so it will, if it sails to him in a sea of penitential tears or
sorrows that it is so little, and that it is so late.

6. Let the sick man's charity be so ordered that it may not

---

[8] Man, the behobpth oft to habe this in mind,
That thow gebeth wpth thin hond, that sall thow fynd.
For widowes be sloful, and chpldren beth unkpnd,
Executors beth cobctos, and kep al that thep fynd.
If enp bodp esk wher the deddps goodps becam.
                    They answer,
So God me help and Halidam, he died a poor man.
                    Think on this.
Written upon a wall in St. Edmund's Church in Lombard Street
                    Contra Avaritiam.

come only to deck the funeral and make up the pomp, charity waiting like one of the solemn mourners; but let it be continued, that, besides the alms of health and sickness, there may be a rejoicing in God for his charity long after his funerals, so as to become more beneficial and less public; that the poor may pray in private, and give God thanks many days together. This is matter of prudence, and yet in this we are to observe the same regards which we had in the charity and alms of our lives; with this only difference, that, in the funeral alms also of rich and able persons, the public customs of the church are to be observed, and decency and solemnity, and the expectations of the poor, and matter of public opinion, and the reputation of religion; in all other cases let thy charity consult with humility and prudence, that it never minister at all to vanity, but be as full of advantage and usefulness as it may.

7. Every man will forgive a dying person; [10] and therefore let the sick man be ready and sure, if he can, to send to such persons whom he hath injured, and beg their pardon, and do them right; for in this case he cannot stay for an opportunity of convenient and advantageous reconcilement; he cannot then spin out a treaty, nor beat down the price of composition, nor lay a snare to be quit from the obligation and coercion of laws; but he must ask forgiveness downright, and make him amends as he can, being greedy of making use of this opportunity of doing a duty that must be done, but cannot any more, if not now, until time returns again and tells the minutes backwards, so that yesterday shall be reckoned in the portions of the future.

8. In the intervals of sharper pains, when the sick man amasses together all the arguments of comfort and testimonies of God's love to him and care of him, he must needs find infinite matter of thanksgiving and glorification of God; and it is a proper act of charity and love to God, and justice too, that he do honour to God on his death-bed for all the blessings of his life, not only in general communications, but those by which he hath been separate and discerned from others, or supported and blessed in his own person; such as are, "In all my life-time I never broke a bone; I never fell into the

---

[10] Πρὸς τὸν τελευτήσανθ' ἕκαστος, κἂν σφόδρα ἂν ἐχθρὸς ᾖ τις, γίγνεταί φίλος τότε.

hands of robbers, never into public shame, or into noisome
diseases; I have not begged my bread, nor been tempted by
great and unequal fortunes; God gave me a good understanding, good friends, or delivered me in such a danger, and heard
my prayers in such particular pressures of my spirit." This
or the like enumeration and consequent acts of thanksgiving
are apt to produce love to God and confidence in the day of
trial; for he that gave me blessings in proportion to the state
and capacities of my life, I hope also will do so in proportion
to the needs of my sickness and my death-bed. This we find
practised, as a most reasonable piece of piety, by the wisest of
the heathens. So Antipater Tarsensis gave God thanks for
his prosperous voyage into Greece; and Cyrus made a handsome prayer upon the tops of the mountains when, by a fan-
tasm, he was warned of his approaching death. "Receive, O
God my Father, these holy rites, by which I put an end to
many and great affairs; and I give thee thanks for thy celestial signs and prophetic notices, whereby thou hast signified
to me what I ought to do, and what I ought not. I present
also very great thanks that I have perceived and acknowledged your care of me, and have never exalted myself above
my condition for any prosperous accident. And I pray that
you will grant felicity to my wife, my children, and friends,
and to me a death such as my life hath been." But that of
Philagrius, in Gregory Nazianzen, is eucharistical; but it relates more especially to the blessings and advantages which
are accidentally consequent to sickness. "I thank thee, O
Father, and Maker of all thy children, that thou art pleased
to bless and to sanctify us even against our wills, and by the
outward man purgest the inward, and leadest us through
cross-ways to a blessed ending, for reasons best known unto
thee." However, when we go from our hospital and place of
little intermedial rest in our journey to heaven, it is fit that
we give thanks to the Major-domo for our entertainment.—
When these parts of religion are finished according to each
man's necessity, there is nothing remaining of personal duty
to be done alone, but that the sick man act over these virtues
by the renewings of devotion and in the way of prayer; and
that is to be continued as long as life, and voice, and reason
dwel' with us.

SECT. X. *Acts of Charity by way of Prayer and Ejaculation: which may also be used for Thanksgiving in case of Recovery.*

O MY soul, thou hast said unto the Lord, Thou art my Lord; my goodness extendeth not to thee, but to the saints that are in the earth, and to the excellent, in whom is all my delight. The Lord is the portion of my inheritance and of my cup; thou maintainest my lot. Psalm xvi. 2, 3, 5.

As for God, his way is perfect: the word of the Lord is tried; he is a buckler to all those that trust in him. For who is God, except the Lord? or who is a rock, save our God? It is God that girdeth me with strength and maketh my way perfect. Psalm xviii. 30—32.

Be not thou far from me, O Lord; O my strength, haste thee to help me. Psalm xxii. 19.

Deliver my soul from the sword, my darling from the power of the dog. Save me from the lion's mouth; and thou hast heard me, also, from among the horns of the unicorns Ver. 20, 21.

I will declare thy name unto my brethren; in the midst of the congregation will I praise thee. Ver. 22.

Ye that fear the Lord, praise the Lord; ye sons of God, glorify him, and fear before him, all ye sons of men. For he hath not despised nor abhorred the affliction of the afflicted, neither hath he hid his face from him; but when he cried unto him, he heard. Ver. 23, 24.

As the hart panteth after the water-brooks, so longeth my soul after thee, O God. Psalm xlii. 1.

My soul thirsteth for God, for the living God; when shall I come and appear before the Lord? Ver. 2.

O my God, my soul is cast down within me. All thy waves and billows are gone over me. As with a sword in my bones I am reproached. Yet the Lord will command his loving-kindness in the day-time; and in the night his song shall be with me, and my prayer unto the God of my life. Ver. 6—8, 10.

Bless ye the Lord in the congregations; even the Lord from the fountains of Israel. Psalm lxviii. 26.

My mouth shall show forth thy righteousness and thy salvation all the day; for I know not the numbers thereof. Psalm lxxi. 15.

I will go in the strength of the Lord God; I will make mention of thy righteousness, even of thine only. O God, thou hast taught me from my youth; and hitherto have I declared thy wondrous works. But I will hope continually, and will yet praise thee more and more. Ver. 16, 17, 14.

Thy righteousness, O God, is very high, who hast done great things. O God, who is like unto thee? Thou which hast showed me great and sore troubles, shalt quicken me again, and shalt bring me up again from the depths of the earth. Ver. 19, 20.

Thou shalt increase thy goodness towards me, and comfort me on every side. Ver. 21.

My lips shall greatly rejoice when I sing unto thee; and my soul which thou hast redeemed. Blessed be the Lord God, the God of Israel, who only doth wondrous things. And blessed be his glorious name for ever; and let the whole earth be filled with his glory. Amen, Amen. Ver. 23. Psalm lxxii. 18, 19.

I love the Lord because he hath heard my voice and my supplication. The sorrows of death compassed me: I found trouble and sorrow. Then called I upon the name of the Lord; O Lord, I beseech thee, deliver my soul. Gracious is the Lord and righteous; yea, our God is merciful. Psalm cxvi. 1, 3—5.

The Lord preserveth the simple; I was brought low and he helped me. Return to thy rest, O my soul: the Lord hath dealt bountifully with me. For thou hast delivered my soul from death, mine eyes from tears, and my feet from falling. Ver. 6—8.

Precious in the sight of the Lord is the death of his saints. O Lord, truly I am thy servant; I am thy servant, and the son of thine handmaid: thou shalt loose my bonds. Ver. 15, 16.

He that loveth not the Lord Jesus, let him be accursed. 1 Cor. xvi. 22.

O that I might love thee as well as ever any creature loved thee! He that dwelleth in love dwelleth in God. There is no fear in love. 1 John iv. 16, 18.

The Prayer.

O most gracious and eternal God and loving Father, who

hast poured out thy bowels upon us, and sent the Son of thy love unto us to die for love, and to make us dwell in love, and the eternal comprehensions of thy Divine mercies, O, be pleased to inflame my heart with a holy charity towards thee and all the world. Lord, I forgive all that ever have offended me, and beg that both they and I may enter into the possession of thy mercies, and feel a gracious pardon from the same fountain of grace; and do thou forgive me all the acts of scandal whereby I have provoked, or tempted, or lessened, or disturbed any person. Lord, let me never have my portion amongst those that divide the union, and disturb the peace, and break the charities, of the church and Christian communion. And though I am fallen into evil times, in which Christendom is divided by the names of an evil division, yet I am in charity with all Christians, with all that love the Lord Jesus and long for his coming; and I would give my life to save the soul of any of my brethren; and I humbly beg of thee that the public calamity of the several societies of the church may not be imputed to my soul to any evil purposes.

II.

Lord, preserve me in the unity of thy holy church, in the love of God and of my neighbours. Let thy grace enlarge my heart to remember, deeply to resent, faithfully to use, wisely to improve, and humbly to give thanks to thee for all thy favours with which thou hast enriched my soul, and supported my estate, and preserved my person, and rescued me from danger, and invited me to goodness in all the days and periods of my life. Thou hast led me through it with an excellent conduct; and I have gone astray after the manner of men; but my heart is towards thee. O, do unto thy servant as thou usest to do unto those that love thy name: let thy truth comfort me; thy mercy deliver me; thy staff support me; thy grace sanctify my sorrow; and thy goodness pardon all my sins; thy angels guide me with safety in this shadow of death, and thy most Holy Spirit lead me into the land of righteousness, for thy name's sake, which is so comfortable, and for Jesus Christ's sake, our dearest Lord and most gracious Saviour. Amen.

CHAP. V. THE VISITATION OF THE SICK; OR THE
    ASSISTANCE THAT IS TO BE DONE TO DYING
    PERSONS BY THE MINISTRY OF THEIR CLERGY
    GUIDES.

SECTION I.

GOD, who hath made no new covenant with dying persons
distinct from the covenant of the living, hath also appointed
no distinct sacraments for them, no other manner of usages
but such as are common to all the spiritual necessities of living
and healthful persons. In all the days of our religion, from
our baptism to the resignation and delivery of our soul, God
hath appointed his servants to minister to the necessities, and
eternally to bless, and prudently to guide, and wisely to judge
concerning souls; and the Holy Ghost, that anointing from
above, descends upon us in several effluxes, but ever by the
ministries of the church. Our heads are anointed with that
sacred unction, baptism, (not in ceremony, but in real and proper effect,) our foreheads in confirmation, our hands in ordin-
ations, all our senses in the visitation of the sick; and all by
the ministry of especially deputed and instructed persons;
and we, who all our life-time derive blessings from the fountains of grace by the channels of ecclesiastical ministries, must
do it then especially, when our needs are most pungent and
actual. 1. We cannot give up our names to Christ, but the
holy man that ministers in religion must enrol them, and present the persons and consign the grace: when we beg for
God's Spirit, the minister can best present our prayers, and
by his advocation hallow our private desires and turn them
into public and potent offices. 2. If we desire to be established and confirmed in the grace and religion of our baptism,
the holy man whose hands are anointed by a special ordina-
tion to that and its symbolical purposes, lays his hands upon
the catechumen, and the anointing from above descends by
that ministry. 3. If we would eat the body and drink the
blood of our Lord, we must address ourselves to the Lord's
table, and he that stands there to bless and to minister can
reach it forth and feed thy soul; and without his ministry
thou canst not be nourished with that heavenly feast, nor thy
body consigned to immortality, nor thy soul refreshed with

the sacramental bread from heaven except by spiritual suppletories in cases of necessity and an impossible communion.
4. If we have committed sins, the spiritual man is appointed
to restore us, and to pray for us, and to receive our confessions, and to inquire into our wounds, and to infuse oil and
remedy, and to pronounce pardon. 5. If we be cut off from
the communion of the faithful by our own demerits, their holy
hands must reconcile us and give us peace; they are our appointed comforters, our instructors, our ordinary judges: and,
in the whole, what the children of Israel begged of Moses,[1]
—that God would no more speak to them alone, but by his
servant Moses, lest they should be consumed,—God, in compliance with our infirmities, hath of his own goodness established as a perpetual law in all ages of Christianity, that God
will speak to us by his ministers, and our solemn prayers
shall be made to him by their advocation, and his blessings
descend from heaven by their hands, and our offices return
thither by their presidencies, and our repentance shall be
managed by them, and our pardon in many degrees ministered
by them; God comforts us by their sermons, and reproves us
by their discipline, and cuts off some by their severity, and
reconciles others by their gentleness, and relieves us by their
prayers, and instructs us by their discourses, and heals our
sicknesses by their intercession presented to God, and united
to Christ's advocation: and in all this they are no causes, but
servants of the will of God, instruments of the Divine grace
and order, stewards and dispensers of the mysteries, and appointed to our souls to serve and lead, and to help in all accidents, dangers, and necessities.

And they who received us in our baptism are also to carry
us to our grave, and to take care that our end be as our life
was or should have been:[2] and therefore it is established as
an apostolical rule, "Is any man sick among you? let him
send for the elders of the church, and let them pray over
him," &c.[3]

The sum of the duties and offices respectively implied in
these words is in the following rules.

---

[1] Exod. xx. 19.   [2] Οἷόν περ αἰῶνα δεδώκατε, τοιαύτην και
τελευτὴν δοῦναι.—Xenoph. περὶ παιδ. lib. viii.   [3] James v. 14.

SECT. II. *Rules for the Manner of Visitation of Sick Persons.*

1. LET the minister of religion be sent to, not only against the agony or death, but be advised with in the whole conduct of the sickness; for in sickness indefinitely, and therefore in every sickness, and therefore in such which are not mortal, which end in health, which have no agony or final temptations, St. James gives the advice; and the sick man, being bound to require them, is also tied to do it, when he can know them, and his own necessity. It is a very great evil, both in the matter of prudence and piety, that they fear the priest as they fear the embalmer or the sexton's spade; and love not to converse with him unless they can converse with no man else; and think his office so much to relate to the other world that he is not to be treated with while we hope to live in this; and, indeed, that our religion be taken care of only when we die: and the event is this, (of which I have seen some sad experience,) that the man is deadly sick, and his reason is useless, and he is laid to sleep, and his life is in the confines of the grave, so that he can do nothing towards the trimming of his lamp; and the curate shall say a few prayers by him, and talk to a dead man, and the man is not in a condition to be helped, but in a condition to need it hugely. He cannot be called upon to confess his sins, and he is not able to remember them, and he cannot understand an advice, nor hear a free discourse, nor be altered from a passion, nor cured of his fear, nor comforted upon any grounds of reason or religion, and no man can tell what is likely to be his fate; or, if he does, he cannot prophesy good things concerning him, but evil. Let the spiritual man come when the sick man can be conversed withal and instructed, when he can take medicine and amend, when he understands or can be taught to understand the case of his soul, and the rules of his conscience; and then his advice may turn into advantage: it cannot otherwise be useful.

2. The intercourses of the minister with the sick man have so much variety in them that they are not to be transacted at once; and therefore they do not well that send once to see the good man with sorrow, and hear him pray, and thank him, and dismiss him civilly, and desire to see his face no more.

To dress a soul for funeral is not a work to be despatched at one meeting: at first he needs a comfort, and anon something to make him willing to die; and by and by he is tempted to impatience, and that needs a special cure; and it is a great work to make his confessions well and with advantages; and it may be the man is careless and indifferent, and then he needs to understand the evil of his sin, and the danger of his person; and his cases of conscience may be so many and so intricate that he is not quickly to be reduced to peace, and one time the holy man must pray, and at another time he must exhort, a third time administer the holy sacrament; and he that ought to watch all the periods and little portions of his life, lest he should be surprised and overcome, had need be watched when he is sick, and assisted and called upon and reminded of the several parts of his duty in every instant of his temptation. This article was well provided for among the easterlings, for the priests in their visitations of a sick person did abide in their attendance and ministry for seven days together. The want of this makes the visitations fruitless, and the calling of the clergy contemptible, while it is not suffered to imprint its proper effects upon them that need it in a lasting ministry.

3. St. James advises that when a man is sick he should send for the elders,[4] one sick man for many presbyters; and so did the eastern churches,[5] they sent for seven: and, like a college of physicians, they ministered spiritual remedies, and sent up prayers like a choir of singing clerks. In cities they might do so while the Christians were few and the priests many. But when they that dwelt in the *pagi* or villages ceased to be pagans, and were baptized, it grew to be an impossible felicity, unless in few cases, and to some more eminent persons: but, because they need it most, God hath taken care that they may best have it; and they that can, are not very prudent if they neglect it.

4. Whether they be many or few that are sent to the sick person, let the curate of his parish, or his own confessor, be amongst them: that is, let him not be wholly advised by strangers who know not his particular necessities; but he that is the ordinary judge cannot safely be passed by in his extraordinary necessity, which in so great portions depends upon his whole life past: and it is a matter of suspicion, when

[4] James v. 14.   [5] Gabriel in iv. sent. dist. 23.

we decline his judgment that knows us best, and with whom
we formerly did converse either by choice or by law, by private election or public constitution.   It concerns us then to
make severe and profitable judgments, and not to conspire
against ourselves, or procure such assistances which may
handle us softly, or comply with our weaknesses more than
relieve our necessities.

5. When the ministers of religion are come, first let them
do their ordinary offices, that is, pray for grace to the sick
man, for patience, for resignation ; for health, if it seems good
to God in order to his great ends.   For that is one of the
ends of the advice of the apostle.   And therefore the minister is to be sent for not while the case is desperate, but before
the sickness is come to its crisis or period.   Let him discourse
concerning the causes of sickness, and by a general instrument move him to consider concerning his condition.   Let
him call upon him to set his soul in order ; to trim his lamp ;
to dress his soul ; to renew acts of grace by way of prayer,
to make amends in all the evils he hath done ; and to supply
all the defects of duty as much as his past condition requires,
and his present can admit.

6. According as the condition of the sickness or the weakness of the man is observed, so the exhortation is to be less,
and the prayers more, because the life of the man was his main
preparatory: and, therefore, if his condition be full of pain
and infirmity, the shortness and small number of his own acts
is to be supplied by the acts of the ministers and standers-by,
who are in such case to speak more to God for him than to
talk to him.   For the prayer of the righteous,[6] when it is fervent, hath a promise to prevail much in behalf of the sick
person.   But exhortations must prevail with their own proper weight, not by the passion of the speaker.   But yet this
assistance by way of prayers is not to be done by long offices,
but by frequent, and fervent, and holy: in which offices if
the sick man joins, let them be short and apt to comply with
his little strength and great infirmities : if they be said in his
behalf without his conjunction, they that pray may prudently
use their own liberty, and take no measures but their own devotions and opportunities, and the sick man's necessities.

When he hath made this general address and preparatory

* James v. 16.

entrance to the work of many days and periods, he may descend to particulars by the following instruments and discourses.

SECT. III. *Of ministering in the Sick Man's Confession of Sins and Repentance.*

THE first necessity that is to be served is that of repentance, in which the ministers can in no way serve him but by first exhorting him to confession of his sins, and declaration of the state of his soul. For unless they know the manner of his life, and the degrees of his restitution, either they can do nothing at all, or nothing of advantage and certainty. His discourses, like Jonathan's arrows, may shoot short or shoot over, but not wound where they should, nor open those humours that need a lancet or a cautery. To this purpose the sick man may be reminded :—

Arguments and Exhortations to move the Sick Man to Confession of Sins.

1. That God hath made a special promise to confession of sins. " He that confesseth his sins, and forsaketh them, shall have mercy ;"[1] and, " If we confess our sins, God is righteous to forgive us our sins, and to cleanse us from all unrighteousness."[2] 2. That confession of sins is a proper act and introduction to repentance. 3. That when the Jews, being warned by the sermons of the Baptist, repented of their sins, they confessed their sins to John in the susception of baptism.[3] 4. That the converts in the days of the apostles, returning to Christianity, instantly declared their faith and their repentance by confession and declaration of their deeds,[4] which they then renounced, abjured, and confessed to the apostles. 5. That confession is an act of many virtues together. 6. It is the gate of repentance. 7. An instrument of shame and condemnation of our sins. 8. A glorification of God so called by Joshua, particularly in the case of Achan. 9. An acknowledgment that God is just in punishing: for by confessing of our sins we also confess his justice, and are assessors with God in this condemnation of ourselves. 10. That by such an act of judging ourselves, we escape the more angry judgment of

: Prov. xxviii. 13.   [2] 1 John i. 9.   [3] Matt. iii. 6.
[4] Acts xix. 18.

God; St. Paul expressly exhorting us to it upon that very
inducement.[5]   11. That confession of sins is so necessary a
duty, that, in all scriptures, it is the immediate preface to
pardon, and the certain consequent of godly sorrow, and an
integral or constituent part of that grace which, together with
faith, makes up the whole duty of the gospel.   12. That in
all ages of the gospel it hath been taught and practised respectively, that all the penitents made confessions proportionable to their repentance, that is, public or private, general or
particular.   13. That God, by testimonies from heaven, that
is, by his word, and by a consequent rare peace of conscience,
hath given approbation to this holy duty.   14. That by this
instrument those whose office it is to apply remedies to every
spiritual sickness can best perform their offices.   15. That it
is by all churches esteemed a duty necessary to be done in
cases of a troubled conscience.   16. That what is necessary
to be done in one case, and convenient in all cases, is fit to be
done by all persons.   17. That without confession it cannot
easily be judged concerning the sick person, whether his conscience ought to be troubled or no, and therefore it cannot be
certain that it is not necessary.   18. That there can be no reason against it, but such as consults with flesh and blood, with
infirmity and sin, to all which confession of sins is a direct
enemy.   19. That now is that time when all the imperfections of his repentance and all the breaches of his duty are
to be made up, and that, if he omits this opportunity, he can
never be admitted to a salutary and medicinal confession.
20. That St. James gives an express precept that we Christians should confess our sins to each other,[6] that is, Christian
to Christian, brother to brother, the people to their minister;
and then he makes a specification of that duty which a sick
man is to do when he hath sent for the elders of the church.
21. That in all this there is no force lies upon him; but "if
he hides his sins he shall not be directed," so said the wise

---

[5] 1 Cor. xi. 31.   [6] Si tacuerit qui percussus est, et non egerit
poenitentiam, nec vulnus suum fratri et magistro voluerit confiteri, ma-
gister qui linguam habet ad curandum, facilè ei prodesse non poterit. Si
enim erubescat aegrotus vulnus medico confiteri, quod ignorat medicina
non curat.—St. Hieron. ad caput. 10. Eccles. Si enim hoc fecerimus, et
revelaverimus peccata nostra non solùm Deo, sed et his qui possunt me-
deri vulneribus nostris atque peccatis, delebuntur peccata nostra.—Orig.
Hom. 17. in Lucam

man: but ere long he must appear before the great Judge of
men and angels; and his spirit will be more amazed and confounded to be seen among the angels of light with the shadows
of the works of darkness upon him, than he can suffer by confessing to God in the presence of him whom God hath sent
to heal him. However, it is better to be ashamed here than
to be confounded hereafter. "Pol pudere præstat quam
pigere, totidem literis."[7] 22. That confession being in order
to pardon of sins, it is very proper and analogical to the nature of the thing, that it be made there where the pardon of
sins is to be administered, and that of pardon of sins God hath
made the minister the publisher and dispenser: and all this
is besides the accidental advantages which accrue to the conscience, which is made ashamed and timorous, and restrained
by the mortifications and blushings of discovering to a man
the faults committed in secret. 23. That the ministers of the
gospel are the ministers of reconciliation, are commanded
to restore such persons as are overtaken in a fault; and to
that purpose they come to offer their ministry, if they may
have cognizance of the fault and person. 24. That in the
matter of prudence it is not safe to trust a man's self in the
final condition and last security of a man's soul, a man being
no good judge in his own case. And when a duty is so useful
in all cases, so necessary in some, and encouraged by promises
evangelical, by Scripture precedents, by the example of both
Testaments, and prescribed by injunctions apostolical, and by
the canon of all churches, and the example of all ages, and
taught us even by the proportions of duty, and the analogy to
the power ministerial, and the very necessities of every man;
he that for stubbornness, or sinful shamefacedness, or prejudice, or any other criminal weakness, shall decline to do it in
the days of his danger, when the vanities of the world are
worn off, and all affections to sin are wearied, and the sin itself is pungent and grievous, and that we are certain we shall
not escape shame for them hereafter unless we be ashamed of
them here,[8] and use all the proper instruments of their pardon;

---

[7] Plaut. Trinum.
   Tam facile et pronum est superos contemnere testes,
   Si mortalis idem nemo sciat.   Juv. Sat. 13.
[8] Qui homo culpam admisit in se, nullus est tam parvi pretii
   Quin pudeat, quin purget se.   Plaut. Aulul. act. iv sc. 10. 60

this man, I say, is very near death, but very far off from the
kingdom of heaven.

2. The spiritual man will find in the conduct of this duty
many cases and varieties of accidents which will alter his
course and forms of proceedings.   Most men are of a rude
indifferency, apt to excuse themselves,[9] ignorant of their condition, abused by evil principles, content with a general and
indefinite confession ; and, if you provoke them to it by the
foregoing considerations, lest their spirits should be a little
uneasy, or not secured in their own opinions, will be apt to
say they are sinners, as every man hath his infirmity, and he
as well as any man : but, God be thanked, they bear no ill-will
to any man, or are no adulterers, or no rebels, or they have
fought on the right side ; and God be merciful to them, for
they are sinners.   But you shall hardly open their breasts
further ; and to inquire beyond this would be to do the office
of an accuser.

3. But, which is yet worse, there are very many persons
who have been so used to an habitual course of a constant intemperance, or dissolution in any other instance, that the crime
is made natural and necessary, and the conscience hath di-
gested all the trouble, and the man thinks himself in a good
estate, and never reckons any sins but those which are the
egressions and passings beyond his ordinary and daily drunkenness.   This happens in the cases of drunkenness, and intemperate eating, and idleness, and uncharitableness, and in
lying and vain jestings, and particularly in such evils which
the laws do not punish, and public customs do not shame, but
which are countenanced by potent sinners, or evil customs, or
good nature and mistaken civilities.

*Instruments by way of Consideration, to awaken a careless
Person and a stupid Conscience.*

In these and the like cases the spiritual man must awaken
the lethargy, and prick the conscience, by representing to him,
1. That Christianity is a holy and a strict religion.   2. That
many are called, but few are chosen.   That the number of
them that are to be saved is but a very few in respect of those

---

9   ———— Verùm hoc se amplectitur uno,
   Hoc amat, hoc laudat Matronam nullam ego tango.
                                   Horat. Ser. l.   sat. 2.

that are to descend into sorrow and everlasting darkness.
That we have covenanted with God in baptism to live a holy
life. That the measures of holiness in the Christian religion
are not to be taken by the evil proportions of the multitude
and common fame of looser and less severe persons ; because
the multitude is that which does not enter into heaven, but
the few, the elect, the holy servants of Jesus. That every
habitual sin does amount to a very great guilt in the whole,
though it be but in a small instance. That if the righteous
scarcely be saved, then there will be no place for the unrighteous and the sinner to appear in but places of horror and
amazement. That confidence hath destroyed many souls, and
many have had a sad portion who have reckoned themselves
in the calendar of saints. That the promises of heaven are
so great that it is not reasonable to think that every man, and
every life, and an easy religion, shall possess such infinite glories. That although heaven is a gift, yet there is a great
severity and strict exacting of the conditions on our part to
receive that gift. That some persons who have lived strictly
for forty years together, yet have miscarried by some one
crime at last, or some secret hypocrisy, or a latent pride, or a
creeping ambition, or a fantastic spirit ; and therefore much less
can they hope to receive so great portions of felicities, when
their life hath been a continual declination from those severities which might have created confidence of pardon and acceptation through the mercies of God and the merits of Jesus.
That every good man ought to be suspicious of himself, and
in his judgment concerning his own condition to fear the worst,
that he may provide for the better. That we are commanded
to work out our salvation with fear and trembling. That this
precept was given with great reason, considering the thousand
thousand ways of miscarrying. That St. Paul himself, and
St. Arsenius, and St. Elzearius, and divers other remarkable
saints, had at some times great apprehensions of the dangers
of failing of the mighty price of their high calling.[10] That
the stake that is to be secured is of so great an interest that
all our industry, and all the violences we can suffer in the prosecution of it, are not considerable. That this affair is to be
done but once, and then never any more unto eternal ages.
That they who profess themselves servants of the institution,

[10] Apud Surium, die 27 Sept.

and servants of the law and discipline of Jesus, will find that
they must judge themselves by the proportions of that law by
which they were to rule themselves.   That the laws of society
and civility, and the voices of my company, are as ill judges
as they are guides; but we are to stand or fall by his sentence
who will not consider or value the talk of idle men or the
persuasion of wilfully abused consciences, but of Him who hath
felt our infirmity in all things but sin, and knows where our
failings are unavoidable, and where and in what degree they
are excusable ; but never will endure a sin should seize upon
any part of our love and deliberate choice or careless cohabit-
ation.   That if our conscience accuse us not,[11] yet are we not
hereby justified; for God is greater than our consciences.[12]
That they who are most innocent have their consciences most
tender and sensible.   That scrupulous persons are always most
religious; and that to feel nothing is not a sign of life, but of
death.   That nothing can be hid from the eyes of the Lord,
to whom the day and the night, public and private, words and
thoughts, actions and designs, are equally discernible.   That
a lukewarm person is only secured in his own thoughts, but
very unsafe in the event, and despised by God.   That we live
in an age in which that which is called and esteemed a holy
life, in the days of the apostles and holy primitives would have
been esteemed indifferent, sometimes scandalous, and always
cold.   That what was a truth of God then is so now ; and to
what severities they were tied, for the same also we are to be
accountable ; and heaven is not now an easier purchase than
it was then.   That if he will cast up his accounts, even with
a superficial eye, let him consider how few good works he
hath done; how inconsiderable is the relief which he gave
to the poor; how little are the extraordinaries of his religion ;
and how inactive and lame, how polluted and disordered, how
unchosen and unpleasant were the ordinary parts and periods
of it ; and how many and great sins have stained his course
of life: and till he enters into a particular scrutiny, let him
only revolve in his mind what his general course hath been ;
and, in the way of prudence, let him say whether it was
laudable and holy, or only indifferent and excusable : and
if he can think it only excusable, and so as to hope for pardon
by such suppletories of faith and arts of persuasion which he

[11] 1 John iii. 20.   [12] 1 Cor. iv. 4.

and others used to take in for auxiliaries to their unreasonable confidence, then he cannot but think it very fit that he search into his own state, and take a guide, and erect a tribunal, or appear before that which Christ hath erected for him on earth, that he may make his access fairer when he shall be called before the dreadful tribunal of Christ in the clouds.[13] For if he can be confident upon the stock of an unpraised or a looser life, and should dare to venture upon wild accounts, without order, without abatements, without consideration, without conduct, without fear, without scrutinies, and confessions, and instruments of amends or pardon, he either knows not his danger or cares not for it, and little understands how great a horror that is that a man should rest his head for ever upon a cradle of flames, and lie in a bed of sorrows, and never sleep, and never end his groans or the gnashing of his teeth.

This is that which some spiritual persons call a wakening of the sinner by the terrors of the law, which is a good analogy or tropical expression to represent the threatenings of the gospel, and the dangers of an incurious and a sinning person; but we have nothing else to do with the terrors of the law, for, blessed be God, they concern us not. The terrors of the law were the intermination of curses upon all those that ever broke any of the least commandments once or in any instance; and to it the righteousness of faith is opposed. The terrors of the law admitted no repentance, no pardon, no abatement, and were so severe that God never inflicted them at all according to the letter, because he admitted all to repentance that desired it with a timely prayer, unless in very few cases, as of Achan, or Korah, the gatherer of sticks upon the sabbath day, or the like; but the state of threatenings in the gospel is very fearful, because the conditions of avoiding them are easy and ready, and they happen to evil persons after many warnings, second thoughts, frequent invitations to pardon and repentance, and after one entire pardon consigned in baptism. And in this sense it is necessary that such persons as we now deal withal should be instructed concerning their danger.

4. When the sick man is, either of himself or by these considerations, set forward with purposes of repentance and con-

[13] Illi mors gravis incubat,
Qui, notus nimis omnibus,
Ignotus moritur sibi.—Thyest. 401.

fession of his sins, in order to all its holy purposes and effects,
then the minister is to assist him in the understanding of the
number of his sins, that is, the several kinds of them, and the
various manners of prevaricating the Divine commandments:
for as for the number of the particulars in every kind, he will
need less help; and, if he did, he can have it no where but in
his own conscience and from the witnesses of his conversation.
Let this be done by prudent insinuation, by arts of remembrance, and secret notices, and propounding occasions and instruments of recalling such things to his mind, which either
by public fame he is accused of, or by the temptations of his
condition it is likely he might have contracted.

5. If the person be truly penitent, and forward to confess
all that are set before him, or offered to his sight at a half
face, then he may be complied withal in all his innocent circumstances, and his conscience made placid and willing, and
he be drawn forward by good-nature and civility, that his repentance in all the parts of it, and in every step of its progress and emanation, may be as voluntary and chosen as it
can.   For by that means, if the sick person can be invited to
do the work of religion, it enters by the door of his will and
choice, and will pass on toward consummation by the instrument of delight.

6. If the sick man be backward and without apprehension
of the good-natured and civil way, let the minister take care
that by some way or other the work of God be secured; and
if he will not understand when he is secretly prompted, he
must be hallooed to, and asked in plain interrogatives concerning the crime of his life.   He must be told of the evil
things that are spoken of him in markets and exchanges, the
proper temptations and accustomed evils of his calling and
condition, of the actions of scandal; and in all those actions
which were public, or of which any notice is come abroad, let
care be taken that the right side of the case of conscience be
turned toward him, and the error truly represented to him by
which he was abused, as the injustice of his contracts, his op-
pressive bargains, his rapine and violence; and if he hath
persuaded himself to think well of a scandalous action, let him
be instructed and advertised of his folly and his danger.

7. And this advice concerns the minister of religion to follow without partiality, or fear, or interest, in much simplicity

and prudence, and hearty sincerity; having no other consideration but that the interest of the man's soul be preserved,
and no caution used but that the matter be represented with
just circumstances and civilities, fitted to the person with pre-
faces of honour and regard : but so that nothing of the duty
be diminished by it, that the introduction do not spoil the
sermon, and both together ruin two souls, of the speaker and
the hearer. For it may soon be considered, if the sick man
be a poor or an indifferent person in secular account, yet his
soul is equally dear to God, and was redeemed with the same
highest price, and therefore to be highly regarded ; and there
is no temptation but that the spiritual man may speak freely
without the allays of interest, or fear, or mistaken civilities.
But if the sick man be a prince, or a person of eminence or
wealth, let it be remembered it is an ill expression of reverence to his authority, or of regard to his person, to let him
perish for the want of an honest, and just, and a free homily.

8. Let the sick man, in the scrutiny of his conscience and
confession of his sins, be carefully reminded to consider those
sins which are only condemned in the court of conscience, and
no where else. For there are certain secrecies and retirements,
places of darkness and artificial veils, with which the devil
uses to hide our sins from us, and to incorporate them into
our affections by a constant, uninterrupted practice before they
be prejudiced or discovered. 1. There are many sins which
have reputation and are accounted honour ; as fighting a duel,
answering a blow with a blow, carrying armies into a neigh-
bour-country, robbing with a navy, violently seizing upon a
kingdom. 2. Others are permitted by law, as usury in all
countries ; and because every excess of it is a certain sin, the
permission of so suspected a matter makes it ready for us, and
instructs the temptation. 3. Some things are not forbidden
by laws ; as lying in ordinary discourse, jeering, scoffing, intemperate eating, ingratitude, selling too dear, circumventing
another in contracts, importunate entreaties, and temptation of
persons to many instances of sin, pride, and ambition. 4. Some
others do not reckon they sin against God if the laws have
seized upon the person ; and many that are imprisoned for
debt think themselves disobliged from payment, and when
they pay the penalty think they owe nothing for the scandal
and disobedience. 5. Some sins are thought not considerable,

but go under the title of sins of infirmity, or inseparable accidents of mortality; such as idle thoughts, foolish talking, looser revellings, impatience, anger, and all the events of evil company. 6. Lastly, many things are thought to be no sins: such as misspending of their time, whole days or months of useless and impertinent employment, long gaming, winning men's money in greater portions, censuring men's actions, curiosity, equivocating in the prices and secrets of buying and selling, rudeness, speaking truths enviously, doing good to evil purposes, and the like. Under the dark shadow of these unhappy and fruitless yew-trees the enemy of mankind makes very many to lie hid from themselves, sewing before their nakedness the fig-leaves of popular and idle reputation and impunity, public permission, a temporal penalty, infirmity, prejudice, and direct error in judgment, and ignorance. Now in all these cases the ministers are to be inquisitive and observant, lest the fallacy prevail upon the penitent to evil purposes of death or diminution of his good; and that those things, which in his life passed without observation, may now be brought forth, and pass under saws and harrows, that is, the severity and censure of sorrow and condemnation.

9. To which I add, for the likeness of the thing, that the matter of omission be considered, for in them lies the bigger half of our failings; and yet, in many instances, they are undiscerned, because they very often sit down by the conscience, but never upon it; and they are usually looked upon as poor men do upon their not having coach and horses, or as that knowledge is missed by boys and hinds which they never had; it will be hard to make them understand their ignorance—it requires knowledge to perceive it, and therefore he that can perceive it hath it not. But by this pressing the conscience with omissions, I do not mean recessions, or distances from states of eminency or perfection; for, although they may be used by the ministers as an instrument of humility, and a chastiser of too big a confidence, yet that which is to be confessed and repented of is omission of duty in direct instances and matters of commandment, or collateral and personal obligations, and is especially to be considered by kings and prelates, by governors and rich persons, by guides of souls and presidents of learning in public charge, and by all other in their proportions.

10. The ministers of religion must take care that the sick man's confession be as minute and particular as it can, and that as few sins as may be, be intrusted to the general prayer of pardon for all sins; for by being particular and enumerative of the variety of evils which have disordered his life, his repentance is disposed to be more pungent and afflictive, and therefore more salutary and medicinal; it hath in it more sincerity, and makes a better judgment of the final condition of the man; and from thence it is certain the hopes of the sick man can be more confident and reasonable.

11. The spiritual man that assists at the repentance of the sick must not be inquisitive into all the circumstances of the particular sins, but be content with those that are direct parts of the crime and aggravations of the sorrow; such as frequency, long abode, and earnest choice in acting them; violent desires, great expense, scandal of others, dishonour to the religion, days of devotion, religious solemnities, and holy places; and the degrees of boldness and impudence, perfect resolution, and the habit. If the sick person be reminded or inquired into concerning these, it may prove a good instrument to increase his contrition, and perfect his penitential sorrows, and facilitate his absolution and the means of his amendment. But the other circumstances, as of the relative person in the participation of the crime, the measures or circumstances of the impure action, the name of the injured man or woman, the quality or accidental condition; these and all the like are but questions springing from curiosity, and producing scruple, and apt to turn into many inconveniences.

12. The minister in this duty of repentance must be diligent to observe concerning the person that repents, that he be not imposed upon by some one excellent thing that was remarkable in the sick man's former life.[14] For there are some people of one good thing. Some are charitable to the poor out of kind-heartedness; and the same good nature makes them easy and compliant with drinking persons: and they die with drink but cannot live with charity; and their alms, it may be, shall deck their monument, or give them the reward of

[14] Nunc si depositum non inficiatur amicus,
Si reddat veterem cum totâ ærugine follem,
Prodigiosa fides, et Tuscis digna libellis.
Juven. Sat. xiii. 62.

loving persons, and the poor man's thanks for alms, and procure many temporal blessings; but it is very sad that the reward should be soon spent in this world.   Some are rarely
just persons and punctual observers of their word with men,
but break their promises with God, and make no scruple
of that.   In these and all the like cases, the spiritual man
must be careful to remark, that good proceeds from an entire
and integral cause, and evil from every part; that one sickness can make a man die, but he cannot live and be called a
sound man without an entire health; and therefore, if any confidence arises upon that stock, so as that it hinders the strictness of the repentance, it must be allayed with the representment of this sad truth, "that he who reserves one evil in his
choice hath chosen an evil portion," and coloquintida and
death is in the pot; and he that worships the God of Israel
with a frequent sacrifice, and yet upon the anniversary will
bow in the house of Venus, and loves to see the follies and the
nakedness of Rimmon, may eat part of the flesh of the sacrifice and fill his belly, but shall not be refreshed by the holy
cloud arising from the altar, or the dew of heaven descending
upon the mysteries.

13. And yet the minister is to estimate, that one or more
good things is to be an ingredient into his judgment concerning the state of his soul, and the capacities of his restitution,
and admission to the peace of the church; and according as
the excellency and usefulness of the grace hath been, and according to the degrees and the reasons of its prosecution, so
abatements are to be made in the injunctions and impositions
upon the penitent.   For every virtue is one degree of approach to God; and though in respect of the acceptation it is
equally none at all, that is, it is as certain a death if a man
dies with one mortal wound as if he had twenty; yet in such
persons who have some one or more excellences, though not
an entire piety, there is naturally a nearer approach to the
estate of grace than in persons who have done evils and are
eminent for nothing that is good.   But in making judgment
of such persons, it is to be inquired into, and noted accordingly, why the sick person was so eminent in that one good
thing; whether by choice and apprehension of his duty, or
whether it was a virtue from which his state of life ministered
nothing to dehort or discourage him, or whether it was only a

consequent of his natural temper and constitution. If the first, then it supposes him in the neighbourhood of the state of grace, and that in other things he was strongly tempted. The second is a felicity of his education, and an effect of Providence. The third is a felicity of his nature, and a gift of God in order to spiritual purposes. But yet of every one of these advantage is to be made. If the conscience of his duty was the principle, then he is ready formed to entertain all other graces upon the same reason, and his repentance must be made more sharp and penal; because he is convinced to have done against his conscience in all the other parts of his life; but the judgment concerning his final state ought to be more gentle, because it was a huge temptation that hindered the man and abused his infirmity. But if either his calling or his nature were the parents of the grace, he is in the state of a moral man, (in the just and proper meaning of the word,) and to be handled accordingly; that virtue disposed him rarely well to many other good things, but was no part of the grace of sanctification: and therefore the man's repentance is to begin anew, for all that, and is to be finished in the returns of health, if God grants it; but if he denies it, it is much, very much, the worse for all that sweet-natured virtue.

14. When the confession is made, the spiritual man is to execute the office of a restorer and a judge in the following particulars and manner.

SECT. IV. *Of the ministering to the Restitution and Pardon, or Reconciliation of the Sick Person, by administering the Holy Sacrament.*

"IF any man be overtaken in a fault, ye which are spiritual restore such a one in the spirit of meekness;"[1] that is the commission: and, "Let the elders of the church pray over the sick man; and if he have committed sins they shall be forgiven him;"[2] that is the effect of his power and his ministry. But concerning this some few things are to be considered.

1. It is the office of the presbyters and ministers of religion to declare public criminals and scandalous persons to be such, that, when the leprosy is declared, the flock may avoid the infection; and then the man is excommunicate,

---

[1] Gal. vi. 1.　　　[2] James v. 14, 15.

when the people are warned to avoid the danger of the man or the reproach of the crime, to withdraw from his society, and not to bid him God speed, not to eat and celebrate synaxes and church-meetings with such who are declared criminal and dangerous. And therefore excommunication is, in a very great part, the act of the congregation and communities of the faithful: and St. Paul said to the church of the Corinthians,[3] that they had inflicted the evil upon the incestuous person, that is, by excommunicating him: all the acts of which are, as they are subjected in the people, acts of caution and liberty; but no more acts of direct proper power or jurisdiction than it was when the scholars of Simon Magus left his chair and went to hear St. Peter: but as they are actions of the rulers of the church, so they are declarative, ministerial, and effective too by moral causality, that is, by persuasion and discourse, by argument and prayer, by homily and material representment, by reasonableness of order and the superinduced necessities of men; though not by any real change of state as to the person, nor by diminution of his right, or violence to his condition.

2. He that baptizes, and he that ministers the holy sacrament, and he that prays, does holy offices of great advantage; but in these also, just as in the former, he exercises no jurisdiction or pre-eminence after the manner of secular authority;[4] and the same is also true if he should deny them. He that refuseth to baptize an indisposed person hath, by the consent of all men, no power or jurisdiction over the unbaptized man; and he that, for the like reason, refuseth to give him the communion, preserves the sacredness of the mysteries, and does charity to the undisposed man, to deny that to him which will do him mischief; and this is an act of separation, just as it is for a friend or physician to deny water to an hydropic person, or Italian wines to a hectic fever, or as if Cato should deny to salute Bibulus, or the censor of manners to do countenance to a wanton and a vicious person. And though this thing was expressed by words of power, such as separation, ab-

---

[3] 1 Cor. v. 5, 12, 13; 2 Cor. ii. 6.   [4] Homines in remissione peccatorum ministerium suum exhibent, non jus alicujus potestatis exercent: Neque enim in suo, sed in nomine Patris, Filii, et Spiritûs Sancti, peccata dimittuntur: Isti rogant, Divinitas donat.—St. Amb. de Spir. S. l. iii. c. 10.

stention, excommunication, deposition; yet these words we understand by the thing itself, which was notorious and evident to be matter of prudence, security, and a free, uncon-strained discipline; and they passed into power by consent and voluntary submission, having the same effect of constraint, fear, and authority, which we see in secular jurisdiction : not because ecclesiastical discipline hath a natural proper coercion, as lay tribunals have, but because men have submitted to it, and are bound to do so upon the interest of two or three Christian graces.

3. In pursuance of this caution and provision, the church superinduced times and manners of abstention, and expres-sions of sorrow, and canonical punishments, which they tied the delinquent people to suffer before they would admit them to the holy table of the Lord. For the criminal having obliged himself by his sin, and the church having declared it, when she should take notice of it, he is bound to repent, to make him capable of pardon with God ; and to prove that he is penitent he is to do such actions which the church, in the virtue and pursuance of repentance, shall accept as a testi-mony of it sufficient to inform her ; for as she could not bind at all (in this sense) till the crime was public, though the man had bound himself in secret ; so neither can she set him free till the repentance be as public as the sin, or so as she can note it and approve it. Though the man be free, as to God, by his internal act, yet, as the publication of the sin was accidental to it, and the church-censure consequent to it, so is the publication of repentance and consequent absolution ex-trinsical to the pardon, but accidentally and in the present circumstances necessary. This was the same that the Jews did, (though in other instances and expressions,) and do to this day to their prevaricating people ; and the Essenes in their assemblies, and private colleges of scholars, and public universities. For all these being assemblies of voluntary per-sons, and such as seek for advantage, are bound to make an artificial authority in their superiors, and so to secure order and government by their own obedience and voluntary sub-ordination, which is not essential and of proper jurisdiction in the superior; and the band of it is not any coercitive power, but the denying to communicate such benefits which they seek in that communion and fellowship.

4. These, I say, were introduced in the special manners and instances by positive authority, and have not a Divine authority commanding them; but there is a Divine power that verifies them, and makes these separations effectual and formidable: for because they are declarative and ministerial in the spiritual man, and suppose a delinquency and demerit in the other, and a sin against God, our blessed Saviour hath declared that "what they bind on earth shall be bound in heaven;" that is, in plain signification, the same sins and sinners which the clergy condemn in the face of their assemblies, the same are condemned in heaven before the face of God, and for the same reason too.   God's law hath sentenced it, and these are the preachers and publishers of his law by which they stand condemned; and these laws are they that condemn the sin or acquit the penitent there and here; whatsoever they bind here shall be bound there, that is, the sentence of God at the day of judgment shall sentence the same men[s] whom the church does rightly sentence here.   It is spoken in the future, *it shall be bound in heaven;* not but that the sinner is first bound there or first absolved there; but because all binding and loosing in the interval is imperfect and relative to the day of judgment, the day of the great sentence, therefore it is set down in the time to come; and says this only, the clergy are tied by the word and laws of God to condemn such sins and sinners; and that you may not think it ineffective, because after such sentence the man lives and grows rich, or remains in health and power, therefore be sure it shall be verified in the day of judgment.   This is hugely agreeable with the words of our Lord and certain in reason; for that the minister does nothing to the final alteration of the state of the man's soul by way of sentence, is demonstratively certain, because he cannot bind a man but such as hath bound himself, and who is bound in heaven by his sin before his sentence in the church; as also because the binding

---

[s] Summum futuri judicii præjudicium est, si quis ita deliquerit ut à communicatione orationis, et conventûs, et omnis sancti commercii relegetur.—Tertul. Apol. cap. 39.

Atque hoc idem innuitur per summam Apostoli censuram in reos maximi criminis: sit ἀνάθεμα μαραινάθα, id est, excommunicatus majori excommunicatione; Dominus veniet, scil. ad judicandum eum: ad quod judicium hæc censura ecclesiæ est relativa et in ordine.   Tum demum pœnas dabit: ad quas, nisi resipiscat, hic consignatur.

of the church is merely accidental and upon publication only:
and when the man repents he is absolved before God, before
the sentence of the church, upon his contrition and dereliction
only; and if he were not, the church could not absolve him.
The consequent of which evident truth is this, that whatsoever impositions the church-officers impose upon the criminal,
they are to avoid scandal, to testify repentance and to exercise it, to instruct the people, to make them fear, to represent
the act of God and the secret and the true state of the sinner:
and although they are not essentially necessary to our pardon, yet they are become necessary when the church hath
seized upon the sinner by public notice of the crime; necessary (I say) for the removing the scandal and giving testimony of our contrition, and for the receiving all that comfort
which he needs and can derive from the promises of pardon as
they are published by him that is commanded to preach them
to all them that repent.   And therefore, although it cannot
be necessary as to the obtaining pardon that the priest should
in private absolve a sick man from his private sins, and there
is no loosing where there was no precedent binding, and he
that was only bound before God, can before him only be
loosed: yet as to confess sins to any Christian in private may
have many good ends, and to confess them to a clergyman may
have many more, so to hear God's sentence at the mouth of
the minister, pardon pronounced by God's ambassador, is of
huge comfort to them that cannot otherwise be comforted, and
whose infirmity needs it; and therefore it were very fit it
were not neglected in the days of our fear and danger, of our
infirmities and sorrow.

5. The execution of this ministry being an act of prudence
and charity, and therefore relative to changing circumstances,
it hath been, and in many cases may, and in some must, be
rescinded and altered.   The time of separation may be lengthened and shortened, the condition made lighter or heavier,
and for the same offence the clergyman is deposed, but yet admitted to the communion for which one of the people who
hath no office to lose is denied the benefit of communicating;
and this sometimes when he might lawfully receive it: and a
private man is separate when a multitude or a prince is not,
cannot, ought not; and at last, when the case of sickness and
danger of death did occur, they admitted all men that desired

it; sometimes without scruple or difficulty, sometimes with some little restraint in great or insolent cases, (as in the case of apostacy, in which the council of Arles denied absolution[6] unless they received and gave public satisfaction by acts of repentance ; and some other councils denied at any time to do it to such persons,) according as seemed fitting to the present necessities of the church. All which particulars declare it to be no part of a Divine commandment that any man should be denied to receive the communion, if he desires it, and if he be in any probable capacity of receiving it.

6. Since the separation was an act of liberty and a direct negative,[7] it follows that the restitution was a mere doing that which they refused formerly, and to give the holy communion was the formality of absolution, and all the instrument and the whole matter of reconcilement; the taking off the punishment is the pardoning of the sin; for this without the other is but a word; and if this be done, I care not whether any thing be said or no. *Vinum Dominicum ministratoris gratia est,* is also true in this sense; to give the chalice and cup is the grace and indulgence of the minister; and when that is done, the man hath obtained the peace of the church; and to do that is all the absolution the church can give. And they were vain disputes which were commenced some few ages since, concerning the forms of absolution, whether they were indicative or optative, by way of declaration or by way of sentence; for at first they had no forms at all, but they said a prayer, and, after the manner of the Jews, laid hands upon the penitent when they prayed over him, and so admitted him to the holy communion; for since the church had no power over her children but of excommunicating and denying them to attend upon holy offices and ministries respectively, neither could they have any absolution but to admit them thither from whence formerly they were forbidden; whatsoever ceremony or forms did signify, this was superinduced and arbitrary, alterable and accidental; it had variety, but no necessity.

7. The practice consequent to this is, that if the penitent be bound by the positive censures of the church, he is to be reconciled upon those conditions which the laws of the church tie him to in case he can perform them: if he cannot, he can

<hr>

[4] Arelat. cap. 3.   [7] Vide 2 Cor. ii. 10; et S. Cyprian. ep. 73.

no longer be prejudiced by the censure of the church,[8] which had no relation but the people, with whom the dying man is no longer to converse; for whatsoever relates to God is to be transacted in spiritual ways by contrition and internal graces; and the mercy of the church is such as to give him her peace and her blessing upon his undertaking to obey her injunctions, if he shall be able: which injunctions, if they be declared by public sentence, the minister hath nothing to do in the affairs but to remind him of his obligation and reconcile him, that is, give him the holy sacrament.

8. If the penitent be not bound by public sentence, the minister is to make his repentance as great, and his heart as contrite, as he can; to dispose him by the repetition of acts of grace in the way of prayer, and in real and exterior instances, where he can; and then to give him the holy communion in all the same cases in which he ought not to have denied it to him in his health: that is, even in the beginnings of such a repentance which by human signs he believes to be real and holy; and after this the event must be left to God. The reason of the rule depends upon this, because there is no Divine commandment directly forbidding the rulers of the church to give the communion to any Christian that desires it and professes repentance of his sins. And all church-discipline, in every instance, and to every single person, was imposed upon him by men who did according to the necessities of this state and constitution of our affairs below: but we, who are but ministers and delegates of pardon and condemnation, must resign and give up our judgment when the man is no more to be judged by the sentences of man, and by the proportions of this world, but of the other: to which, if our reconciliation does advantage, we ought in charity to send him forth with all the advantages he can receive; for he will need them all. And therefore the Nicene council commands[9] that no man be deprived of this necessary passport in the article of his death, and calls this the ancient and canonical law of the church; and to minister it only supposes the man in the communion of the church, not always in the state, but ever in the possibilities, of sanctification. They who in the article and danger of death were admitted to the communion, and tied to penance if

* Caus. 26. Q. 6, et q. 7.
* Can. 13. Vide etiam Con. Ancyr. cap. 6. Aurel. 2. cap. 12.

they recovered, (which was ever the custom of the ancient
church, unless in very few cases,) were but in the threshold
of repentance, in the commencement and first introductions to
a devout life ; and, indeed, then it is a fit ministry that it be
given in all the periods of time in which the pardon of sins is
working, since it is the sacrament of that great mystery,[10] and
the exhibition of that blood which is shed for the remission
of sins.

9. The minister of religion ought not to give the communion to a sick person if he retains the affection to any sin, and
refuses to disavow it, or profess repentance of all sins whatsoever, if he be required to do it.   The reason is, because it is
a certain death to him,[11] and an increase of his misery, if he
shall so profane the body and blood of Christ as to take it
into so unholy a breast, where Satan reigns, and sin is principal, and the Spirit is extinguished, and Christ loves not to
enter, because he is not suffered to inhabit.   But when he
professes repentance,[12] and does such acts of it as his present
condition permits, he is to be presumed to intend heartily what
he professes solemnly ; and the minister is only the judge of
outward act, and by that only he is to take information concerning the inward.   But whether he be so or no, or if he
be, whether that be timely, and effectual, and sufficient toward
the pardon of sin before God, is another consideration of which
we may conjecture here, but we shall know it at doomsday.
The spiritual man is to do his ministry by the rules of Christ,
and as the customs of the church appoint him, and after the
manner of men : the event is in the hands of God, and is to
be expected, not directly and wholly according to his ministry,
but to the former life, or the timely internal repentance and
amendment,[13] of which I have already given accounts.   These
ministries are acts of order and great assistances, but the sum

[10] O sacrum convivium in quo Christus sumitur, recolitur memoria pas-
sionis ejus, mens impletur gratiâ, at futuræ gloriæ nobis pignus datur !
[11] Ita vide, ut prosit, illis ignosci, quos ad pœnam ipse Deus deduxit :
quod ad me attinet, non sum crudelis, sed vereor, ne, quod remisero,
patiar.   Tryphæna dixit apud Petronium, 106. 3.
[12] Sævi quoque et implacabiles domini crudelitatem suam impediunt,
si, quando pœnitentia fugitivos reduxit, dedititiis hostibus parcimus.
[13] Quæcunque ergò de pœnitentiâ jubendo dicta sunt, non ad exterio-
rem, sed ad interiorem referenda sunt, sine quâ nullus unquam Deo re
conciliari poterit.—Gratian. de Pœnit. d. 1. Quis aliquando.

of affairs does not rely upon them. And if any man puts his whole repentance upon this time, or all his hopes upon these ministries, he will find them and himself to fail.

10. It is the minister's office to invite sick and dying persons to the holy sacrament; such whose lives were fair and laudable, and yet their sickness sad and violent, making them listless and of slow desires, and slower apprehensions; that such persons who are in the state of grace may lose no accidental advantages of spiritual improvement, but may receive into their dying bodies the symbols and great consignations of the resurrection, and into their souls the pledges of immortality, and may appear before God their Father in the union and with the impresses and likeness of their elder Brother. But if the persons be of ill report, and have lived wickedly, they are not to be invited ; because their case is hugely suspicious, though they then repent and call for mercy : but if they demand it, they are not to be denied; only let the minister in general represent the evil consequence of an unworthy participation ; and if the penitent will judge himself unworthy, let him stand candidate for pardon at the hands of God, and stand or fall by that unerring and merciful sentence, to which his severity of condemning himself before men will make the easier and more hopeful address. And the strictest among the Christians who denied to reconcile lapsed persons after baptism, yet acknowledged that there were hopes reserved in the court of heaven for them, though not here ; since we, who are easily deceived by the pretences of a real return, are tied to dispense God's graces, as he hath given us commission, with fear and trembling,[14] and without too forward confidences ; and God hath mercies which we know not of; and therefore because we know them not, such persons were referred to God's tribunal, where he would find them if they were to be had at all.

11. When the holy sacrament is to be administered, let the exhortation be made proper to the mystery, but fitted to the man ; that is, that it be used for the advantages of faith, or love, or contrition : let all the circumstances and parts of the Divine love be represented, all the mysterious advantages of the blessed sacrament be declared; that it is the bread which came from heaven ; that it is the representation of Christ's death to all the purposes and capacities of faith, and the rea

[14] 1 Cor. ii. 3.

exhibition of Christ's body and blood to all the purposes of the Spirit; that it is the earnest of the resurrection, and the seed of a glorious immortality; that as by our cognation to the body of the first Adam we took in death, so, by our union with the body of the second Adam we shall have the inheritance of life; (for as by Adam came death, so by Christ cometh the resurrection of the dead;[15]) that if we, being worthy communicants of these sacred pledges, being presented to God with Christ within us, our being accepted of God is certain, even for the sake of his Well-beloved that dwells within us; that this is the sacrament of that body which was broken for our sins, of that blood which purifies our souls, by which we are presented to God pure and holy in the Beloved; that now we may ascertain our hopes and make our faith confident: " for he that hath given us his Son, how should not he with him give us all things else?"[16]   Upon these or the like considerations the sick man may be assisted in his address, and his faith strengthened, and his hope confirmed, and his charity be enlarged.

12. The manner of the sick man's reception of the holy sacrament hath in it nothing differing from the ordinary solemnities of the sacrament,[17] save only that abatement is to be made of such accidental circumstances as by the laws and customs of the church healthful persons are obliged to, such as fasting, kneeling, &c.   Though I remember that it was noted for great devotion in the legate that died at Trent, that he caused himself to be sustained upon his knees when he received the *viaticum* or the holy sacrament before his death; and it was greater in Huniades, that he caused himself to be carried to the church, that there he might receive his Lord in his Lord's house; and it was recorded for honour, that William, the pious archbishop of Bourges, a small time before his last agony, sprang out of his bed at the presence of the holy sacrament, and, upon his knees and his face, recommended his soul to his Saviour.   But in these things no man is to be prejudiced or censured.

13. Let not the holy sacrament be administered to dying persons, when they have no use of reason to make that duty

---

[15] 1 Cor. xv. 22.   [16] Rom. viii. 32.
[17] Vide Rule of Holy Living, chap. iv. sect. 10; and Hist. of the Life of Jesus, part iii. disc. 18.

acceptable, and the mysteries effective to the purposes of the soul. For the sacraments and ceremonies of the gospel operate not without the concurrent actions and moral influences of the suscipient. To infuse the chalice into the cold lips of the clinic may disturb his agony, but cannot relieve the soul, which only receives improvement by acts of grace and choice, to which the external rites are apt and appointed to minister in a capable person. All other persons, as fools, children, distracted persons, lethargical, apoplectical, or any ways senseless and incapable of human and reasonable acts, are to be assisted only by prayers; for they may prevail even for the absent, and for enemies, and for all those who join not in the office.

SECT. V. *Of ministering to the Sick Person by the Spiritua Man, as he is the Physician of Souls.*

1. IN all cases of receiving confessions of sick men, and the assisting to the advancement of repentance, the minister is to apportion to every kind of sin such spiritual remedies which are apt to mortify and cure the sin: such as abstinence from their occasions and opportunities, to avoid temptations, to resist their beginnings, to punish the crime by acts of indignation against the person, fastings and prayer, alms and all the instances of charity, asking forgiveness, restitution of wrongs. satisfaction of injuries, acts of virtue contrary to the crimes. And although, in great and dangerous sicknesses, they are not directly to be imposed unless they are direct matters of duty ; yet where they are medicinal, they are to be insinuated, and in general signification remarked to him, and undertaken accordingly : concerning which, when he returns to health, he is to receive particular advices. And this advice was inserted into the penitential of England, in the time of Theodore, archbishop of Canterbury, and afterwards adopted into the canon of the western churches.[1]

2. The proper temptations of sick men, for which a remedy is not yet provided, are unreasonable fears and unreasonable confidences, which the minister is to cure by the following considerations.

---

[1] Caus. 2b. Q. 7. ab infirmis.

Considerations against Unreasonable Fears of not having ou˙ Sins pardoned.

Many good men, especially such who have tender con-sciences, impatient of the least sin, to which they are arrived by a long grace and a continual observation of their actions, and the parts of a lasting repentance, many times overact their tenderness, and turn their caution into scruple, and care of their duty into inquiries after the event, and askings after the counsels of God and the sentences of doomsday.

He that asks of the standers-by, or of the minister, whether they think he shall be saved or damned, is to be answered with the words of pity and reproof. Seek not after new light for the searching into the private records of God: look as much as you list into the pages of revelation, for they concern your duty ; but the event is registered in heaven, and we can expect no other certain notices of it, but that it shall be given to them for whom it is prepared by the Father of mercies. We have light enough to tell our duty ; and if we do that, we need not fear what the issue will be; and if we do not, let us never look for more light, or inquire after God's pleasure concerning our souls, since we so little serve his ends in those things where he hath given us light. But yet this I add, that as pardon of sins in the Old Testament[2] was nothing but re-moving the punishment, which then was temporal, and there-fore many times they could tell if their sins were pardoned ; and concerning pardon of sins, they then had no fears of con-science but while the punishment was on them, for so long indeed it was unpardoned, and how long it would so remain it was matter of fear and of present sorrow : besides this, in the gospel pardon of sins is another thing ; pardon of sins is a sanctification ; Christ came to take away our sins, by turning every one of us from our iniquities ;[3] and there is not in the nature of the thing any expectation of pardon, or sign or sig-nification of it, but so far as the thing itself discovers itself. As we hate sin, and grow in grace, and arrive at the state of holiness, which is also a state of repentance and imperfection, but yet of sincerity of heart and diligent endeavour ; in the same degree we are to judge concerning the forgiveness of sins ; for indeed that is the evangelical forgiveness, and it

[2] Matt. ix. 6. [1] [3] Acts iii. 26.

signifies our pardon, because it effects it, or rather it is in the nature of the thing; so that we are to inquire into no hidden records: forgiveness of sins is not a secret sentence, a word, or a record; but it is a state of change, and effected upon us; and upon ourselves we are to look for it, to read it, and understand it.   We are only to be curious of our duty, and confident of the article of remission of sins;[4] and the conclusion of these premises will be, that we shall be full of hopes of a prosperous resurrection; and our fear and trembling are no instances of our calamity, but parts of duty; we shall sure enough be wafted to the shore, although we be tossed with the winds of our sighs, and the unevenness of our fears, and the ebbings and flowings of our passions, if we sail in a right channel, and steer by a perfect compass, and look up to God, and call for his help, and do our own endeavour.   There are very many reasons why men ought not to despair; and there are not very many men that ever go beyond a hope, till they pass into possession.   If our fears have any mixture of hope, that is enough to enable and to excite our duty; and if we have a strong hope, when we cast about we shall find reason enough to have many fears.   Let not this fear weaken our hands;[5] and if it allay our gaieties and our confidences, it is no harm. In this uncertainty we must abide if we have committed sins after baptism; and those confidences which some men glory in are not real supports or good foundations.   The fearing man is the safest; and if he fears on his death-bed, it is but what happens to most considering men, and what was to be looked for all his life-time: he talked of the terrors of death, and death is the king of terrors; and therefore it is no strange thing if then he be hugely afraid; if he be not, it is either a great felicity, or a great presumption.   But if he want some degree of comfort, or a greater degree of hope, let him be refreshed by considering,

1. That Christ came into the world to save sinners.[6]   2. That God delights not in the confusion and death of sinners.[7] 3. That in heaven there is great joy at the conversion of a

[4] Est modus gloriandi in conscientia, ut noveris fidem tuam esse sinceram, spem tuam esse certam.—August. Psalm cxlix.
[5] Una est nobilitas, argumentumque coloris
    Ingenui, timidas non habuisse manus.
[6] 1 Tim. i. 15.   [7] Ezek. xxxiii 11.

sinner.[8]   4. That Christ is a perpetual advocate, daily in-
terceding with his Father for our pardon.[9]   5. That God
uses infinite arts, instruments, and devices, to reconcile us
to himself. 6. That he prays us to be in charity with him,
and to be forgiven.[10] 7. That he sends angels to keep us
from violence and evil company, from temptations and surprises, and his Holy Spirit to guide us in holy ways, and
his servants to warn us and remind us perpetually: and
therefore since certainly he is so desirous to save us, as appears by his word, by his oaths, by his very nature, and his
daily artifices of mercy, it is not likely that he will condemn
us without great provocations of his majesty, and perseverance in them. 9. That the covenant of the gospel is a covenant of grace and of repentance, and being established with
so many great solemnities and miracles from heaven, must
signify a huge favour and a mighty change of things; and
therefore that repentance, which is the great condition of it,
is a grace that does not expire in little accents and minutes,
but hath a great latitude of signification, and large extension
of parts, under the protection of all which persons are safe
even when they fear exceedingly. 9. That there are great
degrees and differences of glory in heaven; and therefore, if
we estimate our piety by proportions to the more eminent
persons and devouter people, we are not to conclude we shall
not enter into the same state of glory, but that we shall not go
into the same degrees. 10. That although forgiveness of sins
is consigned to us in baptism, and that this baptism is but
once, and cannot be repeated; yet forgiveness of sins is the
grace of the gospel, which is perpetually remanent upon us,
and secured unto us so long as we have not renounced our
baptism; for then we enter into the condition of repentance;
and repentance is not an indivisible grace, or a thing performed at once, but it is working all our lives; and therefore
so is our pardon, which ebbs and flows according as we discompose or renew the decency of our baptismal promises;
and therefore it ought to be certain that no man despair of
pardon but he that hath voluntarily renounced his baptism or
willingly estranged himself from that covenant. He that
sticks to it, and still professes the religion, and approves the
faith, and endeavours to obey and to do his duty, this man

* Luke xv. 7.   9 1 John ii. 1.   10 2 Cor. v. 20.

hath all the veracity of God to assure him and give him confidence that he is not in an impossible state of salvation, unless God cuts him off before he can work, or that he begins to work when he can no longer choose. 11. And then let him consider, the more he fears the more he hates his sin that is the cause of it, and the less he can be tempted to it, and the more desirous he is of heaven; and therefore such fears are good instruments of grace, and good signs of a future pardon. 12. That God in the old law, although he made a covenant of perfect obedience, and did not promise pardon at all after great sins, yet he did give pardon, and declared it so to them for their own and for our sakes too. So he did to David, to Manasses, to the whole nation of the Israelites, ten times in the wilderness, even after their apostacies and idolatries. And in the prophets [11] the mercies of God and his remissions of sins were largely preached, though in the law of God put on the robes of an angry judge and a severe lord. But therefore in the gospel, where he hath established the whole sum of affairs upon faith and repentance, if God should not pardon great sinners that repent after baptism with a free dispensation, the gospel were far harder than the intolerable covenant of the law. 13. That if a proselyte went into the Jewish communion, and were circumcised and baptized, he entered into all the hopes of good things which God had promised or would give to his people; and yet that was but the covenant of works. If, then, the Gentile proselytes, by their circumcision and legal baptism, were admitted to a state of pardon, to last so long as they were in the covenant, even after their admission, for sins committed against Moses's law, which they then undertook to observe exactly; in the gospel, which is the covenant of faith, it must needs be certain that there is a greater grace given, and an easier condition entered into, than was that of the Jewish law: and that is nothing else but that abatement is made for our infirmities, and our single evils, and our timely repented and forsaken habits of sin, and our violent passions, when they are contested withal, and fought with, and under discipline, and in the beginnings and progresses of mortification. 14. That God hath erected in his church a whole order of men, the main part and dignity of whose work it is to remit and retain sins by a perpetual and

[11] Ezek. xvii ; Joel ii.

daily ministry: and this they do, not only in baptism, but in all their offices to be administered afterwards, in the holy sacrament of the eucharist, which exhibits the symbols of that blood which was shed for pardon of our sins, and therefore, by its continued ministry and repetition, declares that *all that while* we are within the ordinary powers and usual dispensations of pardon, even so long as we are in any probable dispositions to receive that holy sacrament. And the same effect is also signified and exhibited in the whole power of the keys, which, if it extends to private sins, sins done in secret, it is certain it does also to public. But this is a greater testimony of the certainty of the remissibility of our greater sins; for public sins, as they always have a sting and a superadded formality of scandal and ill example, so they are most commonly the greatest; such as murder, sacrilege, and others of unconcealed nature, and unprivate action; and if God, for these worst of evils, hath appointed an office of ease and pardon, which is and may daily be administered, that will be an uneasy pusillanimity and fond suspicion of God's goodness to fear that our repentance shall be rejected, even although we have committed the greatest or the most of evils. 15. And it was concerning baptized Christians that St. John said, "If any man sin, we have an advocate with the Father, and he is the propitiation for our sins;" and concerning lapsed Christians St. Paul gave instruction, that "if any man be overtaken in a fault, ye which are spiritual restore such a man in the spirit of meekness; considering lest ye also be tempted." The Corinthian Christian committed incest, and was pardoned; and Simon Magus, after he was baptized, offered to commit his own sin of simony, and yet St. Peter bid him pray for pardon: and St. James tells, that "if the sick man sends for the elders of the church, and they pray over him, and he confess his sins, they shall be forgiven him." 16. That only one sin is declared to be irremissible, "the sin against the Holy Ghost, the sin unto death," as St. John calls it, for which we are not bound to pray—for all others we are; and certain it is no man commits a sin against the Holy Ghost if he be afraid he hath, and desires that he had not; for such penitential passions are against the definition of that sin. 17. That all the sermons in the Scripture written to Christians and disciples of Jesus, exhorting men to repentance, to be afflicted, to

mourn and to weep, to confession of sins, are sure testimonies
of God's purpose and desire to forgive us, even when we fall
after baptism; and if our fall after baptism were irrecoverable,
then all preaching were in vain, and our faith were also vain,
and we could not with comfort rehearse the creed, in which,
as soon as ever we profess Jesus to have died for our sins, we
also are condemned by our own conscience of a sin that shall
not be forgiven; and then all exhortations, and comforts, and
fasts, and disciplines, were useless and too late if they were
not given us before we can understand them; for, most commonly, as soon as we can, we enter into the regions of sin,
for we commit evil actions before we understand, and together
with our understanding they begin to be imputed. 18. That
if it could be otherwise, infants were very ill provided for in
the church who were baptized, when they have no stain upon
their brows but the misery they contracted from Adam; and
they are left to be angels for ever after, and live innocently
in the midst of their ignorances, and weaknesses, and temptations, and the heat and follies of youth, or else to perish in
an eternal ruin.   We cannot think or speak good things of
God if we entertain such evil suspicions of the mercies of the
Father of our Lord Jesus.   19. That the long-sufferance and
patience of God is indeed wonderful; but therefore it leaves
us in certainties of pardon, so long as there is a possibility to
return, if we reduce the power to act.   20. That God calls
upon us to forgive our brother seventy times seven times, and
yet all that is but like the forgiving a hundred pence for his
sake who forgives us ten thousand talents; for so the Lord
professed that he had done to him that was his servant and
his domestic. 21. That if we can forgive a hundred thousand
times, it is certain God will do so to us, our blessed Lord
having commanded us to pray for pardon as we pardon our
offending and penitent brother.   22. That even in the case
of very great sins, and great judgments inflicted upon the
sinners, wise and good men and presidents of religion have
declared their sense to be, that God spent all his anger, and
made it expire in that temporal misery; and so it was supposed to have been done in the case of Ananias: but that the
hopes of any penitent man may not rely upon any uncertainty,
we find in Holy Scripture that those Christians who had for
their scandalous crimes deserved to be given over to Satan to

be buffeted, yet had hopes to be saved in the day of the Lord.
23. That God glories in the titles of mercy and forgiveness,
and will not have his appellatives so finite and limited as to
expire in one act, or in a seldom pardon. 24. That man's
condition were desperate, and like that of the fallen angels,
equally desperate, but unequally oppressed, considering our
infinite weaknesses and ignorances, (in respect of their excellent understanding and perfect choice,) if he could be admitted to no repentance after his infant-baptism; and if he may
be admitted to one, there is nothing in the covenant of the
gospel but he may also to a second, and so for ever, as long
as he can repent and return and live to God in a timely religion. 25. That every man is a sinner—" in many things we
offend all ;"[12] and "if we say we have no sin, we deceive
ourselves ;"[13] and therefore either all must perish, or else
there is mercy for all; and so there is, upon this very stock,
because " Christ died for sinners,"[14] and " God hath comprehended all under sin, that he might have mercy upon all."[15]
26. That if ever God sends temporal punishments into the
world with purposes of amendment, and if they be not all of
them certain consignations to hell, and unless every man that
breaks his leg, or in punishment loses a child or wife, be certainly damned, it is certain that God in these cases is angry
and loving, chastises the sin to amend the person, and smites
that he may cure, and judges that he may absolve. 27. That
he that will not quench the smoking flax, nor break the
bruised reed, will not tie us to perfection and the laws and
measures of heaven upon earth; and if, in every period of
our repentance, he is pleased with our duty, and the voice of
our heart and the hand of our desires, he hath told us plainly
that he will not only pardon all the sins of the days of our
folly, but the returns and surprises of sins in the days of repentance, if we give no way, and allow no affection, and give
no place to any thing that is God's enemy; all the past sins,
and all the seldom-returning and ever-repented evils, being
put upon the accounts of the cross.

An Exercise against Despair in the Day of our Death:

To which may be added this short exercise, to be used for

---

[12] James iii. 2.   [13] 1 John i. 8   [14] Rom. v. 8.   [15] Rom. xi. 32

tue curing the temptation to direct despair, in case that the
hope and faith of good men be assaulted in the day of their
calamity.

I consider that the ground of my trouble is my sin ; and if
it were not for that, I should not need to be troubled ; but
the help that all the world looks for is such as supposes a man
to be a sinner. Indeed, if from myself I were to derive my
title to heaven, then my sins were a just argument of despair ;
but now that they bring me to Christ, that they drive me to
an appeal to God's mercies and to take sanctuary in the cross,
they ought not, they cannot, infer a just cause of despair. I
am sure it is a stranger thing that God should take upon him
hands and feet, and those hands and feet should be nailed
upon a cross, than that a man should be partaker of the
felicities of pardon and life eternal ; and it were stranger yet
that God should do so much for man, and that a man that
desires it, that labours for it, that is in life and possibilities of
working his salvation, should inevitably miss that end for
which that God suffered so much. For what is the meaning,
and what is the extent, and what are the significations, of the
Divine mercy in pardoning sinners ? If it be thought a great
matter that I am charged with original sin, I confess I feel
the weight of it in loads of temporal infelicities and proclivi-
ties to sin ; but I fear not the guilt of it, since I am baptized,
and it cannot do honour to the reputation of God's mercy that
it should be all spent in remissions of what I never chose, never
acted, never knew of, could not help, concerning which I received no commandment, no prohibition. But, blessed be God,
it is ordered in just measures that that original evil which I
contracted without my will should be taken away without my
knowledge ; and what I suffered before I had a being was
cleansed before I had a useful understanding. But I am taught
to believe God's mercies to be infinite, not only in himself but
to us ; for mercy is a relative term, and we are its correspondent : of all the creatures which God made, we only, in a proper sense, are the subjects of mercy and remission. Angels
have more of God's bounty than we have, but not so much of
his mercy ; and beasts have little rays of his kindness, and
effects of his wisdom and graciousness in petty donatives,
but nothing of mercy ; for they have no laws, and therefore
no sins, and need no mercy, nor are capable of any. Since

therefore man alone is the correlative or proper object and
vessel of reception of an infinite mercy, and that mercy is in
giving and forgiving, I have reason to hope that he will so
forgive me that my sins shall not hinder me of heaven; or
because it is a gift, I may also, upon the stock of the sam
infinite mercy, hope he will give heaven to me; and if I have
it either upon the title of giving or forgiving, it is alike to me,
and will alike magnify the glories of the Divine mercy.   And
because eternal life is the gift of God,[16] I have less reason to
despair; for if my sins were fewer, and my disproportions
towards such a glory were less, and my evenness more, yet it
is still a gift, and I could not receive it but as a free and a
gracious donative, and so I may still: God can still give it
me; and it is not an impossible expectation to wait and look
for such a gift at the hands of the God of mercy; the best
men deserve it not, and I who am the worst may have it given
me.   And I consider that God hath set no measures of his
mercy, but that we be within the covenant, that is, repenting
persons endeavouring to serve him with an honest, single
heart; and that within this covenant, there is a very great
latitude, and variety of persons, and degrees, and capacities;
and therefore that it cannot stand with the proportions of so infinite a mercy, that obedience be exacted to such a point, which
he never expressed, unless it should be the least, and that to
which all capacities, though otherwise unequal, are fitted and
sufficiently enabled.   But, however, I find that the Spirit of
God taught the writers of the New Testament to apply to us
all in general, and to every single person in particular, some
gracious words which God in the Old Testament spake to one
man upon a special occasion in a single and temporal instance.
Such are the words which God spake to Joshua; "I will
never fail thee, nor forsake thee:" and upon the stock of that
promise St. Paul forbids covetousness and persuades contentedness,[17] because those words were spoken by God to Joshua
in another case.   If the gracious words of God have so great
extension of parts, and intention of kind purposes, then how
many comforts have we upon the stock of all the excellent
words which are spoken in the prophets and in the Psalms!
and I will never more question whether they be spoken concerning me, having such an authentic precedent so to expound

<hr>

[16] Rom. vi. 23.   [17] Heb. xiii. 5.

the excellent words of God; all the treasures of God which
are in the Psalms are my own riches, and the wealth of my
hope; there will I look, and whatsoever I can need, that I
will depend upon. For certainly, if we could understand it,
that which is infinite (as God is) must needs be some such
kind of thing: it must go whither it was never sent, and signify what was not first intended, and it must warm with its
light, and shine with its heat, and refresh when it strikes,
and heal when it wounds, and ascertain where it makes afraid,
and intend all when it warns one, and mean a great deal in a
small word. And as the sun, passing to its southern tropic,
looks with an open eye upon his sun-burnt Ethiopians, but at
the same time sends light from its posterns, and collateral influences from the back side of his beams, and sees the corners
of the east when his face tends towards the west, because he
is a round body of fire, and hath some little images and re-
semblances of the Infinite; so is God's mercy: when it looked
upon Moses, it relieved St. Paul, and it pardoned David, and
gave hope to Manasses, and might have restored Judas if he
would have had hope, and used himself accordingly. But as
to my own case, I have sinned grievously and frequently;[18]
but I have repented it; but I have begged pardon; I have
confessed it and forsaken it. I cannot undo what was done,
and I perish if God hath appointed no remedy, if there be no
remission; but then my religion falls together with my hope,
and God's word fails as well as I. But I believe the article
of forgiveness of sins; and if there be any such thing I may
do well, for I have, and do, and will do that which all good
men call repentance, that is, I will be humbled before God,
and mourn for my sin, and for ever ask forgiveness, and judge
myself, and leave it with haste, and mortify it with diligence,
and watch against it carefully. And this I can do but in the
manner of a man; I can but mourn for my sins, as I apprehend grief in other instances, but I will rather choose to suffer all evils than to do one deliberate act of sin. I know my
sins are greater than my sorrow, and too many for my memory,
and too insinuating to be prevented by all my care; but I
know also that God knows and pities my infirmities, and how
far that will extend I know not, but that it will reach so far
as to satisfy my needs is the matter of my hope. But this I

[18] Vixi, peccavi, pœnitui, naturæ cessi.

2 k

am sure of, that I have in my great necessity prayed humbly
and with great desire, and sometimes I have been heard in
kind, and sometimes have had a bigger mercy instead of it;
and I have the hope of prayers, and the hope of my confession, and the hope of my endeavour, and the hope of many
promises, and of God's essential goodness; and I am sure
that God hath heard my prayers, and verified his promises in
temporal instances, for he ever gave me sufficient for my life;
and although he promised such supplies, and grounded the
confidences of them upon our first seeking the kingdom of
heaven and its righteousness, yet he hath verified it to me
who have not sought it as I ought; but therefore I hope he
accepted my endeavour, or will give his great gifts and our
great expectation even to the weakest endeavour, to the least,
so it be a hearty piety. And sometimes I have had some
cheerful visitations of God's Spirit, and my cup hath been
crowned with comfort, and the wine that made my heart glad
danced in the chalice, and I was glad that God would have
me so; and therefore I hope this cloud may pass; for that
which was then a real cause of comfort is so still if I could
discern it, and I shall discern it when the veil is taken from
mine eyes. And, blessed be God, I can still remember that
there are temptations to despair; and they could not be temptations if they were not apt to persuade, and had seeming probability on their side; and they that despair think they do it
with the greatest reason; for if they were not confident of the
reason, but that it were such an argument as might be opposed or suspected, then they could not despair. Despair
assents as firmly and strongly as faith itself; but because it
is a temptation, and despair is a horrid sin, therefore it is certain those persons are unreasonably abused, and they have no
reason to despair, for all their confidence; and, therefore,
although I have strong reasons to condemn myself, yet I have
more reason to condemn my despair, which therefore is unreasonable because it is a sin, and a dishonour to God, and
a ruin to my condition, and verifies itself if I do not look to
it. For as the hypochondriac person that thought himself
dead, made his dream true when he starved himself because
dead people eat not; so do despairing sinners lose God's
mercies by refusing to use and to believe them. And I hope
it is a disease of judgment, not an intolerable condition, that

I am falling into; because I have been told so concerning others who therefore have been afflicted, because they see not their pardon sealed after the manner of this world; and the affairs of the Spirit are transacted by immaterial notices, by propositions and spiritual discourses, by promises which are to be verified hereafter: and here we must live in a cloud, in darkness under a veil, in fear and uncertainties; and our very living by faith and hope is a life of mystery and secrecy, the only part of the manner of that life in which we shall live in the state of separation. And when a distemper of body or an infirmity of mind happens in the instances of such secret and reserved affairs, we may easily mistake the manner of our notices for the uncertainty of the thing; and therefore it is but reason I should stay till the state and manner of my abode be changed before I despair: there it can be no sin nor error, here it may be both; and if it be that, it is also this, and then a man may perish for being miserable, and be undone for being a fool. In conclusion, my hope is in God, and I will trust him with the event, which I am sure will be just, and I hope full of mercy. However, now I will use all the spiritual arts of reason and religion to make me more and more to love God, that if I miscarry, charity also shall fail, and something that loves God shall perish and be damned; which if it be impossible, then I may do well.

These considerations may be useful to men of little hearts and of great piety; or if they be persons who have lived without infamy, or begun their repentance so late that it is very imperfect, and yet so early that it was before the arrest of death. But if the man be a vicious person, and hath persevered in a vicious life till his death-bed, these considerations are not proper. Let him inquire, in the words of the first disciples after Pentecost, "Men and brethren, what shall we do to be saved?" and if they can but entertain so much hope as to enable them to do so much of their duty as they can for the present, it is all that can be provided for them; an inquiry, in their case, can have no other purpose of religion or prudence. And the minister must be infinitely careful that he do not go about to comfort vicious persons with the comforts belonging to God's elect, lest he prostitute holy things, and make them common, and his sermons deceitful, and vices

be encouraged in others, and the man himself find that he was
deceived, when he descends into his house of sorrow.

But because very few men are tempted with too great fears
of failing, but very many are tempted by confidence and presumption, the ministers of religion had need be instructed
with spiritual armour to resist this fiery dart of the devil,
when it operates to evil purposes.

Sect. VI. *Considerations against Presumption.*

I have already enumerated many particulars to provoke a
drowsy conscience to a scrutiny and to a suspicion of himself,
that by seeing cause to suspect his condition he might more
freely accuse himself, and attend to the necessities and duties
of repentance; but if either before or in his repentance he
grow too big in his spirit, so as either he does some little
violences to the modesties of humility, or abates his care and
zeal of his repentance, the spiritual man must allay his forwardness by representing to him, 1. That the growths in grace are
long, difficult, uncertain, hindered, of many parts and great
variety. 2. That an infant grace is soon dashed and discountenanced, often running into an inconvenience and the
evils of an imprudent conduct, being zealous and forward,
and therefore confident, but always with the least reason and
the greatest danger; like children and young fellows, whose
confidence hath no other reason but that they understand not
their danger and their follies. 3. That he that puts on his
armour ought not to boast as he that puts it off; and the
apostle chides the Galatians for ending in the flesh after they
had begun in the spirit. 4. That a man cannot think too
meanly of himself, but very easily he may think too high.
5. That a wise man will always, in a matter of great concernment, think the worst, and a good man will condemn himself with hearty sentence. 6. That humility and modesty of
judgment and of hope are very good instruments to procure
a mercy and a fair reception at the day of our death; but
presumption or bold opinions serve no end of God or man,
and is always imprudent, ever fatal, and of all things in the
world is its own greatest enemy: for the more any man pre-
sumes, the greater reason he hath to fear. 7. That a man's
heart is infinitely deceitful, unknown to itself, not certain in

his own acts, praying one way and desiring another, wandering and imperfect, loose and various, worshipping God and entertaining sin, following what it hates, and running from what it flatters, loving to be tempted and betrayed; petulant, like a wanton girl running from, that it might invite the fondness and enrage the appetite of the foolish young man, or the evil temptation that follows it; cold and indifferent one while, and presently zealous and passionate, furious and indiscreet; not understood of itself, or any one else, and deceitful beyond all the arts and numbers of observation. 8. That it is certain we have highly sinned against God, but we are not so certain that our repentance is real and effective, integral and sufficient. 9. That it is not revealed to us whether or no the time of our repentance be not past; or, if it be not, yet how far God will give us pardon, and upon what condition, or after what sufferings or duties, is still under a cloud. 10. That virtue and vice are oftentimes so near neighbours that we pass into each other's borders without observation, and think we do justice when we are cruel; or call ourselves liberal when we are loose and foolish in expenses; and are amorous when we commend our own civilities and good nature. 11. That we allow to ourselves so many little irregularities, that insensibly they swell to so great a heap that from thence we have reason to fear an evil; for an army of frogs and flies may destroy all the hopes of our harvest. 12. That when we do that which is lawful, and do all that we can in those bounds, we commonly and easily run out of our proportions. 13. That it is not easy to distinguish the virtues of our nature from the virtues of our choice; and we may expect the reward of temperance, when it is against our nature to be drunk; or we hope to have the coronet of virgins for our morose disposition, or our abstinence from marriage upon secular ends. 14. That it may be we call every little sigh or the keeping a fish-day the duty of repentance, or have entertained false principles in the estimate and measures of virtues; and, contrary to the steward in that Gospel, we write down fourscore when we should set down but fifty. 15. That it is better to trust the goodness and justice of God with our accounts than to offer him large bills. 16. That we are commanded by Christ to sit down in the lowest place till the master of the house bids us sit up higher. 17. That " when we have done all that we can, we are unprofitable servants:" and yet no man does all that he can do, and therefore is more to be despised and undervalued.   18. That the self-accusing publican was justified rather than the thanksgiving and confident Pharisee.   19. That if Adam in Paradise, and David in his house, and Solomon in the temple, and Peter in Christ's family, and Judas in the college of apostles, and Nicolas among the deacons, and the angels in heaven itself, did fall so foully and dishonestly, then it is prudent advice that we be not high-minded, but fear ; and when we stand most confidently take heed lest we fall : and yet there is nothing so likely to make us fall as pride and great opinions, which ruined the angels, which God resists, which all men despise, and which betrays us into carelessness, and a reckless, undiscerning, and an unwary spirit.

4. Now the main parts of the ecclesiastical ministry are done ; and that which remains is, that the minister pray over him and remind him to do good actions as he is capable; to call upon God for pardon ; to put his whole trust in him; to resign himself to God's disposing; to be patient and even ; to renounce every ill word or thought, or indecent action, which the violence of his sickness may cause in him ; to beg of God to give him his Holy Spirit to guide him in his agony, and his holy angels to guard him in his passage.

5. Whatsoever is besides this, concerns the standers-by ; that they do all their ministries diligently and temperately ; that they join with much charity and devotion in the prayer of the minister ; that they make no outcries or exclamations in the departure of the soul ; and that they make no judgment concerning the dying person, by his dying quietly or violently, with comfort or without, with great fears or a cheerful confidence, with sense or without, like a lamb or like a lion, with convulsions or semblances of great pain, or like an expiring and a spent candle ; for these happen to all men without rule, without any known reason, but according as God pleases to dispense the grace or the punishment, for reasons only known to himself.   Let us lay our hands upon our mouth, and adore the mysteries of the Divine wisdom and providence, and pray to God to give the dying man rest and pardon, and to ourselves grace to live well, and the blessing of a holy and a happy death.

§ECT. VII. *Offices to be said by the Minister in his Visitation of the Sick.*

IN the name of the Father, of the Son, and of the Holy Ghost.

"Our Father, which art in heaven," &c.

Let the Priest say this Prayer secretly.

O eternal Jesus, thou great lover of souls, who hast constituted a ministry in the church to glorify thy name, and to serve in the assistance of those that come to thee, professing thy discipline and service, give grace to me the unworthiest of thy servants, that I, in this my ministry, may purely and zealously intend thy glory, and effectually may minister comfort and advantages to this sick person (whom God assoil from all his offences): and grant that nothing of thy grace may perish to him by the unworthiness of the minister; but let thy Spirit speak by me, and give me prudence and charity, wisdom and diligence, good observation and apt discourses, a certain judgment and merciful dispensation, that the soul of thy servant may pass from this state of imperfection to the perfections of the state of glory, through thy mercies, O eternal Jesus. Amen.

The Psalm.

Out of the depths have I cried unto thee, O Lord. Lord, hear my voice; let thine ears be attentive to the voice of my supplications. Psalm cxxx.

If thou, Lord, shouldest mark iniquities, O Lord, who should stand?

But there is forgiveness with thee, that thou mayest be feared.

I wait for the Lord; my soul doth wait; and in his word do I hope.

My soul waiteth for the Lord, more than they that watch for the morning.

Let Israel hope in the Lord; for with the Lord there is mercy, and with him is plenteous redemption.

And he shall redeem his servants from all their iniquities. Psalm cxxx.

Wherefore should I fear in the days of evil, when the

wickedness of my heels shall compass me about? Psalm xlix. 5.

No man can by any means redeem his brother, nor give to God a ransom for him. Ver. 7:

For the redemption of their soul is precious, and it ceaseth for ever. Ver. 8.

That he should still live for ever, and not see corruption. Ver. 9.

But wise men die, likewise the fool and the brutish person perish, and leave their wealth to others. Ver. 10.

But God will redeem my soul from the power of the grave: for he shall receive me. Ver. 15.

As for me, I will behold thy face in righteousness: I shall be satisfied when I awake in thy likeness. Psalm xvii. 15.

Thou shalt show me the path of life: in thy presence is the fulness of joy; at thy right hand there are pleasures for evermore. Psalm xvi. 11.

Glory be to the Father, &c.

As it was in the beginning, &c.

Let us pray.

Almighty God, Father of mercies, the God of peace and comfort, of rest and pardon, we thy servants, though unworthy to pray to thee, yet, in duty to thee and charity to our brother, humbly beg mercy of thee for him to descend upon his body and his soul; one sinner, O Lord, for another, the miserable for the afflicted, the poor for him that is in need; but thou givest thy graces and thy favours by the measures of thy own mercies, and in proportion to our necessities. We humbly come to thee in the name of Jesus, for the merit of our Saviour, and the mercies of our God, praying thee to pardon the sins of this thy servant, and to put them all upon the accounts of the cross, and to bury them in the grave of Jesus; that they may never rise up in judgment against thy servant, nor bring him to shame and confusion of face in the day of final inquiry and sentence. Amen.

II.

Give thy servant patience in his sorrows, comfort in this his sickness, and restore him to health, if it seem good to thee, in order to thy great ends and his greatest interest. And however thou shalt determine concerning him in this affair, yet make his repentance perfect, and his passage safe, and his faith strong, and his hope modest and confident; that when thou shalt call his soul from the prison of the body, it may enter into the securities and rest of the sons of God in the bosom of blessedness and the custodies of Jesus. Amen.

III.

Thou, O Lord, knowest all the necessities and all the infirmities of thy servant, fortify his spirit with spiritual joys and perfect resignation, and take from him all degrees of inordinate or insecure affections to this world, and enlarge his heart with desires of being with thee, and of freedom from sins, and fruition of God.

IV.

Lord, let not any pain or passion discompose the order and decency of his thoughts and duty; and lay no more upon thy servant than thou wilt make him able to bear; and together with the temptation do thou provide a way to escape, even by the mercies of a longer and a more holy life, or by the mercies of a blessed death; even as it pleaseth thee, O Lord, so let it be.

V.

Let the tenderness of his conscience and the Spirit of God call to mind his sins, that they may be confessed and repented of; because thou hast promised that if we confess our sins we shall have mercy. Let thy mighty grace draw out from his soul every root of bitterness, lest the remains of the old man be accursed with the reserves of thy wrath; but in the union of the holy Jesus, and in the charities of God and of the world, and the communion of all the saints, let this soul be presented to thee blameless, and entirely pardoned, and thoroughly washed, through Jesus Christ our Lord.

Here also may be inserted the Prayers set down after the Holy Communion is administered.

The prayer of St. Eustatius the Martyr, to be used by the sick or dying man, or by the priests or assistants in his behalf, which he said when he was going to martyrdom.

I will praise thee, O Lord, that thou hast considered my low estate, and hast not shut me up in the hands of mine enemies, nor made my foes to rejoice over me; and now let thy right hand protect me, and let thy mercy come upon me; for my soul is in trouble and anguish because of its departure from the body.   O let not the assemblies of its wicked and cruel enemies meet it in the passing forth, nor hinder me by reason of the sins of my past life.   O Lord, be favourable unto me, that my soul may not behold the hellish countenance of the spirits of darkness, but let thy bright and joyful angels entertain it.   Give glory to thy holy name and to thy majesty; place me by thy merciful arm before thy seat of judgment, and let not the hand of the prince of this world snatch me from thy presence, or bear me into hell.   Mercy, sweet Jesu. Amen.

A prayer taken out of the Euchologion of the Greek church, to be said by, or in behalf of, people in their danger, or near their death.

Βεβορβορωμένος ταῖς ἁμαρτίαις, &c.

I.

Bemired with sins and naked of good deeds, I, that am the meat of worms, cry vehemently in spirit; cast not me a wretch away from thy face; place me not on the left hand, who with thy hands didst fashion me; but give rest unto my soul, for thy great mercy's sake, O Lord.

II.

Supplicate with tears unto Christ, who is to judge my poor soul, that he will deliver me from the fire that is unquenchable.   I pray you all, my friends and acquaintance, make mention of me in your prayers, that in the day of judgment I may find mercy at that dreadful tribunal.

III.

Then may the Standers-by pray.

When in unspeakable glory thou dost come dreadfully to judge the whole world, vouchsafe, O gracious Redeemer, that this thy faithful servant may in the clouds meet thee cheerfully. They who have been dead from the beginning, with terrible and fearful trembling stand at thy tribunal, waiting thy just sentence. O blessed Saviour Jesus! none shall there avoid thy formidable and most righteous judgment. All kings and princes with servants stand together, and hear the dreadful voice of the Judge condemning the people which have sinned into hell; from which sad sentence, O Christ, deliver thy servant. Amen.

Then let the sick man be called upon to rehearse the articles of his faith; or, if he be so weak he cannot, let him (if he have not before done it) be called to say Amen when they are recited, or to give some testimony of his faith and confident assent to them.

After which it is proper (if the person be in capacity) that the minister examine him, and invite him to confession, and all the parts of repentance, according to the foregoing rules; after which he may pray this prayer of absolution :—

Our Lord Jesus Christ, who hath given commission to his church, in his name to pronounce pardon to all that are truly penitent, he of his mercy pardon and forgive thee all thy sins, deliver thee from all evils past, present, and future, preserve thee in the faith and fear of his holy name to thy life's end, and bring thee to his everlasting kingdom, to live with him for ever and ever. Amen.

Then let the sick man renounce all heresies, and whatsoever is against the truth of God or the peace of the church, and pray for pardon for all his ignorances and errors known and unknown.

After which let him (if all other circumstances be fitted) be disposed to receive the blessed sacrament, in which the curate is to minister according to the form prescribed by the church.

When the rites are finished, let the sick man, in the days of his sickness, be employed with the former offices and exercises before described ; and when the time draws near of his dissolution, the minister may assist by the following order of recommendation of the soul.

I.

O holy and most gracious Saviour Jesus, we humbly recommend the soul of thy servant into thy hands, thy most merciful hands ; let thy blessed angels stand in ministry about thy servant, and defend him from the violence and malice of all his ghostly enemies ; and drive far from hence all the spirits of darkness.　Amen.

II.

Lord, receive the soul of this thy servant ; enter not into judgment with thy servant ; spare him whom thou hast redeemed with thy most precious blood ; deliver him from all evil, for whose sake thou didst suffer all evil and mischief ; from the crafts and assaults of the devil, from the fear of death, and from everlasting death, good Lord, deliver him. Amen.

III.

Impute not unto him the follies of his youth, nor any of the errors and miscarriages of his life ; but strengthen him in his agony ; let not his faith waver, nor his hope fail, nor his charity be disordered ; let none of his enemies imprint upon him any afflictive or evil phantasm ; let him die in peace, and rest in hope, and rise in glory.　Amen.

IV.

Lord, we know, and believe assuredly, that whatsoever is under thy custody cannot be taken out of thy hands, nor by all the violences of hell robbed of thy protection : preserve the work of thy hands ; rescue him from all evil ; take into the participation of thy glories him to whom thou hast given the seal of adoption, the earnest of the inheritance of the saints.　Amen.

V.

Let his portion be with Abraham, Isaac, and Jacob ; with Job and David, with the prophets and apostles, with martyrs and all thy holy saints, in the arms of Christ, in the bosom of felicity, in the kingdom of God, to eternal ages. Amen.

These following prayers are fit also to be added to the foregoing offices in case there be no communion or intercourse but prayer.

Let us pray.

O almighty and eternal God, there is no number of thy days, or of thy mercies; thou hast sent us into this world to serve thee, and to live according to thy laws; but we by our sins have provoked thee to wrath, and we have planted thorns and sorrows round about our dwellings: and our life is but a span long, and yet very tedious, because of the calamities that enclose us in on every side: the days of our pilgrimage are few and evil; we have frail and sickly bodies, violent and distempered passions, long designs and but a short stay, weak understandings and strong enemies, abused fancies, perverse wills. O dear God, look upon us in mercy and pity; let not our weaknesses make us to sin against thee, nor our fear cause us to betray our duty, nor our former follies provoke thy eternal anger, nor the calamities of this world vex us into tediousness of spirit and impatience; but let thy Holy Spirit lead us through this valley of misery with safety and peace, with holiness and religion, with spiritual comforts and joy in the Holy Ghost; that, when we have served thee in our generations, we may be gathered unto our fathers, having the testimony of a holy conscience in the communion of the catholic church, in the confidence of a certain faith, and the comforts of a reasonable, religious, and holy hope, and perfect charity with thee our God and all the world; that neither death, nor life, nor angels, nor principalities, nor powers, nor things present, nor things to come, nor height, nor depth, nor any other creature, may be able to separate us from the love of God, which is in Christ Jesus our Lord. Amen.

II.

O holy and most gracious Saviour Jesus, in whose hands the souls of all faithful people are laid up till the day of recompence, have mercy upon the body and soul of this thy servant, and upon all thy elect people who love the Lord Jesus and long for his coming; Lord, refresh the imperfection of

their condition with the aids of the Spirit of grace and comfort, and with the visitation and guard of angels, and supply
to them all their necessities known only unto thee; let them
dwell in peace, and feel thy mercies pitying their infirmities
and the follies of their flesh, and speedily satisfying the desires of their spirits; and when thou shalt bring us all forth
in the day of judgment, O then show thyself to be our Saviour Jesus, our advocate, and our judge. Lord, then remember that thou hast for so many ages prayed for the pardon of
those sins which thou art then to sentence. Let not the accusations of our consciences, nor the calumnies and aggravation of devils, nor the effects of thy wrath, press those souls
which thou lovest, which thou didst redeem, which thou dost
pray for; but enable us all, by the supporting hand of thy
mercy, to stand upright in judgment. O Lord, have mercy
upon us, have mercy upon us; O Lord, let thy mercy lighten
upon us, as our trust is in thee. O Lord, in thee have we
trusted, let us never be confounded. Let us meet with joy,
and for ever dwell with thee, feeling thy pardon, supported
with thy graciousness, absolved by thy sentence, saved by thy
mercy, that we may sing to the glory of thy name eternal
hallelujahs. Amen. Amen. Amen.

Then may be added in the behalf of all that are present
these ejaculations.

O spare us a little, that we may recover our strength before
we go hence and be no more seen. Amen.

Cast us not away in the time of age; O forsake us not
when strength faileth. Amen.

Grant that we may never sleep in sin or death eternal, but
that we may have our part of the first resurrection, and that
the second death may not prevail over us. Amen.

Grant that our souls may be bound up in the bundle of life;
and in the day when thou bindest up thy jewels remember
thy servants for good, and not for evil, that our souls may be
numbered amongst the righteous. Amen.

Grant unto all sick and dying Christians mercy and aids
from heaven; and receive the souls returning unto thee,
whom thou hast redeemed with thy most precious blood.
Amen.

Grant unto thy servants to have faith in the Lord Jesus, a

daily meditation of death, a contempt of the world, a longing desire after heaven, patience in our sorrows, comfort in our sicknesses, joy in God, a holy life, and a blessed death; that our souls may rest in hope, and my body may rise in glory, and both may be beatified in the communion of saints, in the kingdom of God, and the glories of the Lord Jesus. Amen.

The Blessing.

Now the God of peace,[19] that brought again from the dead our Lord Jesus, that great Shepherd of the sheep, through the blood of the everlasting covenant, make you perfect in every good work, to do his will, working in you that which is pleasing in his sight; to whom be glory, for ever and ever. Amen.

The Doxology.

To the blessed and only Potentate, the King of kings,[20] and the Lord of lords, who only hath immortality, dwelling in the light which no man can approach unto, whom no man hath seen, nor can see, be honour and power everlasting. Amen.

After the sick man is departed, the minister, if he be present, or the major-domo, or any other fit person, may use the following prayers in behalf of themselves :—

I.

Almighty God, with whom do live the spirits of them that depart hence in the Lord, we adore thy majesty, and submit to thy providence, and revere thy justice, and magnify thy mercies, thy infinite mercies, that it hath pleased thee to deliver this our brother out of the miseries of this sinful world. Thy counsels are secret, and thy wisdom is infinite; with the same hand thou hast crowned him and smitten us; thou hast taken him into regions of felicity, and placed him among saints and angels, and left us to mourn for our sins, and thy displeasure, which thou hast signified to us by removing him from us to a better, a far better place. Lord, turn thy anger into mercy, thy chastisements into virtues, thy rod into comforts; and do thou give to all his nearest relatives comforts from heaven, and a restitution of blessings equal to those which thou hast taken from them. And we humbly beseech

[19] Heb. xiii. 20, 21.   [20] 1 Tim. vi. 15, 16.

thee of thy gracious goodness shortly to satisfy the longing desires of those holy souls who pray, and wait, and long for thy second coming. Accomplish thou the number of thine elect, and fill up the mansions in heaven which are prepared for all them that love the coming of the Lord Jesus; that we, with this our brother, and all others departed this life in the obedience and faith of the Lord Jesus, may have our perfect consummation and bliss in thy eternal glory, which never shall have ending. Grant this for Jesus Christ's sake, our Lord and only Saviour. Amen.

II.

O merciful God, Father of our Lord Jesus, who is the first-fruits of the resurrection, and by entering into glory hath opened the kingdom of heaven to all believers, we humbly beseech thee to raise us up from the death of sin to the life of righteousness; that being partakers of the death of Christ, and followers of his holy life, we may be partakers of his Spirit, and of his promises; that when we shall depart this life we may rest in his arms, and lie in his bosom, as our hope is this our brother doth. O suffer us not, for any temptation of the world, or any snares of the devil, or any pains of death, to fall from thee. Lord, let thy Holy Spirit enable us with his grace to fight a good fight with perseverance, to finish our course with holiness, and to keep the faith with constancy unto the end, that at the day of judgment we may stand at the right hand of the throne of God, and hear the blessed sentence of, " Come, ye blessed children of my Father, receive the kingdom prepared for you from the beginning of the world." O blessed Jesus, thou art our judge, and thou art our advocate; even because thou art good and gracious, never suffer us to fall into the intolerable pains of hell, never to lie down in sin, and never to have our portion in the everlasting burning. Mercy, sweet Jesu, mercy. Amen.

A Prayer to be said in the Case of a sudden Surprise by Death, as by a mortal Wound, or evil Accidents in Childbirth, when the Forms and Solemnities of Preparation cannot be used.

O most gracious Father, Lord of heaven and earth, Judge of the living and the dead, behold thy servants running to

thee for pity and mercy in behalf of ourselves and this thy
servant, whom thou hast smitten with thy hasty rod and a
swift angel; if it be thy will, preserve his life that there may
be place for his repentance and restitution; O spare him a
little, that he may recover his strength before he go hence and
be no more seen. But if thou hast otherwise decreed, let the
miracles of thy compassion and thy wonderful mercy supply to
him the want of the usual measures of time, and the periods
of repentance, and the trimming of his lamp; and let the
greatness of the calamity be accepted by thee as an instrument
to procure pardon for those defects and degrees of unreadiness
which may have caused this accident upon thy servant. Lord,
stir up in him a great and effectual contrition, that the greatness of the sorrow, and hatred against sin, and the zeal of his
love to thee, may in a short time do the work of many days.
And thou, who regardest the heart and the measures of the
mind more than the delay and the measures of time, let it be
thy pleasure to rescue the soul of thy servant from all the
evils he hath deserved, and all the evils that he fears; that in
the glorifications of eternity, and the songs which to eternal
ages thy saints and holy angels shall sing to the honour of thy
mighty name and invaluable mercies, it may be reckoned
among thy glories that thou hast redeemed this soul from the
dangers of an eternal death, and made him partaker of the
gift of God, eternal life, through Jesus Christ our Lord.
Amen.

[If there be time, the prayers in the foregoing offices may be
added, according as they can be fitted to the present circumstances.]

SECT. VIII. *A Peroration concerning the Contingencies and
Treatings of our departed Friends after Death, in order to
their Burial, &c.*

WHEN we have received the last breath of our friend,[1] and
closed his eyes, and composed his body for the grave, then
seasonable is the counsel of the son of Sirach: "Weep bitterly, and make great moan, and use lamentation, as he is
worthy; and that a day or two, lest thou be evil spoken of;

---

[1] Τάδε δ' ἀμφιπονησόμεθ' οἷσι μάλιστα
Κήδεός ἐστι νέκυς.—Iliad. ψ'.

and then comfort thyself for thy heaviness. But take no grief to heart: for there is no turning again: thou shalt not do him good, but hurt thyself."[2] Solemn and appointed mournings are good expressions of our dearness to the departed soul, and of his worth, and our value of him; and it hath its praise in nature, and in manners,[3] and in public customs; but the praise of it is not in the gospel, that is, it hath no direct and proper uses in religion. For if the dead did die in the Lord, then there is joy to him; and it is an ill expression of our affection and our charity to weep uncomfortably at a change that hath carried my friend to the state of a huge felicity. But if the man did perish in his folly and his sins, there is indeed cause to mourn, but no hopes of being comforted; for he shall never return to light, or to hopes of restitution: therefore, beware lest thou also come into the same place of torment; and let thy grief sit down, and rest upon thy own turf, and weep till a shower springs from thy eyes to heal the wounds of thy spirit; turn thy sorrow into caution, thy grief for him that is dead to thy care for thyself who art alive, lest thou die and fall like one of the fools whose life is worse than death, and their death is the consummation of all felicities. The church in her funerals of the dead used to sing psalms,[4] and to give thanks for the redemption and delivery of the soul from the evils and dangers of mortality; and therefore we have no reason to be angry when God hears our prayers, who call upon him to hasten his coming, and to fill up his numbers, and to do that which we pretend to give him thanks for. And St. Chrysostom asks, "To what purpose is it that thou singest, 'Return unto thy rest, O my soul,' &c., if thou dost not believe thy friend to be in rest? and if thou dost, why dost thou weep impertinently and unreasonably?" Nothing but our own loss can justly be deplored;[5] and him that is passionate for the loss of his money or his ad-

---

[2] Ecclus. xxxviii. 17, 20.   [3] Ὡς γενναίως ἀποδεδάκρυκέ με, dixit Socrates de Ergastulario lugente.

Nemo me lacrymis decoret, nec funera fletu
    Faxit: cur? volito vivu' per ora virûm.—Ennius.

Πέρσας μέντοι πάντας ἐπὶ τὸ μνῆμα τοὐμὸν παρακαλεῖτε, συνησθησομένους ἐμοὶ, ὅτι ἐν τῷ ἀσφαλεῖ ἤδη ἔσομαι, ὡς μηδὲν ἂν ἔτι κακὸν παθεῖν, μήτε ἦν μήτὰ τοῦ θείου γένωμαι, μήτε ἦν μηδὲν ἔτι ὦ.—Cyrus apud Xenoph. viii. 7, 27.   [4] St. Chrysost. Hom. 4. Heb.

[5] Πάτροκλον κλαίωμεν· ὁ γὰο γέρας ἐστὶ θανόντων.—Il. ψ'.

vantages we esteem foolish and imperfect; and therefore
have no reason to love the immoderate sorrows of those who
too earnestly mourn for their dead, when, in the last resolution of the inquiry, it is their own evil and present or feared
inconveniences they deplore: the best that can be said of
such a grief is, that those mourners love themselves too well.
Something is to be given to custom, something to fame, to
nature, and to civilities, and to the honour of the deceased's
friends, for that man is esteemed to die miserable for whom
no friend or relative sheds a tear[6] or pays a solemn sigh. I
desire to die a *dry death*, but am not very desirous to have a
dry funeral: some flowers sprinkled upon my grave would
do well and comely; and a soft shower to turn those flowers
into a springing memory, or a fair rehearsal, that I may not
go forth of my doors as my servants carry the entrails of
beasts.

But that which is to be faulted in this particular is, when
the grief is immoderate and unreasonable; and Paula Romana
deserved to have felt the weight of St. Jerome's severe reproof, when, at the death of every of her children, she almost
wept herself into her grave. But it is worse yet, when people, by an ambitious and a pompous sorrow, and by ceremonies invented for the ostentation of their grief,[7] fill heaven
and earth with exclamations,[8] and grow troublesome because
their friend is happy, or themselves want his company. It
is certainly a sad thing in nature to see a friend trembling
with a palsy, or scorched with fevers, or dried up like a potsherd with immoderate heats, and rolling upon his uneasy bed
without sleep, which cannot be invited with music,[9] or plea-

---

[6] Mors optima est, perire dum lacrymant sui.—Sen. Hippol.
Μηδέ μοι ἄκλαυστος θάνατος μόλοι, ἀλλὰ φίλοισι]
Καλλείποιμι θανὼν ἄλγεα καὶ στοναχάς.
[7] Expectavimus lacrymas ad ostentationem doloris paratas; ut ergò
ambitiosus detonuit, texit superbum pallio caput, et manibus inter se
usque ad articulorum strepitum contritis, &c.—Petron. 17. 3.
Ὡς δὲ πατὴρ οὗ παιδὸς ὀδύρεται ὀστέα καίων
Νυμφίου, ὅς τε θανὼν δειλοὺς ἀκάχησε τοκῆας·
Ὡς, Ἀχιλεὺς ἑτάροιο ὀδύρετο ὀστέα καίων,
Ἑρπύζων παρὰ πυρκαϊὴν, ἀδινὰ στεναχίζων.—Il. ψ.
[8] ——— Non Siculæ dapes
Dulcem elaborabunt saporem,
Non avium citharæque cantus
Somnum reducent.   Hor. Od. iii. 1. 18.
2 L 2

sant murmurs, or a decent stillness; nothing but the servants
of cold death, Poppy and Weariness, can tempt the eyes to
let their curtains down; and then they sleep only to taste of
death and make an essay of the shades below; and yet we
weep not here; the period and opportunity for tears we
choose when our friend is falling asleep, when he hath laid
his neck upon the lap of his mother, and let his head down,[10]
to be raised up to heaven. This grief is ill-placed and indecent. But many times it is worse; and it hath been observed, that those greater and stormy passions do so spend the
whole stock of grief, that they presently admit a comfort and
contrary affection, while a sorrow that is even and temperate
goes on to its period with expectation and the distances of a
just time. The Ephesian woman that the soldier told of in
Petronius was the talk of all the town, and the rarest example
of a dear affection to her husband. She descended with the
corpse into the vault, and there, being attended with her
maiden, resolved to weep to death, or die with famine or a
distempered sorrow: from which resolution nor his nor her
friends, nor the reverence of the principal citizens, who used
the entreaties of their charity and their power, could persuade
her. But a soldier that watched seven dead bodies hanging
upon trees just over against this monument crept in, and
awhile stared upon the silent and comely disorders of the
sorrow; and having let the wonder awhile breathe out at
each other's eyes, at last he fetched his supper and a bottle
of wine with purpose to eat and drink, and still to feed himself with that sad prettiness. His pity and first draught of
wine made him bold and curious to try if the maid would
drink; who, having many hours since felt her resolution faint
as her wearied body, took his kindness, and the light returned
to her eyes, and danced like boys in a festival; and fearing
lest the pertinaciousness of her mistress's sorrows should
cause her evil to revert, or her shame to approach, assayed
whether she would endure to hear an argument to persuade
her to drink and live. The violent passion had laid all her
spirits in wildness and dissolution, and the maid found them
willing to be gathered into order at the arrest of any new
object, being weary of the first, of which, like leeches, they

[10] —— Tremulumque caput descendere jussit
In cœlum, et longam manantia labra salivam.

had sucked their fill, till they fell down and burst. The weeping woman took her cordial, and was not angry with her maid, and heard the soldier talk: and he was so pleased with the change, that he who first loved the silence of the sorrow was more in love with the music of her returning voice, especially which himself had strung and put in tune: and the man began to talk amorously, and the woman's weak head and heart were soon possessed with a little wine, and grew gay and talked, and fell in love; and that very night, in the morning of her passion, in the grave of her husband, in the pomps of mourning, and in her funeral garments, married her new and stranger guest. For so the wild foragers of Libya, being spent with heat, and dissolved by the too fond kisses of the sun, do melt with their common fires, and die with faintness, and descend with motions slow and unable to the little brooks that descend from heaven in the wilderness; and when they drink they return into the vigour of a new life, and contract strange marriages; and the lioness is courted by a panther, and she listens to his love, and conceives a monster that all men call unnatural, and the daughter of an equivocal passion and of a sudden refreshment. And so also was it in the cave at Ephesus: for by this time the soldier began to think it was fit he should return to his watch, and observe the dead bodies he had in charge: but when he ascended from his mourning bridal-chamber, he found that one of the bodies was stolen by the friends of the dead, and that he was fallen into an evil condition, because, by the laws of Ephesus, his body was to be fixed in the place of it. The poor man returns to his woman, cries out bitterly, and in her presence resolves to die to prevent his death, and in secret, to prevent his shame: but now the woman's love was raging like her former sadness, and grew witty, and she comforted her soldier, and persuaded him to live, lest by losing him who had brought her from death and a more grievous sorrow, she should return to her old solemnities of dying, and lose her honour for a dream, or the reputation of her constancy without the change and satisfaction of an enjoyed love. The man would fain have lived if it had been possible, and she found out this way for him; that he should take the body of her first husband, whose funeral she had so strangely mourned, and put it upon the gallows in the place of the stolen thief: he did so, and escaped

the present danger to possess a love which might change as
violently as her grief had done.   But so have I seen a crowd
of disordered people rush violently and in heaps, till their
utmost border was restrained by a wall, or had spent the fury
of the first fluctuation and watery progress, and by and by it
returned to the contrary with the same earnestness, only because it was violent and ungoverned.   A raging passion is
this crowd, which when it is not under discipline and the
conduct of reason, and the proportions of temperate humanity,
runs passionately the way it happens, and by and by as
greedily to another side, being swayed by its own weight,
and driven any whither by chance in all its pursuits, having
no rule but to do all it can, and spend itself in haste, and expire with some shame and much indecency.

When thou hast wept awhile, compose the body to burial;
which that it be done gravely, decently, and charitably, we
have the example of all nations to engage us, and of all ages
of the world to warrant : so that it is against common honesty,
and public fame and reputation, not to do this office.

It is good that the body be kept veiled and secret, and not
exposed to curious eyes, or the dishonours wrought by the
changes of death discerned and stared upon by impertinent
persons.   When Cyrus was dying he called his sons and
friends to take their leave, to touch his hand, to see him the
last time, and gave in charge, that when he had put his veil
over his face no man should uncover it: and Epiphanius's
body was rescued from inquisitive eyes by a miracle.   Let it
be interred after the manner of the country, and the laws of
the place,[11] and the dignity of the person.   For so Jacob was
buried with great solemnity, and Joseph's bones were carried
into Canaan after they had been embalmed and kept four
hundred years; and devout men carried St. Stephen to his
burial, making great lamentation over him.   And Ælian[12]
tells that those who were the most excellent persons were
buried in purple; and men of an ordinary courage and fortune had their graves only trimmed with branches of olive

---

[11] Νόμοις ἕπεσθαι τοῖσιν ἐγχώροις καλῶς.

Τύμβον δ' οὐ μάλα πολλὸν ἰγὼ πονέεσθαι ἄνωγα,
'Αλλ' ἐπιεικέα τοῖον.   Iliad. ψ'.

[12] Lib vi. Var. Histor. cap. 6. Τοὺς τελίως ἀριστεύσαντας ἐν φοινικίδι
ταφῆναι

and mourning flowers. But when Mark Antony gave the body of Brutus to his freedman to be buried honestly, he gave also his own mantle to be thrown into his funeral pile: and the magnificence of the old funeral we may see largely described by Virgil in the obsequies of Misenus, and by Homer in the funeral of Patroclus. It was noted for piety in the men of Jabesh-Gilead, that they showed kindness to their lord, Saul, and buried him; and they did it honourably. And our blessed Saviour, who was temperate in his expense, and grave in all the parts of his life and death, as age and sobriety itself, yet was pleased to admit the cost of Mary's ointment upon his head and feet, because she did it against his burial; and though she little thought it had been so nigh, yet because he accepted it for that end, he knew he had made her apology sufficient: by which he remarked it to be a great act of piety, and honourable, to inter our friends and relatives according to the proportions of their condition, and so to give a testimony of our hope of their resurrection.[13] So far is piety; beyond it may be the ostentation and bragging of a grief, or a design to serve worse ends. Such was that of Herod, when he made too studied and elaborate a funeral for Aristobulus, whom he had murdered: and of Regulus for his boy,[14] at whose pile he killed dogs, nightingales, parrots, and little horses; and such, also, was the expense of some of the Romans, who, hating their left wealth, gave order by their testament to have huge portions of it thrown into their fires, bathing their locks, which were presently to pass through the fire, with Arabian and Egyptian liquors and balsam of Judea. In this, as in every thing else, as our piety must not pass into superstition or vain expense, so neither must the excess be turned into parsimony, and chastised by negligence and impiety to the memory of their dead.

But nothing of this concerns the dead in real and effective

[13] Nam quid sibi saxa cavata,
Quid pulchra volunt monumenta,
Nisi quòd res creditur illis
Non mortua, sed data somno?
                    Prud. Hymn. in Exeq. Defunct.
[14]   ———— Cupit omnia ferre
Prodigus, et totos Melior succendere census,
Desertas exosus opes.   Statius, lib. ii. Sylvar.

purposes; nor is it with care to be provided for by themselves; but it is the duty of the living.[15] For to them it is all
one[16] whether they be carried forth upon a chariot or a
wooden bier; whether they rot in the air or in the earth;
whether they be devoured by fishes or by worms, by birds or
by sepulchral dogs, by water or by fire, or by delay.   When
Criton asked Socrates how he would be buried, he told him,
I think I shall escape from you, and that you cannot catch
me; but so much of me as you can apprehend, use it as you
see cause for, and bury it; but, however, do it according to
the laws.[17]   There is nothing in this but opinion and the
decency of fame to be served.   When it is esteemed an honour
and the manner of blessed people to descend into the graves
of their fathers, there also it is reckoned as a curse to be buried
in a strange land, or that the birds of the air devour them.[18]
Some nations used to eat the bodies of their friends, and
esteemed that the most honoured sepulture; but they were
barbarous.   The magi never buried any but such as were
torn of beasts.   The Persians besmeared their dead with wax,
and the Egyptians with gums, and with great art did condite
the bodies and laid them in charnel-houses.   But Cyrus the
elder would none of all this, but gave command that his body
should be interred, not laid in a coffin of gold or silver, but
just into the earth,[19] from whence all living creatures receive
birth and nourishment, and whither they must return.   Among
Christians the honour which is valued in the behalf of the
dead is, that they be buried in holy ground; that is, in appointed cemeteries, in places of religion, there where the field
of God is sown with the seeds of the resurrection,[20] that their

---

[15] Totus hic locus contemnendus est in nobis, non negligendus in
nostris.—Cicero.   [16] Id cinerem aut manes credis curare sepultos?
[17] Ὅπως ἂν σοι φίλον ᾖ, καὶ μάλιστα ἡγῇ νόμιμον εἶναι.
[18] Fugientibus Trojanis minatus est Hector:
        Αὐτοῦ οἱ θάνατον μητίσσομαι, οὐδέ νυ τόν γε
        Γνωτοί τε γνωταί τε πυρὸς λελάχωσι θανόντα,
        Ἀλλὰ κύνες ἐρύουσι πρὸ ἄστεος ἡμετέροιο.—Iliad. ο'.
[19] Τ: γὰρ τούτου μακαριώτερον, τῇ γῇ μιχθῆναι, ἢ πάντα μὲν τὰ καλὰ
πάντα τ' ἀγαθὰ φύει τε καὶ τρέφει;—Xenoph. περὶ παιδ.
        Sit tibi terra levis, mollique tegaris arenâ,
        Ne tua non possint eruere ossa canes.—Mart.
        [20] Nam quod requiescere corpus
        Vacuum sine mente videmus,

bodies also may be among the Christians, with whom their hope and their portion is and shall be for ever. "Quicquid feceris, omnia hæc eodem ventura sunt;" that we are sure of; our bodies shall all be restored to our souls hereafter, and in the interval they shall all be turned into dust, by what way soever you or your chance shall dress them. Licinus the freedman slept in a marble tomb,[21] but Cato in a little one, Pompey in none: and yet they had the best fate among the Romans, and a memory of the biggest honour. And it may happen that to want a monument may best preserve their memories, while the succeeding ages shall, by their instances, remember the changes of the world, and the dishonours of death, and the equality of the dead; and James the Fourth, king of the Scots, obtained an epitaph [22] for wanting of a tomb; and King Stephen is remembered with a sad story, because four hundred years after his death his bones were thrown into a river that evil men might sell the leaden coffin. It is all one in the final event of things.[23] Ninus the Assyrian had a monument erected, whose height was nine furlongs, and the breadth ten, saith Diodorus: but John the Baptist had more honour when he was humbly laid in the earth between the bodies of Abdias and Elizeus. And St. Ignatius, who was buried in the bodies of lions, and St. Polycarp, who was burned to ashes, shall have their bones and their flesh again with greater comfort than those violent persons who slept among kings, having usurped their thrones when they were alive, and their sepulchres when they were dead.

Concerning doing honour to the dead, the consideration is not long. Anciently the friends of the dead used to make their funeral orations,[24] and what they spake of greater com-

Spatium breve restat, ut alti
Repetat collegia sensûs.
Hinc maxima cura sepulchris
Impenditur.—Prud. Hymn. in Exeq. Defunct.

[21] Marmoreo Licinus tumulo jacet, at Cato parvo,
Pompeius nullo: credimus esse Deos ?—Varro Atacinus.
[22] Fama orbem replet, mortem sors occulit, at tu
Desine scrutari quod tegit ossa solum.
Si mihi dent animo non impar fata sepulcrum.
Angusta es tumulo terra Britanna meo.
[23] Cernit ibi mœstos et mortis honore carentes
Leucaspim, et Lyciæ ductorem classis Orontem.—Æneid. vi.
[24] Lustravitque viros dixitque novissima verba.—Æneid.

mendation was pardoned upon the accounts of friendship; but
when Christianity seized upon the possession of the world,
this charge was devolved upon priests and bishops, and they
first kept the custom of the world and adorned it with the
piety of truth and of religion ; but they also so ordered it, that
it should not be cheap; for they made funeral sermons only at
the death of princes, or of such holy persons who "shall judge
the angels." The custom descended, and in the channels
mingled with the veins of earth through which it passed; and
now-a-days men that die are commended at a price, and the
measure of their legacy is the degree of their virtue. But
these things ought not so to be; the reward of the greatest
virtue ought not to be prostitute to the doles of common persons, but preserved, like laurels and coronets, to remark and
encourage the noblest things. Persons of an ordinary life
should neither be praised publicly nor reproached in private :
for it is an office and charge of humanity to speak no evil of
the dead (which, I suppose, is meant concerning things not
public and evident): but then neither should our charity to
them teach us to tell a lie, or to make a great flame from a
heap of rushes and mushrooms, and make orations crammed
with the narrative of little observances, and acts of civil, and
necessary, and external religion.

But that which is most considerable is, that we should do
something for the dead,[25] something that is real and of proper
advantage. That we perform their will, the laws oblige us,
and will see to it; but that we do all those parts of personal
duty which our dead left unperformed, and to which the laws
do not oblige us, is an act of great charity and perfect kindness ; and it may redound to the advantage of our friends
also, that their debts be paid even beyond the inventory of
their movables.

Besides this, let us right their causes and assert their
honour. When Marcus Regulus had injured the memory of
Herennius Senecio, Metius Carus asked him what he had to
do with his dead? and became his advocate after death, of
whose cause he was patron when he was alive. And David
added this also, that he did kindness to Mephibosheth for
Jonathan's sake; and Solomon pleaded his father's cause by

the sword against Joab and Shimei. And certainly it is the noblest thing in the world to do an act of kindness to him whom we shall never see,[26] but yet hath deserved it of us, and to whom we would do it if he were present; and unless we do so our charity is mercenary, and our friendships are direct merchandise, and our gifts are brocage: but what we do to the dead or to the living for their sakes is gratitude, and virtue for virtue's sake, and the noblest portion of humanity.

And yet I remember, that the most excellent prince Cyrus, in his last exhortation to his sons upon his death-bed, charms them into peace and union of hearts and designs, by telling them that his soul would be still alive, and therefore fit to be revered and accounted as awful and venerable as when he was alive: and what we do to our dead friends is not done to persons undiscerning as a fallen tree, but to such who better attend to their relatives, and to greater purposes, though in other manner, than they did here below. And therefore those wise persons, who, in their funeral orations, made their doubt with an εἴ τις αἴσθησις τοῖς τετελευτηκόσι περὶ τῶν ἐνθάδε γιγνομένων, "if the dead have any perception of what is done below," which are the words of Isocrates, in the funeral encomium of Evagoras, did it upon the uncertain opinion of the soul's immortality; but made no question if they were living they did also understand what could concern them. The same words Nazianzen uses at the exequies of his sister, Gorgonia, and in the former invective against Julian; but this was upon another reason; even because it was uncertain what the state of separation was, and whether our dead perceive any thing of us, till we shall meet in the day of judgment. If it was uncertain then, it is certain since that time we have had no new revelation concerning it; but it is ten to one but when we die we shall find the state of affairs wholly differing from all our opinions here, and that no man or sect hath guessed any thing at all of it as it is. Here I intend not to dispute, but to persuade; and therefore, in the general, if it be probable that they know or feel the benefits done to them, though but by a reflex revelation from God,

---

[26] Χρὴ δὲ καὶ τῶν προγόνων ποιήσασθαί τινα πρόνοιαν, καὶ μὴ παραμελῆσαι, μηδὲ τῆς περὶ ἐκείνους εὐσεβείας.—Isoc. Plataic. c. 24. Lange, p 354.

—— Misenum in littore Teucri
Flebant, et cineri ingrato suprema ferebant.—Æneid. vi.

or some under-communication from an angel, or the stock of
acquired notices here below, it may the rather endear us to
our charities or duties to them respectively; since our virtues
use not to live upon abstractions and metaphysical perfections, or inducements, but then thrive when they have material arguments, such which are not too far from sense.
However it be, it is certain they are not dead:[27] and though
we no more see the souls of our dead friends than we did
when they were alive, yet we have reason to believe them to
know more things and better; and if our sleep be an image
of death, we may also observe concerning it, that it is a state
of life so separate from communications with the body, that
it is one of the ways of oracle and prophecy[28] by which the
soul best declares her immortality, and the nobleness of her
actions and powers, if she could get free from the body, as
in the state of separation, or a clear dominion over it, as in
the resurrection. To which also this consideration may be
added, that men a long time live the life of sense before they
use their reason; and till they have furnished their head
with experiments and notices of many things, they cannot at
all discourse of any thing: but when they come to use their
reason, all their knowledge is nothing but remembrance,[29]
and we know by proportions, by similitudes and dissimili-
tudes, by relations and oppositions, by causes and effects, by
comparing things with things, all which are nothing but
operations of understanding upon the stock of former notices,
of something we knew before, nothing but remembrances:
all the heads of topics, which are the stock of all arguments
and sciences in the world, are a certain demonstration of this;
and he is the wisest man that remembers most, and joins those
remembrances together to the best purposes of discourse.
From whence it may not be improbably gathered, that in the
state of separation, if there be any act of understanding, that
is, if the understanding be alive, it must be relative to the

[27] Ἦλθε δ' ἐπὶ ψυχὴ Πατροκλῆος δειλοῖο,
—— καί μιν πρὸς μῦθον ἔειπεν,
Εὕδεις, αὐτὰρ ἐμεῖο λελασμένος ἔπλευ, Ἀχιλλεῦ;
Οὐ μέν μευ ζώοντος ἀκήδεις, ἀλλὰ θανόντος.—Iliad. ψ'.
[28] Ἡ δὲ τοῦ ἀνθρώπου ψυχὴ τότε δήπου θειοτάτη καταφαίνεται, καὶ τότε
τι τῶν μελλόντων προορᾷ, τότε γὰρ ὡς ἔοικε μάλιστα ἐλευθεροῦται.—
Cyrus apud Xenoph. lib. viii. Instit.
[29] —— Τίς ἐστὶ καὶ εἰν ἀΐδαο δόμοισι
Ψυχὴ καὶ εἴδωλον, ἀτὰρ φρένες οὐκ ἔνι πάμπαν.—Iliad. ψ'.

notices it had in this world; and therefore the acts of it must be discourses upon all the parts and persons of their conversation and relation, excepting only such new revelation which may be communicated to it; concerning which we know nothing. But if by seeing Socrates I think upon Plato, and by seeing a picture I remember a man, and by beholding two friends I remember my own and my friend's need (and he is wisest that draws most lines from the same centre, and most discourses from the same notices); it cannot but be very probable to believe, since the separate souls understand better if they understand at all, that from the notices they carried from hence, and what they find there equal or unequal to those notices, they can better discover the things of their friends than we can here by our conjectures and craftiest imaginations; and yet many men here can guess shrewdly at the thoughts and designs of such men with whom they discourse, or of whom they have heard, or whose characters they prudently have perceived.—I have no other end in this discourse, but that we may be engaged to do our duty to our dead; lest peradventure they should perceive our neglect, and be witnesses of our transient affections and forgetfulness. Dead persons have religion passed upon them, and a solemn reverence; and if we think a ghost beholds us, it may be we have upon us the impressions likely to be made by love, and fear, and religion. However, we are sure that God sees us, and the world sees us: and if it be matter of duty towards our dead, God will exact it; if it be matter of kindness, the world will: and as religion is the band of that, so fame and reputation are the endearment of this.

It remains, that we who are alive should so live, and by the actions of religion attend the coming of the day of the Lord, that we neither be surprised nor leave our duties imperfect, nor our sins uncancelled, nor our persons unreconciled, nor God unappeased; but that, when we descend to our graves, we may rest in the bosom of the Lord, till the mansions be prepared where we shall sing and feast eternally. Amen.

Te Deum laudamus!

THE END.

LONDON:
PRINTED BY WILLIAM CLOWES AND SONS, LIMITED,
STAMFORD STREET AND CHARING CROSS.

COSIMO

COSIMO is a specialty publisher of books and publications that inspire, inform, and engage readers. Our mission is to offer unique books to niche audiences around the world.

COSIMO BOOKS publishes books and publications for innovative authors, nonprofit organizations, and businesses. COSIMO BOOKS specializes in bringing books back into print, publishing new books quickly and effectively, and making these publications available to readers around the world.

COSIMO CLASSICS offers a collection of distinctive titles by the great authors and thinkers throughout the ages. At COSIMO CLASSICS timeless works find new life as affordable books, covering a variety of subjects including: Business, Economics, History, Personal Development, Philosophy, Religion & Spirituality, and much more!

COSIMO REPORTS publishes public reports that affect your world, from global trends to the economy, and from health to geopolitics.

FOR MORE INFORMATION CONTACT US AT
INFO@COSIMOBOOKS.COM

❋ if you are a book lover interested in our
current catalog of books

❋ if you represent a bookstore, book club, or
anyone else interested in special discounts
for bulk purchases

❋ if you are an author who wants to get published

❋ if you represent an organization or business
seeking to publish books and other publications
for your members, donors, or customers.

COSIMO BOOKS ARE ALWAYS
AVAILABLE AT ONLINE BOOKSTORES

VISIT COSIMOBOOKS.COM
BE INSPIRED, BE INFORMED

CPSIA information can be obtained
at www.ICGtesting.com
Printed in the USA
BVHW03s2242290318
512000BV00001B/32/P

9 781602 065505